THE BLACK WORKER

Vol. III

The Era of the Knights of Labor
and the Colored Farmers' Alliance

Other volumes in this series:

I The Black Worker to 1869

II The Era of the National Labor Union

IV The Era of the American Federation of Labor,
the United Mine Workers, and the Railway
Brotherhoods

The Black Worker

A Documentary History from Colonial
Times to the Present

Volume III

The Black Worker During the Era of the Knights of Labor

Edited by
Philip S. Foner and Ronald L. Lewis

Temple University Press, Philadelphia

Temple University Press, Philadelphia 19122
© by Temple University. All rights reserved
Published 1978
Printed in the United States of America

Library of Congress Cataloging in Publication Data
 Main entry under title:

The Black Worker.

   Includes index.
   CONTENTS: v.1. The Black worker to 1869.--v.2. The era of the national
labor union.--v.3. The era of the Knights of Labor and the colored farmers'
alliance, 1880-1890.
   1. Afro-Americans--Employment. 2. Afro-Americans--Economic conditions.
3. United States Race relations. I. Foner, Philip Sheldon, 1910-   II.
Lewis, Ronald L., 1940-
E185.8.B553   331.6'3'96073   78-2875
ISBN 0-87722-136-7 (v. 1)
ISBN 0-87722-137-5 (v. 2)
ISBN 0-13-208512-7 (v. 3)

TABLE OF CONTENTS

PART I

THE CONDITION OF BLACK WORKERS IN THE SOUTH

Introduction   2

BLACKS TESTIFY BEFORE THE SENATE COMMITTEE ON RELATIONS BETWEEN LABOR
AND CAPITAL, 1883   3

    1. Testimony   3

PART II

SHOULD BLACKS JOIN THE RANKS OF LABOR?

Introduction   34

CONFLICTING VIEWS   35

    1. Frederick Douglass on the Labor Question   35
    2. The Vital Labor Problem   35
    3. Proscribed   37
    4. Labor Upheavals   38
    5. Growth of the Colored Press   39
    6. John R. Lynch on the Color Line in the Ranks of Labor 40
    7. Land-Labor Problem   41
    8. The Colored Laborer Must Look to Himself   43
    9. A Word on the Labor Question   44
   10. A Case in Point   44
   11. A Knight is a Knight   45

A BLACK LEADER'S ADVICE TO NEGRO WORKING MEN   45

   12. The Negro Laborer: A Word to Him   45

PART III

BLACK LABOR MILITANCY AND THE KNIGHTS OF LABOR

Introduction   52

BLACK LABOR UNREST IN THE SOUTH   53

    1. Negro Strikers in Louisiana   53
    2. Labor Troubles   53
    3. The Labor Troubles   59
    4. The St. John Strikers   63
    5. Louisiana Strike   64
    6. Strike in Florida   65
    7. A Labor Riot in Missouri   66
    8. Working in Unison   66
    9. Labor vs. Capital   66
   10. The Labor Riots   68
   11. Another Police Murderer   70
   12. Cheering Words   70
   13. Murdered by a Mob   71

THE KNIGHTS ORGANIZE SOUTHERN BLACKS   71

    14. Assemblies of Colored Men   71
    15. Constitution for the Local Assemblies of the Order
           of the Knights of Labor in America   72
    16. Knights of Labor Meeting in Washington, D.C.   72
    17. Plain Talk to Workingmen   73
    18. Description of a Public Meeting   73
    19. Social Affair   73
    20. Baltimore Labor Parade   73
    21. First Black Assembly   74
    22. Black Cooperative Ventures   74
    23. The Richmond Co-Operative Soap Company   75
    24. Letter from a Black Knight   76
    25. Strides in the South   76

BLACK WORKERS AND KNIGHTS OF LABOR STRIKES, 1885 - 1886   77

    26. Paralyzed   77
    27. A General Strike   78
    28. Arbitrators at Work   81
    29. Labor Troubles at Galveston   82
    30. Arbitration in Galveston   83
    31. Boycott Renewed   83
    32. Congressional Report on the Labor Troubles in Missouri   84
    33. The Dangers of Organizing Blacks   90
    34. Colored Knights of Labor   91
    35. Striking Negro Knights   92
    36. Colored Knights of Labor in Arkansas   92
    37. The Futility of Strikes and Boycotts   93
    38. In Case of Necessity   94
    39. Stirred Up   95
    40. Sheriff R. W. Worthen   96
    41. Discharged   96
    42. Anonymous Threats   98
    43. A Card From the Fox Brothers   98
    44. War in Young   99

                               PART IV

              THE KNIGHTS OF LAVOR CONVENTION IN RICHMOND, 1886

Introduction   104

TERENCE V. POWDERLY, FRANK J. FERRELL, AND THE INTEGRATED
CONVENTION IN RICHMOND, 1886   105

    1.   Knights of Labor in Their Mettle   105
    2.   Frank J. Ferrell's Introduction of Powderly   106
    3.   Powderly's Address   106
    4.   Powderly to the Richmond Dispatch   106
    5.   The Colored Brother   107
    6.   He Sits Among the Whites   107
    7.   Social Equality of the Races   109
    8.   Colored Knight Ferrell   109
    9.   A Sample of National Reactions to the Knights
           Position on Social Equality   111
    10. The Mozart Association in Connection With the
           Color Question   112
    11. The Knights and Southern Prejudice   113
    12. J. M. Townsend to Terence Powderly   113
    13. Samuel Wilson to Terence Powderly   114
    14. James Hirst to Terence Powderly   114

15. D. H. Black to Terence Powderly   114
16. "Tradesman" to Terence Powderly   115
17. Negro Press Committee to Terence Powderly   115
18. A. O. Hale to Terence Powderly   115
19. Letter From a White Virginia Knight   116
20. At Work at Last   116
21. Richmond and the Convention Held Up   123
22. Resolutions of the Equal Rights League, Columbus, Ohio   125
23. Resolution Adopted By an All-Black Local Assembly,
       Rendville, Ohio   126
24. A Peaceful Parade   126
25. Powderly on Race Rights   126
26. They Will Find Out Facts   127
27. Banquet in Honor of District Assembly 49   128
28. The Mixed Banquet at Harris's Hall   128
29. Disaffection   129
30. How Their Stand Against Prejudice is Regarded
       By the Colored Press   129
31. Mr. Powderly and Social Equality   131
32. The Knights of Labor Show the White Feather   132
33. An Imprudent Position on Social Equality   133
34. Powderly's Straddling   133
35. Importance of the Richmond Convention   134
36. A Footnote on Frank J. Ferrell   134

PART V

SUPPRESSION OF THE BLACK KNIGHTS

Introduction   136

OPPOSITION TO THE KNIGHTS OF LABOR IN SOUTH CAROLINA   137

1. Industrial Slavery in the South   137
2. Fighting the Knights   138
3. Much Bitter Feeling   139
4. The Trouble in the South   140
5. Hoover's Negro Dupes   141
6. Free Speech in the South   142

AN OVERVIEW OF THE KNIGHTS' 1887 SUGAR STRIKE IN LOUISIANA   143

7. The Knights Strike Sugar   143
8. A Planter's View: Excerpts From the William
       Porcher Miles Diary   149
9. Conflict in the Louisiana Sugar Fields   150
10. Sugar Labor - Demands   151
11. Sugar Labor   153
12. Sugar Labor - The Strike Inaugurated   155
13. Protection From Riot and Violence   159
14. Labor Troubles   160
15. Laborers Shot Down   162
16. Backbone of the Strike Broken   166
17. The Teche Troubles   168
18. Deserted Cane Fields   170
19. Labor Troubles in the Sugar Districts   171
20. The Sugar Strike   171
21. The Teche Troubles - Planter Shot by Striker   172
22. Gone to Work   173
23. Nine Men Killed   175

24. The Labor Troubles - Killing of Negroes   177
25. The Sugar Strike - Negroes Threaten Sheriff   179
26. The Sugar Strike   180
27. Labor in the South   184
28. The Louisiana Strikes   185
29. The Knights of Labor   186
30. Sugar Plantation Laborers   187
31. Sugar Planters' Association of Louisiana   189
32. Labor Troubles in Lafourche   189
33. Riot at Thibodaux   191
34. Peace Restored - Troops at Thibodaux   195
35. The Thibodaux Riot   197
36. The Sugar District Troubles   202
37. The Thibodaux Riot - Three More Dead   202
38. Thibodaux - Ringleader's Surrender Not Accepted   204
39. The Thibodaux Troubles   206
40. The Militia in Thibodaux   207
41. The Sugar Strike   208
42. A Northern View of the Thibodaux Troubles   208
43. Colored People - Denounce Killings   208
44. Outrages in Louisiana   209
45. The Sugar Riots   210
46. W. R. Ramsay to T. V. Powderly   210
47. Labor's Pageant - Workingmen of New Orleans on Parade   211

CONGRESSIONAL REACTION TO THE LOUISIANA SUGAR STRIKE   217

48. From the Congressional Record   217

PART VI

GRAND MASTER WORKMAN TERENCE V. POWDERLY
AND THE BLACK WORKER

Introduction   242

CORRESPONDENCE RELATING TO THE BLACK WORKER IN THE POWDERLY PAPERS   243

1. Powderly to Wm. J. Stewart   243
2. Powderly to Brother Wright   243
3. Robert D. Dayton and Gilbert Rockwood to Powderly   244
4. Joe B. Kewley to Powderly   244
5. Powderly to M. W. Pattell   245
6. Gilbert Rockwood to Powderly   245
7. Powderly to S. T. Neilson   246
8. John R. Ray to Powderly   246
9. An Open Letter on Race to Powderly   246
10. "The South of To-Day," by Powderly   247
11. John R. Ray to Powderly   251
12. Powderly to J. M. Broughton   251
13. John R. Ray to Powderly   251
14. P. M. McNeal to Powderly   252
15. Powderly to Thomas Curley   252
16. Tom O'Reilly to Powderly   253
17. Powderly to W. H. Lynch   253
18. Alexander Walker to Powderly   254
19. D. B. Allison and Edward Gallagher to Powderly   254
20. R. W. Kruse to Powderly   255
21. H. G. Ellis to Powderly   255
22. R. W. Kruse to Powderly   256
23. J. A. Belton to Powderly   256
24. C. V. Meustin to Powderly   256

25. V. E. St. Cloud to Powderly 257
26. W. H. Sims, M.D., to Powderly 257
27. J. M. Broughton to Powderly 257
28. Frank Johnson to Powderly 258
29. S. F. S. Sweet to Powderly 258
30. George H. Williams to Powderly 259
31. Petition to Powderly 259
32. Fourth of July Celebration Announcement 259
33. Powderly to J. M. Bannan 260
34. Powderly to J. O. Parsons 260
35. Powderly to C. A. Teagle 260
36. Andrew McCormack to Powderly 261
37. B. W. Scott to Powderly 261
38. Powderly to B. W. Scott 261
39. B. Stock to Powderly 262
40. Hillard J. McNair to Powderly 262
41. J. A. Bodenhamer to Powderly 263
42. C. C. Mehurin to Powderly 264
43. C. E. Yarboro to Powderly 264
44. John Derbin to Powderly 265
45. Powderly to Rev. P. H. Kennedy 265
46. Samuel G. Searing to Powderly 266
47. Powderly's Open Letter to Secretary of the Treasury
    Charles Foster 266

PART VII

RACE RELATIONS WITHIN THE KNIGHTS OF LABOR

Introduction 272

RELATIONS BETWEEN BLACK AND WHITE KNIGHTS FROM THE 1886 CONVENTION
TO 1889 273

1. No Color Line Wanted 273
2. Ida B. Wells Describes a Knights of Labor Meeting
   in Memphis 273
3. A Florida Strike 273
4. Persecution 273
5. Knightsville is Solid 274
6. Glorious 4th 275
7. He Is On Our Side 275
8. A Cruel Negro 275
9. A Pittsburgh Strike 276
10. Letter From A Colored Knight 277
11. Mustering Up Courage 277
12. An Active Part 278
13. Lively Southern Knights 278
14. Knights of Labor 278

DEPORTATION: THE KNIGHTS' SOLUTION TO THE PROBLEMS OF THE
BLACK WORKER 281

15. Speak Out 281
16. A Black Worker to James R. Sovereign 281
17. Opinion of the Chicago Colored Women's Club 282
18. Our Labor Problem 282
19. On Deportation 283
20. Epitaph 283

PART VIII

BLACK FARMERS ORGANIZE BLACK ALLIANCES

Introduction   286

THE COLORED FARMERS NATIONAL ALLIANCE AND COOPERATIVE UNION,
1890 - 1891   287

1. History of the Colored Farmers' National Alliance
       and Cooperative Union   287
2. The Order System   290
3. Southern Grangers   291
4. Why Has the Negro of the Plantation Made So Little
       Progress?   292
5. Laying Out the Work   293
6. Farmers of West Florida   294
7. H. H. Perry to Elias Carr, President, Colored
       Alliance of North Carolina   294
8. *The National Alliance* Advises   295
9. Gen. R. M. Humphrey Writes From Pulaski, Tennessee   295
10. *The National Alliance* Organ of the Colored Alliance   295
11. *The Alabama Mirror* Notes a Gratifying Fact   296
12. *The National Alliance*   296
13. Election Bill   296
14. The Colored Alliance: Annual Address of the
       National Superintendent   297
15. Unsavory Senator   299
16. The Race Problem   300
17. J. J. Rogers to Elias Carr   305
18. W. A. Patillo to Elias Carr   305
19. J. J. Rogers to Elias Carr   305
20. People's Party Convention   305
21. A Great Absurdity   306
22. Colored Farmers Alliance Meets   306
23. The Convict Lease System   310
24. Camp Meetings   312
25. Notice   312
26. Afro-Americans and the People's Party   313
27. Split Among Whites   314
28. The Rankest Bourbon   314
29. When Thine Enemy Speaks Well of You   314
30. The Southern Alliance--Let the Negro Take a Thought   315
31. Social Equality   317
32. Endorsed By the Colored Farmers   319

THE 1891 COTTON PICKERS' STRIKE   330

33. The Cotton Pickers--A Formidable Organization   330
34. Negroes Form a Combine   331
35. Colored Cotton Pickers   331
36. Not a Bit Alarmed   332
37. The Cotton Pickers' League   332
38. Won't Hurt Georgia   333
39. This State is Safe   336
40. Gathering Cotton   337
41. The Georgia Pickers   338
42. President Polk's Menace   339
43. Still Snatching Cotton   339
44. It Did Not Develop   340
45. A Flash in the Pan   341

46. President L. L. Polk - Probability of a Third Party   345
47. The Exodus of Negroes   346
48. Negro Cotton Pickers Threatening   347
49. Delta Troubles   347
50. A Bloody Riot in Arkansas   348
51. Blood and Terror   348
52. The Cotton Pickers' Strike   349
53. Blacks in Brakes--Lee County Riots   350
54. Race Riot in Arkansas   351
55. Nine Negroes Lynched   352
56. Prisoners Lynched   354
57. The Arkansas Man Hunt   356
58. Force Against Force   358
59. Wholesale Lynching   359
60. The Arkansas Butchery   359
61. Frightful Barbarities   360
62. Those Wholesale Murders   360
63. Peace Prevails   361
64. All Serene Now   362
65. There Was No Lynching   363

PART IX

OTHER EXPRESSIONS OF BLACK LABOR MILITANCY

Introduction   366

THE SAVANNAH WHARF WORKERS' STRIKE, 1891   367

 1. They Strike Today   367
 2. To Patrol Under Arms   367
 3. One Thousand Men Out   368
 4. The Strike Ordered On   372
 5. The Strike Spreading   375
 6. To The Public   379
 7. Progress of the Strikers   380
 8. Strikers Won't Give In   381
 9. Bringing in Labor - Strikers' Places Being Filled   385
10. The Mistake of the Strikers   391
11. The Strike is Settled   391
12. Strikers to Resume Work This Morning   392
13. Badly Advised   395
14. Strikers Splitting Up   396
15. Strikers Are Still Out   400
16. The Strike At An End   401
17. The Strike Ended   403
18. Looking Over Things   403
19. The Alliance in Line   404

BLACK AND WHITE UNITY: THE CHICAGO CULLINARY ALLIANCE   405

20. Limited Options   405
21. The Limited Movement   406
22. The Chicago Waiters' Strike   406
23. History of the Union Waiters' Strike   406
24. Leaders of the Cullinary Alliance   408

NOTES   413
INDEX   429

This is the third volume in *The Black Worker: A Documentary History From Colonial Times to the Present,* the first compilation of original materials to encompass the entire history of Afro-American labor. Recently there has been a revived interest among historians in the relations between black workers and the Noble Order of the Knights of Labor. But this is the first presentation of historical documents, relating to black and white relations within this most significant of nineteenth-century labor organizations.[1]

The Black Worker During the Era of the Knights of Labor begins with the testimony of seven black workers before the Senate Committee on the Relations Between Labor and Capital (1883). While their assessments regarding the conditions of Negro life and labor in the South varied, they generally agreed that black workers languished at the bottom of the economic pyramid. Whether the labor movement was the answer to these woes, however, remained a question of paramount importance among black leaders, and during the 1880s a lively debate was conducted on the issue in the black press. The time for union organization was propitious, for black workers had innumerable economic grievances and throughout the era demonstrated an interest in labor solidarity unparalleled in the past. Large numbers of black workers joined the Knights of Labor, and startled the South by conducting strikes which were impressive in their execution. Faith in the Knights of Labor seemed justified when, at the 1886 convention in Richmond, the Order challenged Southern racial etiquette regarding the segregation of black delegates. This faith was misplaced, however, for the national leadership proved to be ambivalent on the race issue and failed to assist several crucial local black struggles, dooming them to failure. In any case, given the opposition to integration among southern white workers, there was little that the national leadership could do. Consequently, the Knights of Labor acquiesced to segregated local assemblies. Nor could the Order prevent the vicious suppression of black Knights in the South.

While the bulk of Volume III is devoted to the Knights of Labor, the materials on the Colored Alliance, the Cotton Pickers' Strike of 1891, and the Savannah Longshoremen's Strike of 1891, occur during the same era and were related, either directly or indirectly, to the Knights of Labor. They also constitute singular examples of militant activism among working-class blacks and, therefore, are included in this volume.

It is worthwhile to draw the reader's attention to the numerous black newspapers which have been used as sources for this book, especially since their perspective on daily affairs is often conspicuously different from that presented in white newspapers. The following are black periodicals used in Volume III: *New York Freeman, New York Age, Washington Bee, The Christian Recorder* (Philadelphia), *New Orleans Weekly Louisianian, People's Advocate* (Washington, D.C.), *Cleveland Gazette, The Freeman* (Indianapolis), *The Weekly Pelican* (New Orleans), *Richmond Planet, The Appeal* (St. Paul), and the *Detroit Plaindealer.*

Like the other volumes in this series, the documents presented are accompanied by introductions and notes, and original spellings have been retained except in cases where they obscure the intended meaning.

The editors wish to express their gratitude to those who have been generous in their assistance toward the completion of this book. Once again, Miss Lila Prieb demonstrated her expertise at the typewriter and patiently deciphered some very difficult copy. We also take pleasure in acknowledging the assistance of the manuscript departments at the Catholic University of America Library, Washington, D.C.; East Carolina University Library, Greenville, North Carolina; Howard University Library, Washington, D.C.; Tulane University Library, New Orleans, Louisiana; University of North Carolina Library, Chapel Hill, North Carolina. Finally, we thank Roslyn Foner for designing the books in this series, and Susan Lewis for her countless hours of tedious proofreading.

Philip S. Foner   Ronald L. Lewis
Lincoln University,   University of Delaware
  Pennsylvania

I

THE CONDITION OF BLACK WORKERS

THE CONDITION OF BLACK WORKERS IN THE SOUTH

In the spring of 1882, John T. Morgan, Senator from Alabama, submitted a resolution calling for the establishment of a committee to investigate the causes behind the numerous industrial strikes which wracked American industry during the 1870s and 1880s. Southern senators, led by Morgan, planned to use these hearings to demonstrate to the average industrial worker of the North that he, too, was financially penalized by the contemporary high tariff schedule. They believed that the hearings would convince northern laboring men to pressure their congressional representatives into supporting the lower tariff schedules demanded by southern senators. The southern senators also hoped to reveal cases of northern industrial employers who used political coercion against their employees. If it could be shown that the industrialists controlled the voting behavior of their employees through job coercion, then Republican charges that southerners were subverting the political rights of Negroes would be effectively countered.

In order to undermine Morgan's strategy, the Republicans urged that the Senate Committee on Education and Labor undertake a broad examination of the entire range of relations between labor and capital. In effect, the Republicans challenged the southern Democrats, believing that the evidence would in fact vindicate the industrialists' high duty structure, and show workingmen that these duties were necessary to their own well-being. On August 7, 1882, the resolution was unanimously adopted.

Despite the initially partisan intentions, however, the hearings evolved into a genuine attempt to arrive at a fair assessment of industrial labor relations. Much of the credit for the exemplary conduct of the hearings goes to the chairman, Henry W. Blair of New Hampshire (1834-1920). A conservative on most social issues, Blair was genuinely concerned for the welfare of industrial workers and sought to get an impartial hearing for every witness, whatever his views. Surprisingly, the southern Democrats also adopted this general attitude and chose not to utilize the plight of northern workers as a vehicle to justify the treatment of Negroes in the South. The most important southern member of the committee was James Z. George of Mississippi (1827-1896). Even though George was an ex-confederate colonel, and had played an integral role in the restoration of white supremacy in his home state, he, too, had a genuine interest in the welfare of workingmen.

Before the committee passed a parade of employers, union leaders, all kinds of workmen, and ordinary citizens, all of whom spoke their minds. Even though the hearings produced few immediate results, for the first time in history a broad sample of opinion on industrial problems was collected and recorded. Relatively few blacks were asked to appear before the committee, but the seven whose testimony is reproduced in Part I reflect a variety of non-agricultural occupations: sleeping-car porter, minister, lawyer, carpenter, barber, bricklayer, and teacher. Their perspectives varied according to their social class, but some common concerns emerge from their collective testimony.

One of the primary concerns was for improved educational opportunities. Most agreed that both blacks and whites preferred segregated schools because this freed them from the fear of racial conflict. Blacks considered industrial education of primary importance because whites would not work with blacks in the mills and factories; therefore, youths could not obtain training in the skilled trades. Nor must a sound education in the basics of reading, writing, and arithmetic be ignored, for the masses of freedmen could only become good citizens when they were able to understand the world in which they lived. Moreover, blacks believed that the states could not, or would not, fund their education and, therefore, the freedmen looked to the federal government as a source of financial aid. In that they were to be disappointed. Nevertheless, those blacks who testified revealed how well assimilated they had become by their strong affirmations of self-reliance and the American "work ethic." Blacks simply asked that the barriers of racial discrimination be lowered in the race for economic advancement.

BLACKS TESTIFY BEFORE THE SENATE COMMITTEE ON RELATIONS
BETWEEN CAPITAL AND LABOR, 1883

1. TESTIMONY

On The Train, Near Bristol, Tenn., *November* 11, 1883.

FLOYD THORNHILL sworn and examined.

By the CHAIRMAN:

Question. Where were you born?--A. In Campbell County, Virginia, 8
miles from Lynchburg. I was born and raised a slave.
Q. Where have you lived from your birth until now?--A. Lynchburg has
been my principal home. I worked at another place near there for about a
year. Then I worked off and on for about two years on the Chesapeake and
Ohio Railroad. Then for about two years I worked in Lynchburg in a tobacco
factory, and since that time I have been working as porter on these cars.
Q. How old are you?--A. I am going on thirty-four years of age. I
was sixteen years old when Lee surrendered.
Q. Are you a man of family?--A. Yes, sir; I have four children.
Q. Where do your family live now?--A. In Lynchburg.
Q. What do you call your present business?--A. Sleeping-car porter,
running between Washington and New Orleans.
Q. Is this an important route between the North and the South?--A.
Yes, sir; it is called the boss route--the boss Southern railroad.
Q. How long have you worked at your present business?--A. About three
years.
Q. What pay do you get?--A. Twelve dollars a month.
Q. In addition to that you get something from the passengers, I sup-
pose?--A. Yes, sir.
Q. How much does that amount to, on an average?--A. Well, I reckon,
from time to time, I make here about $30 a month.
Q. Do you mean besides the $12 a month wages that you get regularly?--
A. Yes, sir; I don't average so much as that, though, because sometimes from
New Orleans I don't have but perhaps two passengers--sometimes one, sometimes two, and sometimes three. Pretty much all the travel I have now is
going southward.
Q. What is the distance between Washington and New Orleans by this
route?--A. One thousand two hundred and thirteen miles.
Q. How long does it take to make the trip one way?--A. Two days and
two nights and until 9.20 the next night.
Q. What chance have you to see your family?--A. When I get to Lynch-
burg, they have two extra porters there, and the superintendent allows me to
put one of these extra men on, and that gives me two days and two nights.
He only allows that once or twice a month, but he is more lenient in that
way than any other superintendent of the company.
Q. You and the conductor go over the route together, of course?--A.
Yes, sir.
Q. What pay does he get, or what do the conductors generally receive?
--A. The old conductors on this line get about $75; the other conductors
get, some $75, some $65, and some $60.
Q. I suppose you have been a good deal among the negroes who work in
the city, and also among those who work in the country, on the land?--A.
Yes, sir; right smart.
Q. What do they work at in Lynchburg?--A. The principal thing at
Lynchburg is the tobacco business; some of the factories make smoking tobac-
co and some shipping tobacco.
Q. What are the prominent tobacco manufacturing points in Virginia?--
A. Lynchburg, Danville, Richmond, and Petersburg are great tobacco points;
but I don't think there is any of them ahead of Lynchburg for tobacco. They
put up more there than they do in Danville or Petersburg; I don't know so

much about Richmond, but I think Lynchburg beats Richmond, too.

Q. You have worked at the tobacco business for several years; is it hard work?--A. Yes, sir; right hard work, the part that I have done; I worked in the price-room, the last finishing. Some of the tobacco is made by machine and wrapped by hand, then put in the drying-room, then steamed, then packed until it comes to be tough; then after it comes to be tough it is let down into the price-room and run under 12-inch rollers of all shape.

Q. What pay did you get when you worked at that business?--A. I got 60 cents a hundred.

Q. How much could you earn in a day or a week?--A. Some weeks $12.50, some weeks $10.50, some weeks as low as $9, and some weeks as high as $14.50.

Q. Did you save any money while you were at that business?--A. Yes, sir; I saved some money.

Q. How much?--A. Well, in that time I bought me a lot 55 feet by 100 feet. That lot cost me about $200 at the time I bought it, but I suppose it would be worth a good deal more now, because the place is so much built up.

Q. Have you got a house on it?--A. Oh, yes.

Q. Did you build the house yourself?--A. Yes, sir; It cost me $800.

Q. Do your family live in that house now?--A. Yes, sir; in that house.

Q. Are the house and lot fully paid for?--A. No, sir; not altogether; I owes nearly $150 on them.

Q. You have some furniture, of course?--A. Yes, sir; no costly furniture; good common furniture.

Q. How much do you think you are worth altogether?--A. Well, if my place was sold I don't think I would get the full value of it, but I would not like to take less than $1,000 for it.

Q. Do you mean for the place and the things you have in it and upon it?--A. Yes, sir.

Q. Have you earned all that money yourself?--A. Yes, sir.

Q. Are you an expert hand at the tobacco business?--A. Yes, sir. I was the boss hand in Lynchburg. I am the boss hand that was ever known there. I have done more than anybody else ever did in that business; that can be proved by the tobacco men; they will back me up in it. I have done well in that town. I have worked for some of the biggest manufacturers, and I have never been turned off in my life.

Q. Do your wife or children work at tobacco making?--A. Yes; my boy worked during the summer. He is about eight years old now, and he wanted to work and they gave him $1.50 a week.

Q. Is he getting that pay now?--A. No; he is going to school now, but when he works he can get that.

Q. Your wife does not work in the factory?--A. No, sir; she washes and sews some. The white people that raised her showed her how to sew, and she can make any kind of a dress.

Q. How long have you been married?--A. Ten years.

Q. Have you lost any children?--A. Yes, sir; six. But there didn't none of them come to time. My wife is not very strong.

Q. Is your wife growing stronger?--A. Yes, sir; she is stronger than when she was young; but she was always very delicate, and the white people that raised her kept her in the house and learned her to sew. She has had whooping-cough and asthma; she had asthma when I married her, but she does not have it now but once a year.

Q. Do the colored people generally have large families?--A. Generally so.

Q. How about their losing a good many of their children?--A. Some is that way and some not. All women is not weakly alike, you know; some is stronger.

Q. Do your children go to school?--A. One of them does; the one that is eight years old.

School Attendance in Lynchburg.

Q. How is it generally as to the attendance at school of the children, white and colored, in and about Lynchburg?--A. Well, they both seem to attend school pretty well, both colors.

Q. How long are the schools kept open each year?--A. I think the session is about nine months in the year. They have a vacation of about three
months, I think; I don't believe now but it is only two months, because I
kind of remember that my little boy didn't stop going to school till some
time in June.

Q. Are the teachers white or colored?--A. Some white and some colored.

Q. Do you have colored teachers in the schools for the colored people?
--A. There is one part white and another part colored.

Q. Are the schools mixed or separate?--A. They are separate.

Q. There are no white children in the colored schools, nor colored
children in the white schools?--A. No, sir; not one.

The Colored People Want Separate Schools.

Q. You don't want to have any white children in your schools, I suppose?--A. No, sir.

Q. How do the colored people generally feel about that?--A. They want
their children to go to their own schools. I never heard one colored man
say that he wanted his children to go to a white school.

Q. Why not?--A. Well it's just this: them children would not do to
go to school together anyhow.

Q. Why not?--A. Well, now, I'll tell you. The white children, them
that is big enough, knows we have been slaves that belonged to their parents,
and there comes a great 'sturbment out of that. The white children *will*
show authority over the nigger, and I don't believe they have any business
to go to school together. That is my idea. Now, I am a mighty strange man.
If I am working for you and you treat me good and pay me, that is all right,
but you could not have me come and sit down in your dining-room, because I
never been used to it, and I don't look to it, and the dinner is just as
good after you are gone, and my feelings would feel freer to sit down by myself. Now them is facts.

Q. Is it so among the children?--A. Yes, sir.

Q. But still the white children and the colored children get along
well enough elsewhere don't they?--A. Certainly they do.

Q. Do they agree pretty well generally outside the schools; do they
get into quarrels on the street, for instance?--A. There is not much of
that at Lynchburg. Sometimes, of course, a bad one may throw a rock at some
of the others, but there is not much of that at Lynchburg.

Q. Do the white and colored children quarrel more than the white children quarrel among themselves?--A. No, sir; I don't think they do. Sometimes you will hear one say something about the other or talking about what
they are going to do to each other, but that is the way children will do,
you know.

Q. And, on the whole, you don't think that the white children and the
colored children quarrel more than the children of the same color do?--A.
No, sir; they get along very well together.

Advantages of Education.

Q. Do you think it is of any consequence whether the children go to
school or not?--A. Certainly; I tell you I believe in doing the best you
can for the children. When a boy comes to be a man he will need it. I have
managed to get along pretty well, but sometimes I imagine that if I could
read and write it would be better. Many a time a passenger hands me a ticket; wants to know which way he is going, and I have to tell him, "I can't
read, but if you will read it along I will tell you whether it is the Kene-
saw route or not?" I might take it myself and hum over it and make it out
in a kind of a way, but not satisfactory. So I believe in children being
educated and elevated somehow, because when they come to be men it is great
help.

Q. Then you mean to keep your children at school, I suppose?--A. Yes,
sir.

Q. Is that the feeling of the colored people generally?--A. Well, they
seem to be tolerable earnest to keep the children going to school.

Wages of Farm Hands.

Q. What wages do colored men generally receive for working on the land in this part of the country or about Lynchburg?--A. They get from $10 to $12 a month and board.

Q. Do they also have houses and garden plots?--A. Yes, sir; they generally have as much land as they want.

Q. Do the women have anything to do?--A. Yes, sir; they sometimes works for wages; sometimes they does washing, and sometimes they works out in the field.

Q. How many hours do the men and women work generally?--A. The women works along with the men, except that sometimes they have to stop and go home and get the meals.

Q. What pay do the women get?--A. About 50 cents a day.

Q. Do the girls work on the land at all?--A. Yes, sir; some of the girls work at it, and some of them go to school. When they aint going to school they work.

Q. What sort of work do most of the girls do?--A. The girls works the same as the old people do, weedin' corn or suckerin' tobacco or hoein' corn or bindin' wheat in the harvest field--most any kind of work.

Colored Land-Owners in Virginia.

Q. Do the colored people own much land?--A. Yes, sir; a great many colored people have right smart little farms in Virginia. I don't know how many, but I know there is a good many. I know a man named Jackson that has had three farms, and he has two now.

Q. Do you know what he paid for them?--A. No; I don't know what they cost him, but I know one of them is 300 acres. It is in Campbell County, beyond Campbell's Mountain, 7 or 8 miles from Lynchburg.

Q. Has that man paid for his land?--A. Yes, sir.

Q. Did he have anything twenty years ago?--A. No, sir; certainly he did not.

Q. He was a slave then, I suppose?--A. Yes, sir.

Q. He did not have even himself then?--A. No sir, he did not have himself then.

Q. Have you any brothers?--A. Yes, sir; I have one brother in Prince Edward County. He has got forty acres of land and a team. He has got good, rich land. He raises wheat and tobacco and corn.

Q. How much wheat can he raise to the acre?--A. Eight or ten bushels.

Q. What is it worth a bushel there?--A. Sometimes they get $1 for it, and sometimes $1.25.

Q. I suppose they eat it themselves mostly?--A. They don't sell much wheat. My brother has his wheat ground up into flour, but he always keeps enough for himself.

Q. I see that these colored people about the railroad station dress about as well as the rest of the folks. Is that the case generally through this part of the country?--A. Yes, sir.

The Colored People Well Off in Virginia.

Q. On the whole, how are the colored folks generally getting on in Virginia?--A. Well, some parts of Virginia is very poor, you know, but I believe that generally the colored people in Virginia beats them in any of the other States. I may be wrong about it, but that is my opinion. I mean any other State where there is so many colored people. Some parts of Virginia is good and some parts is poor. I know two colored men about 5 miles from where my brother lives, and each one of them fellows has a good, big farm, and an orchard, and two or three horses and buggies and all those things. They are doing well.

Q. Then you think that the colored people generally in Virginia are getting along very well and are pretty happy?--A. Yes, sir; they are getting along very well generally.

Q. Better than they used to?--A. Oh, yes; I think they get along now a good deal better than they used to. I think the people in the country,

the farmers, know better how to go to work and how to live, and at the end
of the year now they have got something. There is very few of them now
that hasn't got something at the end of the year.

Q. Do they save it?—A. Yes, sir.

Q. What do they do with it?—A. Well, some of them that has enough
to do it with gets them little places. They have got a good many places now
in Virginia—the colored folks. But some of them undertook to buy places,
and they have lost them because the crops have failed; they have had bad
crops sometimes.

Q. What did you do before you worked at the tobacco business?—A. The
first work that I did after emancipation was for the man that I belonged to.
I staid with him about a year. Then I came to Lynchburg, and tended a garden
for a gentleman that now lives in Danville. I worked in Lynchburg at that
about a year. I was going on to about seventeen years of age then, and he
gave me $5 a month and board. After that summer I went out on the Manassas
Railroad, and worked there from Mount Jackson to Harrisonburg. Then after
that I went to Lynchburg at Christmas, and I went down to —————— depot, and
worked there about nine months. Then I came back to Lynchburg, and went into the tobacco factory, and I worked there, off and on, about twelve years.
The tobacco factory commenced business shortly after the surrender, and it
was run up to about October; then the tobacco business was dull and there
could not be nothing done for three months or better, in the year, and I
would go out on the railroad to work and come back to the factory in the
spring. I done that to pay expenses, and in that time I saved up a good deal
of money.

Q. What did you do with that?—A. That was money that I kept bad company with and throwed away. I was making ten or twelve dollars a week and I
throwed that away along with it. After I got married I commenced saving up
some money, and as soon as I got a couple of hundred dollars ahead—of course
it took me some little time to save up $200 and keep my little expenses
going. When I got a couple of hundred dollars ahead I bought this lot that
I told you about. I bought it on payments of $6, $12, and $18, and I paid
for it and got the deed. I gave a deed of trust after I made the first payment and then after I made my last payment I got a deed of release. There
was a lot of white people that carried on a building association, and I got
into that as well as other people. I borrowed $250 out of that, and I stint
myself in the way of eating and clothes and everything of that sort to save
money. Of course I had a suit of clothes to go to church, but my working
clothes was pretty bad. I paid my $250 and I reckon nearly $50 interest, and
the man got me to sign some papers that was all wrong. That is where a man
that has got an education can take advantage of a man that hasn't. I got
along so well with that man that I thought it was all right, but it was not.
That building loan association not only robbed the poor men but it robbed
the rich men too. They got me to sign some papers, and they wanted to take
my place, and they would have taken it only that I got another man to pay
the $270. I paid that man up, and now I have got a house that cost me about
$800, and I suppose I have paid nearly $1,000 for that place, and I owe about
$150 on it now.

Q. But, as the result of it all, you have got your home?—A. Yes, sir.

Q. You are a little over thirty years of age?—A. Yes, sir; nearly
thirty-four.

Freedom Better Than Slavery With a Good Master.

Q. I suppose you have had a pretty hard time since the surrender. Do
you think you would have been better if you had staid a slave and let somebody else take care of you?—A. Well, I would not like to say that, because
I like to be honest in what I say, and of course a man that is free is better
off than a slave. I had a good master when I was a slave, as many others
perhaps did not. He had a number of old people on his place, and he would
give them a house or anything they wanted. I suppose he had about five hundred people altogether, and he had about fourteen or fifteen sons and daughters, and all these had slaves, and they was all considered to be good people. But other people was not like them. He didn't put none of the boys

out in the field to work until they were seventeen years old; he kept them doing light work around the yard. I was not old enough to be put to hard work, but even if I had been, my master would not have put me to it, because he was a good man. He would not allow the overseers to whip nary one of the slaves. He said he knew how to treat them right, and if he didn't punish them, he wouldn't allow anybody else to do it.

Q. Still, you think you are better off on the whole than you were in slavery?--A. Yes, sir.

Q. Is that the feeling of the colored people generally?--A. Well, yes, sir. Some of the colored people in the towns and in the country, too, aint smart; they don't work; they lay around and get a suit of clothes wherever they can--hardly that sometimes--but I don't call them people smart. They don't deserve anything. If I had been a slave I could not have done harder work than I have done since I have been free. The inspector says that I am the boss porter on this company's cars, and he knows them all.

Q. You have always contrived to keep at the head of your profession?--A. Yes, sir; that is the way I do. That is the way I done at the tobacco business. If I aint going to work honest, I aint going to hire myself to a man. I have got to work. I haven't got no education, and if anybody was to give me an office at $3,000 a year I could not fill it.

Q. Do you think that if you had education you would be better off?--A. Well, I don't know. I see some people that have tolerably fine educations and they are no better off than I am; in fact they are worse off than I am.

Q. Do you suppose that if they were like you in other respects they would be better off for having education?--A. Well, I suppose so. Of course I would have known better what I was signing for that man if I had an education. I thought he was doing honest with me, but he wasn't.

Q. You speak of having some good clothes to go to church; do you go to church right along?--A. Yes, sir; I never fail to go to church three times on Sunday.

Q. What church do you go to?--A. The First Baptist Church. If I did not go to church three times on Sunday I would feel that there was something that I hadn't done. I know very well that if it doesn't do me no good it will not do me no harm certainly.

Q. What is all this noise about that I notice at these stations as we pass along--this shouting and music and general excitement?--A. I think it is about the election. They have gained Virginia, you know, and it is natural, you know, on either side to give a little toss about it. If the opposite party gets a man of course there is just as much joy on that side.

Q. Which way has it gone here?--A. I think it is Democratic.

Q. There used to be a good deal of trouble here ten or fifteen years ago about politics, I believe?--A. Yes, sir; but the people now, they have come to have more sense as a general thing. You know the colored people is very ignorant people about Congress and all the business that may be passed there; they don't know it because they haven't sufficient knowledge to read and understand it. Some of them do know how to read about it now, but I don't know whether they understand it altogether or not. A heap of them reads that doesn't understand.

Q. Well, you don't have such disturbances here as you used to have, I suppose?--A. No, sir. This thing at Danville this last time was the first 'sturbance for a long time. Elections is always very quiet now. I run on the cars, you know, and I don't have much chance to get out and stop along the way, and I haven't had much chance to know about this election. Of course there is always plenty of papers in the cars, but, then, I can't read them with much understanding to myself, so I don't know much about such things since I have been on the cars. I don't stay long enough in any one place to find out much about it.

Q. The point I want to get at is whether you have any trouble of late about elections such as you used to have some years ago?--A. No, sir; we do not.

Q. Everybody votes as he pleases now, and that is the end of it, I suppose?--A. Yes; the generality of them votes. Some don't vote; they don't care which way the election goes. I believe in a man voting like he wants to vote, but it is well enough for the voters to understand how they want to vote. A great many voters don't understand how they want to vote. A man makes a speech on the stump and they work by him; they go by what he says; they don't really go by themselves; they go by that man on the stump; they just vote because they have got that privilege, but they don't know what they are voting for. One of those stump speakers says to the voter, "This is the right one," and then that voter will go and vote that way; otherwise perhaps he will vote on the other side. If the colored people ever get enlightened there won't be so much trouble about elections, because they will understand. There is one-third of the colored people at least that don't understand what they are voting for. It makes no difference who comes out, if their leader says, "That is the right man," and a man comes and makes a stump speech to them they guide that way; they don't know themselves whether they are going right or wrong.

Q. So you think they had better go to school in order to get enlightened?--A. Yes; I think that would be better.

Q. You run on this route all the way to New Orleans, I understand?--A. Yes, sir.

The Colored People Generally Doing Well.

Q. Of course you see a good many colored people along the way?--A. Oh, yes.

Q. You remember pretty well, I suppose, the condition of the colored people ten or fifteen years ago; are they improving or getting worse, in your opinion?--A. From what I can see in passing along on the railroads, I think the people are getting on pretty well. I was passing along through Georgia last year and I recollect there was a big camp-meeting at a place called La Grange. There was about two thousand people there, I think, and it seems to me they had a good time; they seemed to be getting along well. There was one gentleman on the cars, a passenger, who lived at Montgomery, Ala., and he says to me, "Porter, you see all this cotton here?" I says, "Yes." "Well," says he, "all this is the colored people's cotton; they rent the farms from the white people and most every man's farm clears $800 this year." Now that man lives in Alabama and he knows. He said they made from $700 to $800 clear of all expenses.

Q. He was speaking, I suppose, of what was made by the farmer and his family working together?--A. Yes, sir; these people get groceries and things at the stores through the year, and at the end of the year after they settle up, if they have got much clear I think they have done very well indeed.

Q. What have you observed as to the condition of the colored people in Louisiana?--A. As to Louisiana I can't say very much, because I go right through the swampy part of the country, where there is not much farming, but I notice that the colored people at New Orleans seem to get along very well. The "travelers," wagoners, and draymen there get more pay than anybody else that I know of. They get from $15 to $18 a week, and the fellows that work along the wharves makes sometimes from $18 to $20 a week in the spring and fall. But in the part of the State that I go through on the cars there's not much farming; it seems to be all swamp.

Q. How is it with the colored people in Alabama?--A. They seem to be doing very well in Alabama. I have seen colored men that farmed down there come to Lynchburg, and they had more money than anybody that farmed about Lynchburg. I remember one that had his mother there at Lynchburg and he had some $800 or $1,000. He was sold down in Alabama in slavery time and he lives there now. I know of another man in Montgomery, Ala., that makes money. He was sold down there in slavery time and he stays there yet. But in Virginia the colored people seem to get on very well. I am sorry about that little 'sturbance at Danville, but that could have been done without, and that is the only 'sturbance in Virginia for some time past. This is a rich part of Virginia along here and the people get along very well.

Q. What part of Virginia is this?--A. This is Southwest Virginia.

Q. About how far are we from Bristol, Tenn.?--A. We are about 60 miles from Bristol, now.

Q. Do you think of anything else you can state as to the condition of the colored folks?--A. No, sir; I don't think of anything else just now.

Q. What are the young colored men doing, generally?--A. Some of them is at work, some teaching school, some turns out to be ministers, some mail agents, and some in the Departments at Washington.

Q. Do many of them work on the farms or plantations?--A. Yes, sir; there is a lot of colored people working on plantations around Lynchburg.

Q. Are they generally of steady habits? Do they save their money generally?--A. Some of them is very saving, and again there is others that waste what they makes.

Q. How is it about the young women?--A. Well, they don't do very well in the town; in the country they are much better. They like to dress in the town. Some of them goes to school, some takes in Washington, and some goes to service.

Wages and Morals of Young Colored Women.

Q. What wages can they get in service?--A. Some of them in Lynchburg gets $8 a month; some $6, some $5, and some about $4. When they work by the day they get 50 cents a day; most all of them are with some family in town.

Q. Are the young colored women generally inclined to work?--A. Yes. Pretty much all of them works at service in private families. Them that doesn't, their mothers take in washing and they help them to wash. Then, some of them work in the tobacco factories.

Q. Do the young folks marry and settle down, generally?--A. A great many gets married, but a great many lives single, too. Some of them "breaks the cane down" (as the old man said), and everybody is down on them for a long time. A girl like that doesn't get any respectable people to pay any attention to her, so she often goes where she can be paid attention to. Some of them recover from that step after awhile and get married. I blame the colored people themselves for a heap of their girls turning out badly. A man must try to raise his child like he expects for her to live. If I had a daughter and I didn't think a man was goin' to pay genteel respect to her, I would not let her go to church with him or loll round the fence and talk. If you suffer your daughter to go to church with every man that has got on a stiff collar, and every time she goes to church, if she has to go and come by a round-about way, and then stand out round the corners and round the gate, that is not genteel at all. I believe in lettin' girls and boys have privileges in a respectable way, and if you start children right, they'll go ahead right, as a general thing, though sometimes, of course, one will go off anyhow. But its too late to teach children after they have grown up. That's the way with the colored people. They think so much of their child that they hate to keep him "crank," as they call it, and the first thing they know he's gone. Now, I have never been accused of anything in my life--never had any trouble. The firm I worked with gave me a recommendation for this place, and then I got a pass to go down to New Orleans. It requires an honest man in a place like this, because many and many a time I pick up a pocket-book or some other valuable thing, and if there is no owner for it, I turn it in to the office. I haven't lost a week since I've been working for this company. I lost very little time during the twelve years I worked at the tobacco business.

Q. I infer from what you say that if a colored man sets out to work in this part of the country he can get along and make a comfortable living for himself and his family?--A. Oh, yes.

Q. Well, people have to work for a living, wherever they are. A man has to do that up North, and I believe that most of them work harder there than you do down here.--A. Yes, sir; I reckon so. I have got a brother in Jersey City. He waits on a gentleman up there, and that gentleman is mighty good to my brother. He gives him $50 a month and the privilege of selling the manure, and then he gives him the privilege of riding white people out in his conveyance (to give the horses exercise), and they pay him the same as they would any other hackman. So my brother, I suppose, is making nearly $80 a month. He has been with that gentleman nearly eight years now.

Q. Do you think the colored people generally are pretty well contented? --A. Oh, yes; pretty well contented, and they get along very well, the most of them--them that tries to get along, gets along very well.

Q. I suppose you have about as good a chance as anybody to see how they are getting along all through this part of the country. You see about as many colored folks as any one, and you keep your eyes open, I judge.--A.

Yes, sir; somtimes I ask them at different places how they are gettin'
along, and they generally seem to be doin' pretty well. Down in Georgia
there was two colored men hung, and I was talkin' to a colored man about it,
and he said, "Those two colored men done wrong and it's right that they
should be hung." So I said no more. Them that belongs in a State, that's
their home, and I believe that if I was to go down into Georgia and get into
a fuss with one of the white people there, the colored men would beat me.
Down at Opelika when they had a 'sturbance there and the governor of Alabama
had to send troops, I asked one colored man, "What's the matter, you are so
bad down here?" and he says, "This is my home, and we are gettin' along here
as well as you are in your own home." He didn't want me to talk anything
against the folks down there, so I never said any more. If they have a
little fuss they don't want anybody else to interfere.

BIRMINGHAM, ALA., *November* 16, 1883.

Rev. ISAIAH H. WELSH (colored) sworn and examined.

By the CHAIRMAN:

Question. You are a clergyman of what denomination?—Answer. I am a
clergyman of the African Methodist Episcopal Church, the first colored independent organization in this country.

Q. You are a settled pastor over a church of that denomination in this
city?—A. I am.

Q. How long is it since your church was organized in this city?—A.
It has been nearly fifteen years.

Q. How long have you been pastor of it?—A. Seven months.

Q. From what point did you come here?—A. Selma, Ala.

Religion Among the Negroes.

Q. How large is your church in numbers?—A. We have a membership of
over three hundred. The congregation is nearly five hundred or six hundred.

Q. Are there other colored congregations in this city?—A. Yes, sir.

Q. How many?—A. There are five in all, but some of them are very
small.

Q. What is their aggregate attendance, do you think?—A. I think the
average is about two hundred and fifty.

Q. Are there six in all, including yours?—A. Yes, sir.

Q. How many white churches are there here?—A. Nearly every denomination of whites is represented here by a church organization.

Q. Is there a Catholic church here?—A. Yes, sir.

Q. White and colored both?—A. White only.

Q. Does the Catholic Church organize the races separately or together?
—A. Sometimes they are allowed to worship together, I believe. Here, I
understand the priest has extended a very cordial invitation to colored
Catholics to unite with the whites in worship; but in larger cities, such as
Washington City, they are organized separately.

Q. The tendency of both races is to organize separately where they exist in sufficient numbers, is it not?—A. Yes, sir.

Q. Is it not generally the preference of both races to do that?—A.
It appears to be so.

Q. You find it so on the part of the colored people, do you not?—A.
Yes, sir; there is a strong tendency to be separate.

Q. In school and in church and in social gatherings?—A. Yes, sir.

The Color Line.

Q. There is a social line of demarkation distinctly drawn between the
races in accordance with the wishes of both races?—A. Yes, sir.

Q. That does not lead to any ill feeling between the races, I suppose,
because it is a thing that each desires for itself; a separation that is

meant for their mutual pleasure and their mutual good?--A. Yes, sir; we
think it is better not to thrust ourselves upon the other race, and to
avoid race-clashing as much as possible; we prefer that way both in worship
and in social gatherings.

Q. Is that feeling increasing or lessening among your people?--A.
Well, I think it is increasing slowly.

Q. Along with that, is good nature preserved, or is there a tendency
toward acrimony and hostility of feeling between the races?--A. Good nature
and good feeling seem to be cherished quite generally.

Q. And you think that is the way to preserve good feeling; to keep
the races separate?--A. Yes, sir; I think so.

Q. How long have you been a clergyman?--A. Thirteen years.

Condition and Prospects of the Colored People.

Q. I wish you would state to the committee, in your own way, such
things as you would like to say about your own race and the white race in
this part of the country--the relations that exist between them, the condition of both races here, past, present, and prospective, how you feel about
the future of your people, and how the colored people themselves, generally,
and also the white people, feel about it.--A. Well, in the past our people
have been placed under very discouraging circumstances, and most of the
trouble that has arisen can be attributed, I presume, to the manner in which
they have been treated on the farms. Soon after emancipation a great many
of the colored people were forced to leave the farms and flock to the cities.
That, of course, compelled a great many of them to herd together in the
cities, and sometimes large to accommodate one good-sized family. This
herding together has had a very injurious effect upon the health of the people; but a great many of them were disposed to remain in the city for want
of protection elsewhere, thinking that they could be better protected in the
city than in the country. That was largely the case some time ago, when
there was a great deal of bitter feeling between the races, which resulted
in the death of a goodly number of our people. Then there was a class of
men that came down to this country some years back, and gave us very bad
advice and instruction. That instruction was of a political nature, and its
tendency was to produce unpleasant feeling between the races. Our people
were instructed and led by men who really did not feel very much interested
in us, and when we were exposed to danger and death they, to a very great
extent, deserted us in the time of our greatest need.

Q. Who were those men? I do not ask for names, but merely for an indication of the class to whom you refer.--A. Well, some were running for
Congress, and some were striving for the legislature and for various elec-
tive offices.

Q. They were candidates for political positions?--A. Yes, sir.

The Exodus and its Causes.[2]

Q. About what time do you refer to in that statement?--A. Along about
1870, 1871, 1872, and 1873. During the period of political excitement most
of the people who were employed on farms were induced by these men to leave
their work and engage in politics--stumping, and that sort of thing--with
the promise of pay. Of course, that business had a tendency to unsettle the
laboring class of people, and to enrage the land holders against them, and
in many instances, under the contract system, of which I have some knowledge,
especially in South Carolina and Virginia, from my acquaintance with the
Freedmen's Bureau, the land owners failed to keep their contracts, and that
had a discouraging effect upon the laborers, and that fact accounts to a
great extent for the exodus, of which you have probably heard a good deal--
more, perhaps, than I am able to tell you. The colored people felt compelled
to seek new homes where they could have some certainty of getting what they
worked for. However, the complexion of things has changed very much since
that time, and has improved very much, and while we still have some matters
to lament, there are many things of which we feel proud.

Colored People Excluded From Most Trades.

With regard to our race, generally, I can say that it is making some advancement in many respects, and would make more if the trades were open to our young men. The entrances to the different trades seem, however, to be closed against them to a very great extent. There seems to be a disposition on the part of some laborers in some localities to shut our people out. While some colored parents, fathers especially, are anxious to have their sons learn trades, believing that to be the best means by which they can provide for their future usefulness, there are very few trades outside of the barber's occupation of which our young men have a chance to acquire a knowledge, and therefore they are mostly engaged about here in mining and doing other subordinate work; very few of them are learning trades. There are some labor organizations here which, while they have no definite rules forbidding colored men to enter, yet do practically exclude them. Of course, all this is very discouraging, not only to the young people, but to parents.

Industrial Schools Needed.

If we had industrial schools established among us where these different trades could be learned, it would be very much better, and I think it would have an excellent effect upon our colored people especially.

I am satisfied that if such schools were established and maintained here they would have a very good influence generally, but of course I am unable to say how they should be supported. I presume, however, that they might be maintained the same as any other schools, but I think they would succeed very much better if they were taken under the fostering care of the General Government. The time of study would be lengthened and were there agents of the Government to look after that matter particularly, I think the schools would succeed remarkably well with all classes of people here. Such schools would not only benefit the colored people, but they would also greatly benefit the laboring class of whites.

The School Term Too Short.

We long to see the day when the school terms will be lengthened. They are too short now for the children to make much progress. A child in some instances spends three months in school and nine months out of school, so that when he is in school you may say he is always on review, and is never making any progress. By the time he gets started in the study the school is compelled to close from want of means or some other unavoidable circumstance, and while it is closed the pupils lose as much as they have gained during the short school term. Of course this state of things has a very injurious effect upon both races, especially the laboring classes. People in easy circumstances are able to establish private schools or to patronize such schools where they are already established, and in that way to overcome these difficulties under which the poorer people labor.

Abolish the Liquor Traffic.

So far as intemperance among our people is concerned, of course there is a good deal of it, and we are hoping that there will be an abolishment of the liquor traffic in this country. There seems to be a disposition on the part of the laboring men, especially men who are not able to afford it, to spend their leisure time and their money in drink; this I notice among both races. As Mayor Lane has well stated, it is not confined to one race. I don't know whether the Government could possibly stop that or not; they might possibly abolish the liquor traffic, but I don't believe they feel very strongly inclined to do that; however, it would be a very good thing if it could be done; for, of course, the less drink there is among all classes, but especially the poor, the more means they will have to live comfortably and to educate their children. Very often they will spend enough at one time to furnish their children with books for the whole season in school.

Lack of Thrift.

That class of people have a very limited idea of economy, they are not economical. Of course our people in the past never had to think about economy, they had some one else to think for them and take care of them, but now they have been thrown out upon their own resources and have to do their own thinking; and of course, everything is new to them and they perhaps cannot give as much attention to this matter of economy as they should; still, some of them are doing remarkably well in that regard, some are saving money and living very comfortably and buying homes. There is nothing that tends to unsettle the people more than poverty. Wherever a man has a home you generally find that man temperate and reliable in every respect. There is a class of our people that are anxious to buy homes and settle down, and were the inducements offered to them by the land-holders to purchase lands stronger, I think they would be more ready to do it. The land-holders here can do a great deal to induce the poorer classes to purchase land and to make homes. When our people get homes they will feel that they have an interest in the soil, and it will stimulate them to be more industrious and saving, and they would be better able to support and educate their families. If the body of the people were situated in that way, then, even if the State was not able to support the schools for a sufficiently long term each year, the parents would have sufficient means saved to enable them to employ teachers. In certain districts they do that now. Where there are several families located close together they sometimes unite and employ a teacher during the summer months to instruct their children, and those private schools are very often continued until the public schools reopen. But, of course, a great many of our people are not able to do this.

Q. Are the colored people able to do it to any extent?—A. Only a very few of them.

Private Colored Schools.

Q. How many colored children in this city attend private schools?—A. I presume about thirty-five or forty. There are two private schools. I visited one and found about fifteen children there, and I was reliably informed that in the other colored private school there are about the same number. But the colored people are unable generally to send their children to private schools because of the tax, and in many instances the tax upon the parents for sending their children to the public schools has proved rather a barrier to their attendance. I gleaned from Mayor Lane's statement this morning what I did not know before in regard to the admission of children to the public schools whose parents are not able to pay. I never knew that that was the rule. The general impression in my church is that unless the parent pays for the child it is not allowed to attend school. I am not certain, but I think the principal of our school has left that impression upon the minds of the parents.

Q. Well, that is one of the things we came down here for, to correct that impression.—A. I am pleased to know it. I should have been pleased to have been able to state to my own people what Mayor Lane stated here this morning on that subject.

Q. Well, you can do it now, can't you?—A. If I am authorized by Mayor Lane I will do so with pleasure.

The MAYOR. Of course that is the case. Where the parents are not able to pay, the children will be admitted free of charge.

The CHAIRMAN. Is that the general rule throughout the State?

The MAYOR. No; I speak only of Birmingham.

The WITNESS. The mayor's announcement will have a very good effect hereafter upon the attendance at the public schools. Quite a number of the children have been kept away, especially among members of my church. I have never had to talk with the mayor upon this subject, but I spoke to one member of the school board, from whom I gained very little information, so that I was unable to correct the impression which generally prevails among our people; but in the future I shall take pleasure in doing so. Now, if the school terms could be lengthened it would have a very salutary effect upon the people, and the children would make very much better progress than they possibly can otherwise.

Federal Aid to the Schools.

There is a disposition to ask the Government to appropriate sufficient
money to continue the schools eight or nine months a year, and if that were
done I think they would be very successful.

Q. When you say "the Government" you mean the General Government?--A.
Yes, sir.

Q. You say you find a desire among your people that such an appropriation should be made?--A. Yes, sir; a very strong desire. Inasmuch as the
Freedman's Bank was a failure, and they lost a good deal of money that they
had saved up for the education of their children, some of them are of opinion that it would be well for the Government to take some steps to reimburse
them in some way. [3]

Q. I did not quite understand what you said in regard to the distribution or the expenditure of such a fund, if it were appropriated?--A. Well,
some think that it would be best for the Government if it makes the appropriation to have its own agents to make the distribution, while others are under
the impression that it would be best to turn the money over to the State and
let it make the distribution. But that is a matter upon which the people
have not really decided; they are not particular as to the way, so long as
the thing is done.

Q. From the way in which the State officers administer the State educational fund, do you think that if an appropriation were made by the General Government to aid the cause of education down here, there would be any
difficulty in having it fairly divided between the races?--A. Well, I presume it might be fairly divided; I could not say. I know that some of the
officers of this State are very reliable and very honest, and I believe they
would do their duty in that regard. The country districts, however, I could
not say much about; I am not acquainted with the school officers there or
their character. But the general State officers I should believe would do
their whole duty; especially Mr. Armstrong, the superintendent; I believe he
would do his whole duty in that regard.

Q. And you think if difficulties arose, it would be in the counties and
towns?--A. Yes, sir. From what I can learn, I believe there would be no
difficulty here in our city. Elsewhere there might be some difficulty. Some
people have such an apprehension.

Q. I understood Mr. Armstrong, the State superintendent, to say that in
case of any complaint or of any just cause of complaint existing, there was a
method provided in the law for bringing the abuse to his attention. I did
not understand exactly what power he had to correct any abuse, but I understood him to say that it could be brought to his attention and publicly exposed, so that the power of public opinion could be brought to bear for its
correction.

Mr. PUGH. He has the power of peremptory removal, but he has never exercised it, because there has never been any occasion. [4]

A Colored School Superintendent Wanted.

The WITNESS. In our address, which we presented yesterday, we called
his attention to that question, and asked that there should be a State superintendent selected from our race to superintend the education of our people, and also that there should be district superintendents to attend to the
work in the districts.

By the CHAIRMAN:

Q. You want the rule of unmixed schools carried out to the fullest extent, then?--A. Yes, sir. We do not think that the present superintendent
can do all the work; we don't think that he can give that attention to the
education of our children that its importance demands, and, of course, if we
had a superintendent of our own race in each of these districts it would have
an inspiring effect on the teachers. We need Teachers' Institutes for our
teachers. In many instances the teachers are not at all up to the times;
they are considerably behind; some of them don't study very much, and in fact
are not encouraged to study. Now, in such cases a district superintendent of
our own race would look after them and spur them on, and they would probably

do their work much better than they do now, and introduce progressive modes
and methods of teaching.

Q.   Are there any colored superintendents of schools in any of the
counties of the State, that you know of?--A.   There are none that I know of.
I don't think that there are any.

Q.   The logic runs down, but it does not run up?--A.   No, sir; it
doesn't run up very far.   We are trying, if possible, to give it some encouragement in an upward direction.

Q.   The superintendents are appointed?--A.   Yes, sir.

Q.   But your State superintendent at the head of the matter is, you say,
a man in whom all have confidence?--A.   Yes, sir; a very excellent man.

Q.   Don't you think that by application to him you could have superintendents of your own race appointed in the counties where your people are
numerous?--A.   I think so.   Well, we made a formal application of that
character yesterday.

Q.   In what county?--A.   It was not confined to any particular county.

Q.   You applied for district superintendents?--A.   Yes, sir; one for
each Congressional district, and one for the State.

Q.   I understood the State superintendent to say that there was a
superintendent appointed for each county.--A.   Not from our race.

Q.   But you say you asked for a superintendent of your own race, not for
each county, but for each Congressional district?--A.   Yes, sir.

Q.   Has he power to make such an appointment as that?--A.   We don't know
that he has, but we thought that he might recommend it to the legislature,
and that if it was done it would greatly improve educational matters among
our people.

Q.   Well, it would seem to be but fair that you should have something
to say about the supervision, since you have to support the schools.--A.   The
visit of a superintendent or a member of the school board has a very good
effect, you know, on both teacher and pupils.   I know that from my own experience as a teacher.   It certainly inspires the teacher.   And then the
superintendent always comes with new and improved methods and posts the
teacher in anything that he is deficient in.

Q.   Is there any other matter that you wish to bring to our attention?

A.   There is nothing else that I think of at present.   Having lost considerable rest, I am not prepared, mentally, as well as I might be, under
other circumstances, to make a statement.

Good Feeling Between the Races.

I might add, however, that there is a growing feeling between the races.
I had the pleasure of assuring the governor of that yesterday, and calling
his attention to that one blessing, that there is a good feeling subsisting
between the two races.

Q.   And you say that that feeling is increasing?--A.   Yes, sir; it is
really encouraging.

Q.   You think, I suppose, that the white race will get so by and by,
that they will vote the Republican ticket?--A.   Well, the principles without
the name.

The Negro Vote Divided.

By Mr. PUGH:

Q.   Don't you think the colored people are just as likely to vote the
Democratic ticket as the whites are to vote the Republican ticket?--A.   Well,
they might vote that ticket a little and some will vote it straight out.
They are beginning to think for themselves politically.   They are a little
divided since the decision on the civil rights bill, and I am afraid they
will be more divided.   It is hard to determine the political sentiment among
our people now; a very difficult matter.[5]

By the CHAIRMAN:

Q.   I suppose the same is true of the white people?--A.   Yes, sir; it is
true of both races now.

Q.   I thought so yesterday from what we heard here about the tariff.

A.   Yes, sir; they are very much divided on the tariff.

By Mr. PUGH:

Q. Among the manufacturers there is no division on that subject, is there?--A. No, sir; there is a strong oneness among them.

By the CHAIRMAN:

Q. Then you think the time is coming when the white folks here will be permitted to vote as they please? [Laughter.]--A. I think so; and the colored folks, too. I think the time is coming when they will select the best men for public positions, regardless of politics.

Q. In that case the black folks will help them, won't they?--A. Yes, sir; to a very great extent.

Q. I suppose you fancy that when they adopt that stand-point, the candidates will have to be taken from the colored ranks sometimes?--A. Well, no, sir; except where they are qualified.

By Mr. PUGH:

Q. You say that the Democrats have elected State officers who have your confidence and the confidence of the colored people?--A. I spoke particularly of Mr. Armstrong.

Q. Is there any other State officer in whom you have not confidence; and, if so, have you any reason for having no confidence in him?--A. None whatever. I spoke only of Mr. Armstrong, because I had no occasion to allude to the others. I singled out Mr. Armstrong because I am personally acquainted with him, and have learned considerable about him. But the matter of politics will take care of itself in the South.

The CHAIRMAN: That is the way it should be, and I should rejoice as much as anybody to see the time when the colored people will divide as other people do upon political questions.

The WITNESS. We intend to do that in the future--to think as we please and vote as we please--if the vote is only counted as it is cast; but those matters will all be remedied after awhile, I presume.

The CHAIRMAN. I suppose when the people down here get better educated they can count better. [Laughter.]

The WITNESS. Yes, sir. In some instances others have been doing the counting for them.

The CHAIRMAN. The "others" are the ones that I was thinking of in making that remark.

Mr. PUGH. Both sides have counted in that way, have they not?

The WITNESS. Oh, yes, sir; we have got men on both sides who possess a remarkable faculty for counting. [Laughter.] There is very little difference I find; they all do good counting.

The CHAIRMAN. And make a record accordingly.

The WITNESS. Yes, sir.

Mr. PUGH. Education will obviate the necessity of resorting to false counting to avoid other evils, will it not?

The WITNESS. Yes, sir. I believe that education will remedy that matter.

Mr. PUGH. Education will remedy the evils by keeping bad men out of office.

The WITNESS. That is so; we want better men.

BIRMINGHAM, ALA., *November* 16, 1883.

JAMES A. SCOTT (colored) sworn and examined.

By the CHAIRMAN:

Question. Where do you live?--Answer. In Birmingham, Ala.

Q. How long have you resided here?--A. About nineteen months.

Q. Where did you come from to Birmingham?--A. I came from Montgomery.

Q. You understand the general scope of my inquiry, now go on and make any statement that you desire to make in regard to the condition of your own race here, or in regard to their relation with the white race.

Why The Colored People Crowd Into The Towns.

A. Well, I can say that the advancement and progress of the colored

people has been remarkable. The fact that they have rushed into the towns
in the South has been caused by a desire which took possession of them just
after the surrender and during the days of reconstruction, to obtain protection. The colored people and the poor white people have been two distinct
classes, and they have been antagonistic to each other ever since they have
been together in this country, and that natural antagonism just after the
war was intensified, and all the trouble and disorder that we had in the
South was the result, I believe, of the antagonism and bad feeling which
existed between those two classes. During the days of slavery a colored man
would refer to a poor white man as poor white trash, and there was a natural
antipathy between them, and there always has been bad feeling. The better
class of the white people of the South have never indorsed the lawlessness
that did exist here, and which was the cause of the colored men rushing into
the cities. Those colored men came to the cities and towns, and many of them
who had been industrious before, contracted habits of idleness, and just got
to taking the world as they could find it. That was one reason why a great
many of them left the farms in the South. This is an idea that occurred to
me some years ago, and while I was the editor of a paper in Montgomery I
frequently referred to it, and endeavored to show the people that all of that
bad feeling between the black man and the white man was the result of the
antagonism between these two classes that I have mentioned.

Q. Are you an editor?--A. I was formerly editor of a paper in Montgomery.

Q. What is your business now?--A. I am a practicing lawyer here. I
have said this much by way of preface to the general statement that I desire
to make.

Education--Poor Schools.

The educational facilities for the colored people are not so good now
as they were some years ago--well, they may be just as good, but I fear our
friends do not take that interest in the schools that they ought to take.
I know a county where the superintendent never visits the schools from the
time they open until they close. The schools are open four, five, or six
months. It is a fact that in some of the counties, for instance in Madison--
they have a most excellent superintendent, who takes a great interest in the
schools; but you go into other counties in the lower part of the State and
you will find the case quite different, and particularly is that the fact
with regard to Montgomery County, because I lived there five years and I know
the facts. I know that the schools would open and the superintendent would
never visit them, and he never did take that interest in them that he ought
to have taken.

Q. Montgomery is where Mr. Armstrong lives?--A. Yes, sir.

Q. Don't you think you ought to call his attention to those facts, then,
because he has power to remedy that evil?--A. I frequently called the attention of the superintendent of education to the fact, and at one time he issued
a circular letter to his county superintendents to visit the colored schools.

Q. Men who do not visit the schools are of course unfit to distribute
the school money, and when you make these facts known to Mr. Armstrong I am
confident that he will remove the delinquent superintendents. You have
confidence in Mr. Armstrong?--A. Yes, sir; I believe that Mr. Armstrong is
a conscientious gentleman who desires to see the educational interests of the
State advanced without regard to race or color, and I believe I voice the
sentiment of the colored people of the State when I say that they have the
fullest confidence in every State officer. Referring to Dr. Welch's testimony in regard to the request to the governor to appoint a colored State
superintendent, a mass-meeting of colored citizens was held and also a committee was appointed to visit the railroad commission and lay before them
certain complaints in regard to the treatment received by the colored people
from the various railroads of the State. That committee consisted of Dr.
Welch and myself and three other colored men. In the mean time we drew up an
address to the governor and set forth the fact of this lack of interest in
the work of education, and asked the governor to recommend to the next legislature the enactment of such a law as would secure to the colored people a
State superintendent of their own and an additional superintendent in each

district who would visit their schools and see that the proper methods of education were adopted. That was the object of that visit to the governor. We were received very cordially by the governor and the superintendent of education.

Q. Did the governor indicate any intention to accede to your request?
A. Yes, sir; the governor received the gentlemen cordially and gave them a warm welcome, and assured them that every fact they stated and every complaint they made should be duly considered by himself and by the gentlemen of the cabinet.

Discrimination Against Colored People On Railroads.

We also visited the railroad commission and made certain complaints against the railroads of Alabama. There has been a universal discrimination here in Alabama, and, indeed, all over the South, in the treatment of the colored people as to the cars they are permitted to ride in. The white people have always labored under the impression that whenever a colored man attempted to go into the ladies' car, he did it simply because it was a car for the white people. Now if the white people looked at it as we look at it, taking a common-sense view of it, they would see that that idea is erroneous and false. We go into those cars simply because there are better accommodations there, and because we secure better protection in the ladies' car, for the general sentiment of the white men certainly protects their ladies. But in the cars alloted to the colored people a white man comes in and smokes cigars, and chews tobacco, and curses and swears, and all that kind of thing, and the conductors on the various roads don't exercise their powers for the protection of the colored passengers. We made these complaints to the railroad commission, and the president of the commission told us that it was a matter within their jurisdiction, and that they would take cognizance of it, and would see that those complaints were looked into, and those evils remedied. We asked simply for equal accommodation and protection with the white people in riding on the railroads, and the 22d day of this month was set for a final hearing, and the superintendent of railroads was summoned to be there at the final hearing of the matter, and we have the assurance of the gentlemen of the commission that the subject will be acted upon promptly, and that the vexed question--for this is one of the most vexed questions that we have to deal with in the South--will be settled. We expect, therefore, that so far as Alabama is concerned, the people of both races will have equal accommodation. Our people do not care whether they are put in the front of the train or in the middle or at the tail end, so long as they have proper accommodations and proper protection.

Q. As I understand the case, you simply want the same accommodations that the white people have for the same money?--A. Yes, sir.

The Civil Rights Bill.

Q. And if your request is granted that will settle the civil rights bill, so far as Alabama is concerned?--A. Yes, sir; very satisfactorily to the colored people. By the way, I always regarded the civil rights bill as a humbug and a fraud. I never saw any colored men in the South that exercised the privileges that it conferred on them, and I always regarded it as a piece of political clap-trap.

Q. You have found out that all the protection you could get for your persons and your property was to be got from the State?--A. Yes, sir.

Q. Is there any further statement that you desire to make?--A. I believe not. Dr. Welsh expressed my sentiments on the labor question very elaborately, and I can adopt his statement as my own almost without change.

An Encouraging Prospect.

Q. What is your idea as to the outlook of the colored people of this State for the future?--A. I think the outlook for the colored people is good; I don't see any discouraging signs. They are educating their children, acquiring property, becoming independent in politics, and exercising their thinking powers. I think that is a considerable advance upon the state of things heretofore existing.

Q. What about your schools? Have you sufficient money to maintain them properly?--A. No, sir; that is the great trouble. I am not as well posted on the school question as I ought to be. I am not engaged in teaching and have not been for a long time, and therefore I am not very well posted, but my observation is that the school advantages are not so good as they ought to be. I believe that if they had money, and could have it judiciously applied, our schools could be made more efficient, but I can say here that so far as Birmingham is concerned, we have a very efficient school system here is very good, and a great improvement on that which formerly existed.

Q. Do you desire to make any further statement?--A. No, sir; nothing else occurs to my mind now.

BIRMINGHAM, ALA., *November* 16, 1883.

JESSE CLAXTON (colored) sworn and examined.

By Mr. PUGH:
Question. Do you live in Birmingham?--Answer. Yes, sir.
Q. What is your business?--A. I am a carpenter.
Q. How long have you been a carpenter?--A. Twenty-nine years.
Q. How did you learn your trade?--A. I was bound out in Richmond, Va., by my owner.
Q. Then you learned your trade when you were a slave?--A. Yes, sir.
Q. And you have been at work at it ever since?--A. Yes, sir.
Q. How long have you been living here?--A. About ten years.

A Colored Contractor.

Q. Are you a mechanic working by the day or a contractor?--A. I am a contractor now and have been for a good many years.
Q. Then you employ laborers yourself?--A. Yes, sir.
Q. What wages do you pay the carpenters you employ?--A. From $1.50 to $2.50 per day.
Q. How have you succeeded in your business as a contractor?--A. I have done mighty well. I have had some bad luck, though, but I can blame nobody for it only myself.
Q. Have you been able to save anything?--A. Yes, sir; I have saved a great deal and lost a great deal.
Q. How does your financial condition compare now with what it has been in the past?--A. Well, sir, it is very poor now, but it has been better.
Q. You have been better off than you are now?--A. Oh yes, sir; I have been worth a good deal of property in this place, but I have not got it now. I have some, though.
Q. How did you lose it?--A. My own misfortunes, bad luck, as other men sometimes have.
Q. What are the opportunities here for men in your trade to make money?
A. Good; very good.
Q. Are they better now than they have been?--A. Well, the opportunity has been better than it is right now, but it is good enough now.
Q. In what respect has it been better than it is now?--A. Well, when this place first started we got a little better wages for building a house than we can get now.
Q. There is more competition now?--A. Yes, sir; I worked on this very building (the court-house) making those frames. I was getting $3 a day then, working by the day.
Q. If there is anything further that you want to let us know about the condition of your trade or of the working people generally or anything that you think we can do to improve their condition you may go on and state it.--
A. I don't suppose that I could state anything to you that you could do for me, because the work is here, and if a man can do it the people will give it to him and pay him for it, and if he tries he can make money. There is some that makes a good deal of money here and some that has a chance to make it and don't make it.
Q. Well, that is the case everywhere, is it not?--A. Oh, yes; this is

really about the best part of Alabama for colored people. They can get more
work to do, and they can get better pay for it, I believe. The colored people
generally have no trouble with the better class of white people in this
country; in fact, everywhere that I have been the well raised, wealthy,
respectable white people are generally friends to the colored people, but it
is the class that is nearly on a level with them that oppresses them, if any
at all.

Insufficient School Privileges--Aid Wanted.

In some parts of the State the colored people has no chance to get their
children to school, somehow. In Saint Clair County, a part of the State that
I have been through this year, there is so few colored people living there
that the county superintendent says there is not enough colored children to
pay the teacher, and consequently they do not get any teaching at all. If
they lived in a township where there was a great many colored people then
they could get a school.

Q. Do you think of anything else that you would like to state?--A.
Nothing else that I know of that is worth stating here.

By the CHAIRMAN:

Q. Are there any trades unions among the colored people, or any institutions of that nature?--A. Not here. I belonged to one or two in
Georgia and Virginia.

Q. Were they of any benefit to you?--A. Yes, sir.

Q. I suppose you agree with the other witnesses here in regard to
desiring aid from the General Government for your schools?--A. Yes, sir. If
the colored people had the chance to get their children into shops to learn
trades, it would be a great help to them. The people here that owns the
works, I don't suppose they would have any objection to taking in colored
apprentices, but the class that works there won't work with them as a general
thing. Now, if there was some way to give colored people trades it would be
a great benefit.

BIRMINGHAM, ALA., *November* 16, 1883.

J. G. GOING (colored) sworn and examined.

By the CHAIRMAN:

Question. Do you live in Birmingham?--Answer. Yes, sir.

Q. What is your business?--A. I am a barber by profession.

Q. You understand the subject of our inquiry; go on and make any statement that you desire on the subject.

The Colored People Doing Well.

A. Well, taking everything into consideration, I think the colored
people through this section of the country are doing pretty well. They get
pretty fair wages for their work and there is a good lot of work here to do;
common labor, I think, gets from $1 to $1.25 a day, some more and some less,
and an economical man save something out of that. There is a good number of
colored men here that have acquired homes, and some have got very good
property. I don't know of any section of country in this State where they
are doing as well as they are here.

Q. How badly are they doing anywhere?--A. I don't know that they are
doing overly badly anywhere.

Q. How well are they doing outside of Birmingham?--A. I don't know
much about what is going on outside of this town, because I don't go much to
the country. In the place that I came from the colored men was doing pretty
well, some of them living on good farms and having nice property.

Q. Do you think the colored men are buying land more than they used to?

A. Yes, sir; a good deal more.

Q. You think they have generally the idea that they want to own land?

A. Yes, sir.

Q. There is a good deal of talk of their wasting their money, to what
extent does that go, according to your observation?

Colored Men Thriftless, Just Like White People.

A. Well, colored people are just like white people in that respect.
Plenty of white men work all their lives and don't accumulate anything, and
it is the same way with colored people, but it is more general with them, I
think, because they are not cultured as much as the white people. It is
the more ignorant class of people that are the sufferers in that respect,
both white and colored.

Education The Remedy.

Q. You think that if they knew more they would save more?--A. Oh, yes,
and they would be better citizens in every way. A great amount of the crime
that is committed by both whites and blacks is committed by the more or less
ignorant people.

Q. You all seem to be thoroughly impressed with the idea that it is
well and desirable to be better educated?--A. Yes, sir; that is the thing
that our people need mostly. What they need is a common-school system--not
colleges, but a common-school system that would meet the wants of the poorer
classes, white and black. The colored people, for instance, the poorer
classes, cannot send their children off to be educated, and it is the same
way with the white people; a few colored people and a few white people can,
but the poorer classes cannot.

Q. Have you thought anything about the establishment of the postal
savings bank system here, and whether it would be a good thing?--A. No, sir;
I have not thought much of that.

Q. Which do you think is the best way for a colored man who has no home
to invest his money, in a bank or in a piece of land?--A. Well, the safest
way, I think, is to put it in property.

Q. Then, you think that nobody needs to wait for the establishment of
savings banks in order to save money?--A. Oh, no; they do not need to wait;
but there are very few people who are laying up anything.

Q. Is there any difficulty in their getting land here to buy?--A. None
at all, if they have got the money to pay for it.

Q. Can they get trusted like other folks--can they buy a piece of land,
paying part down, give a mortgage, and get time to pay the balance?--A. Yes,
sir.

Q. Is there any place of which you have knowledge where it is better
to buy land than it is here?--A. Well, the tendency around this country is
for the value of land to go up.

Q. So that if a man buys a piece of land it may increase in value a
great deal faster than his money would increase at interest?--A. Yes, sir.

Q. Is there any other point that you wish to suggest?--A. No, sir;
that is all. About the most important thing for our people is to try to
have good common schools established.

Federal Aid Wanted.

Q. And you want national aid to help that along, do you?--A. Yes, sir.
Our school system here is very poor. The State does not appropriate much
money for the support of the schools, and the result is that there are very
few children in school. The parents are all poor and are not able to send
their children to school in many cases. I reckon there are one thousand
children in this town of school age that are not in school.

The CHAIRMAN. If you are going to elect Democrats to office in Alabama,
you must insist upon it that they shall give you good schools.

The WITNESS. It is always pretty easy to make that bargain, but the
sticking up to it is more trouble.

The CHAIRMAN. You do the voting before you get the schools.

The WITNESS. That is the trouble.

The CHAIRMAN. Well, insist upon it that your Representatives in
Washington shall vote for a national appropriation to aid your school system.

The WITNESS. Well, I suppose some of them do that.

BIRMINGHAM, ALA., *November* 16, 1883.

N. R. FIELDING (colored) sworn and examined.

By the CHAIRMAN.
Question. You live in Birmingham?--Answer. Yes, sir.
Q. What is your business?--. I am a bricklayer.
Q. Are you a good one?--A. Well, you know I might say so without
other people believing it. I pass for one, anyhow.
Q. Do you get plenty of work?--A. Yes, sir.

Another Colored Contractor

Q. Do you ever take contracts and employ others to help you?--A. Yes,
sir.
Q. How many men have you had in your employ at one time?--A. I have
had six or eight bricklayers, apart from laborers. Probably I have had
twenty-five men altogether employed, including laborers.
Q. Then you have yourself superintended the labor of twenty-five men
in your business?--A. Yes, sir.
Q. It is skilled work that you do?--A. Yes.
Q. You understand the general subject of our inquiry. If you have any
ideas that you think would be useful to the committee, just make your own
statement of them.--A. Well, I have not given the subject much thought. I
was just caught up and asked to meet this committee, and I did not know what
they wanted with me.
Q. Well, we want to know, in a general way, how you colored people, and
other laboring people, are getting along here, and how you think you are
getting along--whether you feel that your condition is improving or is getting
worse, and generally how you are situated in this part of the country.--A.
A question like that I will answer first in regard to myself, and then,
perhaps, I can branch out a little about other people. My circumstances are
very good. Since I have been in business I have made quite a success as a
bricklayer, while others that have been more advanced and better workmen than
I am, have not made as much as I have. There is a great many men, you know,
that will make a dollar to-day and spend a dollar, and there is others that
will make only fifty cents, but will save it. Wherever I made any money I
saved a part of it.
Q. Have you a family?--.A. Yes, sir; I have two children.
Q. You have got a home?--A. Yes, sir.
Q. Do you send your children to school?--A. My oldest girl is going
to school, but not in this county. She is going to school at Limestone.
Q. How old is she?--A. She is fourteen.
Q. How old is your other child?--A. He is going on two years of age.
Q. Is your house in this city?--A. Yes, sir.
Q. Do you own it?--A. Yes.
Q. Have you any objection to telling us what your place is worth?--A.
Well, I can get $2,500 cash for it, if I want to sell it.
Q. Is it in a good situation?--A. Yes, sir; I have got a good two-
story house of thirteen rooms.
Q. A brick house?--A. No, sir; it is a frame house.
Q. What did it cost you?--A. It cost me about $900, the way I built
it. I paid $250 for the lot, and now the same lot, with nothing on it, would
be worth $500.
Q. You have made that by saving and managing a little?--A. Yes, sir.
Q. Tell us now about the rest of the colored folks.

Colored Men Who Are Dependent and "Oppressed."

A. Well, the rest suffers themselves to be oppressed in some instances,
but in others they do not. What they earn in the week most of them go on
Saturday and spend it in rowdiness, and don't have anything left on Monday

morning. In old times, you know, we always used to have a living from our
master's smoke-house, and if the master did not have anything for us to eat
we waited until he got it for us, and a good many of the colored people are
of that opinion still--they wait for some one else to provide for them
without trying to provide for themselves. But there is others that do better,
and there is some others that would probably do better only that they are
somewhat oppressed in their labor.

Q. What do you mean by "oppressed:"?--A. Well, they are not permitted
to get the value of their labor.

Q. In what way does that come about?--A. Suppose I was a journeyman,
working for a contractor, he would give me $2.50 a day, and a white man
would come along, and if the contractor wanted another man and employed him
he might give him $3.50 or $4 a day.

Q. For doing the same work?--A. Yes, sir; and sometimes the white man
might not be as good a workman as I was. The highest wages a colored man
gets now is $2.50 a day, while the white men get $3 or $4 a day. They always
get 50 cents or $1 a day more than colored men, even though the colored man
be a better workman.

Q. How does that come to be so?--A. Well, we look at it that it is
all on account of color.

Q. They discount your color?--A. Yes, sir; it is not worth a great
deal to be black.

Q. There is no compound interest on that?--A. No, sir; not a bit.

Q. The main question, after all, is whether you are not improving under
all these difficulties; whether things are not getting better. We have had
a big war and lots of trouble all around, but now the question is whether we
are improving all over the country?--A. If we are getting along at all, it
must be better than it used to be, because it is impossible for us to be in
a worse condition than we were then. If there is any change at all it must
be to the better. All the condition wherein we are not better is this being
oppressed in our labor, in our work, and deprived of being advanced in skilled
labor as we might be. We have no opportunities to learn trades as the whites
have.

Q. Do you take any apprentices?--A. Yes, sir; but I do not have work
enough to keep them. I have had one.

Q. Do you think that the white man has the preference over the black
man as a skilled laborer?--A. Oh, yes; two to one in every respect, in any
kind of work from a saw-mill up.

Q. In what they call common labor, the lowest paid labor, which will
get most wages, the white or the colored?--A. If there is any difference
at all in that, the white man will get from 10 cents to 25 cents a day more
than the colored man. On the railroads they will pay a colored man 80 cents
or 90 cents a day and a white man $1 a day.

Q. Where the work is the same?--A. Yes, sir; the same thing. Take the
same tools and the same work, and the men working side by side.

Q. What reason do they give for that discrimination?--A. Some give the
reason that it takes more for the white man to live on than the colored man,
and that, consequently, they pay him higher wages, so that he may live better.
The colored man, they say, gets board for $2.50 a week, while the white man
has to pay $3.50, and they have to make up the difference in wages to make
the men even.

Q. Do you think that is so?--A. I have some doubt about it. I think
the board bill depends upon where the man boards and what he demands for his
subsistence.

Q. Have you thought of anything which the General Government ought to
do, or that you would like to have it do, for the improvement of your condition here?--A. I really don't know of anything that you could do for us.
I have never given much time to matters outside of what comes directly in
my business of bricklaying. I don't profess to know everything connected
with that, but I don't know whether the Government could improve that or not.
It seems to be a matter left entirely to the contractors.

Poor and Insufficient Schools.

Q. How are your schools here?--A. Well, I am somewhat opposed to the

school system. I don't know who to find fault for it directly, but the
poorer classes of colored people here are deprived of schools. The State
or the county makes a little appropriation to start a school, but, as some
people have already testified, we have very incompetent teachers, a good many
of them; and the poorer children, that are not able to go to school, they
are charged a "supplement," and they are not able to pay that, so they are
not able to go to school on account of the supplement fund. They are
charged 10 cents a week. Now, where a man has to work for $1 a day, and
has to pay from $5 to $10 month, and has five or six children to go to
school, he cannot afford to send them to school and pay 10 cents a week extra
for each of them; and if he is not able to pay that his children are not
allowed to go to school, and he is deprived of the benefit of the public
appropriation which the State makes for that purpose.

Mr. PUGH. You are mistaken about that I think.

The WITNESS. No, sir; I am not.

Mr. PUGH. Well, the mayor differs with you about it. He says that if
the parents are not able to pay, the children are received in the schools
at any rate.

The WITNESS. Well, they do not go, and they are refused admittance to
the schools, and that has been so within the last thirty or sixty days.

Mr. PUGH. The mayor says that if they say that they are unable to pay
they are admitted without pay.

The WITNESS. Well, I have always argued that they could not be deprived
of going to school, but the teachers have undertaken to collect money from
them, and if the parents don't pay they send the children home. I don't know
whether it is done by authority or not, but I know it is done.

The CHAIRMAN. There is nothing to pay the teachers but that fund, is
there?

The WITNESS. My idea is that if a school is being run in the name of
the public, the poor children ought to get the benefit of it even if it does
not run but one month. There is a heap of people that would send their
children if they could pay.

Q. Do you think of anything else that you desire to state?--A. No, sir;
nothing else.

_____

AUGUSTA, GA., *November* 23, 1883.

The Colored Farm Laborers and Farmers of Georgia.

R. R. WRIGHT (colored)sworn and examined.
        By the CHAIRMAN:

Question. You have heard the questions that have been asked other
witnesses here and the testimony they have given, so that you have a general
idea of the kind of information that we are seeking; now you may proceed to
make any statement you please on the subjects to which this investigation
relates.--Answer. Well, since I have been here this evening some thoughts
have occurred to me, suggested by what I have heard said in regard to the
labor question in this State, and I suppose the same may be said to be true
of the South generally. About 75 per cent of the Georgia farm-laborers are
colored, and 25 per cent. of those work for wages at about $8.33-1/3 per
month; between 35 and 40 per cent of them work as tenants, paying a portion
of what accrues from their labor as rental for the land, and probably between
10 and 15 percent own the land, on which they work. The colored people of
Georgia own something over seven acres of land to every colored male voter;
that land, however, is cut up into small farms of between fifty and one hundred acres each, and is, of course, confined in its ownership to a much less
number than the number of voters. Of the farm laborers, probably the most
impoverished and wretched are those that are farm tenants; they till the land
on shares, and in such cases generally the whole family, the mother, as well
as the children, work for wages, and at the end of the year they come out in
debt. This result I think is caused by the small wages they receive; but
partly, perhaps, also by the fact that they do not understand farming. Still
the colored people are accumulating some property. In this State they pay
taxes on something over $6,000,000.

A Saving People.

This last year they made gains to the amount of $111,285, but this does not so much show their prosperity as it does their arduous industry and stinting frugality. The colored people, I suppose, are the most saving people on earth under the circumstances. I have heard it said that the Irishman, I believe can live on what the New Englander throws away; that the Chinaman can live on what the Irishman throws away, and, I believe, that the colored man can live on what the Chinaman would throw away.

Q. And he is the most muscular of them all?--A. That may be true.

Q. It would follow that the others injure themselves by eating, would it not?--A. I don't know whether that would follow or not; it does not seem to be so; they seem to grow fatter while the colored man grows leaner.

Q. Still they are inferior to the colored man in the matter of physical strength, are they not?--A. I think that is true. It was proved by the reports to the Secretary of War a short time ago that the colored man, for all purposes of war and everything else, showed less sickness, less disability from disease or from hard work, or from soldierly duties generally than the white man. That statement is in the official reports, and I make it on that ground and from what I have heard; and it will be generally admitted, I suppose, that I may be called a representative negro.

Q. Have you any white blood in you?--A. No, sir; I have sixteen-sixteenths black blood in me. [Laughter.] When I say that, I may be called a representative negro; I do not mean, of course, in point of education, or in point of intelligence, but I mean racially.

Education--The Negroes Have Made More Progress Than The Whites.

Now, in regard to education, I think the colored people have given more attention to education and have made greater progress in it since the war than the white people have. That may seem a startling proposition, but it is certainly true. Let us take Georgia for example. In 1871 or 1870, when the schools in this State began, there were entered 49,000 white children and 6,000 colored. The white people, of course, had been educated up to the point where they saw the importance of educating their children; the colored people had not. To-day, however, in the schools of Georgia there are only about two white children to one colored. Now, taking into consideration the fact that there is considerable prejudice against the colored people, as has been evinced here to-night, this seems to me to be quite a remarkable showing, and it proves that the colored people are taking hold of education vigorously, and not only that, but also that the white people of the South are beginning to feel that it is right and wise to educate the colored people. I do not believe that the contrary sentiment to which expression has been given here is widely extended throughout this State, or throughout the South. I do not know much about the other portions of the country, but I know something about Georgia, and it is my opinion that the white people generally do not think it is wrong to educate the colored people. I believe that the white people generally understand that education is the very thing the colored people need most, and that the two races will get along better and have a better and more harmonious feeling between them the more they are both educated. That I believe is the general sentiment throughout this State now, and I think it is the same throughout the South generally. There are something over one million colored children in the South, and of that number eight hundred thousand are in the schools. That shows beyond question that they are taking hold of education in earnest.

The Race Question.

There is another question that has come up here to-day, in regard to the comparative superiority and inferiority of races. I do not know that I am capable of talking intelligently upon that subject, but I will venture to say that I think this idea of the inferiority of any race is a mistake. I think that the differences between races are simply matters of education, training, surroundings. Some people think that the white man is inherently superior to the black man. That may be so, but let us look at facts. I believe that very nearly three-fourths of this globe is owned and inhabited

by colored people. I may be a little wrong in stating the proportion, but
I do not think I am very far wrong. Then it is generally admitted that
religion has been a great means of human development and progress, and I
think that about all the great religions which have blest this world have
come from the colored races—all. In other words, what is called the Aryan
race has not originated a single great religion. I believe, too, that our
methods of alphabetic writing all came from the colored race, and I think
the majority of the sciences in their origin have come from the colored
races. I think also that the term Caucasian, if it is taken historically,
is somewhat misleading. The Caucasian race includes the Aryan, the Semitic,
and the Hamitic race, the race to which I claim to belong. Hence, I say,
the expression Caucasian race is misleading. The leading type of the Hamitic
race is the Egyptian. Now I take the testimony of those people who know,
and who, I feel are capable of instructing me on this point, and I find them
saying that the Egyptians were actually woolly-haired negroes. In Humboldt's
Cosmos (vol. 2, p. 531) you will find that testimony, and Humboldt, I presume,
is pretty good authority. The same thing is stated in Herodotus, and in a
number of other authors with whom you gentlemen are doubtless familiar. Now,
if that is true, the idea that this negro race is inherently inferior, seems
to me to be at least a little limping. Again, it was said here to-day that
the white race had never been enslaved or ruled over—by which I understood
the gentlemen to mean that the Aryan race or the Teutonic race had never
been enslaved by a colored race. If what I have already said on this question of race has any foundation, that is evidently a mistake. The Israelites,
I suppose, must be included in the white race, but we all know that Israel
was conquered by Egypt, and hence it follows, it seems to me, that there *have*
been instances in which the white race has been dominated and held in slavery
by a black race.[6]
    Q. How long were the Israelites in Egypt?—A. About four hundred years,
I think.
    Q. How long is it since America was discovered by Columbus?—A. A
little short of four hundred years, and slavery here did not begin as early
as that, and it has already disappeared. Therefore the negro in America has
not been in slavery quite so long as that white race was in slavery in Egypt.
Again, Nimrod, who was a descendant of Ham, and who, I think, will be admitted
to have been an ancestor of the negro race—this same Nimrod founded Nineveh
and founded some other places between the Tigris and the Euphrates. From
Nineveh the race came toward the west, over into the islands of the sea,
over into Greece, and I think it is generally conceded that from that region
we get a great deal of this very civilization which we talk so much about and
boast of as a Caucasian or white civilization. If I have any correct idea
of what history teaches on that subject, almost the first civilization of
which we have record was in the Nile Valley, coming up from Ethiopia and was
a negro civilization. The next civilization was that between the Tigris and
the Euphrates, and in the Indian Peninsula. Some of the people of India were
descendants of this same man of whom I have spoken, and the Arabians, also.
    Now, to say that these races which preceded the Caucasian race, the
Aryan race, and who laid the first foundations of civilization and the arts,
and sciences, were inferior races, does not seem to me quite reasonable.
Possibly it is not to be expected that it should seem reasonable to me, but
certainly it does not. This idea of the inferiority of the colored race is
based upon a theory which seems to have obtained in this country because of
slavery. Now, slavery, as I have just shown, has at different periods of the
world's history prevailed with every race. There is not a race on the top
side of the earth that has not, at one time or another, been subjected to
slavery in some of its members, and really—if you will pardon me for talking
in this general way, for I have not prepared anything, but am just talking
upon general facts—I venture to say that this Aryan race, or this Teutonic
race, is itself an amalgam. It is a composition of nearly all the races on
the top side of the earth. Now, when this subject of inferiority comes up
it strikes me that this is a point to be considered. What is the Teutonic
or the Anglo-Saxon race, or the Aryan race? As gentlemen discuss it, it seems
to be merely a matter of color. Now, I understand that in Madagascar there
are some black Jews. I understand also that in some portions of Africa there
are people with white skin. That may not be true, but it is certainly believed by a good many of the scientists and ethnologists that these differ-

ences of food and climatic influences, and I offer that as testimony to show
that if differences in food and in climate can change the constitution of
man and change his color, then these differences of race, so called, are a
mere matter of color and not of brain. These influences, operating for a
great number of years, may cause these differences to become fixed, and, as
it were, constitutional, and so the different families of man go on, growing
more distinct in these external respects, until in the case of each race the
color becomes a constitutional feature; because if we take the Bible, and it
ought to be good testimony to all Americans, or to the great majority of
them--at any rate, to all who believe that we live in a Christian country--
if we take the Bible as authority, we cannot get around the idea that Adam
was the forefather of all the living, that Noah was descended from him, and
that from the Noachian line we have all descended, and hence that all these
nations are of one blood. It seems to me, therefore, that it becomes us to
acknowledge the fact that difference of color is simply a constitutional
difference, resulting from difference, of climate, different education, and
different circumstances, and that it is those influences that have made me
inferior to you, Senator, or that make me inferior to the gentlemen who gave
us that splendid argument awhile ago on the question of the inferiority of
my race. That is the way it strikes me.

A Danger Ahead.

I have one other thought. It is this: I am a young man, but although
young I have some patriotic feeling which rises in my breast, and some interest in the welfare of this State and of this South land in which I was
born and from which I have drawn all that I am. Having that idea and that
feeling I have thought, in view of the late census, in view of the facts
that are brought out and exhibited there, that attention ought to be given
to the fact that the race to which you gentlemen belong is increasing at the
rate of only 2 per cent, every thirty-five years, while the race to which I
belong is increasing at the rate of 3-1/2 per cent, every twenty years.
Now, at that rate of increase, the race to which I belong will soon be twice
as numerous in these Southern States as the race to which you belong, and,
in view of that fact, I have sometimes asked myself the question what will
become of these two races when there is such a disparity of numbers between
them and when there is inculcated into the minds of the people of both races
a feeling of antipathy toward each other--when I am taught to feel that you
are determined to dominate over me and that I must do all I can to try to
ride over you--what will become of this South land with such a feeling and
such a disparity between the races? I have asked myself that question, and
I have asked whether it would not be best for you and best for me to try to
get rid of this antagonistic feeling and do away with this idea of dividing
on the color line. I do not believe that these two races will ever mix.
There have been fewer mulattoes born within the last year than ever before,
and I think there is no probability of the amalgamation of the races.

Politics.

Now, as to politics, if you make the standard intelligence and respect-
ability, I believe that a majority of the white people and a majority of the
black people will vote to put in office those who are best capable of ruling
wisely and honestly. If I am more capable of ruling than you are why should
I not be elected to the Senate or to fill any other position? And, on the
other hand, if you are more capable than I am, why should not you be elected
instead of me? It seems to me if you come to that conclusion--if the South
comes to that conclusion, if the United States come to that conclusion--it
will do away with the race question and the race problem. Then, when I become more educated and intelligent, I naturally look to the most intelligent
man I can find to advise me, without regard to whether he is black or white.

The Duty of the General Government as to Education at the South.

In respect to education, the South has lost much and suffered much. It
has been too impoverished, and it is still too poor to educate its people

properly. There is a large number of white people and of colored people at
the South who have no means of education, and I believe that illiteracy among
the white people is shown by the census to be greater in proportion than
among the colored people, 28 per cent, as against 11 per cent. Now, the
United States Government has taken a great deal from the South--justly, I
suppose, or unjustly (I do not pronounce upon that)--I refer to this tax
upon cotton and the confiscation of property during the war. Whether justly
or unjustly, the Government has done that, and now it has millions of dollars in its treasury lying idle, as I understand, and why should it not help
the South to take care of the ignorant people, and to bear the burden of this
mass of ignorance that it has turned loose on the Southern people? There is
no doubt that it is a mass of ignorance. The greater portion of our people
are, of course, ignorant, and I believe it is the duty of the United States
Government to help to educate them, and I believe, further, that it will be
for the direct advantage of the Government to do so. Of course, as one who
is engaged in the cause of education, I add my voice to other voices that
have been raised on that subject. I have been teaching for several years;
ever since I was quite a lad I have done nothing but teach school, and I
know something personally about the ignorance among my own people. Therefore, I say, I join with the other gentlemen who have spoken in saying to
the National Government to make that appropriation of $10,000,000 for five
years at least.
     Q. What is your knowledge as to the actual condition of your race and
of the white race throughout this State, in the country portions of the
State, in respect to education?--A. In the country the colored people are
deplorably ignorant. They have a free school for three months, of course,
but they are so poor, as a general thing, that they are hardly able to keep
their children at school even during those three months. For that period
the schools are practically free; there is no doubt about that.
     Q. Are the schools in continuous session for three months?--A. Yes,
sir.
     Q. How much more can a boy learn in three months than he can forget in
nine months?--A. I think he will forget about three times as much as he
learns, if that is possible. That is where the great trouble comes in, and
yet it is wonderful how much they do learn, although it looks as if they
would forget everything. It takes them three or four terms to get along so
that they can retain anything they do learn, but very often they do not make
any progress, because they forget by the next term what they have learned in
this. Still, after about two or three terms you find they have gained something. I have taught school in the country a good deal, and I think the
case is just about the same with the poor white people. They have been
largely neglected. I believe there has been $25,000,000 expended by charit-
able societies in the South among the colored people, while there has been
a very small amount spent among the poor white people, and they are almost
as badly off as the colored people.

Relations Between the Poor Whites and the Negroes.

     Q. How do the poor white people and the colored people who live in the
same neighborhoods feel toward each other, so far as you have observed?--A.
Well, I have had considerable opportunity to judge of that, and I think they
get along very well together. Now and then they have a little trouble.
     Q. Where does the trouble come in?--A. There are two sources of
trouble. One is the political source, and the other is--I reckon it might
be called a social source, or something of that kind. It is true, the
poorer white people are unable to do much more than the poorer colored
people, and I think the farmers usually prefer the colored laborers, because
they are more docile and tractable than the white laborers. Of course that
preference for colored laborers in many cases deprives poor white men of
opportunities of employment, and that brings about some feeling. I have
noticed some feeling about that in some localities. For instance, in Murray
County, Colonel Carter owns a large part of the county--I do not know how
many hundred acres of land--and he has four or five hundred colored men employed, and all around his plantation there are white men living. I taught
school there for awhile, and I found that there was some little trouble

between Colonel Carter's tenants and these poor white people in the neighborhood, whom he would not employ. In that mountain region there is very little
tillable land, and that probably is an additional reason why this feeling
exists.

Q. It was really a competition for life?--A. I think that was really
it. There is some trouble on that ground, and there is also some on political grounds. It is natural though, I think, and I have thought so all along.
There are so many intelligent men among the white people and so few among
the colored people, and it does look hard for a man who owns the property and
has the intelligence to submit to the domineering of those who have not. That
is natural, and it would be so among any other people, I believe. That is
where the trouble comes on that matter, and while I would not justify many
things that have occurred, still, I say, it is natural that there should be
some trouble on that ground. I think, however, that when the people become
generally better educated, and when the idea that Mr. Jackson has advanced
here this evening is done away with, I think there will be no trouble whatever between the races, none in the world.

Rich Colored Men.

Q. So you feel as hopeful about the future as the last witness did?--
A. Oh, yes, sir. I do not know how hopeful he felt, but I am sure I feel
hopeful. I know some colored men who are gaining property--or, to use the
more explicit term that was used here by Mr. Jackson, some *black* men who
have property, and I believe there are some of those black men who are worth
as much as $500,000.
Q. Do you mean that you know a colored man who is worth half a million
dollars?--A. Yes, sir.
Q. Has he any white blood in him?--A. I do not think he has any. He
is a little blacker than I am.
Q. About seventeen-sixteenths, I suppose? [Laughter.]--A. I suppose
so. It is stated that there are some of them who own nearly $1,000,000.
There is one colored lady who lives in Brooklyn who is worth $1,000,000, I
believe.
Q. How did she get it?--A. I am not certain as to how she came by it.
I know of quite a black man in Americus who owns nearly half of that town; I
think he is one of the largest shareholders in the bank there. He furnishes
a house to his old master, and takes good care of him.
Q. How much do you say he is worth?--A. I suppose that Mr. Head is
worth on toward $100,000. That is pretty good for a colored man in Georgia,
or anywhere in the South, who has been free only about eighteen years.
Q. How did that man get his money?--A. He got it by dint of hard labor
and frugality.
Q. How many white men have made $100,000 in Georgia since the war by
dint of hard labor and frugality?--A. I should think there were many. I
suppose that most of the wealth in the South has been made by good bargains
and shrewd investments. This gentleman has made his money by industry and
judicious investments. He has taken all that lower part of the city of
Americus that the people had almost thrown away, and has built houses on it
and made that part of the city very valuable.

America Common Ground. The Negro at Home in the South,
And Going to Stay.

Q. Is there any need of you colored people staying in this country?--
A. Yes, sir; this is our home.
Q. It is ours, too, you know?--A. Yes, sir. I think this whole question of race ought to be done away with. The Irishman need not change his
racial quality to become an American; why, then, should the African change
his? America is common ground. The Creator has set it apart, in my opinion,
for the purpose of bringing over and planting here all the branches of the
human race, and He is going to make this the common ground where they shall
all come and live together as brethren and I think that the colored man, having been brought here by no wish or act of his own, has a right to stay, and
is going to stay, and I think further that he is going to stay right here in
the South, because the South is congenial to him and is just the place for him.

Q. Do you feel at all inclined to move away?--A. I do not think I do; not at all.

Q. What do you think of the idea of colonizing your race in Africa?--A. That was spoken of here, and your question brings it back to my mind. Africa has a large population already, and when they did attempt to set up a colony of our people there they selected a little place in one of the worst parts of Africa--the worst part for civilization--Liberia, a region which is known to be just the place to kill people off rather than to build up a civilized community. However, that has no effect upon us; it does not concern us. We have no desire to go to Africa.

Q. If I understand your view, you do not think there is any probability of race collisions here in the future?--A. No, sir; I do not think there is. I think there is less probability of that now than there has ever been. As people become intelligent they select wiser leaders. The white race being of course in the advance, and likely to continue so for perhaps a century to come, as intelligence spreads throughout the whole community, they will be likely to be selected to take the lead as a general thing. There is no doubt about that at all, and therefore there are not likely to be any race collisions.

There is No Real Race "Problem" in the South.

Q. Don't you think it is well enough for you colored people to let this class of questions alone at present and attend to business and get all the money you can and let everybody else do the same?--A. Yes, sir; that is it. There is really no such "problem" here as has been talked about. All this fuss and furor about it seems to me to be simply an effort to create a problem rather than an attempt to solve one. It is a striving to get together enough disturbing elements to make a problem, rather than an effort to find a solution of any problem that really exists; and if this question is let alone, and the people go on attending to their business it will settle itself, and all the people of this country will have no difficulty in living together in peace and harmony.

Q. What is your age?--A. I am thirty years old.

Q. Where were you born?--A. In Whitfield County, Georgia.

Q. Were you ever a slave?--A. Yes, sir.

Q. What schooling have you had?--A. I have been at school about seven or eight years.

Q. Where?--A. At the Atlanta University.

Q. Are you a graduate?--A. Yes, sir.

Q. When did you graduate?--A. In 1876.

Q. I understand that you have been a teacher ever since?--A. Yes, sir.

Q. In Georgia all the time?--A. Yes, sir.

Q. What pay do you get?--A. I get $75 a month.

Q. How many pupils do you have?--A. Forty.

Q. Where is your school?--A. In this city.

Q. How long have you taught here?--A. I have taught here going on four years.

Q. In the same school all the time?--A. Yes, sir.

Q. Do you teach boys and girls?--A. Yes, sir.

Q. Is yours what is called a common school or a high school?--A. It is the high school, the only one of the kind in the State.

Q. Then a high school for colored children, and the only one in the State, is here in Augusta?--A. Yes, sir.

Q. You have no trouble, you say, in getting along with the white people? --A. None in the world. Some of my best friends are among the white people. I have always expressed my views on almost any subject that I have felt disposed to talk about and have never had any trouble whatever.

Q. And I suppose you are descended direct from those curly-headed people you have told us about?--A. I think I am. My grandfather was a Mandingo brought over to Maryland; a native African; then they drifted down to South Carolina, and my mother came to this country, and I am here.

Q. Where does the Mandingo tribe live now in Africa?--A. On the northeastern coast of Liberia; above that. They are said to be one of the most intelligent tribes. A neighboring tribe, the Vivas, invented an alphabet of their own, similar to the Phoenician, not so very similar, but in some respects similar and answering the same purposes.

Q. How long is it since they invented it?--A. I think it was in the eighth century.

Q. Have they any written literature?--A. I have seen some short poems given in Mr. Williams's history, but I don't know that they have any amount of literature.

Q. They have a religion, I suppose?--A. They have a religion of their own. Their religion, however, is Mohammedan. That is the religion of most of them.

Q. Do you claim that the Phoenicians were a colored people?--A. Yes, sir. I claim that they were the descendants of Ham.

Q. And you claim that Hannibal was a Phoenician?--A. Yes, sir. Hannibal, and Hamilcar the conqueror of Spain.

Q. Hannibal did some fighting with the Romans, I believe?--A. Yes, sir; he made Rome quail as he came across the Alps.

The CHAIRMAN. Well, all I have got to say to you colored people is be as good to us as you can, and give us a fair chance. [Laughter.]

Report of the (Education and Labor) Committee of the Senate Upon the Relations between Labor and Capital, and Testimony Taken by the Committee (Washington, D.C., 1885), vol. III, pp. 3-12, 372-83, 399-405, 811-19.

II

SHOULD BLACKS JOIN THE RANKS OF LABOR?

SHOULD BLACKS JOIN THE RANKS OF LABOR?

The heightened militancy of American laborers during the late 1870s and 1880s rendered it vital to the interest of black workers to form some consensus regarding the advisability of trying to join the labor movement, or to remain apart from it. While the issue had confronted blacks before, the rise of the Noble Order of the Knights of Labor, which reached its membership peak in 1886, agitated the question as never before. The Knights' policy of organizing all workers, except financial speculators and liquor dealers, into one big union was not entirely new; what was unique about the Knights, however, was the constitutional rejection of racial discrimination within the organization.

This public position on racial equality in union membership fueled a heated debate in the black press during the 1880s. The positions expressed in these black newspapers, which are sampled in Part II, break down into several general categories. No doubt there were some Negroes, like one member of the Carpenters' and Joiners' Union, who rejected altogether the notion that blacks were discriminated against at all once they joined existing unions. This black unionman charged that Negroes had demonstrated little interest in learning the skills required to join a craft union, thus laying the blame for low black membership at the door of Negroes themselves (Doc. 2). But most blacks probably held views somewhat less sanguine. Knowledgeable Negroes generally agreed with Frederick Douglass, who believed that all workers had the same economic interests in receiving "an honest day's pay for an honest day's work." He believed that laborers of all races eventually would organize for their own protection, for the poverty of "wage slavery" was only a little less galling than chattel slavery (Doc. 1).

The New York Freeman agreed with Douglass, and generally supported the view that since the Knights were willing to accept all workers regardless of race, and since the organization had the power to shut down the entire economy, blacks should belong. Moreover, blacks were, by and large, laboring people and therefore had a moral obligation to join the struggle for a more equitable distribution of wealth (Doc. 4). Black and white workers had the same economic interests, the Freeman argued, and could not afford to alienate white workers by refusing to join with them (Doc. 10-11).

On the other hand, some Afro-Americans followed the issue with the same suspicion as the New York Age, which pointed out that, at least as early as April 1886, the Knights had not actively attempted to organize black workers. The Age reminded its readers that past experiences with white workers did not justify the belief that the Knights would actually practice their own constitutional principles on racial equality (Doc. 5). John R. Lynch, a former U.S. Senator from Mississippi and one of only three blacks ever to serve in that august body, agreed with the Age and suggested that the Knights only thought of blacks as "tools." As evidence, Lynch alluded to the fact that, even when Negro workers supported unions, many white Knights still refused to work alongside them. Lynch concluded, however, that exclusion itself caused racial prejudice and, rather than remain aloof, blacks must fight for access into the dominant unions (Doc. 6).

Adopting a more nationalistic point of view, the Washington Bee advocated the organization of "all colored labor into one strong fraternity" powerful enough either to force white unions to accept blacks, or to erect an independent black body (Doc. 8).

In a pamphlet published in 1887, William H. Councill, a southern black conservative, expressed views less in keeping with the working classes but quite in tune with the intellectual climate of the day. Espousing a hybrid "social darwinism," Councill believed that labor and capital were not antagonistic forces at all. Stretching sophistry to its limits, he concluded that all people were accumulators of wealth; rich people simply had excelled in this capacity. Envy, not injustice, was the root of the conflict between labor and capital. Anticipating the ideology popularized by Booker T. Washington a decade later, Councill announced that blacks were the "most desirable" of all laborers they were unskilled for the most part, and if they remained so, the laws of the marketplace would forever render them outcasts (Doc. 12).

CONFLICTING VIEWS

1. FREDERICK DOUGLASS ON THE LABOR QUESTION[8]

Not the least important among the subjects to which we invite your earnest attention is the condition of the laboring class at the South. Their cause is one with the laboring classes all over the world. The labor unions of the country should not throw away this colored element of strength. Everywhere there is dissatisfaction with the present relation of labor and capital and today no subject wears an aspect more threatening to civilization than the respective claims of capital and labor, landlords and tenants. . . .

It is a great mistake for any class of laborers to isolate itself and thus weaken the bond of brotherhood between those on whom the burden and hardships of labor fall. The fortunate ones of the earth, who are abundant in land and money and know nothing of the anxious care and pinching poverty of the laboring classes, may be indifferent to the appeal for justice at this point, but the laboring classes cannot afford to be indifferent. What labor everywhere wants, what it ought to have and will some day demand and receive, is an honest day's pay for an honest day's work. As the laborer becomes more intelligent he will develop what capital already possesses, that is the power to organize and combine for its own protection. Experience demonstrates that there may be a wages of slavery only a little less galling and crushing in its effects than chattel slavery, and that this slavery of wages must go down with the other. . . .

Proceedings, National Convention of Colored Men at Louisville, Kentucky, September 24, 1883.

2. THE VITAL LABOR PROBLEM

OUR RELATIONS TO LABOR ORGANIZATIONS, THE VIEWS OF A COLORED MEMBER AND EX-MEMBER OF THE OHIO LEGISLATURE. FROM THE DETROIT PLAIN DEALER.

For twenty-eight years it has been my fortune to be associated with the white mechanics of the United States. . . . A mechanic myself, the many indignities to which colored men were formerly subjected were a portion of my experience. While it is not my intention to appear as a critic, your article contains some charges against organized labor that do not wholly support the facts as they exist in Ohio and the city of Cleveland, Ohio. Farther than this I know no more, except such information as is gleamed from the public press in regard to the work, objects and aims of organized labor societies. A member myself of the Carpenters' and Joiners' Union of Cleveland, Ohio, these facts are perfectly in my knowledge. In this organization, which is subordinate to the National organization, there are several colored members, and no distinction has ever been shown in the election to offices, obtaining employment, sick and death benefits, etc., etc. There are in Cleveland many colored men who are mechanics; and with a very few exceptions they are members of the particular organization formed in the interest of the trade. Bricklayers, plasterers, blacksmiths, cigar makers, machinists, molders, etc., have as members in each of their unions colored men. In the Knights of Labor there are colored men also; and to my certain knowledge in one local assembly, organized a few years ago, a colored man was a charter member. For years I have been importuned to enter into the formation of an assembly to be composed exclusively of colored men, but have persistently refused, believing as I do in mixing and not in isolating and ostracising ourselves, there by fostering and perpetuating the prejudice as existing today.

At no time, since my residence in our "Forest City," over sixteen years, do I recall one instance where white laborers have refused to work with the colored co-laborers. While I do not say that such instances have not occurred, if happening in labor organizations, certainly they would have come to my knowledge.

On the 26th day of January there convened in the city of Columbus the "State Trades and Labor Assembly of Ohio." A delegate to that assembly was a colored man, Robert Gray, Esq., a resident of Akron, O., by occupation a bricklayer and a member of the union in that city. There was no doubt as to his genuineness, as his distinctive color precluded that. In a conversation with the gentleman I learned that he had occupied every station in the local organization, from the lowest to the highest, and that no distinction was or ever had been shown him on account of his color. In reading your article he unhesitatingly said that you certainly must have been misinformed, for no such prejudice had ever been shown during his connection with labor unions, and especially the Knights of Labor. That there were no such distinctions either taught or sanctioned by these organizations in any manner; that if they did **exist** it was of a local nature and totally at variance with the principles of **labor** unions.

I am aware that in certain localities where prejudice against the colored man has had unlimited sway the local atmosphere has become so polluted thereby that it is impossible to eradicate or overcome that prejudice, except by persistent efforts, a new and comprehensive knowledge of one's particular trade, which demonstrates the ability of a master workman and demands admission to the ranks of labor.

Education enters largely into the consideration as to whether a person has reached the necessary point where his labor demands the remuneration and consideration that all labor should receive. In many branches of trade it is an utter impossbility to reach this point without a thorough knowledge of geometrical lines and their practical uses. Some do not require this, but all are benefitted by acquiring a knowledge of a common school education.

Therefore it becomes necessary for those who desire to enter upon mechanical pursuits, that the first requisite steps to be taken by them is that of education. All mechanics of any age admit this to be a settled fact. Your question, "can intelligence alone keep the body alive?" is pertinent, and we answer, No! But education without application is to be taken the same as application without education.

My experience has proven to me conclusively that our boys, or at least a majority of them, have no tendencies to enter into the mechanical pursuits. For years my whole efforts have been directed to educating the youth of my acquaintance to the fact that hard labor was largely on the decrease and a steady downward tendency; that in a few years a master workman, one who thoroughly understands his particular trade, would be able to command the highest remuneration for his labor. But I have often seen my efforts vanish in mid-air and to-day I know of but three colored boys who are apprentices in the city of Cleveland, and this in the face of a large population. One fault lies in the want of foresight, which can only be remedied by teaching the youth the many advantages to be obtained in after years, by an application to the acquirements necessary to enter the pursuit of mechanical trades.

In my immediate vicinity no trouble exists as to gaining admission into shops, factories and other branches of the trades a young man may desire to enter. If our youths prefer to enter into the profession in preference to the trades, we cannot shape their course otherwise but by teaching them the folly of it. Soon, we shall become a race of professional men in whose ranks there does not exist the prejudice that exists in the trades, as education always tends to the eradication of prejudice.

With you I firmly believe that this matter should be plainly and forcibly brought before our race, and to such valuable educators as the *Plaindealer* and others that could be named, we look for such teachings as will tend to benefit us in every manner. There is no influence that will be a greater lever to eradicate all prejudices that may exist than the influence of education, organization and agitation. But no separate organizations can effect what we desire to accomplish; for as we are a component part of this great government, we must have accorded to us such treatment as other citizens have, which can only be obtained by persistant agitation and intermingling. If one applies for admission either as a member of an organization or for an apprenticeship in a workshop, let him not be discouraged by one refusal, but continue, and his aim will eventually be accomplished. Much more could I say, but my advice is summed up in a few words; educate the children; teach them their duties as citizens; that they are inferior to no other race on the face of the globe; to always assert their manhood at all times and places; that all labor is honorable, and that it is far more preferable to be a mechanic than to occupy any menial position.

JERE A. BROWN

CONSIDERED ALMOST UTOPIAN.--You ask, "How can the hostile forces of labor be best combatted and overthrown? Now I cannot answer that question--it is too difficult for me. If I could answer it, I would hold the key that would unlock the secret of the future success and happiness of our proscribed people in the United States. For, once remove the barriers and obstacles in the way which prevent us from enjoying equal facilities in the way of serving an apprenticeship and working on the scaffold, side by side with white men, in all the various trades and avocations in life, and presto, we succeed to wealth, social station and all that they imply. There are thousands and thousands of ambitious young colored men with strong arms and willing hearts, who would jump at the opportunity of going into a work-shop or on a scaffold to learn a trade, could the feat be accomplished, in the ordinary way; and especially if they could be encouraged to believe that the time and labor given to learning a trade would not be in vain; that they would not be ostracised and compelled to wander from "pillar to post" in search of employment on account of their color. Did you ever think that the obstacles placed in our way by caste are more discouraging to the average boy or man than even adverse legislative enactment? There is no status which forbids a dry goods merchant, banker or other dealer in our city from employing colored persons, and yet, to see one in such a position is almost a phenomenon. In fact, the "tyrant custom" seems to have frozen us out so completely, that any thought of attaining to such positions, even by those of our young people who succeed in acquiring a first class education, is considered almost utopian.

What shall we do then to overcome this hostile, discouraging power? We must, at least, continue to aspire, prepare ourselves as best we can, so that when one of us does succeed in attaining any position, its duties will be faithfully and well performed. We must do everything we can to encourage those of our own household.

> "Equity demandeth recompense
> For high place--calumny and care:
>> For State--comfortless splendor eating on the heart of home;
> For warrior fame--dangers and death,
>> For a name among the learned--a spirit over strained;
> For honor of all kinds--the goal of ambition.
>> Upon every acquirement the tax of anxiety."

JOHN P. GREEN[9]

New York Freeman, March 13, 1886.[10]

3. PROSCRIBED

BOSTON, April 6.--The Knights of Labor, not as an organization but as individuals, have, at the workshops, manufactories and in all the trades, proscribed the black man. We have been asked by colored men, "Will the high officials give assurance that we shall not be subjected to a like policy in the future?" We are persuaded that they would. Let a committee of well-known gentlemen be appointed to wait on the master workmen and find out about it.

J. GORDON STREET

New York Freeman, April 10, 1886.

4. LABOR UPHEAVALS

All the world, as far as this country is concerned, appears to have gone
mad, after the Knights of Labor. The newspapers, and the politicians appear
to be as much on the fence as they were forty years ago on the slavery question, doubting which side to take in the conflict impending. The Knights of
Labor have sprung into power like a young giant. Only a few years ago and
the wailings of the toilers of the land were poohpoohed by the press and
unheeded by the politicians, while the lords of capital smiled in their sleeves
at complaints and demands which seemed so utterly absurd as to warrant no
serious reflection. In the last Presidential election the vote of the Labor
party was such a very small thing as actually to have been lost in the great
stack of votes polled by the two national parties. How will it be in the
future? The power of the leaders of the labor unions as demonstrated during
the past six months, puts an entirely new phase on this aspect of the matter.
Labor has heretofore been powerless simply because it was a disorganized,
leaderless mass. Now it is organized; now it has masterful leadership. At
the nod of an authorized person thousands of men in every line of industry
desert their posts of duty and simply paralyze the productive and carrying
agencies of the country. Before this organized power capital, even the great
body of the people, is as powerless as labor once was.
     Political economists have for years snarled at the proposition that
labor was the productive and capital the non-productive force in our sociol-
ogy, and that when labor ceased to produce capital would wither into the
elements out of which it was delved. But the events of the past few months
have gone very far towards vindicating the tenability of the proposition.
The political economist of the future will have largely to reconstruct this
glaring heresy before he has a correct premise upon which to predicate his
deductions and conclusions.
     To become an invincible power the Knights of Labor have wisely concluded
to enlist the support of all grades of labor, barring out no nationality except that of the Chinese. Hence colored men all over the Union, are rapidly
becoming affiliated with the organization. For instance the colored waiters
of New York have formed a strong assembly of the Knights of Labor, and meet
Thursday every week at Garnet Hall, and some of the ablest speakers of the
Central organization are present to instruct them in the requirements of the
parent Union. In most other branches of labor colored men are affiliated
with white organizations, not being strong enough to form a separate assembly. We predicted this result a year ago in the book we published under
the title of "Black and White," but we did not expect so speedy a consum-
mation of the prediction then made.[11]
     We do not hesitate to say we fear the conflict which must result from
organized capital on the one hand and organized labor on the other. The
gravity of such conflict is correctly estimated by those more directly interested pro and con. We believe in that absolute justice which it is so
very difficult to secure in either the social or political relations of men.
Tyranny, some one of its multiform variations, seems far more natural in the
practice than equity. It therefore almost reduces itself to a choice between
the tyrants we shall have, and of which of them is the safer. For centuries
we have had the tyranny of capital, and an odious and unjust tyranny it has
been, and if we are to have the tyranny of labor we shall after awhile be in
position to judge which of them is the more odious, which the more conducive
to the happiness of the greatest number and to the general progress of the
race.
     After all it is a matter of how far forth the masses shall share with
the capitalistic oligarchs and sharks the interest of the fruits of labor--
whether the fellow who develops the gold mine shall sleep on a board and eat
pone cake and hog, while the fellow who claims to own the mine, but does not
work it, shall sleep in a palace and fill his stomach with caramels and ice
cream.
     The revolution is upon us, and since we are largely of the laboring
population it is very natural that we should take sides with the labor forces
in their fight for a juster distribution of the results of labor. We cannot

afford to stand off from or to antagonize the army under whose banners we
labor in the common lot of toil. We do not make conditions. All we can do
is to fall into line on the right or left, and which side it shall be will
depend entirely upon whether we are a capitalist or a laborer.

New York Freeman, March 20, 1886.

5. GROWTH OF THE COLORED PRESS

Scarcely any leaders of public opinion watch the tendency of current
events more closely, or discuss the probable effect upon the interest of
their constituents more plainly than the colored editors of the country.
The Negro press has got to be a firmly established fact; and as the number
of newspapers edited by colored men increases, showing that the number of
colored readers of newspapers is also increasing, its influence and power
for good must grow as its intelligence, discretion and wisdom grows. It is
not longer possible to reckon on any matter affecting the colored race without counting in the influence of the colored press. And it is likely to become more and more an important factor in the reckoning.

This fact finds indorsement in the discussions of two colored papers
last week on the liveliest issues of the day. The Detroit *Plaindealer,* for
example, which boasts of being "the only colored newspaper ever endorsed by
a State convention," debates the question whether colored laborers shall join
or shall be permitted to join the Knights of Labor. The first step toward
removing prejudice and the idea of the colored laborer's inferiority is for
him to make the common cause of the wage workers his own; "and in accomplishing this," says the *Plaindealer,* "no better opportunity is to be had than by
connecting himself with such labor organizations, as show a disposition to
take him in, and who, perhaps influenced by self-interest, more than anything else, are willing in the general movement for the emancipation of the
wage-worker to include him. It is therefore meet that all such overtures
of friendship on their part should be met half way and a unit made for a
common cause."

Such overtures of friendship have already been made to the Afro-American, as the *Plaindealer* calls him, by the Knights of Labor of Detroit, "the
first public attempt" the organization has made "to gather him into its
ranks." There has as yet been no Negro made a Knight of Labor, because on
the part of the organization, "the same effort to enlist the white mechanic
or tradesman in their order was not made to enlist the colored wage worker,"
and, on the part of the colored men themselves, because this organization
was looked upon as something kindred to trades union in objecting to him as
a member of their organization, and, as he has known to his cost, both as
to pocket and personal feeling, in refusing to work with him. Such experience has no tendency to make a man rush blind-folded into meeting insult and
prejudice.

But the invitation having come, the *Plaindealer* advises its acceptance
and recommends the colored men not to form new assemblies, but join the old
ones. "Isolate themselves," it says, "by forming separate assemblies, and
they will foster and encourage the idea of inferiority and thus delay their
emancipation as workmen. Unite with the older, reap the benefit of long
organization, and the stride forward will be more rapid. There is in this
movement of labor much that is to be commended. Its object is a glorious
one. Its accomplishment is not far off, and the Afro-American should take a
hand in the fight and be in at the finish."

It does not greatly matter whether the harmonious assimilation of a
considerable body of colored laborers by the Knights of Labor is practicable
or possible to-day or not. The fact that an organ of Negro opinion, reaching
with its influence a considerable body of Negro workers, can discuss this
question with such intelligence and shrewd appreciation of its salient points
as they pertain to the interest of its people, is the significant thing to
be noted. A people which sustains an honest and intelligent press will not

long lack the knowledge which is the basis of strength and independence.

New York Age, April 10, 1886.

6.   JOHN R. LYNCH ON THE COLOR LINE IN RANKS OF LABOR[12]

Mr. J. S. Woods, president of the Hod Carrier's Union, told me that I
was misinformed about the hod carriers taking part in the parade of May 1.
Said he: "There were only four of our members in the procession out of 275,
and they are the only four of our Union who belong to the Knights of Labor.
The Knights of Labor sent a committee to wait upon our Union asking us to
adopt their charter as our own. We inquired if they would concede the right
of apprenticeship to our children and admit those of us who are mechanics
to full membership in all of their different lodges, allow us to work upon
the same scaffold together as their brother?"
Said he: "What reply do you think that committee gave us? The chairman
of that committee told our Union that these questions would be an after consideration. Isn't that proof that the Knights of Labor intend to use the
colored man as a tool? Suppose our Union had accepted the proposition,
without asking them for equal rights? We would have been duped into a second
slavery. Further than that the Negroes are barred out of the machine shops,
the factories, off of railroad engine and all other mechanical doors are
closed against him controlled by the Knights of Labor."
I asked Mr. Woods if the Hod Carriers' Union was a secret organization?
"No, sir," was his answer, "but the Knights of Labor and trades unions are.
I have no objections to any secret orders that do justice to all nationalities
alike."
He asked me if I had ever heard of a colored society being boisterous
in the strikes of 1877 and 1878. The few colored men who took part were
hunted down, arrested, tried, punished in the courts and kept out of employment by the same white working men who inaugurated the strikes. There were
several colored unions that did not turn out May 1. Among them the Teamster's
Union, which number 200 and over; the Coachman's Union, 160 strong; Hotel
Waiters, Butlers and a number of others that would have added a thousand more
to the procession.
The Trades Unions or the Knights of Labor cannot succeed as long as the
color line exists. Mr. Wood said: "We are well aware of that and there is
an agreement among all the colored Unions of this city to stand aloof from
all white labor organizations that refuse to recognize us as their brother.
These white organizations must concede all rights to the colored man themselves. When they do this then the Hod Carriers' Union will unite with them."
. . . The colored laborers should not allow themselves to be placed
in an antagonistic position towards the laboring classes of other races, unless the hostility and opposition of those classes make such a course on
their part, a necessity.
We all know it to be a fact that labor organizations, in many parts of
the country, among the whites, do not recognize the meritorious claims of
colored people. Why? That race prejudice has something to do with it cannot be truthfully denied, but this, in my opinion, is not the principle
reason. Less than a quarter of a century ago the colored people of this
country had no political, social or industrial status. The laboring people
of that race represented, at the time, contrary to their own wishes, it is
true, opposition to free, intelligent and remunerative labor. This was one
of the principal causes of the late civil war--the war between free and slave
labor. The colored laborers were justly looked upon, at that time, and consequently unjustly looked upon in many localities now, as a degraded and
servile class. It is the present duty of the colored people to do whatever
is necessary to eradicate this erroneous impression. Let them impress the
white laborers with the fact that while they are not disposed to antagonize
their interests, and are determined not to do so, unless it becomes a necessity, yet they insist upon justice themselves--a right to an equal participa-

tion in the enjoyment of the fruits of honest and well paid labor.

I do not wish to be understood as endorsing all the means that are
employed by some labor organizations to secure a recognition of the justice
of their claims. Lawlessness should never be countenanced or encouraged.
The laboring people of the country can, in my opinion, through organization
and cooperation, secure for themselves the just rewards of labor without
resorting to any methods that cannot be sanctioned by the most law abiding
people of the community. . . . Colored men should not identify themselves
with any organization that seeks the accomplishment of its purposes through
a resort of lawlessness and violence. They should maintain their reputation
of being a law-abiding and law-observing people, except so far as may be
necessary for the protection of themselves and their families. They should
discountenance, discourage and condemn lawlessness, violence, communism,
socialism and anarchy. . . .

The laboring people in this country can secure all the rights to which
they are justly entitled without violating law, and there is no better way
to bring about this result than through organization. The legitimate object and purpose of labor organizations should be to call public attention
to the condition and wants of the laboring people with a view to creating a
sentiment that will enforce a recognition of their just and reasonable demands—to unite their efforts and labors in an intelligent direction for
their mutual aid, protection and advancement. Such organizations, created
and organized for such purposes, are entitled to and should receive the
assistance and support of laboring colored people. It is understood, of
course, that I refer to such organizations as do not discriminate on account
of race or color in the admission of persons to membership. I hope it is not
neccessary to advise the laboring colored people to strongly oppose and
antagonize every organization that will exclude persons of color from the
organization without regard to merit. . . . It is the duty of the colored
people of the present generation to give their sons and daughters an industrial education and have them contend for recognition by, and admission
into, reputable and intelligent labor organizations, and take their chances
in the race of life upon terms of equality with the whites.

The A.M.E. Church Review, III (October 1886): 165-67.

7. LAND LABOR PROBLEM
OUR RELATIONS TO THEM DISCUSSED BY PROMINENT COLORED MEN

From the Detroit Plaindealer.

THE REMEDY A POLITICAL ONE.--In discussing the labor problems and the
Negro's connection therewith we must first confess in the question of labor
as with politics we rail against obstructionists in the way of our advancement, while the fault is largely our own; do we take instant hold of our
advantages?

We are the unskilled labor of the country, and unskilled labor is a
close ally to pauperism; pauperism is a communist, and it is into this condition that the customs, discriminations and injustices of the white race
is forcing us. It has been the unwritten law of the land that color dis-
qualifies a man for positions that involve master minds and trained hands,
and it is as absurd as the principles of prejudice which debar the Negro
from acquiring that sort of protection and education; it is tyrannous and
barbaric, as well as injurious to the economies, political and moral.

In the South the Negro will first find a general sympathy for his legitimate advancement, and a personal interest in his prosperity and well being.
The Negro question in the North is merely a theoretical one, which cannot be
appreciated by those of the South where the same is practical. In the North
the Negro is a sentiment, and illegitimate political agitation has been the
bane of the race. In the South he is the most important part of the daily
life and labor of the country; having interests in common with the white race

and bound to it by many ties of friendship, obligation and consanguinity.
The educated Southern people almost as a whole feel the heartiest desire for
the moral and industrial elevation of the Negro, and are doing all they can
to promote the same. They have studied carefully the moral of the census of
1880.
    From the South and from one to the manor born came the first pleading
of our case in equity; and a noble effort it was. It would have been accepted by the South had not Mr. Cable attempted the social status of the
Negro. Here is the cause of where we are today, politically, educationally,
our civil rights and our standing in regard to labor. [13]
    While the Republican party exulted in the achievement of the liberty
of the slave, they turned a deaf ear to the half freed slave's cry of right
and justice, and hoping to woo eternal peace to the heart of the Nation
allowed the helpless citizens born of throes of war to be led away into a
thraldom all the more pitiable and unjust because seemingly sanctified with
mercy and sanctioned with the approval of their natural guardian and pro-
tector.
    That is the cause of our condition.
    I believe that it is folly to try to effect the object of which you and
I and all so much desire, outside of politics.
    If the combination of labor and independentism will smash a Democratic
machine in one State, a Republican ring in another, and make a Republican
administration in Michigan give consolidated labor everything it asks and
more, we should combine and utilize the same for our purpose. We by our
votes make at least three congressmen, hold the balance of power in this
State. Why not use it? And taking the whole country through what can we
not do? We could force a recognition of all our wants. Let an organization
patterned after the Knights of Labor be formed, and every colored man North
and South join it and give it the full weight of his confidence and labor,
and if this combination be true to each other force each of the great political parties to accede us our rights.
    Although we may not at first come up to the highest standard as politi-
cal and labor revolutionists, it will open the way for more advanced positions in the future, this may not be all we desire, but it is in the right
direction, and if such a movement is supported by us solidly it will eventually lead us to all which we desire. As a means of enforcing recognition
of us politically and industrially it is perhaps all that is necessary.
    This principle is a nucleus about which we can all crystalize, it is
no ubiquitous most, inefficient and helpless, but it is a dozing lion which
can awaken to power and glory.
                                        C. FABE MARTIN,

Dowgiac, Mich., March 1, 1886.

    . . . The Detroit *Plaindealer*, . . . which boasts of being "the only
colored newspaper ever endorsed by a State convention," debates the question
whether colored laborers shall join or shall be permitted to join the Knights
of Labor. The first step toward removing prejudice and the idea of the
colored laborer's inferiority is for him to make the common cause of the wage
workers his own, "and in accomplishing this," says the *Plaindealer,* "no
better opportunity is to be had than by connecting himself with such labor
organizations, as show a dispostion to take him in, and who, perhaps influenced by self-interest, more than anything else, are willing in the
general movement for the emancipation of the wage-worker to include him. It
is therefore meet that all such overtures of friendship on their part should
be met half way and a unit made for a common cause."
    Such overtures of friendship have already been made to the Afro-American,
as the *Plaindealer* calls him, by the Knights of Labor of Detroit, "the first
public attempt" the organization has made "to gather him into its ranks."
There has as yet been no Negro made a Knight of Labor, because on the part
of the organization, "the same effort to enlist the white mechanic or "tradesman in their order was not made to enlist the colored wage worker," and, on
the part of the colored men themselves, because "this organization was looked
upon as something kindred to trades union in objecting to him as a member of
their organization, and, as he has known to his cost, both as to pocket and

personal feeling, in refusing to work with him. Such experience has no
tendency to make a man rush blind-folded into meeting insult and prejudice."
     But the invitation having come, the *Plaindealer* advises its acceptance;
and recommends the colored men not to form new assemblies, but join the old
ones. "Isolate themselves," it says, "forming separate assemblies, and
they will foster and encourage the idea of inferiority and thus delay their
emancipation as workmen. Unite with the older, reap the benefit of long
organization, and the stride forward will be more rapid. There is in this
movement of labor much that is to be commended. Its object is a glorious
one. Its accomplishment is not far off, and the Afro-American should take
a hand in the fight and be in at the finish."

New York Freeman, April 10, 1886.

8. "THE COLORED LABORER MUST LOOK TO HIMSELF."

     . . . There is one striking feature, however, of these strikes. . . .
It is the utter dependence of our colored union men upon the disposition of
the whites. For instance, the hod carriers, who are for the most part
colored, by reason of the dissatisfaction of the bricklayers, were forced,
by their dependence, to join the strike, notwithstanding the wages they were
receiving was quite satisfactory. As for colored bricklayers, plasterers,
and the like, they have not taken any considerable part in the strikes.
This grows out of the fact that they have not been invited. These colored
bricklayers and plasterers, in order to insure the proper performance of
their labor, must depend entirely upon colored hod carriers. But these hod
carriers, by reason of their regulations and their dependence upon the whites,
are forced to ignore the demands of colored mechanics, and the consequence
is a corresponding disadvantage to the colored mechanic. Moreover, were the
colored hod carriers less allied with the whites and were there a stronger
attachment on their part to the colored journeymen and mechanic, should the
whites strike for unreasonable demands, an opportunity would be offered to
colored mechanics whereby they could monopolize the trade which would greatly
benefit to both, mechanic and unskilled laborer. But as it is, the colored
mechanic and colored common laborer must suffer together, notwithstanding
the one is not entitled to the benefits, while from the other is withheld
wages which he deems satisfactory. As we said before, our sympathies are
with the working classes; but they are first of all with the colored laborer
which is being discriminated against and crushed wherever it is possible and
made dependent when it can be treated no worse.
     Now the question which occurs to us is, cannot something be done which
will unite all colored labor into one strong fraternity with the view to
establishing an importance and a power which will either force the white
Unions to open wide their doors, or enable sub-fraternities to stand in-
dependently of the white striker? The attitude of the colored laborer in
this country is simply humiliating. Trained mechanics and willing workers are
told that they cannot join a Union formed ostensibly for the purpose of
protecting labor and for defending itself against the impositions and tyranny
of capital. Would it not be wiser to stand aloof and attract attention and
sympathy by filling up the breaks which these strikes occasion, rather than
manifest undue sympathy for a movement which in practice operates against
the interests of colored labor? The time has come when the colored laborer
must look to himself for protection. It is unreasonable in the view of past
history, to suppose that the whites will show any very great interest in our
material welfare and unless we begin to form counter forces to those which
the whites are forming against us, we will find ourselves gradually growing
weaker and weaker until, having no power to defend, we will succumb and be
forced to occupy those grades of labor which are unremunerative and which
the whites decline to perform. When we consider our dependence upon our
labor, we cannot fail to see the importance of striving to protect it, and
of encouraging alliances which will tend to strengthen and develop it. Let

us have a consolidated Colored Craftsmen's Protective Union and see what by
earnest effort wisdom and fraternal co-operation can be accomplished.

Strikes are good things for the whites because they are benefited; they
will become beneficial to us only when we manifest a disposition to oppose
discrimination and determine to protect ourselves.

The Washington Bee, May 8, 1886.

9.   A WORD ON THE LABOR QUESTION

Knights of Labor. You are right in seeking to protect an elevated
labor; but you are wrong if you forget that capital honestly obtained is
labor; it is the stored up energy of labor. Don't overlook your strongest
argument. Here it is: according to the census of 1880 the wealth of this
country increased the ten preceding years from $24,000,000,000 to $43,640,
000,000. In the same time, the same census reveals the average wages of
the laboring man per annum decreased from a little more than $400 to $300.
That is, while the wealth increased some 80 per cent wages decreased one-
fourth. There is something frightfully wrong in this. Machinery and the
competitive system applied to wages are grinding the working man. We must
look this fact in the face. In some way it can be righted and must be
righted. There can be no permanent progress that does not lift society from
the bottom. Free discussion, the force of reason, with patience, will right
the wrong.

The Christian Recorder, April 29, 1886.

10.   A CASE IN POINT

We have taken the position that the colored laborers of the United
States cannot afford to antagonize white laborers when the latter are on
strike for whatever cause. We regret to see so good a man as Mr. T. McCants
Stewart go wrong on this question, as he does in a recent issue of a local
contemporary, basing his article on the views advanced by us in our issue
of May 1. Of course, Mr. Stewart has an American citizen's right to go
wrong on any question it please him to. But despite Mr. Stewart's endorsement of the proposition advanced by the *Enterprise* that colored men should
make themselves officious in taking the places of white strikers, we still
pronounce the doctrine pernicious, the practice of which would intensify
the antagonism between white and colored labor, so long a bone of contention,
but which happily is fast giving way to a more just and reasonable state of
things all over the country.

The best and most forcible endorsement of the position here taken is
furnished by the action of the white workmen of Baltimore, as reported in
the Baltimore *Daily American*, to which Mr. Isaac Myers of that city was so
kind as to call our attention. We advise Mr. Stewart and the editor of the
Enterprise to read the following item from the *American:* [14]

The workmen have a practical illustration of a boycott at the [illegible]
Monday afternoon. Soon after the procession broke up in Scheutzen Park, a
number of the colored men taking part in the festivities, went into the Man-
sion House to get some refreshments. This portion of the building property
on the ground is never included in the privileges and when the thirsty workmen asked for drinks, the man in charge turned them down. Thereupon the
colored men went out and made complaint of the treatment they had received.
The committee in charge without delay placed a sub-committee at the door,
and would not permit any one to patronize that bar or eating saloon. The
means they took were effectual. Business at this end was literally cut off.

It must be borne in mind, to properly appreciate this manly action of the white workmen of Baltimore, that color prejudice is nowhere in the Union more firmly entrenched and rampant than in Baltimore. . . .

New York Freeman, May 22, 1886.

11. A KNIGHT IS A KNIGHT

Does the colored laborer in the South receive less wages than a white laborer does for the same grade of labor? The *Southern Leader* says:

"We claim that, to a large extent, white mechanics are better paid than colored mechanics here for doing the same quality of work, either as carpenters or bricklayers, and that in a majority of cases, colored laborers and mechanics are given employment by white contractors and capitalists simply because they can be had at lower wages than can white laborers and mechanics. We claim that, in a majority of cases, white contractors and capitalists would not employ colored mechanics and laborers if they demanded the same wages paid to white mechanics and laborers. Now, if colored men join the Knights of Labor, they will be compelled to demand the same wages as the white Knights of Labor get, and that, through race prejudice, they will throw themselves out of employment."

We think your logic is frothy. A Knight of Labor is a Knight of Labor, be he black or white. If the inequality in the relative wages paid black and white laborers is to be rectified it is to be accomplished by an understanding with white laborers and a union of forces to compel the equalization. The colored laborer stands on the same footing with the white laborer in point of interest, and to better secure their just rights the two must combine and work together. The colored laborer cannot antagonize the white laborer without jeopardizing his own interest. The proposition is as plain as the nose on your face.

New York Freeman, October 2, 1886.

A BLACK LEADER'S ADVICE TO NEGRO WORKINGMEN

12. THE NEGRO LABORER: A WORD TO HIM

The Morals of Labor

You often hear lawyers and doctors speak about the ethics of their professions. This means nothing more than those rules which should govern the lawyers and doctors in their relation to each other and to their clients and patients. Now, every occupation has its ethics. The workingmen are bound by moral obligations to have regard for the interests of one another; i.e. they are morally bound to give one another equal chance in the great race for bread. Then they must observe all the rules for the government of their relations to the employer. This is very important, as the good of society depends entirely upon the faithful observance of the laws of reciprocity. The Great Teacher has laid down one infallible rule which is ample for all the transactions of life, viz: "Whatsoever ye would that men should do to you, do ye even so to them" I would like for you to regard this divine injunction as your constitution, and then adopt the following by-laws:

1. Decide what you are going to follow for a living.
2. Select an occupation in keeping with your abilities and capabilities.
3. Thoroughly qualify yourself for that calling.
4. Always have a plain understanding with your employer as to wages and hours of work.
5. Carry out your part of the contract "though the heavens fall."
6. Be at the place at the time appointed, do faithfully your work in good spirit, not grumblingly, and then your employer will meet you in a like spirit, and your life will be one of happiness.
7. Consider that for the time being you are the property of your employer, and faithfully obey his instructions and requests.
8. It is better--more honest--to give him an hour or two of labor than to cheat him by idling or work poorly performed.
9. Avoid intoxicants, especially while you are at work, for as your time belongs to your employer, you should strive to render faithful, intelligent, service, which cannot be done under the influence of liquor. Besides, you endanger your own life and the safety of the property you are paid to protect.
10. Be frank, and never under any circumstances deceive your employer. If you have done wrong, or made a mistake, own it like a man. He will respect you more for it.
11. Treat your employer's property as you would your own; and if you are a careless man, treat it better.
12. Be polite and gentle to your fellow workmen and your employer, as coarse jests and ill temper are out of place even on the rock pile, as well as in the parlor. Remember the street scavenger can be a Chesterfield as well as the gentleman of fashion who graces the Richest drawing room.
                    "True politeness is to do and say
                     The noblest things in the kindest way."

I shall next consider Labor, Capital and Wealth.

1. Labor has been defined.
2. Capital is that which is employed to produce wealth.
3. Wealth is accumulated capital at rest.

Society can no more be in a healthful state without the harmonious working of these three elements, governed by ethics, than the human body could without the united action of heart, arteries and veins influenced by the lungs. Let me go a step further and say that labor is capital, or labor and capital are one. Labor is power. That power produces wealth. That wealth in action is called capital, and thus the work of labor, capital and wealth goes on subduing the earth. Every individual with all the powers and capacities of his constitution sound, is a capitalist to the extent of the exercise of those powers. That which such exercise produces and he accumulates is wealth, and if he wish to employ it to produce other wealth, it becomes capital.

The peanut vendor is a capitalist to the extent of his investment in earth nuts, roaster, pans, baskets, etc. The little girl who peddles laces, or newspapers, or pins around the streets, is as much a capitalist to the extent of her investment as Mr. Vanderbilt or Mr. Gould. Mr. Gould and Mr. Vanderbilt have simply by the exercise of more economy, sagacity and energy accumulated more wealth than she. But the peanut vendor may become a greater capitalist as he accumulates more wealth and employs it. It is folly to go point the finger of prejudice and envy at the very rich people and cry: "These men oppress us; these capitalists are sharks; these wealth people have our earnings." It is not only folly, but it is unjust. I see many of you with watches and chains, rings on your fingers, and pins on your breasts. These articles are wealth. They represent so much capital--labor or money--at rest. The man who owns the watch worth $8 and the one with the $100 watch, are men of wealth to the valuation of those useful articles. The poor laborer, who, by industry and frugality, after the exercise of his capital--his muscle--accumulates enough to buy an acre of land and erect a small cottage for his

faithful wife and little ones, was in turn a laborer, capitalist, and is now
a man of wealth to the value of that happy little home, where peace and
virtue reign and upon which the blessings of God rest. Mr. Vanderbilt is a
man of greater wealth than this man, but it is because he operated a larger
capital. Sometimes a spirit of envy creeps in between these two capitalists
and then both suffer--each in proportion to his wealth. This brings me to
consider Agrarianism.[15]
     This form of ownership originated in bloody Rome. It was tried among
the early Christians. Wherever it has been introduced failure and crime
followed. The population of the United States and Territories is 50,155,783;
the value of real estate and personal property is $16,902,993,443. Divide
this according to agrarianism and each person would get $337, which by trade
and speculation would soon again be in the hands of a few. And thus with
each day we should have to re-collect and re-distribute. Out of such a system no good could possibly come. Nature everywhere teaches that differences
and distinctions must exist. Why has she been more lavish with the peafowl
than with the crow? Why has she bedecked the gold finch or the bird of
paradise more gorgeously than the snow bird or the hawk? Why the lily more
fragrant than the sun flower? Why the difference in the magnitude of the
twinkling stars? Why the dissimilarity in the talents of men? Why are some
men born idiots and others with the sparkling gems of genius shining in their
souls? Why do some mountains possess millions of dollars of the precious or
useful minerals and others only sandstone or lime rock? The answers are
secrets locked up in the mystery of the Almighty. The man of talent, of
push, of energy, frugality and sagacity can not help accumulating more of the
results of labor than the individual of opposite qualities. Agrarianism is
a foe to thrift and activity, and encourages idleness and stagnation. It
would paralyze business and cause the wheels of industry to hang dry and
still over the stream of progress.
     Agrarianism is a hydra-headed monster. It has presented itself in many
forms and at various times. To-day it breeds discontent among the common
people which to-morrow bursts into rebellion and revolution. Lawlessness
prevails, property is destroyed and bloody murder stalks boldly abroad. Is
anything gained? No! as loud as heaven's loudest artillery can sound it.
All classes of capitalists are weakened, wealth is destroyed, and fond Hope,
the bright anchor of the soul, sits dark and gloomy in the ashes of ruin.
     Communism. Saint-Simonianism, nihilism, anarchy, socialism, Henry
Georgeism, are all dangerous forms of that hideous monster, agrarianism.
Every capitalist--every man of wealth--whether his muscle is his only stock
in trade or not, or whether he counts his capital and wealth by dimes or by
millions--should seize the bludgeon of reason and justice and strike the
monster--the common foe to the progress and happiness of man--a deadly blow.
It is true that laboring men have their grievances, but strikes are not the
means by which these wrongs may be set right. The appeal to strikes is an
appeal from reason to error, from justice to injustice, from order to disorder, from law to riot, from morality to immorality, from virtue to sin,
from innocence to murder. The strike is a foe to the infant at the mother's
breast; it is an enemy to the happiness of home; it is the howling wolf at
the door of the humble cottage; it is hostile to personal liberty; it is an
enemy to religion, it is the embodiment of riot and murder striding through
the land stamping out the life of the nation, crushing out the manhood of the
citizens, setting a premium upon crime and outlawing virtue and honesty. I
wish I had the power to represent it in its true light. A mass of grumbling,
dissatisfied men who will not work, by desperation and lawlessness deterring
others from honest toil. Business is paralyzed and millions of dollars sunk.
But this is small compared to the suffering and misery and want in the homes
of these frantic men. Could we but lift the curtain which hides their dark
homes, a picture would be presented which would cause the blood to chill and
sicken the soul. These men hang around the saloons and stifle the cries for
bread from their homes by liquor and beer- a morsel of cheese or a cracker
answering for food. But what about the wretched wife and starving child?[16]
     But they do not stop there. The torch, pistol, the knife, the bomb and
infernal machines are brought into play their deadly parts. Then the fire

fiend with his angry tongue laps up wealth and happy homes, the knife and the
pistol start streams of human gore down the gutters of the streets, and the
hellish bomb brings massive edifices cracking, crumbling to the earth.
    The fiend having sated himself in gore and ruin, surveys the field of
desolation. What has been gained? Nothing. If permitted he returns to
work with a weakened constitution, less respect of his family, kept under
the watch of the law, without the confidence of his employer and with the
curse of his own conscience. You ask: "If strikes are not the remedy, what
is the remedy?" Have a clear understanding with your employer. Try to enter
into his interests and feelings. Tell him plainly that you can not afford
to work for him at present rates. If he can not or does not raise your wages,
give him notice that you will quit at a certain time, and then do not interfere with the person engaged in your place. All parties will feel better,
and your employer may soon be able to grant your request and recall you.
You certainly have no right to interfere with others who are willing to work
for him.
    The colored laborer can neither afford to strike nor encourage strikes.
He has felt the baneful effects of them. He has time and time again seen
white labor organizations resort to this method of getting colored men out
of employment. If it is right against the employer for higher wages, it is
right against a fellow-workman on account of race or color. But it is not
right at all. This is a country of law and order, and the negro's salvation
lies in his willing obedience to law--fairly and impartially administered.

                              LABOR ORGANIZATIONS.

    I do not deny labor the right of organization for the advancement of its
interests. This is legitimate and highly proper so long as the general interests of society are protected. There is perhaps, no country upon the
globe which extends greater liberties and protection to labor than the United
States of America. In Alabama and many other states of the union, the
mechanic's lien enables him to compel the employer to fulfill his obligations,
but the employer has no remedy against the mechanic except in rare cases
where bonds have been given by the contractor.
    The cause of the laboring man has kept pace with the march of civili-
zation and progress, until the order of government has been reversed and the
laboring classes have become the rulers. However, they are threatened with
great danger growing out of the slavery entailed by labor organizations.
Few of them are for the real advancement of the interests of labor, but mere
machines for the personal aggrandizement of the politicians who stand behind
the scenes. The laborer, in attempting to avoid the imaginary Scylla of
capital, may dash his life out against the terrible Charybdis of demogogy.
Our laws all favor the laborer, and I make this assertion regardless of
statements of those who see gain in keeping labor in a state of excitement.
In Egypt, many hundreds years ago, the poorer class could not be anything
else. They were not permitted, under heavy penalties, to change their occupations or locations. A hod carrier was doomed to that work during his
natural life. Other countries more recently oppressed labor just as severely.
I mention this in illustration of the depths from which labor has come. Today the laborer may not only change his location but may change his occupation, and ply a dozen if he choose to do so. An organization which has for
its object the moral and intellectual advancement of its members, as well as
their financial welfare, is not objectionable and should be encouraged. But
where prejudice is aroused against other forms of labor (as capital, banking,
etc., etc.,) they are lawless, dangerous, and should be shunned by every good
laboring man. No organization outside of a benevolent institution should be
secret, and I doubt the propriety of all secret societies. Secrecy is too
often the cloak for evil and scheming. The dark clouds of secrecy have ever
been the means of over-awing or misleading the lower classes. Permit me to
introduce here the following extract from an address bearing upon this subject. It is so excellent that I will be pardoned for clipping at length and
endorsing it *in toto:*
    The twenty-fourth annual Grand International Convention of the Brother-
hood of Locomotive Engineers was held in Chicago on the 19th October, with
delegates present from all parts of the Union. The Grand Chief Engineer,
P. M. Arthur, with his usual rare good sense, said in the course of his

annual address: "We are enemies only to wrong in its various devices and
garbs, and can assuredly say that political schemes and aspirations have no
place nor part in our association. A mighty army of men, representing 365
divisions, has gathered about a nucleus of 12 men who, 24 years ago assembled
in the city of Detroit and started an organization destined to be more than
they knew or dreamed. To-day we number 25,000 men, and while our numbers
are great, we would not have you consider only the quantity, but the quality
as well. To be a Brotherhood man, four things are requisite, namely: Sobriety,
truth, justice, and morality. This is our motto, and upon this precept have
we based our practice. Taking all things into consideration, our relations,
both to ourselves and with various railroads, employing Brotherhood men, are
amicable. When we consider the dissatisfaction which is everywhere manifest
about us, our few troubles pale in insignificance. There have been times
and incidents when the 'strike' was the only court of appeals for the workingman, and the evil lay in the abuse of them and not in the use of them. The
methods used to bring about a successful termination of strikes, the abuse
of property and even of persons, have brought the very name into disrepute,
while the troubles of the laboring man are receiving mere cant, and sympathy
for him is dying out. More and more clearly defined is the line becoming
which divides the honest man, satisfied with a just remuneration which he
has truly earned, until by his own effort he can rise to a higher position
in life, and the loud-voiced 'bomb thrower,' who, scarcely able to speak the
English language, seeks to win his own comfortable living from those who have
worked for it, presuming upon the imagination and arousing false hopes in the
hearts of those who are still more ignorant than himself. Among sensible men
the day for all this is past. Let 'mercy season justice, and justice be
tempered with moderation.' A wise arbitration looks to a long result rather
than to immediate satisfaction, and accomplishes more than intimidation ever
can hope to do." [17]

"It is not my intention," said Mr. Arthur, "to impose upon this convention any dogma upon the drink question; but I cannot refrain in honesty to
my own convictions from deploring the sad havoc that intemperance is making
in the ranks of our fellowmen. So great is this evil that no man or woman
who is striving to improve his fellows can help taking it into account. It
is, indeed, an important factor for evil in our midst. Not only from the
physical and moral standpoint is it working mischief, but from the standpoint
of labor. The man who has so little self-control that he cannot resist the
temptation to degrade himself is always in danger of bringing disgrace upon
his brethren. He has lost his self-respect and, to some extent, his independence, thus making an easier victim to the greed of a selfish employer.
I would therefore urge upon you the necessity of abstaining from everything
that will in the slightest degree impair your usefulness as citizens or your
efficiency as locomotive engineers."

THE NEGRO AND THE LABOR QUESTION

Competency is a prerequisite to all occupations. I have alluded to this
above, but I desire to treat it more at length here, and especially in its
relation to the Negro of the South.

In consequence of former conditions, incompetency has been the normal
standard of both employer and employe. The conditions being changed, and
new relations existing between these two classes in the South, the standard
must be changed--must be raised. I shall put aside sentimentalism, and view
the subject in its true light.

What is the "Negro Labor Problem" of the future?

Simply the ability on the part of the Negro to remain in the market as
a laborer, and the ability of the Southern white man to meet the labor complications of the future, which will be developed in the necessity for better
skilled labor, and the desire of the white man to get this superior labor at
the old prices.

Leaving competency and skill out of the question, it will be readily
admitted that the Negro is the most desirable of all races as a laborer. He
is kind, forgiving, and easily understood and managed. He is willing to work
and at almost any price. This is shown in the fact that there is a larger
per cent of breadwinners in the Southern States than any other section, except
in the far West and East. But he is ignorant, improvident and unskilled;

and it is to be regretted that his progress is slow in the cultivation of skill in the industries, but there are fruitful and encouraging signs in this direction.

There are two causes which tend to demand a higher standard of labor qualification in the South:

1.   The more free intermixture of northern and southern people--thereby bringing the southern people in contact with the superior white labor of the North.

2.   The immigration of northern people who have been accustomed to cultivated, free labor.

We do not pretend to hint that the Negro laborer will not improve, but will he do so sufficiently and rapidly enough to meet the heavy demand?

He must be able to compete with the skilled white labor, ready to crowd the South, or he must go to the rear. This is a stern fact, becoming more and more patent daily.

I am not speaking only of the Negro as a domestic servant, carpenter, brick-mason, and other occupations of the cities, but of him as a farmer. Sentimentality, which has had much to do with holding the Negro and white man together in their relation of employer and employee, is fast giving way to business principles which are to govern the future South. If my forty acres can be made to produce more by A's method of farming than by B's, A is a more scientific, skilled and desirable tenant, so B must stand aside. This is the "Negro problem" in its relation to labor, in a nut shell.

William H. Councill, *The Negro Laborer: A Word to Him* (Huntsville, Alabama, 1887), pp. 7-15.

III

THE KNIGHTS OF LABOR AND BLACK MILITANCY

III

BLACK LABOR MILITANCY AND THE KNIGHTS OF LABOR

While the black press debated the desirability of blacks joining the ranks
of labor, Negro workers themselves were demonstrating what was for southern
whites an alarming tendency to organize and fight for higher pay and improved
working conditions. The mythology that blacks were docile and tractable workers came under challenge in the 1880s when those same workers displayed an
assertiveness decidedly uncharacteristic of the straw man created by racial
mythology.

The most dramatic mechanism through which black workers asserted their
militance was the strike. In March 1880, plantation wage laborers in St. John
Parish demanded an increase from 75¢ to $1.00 per day. When the owners refused
to comply, blacks left the fields, and strike leaders travelled from plantation
to plantation enforcing the stoppage. Violence inevitably followed, and the
governor quickly ordered troops to the scene, withdrawing them only after they
had arrested the ringleaders and broken the strike. Typically, the newspapers
reported the troubles with a deliberate planter bias (Doc. 1-5).

In East Atchison, Missouri, whites mobbed black strikers in July 1880,
and the authorities refused to send the militia to protect them (Doc. 7). Another strike conducted at a Jacksonville, Florida, saw mill culminated in a
gun battle between the primarily black strikers and the police (Doc. 6). On
the other hand, during the 1881 New Orleans Cotton Yard strike, 4,000 black and
white workers displayed a high degree of class solidarity (Doc. 8).
Between 2,000 and 3,000 workers of both races attended the funeral of a black
drayman shot by police during the stoppage, and other unions sent representatives as well. The employers brought in scabs from Savannah and, naturally,
the mayor supported the employers. As the police made mass arrests, numerous
non-striking black men and women also were jailed for assisting the workers
(Doc. 10). During the week of disturbances which followed, the police shot
another black man, which prompted one Louisiana newspaper to wonder why, when
thousands of strikers of both races took to the streets, only blacks were shot
(Doc. 11).

In this atmosphere of working class solidarity, the Knights of Labor began
a definite campaign to enlist black members (Doc. 14-25). Southern Negroes
generally responded favorably once it became apparent that the Order was open
to them. But the South was not a homogeneous region and its work force was
fractured by class, race, and provincialism. Consequently, black and white
relations among the working classes varied greatly by locale. In some places
white Knights refused to organize blacks and paid the penalty of defeat. Such
was the case in Galveston, Texas, where between 1,500 and 2,00 Knights went on
strike in November 1888. When black strikebreakers were imported, racial con-
frontation seemed inevitable (Doc. 26). For whites the main issue was the
employer's use of black workers. Since they refused to recognize the needs of
Negro workers, the white laborers chose to view the strike as a struggle for
the "protection of white labor." Trouble appeared imminent when the black
longshoremen announced that they would not "tamely submit" to being replaced.
Tension mounted when the local Master Workman of the Knights attempted to get
three black policemen fired, and when the militia was mustered (Doc. 27-31).

Working conditions for blacks were generally worse in the South than in
the North. The truck system of payment, the leasing of convicts, and other
devices by which tillers of the soil were kept in debt, and sometimes debt
peonage, all provided the landless agricultural workers of the region with a
multitude of grievances which called for organized action. But here employer
resistance to the organization of black farm workers was particularly severe.
Just south of Little Rock, Arkansas, three assemblies of black Knights were
organized, and a strike was called in July 1886 for improved wages and to protest exploitation at the company store. Believing that a rebellion of racial
revenge was underway, planters sent their families away, and an armed posse
assembled to quell this outrage to the planters' sense of racial order (Doc.
34-35).

BLACK LABOR UNREST IN THE SOUTH

1. NEGRO STRIKERS IN LOUISIANA

FORCING OTHER PLANTATION LABORERS TO CEASE WORK--
THE LEADERS IN CUSTODY

NEW ORLEANS, March 19.--Trouble broke out last Monday with the negro
laborers on the Dugan and Whitehead plantations, apparently growing out of a
strike which is now general throughout the parish for higher wages. Laborers
on plantations in that parish are now paid 75 cents a day. They demanded $1.
They were refused. Several of the strikers then banded together, and released
the stock on the Davenport plantation, on Tuesday, while the overseers were
at dinner, and whipped two hands with a bull-whip for endeavoring to prevent
them from so doing. Their next scene of action was the old Killmore, now Hy-
melia plantation, near the line of St. John Parish, where they compelled
workmen to cease labor. They then returned down the river, stopping work on
every plantation for a distance of 10 miles. The people on the Kelly, Ashton,
and Culing plantations were attacked yesterday by an armed band numbering
nearly 250 men. On Ashton plantation one of the miscreants was wounded by
the overseer. The greatest show of resistance was made on the Kelly place.
Kelly and T. J. Harris were surrounded, their lives were threatened, and they
were fired upon while fighting their way through the mob. They escaped with
only a severe bruise on the hip of Mr. Harris, inflicted with a bludgeon.
Mr. Kelly stated that the movement is organized and under the leadership of
Jake Bradley and others equally desperate. Jake Bradley is a tall, burly
negro, who led the attack on the Parish Jail on Sept. 14, 1878, which resulted
in the butchering of Valcour St. Martin, son of the Parish Attorney.
This morning at 4 o'clock, the Louisiana Field Artillery left here on
the Morgan ferry-boat and took the train for the scene of trouble under orders from Gov. Wiltz. At 2:30 o'clock this afternoon, Brig. Gen. John Glynn
received a telegram from Col. Legardour, at the front, saying: "On arrival
of troops, the rioters quietly dispersed. One of the ringleaders, Bradley,
has been arrested, and is at present in custody." Later it was ascertained
that the other leaders were captured. The troops arrived home this evening.

New York Times, March 20, 1880.

2. LABOR TROUBLES

THE STRIKERS IN ST. JOHN PARISH

Governor's Proclamation

A Full Investigation by a Representative of the Picayune

Acting upon the solicitation of the planters, His Excellency, Gov. Wiltz
commissioned Major Strong, Secretary of State, to proceed to St. John, for
the purpose of investigating the labor troubles in that parish.
The idea actuating his Excellency was doubtless to see if the difficulties referred to could not be settled without the inconvenience and trouble
of sending a detachment of the militia, as was the case in the St. Charles
strike. Major Strong was notified to leave yesterday morning by the Morgan

Road, and on Saturday night he was furnished with a proclamation by the
Governor, a large number of copies of which had been printed in the form of
a handbill to be posted in conspicuous places throughout the parish.

The Proclamation

read:

EXECUTIVE DEPARTMENT,
State of Louisiana

Whereas, information has reached me that evil doers and mischievous
persons are wandering about in the parish of St. John the Baptist, in this
State, giving orders to residents of that parish to depart therefrom, and to
others to leave their work, thereby causing disorder, and assuming to themselves a right which is prohibited by law; and,

Whereas, I am determined to protect all citizens of this State in the
enjoyment of their right and of their liberties;

Now, therefore, I, Louis Alfred Wiltz, Governor of the State of Louisiana, by virtue of the authority vested in me by the constitution, do hereby
warn these evil doers and mischievous persons to desist from their evil
doings, and do also call upon the good citizens of the parish of St. John
the Baptist to discountenance such persons, and to aid and assist the law
officer of this State in arresting and bringing to justice all persons who
may disturb the peace and interfere with the rights and privileges of the
people or of any portion of the people of the parish of St. John the Baptist.

Given under my signature and seal of the State of Louisiana, at the city
of New Orleans, this twenty-seventh day of March, A.D. 1880.

LOUIS A. WILTZ,
Governor of Louisiana.

By the Governor:
WILL A. STRONG, Secretary of State.

A reporter of the Picayune was commissioned to

Accompany Major Strong

to the scene of action, and to present an immediate report of the condition
of affairs.

At Gretna Station, Mr. Bradish Johnson, one of the leading planters in
the parish of St. John boarded the train, and a union of the visiting forces
was effected. On the way up it was discovered that the strike in St. Charles
parish is by no means at an end, although the laborers are now working on
the Howard & Morris, the Lulling and the Kelley places, at the old rates,
seventy-five cents a day.

Passing the plantations in the upper portion of the parish one could not
fail to see the evil effects of the strike in the neglect of the crops which
has resulted. The weather now is most favorable for the cultivation of the
growing cane and every day lost in this respect must result in serious de-
preciation of the amount and value of the year's crop. While the negroes
are holding out for an increase of wages and asserting they are almost starving from the low rates paid them the reporter was informed that a neighboring bar-room has been, and is now, doing a thriving business through the
patronage of the strikers. This information, if reliable, would go to show
what has been charged against the colored people is true and that is that
their poverty is due to their recklessness and dissipation.

A pleasant and uneventful ride of forty-four miles brought the party to
St. John Station, where conveyances speedily transported the party to the
court-house. It was evident that something unusual was going on, for the
planters in the vicinity were collected at the hotel, while the negroes were
moving on towards Senator Henry Demas' place, where a mass meeting had been
arranged. Before going into the details of the meeting in which Major Strong,
the planters and the strikers participated, it may be well to prevent the
events which caused it. Where so many conflicting statements were made to
him, the reporter was compelled to sift the evidence for himself, and here
gives the result of his conclusions.

The Strike Began

last Monday in the lower part of the parish and on the Sarpy place, adjoining

St. Charles, who thus became a continuation of the St. Charles strike. The
ground for the strike was the same as in the St. Charles case, a demand for
an increase of wages from seventy-five cents to one dollar a day. The
strikers went from plantation to plantation, inducing others to join them;
and although they deny that force was used to increase their numbers, there
is very good reason to believe that verbal intimidation was a most potent
factor in making the strike general.

The idea the strikers have all along held to was that "the colored people
are a nation" (the words of one of them) and must stand together. Hence,
while no attack was made upon the whites, every colored man was given to
understand that the movement was a race one, and he must, therefore, join
it. They believe negroes have a right to make laws for themselves, and in
carrying out this theory every laborer was brought into the strike either by
suasion or threats.

On Tuesday the strikers drew up a "constitution" as a basis for their
visionary government, which every one signed and took an oath to obey.

The Constitution

declares that for the better protection of themselves the signers agree not
to work for less than a dollar a day, and any violating his oath shall be
punished with a severe thrashing.

One of the prime movers in getting up this document was Lucien Antoine,
a laborer on the Lendiche place. A day or so afterwards Antoine was observed
busily at work in the fields, and his fellow-strikers being anxious to find
out if he was getting his dollar a day, asked the owner what wages Antoine
was getting. The answer ninety cents, whereupon Antoine's fellow-signers
proceeded to give him the severe thrashing provided for in the "constitution"
as a penalty for violating his oath. Antoine after it was over, remarked
he thought he deserved the whipping as he had himself proposed the law.

Two negroes working at Bonnet Carre were also reported to have been
thrashed by the strikers, but in the limited time at the reporter's disposal
it was impossible to either verify or disprove the rumor.

According to the statement of Mr. Halloway, the manager of the Johnson
Plantation, two of the negroes who live on the plantation, worked on the
levee on Tuesday, and that night they were taken from their houses and unmercifully whipped. Mr. Halloway crossed the river after the occurrence was
known and tried to find the parish judge, G. Leche, who had gone fishing and
could not be found. The justice of the peace for Mr. Halloway's ward having
joined the strikers, no local relief could be had from him. The sheriff of
the parish, John Webre, a colored man, either was unwilling, or unable, as
he remarked to Major Strong, to arrest so many men, and the only recourse
left to the planters was to apply to the authorities outside of the parish
for assistance, and the response was the visit of Major Strong.

During His Stay

the reporter mingled almost exclusively among the strikers, for the purpose
of getting at their views and expectations. All who were spoken to declared
they were ignorant of any outrages having been committed, and in fact had
endeavored to keep the peace. They were emphatic in asserting that starvation would soon overtake them if they kept on working for seventy-five cents
a day, as the rise in provisions and clothing was so great. They seemed to
realize that they had no chance of getting away from their present homes,
and when asked what they looked forward to in case their demands were not
complied with, they could find no answer.

To the practical eye of the inquisitor it soon became evident that the
crowd was divided into two classes--the unscrupulous leaders and the well-
meaning but ignorant followers. The majority of the negroes were respectful
and good hearted, and while they were anxious to have their wages raised,
they were opposed to violence in any shape, and if let alone would doubtless
go to work again. The leaders might be sat down upon with advantage to the
general welfare, and the reporter thinks it a personal duty to show how
several of them lied to him, including Andrew Fox and James H. Davis, the
speakers at the meeting.

When these worthies found out that some of the honest negroes were trying

to get the "constitution" for the reporter, they swore up and down that no
such document was in existence or ever had been. This had the effect of
discrediting their assertion that no violence had been used. When Davis was
asked how long the strikers could maintain themselves without working, he
answered: "About eight months, and not steal."

"But I thought you were on the verge of starvation," innocently remarked
the unsophiscated newsman.

"Suppose there were rich men who could help us and didn't want their
names known, suppose the storekeepers would supply us!"

"That's so; in fact they say the storekeepers started this affair."

"But they can't prove it, emphatically rejoined Davis, and the reporter
thought if the storekeepers were innocent their champion displayed unusual
excitement.

With regard to the differences between the laborers and the planters as
to wages, the reporter did not consider it his duty to take sides one way or
the other, since the law of supply and demand cannot be changed by strikes.
On the part of the planters it may be said that in other parishes, such as
St. James and Ascension, the negroes only get sixty cents, and up to this
time have been satisfied that indulgence in bad cigars and worse whisky is
what makes the laborer poor.

On the side of the negroes it is urged that the rise in values has not
been accompanied by an increase of wages and that they are daily getting
behind hand. One old darkey remarked that he was financially better off
before the war than now, and this seems to be the general opinion among the
negroes.

The Mass Meeting

was held in the enclosure before Senator Demas's house. Before going to it
Major Strong sent for Webre the Sheriff, and explained the object of the
meeting, and read him a lecture upon his duty in suppressing rioters, and at
the same time handing over one of the Governor's proclamation.

Webre said he had made no arrests, because no warrants had been issued,
and he knew of no outrages having been committed, also adding the strikers
were too numerous a body to be arrested by one man. He was told that he could
summons a *posse comitatus,* and if that was not sufficient, the militia could
be sent up. Thereupon he promised to suppress all future lawlessness, come
what might. Webre is a farmer, whose hands have struck also and his friends
were very anxious to assure the visitors that he had done all he could.

About three hundred negroes attended the meeting, and the Demas Brass
Band recklessly tackled a number of popular and time-worn airs. Among the
planters present were noticed John A. Stevenson, Bradish Johnson, L. D. Martin, M. A. Bechel, the Scheixnayder brothers, L. Landaiche, P. A. Bechel, E.
L. Bechel, F. Wehre, J. B. Caire, A. Oubre, O. Roussel and E. Ferret. The
small number, comparatively speaking of negroes present was due to the short
notice given of the meeting; as all the parish joined in the strike, the number would have been nearer a thousand if a day's notice had been allowed.

Senator Henry Demas

mounted a high bench and made a very sensible address to the strikers. Being
their Representative in the Legislature and yet a farmer whose twelve hands
had joined them, his position was rather a delicate one. He explained the
difficulty of getting the St. Charles prisoners free and said his mission
was to keep his friends from getting into a similar scrape. He told them that
they had a perfect right to strike but they had no right to force others to
join them. They had the right to meet on the levee and stay as long as they
could maintain themselves, yet they could not go upon private property for the
purpose of inducing the laborers thereon to join them.

"It is reported in the papers," said he,"that you have been marching
aroused armed with cane knives and guns [cries of 'No, no,'] and threatening
the lives of the whites. [Yells of 'It's a lie.'] I don't say you have done
so, but if you have, you have violated the law it's my duty to tell you just
how far you can go and keep within the law. The Governor has sent his
respresentative up here with a proclamation which I will read."

After reading the proclamation Senator Demas went on to say, "I don't

want to have to intercede with the Governor for you. You are charged with
whipping negroes and cutting levees." Cries of "It's not so;" "That's a
lie."

Major Strong--In the name of the Governor I call upon the sheriff to
enforce order; if you don't keep silence I'll have you arrested in a minute.

This command had a soothing effect and Senator Demas pointed out how it
was possible to gain an object such as they had in view by peaceful means.
He advised the planters and laborers to have a mutual sympathy, as each
class contributed to the general good.

He wanted the difficulties settled amicably and satisfactorily. Said
he: "If one man can work for five cents a day, that's his business; if you
can't work for seventy-five cents, that's your business. Sometimes people
do things which they think are right, but which are wrong, and their leaders
are unable to protect them." In closing, he advised them to appoint committees to confer with the planters, as he was satisfied an adjustment of
the troubles would result.

Major Strong was then introduced as the
                    Representative of the Governor,

and without delay expounded the law of individual rights, reading for the
purpose a portion of the fourteenth amendment.

"This," he remarked, " gives you the right to do what you please so long
as you do not abridge the rights or interfere with the property of others.
For instance, you signed an agreement which provided that any one who broke
it should receive forty lashes. You had no right to sign such a document,
and the Governor will not allow any one to be punished who breaks that
agreement. I know more about negroes than you think. I was born among them,
played with them, taught many of them to read, and all our old slaves live
with me still. I know many of you are ignorant, while some have a smattering
of knowledge, who are leading you astray. Now, on every plantation there is
one negro who is respected and has the confidence of all the others. I
advise you to select such a man from each place and let him meet the planter
and confer with him upon your troubles. I guarantee if you do this the
planters will meet you half way. If they can't pay you more than seventy-five
cents, then you can leave and they can get others. I have come in my uniform
today, but without the emblem of war, but if there is to be any trouble I can
get that emblem and 10,000 men within four hours from the city. The Governor
says bulldozing must stop in this State, and he means what he says."

A voice--"Boss, I axes you if we 'plut dat committee, won't de planters
kick 'em out as sassy niggers?"

"I'll guarantee not," answered Major Strong, while Mr. Johnson arose and
corroborated the assurance. Continuing, Major Strong said:

"I understand that you believe the Governor pardoned the St. Charles
prisoners because they did no wrong. That's not so. They acknowledged they
did wrong before they were pardoned."

A voice--"Well, boss, I begin de year wid nothin' and end with nothin."

Major Strong-- "I'll ask you candidly if the corner grocery isn't to blame
for that [laughter]. With $20 a month, cabin and fuel free, you are getting
better wages than any laborers in the world.

At this point one of the leaders handed in a petition which had been
prepared on Saturday to be handed to the planters on Monday.

                      The Petition,

To Farmers and Planters of St. John Baptist:

Sir--in consideration of the general advance of the price of provisions,
clothing and food, and everything which constitutes materially the cost of
living, taken in connection with the revival of business and returning pro-
perity in all the channels of trade, the increased demand for labor, skilled
and unskilled, in all the industrial pursuits, and also the flourishing condition of present crops and the low rate of State and parish taxes, etc.,

We, the undersigned laborers, do herein respectfully petition you for
an increase in our pay from present rates to the following figures: All
plantation work, such as field labor for making a crop of cane, corn, rice,
etc., one dollar per day ($1) for ten hours labor.

Believing our request is just and consistent and, that the reward for

our toils should keep pace with the demands of the cost of living, we
earnestly desire you to give our petition your careful consideration. Hoping
it may meet with a favorable response, we further ask that you will, after
having duly considered the same, grant us a reply.

Major Strong having read the petition, made some remarks upon it and
warned the crowd if there was any trouble he would hold the sheriff responsible, and if he didn't do his duty he would be impeached by the Legislature.

Messrs. Johnson and Stevenson made short addresses, in substance stating
that if no arrangement could be made as to wages, the planter and laborer
should part company in peace.

Both gave excellent advice, which was well received and applauded by
the negroes.

Andrew Fox, one of the colored leaders, spoke for the strikers. He
denied most stoutly that the negroes had resorted to violence, as their
intention was to keep within the law. He said if the negroes attempted to
go to Kansas, the bulldozers would stop them.

He "wished to God" men would stop running down to New Orleans and telling stories about disturbances in St. John. The people were starving and
wanted relief. He read from the constitution of 1879 the article which
provides that "no law shall be passed fixing the price of manual labor," and
by weak sophistry tried to convince his followers the article referred to
the rights of strikers. He closed a demagogical speech by remarking:

"I fought in the United States Army and 10,000 militia wouldn't change
my opinion. If you go to leave I ask if the whites would not bushwhack you
and burn your homes?" [Shouts of "That's so," "Yes," "True as Gospel."]

Major Strong here interposed and informed the burning orator he would
have to cease such incendiary and ridiculous assertions, as he would be
summarily arrested.

Fox was heard to mumble something about not being afraid to be arrested,
and then stepped down.

Evan Colvin another negro, spoke sensibly enough, advising the negroes
to be quiet and if they did not get their $1 a day to emigrate to Kansas.

James H. Davis, another colored head centre, who has been alluded to
before, followed in the strain of Fox. He also denied any violence had been
used and advised the Sheriff to come forward and arrest any one who had
broken the law and he promised there would be no resistance. He didn't see
the use of calling on the militia when everybody was so law-abiding.

He said that the negroes had appointed a committee of twenty-seven to
meet the planters on Monday and Tuesday, at the court-house. The planters
present asked if the crowd would stand by the committee's action if the conference was held. The reply was in the affirmative if the action was satisfactory. This did not suit the planters, and the crowd agreed to abide the
committee's action, whereupon the planters consented to the conference Jim
Lee, a colored divine, made some humorous remarks, which placed matters in
a more satisfactory light, and the meeting dissolved.

From the opinion expressed by planters and laborers there seems every
chance that the meeting to-day will result in a compromise being effected,
by which the wages will be increased, but not to a dollar.

During the afternoon it was rumored that the negroes in St. James had
started on their strike, and the probabilities are that, like an epidemic,
the strike will spread from parish to parish.

Major Strong will remain in St. John for several days to see if any
trouble occurs, but the good effect produced by his speech, in conjunction
with the Governor's proclamation, will doubtless smooth the way for a peaceable compromise.

New Orleans *Daily Picayune, March 29, 1880.*

3. THE LABOR TROUBLES

A FULL REPORT OF THE PROCEEDINGS IN ST. JOHN PARISH--
CONDUCT OF THE NEGROES--ARRIVAL OF THE MILITIA

[Special Correspondence of the Picayune.]

St. John, March 31, 1880, 3 P.M.

When the Picayune correspondent left on Sunday afternoon for the city the labor troubles in St. John Parish seemed in a fair way of settlement.

The mass of negroes exhibited a disposition to go to work, if they were assured of protection from the assaults of the strikers, headed by the preacher, S. Andrew Fox, James Davis and Bill Lee. These unscrupulous men professed to be anxious to terminate the strike, and in their speeches at the mass meeting Sunday advised their followers to commit no outrages and to keep within the law. Under these circumstances it was natural to believe that the end of the difficulties was near, and that at the conference between the planters and the committee representing the negroes arranged for Monday, a satisfactory settlement would be agreed on.

These expectations, however, proved ill-founded. When the conference came off Col. John A. Stevenson, acting as the spokesman for the planters, made a very sensible address, which, if the strikers had been so disposed, would have opened the way for a compromise. But the negroes, led on by the men before mentioned, were in no humor to think of a compromise, and at the outset proclaimed an ultimatum.

"A dollar a day or Kansas."

It was in vain that the planters tried to reason with them, or to show them how useless it was to think of going to Kansas without money or provisions.

The patience of Col. Stevenson and his associates entirely gave way when Fox made a most incendiary speech, during which he said that when the United States Government saw the fields going to waste, because of the strike, it would take them away from the planters and parcel them out among the strikers. The cheers that greeted the assertion showed how freely the gullible blacks believed it, in fact, it is the writer's belief they would swallow anything as Gospel Truth that the leaders would tell them, and some facts will be given to show this belief has good foundation. From this point Fox and his colleagues went on with the wildest declaration. They posed as martyrs and said if any outrages had been committed they were responsible, and wished to suffer whatever punishment the law might inflict.

Later in the day, finding the temper of the negroes growing worse, it was determined to take some decisive steps, and accordingly a number of affidavits were sworn out against those who had been most prominent committing outrages.

The most serious charge related to the whipping of two negroes on Mr. Bradish Johnson's place, and the arrests were made upon the affidavit of Mr. Holloway.

All of the parties implicated were promptly scored and locked up in the court-house jail. Henry May, a dusky bulldozer, who whipped Lucien Antoine for working for eighty cents a day, was arrested, but the kind-hearted Judge Leche released him on bail of $50. On the charge of trespass, preferred by Col. Stevenson, Floren Taylor, Felice Bethencourt and Valeour Brown were taken into custody.

Although the names are rather high-sounding and trifle romantic, the color would not suffice by comparison with the best brand of May & Day. Auguste Deviesin, another striker, was arrested for carrying concealed weapons, on the affidavit of Lucien Antoine.

As might be imagined, these arrests created some consternation among the strikers, who had previously been under the impression that the law could not touch them. Major Strong who had arrived on Sunday, did all in his power to make the negroes understand that he really represented the Governor, who was determined to protect every colored man who wanted to work. While he would give this assurance to those who wanted to resume work the leaders would move around and caution them not to take his advice, insinuating that he represented no one and his power was merely imaginary. Through fear of the strikers and belief in their statement that the Major had no power to bring the militia up to protect them, the weak-minded negroes informed their employers that they could not go to work until they saw some tangible evidence of Major Strong's assurance of protection. The strikers to still further carrying out their scheme of intimidation, tore up the printed copies of the Governor's proclamation and trampled the pieces under their feet.

It then became evident that if any crop was to be made during the year it would be necessary to bring the corps to protect the laborers who wanted to resume work. The story of how Major Strong communicated the facts to the Governor may bear recital, as showing the difficulties of communication between St. John and New Orleans, points only forty odd miles apart.

It was midnight Monday when he started for the city.

The train on the Morgan road has stopped running and no steamboat was to be seen. There was only one way to make the trip and that was by hand car and through the friendly aid of the section bosses on the railroad.

The night was quite cold and there were no overcoats in the party. A kind-hearted old woman observing the condition of affairs, lent one of her blankets which kept the State from losing its Secretary through freezing.

The ride was terribly monotonous, for everytime the brakes went up the Major received a dig in the back, and the digs came at the rate of about sixty a minute. At Westwego the hand car stopped and the traveler had to cast around for a conveyance to the city, and in the darkness and solitude the prospects were anything but encouraging. Wandering along the marshy ground he finally stumbled against a cabin and roused its owner, a burly negro. The colloquy between the two men was short and to the point.

"How much?" queried the Secretary of State, "will you take to row me to Jackson street?"

"How much, boss, will yer give?" was the non-commital reply.

"Five dollars," was the answer.

"I'll ask the old woman fust."

"If you have to ask your wife, I'm off," responded the representative of the Governor.

"Never mind, boss, I'll go."

In a weak and leaky skiff the two headed for Jackson street, which was reached about 3 o'clock in the morning.

The Major's trouble were by no means at an end and for two hours he hunted for a telephone or telegraph office to summon a cab. By daybreak a cab was procured and the driver directed to go straight to the Governor's residence. Even while His Excellency was soundly sleeping, forgetful of Supreme Court appointments and the demand of politicians, he was aroused by a ring of the bell and soon found himself giving audience to his representative. The result of the interview was seen in the order to the Washington Artillery and Crescent City Battalion, published in yesterday's Picayune.

The troops so ordered to proceed to St. John were under the command of Capt. Frank McElroy, of the Washington Artillery. The detachment of the C. C. Battalion was officered by Lieut. B. H. Baker, and Lieut. J. G. Woods, part of the Washington Artillery by Lieut. Beebe and Lieut. Dudley Selph, acting Adjutant.

It was given out that four days' rations were locked up in the freight car, and this, enabled with the assurance of the commission . . . Lieut. M. Montgomery, that tables would be set immediately on arriving at St. John conjured up pictures of Epicurean Feasts in the minds of the hungry soldiers. St. John was reached at 3 o'clock and the boys marched to the Court-House, where they executed a series of military manoeuvres in the presence of the awe-stricken darkies looking.

In the temple of justice the trial of the men charged with whipping the negroes on the Johnson place was progressing slowly, probably fifty negroes watching the proceedings with absorbing interest. The evidence of the case is appended further on.

After consultation the troops were ordered to pitch a Guard Tent in the Court-House square and quarter themselves in the court-house. The epicurean feasts expected by the boys were abundantly real when the crackers and corned beek was dealt out for supper, and the bread and breakfast bacon for breakfast. What the bill of fare may be for dinner is a matter of supposition.

The Picayune's young man acknowledges himself a failure as a war correspondent--he never played poker. So when he was invited to "bunk" in the court-house with the militia, with all that the term implied, he declined sorrowfully but firmly and accepted an invitation from Mr. Holloway to visit Carroll Plantation, owned by Mr. Bradish Johnson.

Interviews with the negroes show how thoroughly they have been misled by Fox and his crowd.

"How", asked the correspondent of a quiet and intelligent looking Creole negro, "do you expect to get to Kansas without money?"

"The Governor," he replied in very good English, "will send us there. Isn't it the duty of the Government to protect its citizens in their rights, and ain't we citizens?"

"Certainly," responded the news gatherer, "but not only does the law not authorize the Governor to transport strikers to Kansas, but even if it did, he has no money to do it with."

The negro looked perplexed at this and could only reply, "How is it, boss, all you whites take up for one another?"

The opinion held by this man is the opinion of the entire batch of the deluded laborers. They expect that one of three things will happen; that the Government will divide out land among them; that the Governor will send them to Kansas, or that Grant will come up and make the planters pay the extra wages demanded. Some amusing incidents happen every day. Yesterday one of the negroes on the Carroll plantation agreed to go to work at seventy-five cents, but when night came he had not touched a plow. When he was asked why he had broken his agreement, he replied:

"Well, boss, when I got into dat big field and no udder nigger 'round, my heart failed me. I just quit."

So it is with all of the laborers. They are afraid of their own associates.

Your correspondent after hearing both sides of the question, has reached the conclusion that seventy-five cents a day is sufficient for the laborers to live on except where there is a very large family of children who are too young to work. . . .

They have land to plant corn and vegetables, and can raise chickens and hogs, but it is said they are nearly all too lazy to cultivate the patch given them. On Saturday afternoons they have a holiday, and are allowed to use plantation mules to work their crop.

Gambling is one vice which many indulge in, and the greater part of their wages are lost in throwing dice. Whisky and cigars are dear to the negro heart, and some of the most experienced planters assert that at least one-half of their earnings go for such luxuries.

The credit system which prevails is one that directly encourage the negro to buy whatever his fancy may covet, whether he needs it or not.

With all these habits against him, it is no wonder the ignorant darkey continues poor, and were he to receive $5 a day he would have more whisky, more cigars and more trinkets, and would save nothing. At least this is the opinion of those who know him best.

As to the ability of the planter to give one dollar a day, your correspondent is assured that the result would be a loss to the employers. Last year was a successful one, and yet in this parish very little above expenses was made by the mass of the planters, and they are convinced that they cannot afford an increase to a dollar and make anything.

The Court House Wednesday morning, was the centre of attraction. The militia were removed and spread their tents some distance away. About nine o'clock, crowd of negro men and women began gathering and discussing the situation of affairs. The presence of the militia seemed to have a depressing effect and they were unusually quiet and respectful although they persisted in asserting that there was no reason for sending up the troops. In the cells below the court room, the prisoners were interviewed, and of course protested their innocence.

One particularly bad looking fellow said he would rather hang than confess he had done anything wrong. Of course he was in earnest.

The trial of the whipping cases was continued at 10 o'clock, L. Depoota, District Attorny pro tem, acting for the State.

Mr. Holloway, of the Carroll plantation, testified to the facts in a case of bulldozing perpetrated by the strikers against a negro on the said plantation.

William Wallis, a negro, recognized the prisoner as being a part of the attacking crowd, but could not swear that they took a hand in the whipping. On the cross examination he stated that he did not go to work because he was afraid of another whipping.

John Joseph, the other laborer, who was whipped, lives in the next room to Wallis. The attacking party called upon him to come out, but his wife went to the door, and, peeping through, saw a lot of men disguised in women's clothes. He then refused to come out, and went to get his gun to defend himself, but before he could make any use of it the party broke in the door and captured him. They dragged him out twice and gave him a severe beating with whips and hoops. He exhibited a scar on his cheek caused by one of the blows. He identified the prisoner as being among the attackers, and recognized several by their voices.

At the conclusion of the evidence, the Judge decided to remand the prisoners to jail to stand trial before the District Court. The decision was not well received by the strikers. In the cases of Devesin and the four negroes for trespass, a preliminary examination was waived and the accused remanded to the District Court.

Affidavits are now being made out against Fox, Lee, Davis, and others for inciting the laborers to riot and disturbing the peace and using incendiary language. If they can be disposed of the trouble will be at an end.

If they have enough influence they may arouse the negroes to riot, and it is needless to say who will suffer if such a thing should occur. When arrested, they will likely be brought to the city for safe keeping. In the meanwhile intelligence comes from St. James that the labor troubles have begun in earnest, and Major Strong is now waiting for news which, if unfavorable, will cause him to step aboard the special train held with a part of his command and hasten to the scene of action.

The planters have found out that the best protection is a militia company of their own, and on both banks of the river they have formed companies, and will apply to the Governor for commissions.

The officers for the right bank are: L. Bechel, Captain; L. D. Martin, First Lieutenant; S. L. Giuol, Second Lieutenant; Gustave Roussel, Third Lieutenant.

For the left bank: Capt. Frank Reid, First Lieut. Lucien Montegut, Jr., Second Lieut. Jos. L. Bourgeois, Third Lieut. Burris Edrinton.

It would not do to close this letter without referring to the gallant conduct of the militia. Although many are here to the neglect of their private business, they responded promptly when called upon, and have behaved splendidly since their arrival.

Waiting For Orders.

A rumor was circulated yesterday that the colored strikers in the parish of St. John had refused to surrender the ringleaders to the militia when desired to do so by Major Strong, and that the latter had dispatched a special messenger to the Governor with this statement, and a request for more troops, as an attack upon the militia was feared, as the strikers were said to number four thousand.

This rumor, although apparently having no foundation in fact, caused considerable excitement in and around the several armories, the Washington Artillery, two companies of the German Battalion, twenty-five men of the Vaudry Rifles, and twenty-five men of Capt. Pinckard's company, having assembled at their respective armories waiting orders from headquarters.

Up to 10 o'clock last night, however, Major Gen. Behan had received no orders from the Governor to send an additional force to the parish of St. John and the information from there received by his Excellency being of a satisfactory nature the severe commands were relieved for the night. Gen. Behan,

however, made the request that inquiry be made at the armories in the
morning, as announcements or orders would appear on the bulletin boards in
case a demand for more troops is made.

New Orleans *Daily Picayune,* April 1, 1880.

4. THE ST. JOHN STRIKERS

RINGLEADERS ARRESTED AND THE MILITARY RETURN TO NEW ORLEANS-- THE NEGROES GO TO WORK AGAIN--AMUSING EPISODES

The labor troubles in St. John parish may now be regarded as settled.
The militia sent up to quell the disturbances there returned yesterday afternoon, bringing with them the ringleaders in the strike, who were taken to
the Parish Prison to be kept until the proper legal proceedings can be instituted against them.

The account of the event which occurred upon the arrival of the troops
at St. John Court-House, published in yesterday's Picayune, gave the condition of affairs up to 3 o'clock on the afternoon of Wednesday, and very
clearly foreshadowed what result might be anticipated.

The negroes who had gathered at the court-house to attend the preliminary
examination of their fellow-strikers for whipping the two laborers on the
Johnson plantation, were much dissatisfied when the prisoners were remanded
to stand trial before the District Court.

The presence of the militia, however, had a most salutary effect and
prevented any resistance being made. As the afternoon wore on a band of
strikers came from across the river, bearing a white flag labeled Peace--
One Dollar A Day.

This accession to their forces made the negroes assume a strong numerical
appearance which inspired the leaders to hold a mass meeting upon the levee.

Speeches were made by Fox, Lee and others, who spoke to the same effect
as on the previous Sunday. While advising that the strike should continue,
they were particularly careful to caution their followers against committing
any outrages, or to do anything which might be construed as a violation of
the law.

But even these peaceful counsels were not sufficient to protect the men
who had hitherto given nothing but incendiary advice. So when Fox and his
colleagues stopped their glowing remarks the sheriff tapped them on the
shoulders and arrested them on the charge of being accessories before and
after the fact to the whipping of Wallis and Joseph. This was the critical
moment of the strike. Either the arrests would settle the strike, as predicted in the Picayune, or else the influence of the leaders would incite a
riot. Major Strong and Capt. McElroy showed their appreciation of the importance of the situation by drawing up the troops in line ready for instant
action. This movement had the desired effect upon the strikers, and it could
be seen in a moment that they had weakened most perceptibly. Fox, Lee and
May, the latter the brother-in-law of Senator Demas, at once signified their
willingness to go to jail, with the Sheriff without the coercion of the militia, and taking them at their word Sheriff Webre escorted them to the cells
beneath the Court-House. To further impress the negroes with the importance
of the militia, Capt. McElroy put the boys through a series of war-like movements, such as loading and firing, and the promptness with which they were
executed as well calculated to show the ignorant strikers how hopeless it was
to think of rescuing their leaders. Later on Senator Demas addressed a
meeting in the Court-House, and advised his constituents to return to their
homes and to go to work on the best terms they could.

His hearers were in a mood to obey such good advice, and lost no time in
following it out, so far as dispersing to their homes was concerned. The
evening thus closed quietly enough, and the guardian of the peace, in the shape
of the militia, soon lit the camp up, and made preparations for the evening
banquet.

During the night a wandering canine stole into the tent of a Washington Artillery mess, and ran off with half the rations, consisting of a piece of bacon. No other tent suffered from such a depredation, as the inmates were awake and engaged in a game played with cards and grains of corn, the latter being valued at five cents a piece. Yesterday morning, however, the provisions increased both in quantity and attractiveness as the good people of the neighborhood had contributed chickens, wine and other delicacies in profusion.

In this connection it may be well to say that the troops feel very grateful to Father Ravoire, Messrs. Laurent Martin, E. Leger, M. Pecnel, Joseph, J. B. Caire, and Gaiol, for attentions such as soldiers never fail to appreciate.

The events of Wednesday were singularly devoid of interest. In the camp the most notable incident happened to Lieut. Dudley Selph, who was officer of the day. He, in a fit of absent-mindedness, mounted a war horse, which imbued with military ardor took to his heels and ran off with the gallant sharpshooter. At least this was the explanation given by the officer of the day when he was captured about a mile and a half from camp, enjoying himself in the limited amusements of the adjoining country. Two privates, belonging respectfully to the Washington Artillery and Crescent City Batallion, started off on a tour of exploration on their own account without the necessary leave and failed to escape the argus eye of the sentinel. Their punishment was two hours of extra guard duty.

Such escapades, however, were rather laughed at, as the presence of the militia had already done the good which was anticipated. The negroes were no longer to be seen at the court-house, and it was very soon found out that on most of the plantations the laborers had agreed to go to work, and many could then be seen in the fields busily plowing or hoeing the long-neglected ground.

At the Carroll Plantation the prospects were cheering, and although a few persisted in saying they would hold out, it was evident the backbone of the strike was broken. This was the case substantially on all the plantations between the Carroll Plantation and the court-house. Even in cases where the strikers would not yield it was understood that they would be turned out from the plantations on which they were working, and would ask employment on other places, at the old rates. In this way an exchange of labor would be had and when a plantation lost some of its hands it made up for the deficiencies by recruits from other places.

Affairs being so satisfactory, Major Strong decided to return to the city with the troops, and to bring Fox, Lee and the seven negroes who were sent before the District Court, to the city.

The necessary affidavits to effect this were made by citizens, stating that the force at the command of the sheriff would be insufficient to maintain the prisoners in jail in case an attempt to release them was made. Judge Leach declined to order them taken to St. Charles or St. James, as there were similar troubles in those parishes, and he accordingly made out the commitment for the Parish Prison. May was released on a peace bond, signed by Senator Demas, and the nine others were brought to the city and locked up in the Parish Prison.

On Monday next, Mr. Sewell of St. Charles, will apply for a writ of habeas corpus, and will endeavor to have them released.

Last night, after the militia had disbanded, Major Strong entertained the officers of the command at dinner at Victor's and a very pleasant time was spent discussing the events of the trip.

New Orleans *Daily Picayune*, April 2, 1880.

5.   LOUISIANA STRIKE

There were strikes in some parts of this State, but they were similar to the labor troubles elsewhere, and were devoid of race antagonism. It was not

a rising of blacks against whites, but of employees against employers. In
the parishes of St. James, St. John the Baptist, and St. Charles, during the
month of March, negroes went from plantation to plantation, requiring others
who had not joined in their movement to desist from work, and even to leave
these parishes. They rode about in armed bands, broke into cabins, frightened the inmates, took quiet laborers from their work in the fields, and
whipped them. No outrages were committed except on colored persons. The
Governor's proclamation produced no effect upon the rioters, and the militia
was called out and sent to the two or three points of disturbance. The
ringleaders were arrested without bloodshed or difficulty, and were brought to
New Orleans, tried, and imprisoned. The other strikers appointed a conference committee to arrange their difficulties with the planters. A colored
Senator, Demas, wrote out the following petition in behalf of the St. Charles
strikers, which shows the misconception of their rights under which they acted:

New Orleans, *March 23, 1880.*

To His Excellency Governor Wiltz, *of the State of Louisiana.*

The undersigned, having pleaded guilty to trespass before Judge Augustin,
holding court at St. Charles Court-House on Saturday, March 20th, and having
been brought to New Orleans to serve out their sentence, ask you for a
remission of the same on the following grounds:
We, as well as the majority of our people, were misled as to our rights
when we acted as we did in the recent strike; and when we were guilty of
trespass, we did not know we were exceeding our rights; we really thought we
had a right to go where other laborers were working, even though it was on
the property of an individual, and induce those laborers to join us.
We now understand we have no such rights; we understand we have no right
to go on the property of other people against their will, and we propose to
obey this law hereafter.
We feel sure the laborers in our parish understand this question now,
and are equally certain they never understood it before.
We feel sure the laborers in our parish will respect the law, as we
intend to hereafter, and believe quietness and peace will continue from this
time, and that when laborers differ with their employers hereafter about
the price of their labor, it will be in a peaceable manner, and with law
always on their side.
For these reasons, your Excellency, we would ask a remission of our
sentence, and allow us to return to our wives, our children, and our work.
This was signed by the prisoners, and the Judge and the militia officers
concurred in recommending that Executive clemency be extended. They were
accordingly released, and quiet was restored.

Appletons' Annual Cyclopedia, 1880, p. 482.

6. STRIKE IN FLORIDA

COLLISION WITH SPECIAL POLICEMEN

A strike of the workmen in the saw mills, situated just below Jacksonville, Fla., has been going on for some days. Last Friday night it culminated
in a collision between some special police detailed for duty by the Mayor
of the city and the strikers who had assembled to interview the men who had
been induced to continue their work. In the collision one policeman was shot.
The ball struck him on a lower rib on his right side, and, glancing lodged in
his back. Three of the strikers were wounded, but none killed. Twenty-five
or thirty shots were fired before the riot was quelled. Saturday morning
the fight was renewed to some extent, and a policeman received three shots,
but without serious damage. Some of the strikers were seriously clubbed,
but none killed. More trouble is anticipated, but preparation is being
made for all emergencies. The mills shut down at first but they are

now running short-handed.

Labor Standard (Fall River, Mass.), July 3, 1880.

7.   A LABOR RIOT IN MISSOURI

COLORED LABORERS DRIVEN FROM THEIR WORK

THE AUTHORITIES UNABLE TO SUPPRESS THE RIOT--THE SHERIFF OF ST. JOSEPH REFUSES TO INTERFERE.

C. A. Parker, contractor for the excavation work of the packing house of J. M. Smith, East Atchison, Mo., having engaged several colored men, to whom he was paying a dollar and a quarter per day, a furious mob armed with revolvers and knives, made its appearance Wednesday and compelled them to quit work. From there, the crowd increasing, proceeded to the brick yard of Seth & Co., where seven colored men were employed, and compelled a suspension of all work, and drove the colored men over the river. The mob then, numbered several hundred, and it was addressed by the Mayor of Atchison and others, urging peace and order, but without avail. The colored drivers of transfer teams were compelled to turn back over the bridge, and the colored porters at the various freight depots and other darkies in town hunted up and sent over into Kansas. The authorities, finding all efforts to quiet the mob useless, telegraphed to Sheriff Spencer at St. Joseph, to come and exercise his authority, but he refused to come. The mobs have possession of East Atchison and defy the law and the militia.

Labor Standard, (Fall River, Mass.), July 14, 1880.

8.   "WORKING IN UNISON."

On the first of September a strike for higher wages will be inaugurated by the combined labor of the city. The cotton yard men and those connected with the handling of cotton, have made a tariff which will not be agreed to by press owners and others. The different organizations will parade about the 15th of September with over four thousand men in line. The white and colored laborers are working in unison and are governed by the same rules and regulations.

New Orleans *Weekly Louisianian, August 13, 1881.*

9.   LABOR VS. CAPITAL.

One of the greatest questions which confronts the South is the labor question. It is a problem which if not met by some practical solution, it must eventually entail agricultural and commercial ruin. It is essential to New Orleans especially, because of its great importance, situated as it is upon the greatest commercial highway, it must necessarily be a great centre of trade, and its importance is being considered by other large metropolists, and the natural competition for supremacy makes New Orleans a target for all kind of scandal; and everything will be resorted to to obstruct its agricultural and commercial facilities. The labor of the South is a peculiar one.

Notwithstanding all of the theories, and speculations in connection with this
great question, we assert without successful contradiction that nature has
decreed, that colored labor is the only labor that can give satisfaction in
this section. That labor must be contented and retained. The North and
West have found out that it can be successfully utilized in all of their
industries, and it is being utilized. To-day we have ten thousand colored
laborers from the South successfully employed, in the mines, upon the railroads, and in other industries in the North and West, and the great railroad
centers which will soon lead out of New Orleans, traveling all over the
country, will be a great source of temptation, to bereft this State of its
vitality if the colored labor is not contented. It is very good for our
political journals to say "let them go, they can be replaced by others," but
in reality our planters know that if they are forced to go, the State is
necessarily ruined, hence this labor must be contended. It must be guaranteed
all of its educational, its civil, and its political rights. The LOUISIANIAN
as the defender of this labor, must call the attention of our business men to
the great trouble now before us as far as colored labor is concerned. It is
an unfortunate and lamentable spectacle to see the present conflict between
labor and capital which threatens to seriously embarrass the commercial relations of this city. Some method must be brought about to prevent the
occurrence of these labor strikes which must eventual drive our shipping
away to other ports where they will not be detained by these periodical upheavals. Whilst we cannot antagonize capital we must admit that the laborer
has some right which the capitalists are bound to respect. By a careful
analysis of this matter, it will be found that the seeming exorbitant rates
exacted by strikers lies in the fact of the uncertainty of employment. The
laborer who handles the great cotton staple of this State can only find
employment for six or seven months during the year, there being no equalization tariff throughout the year they must earn sufficient during these six
or seven months to support themselves and families during the rest of the
year. The question to be solved is, can the merchant or cotton factors by
any process whatever bring about an equalization tariff which will give a
reasonable compensation the year round for these men in whose hands are
placed the destinies of the city and State? Upon calculation it will be
found that six dollars a working day will aggregate the large sum of one
hundred and forty-four dollars per month, making the amount of eight hundred
and sixty-four dollars earned per laborer for six months. This is true to a
greater or less extent with all of our industries in connection with the
cotton trade. Suppose the same number of men who are now employed in handling the staple could be guaranteed regular employment throughout the whole
year upon averaged salaries. We find that two dollars and a half per day
which would be an averaged salary would be sixty dollars per month, making
seven hundred and twenty dollars per year, a gain of one hundred and forty-
four dollars. If such a system could be established the laborer would have
no just cause to complain, and the merchant, the ship owner and in fact, all
parties concerned would be free from the serious complications which now
confronts us. This seems to be a question worthy of consideration and we
submit it to the consideration of all parties concerned. It will guarantee
to the laborer permanent support for his family during the whole year, it
will secure to the merchant a contented and stable labor, it will pass out of
existence these associations which are continually menacing the capitalists,
and it will place New Orleans upon the highway to success. We trust that
the matter be thoroughly investigated and in short we will have a compromise
of the serious trouble now upon us.

New Orleans *Weekly Louisianaian, September 10, 1881.*

10. THE LABOR RIOTS.

MAYOR SHAKESPEARE'S PROMPT AND DETERMINED COURSE--THE PLANS OF THE
STRIKERS AND THE WORK OF THE POLICE--THE BURIAL OF THE FIRST VICTIM--
EFFORTS FOR ADJUSTMENT

Between two and three thousand persons attended the funeral of James
Hawkins, the negro teamster who was shot and instantly killed by Sergeant
Reynolds on Saturday morning at 9 o'clock, at No. 337 Tehoupitoulas street.
After the autopsy had been held by the Coroner, the body was removed to the
colored church on Levee, between Gafennie and Erato streets, where it was
laid out, and the church was visited by numerous persons, white and black,
male and female, adults and children, all curious to see the first victim of
the war between capital and labor. The crowds were not demonstrative or
boisterous, and what conversation passed between them was carried on in a
subdued tone of voice far more impressive and ominous than loud threats of
vengeance or wails of grief.

At 9 o'clock quite a number of the members of the different labor organizations, mostly colored, who had determined to attend the funeral, had
arrived, and at 11 o'clock the cortege moved.

After the hearse, which was escorted by pall bearers selected from the
different societies in the line, came seven carriages containing relatives
and friends of the deceased. The St. Joseph Colored Society, the Teamsters'
and Loaders' Union, the colored cotton yard men, the colored longshoremen,
a delegation from the white cotton yard men, and one also of the white
screwmen, followed in the above order, and constituted the procession, which
was several blocks long.

Out Gafennie to Magazine, to Washington Avenue, thence to Lafayette
Cemetery No. 2, moved the procession without any interference whatever. Perfect order prevailed, both in the ranks and on the sidewalks, where large
crowds of colored people were following the cortege on foot.

Each society was headed by a brass band, and when the cemetery was
reached, the coffin was carried through the open ranks of the societies to the
tomb of the St. James Society, where it was placed in the vault, after the
sermon had been preached and the ceremonies incidental were performed.

The programme as mapped out by both sides for Monday promises to be one
prolific of excitement, bloodshed and riot.

The Factors' and Employers' Union appear to be determined to compel the
labor organizations to surrender unconditionally, while on the contrary, the
laborers are more determined than ever that they will not be whipped into
submission without raising an arm of defense of their cause.

If the issue comes, they say, and blood is spilled, no one is to blame
but the cotton factors and their allies who refused peremptorily to accept
any of their propositions looking towards a compromise, although they made
all the concessions they possibly could. On Saturday morning, prior to the
news of Hawkin's death at the hands of Sergeant Reynolds, they took things
in good part, and were more than anxious to come to terms; but now blood had
been spilled, and unless some unforeseen obstacle in the shape of effectual
settlement arises, more will follow. [18]

The Labor Bureau, under whose auspices the Savannah Screwmen were brought
to the city, are determined that those men shall go to work on Monday morning,
and it is believed that the British steamship Cella is the objective point
where services will be utilized. Per contract, the longshoremen and others
are equally determined that those importations shall not work in the ships,
and if the attempt is made trouble is bound to follow.

They also threaten to keep any of the boss draymen from sending out teams,
and say that they will stop them at the gates and drive them back into the
yards. The boss draymen, or at least some of them, express a firm determination of sending out their floats, no matter what the result may be.

The cotton presses will also be debarred from delivering cotton aboard
vessels, if the plans of the laborers are carried into effect. The Liverpool
Shippers and Orleans Presses all have deliveries to make this morning, and

it is the intention of the cotton press owners to carry out their contracts
even if they are compelled to place an armed squad on every float.

The various precinct commanders were all ordered to report at Chief
Boylan's office at 7 o'clock last night and were promptly on hand. The
state of affairs was discussed at length among them and orders given for
their various forces to be on hand at an early hour this morning.

Mayor Shakespeare seems to be determined if possible, to put an end to
the existing troubles to-day, and will put forth every effort in that direction. He last evening issued the following order to the Chief of Police:

T. N. Boylan, Esq., Chief of Police:
   Sir: You will give instructions to your force to keep all idlers off
the wharves where vessels are loading. Respectfully,
                              JOSEPH A. SHAKESPEARE, Mayor.

This order is intended as a precautionary measure, as presumably the
strikers will move towards the vessels in small squads, when it will be much
easier to manage them than if they came in force. At the different Armories
and Arsenals of the militia a guard was kept all night, to protect the State
property, and signals will be agreed upon.

At Exposition Hall Mayor Shakespeare, Generals Behan, Glynn and Meyer,
Major Williams, Chief of Police Boylan, and Police Commissioner Schomberg
met at 8 o'clock, in conference, the subject being the plan of action, in
anticipation of the troubles to-day. It was determined that the police force
in its full strength was to be concentrated somewhere in the vicinity of the
expected troubles, and would move in solid phalanx at the very first intimation of any interference on the part of the laborers.

A general order was also issued calling the militia to their respective
armories at 1 o'clock this morning, there to be held in readiness in case of
emergency.

Those members of the police force who were ordered to report in the
morning were sent home off their beats at midnight, and the necessary orders
given them.

It appears to be the policy of the officials to bring matters to a
crisis at once, and effectually settle the question.

THE ROLL OF RIOTERS

How the Police Force "Overpowered" Themselves on Saturday.

The following named negroes will be brought up before Judge Davey, of
the upper districts, to-day, for attempting to incite a riot and disturbing
the peace:

Perry Jones, a laborer, arrested at the corner of Richard and Chippewa
streets by Officers Garney and Abadie.

Humphrey Mitchell, arrested by Officers W. Murphy and Tully at the
corner of Chippewa and Terpsichore streets.

John P. Colbert, a white laborer, arrested at the corner of Richard and
Chippewa streets by Officers J. T. Gallagher and J. D. Donovan.

The negro driver, Henry Williams, arrested at the corner of Tehoupitoulas
and Thalia streets, by officers Knapp and Tholemer, for interferring with
drivers of cotton floats and attempting to incite a riot, will soon make his
appearance before the bar.

The next in line will be the negroes who showered the cooking utensils
upon the police when they attempted to make an arrest at the corner of Thalia
and Tehoupitoulas street. It took seven officers of the law to arrest the
following named negro women and lock them up in the Second Precinct Station:
Edwina Thomas Manly Richards, Winnie White, Ellen Alexander, Annie Williams,
Letty Bailey and Isabel Wilkinson.

Three prisoners were subsequently transferred to the Central Station, in
the Black Maria, on account of the rickety condition of the Second Station
House. It had been repaired several times as being in an unsafe condition,
but no attention has ever been paid to it.

New Orleans *Daily Picayune,* September 12, 1881.

11.   ANOTHER POLICE MURDERER

During the past week another of those horrible crimes which causes
honest men to blush, was perpetrated by officer Reynolds, who shot down the
man Hawkins with the same deliberation that he would use in shooting down a
mad dog, and the strangest thing about the whole affair is that a few hours
afterwards, before any testimony had been taken in the case, officer Reynolds
was turned scott free upon a nominal bail under the same old pretense, self-
protection. It is evident that if justice was done in ferreting out the
facts, officer Reynolds could give no reasonable excuse for washing his hands
in the blood of this poor colored man, every inquiry about Hawkins shows that
he was a law-abiding, peaceful man, with honest convictions and a christian
character, and was shot down for no other cause than that a negro has no
rights which a police officer is bound to respect. The nature of the affair
is well known to the community. Thousands of men had banded themselves together, white and colored, to conduct a strike for higher wages and other
demands, we are not here to say whether they were right or wrong, but we do
say that the colored portion of the strikers should not have been selected by
the police as chosen objects for personal violence. The daily papers which
really took no position in the strike neither for or against labor nor capital
passed the most of their time discussing about excited Negroes and Negro women
whilst the white men and women belonging to the strike numbered three to one
and was more violent in their demonstration than the Negro dared be. Yet the
policemen could find naught to say against the white strikers, but the colored
portion must be beaten and killed. Every individual both white and colored
who witnessed this awful tragedy states that it was one of the most deliberate
and cold-blooded murders on record. The greatest offence alleged is, that
Hawkins protested against being arrested, he was not armed, he had nothing with
which to defend himself, notwithstanding this he was shot down by officer
Reynolds, and with hardly a protest from our public journals. Is it strange
that we should have strikes, upheavals, lawlessness, opposition to commerce
and every other kind of deviltry whilst the authorities and our merchants are
blind to these barbarous outrages? If an officer of the law cannot make an
arrest without taking a life, then it would be better for the commonwealth
for such an officer to resign his charge. If the judges cannot protect the
sacrecy of the law, let them relegate back to the people that responsibility,
and let it be bestowed upon some one who can fill it with dignity and with
safety. The Democratic party is making for itself a record, by the toleration
of these crimes from which its representatives cannot shield them. There seem
to be no law in this community with which to punish the murderer of a Negro.
   Here stands before us three peace officers with their hands dyed in the
blood of colored men with no condemnation whatever. Must we strike back, or
shall we be protected by the law? The solution cannot be delayed much longer.
We appeal to the tribunal of justice again in this case and ask a redress for
the murder of Hawkins. Let the murderer be brought to trial and hung as a
living example to those who seem determined to ruin the reputation of this
City.
   It was a source of satisfaction to see the sympathy expressed by the
white laborers association. Their popular indignation were expressed by the
large numbers who turned out to pay their last tribute of respect to the
unfortunate man. More than two thousand souls formed the funeral train.
We trust that this public demonstration will be an incentive to the authorities in meeting out justice to officer Reynolds.

New Orleans *Weekly Louisianaian,* September 17, 1881.

12.   CHEERING WORDS.

LEADING SOUTHERN PAPER ON THE NEGRO AS A MANUFACTURER AND MINER

It is an undeniable fact that the Negro is making his way, and is winning

a more forward position than had been thought possible in the same generation
that saw him a slave. While that people can produce a Douglass and a Senator
Bruce, it is impossible utterly to despise them. Their children are absorbing
education with a power of assimilation they had never been credited with
possessing, and events are proving that as working men they are not to be
tied down to the position of mere hewers of wood and drawers of water. The
Iron Age has an article upon "The Negro as an Iron Worker and Miner," that
shows there are decided powers of progress among them. It remarks upon the
prevalent belief in the South that the Negro could never become a skilled
workman, able to accomplish results requiring judgment, dexterity, and a
shrewd application of human powers. In the iron business, however, he has
become a skilled puddler, heater and roller. He fills those occupations at
the Tradegar and Old Dominion works in Richmond, Virginia; as a puddler he
proves very efficient. At Pittsburgh he first was introduced during a strike
and proved a success. At the Knoxville, Tennessee Ironworks, he is a puddler,
heater, roller and shearer, and whatever else is required in the iron mani-
pulation. At Atlanta, Ga., he is at work in similar departments. The better
wages these men get is arousing ambition and, as the Negroes become more
widely educated, they desire comforts that a better income wins. They do not
all make good skilled workmen, no more do all the whites, but they are pronounced teachable and are strong, they understand the heat well and are
competent for duties it had been thought they had not the brain to perform.
In the coal mines and in ore mining they are pronounced to be excellent,
faithful, steady and not given to "sprees." Whatever may come in the future,
however--when education is more general among the Negroes and they come to
have the discipline and other benefits that come from experience--the Negro
does not yet become a superintendent, plan how work is to be done, allot it
among the men, and oversee its accomplishment; that is done by whites. All
this is a beginning with the Negro, he has proved that he can handle tools,
work among machinery, and attain skill in manufacturing operations, the
question is how far may a race that has made such amazing strides in one
generation attain; in how many trades and occupations may he be--not a mere
fag, a helper, a sweeper out of rooms, a blacker of boots--but a competent
steady, and valued workman? Should he fulfill present promise, the Negro as
a citizen is likely to take a more prominent place than has usually been
anticipated. [19]

People's Advocate, (Washington, D.C.,), October 1, 1881.

13. MURDERED BY A MOB

We learn that a colored man named Ben was killed at Jeanerette, a few
days ago under circumstances which deserve investigation. It seems he had
been arrested for stealing chickens, was confined in the town jail, but was
assaulted by a mob, taken from the jail, and whipped, and when he ran, was
shot and killed. . . .

New Orleans *Daily Picayune,* October 8, 1881.

THE KNIGHTS ORGANIZE SOUTHERN BLACKS

14. ASSEMBLIES OF COLORED MEN

We are often asked, "Are colored men admitted to this Order and can we
form colored Assemblies?" We answer yes. We have already several Assemblies
composed exclusively of colored men, and many other Assemblies have colored

members, and the testimony is, that for fidelity to their obligations, strict
attendance on all meetings, prompt payment of dues, good conduct, and all
that goes to make good members and good citizens, they are not excelled by
any other class of men in the Order.

We should be false to every principle of our Order should we exclude from
membership any man who gains his living by honest toil, on account of his
color or creed. Our platform is broad enough to take in all.

In every portion of our broad land, whenever a strike is resorted to, as
the only means of resisting a further reduction of wages, already below living
rates, what is the first thing done by the employer? Does he not seek far
and near for those who will take the place of the men on strike, without inquiring their nationality, color, or creed? Certainly he does. The only
question asked is, "Will he work for less wages?", and if he will, he can go
to work at your job, and you can go tramping. Why, then, should workingmen
allow a foolish prejudice against the color to keep out of our organization
any one who might be used as a tool to aid the employer in grinding down
wages? In the coal regions of Illinois, Kansas, Indiana, Ohio, and West
Virginia, during the strikes of the past winter, colored men were put into
the mines to take the place of the strikers, and we ask any white miner who
objects to the admission of colored men into our Order, this question: If
you are forced to strike against a reduction of wages, will your employer
stop to inquire the color or nationality of any man who will take your place
at the reduction offered?

Journal of United Labor, August 15, 1880.

15.   CONSTITUTION FOR THE LOCAL ASSEMBLIES OF THE
ORDER OF THE KNIGHTS OF LABOR OF AMERICA

Preamble

The Local Assembly is not a mere Trade Union, or Beneficial Society; it
is more and higher. It gathers into one fold all branches of honorable toil,
without regard to nationality, sex, creed or color. . . .

Proceedings, General Assembly, Knights of Labor, 1884, p. 780.

16.   KNIGHTS OF LABOR MEETING IN WASHINGTON, D.C.

The platform was occupied by white and colored representatives of every
labor organization in the District. The Committee representing all trade
unions presented the following resolutions which were unanimously adopted.

Whereas the only hope for the masses, in bringing about a more equitable
and just distribution of the wealth of this country, consists in the more
thorough and complete organization and harmonious affiliation of the classes
of wage-paid labor, regardless of caste, creed, color, or sex; therefore, be
it

Resolved, That the efforts of all working men and women should first be
devoted to the compact, thorough organization of all trades or callings whatsoever, regardless of sex, creed or color, with the single purpose of elevating
and protecting labor, and to this end ceaseless agitation and education must
be conducted.

National Republican, (Washington, D.C.), February 5, 1884.

17. PLAIN TALK TO WORKINGMEN

The Central Committee of the Austin, Texas Labor Organizations has
issued the following circular to workingmen:

Are you a workingman?
If so, sit down and for ten minutes think, even if you never thought be-
fore in your life. . . .
Join some organization in the interest of labor.
Organization is strength through union, it is education through discussion, it is efficiency through intelligent effort. Without organization
nothing can be accomplished. Organization is life, development, progress.
If there is a union of your particular trade then join it. If there is none
then endeavor to organize one. If you cannot succeed then seek to join the
Knights of Labor, an order which admits every man of good, moral character,
who is a bonafide worker and producer. It makes no other distinction, but
recognizes in every worker a man and a brother, without reference to race or
creed, section, condition, or occupation.
Its motto is, "AN INJUSTICE DONE ONE IS THE CONCERN OF ALL." No matter
where destiny or choice may place a toiling brother; no matter what race he
belongs to, what section he hails from, what altar he bows to; no matter how
heavy his labor, hard his lot, and lowly his position, he is equally welcome,
equally respected. . . .
                              Central Committee of the Austin Labor Organizations

Irish World and American Industrial Liberator, July 12, 1884.

18. DESCRIPTION OF A PUBLIC MEETING HELD BY THE KNIGHTS OF LABOR AT HAMILTON, ONTARIO, DURING THE 1885 CONVENTION

A large audience was assembled and great enthusiasm was manifest. Upon
the platform was assembled several of the more prominent members of the Order.
Among them was Johnson from Virginia, the only colored delegate in the General
Assembly. As Master Workman Powderly was speaking, he turned to the brother
from Virginia, and taking him by the hand, pledged him the services of the
Order for his race to fulfill for them their complete enfranchisement in common with those whose faces were white. The applause was tremendous.

Frank K. Foster in *John Swinton's Paper,* October 25, 1885.

19. SOCIAL AFFAIR

The entertainment and ball at Fort Worth sponsored by the colored K.
of L. Tawani Assembly No. 4000, was a very merry affair. The colored brethren covered themselves with great credit, and the occasion will long be
remembered as one of the most enjoyable of the season.

John Swinton's Paper, November 8, 1885.

20. BALTIMORE LABOR PARADE

COLORED AND WHITE WORKERS FRATERNIZING IN THE PROCESSION--SHAMEFULLY CROWDED
SCHOOLS--OBITUARY--PERSONAL MENTION.
Baltimore, Sept. 7.--The labor parade here on Monday far exceeded in

magnitude the expectations of the promoters, there being fully twenty-five
thousand persons in line. It was a very imposing procession, and was re-
viewed by Grand Master Workman Powderly from the balcony of Ford's Opera
House. The procession was just one and a half hours passing a given spot.
Nearly every trade and branch of labor was well represented, many of them
carrying the implements of their craft or a representation of their skill.
Many of the assemblies carried handsome banners. Among the most handsome
was that of the T. V. Powderly Assembly 2397 of Colored Knights. Colored men
were well mixed in and through the procession. In some instances you would
see an assembly composed entirely of colored Knights; another assembly would
be perhaps half colored, and in some instances one solitary colored individual would be marching with any number of his white trades-brothers. After
marching to Druid Hill Park, where the parade was dismissed, addresses were
made by Grand Master Workman Powderly, M. A. B. Gantt of Washington, Mr.
Charles H. Litcheman of Massachusetts and others. The procession was a very
orderly one, the colored and white fraternizing as if it had been a common
thing all their lives. I wondered how much of that fraternity would be left
in the park and how much would be brought back to the city. The hod carriers
did not take any part in the procession, but went on an excursion to Harper's
Ferry. They took a large crowd with them as usual.[20]

New York *Freeman*, Sept. 11, 1886.

21. FIRST BLACK ASSEMBLY

The first Local Assembly in the world composed wholly of colored people
was organized and instituted at Hot Springs, January 11, 1883, and is known
as Freedom Assembly, No. 2447.
For about two years no progress was made in the State outside of Hot
Springs and vicinity. L. A. 2677 was organized at Pine Bluff in May, 1883,
but very soon after lapsed.

Journal of United Labor, September 25, 1886.

22. BLACK COOPERATIVE VENTURES

The State Assembly of Arkansas was temporarily organized November 26,
1885, the law authorizing State Assemblies not coming into effect until January following; and on January 6, 1886, the charter was issued and the permanent organization effected. Prior to this time all local assemblies of the
State were attached directly to the General Assembly, but most all of them
joined in its formation, and became at once attached to the State Assembly.
The recent semi-annual session of the State Assembly at Hot Springs
showed an increase in new Assemblies added since the regular annual session
in January of five to one, and in the membership of Assemblies previously
organized of about one third the establishment of a State journal--the
Industrial Liberator--on the co-operative plan of and by the Order, and otherwise demonstrated a healthy growth and interest throughout the State, almost
unparalleled in labor organization. A plan for a co-operative wagon factory
at Malvern was submitted and recommended and the colored Delegates spoke of a
project to establish a co-operative steam gin in a rich cotton district below
Little Rock, east of the river. All this, in connection with other evidences
of increased and increasing interest and prosperity in the face of a great
railroad strike, and other reverses; the disposition and vigorous effort of
its enemies to slander, misrepresent and in every way damage the Order, evidences the purity of its principles and the utter impossibility to shake its
foundations--most, convincing to skeptics and most gratifying to the workers

who have put forth such noble and earnest efforts in its behalf.
    The organization of the colored people on the plantation was a new as
well as an important feature for consideration by the State Assembly. To
this State Organizer Tomson has devoted particular pains and care. Due
caution in selecting the material from the thousands of colored planters and
plantation hands who make application has been exercised, realizing that
the task is a delicate one. This feature in fact is almost a new departure
in the Order--not because our platform has not always been broad enough to
admit those of every race, creed, sex and color, but because such great care
is required that Organizers have been loathe to undertake the work and assume
the responsibility. Scarce more than a score of years ago slavery was
abolished, and these people, illiterate, ignorant, even superstitious, and
entirely without culture, imported from a semi-barbarious land in a semi-
civilized condition; bred slaves and reared in hovels; directed by the lash
of a master and cut off from every privilege of citizenship, were set free
in a land made desolate by war and demoralized by adventurers, renegades and
scoundrels, who sought self-aggrandizement on the misfortunes of others and
fortune from the spoils of revolution. Almost naturally these colored people
were devoid of ambition, improvident and sadly lacking that independence
characteristic of an American citizen. In this condition, without means,
they were made citizens of a country in which each individual [is responsible
to the body politic].
    Appreciating these facts, other organizers have felt a reluctance to
clothe the colored people with the power that organization gives; but our
organizer, who is a Southern man born and bred, having had a lifetime of
experience among them, was satisfied that thousands could be found among their
ranks who were capable of exercising their power with the caution enjoined by
the Order, and who would not only be benefitted by its teachings, but would
be enabled to benefit others, less fortunate, of their race. He undertook
the work as an experiment, fully convinced of its ultimate success. The
result so far is most gratifying. A short time since an effort was made to
involve the colored Assemblies in this county in trouble. The Sheriff of
the county, during the progress of a petty strike undertaken by a few plantation hands, made a raid on the house of an inoffensive colored man, who was
shot by one of his deputies. A large number of deputies were then hurried
to the scene to attack any party of colored men who might congregate in the
vicinity. They made one such attack, but fortunately no one was injured,
although they fired several shots, the colored men forbearing to return the
fire. There is no doubt that these outrages were committed in the hope that
the colored people, being organized, would resist, and that, this would serve
as a pretext to break up organization among them. But the colored people
proved equal to the emergency and kept within the bounds of law, even under
such trying circumstances. After this test Mr. Tomson is more convinced than
ever that the colored men can be relied upon, that they will profit by the
teachings of the Order, and with their white brothers march onward in the
army of progress and eventually raise themselves to that high and efficient
standard of industrious and dignified citizenship, that must be obtained
before the masses can assert and maintain their right to the full product of
their labor. [21]

Journal of United Labor, September 25, 1886.

23. THE RICHMOND CO-OPERATIVE SOAP COMPANY

    The members of the Order in D.A.'s 84 and 92 (white and colored) have
succeeded in establishing a soap factory on the co-operative plan, and have
now established the fact that they have come to stay. They make a first-
class article, and our members should help it along by demanding from their
grocers the soap made by the Co-operative Soap Co., of Richmond, Va. They
have a brand called "Knights of Labor," which is imitated by a firm in Phila-

delphia, named Chas. W. Young & Co., who do not employ a Knight of Labor.

Journal of United Labor, August 25, 1886.

24. LETTER FROM A BLACK KNIGHT

I am a colored man. I had a letter sent me from Georgia by a colored man asking if colored men would be recognized in the K. of L., and I have had similar questions from others of my race, both in New York and Brooklyn. My answer is yes and I especially refer to the case of the colored delegates to Richmond from District 49. I myself belong to a local that is wholly composed of white men, with two exceptions, and I hold a very high position of trust in it. I was elected junior delegate to the District Assembly, and there is no office in the organization that I could not be elected to. I will say to my people, Help the cause of labor. I would furthermore say to colored men, Organize. I also appeal to you to support Henry George and the Knights of Labor. You will never gain anything from the Republican Party but the titles of "Mrs. Johnson" or "Mr. Johnson." You are a man. Let us break this race prejudice which capital likes. Let us put our shoulders to the wheel men, and victory is ours.

John Swinton's Paper, October 10, 1886.

25. STRIDES IN THE SOUTH

Our Order is now established in every State and Territory of the United States. Rapid strides have been made in the South, especially in the States of Virginia, the Carolinas, Georgia and Alabama. One year ago South Carolina had no Assembly within its borders.

The colored people of the South are flocking to us, being eager for organization and education, and when thoroughly imbued with our principles, are unswerving in their fidelity.

Report of General Secretary-Treasurer to the 1886 General Assembly, Knights of Labor, *Proceedings,* General Assembly, Knights of Labor, 1886, p. 44.

BLACK WORKERS AND KNIGHTS OF LABOR STRIKES, 1885-1886

26. PARALYZED

GALVESTON, Nov. 3.--A general strike of Knights of Labor in this city was inaugurated this afternoon, seriously affecting every branch of commerce and completely paralyzing the movement of cotton and other freight. The longshoremen, the screwmen, the freight handlers and switchmen, the cotton handlers in the presses, the printers, and other members of the Knights of Labor all quit work at 1:30 o'clock. It is estimated that 1,500 men went out, but they are so widely scattered from one end of the city to the other that it is impossible to enumerate the exact number by trades. The strike was planned and carried out so quietly and orderly, that not over a dozen people outside of the Knights themselves knew what was coming. So united are the labor organizations of Galveston that it may be truly said they have the city in their grasp, for there is no force here able to cope with them if they get ugly.

The present general strike is the outgrowth of a small strike inaugurated on Oct. 12 by the 150 longshoremen employed by the Mallory Steamship Company on their wharves here. These longshoremen were getting 40 cents an hour for daylight labor and 60 cents for night and Sunday work. But very little work is done at night, and they struck for 50 cents an hour all around, Sundays included. Capt. Sawyer, agent for the Mallory Line, resisted this demand, and employed colored laborers, allowing them 50 cents an hour night and day, the same rate demanded by the strikers. Very few of the original 150 striking longshoremen were members of the Knights of Labor organization at the time they struck, but all have since become members. Various attempts at arbitration were made between the white and colored longshoremens' associations, the colored men even agreeing to divide the labor equally, but the Mallory folks would not be dictated to, and Sawyer stubbornly refused to reinstate the strikers, even on half time. At this juncture the Knights of Labor quietly stepped in, and attempted to arbitrate matters, but were also rebuffed by the Mallory Company. On Monday last, P. H. Golden, Chairman of the State Executive Board of the Knights of Labor, addressed a letter to J. N. Sawyer, stating that whereas it had been made known to the Executive Board of the Knights of Labor of Texas that the Mallory Line of Steamships was discriminating against members of their order by discharging and refusing to allow them to work upon the Mallory wharves, therefore this committee had adopted a resolution requesting the reinstatement of the strikers, and that the Mallory Line allow the Knights of Labor equal representation upon their wharves. Golden requested an answer at 12 o'clock to-day.

In his reply Agent Sawyer says that he was informed by a member of the Knights of Labor on Oct. 18 that "the striking longshoremen were not members of that order." After reciting the fact that the men were not discharged, but voluntarily abandoned their positions, Sawyer concludes: "Compliance with your request would compel us to enact the injustice, of which you unwarrantably complain, of discharging laborers who are performing their duties faithfully. We therefore decline to disturb the present status of labor on the Mallory wharf." This reply precipitated the strike of 1,500 Knights of Labor. Marine commerce suffers greatly by the strike. There are a dozen large foreign steamers in port loading with cotton, and not a bale can go aboard until the strike is ended. All freight handling at the Missouri Pacific and Santa Fe depots is at a standstill. Even the job printing offices are closed. Golden and other members of the State Executive Committee declare that unless the Mallory Company immediately yields the strike will be made general all over Texas and Louisiana in which it would be impossible to move even by train. If that don't bring them to time, the strike will reach to New York. This is what high officials in the order declare.

The most serious feature of the strike is the race hatred which it

engenders. Both races are strongly and nearly evenly represented in the
laboring element of Galveston. Some trifling incidents may turn the issue
into a race conflict with terrible and sanguinary results.

New York Times, November 4, 1885.

27. A GENERAL STRIKE

ABOUT FACE OR 2,000 LABORERS QUIT WORK IN GALVESTON--THE KNIGHTS OF LABOR
MAKE AN ISSUE WITH THE MALLORY STEAMSHIP COMPANY, AND ORDER A GENERAL STRIKE
OF THEIR ORDER--A SUSPENSION OF WORK.

The recent strike of white laborers on the New York wharf, and their
substitution by colored laborers, is of too recent occurrence to require any
recapitulation here, and is merely referred to as the cause which has resulted in one of the most general labor upheavings ever known in the history
of Galveston. The Knights of Labor on Sunday held in this city an important
meeting of their executive committee. This meeting was followed up by another
held on Monday night, and rumors were then afloat that the result would be a
general strike ordered by the association of Knights of Labor. These were
merely rumors, but they culminated yesterday in a very serious reality when,
at 1 p.m., a general strike was ordered throughout the city by which some
1,500 or 2,000 men employed in various capacities throughout the city quit
work, creating a general excitement, as the facts in the case became known.
The strike permeated every department of work where Knights of Labor are
employed, including the men at the cotton presses, on railroads, along the
docks, screwmen and longshoremen, printing offices and even the barber shops.
A general stagnation of business was the result, but matters were in such a
confused state during the afternoon, and the actual situation so little known,
that it was difficult to ascertain accurately the extent of the movement.
About 500 men employed in the four compresses quit work almost to a man, excepting probably the clerical force, all employed in the yards and at the
freight depot of the Gulf, Colorado and Santa Fe Railway company, while the
work along the docks was almost completely suspended.

THE CAUSE OF THE MOVEMENT.

The cause of the present movement is briefly stated by the following
correspondence between the Knights of Labor and Captain Sawyer, representing
the Mallory Line in this city:

GALVESTON, Tex., November 1, 1885.--J. N. Sawyer, Esq., Agent Mallory
Line Steamships, -- Dear Sir: At a meeting of the executive board of Knights
of Labor of the state of Texas, held in this city on this day, the following
resolution was adopted:

Whereas it has been made known to the executive board of the Knights of
Labor of the state of Texas at the Mallory Line of steamships and its agents
are discriminating against this order by discharging and refusing to allow
them to work upon the Mallory or New York wharf, therefore be it

Resolved that we, as the executive board of the Knights of Labor do
hereby request that you reinstate said men and also allow the Knights of
Labor of the city of Galveston an equal representation upon said wharf. This
board will be very much gratified to receive an answer from you by Tuesday,
the 3d day of November, A.D. 1885, at 12 o'clock m. Very respectfully,
                                                            P. H. GOLDEN

D.M.W.D.A. No. 18, of the State of Texas, and Chairman of the Executive Board.

This communication was submitted yesterday morning, the committee stating
that they would return at noon for an answer. Promptly at noon the executive
committee returned and were handed the following reply:

Galveston, Tex.--Dear Sir: Your favor of the 1st ultimo, covering preamble and resolutions as adopted by your board on that date, as follows:
"Whereas it has been made known to the executive board of the Knights

of Labor of the state of Texas that the Mallory line of steamships and the
agents are discriminating against this order by discharging and refusing to
allow them to work upon the Mallory or New York wharf; therefore be it
     "Resolved that we, as the executive board of the Knights of Labor, do
hereby request that you reinstate said men, and also allow the Knights of
Labor of the city of Galveston an equal representation upon said wharf," is
received, and replying thereto we desire to say that the charges presented
in the preamble to your resolution is without foundation, inasmuch as we have
not, to our knowledge, discharged any member of your order, or any other well
behaved laborer.
     In a conference held in this office October 18, 1885, we were informed
by Mr. Patrick Nugent, a representative of your order, acting in an advisory
capacity, that the men who had been employed at discharging and loading the
Mallory steamers were not members of the order of Knights of Labor.
     These men were not discharged, but (excepting nine white men who did not
leave, and who are now working on the wharf) they of their own volition
abandoned their positions as laborers for the Mallory line. Compliance with
your request would compel us to enact the injustice of which you unwarrantably
complain, of discharging laborers who are performing their duties faithfully
to employ others in their stead. So, conforming to our reply to the joint
committee of October 27, 1885, we decline to disturb the present status of
labor on the Mallory line wharf, and are, sir, yours very truly,
                              J. N. SAWYER & CO., Agents.

     The committee, after considering the above, asked Captain Sawyer if this
was his final answer, and he replied in the affirmative; when they informed
him that they would be at their meeting-room until 1 p.m., where he could
communicate with them if he had anything further to say upon the subject. No
further conference took place, and at 1 p.m. sharp the strike was ordered.
     Matters were thrown into such confusion for the time being, that no very
intelligent opinions could be expressed, and but few seemed to know the cause
or the extent of the movement. The corner of Market and Twenty-second streets
in the Alvey building, where the Knights of Labor have their meeting-room,
seemed to be the general rendezvous, and being the headquarters of the executive committee, it was here that large numbers of the striking laborers
congregated causing quite an animated scene. The Knights of Labor generally
were reticent as to the details of the movement and a reporter of THE NEWS,
with a view of ascertaining the extent of the strike, called upon Captain
Sawyer and the management of the different roads and compresses to ascertain
to what extent they were affected. Captain Sawyer kindly furnished the above
correspondence, which is unquestionably the basis of the strike. In recapi-
tulating the recent trouble out of which the present one has grown he referred
to his letter as published above defining his position in the matter. He
referred to the recent tacit agreement between the white and colored laborers
as to a division of the work, but the Mallory company was under moral obligations to continue the colored laborers so long as they gave satisfaction.
He had been further advised subsequent to the recent strike that the Knights
of Labor would take no definite steps in the matter, merely acting in an
advisory capacity to secure, if possible, an amicable adjustment of the difficulties. He could not say at the time what effect the strike would have on
the Mallory business. The colored laborers were still at work there, and
while work had been stopped at the presses, the cotton already compressed
there was being hauled to the wharf. At the four compresses work was at a
standstill, and none of them were running in the afternoon, in all about 500
laborers had quit work here. Along the docks members of the Screwmen's and
Longshoremen's associations who are members of the Knights of Labor had quit
work, disabling the crews to that extent that work was virtually suspended.
All the men in the yards and at the shops and freight depot of the Gulf,
Colorado and Santa Fe quit work, and until the matter is settled it is a
matter of doubt whether any freights will be permitted to move. The forces
of the Missouri Pacific railway had not quit, at least up to a later hour,
the cause assigned for this being that these laborers are under a different
jurisdiction, and were awaiting orders from their assembly. In all, it is
estimated that about 1500 or 2000 laborers of this city have obeyed the mandate of the Knights of Labor. It applies to every interest where members of

their order are employed, and the printing offices generally were deserted
during the afternoon, and in one instance even a hand in a barber shop knocked
off work. This instance is cited merely to show how general is the present
movement.

THE TYPOGRAPHICAL UNION.

The movement, as applied to the printers, called off all who were employed either in job offices or the newspaper establishments of the city.
The printers on THE NEWS, however, resumed work last night under the following resolution, passed by the local lodge of the Typographical union, of
Galveston:

Believing the order of the Trades assembly in ordering all working people
to quit work, as far as it affects the status of the Typographical union,
unwise and inapplicable to the purpose for which it was promulgated (the boycotting of the Mallory Steamship line), inasmuch as the strike was not ordered
by the Trades assembly, and that the strikers came under the jurisdiction of
the Trades assembly subsequent to the strike, and not previously; therefore,
it is hereby

Resolved, that on account of the short notice given and the above cited
reasons, we do not concur as a body in the action of the Trades assembly as
far as to quit work, but that we will boycott and aid and assist the said
Trades assembly, financially and otherwise, as far as is in our power, further, that the calling of all workingmen from the different offices under the
jurisdiction of the union is virtually boycotting the establishment in which
they work, and that there exists at present a state of feeling between the
union and the employers that will not justify such action.

Resolved, that the delegates from Galveston Typographical Union No. 28,
to the Trades assembly, be instructed to use their best endeavors to avoid
difficulty in labor organizations outside those interested in the Mallory
wharf strike; that in case a strike is ordered in the printing offices under
this jurisdiction, the proprietors first be notified of what is required of
them to avoid a boycott, and replies be received from them to the demands
made upon them.

THE ISSUES INVOLVED.

While the employment of the colored labor on the New York wharf is
the main issue upon which the strike is based, some of the strikers claim
that it is a movement of organized labor against unorganized labor and a protection of white labor as against a substitution of colored labor in this
city. Besides citing the condition of affairs on the New York wharf, it was
very generally rumored yesterday that two carloads of colored laborers had
been brought in the night previous from Brasoria, and that a boat had brought
in some forty or fifty more during the day from the mouth of the Brasoe.
These rumors could not be verified, and in conversation with N. W. Cubey,
last night, he informed a reporter of THE NEWS that such was not the case,
and that there was no foundation for the statement very generally made that
there was a movement on foot to substitute colored for white labor in the cotton presses and other positions now occupied by white labor, and in connection
with which his name was mentioned. He says that if such an importation of
colored labor had been made he would surely have known of it, and his denial
of the charge was quite positive and emphatic.

Mr. Golden, the master workman of the Knights of Labor, and as such the
leader of the present movement, stated to a reporter during the afternoon
that it was a matter of self-preservation. A means of adjustment of the late
strike on the New York wharf had been submitted to the Mallory company, but
they had not accepted it and the white laborers at Galveston who had their
families to support, and whose interests are here, could not afford to and
their subsistence thus taken from them. The Knights of Labor had done all in
their power to settle the differences today and without a resort to extreme
measures they had notified Captain Sawyer, of the Mallory line; Captain Fowler,
of the Morgan line; President Sealy, of the Santa Fe, and several prominent
ship brokers that men of their order, who were not in the strike, were being
discriminated against and would not be allowed to work. He had hoped that
the present trouble might be averted, but unless the matter were settled the
strike would be made general.

HOW IT IS REGARDED

While public opinion has not yet had time to be thoroughly or definitely fixed as to the causes and the extent of the means used to accomplish results, the present trouble is very generally deprecated as a blow that Galveston can ill afford to sustain at this particular season. The means resorted to are also considered too general and violent to be justified in the accomplishment of the results expected to be brought about. This is the conservative view of the situation and the principle that seems to prevail in the present instance in calling upon every department of labor to redress a grievance where no interests in common exists is generally considered as illogical. The remedy seems to rest altogether with the Mallory people in submitting to a division of labor between the white and colored element in the handling of their business here, and the universality of the strike appears to have been determined upon for the purpose of bringing to bear every influence possible to the accomplishment of this end, however extraneous may be the interests that are made to suffer.

NO SETTLEMENT REACHED

A general meeting of the Knights of Labor, held at their hall last night, was attended by some 500 or 600 laborers, and the meeting was regarded with much interest, as it was thought that through it a settlement might be reached. While the details of this meeting could not be learned, it is generally regarded as a settled fact that the end is not yet reached. A reporter of THE NEWS sought Mr. Golden after the meeting, but was informed that it had been decided to give no information to the press. From this it may be inferred at least that no settlement has been reached.

NOTES

The colored laborers engaged on the New York wharf were also in session last night considering the present situation, in which they are incidentally interested.

The present strike continuing will result in a general blockade of freight, as no trains can move out under the present circumstances except the passenger trains, which will not be interfered with. The strike as applied to the railroads is quite as general as the late strike against the Santa Fe, but as the railroads are not the direct cause of the trouble it is not thought that such extreme measures will be resorted to as were applied against the Santa Fe in that strike.

The Mallory ship was loaded yesterday by the colored laborers without any hindrance or interference.

It is learned that the result of last night's meeting was to order the strike to be general throughout the State.

Galveston (Texas) *Daily News,* November 4, 1885.

28. ARBITRATORS AT WORK

THE GALVESTON COMMITTEE CONSIDERING THE TROUBLES IN THAT CITY

GALVESTON, Nov. 9.--The results of yesterday's agreement between the Citizens Committee and the State Executive Committee of the Knights of Labor were manifest on all sides to-day. Every Knight being at his post, the wharves, railroad yards, and cotton presses presented scenes of the great activity.

The Arbitration Committee of Ten was announced this morning, and the first meeting held at 10 o'clock. W. L. Moody, President of the Cotton Exchange, was chosen Chairman by his associate arbitrators. Rules were adopted for the hearing of evidence on both sides, and George Sealy, President of the Santa Fe Railway, appeared before the committee and formally answered for Capt. Sawyer, agent of the Mallory Company, pledging that Sawyer would abide

the result of the arbitration.   The Knights submitted their grievances in
writing.   An afternoon session was held at which Capt. Sawyer gave the
Mallory side of the case.   The committee then adjourned until to-morrow
morning.

The colored laborers are watching the outcome of arbitration with a
great deal of interest.   Prominent colored men, reviewing the situation today, declared that the colored longshoremen employed on the Mallory wharf
would not tamely submit to being replaced by strikers, no matter what the
outcome of arbitration might be.   They hold that the Mallory Company made a
contract to employ them so long as they gave satisfaction.   The Mallorys
admit that the negroes are giving good satisfaction, and indications point to
further trouble, no matter how the arbitration results.

Adjt. Gen. King arrived in the city to-night from Austin.   He has been
ordered by Gov. Ireland to make personal inquiry into the situation both here
and at Houston, and instructed to take such action in the premises as shall
seem best to him.   Under this authority the Adjutant General could call out
the militia on short notice.   His presence at this juncture is not calculated
to improve the situation.

New York Times, November 10, 1885.

29.   LABOR TROUBLES AT GALVESTON

FEARS THAT AN AMICABLE ADJUSTMENT WILL NOT BE REACHED

GALVESTON, TEXAS. Nov. 10.--The situation to-night touching the settlement of the recent strike does not promise an amicable adjustment.   Adjt.
Gen. King arrived in the city last night from Austin to personally investigate the causes which led to the recent boycott.   Gov. Ireland has ordered
Gen. King to take such action in the premises as the result of his investigations may warrant.   The feeling of hatred between the Knights of Labor and
the colored workmen was greatly intensified to-day when it became known that
the local Assembly of Knights of Labor had addressed a formal request to
Mayor Fulton, asking him to dismiss Patrolmen Davis, De Bruhl, Warren, and
Sparks, alleging that "They have been using their best endeavors to incite
the colored people to violence." The three last named policemen are colored
men.   The Mayor replied that he could not comply with their wishes, as an
investigation proved the accused policemen were quiet and efficient officers.
This incident has aroused the colored laborers to open and avowed hostility
toward the Knights.

The Committee of Arbitration passed the day in secret session taking
testimony.   Their proceedings are invested with the air of an important
court sitting in a momentous case.   All evidence is reduced to writing.   It
is the general belief that the committee stand 5 to 5 on the final questions
of settlement and that some outside civilian will be called in as an eleventh
juror to cast the deciding vote as to whether the negroes shall be ejected
from the Mallory wharf.   Human lives hang on that vote.   There is reason to
believe that the military and city authorities are quietly preparing to
suppress by force any outbreak that may follow the rendering of a decision
unfavorable to the Knights of Labor.   Adjt. Gen. King is privately inspecting
the military companies to-night, and in his charge to the United States Grand
Jury to-day Judge Sabin called their attention to the gravity of the situation, and bade them examine closely into any violation of the United States
statutes.   An impression is growing that the Mallory Company was forced
against their wishes to recognize the arbitration court, and a good deal of
doubt exists as to whether they will really abide its decision if their
colored laborers are ordered to quit.   Henry R. Mallory is quoted here as
having said he would lay up his shins rather than submit to be dictated to in
this matter.

New York Times, November 11, 1885.

30.   ARBITRATION IN GALVESTON

GALVESTON, Texas, Nov. 11.--The Committee of Arbitration appointed to settle
the differences between the Knights of Labor and the Mallory Steamship Company concluded its labors this evening by adopting, upon motion of Julius
Runge, of the Citizens Committee, the following preamble and resolution:

   Whereas, It is the sense of the Committee of Arbitration that in the
employment of labor there should be no discrimination against any one on
account of race, color, or organization, as is maintained by the Knights of
Labor and recognized by Capt. Sawyer in his letter of this date; therefore,
   Resolved, That in consideration of the fact that the strike originated
in consequence of mutual misunderstandings, we recommend and request Capt.
Sawyer, agent of the Mallory Company, that whenever he needs labor in addition to the number of men on his payroll this day, that he give the preference to the men who were at work on the wharf at the time of the strike on
Oct. 15.

   This resolution was passed by a vote of 8 to 2. Messrs. Moody and Miller
of the Citizens Committee, voting against its adoption. It will be observed
that the language of the resolution is merely recommendatory and not in any
sense mandatory upon the Mallory Company. The result is unsatisfactory to
all, and is looked upon as merely an excuse on the part of the Arbitration
Committee to enable it to disband and thereby get rid of a bad job. They
must make some report to the waiting public, so they adopt this watery resolution. Leading members of the Knights of Labor claim the result of the
arbitration as a victory for the Knights. They claim that the journal of the
arbitration court shows that the Mallorys are bound by the Citizens Committee to employ the late white strikers whenever they desire to increase
their present force or supply vacancies. In other words, no colored men are
to be discharged by the Mallory Company, but each side is furnished with a
payroll of the present laborers and of the striking white longshoremen on
Oct. 15, so that whenever Mallory's agent wants a new man he must take him
from that old payroll, and by this means the Kinghts claim they will again
have possession of the wharf in a few months. Any violation of this understanding, say the Knights, will result in immediate trouble.

   Agent Sawyer, on the other hand, it is reliably reported to-night, does
not interpret the result of arbitration as being at all binding on his company. He says if the committee meant it to be binding, they would have said
so, and not used the words "recommend and request." Inasmuch as Agent Sawyer
tacitly stood by George Sealy's pledge in his name to abide the result of
the arbitration, it would seem that the committee had full power to use
stronger and binding language had they seen fit to do so. The result of the
committee's labor is not generally known on the streets to-night; therefore,
the effect of the verdict upon the great body of the Knights and colored
workmen cannot be given, but every indication points to intense dissatisfaction.

   Under the auspices of the merchants of this city a committee of six
prominent business men has been permanently organized and empowered to increase its membership to 100 for the prosecution of the commerce of the city,
should occasion require, and this committee has been in close consultation
with Adjt. Gen. King to-day, who posted them on the law, and apprised them
at just what point the military could and would interfere.

New York Times, November 12, 1885.

31.   BOYCOTT RENEWED.

GALVESTON, Texas, Jan. 28.--The general public was very much surprised
to-day by the official announcement that the Knights of Labor had promulgated
another boycotting mandate against the Mallory Steamship Company. The order

came from Fort Worth by mail, the Executive Committee of District Assembly
No. 78 having met there several days ago and secretly determined upon its
issuance. District Master Workman P. H. Golden, who resides in this city,
is absent in North Texas, and the promulgation of the order to boycott before
his return to the city occasions a good deal of comment even among the Knight
who say that some special reason exists for putting on the boycott at this
particular time. The seriousness of this move will be appreciated when it is
stated that the former boycott against the Mallory Company, which lasted only
some 10 days, from Nov. 1 to 11, cost the commerce of the city of Galveston
an even $500,000. The difficulties in the way of a settlement of the present
differences are far more stubborn than at the outbreak of the November boycott, and every indication points to a prolonged and bitter struggle between
the giant labor organization and the great corporations that supply the
Mallory Line with freight.

The history of the difficulty dates from the middle of last October,
when the 150 white longshoremen employed on the Mallory wharves demanded an
increase of wages, from 40 cents per hour for daylight labor and 60 cents for
night and Sunday work to 50 cents an hour all around. They made this demand
under a claim that the Mallory Company had promised, on the revival of business, to increase wages. Capt. Sawyer, agent for the Mallory Line, refused
their request, whereupon the longshoremen struck and Sawyer promptly filled
their places with colored laborers, but paid them the very wages demanded by
the striking whites. The Knights of Labor took up the cause of the white
longshoremen, and from that day they have never ceased in their efforts to
displace the negroes from the Mallory wharves. The November boycott failed
to effect the desired expulsion of the negroes, and after its disastrous
effect has paralyzed the trade of Galveston and a large portion of Texas,
about a dozen business and railroad men of this city, including George Sealy,
President of the Gulf, Colorado and Santa Fe Railroad; W. L. Moody, President
of the Cotton Exchange, Julius Runge, and a score of other very rich men, got
together and effected a temporary compromise of the difficulty by agreeing to
the following resolutions while sitting in joint conference with the labor
delegates:

Resolved, That it is the sense of this Committee of Arbitration that in
the employment of labor there should be no discrimination against any one on
account of race, color, or organization.

Resolved, That in consideration of the fact that this strike originated
in consequence of mutual misunderstandings, we recommend and request Capt.
J. N. Sawyer that whenever he needs labor in addition to the number of men
on the rolls this day he give the preference to the men who were on the wharf
at the time of the strike.

The present boycott is simply the outgrowth of the open violation of
this agreement, for such it was, as Mr. Sealy openly pledged the good faith
of Capt. Sawyer in observance of whatever result the arbitration reached.
Although three busy months have elapsed since that agreement and hundreds of
men have been employed by the Mallorys, not a single Knight of Labor has ever
been called. Mr. Sawyer, being interviewed to-day, denied any violation of
the agreement, stating that the names of all men employed since the arbitration were taken from his rolls. He refers to old payrolls which contain the
names of nearly every workingman in the city at some period in their order.[22]

New York Times, January 29, 1886.

32. CONGRESSIONAL REPORT ON THE LABOR TROUBLES IN MISSOURI[23]

JASPER WILLIAMS (colored) sworn and examined.

By the CHAIRMAN:

Question: Where were you born?
Answer: In Texas.
Q. What is your occupation?

A. I am a section man.
Q. On what road?
A. On the Missouri Pacific.
Q. Are you working on that road now?
A. I was before the strike.
Q. Did you go out on the strike?
A. Yes, sir.
Q. Are you a Knight of Labor?
A. Yes, sir.
Q. Do you belong to a colored organization or a white organization?
A. To a colored organization.
Q. Were there other colored men working on the road besides you?
A. Yes, sir; there were.
Q. Did they all go out?
A. Yes, sir.
Q. Have you been working for the road since the strike?
A. No, sir.
Q. How long had you been working for the road before the strike took place?
A. About four years.
Q. How old are you?
A. I allow I am twenty-eight passed.
Q. Did you ever work in the water?
A. Yes, sir.
Q. For the road?
A. Yes, sir.
Q. Did you receive extra pay for it?
A. No, sir.
Q. Did you demand pay for it?
A. Of course, I spoke to the section foreman about it, and he said he did not know, but guessed they would give us some extra pay. He told us to go to the road-master about it, and, of course, we could get no understanding about it from the road-master.
Q. Did you go to the road master?
A. Yes, sir, we did go to him.
Q. Whom did the foreman send you to?
A. He said go to the road-master. He said, of course, he couldn't do anything about it.
Q. So you failed to get your extra pay. Is that what you mean to say?
A. No, sir; we did not get it.
Q. (By Mr. BUCHANAN.) What is the name of this road-master?
A. Mr. Courtney.
Q. What is the name of the foreman?
A. Peter John.
Q. What is this "working in the water," and what did you do?
A. There was a big overflow that washed the track off the dump, and we section men had to go and get it on the dump.
Q. Where did this happen?
A. Down in the Nation.
Q. When was that?
A. I do not know. I guess it was some time in the latter part of last year. Along about the last of the year; but I do not know exactly.
Q. How many days were you at that kind of work?
A. I believe it was about two or three days, as near as I remember.
Q. How much extra pay did you think you ought to have for that extra work?
A. I thought we ought to have had time and a half. It was the understanding that we were to have that time.
Q. You said that was your understanding. Had you that understanding with the road-master or the foreman?
A. The foreman told us after the strike of last year we were to get time and a half for all overtime we worked.
Q. Was this work in the water "overtime?"
A. Why, yes; in cases of that kind, when the track was washed off the dump, you have to be there all the time. We scarcely got anything to eat.

Q. Do you mean to say that during this time you worked overtime and you only got regular pay, and that you did not get time and a half for that time?

A. No, sir. we did not.

Q. You are certain that you did not get time and a half for the overtime?

A. Yes, sir; I am certain of it. Back last winter, I believe last December, we were taken down in the Nation to shovel snow. They tried to get men down there for $1.10 a day, and men would not agree to go. Well, then the road-master he went around and told the section men to go around and see if they could not get men to go and they would give them time and a half to go and shovel snow. Well, we got several men, and went down, and the agreement was that we were to get time and a half for all the time we were out, and we were out three days, I believe--if anything, a little more --and we scarcely got anything to eat at all. We got two meals during the whole time we were out.

Q. Did you get time and a half for the time you were out?

A. No, sir.

Q. Did you present any of these grievances to your assembly?

A. Yes, sir.

Q. Do you know whether they presented them to the managers of the road or not?

A. I do not know; they said they did.

Q. Do you know whether these grievances were among those which led to the strike?

A. I suppose so, they said they were.

Q. (By the CHAIRMAN.) Who paid your board while working in the water and snow?

A. The road-master; he got what was bought; I guess the company paid for it. I did not.

Q. They paid you ordinary wages and paid the board?

A. They paid us $1.10 a day.

Q. And boarded you?

A. I did not consider that board.

Q. You all ate together?

A. No, sir; we did not. Of course I was not with the boss all the time I did not get but one meal a day, and of course I did not get half enough.

Q. Was it customary to furnish board while off with your gang?

A. No, sir.

WYATT OWENS (colored) sworn and examined.

By the CHAIRMAN:

Question: How long have you lived in Denison?

Answer. Ever since 1875.

Q. Have you worked for the Missouri Pacific Railroad Company?

A. Yes, sir.

Q. How long?

A. About seven or eight or nine years.

Q. In what capacity?

A. The first work I did was on the work train.

Q. Were you at work for the railroad company on the 6th of March?

A. Yes, sir.

Q. What were you doing?

A. I was a laborer up in the car department.

Q. Were you a Knight of Labor?

A. Yes, sir.

Q. Are you one now?

A. Yes, sir.

Q. Do you belong to the colored organization of the Knights of Labor?

A. Yes, sir.

Q. Did you go out on the strike?

A. Yes, sir; I went out on the strike.

Q. Why?

A. For the rates of wages. I cannot live on what I was getting--$1.25 a day.

Q. Was the only reason for your going out on a strike the fact that you were getting $1.25 a day and could not live on that?

A. No, sir; it was not the only question; because in 1885 they promised to restore our wages to the September, 1884, rate. To the best of my knowledge, they promised to give us $1.45 a day. When the pay-car came around they did not pay us $1.40, and the question was raised; and they said they could not pay that, and that the rate was $1.25 in September, 1884. I told them that I was getting $1.40 for the same work, and other men were getting $1.25. Mr. Bailey cut us down to the same as they paid these other men.

Q. When was this cut-down in the wages?

A. It was in 1885.

Q. What time in 1885?

A. I cannot remember exactly what time.

Q. Was it not in the spring?

A. Yes, sir; it was in the spring.

Q. Did you work from that time until the 6th of March, 1886, for $1.25?

A. Yes, sir.

Q. Why did you not strike during that period of time if you could not live on $1.25 a day?

A. I thought they would restore our wages according to the agreement. They said they were working on it.

Q. Who said?

A. Some of the members; I do not know exactly who said so.

Q. Working on what?

A. Working to get our wages restored.

Q. You mean that you were living in hope?

A. I was living in hope.

Q. Did you return to work?

A. Yes, sir.

Q. When?

A. I do not exactly know when it was.

Q. Did you go back when Mr. Powderly issued his order?

A. Yes, sir.

Q. Ordering, or directing Mr. Irons to order, the men back to work? [24]

A. Yes, sir.

Q. How long did you work?

A. I worked five days.

Q. When did you stop work?

A. Well, they arrested me.

Q. Who arrested you?

A. Mr. Whiteside; I believe that is his name.

Q. What position did he hold?

A. He is Mr. Douglass's deputy.

Q. Deputy sheriff?

A. Yes, sir.

Q. Upon what charge did he arrest you?

A. For being in the raid upon the shop that night.

Q. What night do you mean?

A. That night that the raid was made upon the roundhouse. They took me to jail, and they put me in irons and forced me to tell something, and to say something to the jailer.

Q. What did he question you about?

A. They tried to make me say I was down there. They went out and staid about fifteen minutes and the jailer was out in the yard talking, and Whiteside told the jailer to chain me down. He chained me down with irons all night, and kept me that way all night.

Q. Who told the jailer to do that?

A. I understood the deputy sheriff to do that.

Q. Did you resist the jailer?

A. No, sir; I never resisted any at all; I told him "all right."

Q. How did he chain you?

A. He chained both legs, and by a chain right around me, and I could not do anything but lie down on my right side all night.

Q. Did you rest?

A. No, sir; I did not rest a bit.
Q. What kind of a jail was it; was it a safe jail?
A. It was a safe jail; built of rock.
Q. What reason did he assign for that treatment?
A. I do not know, sir, except to make me tell something I did not know anything about.
Q. You were not a convict?
A. No, sir, I am not a convict.
Q. Have you been tried?
A. No, sir, I have not been tried.
Q. Are you out on bond?
A. I am out on bond now.
Q. Did Mr. Whiteside come back and converse with you after you were chained?
A. He came back the next morning and cursed me around a little.
Q. State what he said.
A. He said that he wanted to get any evidence that I could give. He said, "I am not after you colored men; I am after those white sons of bitches." I told him I did not know anything about it; but that I would tell him the truth, and directly he kept pumping around, and I told him something, and he took me out of there and took the chain off one leg. He would not allow me bond before my trial. He took me from the roundhouse and took me to jail.
Q. (By Mr. BUCHANAN.) How long did you stay in that jail with a chain on?
A. From half past 6 to half past 10; and from Thursday to Saturday night I staid in jail and had chain around one leg all the time.
Q. You say that you could not live on $1.25 a day; how much family have you?
A. A wife and one child.
Q. What rent have you to pay?
A. I have no rent to pay now.
Q. Were you in the employ of the company in September, 1884?
A. Yes, sir.
Q. And you got how much then?
A. I don't remember, but about $1.40.
Q. They cut that pay when?
A. In the spring of 1885, some time.
Q. Did you agree to have it reduced from $1.40 to $1.25, or was it done without your consent?
A. It was done without my consent.
Q. Were you in the strike of 1885?
A. Yes, sir.
Q. Did you strike against that reduction then?
A. Yes, sir.
Q. And after the strike was over did you get your $1.40 back again?
A. No, sir.
Q. You never did get it?
A. No, sir; I never got it.
Q. (By Mr. PARKER.) What was the name of the jailer that chained you?
A. I do not know his name.
Q. Do you know whether he is in town now?
A. He is jailer now.
Q. (By the CHAIRMAN.) Have you made any complaint against him for it?
A. No, sir; I have made no complaint against him.
Q. (By Mr. OUTHWAITE.) I am requested to ask you whether you were ever arrested before?
A. I was never arrested before, and was never in the court-house as a witness.
Q. Are you certain that you were paid $1.40 in 1884?
A. Yes, sir.
Q. You signed the pay-roll?
A. I do not know about signing the pay-roll.
Q. In September, 1884, you signed the pay-roll for some amount?

A. I disremember now.

Q. Did you ever sign any papers when you got your money?

A. I touched the pen.

Q. You signed the pay-roll for the amount of wages which were coming to you?

A. I do not remember.

Q. Well, did you make your mark, or do you write your own name when you get your pay at any time?

A. I always touch the pen; that is all I can do.

Q. And you afterward got all the money that was coming to you?

A. All that was promised me.

Q. Did you ever work without getting your time and a half?

A. I never have got time and a half.

Q. Where were you working?

A. Round about the round-house and car shops.

Q. Didyou ever go to your boss and complain about not having received the amount of wages that you ought to get?

A. No, sir; not as I remember of; I cannot remember now.

Q. Had you any talk with any officers of the road about not getting the pay that was coming to you?

A. I told Mr. Bailey that I was not getting the pay that I was paid before; that is, I was not getting $1.40 a day.

Q. After that you went to the local assembly of the Knights and complained to them?

A. Yes, sir.

Q. (By the CHAIRMAN.) Were you not working on the road on work trains in September, 1884 when you were getting $1.40 a day?

A. I was working down at the round-house in 1884.

Q. Were you not working out on the road in September, 1884, and getting $1.40 a day; was that not the regular pay for that work?

A. I got $1.40 a day all the time I worked on the work train.

OBADIAH ORGAN (colored) sworn and examined.

By Mr. BUCHANAN:

Question: Where do you reside?

Answer. I live out here east of town, about the Fourth ward.

Q. How long have you lived there?

A. About two and a half years.

Q. Have you been in the employ of the Missouri Pacific road?

A. Yes, sir.

Q. For how long?

A. Ever since I have been here.

Q. What did you do?

A. I am a laborer in the car shop and handle lumber.

Q. When you first went to work what were your wages?

A. One dollar and forty cents a day.

Q. Do you remember the strike of 1885?

A. Yes, sir.

Q. What were your wages up to that time?

A. Along about September $1.40, and I think it was October $1.25, and running down to January some time when they were cut down to $1.25.

Q. And January of what year?

A. January a year ago.

Q. They were then cut down to $1.25?

A. Yes, sir.

Q. What were your wages at the time of the strike in March, 1885?

A. I got $1.25. I believe the strike was in March. In January, I think, they cut us to $1.25.

Q. And in March there was a still further reduction?

A. I think it was. There were four or five of them and they cut down to $1.10.

Q. And then you struck?

A. Yes, sir.

Q. After you went to work after the strike of 1885, what wages did you get?

A. One dollar and twenty-five cents.
Q. How long have you been receiving $1.25?
A. I have been receiving it ever since.
Q. Up to the time of the last strike?
A. Yes, sir.
Q. Did you go out on the last strike?
A. Yes, sir.
Q. Are you a member of the Knights of Labor?
A. Yes, sir.
Q. Are you now working for the company?
A. Yes, sir.
Q. When did you begin to work for them again?
A. Three or four weeks ago.
Q. About the time Mr. Powderly's letter came out?
A. Yes, sir.
Q. Have you been at work for them ever since?
A. Yes, sir.
Q. At what rate?
A. One dollar and twenty-five cents a day.
Q. Did you ever work Sunday work?
A. Yes, sir.
Q. How often?
A. About every Sunday. Some Sundays I have got a lay-off.
Q. How many hours do you work on Sunday.
A. Ten hours a day.
Q. What do you get for that?
A. One dollar and twenty-five cents.
Q. Do you only get $1.25 for Sunday work?
A. I never received any more.
Q. Are you certain that is all you get?
A. When I work thirty days I get $37.50.
Q. Who is your foreman?
A. Mr. Tuley.
Q. Who pays you?
A. I get my pay from the pay-car.

House Document No. 4174, "Report of the House Select Committee on Labor Troubles in Missouri, Arkansas, & Texas," 49th Congress, 2d Session, 1886-7, pp. 62-63, 115-17, 123-24.

33. THE "DANGERS" OF ORGANIZING BLACKS

It is apparent to the most hearty sympathizer of the labor organization known as the Knights of Labor, that in their conflict with the Gould system of railroads they were all wrong in the question at issue, and that the outcome of the strike has been a deplorable failure all along the line. It is plainly apparent that the organization was seduced into ordering the strike by short-sighted leaders of a local organization, and that those persistently refused to listen to the wiser and maturer counsels of better informed men of the National organization. . . .

Early in the progress of the strike last spring upon the Texas and Pacific Railroad, the Knights of Labor in the southwest discovered that many Negroes were obtained without much difficulty to do the work which they had supposed must be done by themselves if at all. Soon afterward a dispatch from some point on the Gould system [Union Pacific] Texarkana, we think it was, stated that the colored men of Western Arkansas were being organized as Knights of Labor. It was added that the movement was exciting "grave apprehension." Now it appears that the landowning class of whites are in a painful state of excitement in that region, owing to the turbulent strike of certain colored Knights working on two or three plantations. In the end, this strike may amount to much or little, probably the latter judging by yesterday'

dispatches, but it is still an extremely interesting suggestion. It needs
only a passing glance at the possibilities of the organization of the colored
laborers of the South as Knights of Labor to convince any intelligent person
that the most tempestuous industrial disturbances of the last 6 months in
the North may be totally cast in the shade before long by greater disturbances
in the former slave states. First of all, the grievances of the colored
laborers of the south, especially those who work on plantations, are much
greater than any of which northern working men complain. The truck system of
payment, the renting out of convicts, and the ingenious devices whereby the
tiller of the soil is kept always in debt to its owner, make the condition
of a large part of the southern Negroes, little better than slavery, and
their social and political oppression adds its weight to their crushing
burdens. Desperate diseases are often met by a resort to desperate remedies,
and in that fact lies one reason why the Knights of Labor movement among the
colored laborers of the South may cause startling results. Another very
significant point is the intolerance with which any organized effort on the
part of the Negroes to coerce or resist the employing class will surely be
met. The guilty conscience of the South told its dominant class before
slavery fell, and tells them still, that there are crimes against the colored
race which the wildest carnival of rapine and slaughter will hardly avenge.
This alone is enough to make the white capitalists recoil in terror and rage
from any organization which may embolden and strengthen the Negro race. The
authors of political, social and industrial oppression are never inclined
to deal quietly and reasonably with anything which seems likely to make an
end to that oppression and possibly punish it besides. And it must be admitted, on the other hand, that the Negro laborers of the South are possibly
very unfit as yet to use the power of an organization like the Knights of
Labor prudently, wisely and justly. During the existence of slavery they
were without any semblance of organization, a fact which was largely the
cause of their quiet submission to great wrongs. . . . If the Southern
Negroes, finding themselves for the first time in a powerful organization
which promised them the pecuniary support of hundreds of thousands of white
men, besides that of their own race, and should be intoxicated to the point
of serious mistakes and wrongs, it would not be at all surprising, and herein
lies another highly significant feature of the situation in Arkansas. At
every turn the natural friction between employers and labor organizations
is sure to be so complicated and intensified by race feelings, old fears and
hates and by the differences both social and political which do not exist in
the North, that the Southern whites may well look with apprehension upon the
spread of the Order of the Knights of Labor among the colored people of the
section, and yet it may prove in the end the long-sought wedge which shall
split the solid South industrially, socially, and politically.

Cleveland *Gazette,* July 17, 1886.

34. COLORED KNIGHTS OF LABOR

PLANTATION HANDS BECOME RIOTOUS AND ONE OF THEM IS SHOT

LITTLE ROCK, Ark., July 6.--Thursday last colored laborers on the Tate
plantation, nine miles below here, on the Arkansas River, struck for an advance in the wages generally paid in the neighborhood. They then, by intimidation, prevented others from taking their places. Sheriff Worthen was
called on by the planters for protection, and went down early yesterday
morning. About 150 colored men assembled from neighboring places, and began
making threats that nobody should go to work or be arrested. The Sheriff
attempted to arrest Gill, a ringleader, who resisted and was shot by a Deputy
in both arms. During the afternoon a posse went down from Little Rock heavily
armed, when the Sheriff succeeded in dispersing the mob and averted what
threatened to prove a general uprising. Gill, who was taken to jail, says
he is a Knight of Labor, and it is understood that all the strikers are

Knights, there being three assemblies in that portion of the country.

New York Times, July 7, 1886.

35. STRIKING NEGRO KNIGHTS.
FEARS THAT THEY WILL REDRESS THEIR WRONGS BY FORCE.

LITTLE ROCK, Ark., July 8,--It was supposed that the trouble at the
Tate plantation had ended, and that the striking negro Knights of Labor had
become pacified and would return to work, their Master Workman having so
advised. Just the reverse, however, seems now to be the condition of affairs,
and many believe that this county is on the verge of one of the bloodiest
race conflicts that has occurred since the war. Intelligence has arrived
from the neighborhood of the late trouble that the striking negroes, reinforced by many sympathizers from the surrounding farms and plantations,
numbering fully 1,000 in all, have made complete preparations for a general
uprising; that, fully armed, they will attempt to redress their wrongs and
grievances, directing their attention first to Sheriff Worthen, who recently
subdued the striker. They will next advance upon the farms of Morey and Fox,
with the intention of burning their crops, barns, and houses. Others who
have incurred their enmity will be visited and treated in a like manner.
The negroes have been openly buying arms and ammunition within the past few
days, and they state that if they are opposed in their campaign of revenge
they will be freely used. Sheriff Worthen called a public meeting last night
and stated these facts, at the same time requesting those who were willing
to join his posse to hand him their names. About 100 men responded to his
call and were sworn in a special deputies. At the first intimation of an
outbreak among the blacks the posse will proceed to the scene of trouble and
attempt to quell the disturbance, and bloodshed will doubtless follow. The
Governor has been called upon to order out the militia, but he refuses to do
so until some actual trouble shall have occurred. Some of the farmers in
the vicinity of the Tate plantation have prepared to resist the negroes,
while others have removed their families and valuables to places of safety.

New York Times, July 9, 1886.

36. COLORED KNIGHTS OF LABOR IN ARKANSAS

Last week there was an uprising of colored men (who are Knights of
Labor) on a large plantation in Arkansas, and for sometime very serious
trouble was feared. These colored farm laborers struck for higher wages.
There were only a few hundred of these colored men, and yet they threw
the entire county into a state of nervous excitement. A large number of
planters immediately removed their families without the vicinity of the
trouble; and frantic appeals were made to the county and State authorities
to put down the strikers, before any violence was shown, and to protect the
lives of innocent planters and their vested rights, when it does not appear
that these were in any great danger.

It is truly remarkable, how a Southern white grows blue in the face, in
the presence of a real or expected Negro uprising, and how frantically he
appeals to the lawful authorities for protection! And he usually get all the
protection he wants. But when these same white rascals arm themselves with
rifles and shoot down unoffending blacks by the score in the very temple of
justice, as at Carrollton, the Negro appeals in vain to lawful authority, of
country or of State. His cries are unheard!

In its treatment of this matter--deploring the threatened danger to the
amicable relations of the blacks and whites of Arkansas--the able New York

Evening Post failed to note this propensity of the Southern whites to rise
above the law when they feel in a mobocratic humor, and their reliance upon
and frantic appeal to the protection of the law whenever the Negro feels like
taking the law in his hands. What is sauce for the goose is not sauce for
the gander in the South. The Negro must abide by the law; the white man
consults his lordly pleasure about obeying or breaking the law.

In the book, "Black and White," published last year by the editor of
this paper, the position was there taken that all the future trouble in the
South would arise out of industrial complications, not out of political complications, as in the past. Everything tends towards a confirmation of that
view. Indeed, the industrial condition is more vital at all times than the
political, since the former hinges upon the latter. And we may henceforth
expect to hear of more trouble arising out of the industrial than out of the
political relations of the whites and blacks of the South; for we assert,
without fear of successful contradiction, that nowhere else in the world can
there be found a more odious, unjust and tyrannical landlord system than
that which obtains in the South. It is a virtual continuation of the slave
system, with the landlord relieved of the obligations and responsiblities
to the laborer imposed upon him by the laws of the slave system and his right
in the person as well as the labor of the slave.

All the land laws in the South are made in favor of the planters, and
it is notorious that the wages paid by them to their employees are simply
pauper wages; and this is aggravated by the store account and order system
by which the laborer seldom ever sees a dime of cash and is frequently
allowed to overdraw his account, or is overcharged, for the purpose of being
held at the pleasure of the planter. There is more direct and indirect
robbery of the colored laborers of the South than is practiced anywhere else
on earth. The thing is simply infamous, and will cause infinite trouble in
the future.

New York *Freeman,* July 17, 1886.

37. THE FUTILITY OF STRIKES AND BOYCOTTS

The restlessness of all the labor elements of the country becomes more
and more evident and embarrassing to all industrial interests. Never before
in the history of the country was the antagonism between labor and capital
more decided and determined. In times past organized capital has had things
all its own way; the conflict has come which must settle one way or the other
these questions or interest on capital and wages of superintendence on the
one hand and the wages of labor on the other. The whole land is convulsed
with the conflict and every species of business is more or less affected.

One of the most important demands made by the labor forces, and which
now characterizes the contest, is that eight hours shall constitutes a day's
work. From the universality of the demand the gravest consequences may be
expected to result, especially in such branches of industry as have already
entered into large and important contracts, at estimates based upon the
marketable rate of labor at the time the contracts were made. In such cases,
to concede the eight hour demand when the estimate was made upon a basis of
ten hours' labor cannot but eventuate in great loss in some instances and
bankruptcy in others. The only possible way by which the eight hour demands
could be reasonably acceded to would be a proportionate reduction in the
rate of wages. This would be equitable to all sides, and would give employers an opportunity to make estimates upon future work by anticipating a
demand for an increase in the rate of wages.

This being true, who will suffer most from an increase in the rate of
wages, or, what is the same, a reduction in the hours of labor. The manufacturer will insure himself against loss by increasing the cost of his
products; the rich can afford to stand this increase in the cost of the
necessaries and the luxuries of life; but can the great army of wage working
consumers stand it, and reap any substantial advantage over the old rate of

wages and hours of labor? Or will not the increased cost of living absorb
as before the increased rate of wages? It seems so to us. The iron law of
supply and demand, which regulates the cost of consumption, based logically
upon the cost of production, will admit of no other interpretation.

From this statement of the case it would seem that nothing could be more
absurd as a remedy for the evils which afflict wage workers than the demand
so universally made for higher wages and shorter hours of labor. They gain
nothing in the last resort, but lose millions by ceasing to utilize the
power to produce, which is their stock in trade. When the present conflict
adjusts itself on the demands now made, the philosophers of the labor movement will still have to seek the power remedy through the intricate and
tortuous machinery of legislation and effect a re-adjustment in the rate of
taxation on real and personal property, the interest on invested capital,
and by fixing a reasonable but iron-clad rate of interest on incomes above,
say $5,000. This re-adjustment would be materially remedied, since it
necessarily reduces the rate of taxation and curtails to some extent the
enormous and pernicious aggregation of capital in the hands of a limited
number of men, to the danger and disadvantages of the masses of society.

New York *Freeman,* May 8, 1886.

38.   IN CASE OF NECESSITY

A FORCE ORGANIZED FOR SERVICE IN YOUNG TOWNSHIP IF CALLED UPON--COL. ANDERSON
MILLS CHARGES THE MEETING TO BE FOR POLITICAL PURPOSES--SHERIFF WORTHEN'S REPI

Last night the circuit court-room was crowded with citizens in response
to the call by Sheriff Worthen for men who would be willing to serve as deputies if necessary, to quell any more trouble with the colored men at the
Tate plantation and vicinity. The men who assembled were of all political
parties and there were a number of colored men present.

Sheriff Worthen was called to the chair and stated that the object of
the meeting was to adopt precautionary measures to prevent any disturbance
or violation of the laws. He said he had been informed in the morning that
the colored men had held meetings, at which they had arranged to start a
systematic destruction of property, beginning at his plantation and coming on
to the plantations adjoining until they reached the Fox plantation, where the
trouble of last week occurred. That they then expected him to arrive with
men and would be ready to begin the destruction of life. . . . He therefore
wanted to have all present who would do so to give their names and addresses,
so that, if necessary, he could get a posse speedily in case of emergency.

A CHARGE BY COL. ANDERSON MILLS

Mr. Anderson Mills arose and addressed the meeting. He said he had come
from the neighborhood mentioned late in the evening and that he did not believe there was any truth in the reports. He thought the meeting was entirely
out of place and uncalled for. He said he believed it was simply a political
scheme, and had objects hidden and beyond what had been stated. In regard
to the trouble at the Tate place, he said the Fox brothers who ran it were
to blame. They said they paid their laborers 75 cents a day, but this was
not so. They gave their hands tickets, and when they gave for provisions,
charged them 100 or 200 percent profit on the provisions so that when it was
figured out the hands got nothing, and could not live on such wages. He did
not have any such trouble with his "niggers," and paid them their wages in
money. He denounced the meeting and said it was a great mistake to take such
a step.

Dr. F. M. Chrisman said he had been in the neighborhood during the afternoon and there was not a scintilla of truth in the reports. He agreed with
Anderson Mills.

E. A. Fulton, colored, said that there were some things which Mr. Mills
had said that he agreed to, and was going to say that he believed that there

was politics in the trouble that had taken place on the Tate plantation, when Sheriff Worthen stopped him and made a little speech.

NOT A CANDIDATE

He said he would say right there that there was no foundation for the statements that there was any politics in the meeting. He created a decided sensation by saying that there could be no politics in it, because he was not a candidate for sheriff. He had had as much work as he wanted. If there were other men who wanted to be sheriff he was glad of it. The only thing he had to consider was his duty. He had received these reports and he would be a fine officer if he did not prepare for an emergency that might arise.

Merriman, a colored organizer of these Knights of Labor and D. F. Thomson, the state organizer, had promised to go down to the scene of the trouble and had gone. They said they could control the colored men. Consequently he had not sent an armed force there. He believed that there would be no trouble. But it was a condition in which he as the peace officer of the county would fail in his duty if he did not prepare for duty in case these men could not control the colored people.

After this there was an informal registration of names of those who would be willing to serve if there should be need of their services, and seventy-five men, several of them colored men, put their names down. After this the meeting gradually broke.

Arkansas Gazette, July 8, 1886.

39. STIRRED UP

THE RUMOR OF REPUBLICAN RESPONSIBILITY FOR THE
TATE PLANTATION RIOT BRINGS OUT A CARD

To the Editor of The Gazette:

In your article headed "War in Young", published in your paper the following appears:

"Behind the whole trouble it was freely stated by those with whom *The Gazette* man talked, that this trouble was incited just at this time by politicians who hoped to benefit by the unfortunate prejudices that would be engendered by it. It was openly asserted by men whose integrity cannot be questioned, that republican politicians were at the bottom of the whole matter.

We desire, as this statement is made so broadly by you, to learn through your paper what "republican politicians" have instigated this matter. We ask you to give the names of the Republican politicians who incite not, and, if you are unable to do so, to give the names of the men whose integrity cannot be questioned, who assert that the alleged riot was incited by "republican politicians."

The undersigned are republicans, and, as we think, law-abiding citizens of Pulaski county. We are of opinion that republicans are, as a rule, law-abiding citizens. We object to any wholesale denunciation of republicans as violators of law, and ask for the names of "republican politicians" who incite riot, to the end that we may take steps to cause their expulsion from the party.

W. S. OLIVER,
CHAS. C. WATERS,
A. S. FOWLER

The report that politicans were mixed up in the Tate plantation trouble was stated as a report by THE GAZETTE and was made by a number of gentlemen with whom THE GAZETTE representative talked at the plantation. It was the general impression that such was the case. It is natural that the republicans should desire to disclaim the responsibility for inciting such a deplorable riot.--[City Editor.]

Arkansas Gazette, July 8, 1886.

40 . SHERIFF R. W. WORTHEN

DECLARES THAT HE DOES NOT DESIRE TO BECOME A CANDIDATE FOR SHERIFF

To the Editor of The Gazette:
    You were mistaken Sunday morning in announcing me a candidate for sher-
iff. It is true, I have allowed myself to say to a few friends that I would
run, it being understood there would be no opposition to me.
    That I do not want to run is well known to many of my personal friends,
and it was a long time before I would say to a number of them who thought
there would not or should not be any opposition for the nomination. I am
glad to see men now announced and unannounced as wanting to be sheriff. I
have had an office for many years, and will be glad to give way to other
democrats wanting to try political life.
    I don't feel any doubt about either the nomination or election. Of
course the usual "kick" against Worthen being nominated is on hand and were
I a candidate, would result as heretofore in my nomination. I have been
very highly complimented by the democrats of this county, having received
practically unanimous nominations except for sheriff in 1884, when I was not
a candidate until thirty-six hours before the convention made the nomination.
But I think I can use the same amount of brains and energy that I have given
to the politics of this county and make more money. What I make in some
other business may be less, but it certainly will be mine and not belong to
everybody asking it, as has been the case for the past ten years.
    I desire to say that I shall not "sulk in my tent" as I have known men
who didn't get a nomination to do. I shall be on hand during the election
as heretofore, and do my duty. Thanking the people for past favors, I am
very respectfully,

                                            ROBT. W. WORTHEN.

Arkansas Gazette, July 8, 1886.

41. DISCHARGED.

EXAMINATION BEFORE MAGISTRATE J. G. YEISER

OF HUGH GILL, WOUNDED LAST WEEK ON THE TATE PLANTATION

    Yesterday morning before Magistrate Yeiser, the examination was begun
of Hugh Gill, colored, who was wounded last week on the Tate plantation by
Deputy Sheriff Kinkaid. The examination of the prisoner was on the charge
of assault with intent to kill Worthen, who called at Gill's estate last
Saturday morning to talk with him about the plantation troubles, having heard
that Gill was one of the leaders of the colored hands. The shooting was done
by the deputy, when he saw Gill reaching up for his gun, thinking that the
colored man was trying to get the drop on the sheriff.
    The state was represented by T. C. Trimble and the defendant by Mr.
Thomas, one of the few colored lawyers of the city.
    Sheriff Worthen was the first witness called, and he related the story
of the shooting. He had been called to the Tate plantation, which was run
by the Fox brothers, to assist in preservation of the peace. He went there
for the purpose of quieting any disorder that might arise. When he arrived
at the Fox house, he was told that Hugh Gill had threatened that he should
not come on the plantation. He inquired where Gill lived, and went at once
to his house to talk with him and explain the law to him. It was just daylight, and nearly everybody was asleep. He dismounted at Gill's house, and
knocked on the door, asking Gill to get up. The latter replied from the inside of the cabin who it was that wanted him. The sheriff replied that it
was Worthen, sheriff of Pulaski county. The sheriff asked him why he could
not come on the place and why other men could not work.
    Gill replied, excusing himself from any hand in any trouble and wanted

to shut the door. The sheriff objected and got in the doorway. Gill went
towards the bed and Worthen told him to keep away from the bed. Gill then
started diagonally across the room and raising his hands jumped up for his
gun, which was across the joists. He jumped twice and just then Kinkaid,
whom he thought was at the gate, shot. The shot struck Gill in the arms and
disabled them. He shouted, "I'll quit, I'll give up," and came out of the
house on being requested to do so, saying, "I am sorry I did it." He was
then taken to the Fox house. Mr. Worthen was cross-examined but no additional
facts were developed.

Deputy Kinkaid was next examined. He said: "I went to the Gill house
as a deputy sheriff. Mr. Worthen got off his horse and knocked at the door.
Some one answered; I walked to the door. The first conversation I heard was
Worthen asking Gill not to go near the bed. I understood from that the man
was aiming to make some resistance and I watched him very closely. I was a
little to the rear and nearly opposite Worthen. I could see in the house.
Very soon after he made a spring for his gun. I saw his hands on his gun,
which was on the joists of the house, and I fired on him. I could not see
the gun. I fired one barrel of the double barreled shot gun. The first remark he made after I fired was: "I will quit, I will give up." The very
language he used as I recollect. I then said to him: "Throw up your hands
and back out." He did so. I then said: "You fool you, what did you undertake to get your gun for?" He answered: "I am sorry I did it. I wish I
hadn't done it." I then marched up to Mr. Fox's house in company with the
sheriff and Mr. Carmichael, a deputy sheriff."

Mr. Kinkaid was closely cross-examined. In his cross-examination he
explained the situation more in detail, but no new facts were elicited. He
saw Gill jumping for his gun, heard it rattle and he had no doubt but that
he was trying to get it.

There were several witnesses examined, one by the state, Osborne Austin,
and Henry Hill and Walker Evans by the defense in regard to a conversation
which was said to have been held Saturday morning, in which the threats
against Worthen were said to have been made. Austin swore he did say that
the sheriff should not come on the place while the other two swore that no
such conversation took place.

Then Hugh Gill was placed on the stand. His arms were bandaged, and
since he could not use them freely, he was continually moving them about to
keep the flies away from him. His testimony was as follows:

"I never had expressed any ill-will toward Mr. Worthen. I didn't know
Worthen was on the place. My wife woke me up. I heard some one say, 'Wake
up, there.' It wasn't good light. The man said it was Wat Worthen, sheriff
of Pulaski county."

"I said all right, sir. I gets up and gets my pants. I opened the
door, but he had done knocked in the door until it was nearly open. I pulled
the keg away and opened the door, "how is it you don't let these people go
to work down here?" I says how do you know that I am the cause of this? He
vowed 'by God, I know you are the cause of it.' I says I guess not. He said
'oh yes you are. Come on out here. You're the very man we want.' I says
wait til I get my hat on and I'll be right out. When I went to reach up to
get my hat, it hung right again the gun, it slipped; I reached up the other
hand, and before I knowed anything I was shot. I don't know Wat Worthen.
After I was shot he jumped in and threw the doors open and some one says,
'throw up your hands.' I says yes, sir, I will come; I'm coming. I had no
intention of even defending myself against Worthen."

The facts as related above are the principal points in the examination.
These were all the witnesses examined. The counsel made an argument before
the magistrate, at the conclusion of which he discharged the prisoner from
the charge of assault with intent to kill.

Arkansas Gazette, July 10, 1886.

42. ANONYMOUS THREATS

A Pleasant Note Found On a Gatepost

Tuesday morning a planter named Roberts, living six miles below Little
Rock, found the following note on the gatepost in front of his house:
Mr. Roberts as you think it is Best for the Knights to keep off ov your
Place and Let youre Hands alone We think you had Better take your Place and
go Whare your Wife is our men wil go Where they want to go and if you Dont
want us to talk to hands you had Better turn them of, if we take you in han
it will Bee to Late for Wat Worthen to Come to help you and we wont Bee Long
about it.

Arkansas Gazette, July 10, 1886.

43. A CARD FROM THE FOX BROTHERS.

To the Editor of The Gazette:
We have seen in your report of the proceedings of a meeting held in
Little Rock last night, that Mr. Anderson Mills, in speaking of the trouble
on the Tate plantation, between us and our colored hands, said that we
cheated our hands by charging them an exorbitant price for supplies. Also,
that while we agreed to give the 75¢ per day for their services, we paid them
off in chips and forced them to trade them out for supplies at this exorbitant profit so that nothing was left to them. Also, that we were responsible
for the trouble on the plantation, owing to these facts.
We desire to say that we buy a good quality of supplies from Messrs.
McCarthy & Joyce of Little Rock, which can be ascertained by any one who
applys to them. These supplies are purchased at cash prices, and are sold
as reasonably to the hands as by any planter in the state.
We pay our hands in time checks for every day's work, and the checks are
good to buy anything at the store during the week if they wish to buy of us.
But we do not force them to buy of us, and as a matter of fact, a number of
our hands buy their supplies from different stores in the country. These
time checks are cashed by us every Saturday evening without fail.
The reason we adopted this plan was to save bookkeeping, and because it
was better for the hands, as they saw each day what they had. We believe
we are justified in saying that we treat our hands as fairly and honorably as
any planters in the county, and that the statements of Mr. Mills are without
foundation. We do not understand why Mr. Mills should try to injure us in
the estimation of the public by statements that are not true.
                                        D. H. FOX,
                                        C. G. FOX,
                                        J. C. FOX.

Arkansas Gazette, July 11, 1886.

44. PLANTATION WORKERS ORGANIZE

Some weeks ago Organizer Tomson decided to undertake the organization of
the colored people on the plantations below Little Rock. This was a new
departure for the Order, but the work was not undertaken without deliberation
and a careful survey of the field. Opposition was met within the very beginning. The landlords and planters were so bitterly opposed to the project
that they refused the poor fellows their rations and circulated threats of
violence. The Organizer proceeded with his work, calling to his assistance
a very intelligent and honorable colored brother, Mr. G. W. Merriman, for

two terms Master Workman of L. A. 4225, at Argenta. This colored brother not
only proved himself as an apt student and competent for the work, but far
above the average in the exercise of proper judgment where the souls of men
are put to the test, for, when a few men upon a single plantation below
Little Rock asked for a little more to be added to their meagre pay, temporarily, because of an unusually tough piece of work in the cotton fields,
and quit work because they were refused it, and the Sheriff notified of the
fact that such was the case, and appearing upon the ground with armed deputies, went to an innocent negro's house about daylight, called him out of
bed and to the door, where one of his deputies shot the poor fellow, when
the news was narrated throughout the neighborhood and a thousand excited and
armed colored men were upon the ground, and the Sheriff and his deputies
after having shot down one of them at their mercy, the excellent judgment
and generalship of this colored Knight prevented the slightest violence to
any one. Not a hair on the head of the Sheriff nor of his deputies was
harmed; not a particle of the property of any one in the least molested but
the men promptly dispersed, and, being fired upon by a posse sent out from
the city to the relief of the Sheriff and his deputies, while peaceably and
quietly returning to their homes, they refused to return the fire, under the
direction of their instructor, preferring death rather than to violate the
law or resort to violence, under the teachings of their preceptor.

State Assembly of Arkansas, Pine Bluff, Ark., Sept. 15, 1886
E. M. Ritchie, S.M.W.
Journal of United Labor, October 10-25, 1886.

45. WAR IN YOUNG

COLORED KNIGHTS OF LABOR ON THE TATE PLANTATION STRIKE
FOR HIGHER WAGES AND PREVENT OTHERS FROM WORKING

A messenger from the Tate plantation, nine miles below Little Rock arrived in the city yesterday at 1 o'clock, stating that Sheriff Worthen was
hemmed in by colored people, and needed assistance. The sheriff asked for
twenty-five men, and a posse of twenty-seven were soon ready, and started.
Some were on horseback, and the others in two canvass-back omnibusses. THE
GAZETTE's war correspondent was one of the posse, and as the warlike detachment clattered through the streets people stared and wondered what was the
matter. It took the posse two hours to reach the plantation, and while that
sandy journey took place, the reason for its being taken may be set forth.
Last Thursday about thirty of the forty hands at work on the Tate plantation struck for higher wages. The plantation is run by D. H. Fox & Bros.
The brothers C. G. Fox and J. C. Fox. The strikers came to Mr. C. G. Fox
and presented a paper to him asking for an increase from 75 cents a day to
$1 a day until the crop was out of the grass.
Mr. Fox told the men, the spokesman being Harrison Goble, that their
demand was unreasonable. That there was no more grass in his crop than on
any plantation in the township. That there was no demand for higher wages on
any of the surrounding plantations. That they were paying the usual price,
and more, because they were paying the women who worked just as much as the
men, while on many adjoining plantations the wages of the latter were cut
down to 60 and 65 cents a day. He told them that he was willing to pay them
$1 a day when the neighboring planters would do so. But with 75 cents a day
for labor and 75 cents a hundred pounds for picking he could not afford to
increase the wages at the prices cotton brought. He told them he would let
the cotton stand as it was and not increase the wages for the reasons given,
and if they did not wish to work, they could quit and give up their houses.

A STRIKE

On Friday the men would not go to work, and tried threats to keep the
ten men who had refused to quit from working. Strikers went to them in the

field and told them they had better quit, but they refused to be intimidated and continued their work. This state of affairs continued until Saturday evening. Late in the evening some men came down from Little Rock with supplies for the strikers. The supplies consisted of meat, flour and meal. This put courage into the hearts of the disaffected men, and they became rampant. The threats grew more frequent and the ringleaders became dictatorial and swore that no one should work and that if Sheriff Worthen came down he would never leave there alive. The ringleaders were three colored men named Hugh Gill, Tom Auberry and John Larkin. Henry Hill was also one of the leading men in the matter, though not so rampant as the others.

This was the state of affairs yesterday morning. The men who were willing to work were terrified, and the strikers and their friends were congregating from all parts of the surrounding country.

THE RINGLEADER SHOT

Sheriff Worthen had been notified, and with several deputies arrived at the Tate plantation early in the morning, about 5 o'clock. He was told at the Fox house that Hugh Gill had said he should never set foot in the neighborhood and inquiring the way to Gill's house, rode there immediately with some of the deputies. On arriving at the house he knocked. Gill opened the door and the sheriff told him who he was. Gill reached up for something and Worthen told him to drop his hands. He did so, but made another motion, and Worthen repeated the admonition. Again he dropped his hands, but almost immediately jerked his hands up to get his gun, which was hanging above.

At this moment Deputy Ewing Kinkaid shot at his arms and they dropped helpless. A buck-shot penetrated one arm, and several squirrel shot the other. The man was taken up to the Fox house, and afterwards John Larkin was arrested.

A COURIER FOR HELP

There were in all ten men who assembled at the plantation house. The colored men continued to assemble, and by 10 o'clock there were fully 250, all armed, around in the fields surrounding the house.

It was then that the sheriff, seeing the overpowering numbers that surrounded him, dispatched a horseman to Little Rock with the request for a posse to be sent immediately. The house was turned into a fort, and sentinels stationed at convenient points, while developments were awaited.

Capt. Scruggs rode down and seeing the large crowds of colored people, went among them and asked them what they wanted. They told him they wanted the men who were arrested and tried without going to Little Rock.

They asked for a parley with the sheriff and he went out to them. They stated their request to him, and he said that he did not care how it was settled if the men were tried fairly and legally. Hd did not care whether they went to Little Rock or any other place. This seemed to satisfy the men. John Larkin was taken to Squire Vagine's office, not far from the Tate place, and put under bond, while the wounded man remained at the Tate place. The sheriff then awaited the arrival of the posse from the city.

A FIGHT ALONG THE ROAD

The posse of twenty-seven which started from the city, arrived just above Gov. Churchill's plantation, which is the adjoining plantation to the Tate plantation, about 4 o'clock yesterday afternoon. All along the route few men were seen at work, and the nearer the army approached the scene of conflict the less men were observed following their legitimate occupations.

About half a mile above the Churchill place a gang of colored men were seen along the road by the cavalry in front of the posse. They were all armed.

Capt. Ham Williams ordered them to lay down their guns. Some of them did and others jumped into a cornfield and a shot was fired at Williams, which he returned. Another shot was fired by one of the posse, and that closed the engagement. Three men were captured, and their guns were bundled into the commissary wagons. Ex-Gov. Churchill and Miss Mattie Churchill, who were close to the encounter, stood fire like veterans.

ALL QUIET

The posse proceeded to the Tate plantation and found that information of its approach had preceded it. The armed men had nearly all dispersed and squads could be seen disappearing in the corn fields. Two more men were disarmed, and the posse was directed by the sheriff to return, as all danger had disappeared. But before the cavalcade had gone far on their homeward way, reports of fresh shooting on the Tate place arrived, and all returned post-haste.

Armed men could still be seen in the fields, but no violence was attempted. It was decided best to leave the posse at the plantation, and they proceeded to make themselves as comfortable as the circumstances would allow while the war correspondent of THE GAZETTE, J. J. Johnson and Gabe Jones bestrode fiery steeds and rode back to Little Rock.

KNIGHTS OF LABOR

It was learned that the cause of this outbreak was the Knights of Labor. The colored people have been organized into assemblies of Knights of Labor, and in Young township, where this trouble occurred, there are nearly a hundred in the order. Their brethren in adjoining assemblies were reported arming, and many of them did come armed with shot-guns, squirrel guns, and all the implements of warfare they could rake up.

PROVISIONED BY KNIGHTS

It was also stated to the GAZETTE representative that there was no doubt that a courier from Little Rock notified the colored people of the approach of a law and order posse, and that they were supplied with provisions from Little Rock to continue the fight on their employers of not working themselves or allowing anyone else to work.

POLITICS IN IT

Behind the whole trouble, it was freely stated by those with whom THE GAZETTE man talked, that this trouble was incited just at this time by politicians who hoped to benefit by the unfortunate prejudices that would be engendered by it. It was openly asserted by men whose integrity cannot be questioned that republican politicians are at the bottom of the whole matter.

VISITORS FROM THE CITY

In the evening about dark, Angelo Marre and Billy Flynn, in a spanking double team, arrived at the Tate place, to see what was going on.

Arkansas Gazette, July 6, 1886.

IV

THE KNIGHTS OF LABOR CONVENTION IN RICHMOND, 1886

THE KNIGHTS OF LABOR CONVENTION IN RICHMOND, 1886

By 1886 no fewer than 60,000 blacks were members of the Noble Order of the Knights of Labor. Rapid strides had been made in the South, especially in Virginia, where Negroes constituted half of the 10,000 to 15,000 members in 1886. Black Knights were best organized in Richmond, where a purported 3,125 members in twenty-one local assemblies and one separate black District Assembly had been enrolled. To many Afro-Americans, however, the Knights of Labor stood at a critical crossroads. Would it wage an active battle for racial equality, or simply make a token effort in order to appease white supremacists? This question came to a climax at the 1886 convention in Richmond, Virginia. The forces involved swirled around one man, Frank J. Ferrell, an engineer, and the only black in the New York delegation. Well-suited for the battle, Ferrell, a Socialist and ardent unionist, was recognized in the Negro press as the most able black member in the Knights of Labor.

A few months before the convention opened, it was learned that Ferrell would not be permitted to stay in the same hotel as the white delegates of District 49, known as the "Home Club." The 49ers rejected this arrangement, and in protest came to Richmond with tents. Just before convention business got under way, the New Yorkers informed the Grand Master Workman, Terence V. Powderly (see Part VI), of the incident. As a reprisal the 49ers proposed that Ferrell be chosen to introduce Governor Fitzhugh Lee when he rose to welcome the delegates at the opening session. After some hesitation, Powderly finally agreed to permit the black delegate to follow the governor on the platform and introduce Powderly. He praised the "Home Club" for upholding the Order's principles on racial equality. In an assertion of these principles, the New York contingent and Ferrell upset the local populace by attending a performance at the Academy of Music, becoming the first black in Richmond's history to occupy an orchestra seat in one of the city's theaters (Doc. 1-3, 36). If these events were not unsettling enough, a few thousand black residents actually attended the picnic which brought the convention to a close. It was the largest racially integrated social affair in Richmond's history. For the first time many white northerners actually confronted the insults which black workers experienced in the South, and became convinced that black Knights must be placed on an equal political and economic, if not social, footing (Doc. 24, 27, 28).

The Richmond convention created a **national** sensation. Southerners heaped abuse on the Knights, charging them with forcing "social equality" upon the people who had accepted them as guests, a charge which Powderly felt compelled to rebut in the Richmond Dispatch. The Negro press, as well as many labor and Northern newspapers, applauded the actions of the delegates. But after Powderly's disclaimer regarding social equality, the black press mixed its praise with disappointment and some distrust. Generally, however, blacks saw the events in Richmond as justification for their full support of the Knights of Labor (Doc. 4-23, 25-6, 29-34).

In the North, 1886 was a year marked by a powerful counter-offensive by employers, characterized by lock-outs, blacklists, arrests, imprisonment, and occasional execution. As a result, union membership in the North plummetted. But in the South, blacks flocked to the Order. In fact, after 1886 the Order attracted more black workers than whites. Several explanations account for this development. First, for many months following the Richmond convention, the Knights' national organization remained faithful to the principles of labor solidarity and interracial unity. Equally important was their program, which struck hard at several major grievances particularly affecting southern blacks. Stressing land reform, increased public education, and workers' cooperatives, was bound to appeal to landless and poorly educated Negroes. Moreover, the Knights provided Negro members with a mechanism for the organization of mutual-benefits assistance within the community, as well as social functions, and the means for the training and development of a leadership class.

Finally, in 1886 the Knights of Labor proved their coercive power by winning the so-called Great Southwestern Strike against the powerful railroad magnate, Jay Gould (see Vol. III, Notes 15,23). This demonstration of power presented evidence that the Order could indeed provide black workers with a powerful agency for improving their station in life.

TERENCE V. POWDERLY, FRANK J. FERRELL, AND THE INTEGRATED

CONVENTION IN RICHMOND, 1886

1. KNIGHTS OF LABOR ON THEIR METTLE

The Knights of Labor will soon hold a General Assembly in Richmond, Va. Richmond hotel proprietors are Southern to the backbone, and are sure that while it is natural for colored men to wait on tables and perform other hotel work,--thereby coming into the very closest contact with the patrons of the hotel,--that it is most unnatural for colored men to be entertained as guests in their hostelries. There are sixty delegates of District Assembly 49 of New York who will attend the Richmond convention. One of the delegates happens to be in the nature of a Jonah to a Richmond hotelkeeper, as the following from the New York *Sun* will explain:

Sixty delegates of District Assembly 49 will attend the General Assembly of the Knights of Labor in Richmond, Va. "Every Knight of Labor," said one of these delegates yesterday, "when he enters the order knows that his obligation makes him disregard the color, creed, and nationality of his fellow members. District 49 has among its members a number of colored men. One of these colored men happens to be a delegate. In fact, he was one of the first chosen. When our committee was making arrangements with Col. Murphy of the Merchants Hotel of Richmond, he said he would gladly accommodate 49, but he could not defy the custom and usages of the city by allowing the colored man the equal rights and privileges with those of his fellow white delegates. The colored delegate, when he heard this, secured a place for himself, and said the other delegates could select any hotel they liked. The other delegates, however, by a unanimous vote, declared they would only go where their colored brother was admitted on the same footing.

"The Assembly then looked about to devise a way out of the trouble. It finally sent the colored delegate and a white brother to Richmond to secure board for the entire delegation among colored families in that city. No member of 49 will board anywhere except with a colored family. This action of 49 we hope will work good and be of great benefit to us and to humanity. In Richmond there is a district assembly which ignores the colored Knights. District Assembly 49's act will bring, we hope, these white brothers to their senses and start a breakup of the color line. We are all anxious to begin the work. It may be that the greater part of the session of the General Assembly will be taken up with this question, and not on the Home Club. The Home Club is not very bad, after all. You ought to have heard some of them on the question of color, and they were men who were in Richmond when Lee surrendered."

District Assembly 49 of New York should be placed at the head of the class for a square-toed manifestation of true manhood and most unusual courage. It is a simple matter of justice and fair play which the members of the Assembly have shown in resenting the insult offered a brother member by the narrow, prejudiced keeper of a Southern hotel, but all the race asks for or has ever asked for are justice and fair play. It is the constant denial of these against which we have to labor and protest.

We are free to say that the action of this labor assembly will have its influence on the people of Richmond. The papers of that city will ignore the matter, in all probability, as they cannot very well afford to condemn the course pursued by the New York delegation, since such condemnation might provoke the whole convention, and lead to damage to Richmond newspaper income and to loss of votes to the Democratic party. It is in this taking the bull by the horns which will convince the colored laborers that their interests and those of white laborers are identical. Let the good work go on.

New York Freeman, October 2, 1886.

2. FRANK J. FERRELL'S INTRODUCTION OF GENERAL MASTER WORKMAN
TERENCE V. POWDERLY AT THE 1886 CONVENTION
OF THE KNIGHTS OF LABOR

Governor Lee [of Virginia] and Gentlemen of the Convention: It is with
much pleasure and gratification that I introduce to you Mr. T. V. Powderly,
of the State of Pennsylvania, who will reply to the address of welcome of
Governor Lee, of this State, which is one of the oldest states in the
avenue of political influence of our country. He is one of the thoughtful
men of the nation, who recognizes the importance of this gathering of the
toiling masses in this our growing Republic. As Virginia has led in the
aspirations of our country in the past, I look with much confidence to the
future, in the hope that she will lead in the future to the realization of
the objects of noble Order. It is with extreme pleasure that we, the
representatives from every section of our country, receive the welcome of
congratulation for our efforts to improve the condition of humanity. One of
the objects of our Order is the abolition of these distinctions which are
maintained by creed or color. I believe I present to you a man above the
superstitions which are involved in these distinctions. My experience with
the noble Order of the Knights of Labor and my training in my district, have
taught me that we have worked so far successfully toward the extinction of
these regrettable distinctions. As we recognize and repose confidence in
all men for their worth in society, so can we repose confidence in one of
the noblest sons of labor--T. V. Powderly--whom I now take the pleasure of
presenting to you.[25]

Proceedings, General Assembly, Knights of Labor, 1886, pp. 7-8.

3. POWDERLY'S ADDRESS AT RICHMOND CONVENTION

It is not the negro alone who stands ostracized in the South by the
remnant of the Bourbon element, which still exists to protest against the
progress of the Southern States. The white man who works is held in no
higher esteem than the black man, and his ignorance is taken advantage of
when he is patted on the back and told that he "is better than the negro."
. . . The intellectual status of the black and white laborer must be improved if either one is to prosper. Of the two races in the South at the
present time the negro is making the most energetic struggle for an education.

Terence V. Powderly, *Thirty Years of Labor* (Cincinnati, 1889), p. 662.

4. POWDERLY TO THE RICHMOND *DISPATCH*

My sole object in selecting a colored man to introduce me was to encourage and help to uplift his race from a bondage worse than that which
held him in chains twenty-five years ago--viz., mental slavery. I desired
to impress upon the minds of white and black that the same result followed
action in the field of labor, whether that action was on the part of the

Caucasian or negro. . . .
    While I have no wish to interfere with the social relations which exist
between the races of the South, I have a strong desire to see the black men
educated. Southern cheap labor, regardless of color, must learn to read and
write. Southern cheap labor is more a menace to the American toiler than the
Chinese, and this labor must be educated. Will my critics show me how the
laws of social equality will be harmed by educating the black man so that he
may know how to conduct himself as a gentlemen? Will they explain how a
knowledge of the laws of his country will cause a man to violate the laws of
social equality? Will they in a cool, dispassionate manner, explain to me
whether an education will not advance the moral standard of the colored man,
and will they tell me such a thing is not as necessary with the blacks as
with the whites?
    Will it be explained to me whether the black man should continue to
work for starvation wages? With so many able-bodied colored men in the South
who do not know enough to ask for living wages, it is not hard to guess that
while this race continues to increase in numbers and ignorance prosperity
will not even knock at the door, much less enter the home of the southern
laborer. . . . There need be no further cause for alarm. The colored representatives to this Convention will not intrude where they are not wanted,
and the time-honored laws of social equality will be allowed to slumber undisturbed. . . .
    To the Convention, I say: Let no member surrender an iota of intel-
lectual freedom because of any clamor. Hold fast to that which is true and
right. The triumph of noise over reason is but transient. Our principles
will be better known, if not to-day it may be tomorrow; they can bide their
time, and will some day have the world for an audience. In the field of
labor and American citizenship we recognize no line of race, creed, politics,
or color.

Richmond Dispatch, October 12, 1886.

5. THE COLORED BROTHER

    After Mr. Powderly finished his regular speech he said he desired to add
one word more. He continued by saying that some of the members of the visiting delegations who were of darker hue than their brothers could not find
place in some of the hotels. This was in accordance with what had long been
the custom here, and old customs and prejudices do not readily vanish. There
had been particular mention made of one instance where a delegation numbering
nearly seventy members had only one colored member among them. He was refused
admission to the hotel where they intended to go, and the delegation, standing
by the principles of the order, which recognize no distinctions of creed,
nationality, or color, went with their colored brother. That, he said, was
why he made the selection of that brother to introduce him to them, so that
it might go forth that they "practice what they preached."

Richmond (Va.) Dispatch, October 5, 1886.

6. HE SITS AMONG THE WHITES
The Negro Ferrell Escorted Into the Academy of Music

    Last night just before the performance of "Hamlet" began at the Academy
of Music sixty members of District Assembly 49 of New York, the negro member
(Ferrell) being one of the party and twenty other Knights of Labor, delegates
to the General Assembly, went in a body to that place of amusement, and,

marching up to the box-office, the foremost man bought eighty tickets, for
which he paid $40. These tickets admitted the party to reserved seats on
the left-hand side of the body of the house, about eight rows from the stage.
Thither they wended their way, the negro sitting between two of his white
confreres, near the end of one of the rows. Here he remained undisturbed
during the whole performance. A good-sized audience of ladies and gentlemen was present. Only a few left the hall. In fact, it was not generally
known through the audience what had occurred and who the strange visitor was.

    There was last night among those citizens who knew of the affair severe
criticism of the management for allowing this violation of the long-estab-
lished customs of this part of the country, but Ferrell having been seated,
no doubt the management thought it wiser and better for all concerned not to
make any move which might possibly result in a disturbance.

    It was to presume that "Forty-nine" went to the Academy in a body last
night, and was ready to make a "test case."

    Later on the manager of the Academy, stated that he knew nothing of the
presence of the negro until after his entrance into the hall. Mr. Castine
then consulted some of the men as to the best course to take and on their
advice, rather than cause any excitement, he took no action, and allowed the
man to remain.

Slept in the Same Bed

    Situated on Broad street between Sixth and Seventh is the Central Hotel,
a colored boarding-house, of which _____ Fry is one of the proprietors.
Yesterday morning a *Dispatch* had occasion to visit this place with other
business, and while there asked guests, "are you any delegates to the General
Assembly?

    I have only one, a white northern man from Maine. There is a colored
man from the same State stopping here but he is not a delegate.

    What is the delegate's name?

    I will get you the register.

    He went to a back room and brought out a black book in which the list
of guests is kept; also, the colored female who does the clerical work of
the house. She opened the book and pointed to the name registered "Joe Burns,
Hallowell, Maine," as the white delegate, and directly under it was "C. D.
Freeman, Augusta, Me." who, she said, was the colored visitor.

    The reporter asked: Do these men room together?

    Yes, sir.

    And sleep in the same bed?

    Yes, sir.

    The conversation ended here, and the reporter left.

NUMBERS AND QUARTERS OF THE COLORED DELEGATES

    Secretary Turner says there are about twenty colored delegates in the
Assembly. Three are from Richmond, members of District Assembly No. 92--
Richard Thompson, W. W. Fields, and _____ Mitchel.

    A young colored woman named Scott was appointed as a delegate from this
city, but for some reason she will not act.

    Colored members also come from Augusta, Ga., Florida, Washington,
Baltimore, Pennsylvania, Norfolk, Petersburg, Danville, Charlotte county, Va.,
Alabama, and North Carolina. Most of them are quartered with colored
families.

    The colored brother from Baltimore, James H. Edwards, is stopping at the
St. Charles Hotel, where he arrived with eighteen other Knights from Baltimore
on Monday. He eats in the dining-room with the other guests (although the
proprietors say that a screen hides him from the general view) and sleeps
in as good apartments. His fare is altogether the same as that given white
people, and he pays the same price for it.

    Mr. Gallaghan, the proprietor of the hotel, claims that he did not know
at first that a negro was to be one of the Baltimore party, and that as soon
as he found it out, he told the delegates that the negro could not be given
the first-class accommodations. They said they were not willing to leave their
brother, and so it was arranged they should eat and sleep with their friend.

Richmond Dispatch, October 6, 1886.

7. SOCIAL EQUALITY OF THE RACES

THE OLD VIRGINIA "SUPERSTITION" ON THIS SUBJECT--WHAT KNIGHTS THINK

One of the best-known Knights of Labor in this city--who authorizes the use of his name if necessary--was seen yesterday and asked by a *Dispatch* reporter:

"What do you think of the attitude taken by Assembly 49, of New York, regarding social equality."

"I regard," said he, "the action of these persons who took Ferrell to the Mozart Academy as an outrage upon the people of this city, and an insult to the Knights of Labor of the United States. I feel confident that they do not represent any but themselves."

How do the Knights of Labor of Richmond regard the action of their visiting brethren in this respect?

The Knights of this city are justly indignant, and their position of host only restrains them from an outburst of righteous contempt. Most of them earnestly hope that Master Workman Powderly will avail himself of the first opportunity to administer to 49 the rebuke they merit and justly deserve. The action of 49 will cause a great many to leave the order, and will in a large measure detract from the parade of Monday next. I have yet to meet the first man, white or colored, Knight of Labor or otherwise, who has expressed anything but the severest condemnation of the action of 49. Indeed, all have some respect for Ferrell; for the others contempt.

Does the constitution of the Knights of Labor require social equality? If it does not, upon what ground does "49" rest its claim upon this point?

I cannot find anywhere in the constitution, by-laws, and "work" of the Knights of Labor anything upon which 49 can lay any claim for social equality, unless it is the quotation from the Declaration of Independence--"All men are created equal." People may accept as much of the doctrine as they please; as for myself, I do not in any way accept it as a fact. . . .

Richmond Dispatch, October 7, 1886.

8. COLORED KNIGHT FERRELL

RACE PREJUDICE AROUSED IN RICHMOND

THE KNIGHTS CONDEMNED FOR ABUSING SOUTHERN HOSPITALITY--

NOR ORGANIZATION EFFECTED YET

RICHMOND, Va., Oct. 6.--The Knights of Labor have committed what is considered here an unpardonable mistake since their arrival in Richmond. They are bitterly denounced on all sides, and it's generally conceded that the order will never attain any considerable strength among the white population of the South. The hot Southern temper is at boiling point tonight, and serious trouble was only averted by the prompt action of the city authorities. The objects of the Knights' convention, its very presence, in fact, have been forgotten in the excitement created by the action of some of its members. Although the brunt of the general clamor is borne by the delegates of District Assembly No. 49, of New York, Mr. Powderly is censured for having given that assembly an excuse for outraging public sentiment. The social line dividing the white from the colored population of Richmond is quite as distinct to-day as it was 20 years ago, and the attempt made by New York Knights to obliterate it has aroused a storm of indignation, the intensity of which cannot be appreciated except by those who are thoroughly conversant with the social conditions of the South.

There were widespread mutterings of discontent on Monday when it became known that General Master Workman Powderly was introduced to the tenth annual convention of the Knights of Labor by a colored man Frank Ferrell of

New York, and that Ferrell's introductory remarks immediately followed the
address of welcome delivered by Gov. Fitzhugh Lee. The latter had no idea
that such a programme had been determined upon, and Powderly had been
harshly criticised for taking advantage of Gov. Lee, on the ground that he
should have understood the situation. It is thoroughly understood here
that in the North there would have been nothing deserving or unusual comments
in the fact that white and colored men occupied the same stage at a public
meeting; but it is claimed that Northern men are well aware that the social
relations existing between whites and blacks in the North and South are as
opposite as the poles. It is also claimed that District No. 49 was warned
of the condition of affairs here by Capt. Murphy's refusal to lodge a
colored delegate at his hotel. Assembly No. 49 disregarded all warnings and
its Master Workman boasted soon after his arrival that the colored delegates
should fare exactly the same as his white brethren.
    To make good this boast, No. 49 attended the Academy of Music last
evening in a body. One man bought 80 tickets of admission, and on one of
these Ferrell entered the theatre and occupied an orchestra chair. Ferrell's
presence was not known to all the patrons of the Academy, but several of
those who saw him left the building and interrogated the manager. The latter
at once held a consultation with several friends, who advised him to allow
Ferrell to remain rather than to create a disturbance. Upon leaving the
theatre the Knights boasted that the color line in Richmond had been broken,
and the fact that Ferrell had occupied an orchestra chair soon became public
property, and created as much excitement as if the New York colored man had
committed arson. Few people blamed him, however. All the censure was
leveled at his white companions, who, to make matters worse, said they would
attend the Richmond Theatre tonight in a body and take Ferrell with them.
    Secretary Turner was in the midst of a discussion touching this matter
last night when he was tapped on the shoulder by a Richmond Knight of Labor.
The Richmond Knight was accompanied by a fellow-Knight. "You are all wrong,"
he said to Turner, "and the course you are pursuing will break up the Knights
of Labor here. We have white and colored Knights of Labor here, and they
are members of different assemblies. A colored man has all the rights of a
white man here except socially. They are satisfied with things as they are,
and it is not right for you to come here and tear us all to pieces."
    These utterances were indorsed by Richmond Knight No. 2 who added:
"The forcing of a colored man among white people here has knocked me out of
the order. When my wife heard that Northern white men had come here and
lived with colored people, she said to me, 'You must get out of the order,'
and I must."
    The hotel corridor in which the discussion was held was solidly packed
with excited white citizens and Knights. Several of the former stated, in
language that could not be misunderstood, that Northern Knights must not
undertake to build a new social fabric during a two weeks' visit. Early this
morning it was quietly noised about that the Law and Order League had
determined to show its hand, if an attempt was made to force Ferrell into
the Richmond Theatre, unless he was willing to occupy the gallery devoted
to the use of the colored people. The Law and Order League has a membership
of over 2,000 and it was formed to protect all persons boycotted by the
Knights, and is thoroughly antagonistic to the latter.

New York Times, October 7, 1886.

9. A SAMPLE OF NATIONAL REACTIONS TO THE

KNIGHTS POSITION ON SOCIAL EQUALITY

The workingmen of this country know no color line. They stand together shoulder to shoulder, and the black man to them is as good as any if
he is a true citizen and performs his allotted task faithfully and well.
The color line is fading away like the relic of the confederacy.

Harrisburg *Telegraph,* October 5, 1886.

Let those people who can see no good in the work of the Knights of
Labor now come forward like men and allow that their action upon the color
question in their Richmond convention is magnanimous, consistent, and far
ahead of the age.

Lynn (Mass.) *Bee,* October 6, 1886.

It is well that our people should be warned in time of the new and vile
use to which the Knights of Labor organization is to be put--that is to say,
if the Southern Knights will consent thus to be used. Will they? We don't
believe it.

Raleigh News and Observer, October 7, 1886.

It is reported that the liberal views of the Northern delegates touching the colored members has disgusted the aristocratic workingmen of Richmond.
The latter threaten to withdraw from the order. If that is their view of
the cause of labor, they had better withdraw and stay out until they learn
that honest labor ennobles every doer on the face of the green earth.

Philadelphia *North American,* October 7, 1886.

The Knights who marched to the Richmond theater with the colored delegate at their head said by their action that they had no respect for the
sentiments of the people of Richmond, or of the local white Knights, so far
as the social equality question is concerned. They took it upon themselves
to show the Richmond Knights and the Southern delegates their contempt for
Southern opposition to social recognition of colored people, and they did
it in a very aggressive, not to say offensive, way. It may be well for
Southern Knights to inquire whether it is the purpose of the Knights of
Labor to settle social as well as labor questions.

Savannah News, October 8, 1886.

Laboring men struggling to better their condition have a common cause
which binds them together in a common brotherhood. There can be no color
line. They must stand or fail together, and as this becomes more generally
recognized the labor question in the South will assume a new and more
promising phase.

Philadelphia *Press,* October 8, 1886.

The decision of the assembly from New York to lodge in tents because
one of their number was refused admission to the hotels was right. It would
have been a curious commentary on the doctrine of brotherly love for the
white men to accept accommodations from which their colored brother was debarred, and if they had chosen to stay away from the theaters because Ferrell
could not be admitted with them that would have been an eminently right and
proper protest, and would have had considerable weight with the managerial
pocket-book. But the forcing of Ferrell into the lower part of the theater
among people who did not want him was quite another matter and a move that
could do no good to anybody. Race prejudices fade out slowly; they do not
die of single blows in the head. These Knights do not live in Richmond;

they can not follow up their effort, and when they depart they will have intensified the race prejudices of the city. The matter is, luckily, not big enough to have any lasting effect, but what influence it has works to the prejudice of the weaker race.

Springfield (Mass.) *Republican,* October 8, 1886, reprinted in "Knights of Labor and the Color Line," *Public Opinion,* October 16, 1886.

If the Knights of Labor intend to make the social equality of the races part of their creed they will gain little strength in the South. The white working man has as little taste for that as anybody and understands very clearly that social intermixture is the first and longest step toward miscegenation, which means mongrelization.

August News   (Ga.), October 9, 1886.

The moment Farrell, the colored man, made his appearance in the ranks of "District 49" the Knights were face to face with a very practical and hard-headed problem. It was certainly very loyal in the "Forty-niners" to refuse good quarters which their colored comrade could not share. Everybody appreciates that, and against this fidelity to conviction the hospitable people of Richmond has nothing to say. There was a lesson in the incident, however, which the Knights received very graciously--namely, that not even ardor in a great cause can override old prejudices or fixed customs. They must take the world as it is and not become disheartened because they can not change it in the twinkling of an eye. Therein lies the difference between a true knight and a mere anarchist. The knight, when he finds the wind dead ahead, tacks ship, going where he does not want to go, both the south and the north, but making progress eastward all the time. The anarchist, on the other hand, insists on sailing straight in the eye of the wind, and when he finds he can not do it he brings out his dynamite and wants to blow up the ship and the ocean and everything else.

New York *Herald,* October 12, 1886.

10. THE MOZART ASSOCIATION IN CONNECTION WITH THE COLOR QUESTION

Yesterday afternoon Manager F. M. Castine, of the Mozart Academy, received a letter from Colonel S. B. Paul, chairman of the Finance Committee of the Mozart Association, calling attention to the violation of the contract of the lessees in permitting a colored person to occupy a seat in the body of the house last night.

The letter says the contract provides "that persons of the Caucasian race shall alone be admitted to any part of the house except the gallery, and that is clearly defined in said contract to be what your advertisements call the balcony. Under the circumstances which so unexpectedly arose last night, and in which you took the advice of the chairman of the Hall Committee, I think your action was judicious, but as they forewarn you of a systematic effort to force you to a course which would prejudice the interest you represent, in violation of contract of lease, I shall be compelled to report any recurrence of any infringement of the lease.

We exacted this condition in the lease because our membership was exclusively Caucasian; and, in providing a place where in public entertainments by our lessee persons of another race could go if they pleased, we did not exclude persons of our race who preferred their society, nor give the slightest ground of offence to any person of another race who was not ashamed of his own people."

THE COLORED DELEGATE AT THE ST. CHARLES

Yesterday morning about 8 o'clock James Edwards, the negro Knight quartered at the St. Charles with a Baltimore delegation, came down from his

room puffing a cigar, and, walking into the office, he exclaimed to some
white brethren congregated there: "Have you fellows been into breakfast?"
Some had and some had not, and so replied, "Well, I believe I will go and
get mine," he rejoined, and walked into the dining-room.

The table at which he sits is at the further end of the room from the
door, and in front of it is a screen about as long as the table. This
screen protects him from general view, but any one at the first two tables
on the front side of it can see him. He is quite a black negro--about the
same hue as Ferrell--and the top of his head is slightly inclined to bald-
ness. He sits at the head of the table, and during meals he chats with his
white brethren who eat with him.

MORE SOCIAL EQUALITY

Tuesday afternoon four white members of the General Assembly of the
Knights, accompanied by a colored girl, got into a hack in front of the
post-office and drove down Main street.

The same evening three more white Knights and two colored women--one
very black and one yellow--got into a carriage on Franklin street and directed the driver to take them to town. They were last seen going up Franklin street.

Richmond (Va.,) Dispatch, October 7, 1886.

11. THE KNIGHTS AND SOUTHERN PREJUDICE

The Knights of Labor in session at Richmond, at their opening session
last Monday, took Southern prejudice, arrogance and intolerance by the
throat and gave it the most furious shaking it has had since the war. The
occasion was the action of New York Assembly No. 49 in refusing to sanction
the discrimination made against their colored fellow-member Farrell by a
Richmond hotel-keeper. The honor of introducing Grand Master Workman
Powderly to the Convention and the people of Richmond was assigned to Delegate Farrell, who, in doing this followed Governor Lee in a very neat speech.
Mr. Powderly said the honor had been conferred upon Mr. Farrell to show that
the Knights of Labor recognized neither the race nor the color of its
membership, but that all were brothers possessing equal rights and privileges. The Bourbons of the South may rage to their hearts' content, but the
fact remains that there is one great organization in the land which recognizes the brotherhood of all men and has the courage to practice what it
teaches, even within earshot of the infamously famous Libby Prison. It is
written on the wall: Such high-handed conduct and language as are used and
sanctioned by the Richmond *State* and the Norfolk *Virginian,* produced elsewhere in this issue, are doomed! And Southern prejudice and intolerance will
yet be made to eat grass like an ox.

New York Freeman, October 9, 1886.

12. J. M. TOWNSEND TO TERRENCE POWDERLY

Telegram
                                                    Richmond, Ind. Oct. 4, 1886.

Mr T V Powderly K of L In session

Accept my humble thanks and congratulations for the dignified stand you
have taken on behalf of equal and exact justice for my race especially as
shown by post 49

                                                    J. M. Townsend, Colored.

Powderly Papers, Catholic University of America.

13. SAMUEL WILSON TO TERENCE POWDERLY

October 6, 1886.

I cannot believe that our colored brothers will be set up by our grand order as our social equals . . . when the social problems come in, public sympathy is to be emphatically against it for our order to hold up its head this side of Mason and Dixon line.

Powderly Papers, Catholic University of America.

14. JAMES HIRST TO TERENCE POWDERLY

October 13th, 1886
Galveston, Texas

Sir
    Since you have changed from a Knight of Labor advocate to a nigger social equality man I hereby denounce you as a low, vulgar buffoon than whom there is none more contemptable. A decent nigger should shun you and if you have a daughter she should be taken from you else you may marry here to a nigger. The low Irish will come out.   Yr's in contempt

James Hirst--now and henceforth an
ex-Knight of Labor.

Powderly Papers, Catholic University of America.

15. D. H. BLACK TO TERENCE POWDERLY

Fort Worth, October 15, 1886.

Dear Sir & Bro.
    Your letter on the color line question meets the approval of the colored people in this part of the south and this part of the state as far as heard from by those who do not belong to the organization and has help our cause here a great deal. A good organizer and lectur in this part of the country would increase the membership amonge the colored in this state and adjoining states supprisingly. Of course the prejudice in the south amonge the major-ity of the white laborers is quite stronge against the negro, some places in this state the white assembly will not admit the negro in the pass word travelling card test or anythinge else, this has given the week kneed negro a good chance to leave the order, and those not members to fight it, thereby in my opinion standing in there own light, I am glad to see the proposed plan by which the colored knights will be benefitted by difusing amonge them a knolledge of the true situation of there surroundings. I have been a faith-ful member since June 28th 85 I am highly pleased with its principles.

Powderly Papers, Catholic University of America.

16.   "TRADESMAN" TO TERENCE POWDERLY

Montgomery, Alabama, October 16, 1886.

Mr. Powderly
    . . . there is only one way for you to find out what a nigger is, that
is to come south and stay 3 months, and Montgomery is a good place to come,
where the population is about equal. In the north, Mr. Powderly, one white
girl does all the work for a family of five or six people, while you have
to hire 3 to do the same work. A colored girl that cooks wont wash, and one
that washes wont do the house work. There wages will come to about 25 00
if you think any thing I have written here is not so there is but one way
to find out the truth, come south and see for yourself. You will also see
why the Races ought to be seperated at public places. If you was sat down
amonst several of them at a theatre or table you would get up and leave for
I tell you as a rule 99 out of a hundred have a smell when they get heated
up that is sickening it is a great deal better to keep them seperate at
schools also, it is dangerous to put them together for many Reasons, The
writer of this was born and lived all his life in the north except the last
10 years which I have lived here, and I believe the laboring man here gets
along better than in the north they have less clothes and fuel to buy and
can work the year Round and between the whites and blacks there is no
trouble. The colored people have Fire and military companies, civic societies, and many other things of that kind here, and are never interfered
with, and are treated just as good as any people in the north are treated.

Powderly Papers, Catholic University of America.

17.   NEGRO PRESS COMMITTEE TO TERENCE POWDERLY
Telegram
Little Rock Ark   Oct 19 1886.

T V Powderly,
    The negro press association now in session hail with joy the dispatches
of the morning containing action of Knights of Labor convention now in
session at Richmond in adopting resolution in regard to admission of colored
apprentices in work shops and factories of the country on Equal footing with
white apprentices
                        E. C. Morris, J. H. Garnett, M. W. Gibbs,
                        J. T. Bailey--Committee.

Powderly Papers, Catholic University of America.

18.   A. D. HALL TO TERENCE POWDERLY

Robeson Co., N.C., October 26, 1886.

    Dear Sir haven read a good deal in Regard to the Knights of labor and
thinking it to be the best organasion in existance compells me to write to
you for information and to see if you would grant us a lodge and with what
condsion and so on please write me soon as you get this all a bought it your
friend white.
                        A. D. Hall

    P.S.   can get plentey of signers both blacks and white.

Powderly Papers, Catholic University of America.

19. LETTER FROM A WHITE VIRGINIAN KNIGHT

The membership of labor organizations in Virginia is steadily increasing, and it bodes no good to the political aristocracy of that State, which
has no sympathy for the workingman, and which seeks to perpetuate its
political control by appeals to race prejudice. The angry demonstration at
Richmond was not misunderstood by the Northern Knights, and it opened their
eyes to the true condition of affairs in the South as nothing else could
have done. The white political leaders in the South are hostile to all
labor organizations, but they will be forced to yield. They will be made
to understand, too, that a colored Knight of Labor must be placed on equal
terms with a Knight of Labor who is white, so far as wages and political
rights are concerned, of course with the qualification that the former is
as skillful and efficient as the latter.

New York Tribune, October 10, 1886.

20. AT WORK AT LAST

AFTER FIVE DAYS THE KNIGHTS GET DOWN TO BUSINESS

When the Knights' General Assembly convened at 9 o'clock yesterday
morning the Committee on Credentials, which had been engaged until a late
hour the night before considering the St. Louis case, submitted a report in
favor of seating all six of the delegates from that city. This case involved a question of great importance to the Assembly, and the recommendation to seat all of the St. Louis delegates provoked a heated discussion,
which lasted for more than an hour, when the report was adopted and all six
of the delegates accorded seats.

ISSUING BADGES

The remainder of the morning session, Mr. Powderly said, was consumed
in giving out badges to the delegates. The badges are all alike, and are
very neat and attractive in appearance. Each bears a number, beginning with
No. 1 and going up to the highest, which is the total number of delegates
present. All of the delegates have not yet received their badges, and consequently the exact number is not yet known, the Credentials Committee not
having made a final report. The number of Mr. Powderly's badge is 555.

ALL THE ST. LOUIS DELEGATES SEATED

The Assembly adjourned for the dinner recess at 12 o'clock, but Mr.
Powderly and other members of the Executive Board were detained at the hall
for some time, so that it was nearly 1 o'clock when the grand master workman
reached the veranda of Ford's Hotel, where a number of representatives of
the press were waiting to receive their small quota of information. When
Mr. Powderly had entered the hotel he was asked what had been done, to which
he replied that the report of the Committee on Credentials had been completed
and adopted, and that the remainder of the session had been occupied in
issuing badges to those who called and were entitled to them.
Which delegates from St. Louis were seated? was asked.
All of them were, he replied.
Who are the delegates from there?
There are six of them, but I do not remember their names.
What was the nature of the contest there?
There was no contest. The trouble was that some of the delegates were
elected by a convention or meeting, properly called and held at the time for
which it was called, and that there was some informality in the election of
some of the others; also, that some of the delegates elected had not been,
it was alleged, members of the District from whey they were elected for the
length of time required by the laws of the order which entitle a member to be
elected a delegate.

Then all of the delegates, including those about whose election there
was some informality, were seated?

Yes, that's the idea. There were only six from that city, and all of
them were seated.

How about the Heep delegation?

I know nothing of any such delegation. There is one delegate in the
number named Heep, but he is on both sides and there is no contest about his
seat.

ANOTHER VERSION OF THE CASE

Since the above was written the following explanation of the St. Louis
contest has been made to a *Dispatch* reporter, which is endorsed by several
delegates, and which is doubtless correct; two elections of delegates were
held in St. Louis, each of which was considered illegal. The third election
was ordered, and it was claimed that the hour fixed for this one was 8 o'clock
P.M., but that, without proper authority, and without the majority of the
members being informed of the fact, the meeting was held an hour earlier,
and six delegates elected. When the hour of 8 o'clock arrived the members
who were on hand ready for business were informed of what had been done.
They acting on the theory that the 7 o'clock election was irregular and dis-
regarding what had been done they proceeded to the election of six more
delegates. Of the six chosen at this meeting three were the same as had been
selected at the one held an hour earlier--consequently, the contest was over
only three delegates. The second report of the Committee on Credentials like
the first one recommended seating all six of the delegates chosen at the
8 o'clock meeting. After the first report had been made the committee was
increased by the addition of three members, the matter was recommitted to
the committee, reconsidered, and reported as at first. The report of the
committee was adopted, and the six delegates elected at the 8 o'clock meeting
three of whom were also elected at the 7 o'clock meeting, were seated. So
the other three elected then have to return home.

AFTERNOON SESSION

The Convention, after a recess of two hours, reassembled soon after
2 P.M., and did not adjourn for the evening until 6:30--a half hour after the
usual time. Hitherto Mr. Powderly had been meeting the representatives of
the press on his way into supper, and furnishing the matter which he desired
to give for publication, but last night he decided not to meet them until
8:30 o'clock. Hereafter he will meet them in the reading-room of Ford's
Hotel at 7:30 o'clock, or as soon thereafter as other engagements will permit. This is done because of the fact that when Mr. Powderly gets to the
hotel after the afternoon session there are many persons who wish to see
him, and his supper is ready, so that altogether he has had to furnish the
"news" in a very hurried manner. By the change Mr. Powderly will have much
more time to give to this, and the reports will doubtless be much more satisfactory, both to the delegates and the public, than they have been.

A PRACTICAL JOKE

At 8:30 o'clock the knights of the quill were in full attendance awaiting
the appearance of Mr. Powderly, anxious to learn what had been done in the
secret meeting of the Assembly. He was slow putting in an appearance, so a
scheme was concocted by which an audience could be had. One of the maids was
dispatched to his room with the message that the reporters desired a conference with him. Before the message reached him, by the interference of some
one it was made to appear that one of the clerks desired to see him at the
office at once on imperative business. Mr. Powderly responded promptly, and
seemed much amused when he learned what a practical joke had been perpetrated
on him. He endeavored to ascertain who had intercepted the messenger and
caused the message to be changed, and to this end suggested that a committee
of one is appointed to ascertain and report as to who was the guilty party,
but to no avail.

THE HOME CLUB

When the newspapermen had congregated around a table in the reading-room,
some with seats and other unable to get them, Mr. Powderly proceeded to furnish

them with those proceedings of the Assembly which he could make public
without violating the obligations resting upon him. He said in the offset
that there were many things which he was not at liberty to make public, and
that if by inquiring around the reporters could gain information that ought
not to be given out, the ones who violate their pledge of secrecy must be
held responsible and not he. He said that the committee appointed at the
Cleveland Convention to report upon the charges preferred against the Home
Club submitted their report, which was adopted. The charges preferred
against the Home Club were in effect that it was conspiring to control the
principal offices of the organization. The committee appointed to investigate these charges was given the power to send for persons and papers to
take testimony, &c. Mr. Powderly said that he could not give out what was
in the report; that although it had been acted upon it was still the property
of the committee, and could not be given out except by them. It is understoc
that most of the members of the committee are Home Club men, and that the
report was in their favor.

CHILD-EDUCATION FEATURES OF MR. POWDERLY'S ADDRESS

Mr. Powderly's address, which was published last Wednesday, was read.
In addition to what had been printed, Mr. Powderly had a little to say, which
he stated, was of no great public interest. The following, contained in that
paper, which relates to the education of American children, was referred to
a special committee with instructions to report to the General Assembly some
plan by which the American people may be educated for good businessmen and
women:

The thirteenth article in our declaration of principles reads: "The
prohibition, by law, of the employment of children under fifteen years of
age in workshops, mines, and factories." The end sought for in carrying this
declaration into effect is not that the child may live in idleness; it is
not that more adults may be employed. It is that the child of the poor man
may be enabled to acquire an education to equip him for the duties which will
in future fall upon him as man and citizen. We cannot afford to pass this
question by and legislate on some simple question of trade discipline. The
question of child-labor and education is the most important that can come
before us now or any other time. With an education, all things are easy of
accomplishment; without it hope itself almost dies, and liberty is a farce.

In our organization of labor, and it has been so from the beginning, we
take up the work of reform when the subject has advanced in years--the new
member must be sixteen years before we admit him. We attempt to drive from
his mind the false ideas gathered in from the workshops, or, possibly, the
street-corner. His habits are formed, and the work that should have been
begun at seven years we take up at twenty or later on in life. To attempt to
settle so intricate a question as the one we are grappling with, or to successfully solve the question, is a task so difficult that I do not wonder
that men drop out of the ranks of labor organizations discouraged and hopeless. To make the necessary progress we must begin with the child, and see
to it that he has education. If the principles of the Knights of Labor are
right, and few men question them, we should teach them to the young. It
should be a part of the duty of every Assembly to ascertain the number of
children who do not attend school in its vicinity, learn what the causes are
and take steps to have them attend school.

The sword may strike the shackles from the limbs of the slave, but it is
education and organization that make of him a free man. He is still a slave
whose limbs alone have been freed.

Of what avail is it to say that we are laboring to establish a system o
cooperation when that which is most essential to the success of cooperation
is lacking? A business training is necessary to successfully carry on a
cooperative enterprise. If the management of the large or small concerns in
operation in this country were turned over to us today, we would but run them
in the ground, for we lack the business training necessary to successfully
operate them. Our vanity may prevent us from acknowledging this to be true,
but we cannot deny it. It is through no fault of ours that it is true, but
it continues it will be our fault.

COMMITTEES APPOINTED

The following committees were appointed: Laws, nine members; Appeals a

Grievances, eleven members; State of the Order, nine members. There was
also appointed a Committee on Distribution to look over the resolutions, &c,
introduced, and to mark and refer them to the proper committees without
discussion. This relieves the presiding officer of the trouble of examining
all of these papers to determine to what committees they should be referred.
The other committees will be appointed today.

MUST BE ALLOWED TO VOTE

A motion was adopted providing that a special committee of five be
appointed to send telegrams to Providence, R.I., and to the District of
Columbia in reference to the people there not being permitted to exercise
the right of suffrage. In the former place a person before being allowed to
vote must own $134, and in the latter they are not allowed to vote at all.
Their officers are all appointed by the President. The object of this is to
carry out the intent of the resolution adopted by the Cleveland Convention.
The committee will be appointed today. The exact nature of the telegram
which will be sent is not yet known.

KNEW NOTHING ABOUT IT

Mr. Powderly's attention was called to the following paragraph which
appeared in the telegraphic column of the papers yesterday and asked about
its being correct:
MONTREAL, October 7.--The constitution of the Knights of Labor has been
revised by the members of the clergy of this city, under the auspices of
Archbishop Fabre, with the object of expunging provisions contrary to the
rules of the Roman Catholic Church. Mr. Powderly, the general master workman, when here promised the Archbishop to support the passage of the amendments before the annual Convention. Two delegates from the Knights of Labor
organization have left to attend the Convention in Richmond, Va., and have
taken the revised constitution with them. It is stated that the Archbishop
delayed action until the present time because of the assembling of the Richmond Convention.
After reading it he said: If that is so I know nothing about it.

ONLY A SOCIAL CALL

Mr. Powderly was told that it had been stated that he called on Bishop
Keane a few days ago and had an interview with him concerning Catholics joining the order and asked if such was the case. He said this statement was
entirely erroneous; that he paid the Bishop a social call, as he always does
when he stops where a bishop lives, whether attending a convention or not.
In answer to further questions, Mr. Powderly said that nothing passed between
the Bishop and himself with reference to the question of social equality, but
that they spent a half hour in pleasant conversation on general topics.

SECRETARY-TREASURER'S REPORT

The report of Mr. Frederick W. Turner, general secretary and treasurer,
will be submitted this morning. It has not been customary heretofore to
furnish this report for publication, and it will hardly be done this time.
At the Cleveland Convention the report was gotton hold of by someone without
the permission of the officers of the Convention, and was printed in the
newspapers all over the country. Seven hundred and ten delegates are in
attendance, and forty-five more have reported, but have not arrived yet.

POWDERLY ON SOCIAL EQUALITY

Before leaving the newspapermen last night, Mr. Powderly said that if he
could get time before going to sleep he would write a letter, to be published
over his own signature, on the "social-equality" question, and that if he did
not get time last night he would do so this morning. He promised to have it
ready and to give it out tonight to be published in the morning papers. Mr.
Powderly said that many conflicting reports had been sent out concerning the
social-equality question, all of which were incorrect, and that to furnish
the public with the true position and sentiment of the General Assembly on
this subject he would have to pursue this course and discharge what he con-
ceived to be his duty. He said that it might be bad stuff, but that he felt
it to be his duty to speak plainly on the subject, and he intended to do it.

TELEGRAMS SENT

Mr. Powderly yesterday sent the following telegrams in reply to ones which he had received:

Richmond, Va., October 8th.

J. J. McGuire, Cleveland, O.:
The General Assembly of the Knights of Labor receive with kindly spirits the fraternal greeting extended by the Brotherhood of Carpenters' Association, and extends the right hand of fellowship in the labor movement.

T. V. POWDERLY

William Wright, Pittsburg, Pa.:
The General Assembly of the Knights of Labor received in a fraternal spirit the kindly words of cheer sent by the Amalgamated Association of Iron and Steel-Workers and join with them in praying for the day when labor will be massed into one solid body on the side of suffering humanity.

T. V. POWDERLY

CONVENTION NOTES

In the Assembly yesterday a colored delegate from the South got up to deny that the social-equality question had been discussed in that body. He then took occasion to deplore and deprecate the course of No. 49 in stirring up the race issue here, saying that it could but work harm to the negro. The colored people of the South, said he, understand and appreciate the situation, and don't want the question agitated.

One of the lady members of the Assembly is the district workman of Chicago, and she is said to be one of the best-informed labor leaders in the United States.

The Assembly have had the size of the Armory reduced by putting up cloth partitions. This was done to better the acoustics and to keep outsiders from seeing in there.

Many of the visiting delegates are debilitated, as they think, from change of water.

The Assembly will not sit Monday, and only a part of Tuesday; Monday is the day of the parade; Tuesday night there will be a concert in the Armory, and the Knights have consented to vacate the hall after 1 P.M.

Foster, of Massachusetts, is regarded as the most eloquent delegate.

The youngest delegate on the floor of the Convention is the three-months' old child of Mrs. Elizabeth Rogers, master workman of District Assembly 24, of Chicago. When the badges were distributed it received one also, the number of which was 860, the highest one made.

Mr. Powderly said last night that the election of officers would be about the last thing done by the General Assembly.

THE AMSTERDAM SPINNERS

During his conference with the newspapermen Mr. Powderly was asked if the Assembly had not on Thursday endorsed the Amsterdam (N.Y.) strikers. He replied that the Assembly had not endorsed any strike or lockout, but had decided to support the men who are on a lockout at Augusta, Ga., and other places. He said further that strikes were only endorsed by the Executive Board, not by the Assembly. It is stated that on Thursday the salient features of the strike of the spinners at this point were presented in a report by delegates from the Amsterdam district, after which there was a discussion as to the proper steps to be taken. Some thought it only neces- sary to refer the matter to the Board, while others insisted on some kind of expression from the Convention as a body. It is further understood that the matter was referred to the Executive Board for formal action, and that the Convention showed itself in sympathy with the strikers, and voted to stand by and assist them.

THE FERRELL CASE

The newspapers throughout the country have generally commented on the appearance of Ferrell at the Academy of Music, and while some of the most rabid Republican journals have applauded the course of District No. 49, the

predominant sentiment is against the whole thing as in exceedingly bad taste
and hurtful to the order.

There is comment also on the fact that Mr. Powderly, following upon
the pleasant speech of welcome of Governor Lee, permitted himself to be
introduced to the Assembly by Ferrell, who at once proceeded to discuss the
color-line question.

AIN'T YOU ASHAMED

A postal card was received by one of the members of District 49 at
their headquarters yesterday, from a prominent brother Knight in Philadelphia, saying: "Ain't you fellows ashamed of yourselves for insulting the
people of Richmond, whose guests you are? You are doing injury to the
order and heaping disgrace upon yourself."

THE PARADE MONDAY--LINE OF MARCH, &C.

Mr. L. L. Lynch, chief marshal of the parade of the Knights next
Monday, wishes all assemblies of trade organizations of this city of Man-
chester and visiting organizations and assemblies who expect to take part
in the parade, to meet as follows:

All assemblies and organizations west of Tenth street meet at the corner of Fourth and Broad streets--colored on north side, white on south side.

All assemblies east of Tenth street meet on the corner of Eighteenth
and Main streets--colored on north side, white on south side, at 8 o'clock
sharp.

All local master workmen and officers will wear a white rosette.

The aids to the Chief Marshal a blue sash.

The Chief Marshals a sash of lilac, blue, and white.

Marshals and aids will assemble at Armory committee room, Seventh and
Marshall streets at 7 o'clock A.M., sharp.

The column will be formed at the head of Fourth and Broad streets, and
march down Broad to Nineteenth, down Nineteenth to Main, up Main to Fifth,
up Fifth to Franklin, and thence to Laurel street and out to the Fair Grounds.

MARSHALS AND AIDS

The following are the marshals of the parade; Messrs. L. L. Lynch, R. E.
Jones, John T. Chappell, and Isaiah Peterford.

The aids are: Messrs. G. E. Conway, S. H. Dismond, J. D. Wade, J. H.
Barrett, Colonel D. E. De Clay, Lewis Stewart, Charles De Voto, and Robert
Taylor.

SPECIAL CORRESPONDENTS

NUGGETS OF NEWS TELEGRAPHED ABOUT THE KNIGHTS' PROCEEDINGS

While most of the members of the General Assembly imagine that they are
sitting "in secret session" the press reporters and special correspondents
here are getting almost all the news they want. The Boston men gather up
and telegraph to the Boston journals what is of most interest to the people
of that vicinity; the New York men do the same for New York; the Philadelphia
men the same for Philadelphia, and the *Dispatch* flatters itself that very
little of general interest to the citizens of Richmond escapes it representatives. While Mr. Powderly is giving out scanty and attenuated reports,
there are people in the hall--delegates, it is believed--who are telegraphing
the proceedings from this city, and there are others supplying news to correspondents. So in one way or another it all leaks out, but sometimes in
quite a tangled shape. If the United States Senate, with about seventy-
five members, can't keep their secrets, it is a hopeless undertaking for a
convention of eight hundred. The Assembly is managing this part of its
business miserably bad. A far better plan than they are now pursuing would
be for Mr. Powderly to appoint one of his eight hundred delegates as reporter, and let that reporter furnish the press with a two-column report of
proceedings every day. That would kill off speculation and be far more
satisfactory, to the delegates at least, than the present "open secret"
session. From a great mass of matter sent from Richmond--most of it of no
earthly interest to our people--the following readable extracts from reports
of special telegraphic correspondents are taken:

SOCIAL EQUALITY AND NEGRO MASONS

[Boston Herald.]

A conservative and influential citizen of Richmond, discussing the social equality matter tonight, said: "As long as these members of the Convention chose to sleep and eat with negroes, we did not care--that was their own affair; but when they propose to dictate to us how we shall govern our local affairs, we feel it time to call a halt. At the North there is not a lodge of Masons into which a negro will be allowed to enter. White members of that order in the South could with as much propriety carry a negro Mason into a northern lodge as can these white Knights of Labor carry a negro into the orchestra of our theatres. Why is the negro Mason denied admission into the northern lodge, if not because of his color? The negro Masons in the United States hold their charter from the English Masons, as do the white Masons in the United States. New York and Massachusetts lodges have been the most persistent in their refusal to admit colored Masons into their lodges, and yet a party of New Yorkers undertake to force a social equality upon us that they do not practice themselves."

POWDERLY ENDORSES NO. 49

[Pittsburgh Dispatch, 7th.]

. . . But the greatest blow to the enemies of the Home Club was yet to come. In the midst of the mélée, when crimination and recrimination raged hottest, and when all the damaging lies and truths ever alleged against the Home Club had been rehashed and reembellished, the calm voice of the general master workman hushed the confusion. Deliberately, but forcibly and with feeling, Mr. Powderly put the seal of his condemnation on the abuse that had been heaped on District 49; defended it from the ridiculous slanders that had been circulated in regard to it, and expressed general approval of its course, his admiration for its energy in the cause of oppressed labor and its chanpionship of the victims of race prejudice. It is not putting it too strong to say that his speech was virtually a thorough endorsement of the leaders of District Assembly 49. It was decidely quieting to anti-Home Clubbers, and was received with general applause.

Mr. Powderly's attitude is a subject of much gossip on the quiet, and it is, of course, asserted by the most uncompromising opponents of District 49 that he has been captured, body and breeches, by the Home Club. The truth is, the Home Club is right, and Powderly simply espouses on the side of the right. He would not see an injustice done on account of an antagonism that could give no reason for its own existence. I don't like to talk so much about the Home Club, but the atmosphere is so full of it that I can't get away from it.

A SHOCKING RUMOR

[New York Times.]

The color line as a matter of contention between the Knights of Labor and the white citizens of Richmond has been quietly buried. The Knights found the question a dangerous one to handle, and dropped it after receiving considerable damage. Their attitude has proved a disadvantage to them, even among the colored people, who apparently are not overwhelmed with respect for white men who are willing to consort with colored. The colored man here seemingly entertains the same views on the question of social equality as his white brother, and he does not appear at all willing that the situation should be turned upside down by Knights of Labor possessed of so little discretion and good taste as some of the members of District Assembly No. 49. The local papers are still indignant, but the people at large are satisfied that the trouble is over, and pay little attention to the rumors of further disturbance. The most shocking of these was a story that Mr. Powderly and New York's colored delegate would attend the Theatre this evening. The story naturally made the General Master Workman angry, and he said with a good deal of emphasis tonight that he had never contemplated such a move. He also said that Ferrell had promised him that he would not attend a theatre in Richmond while the Knights are here. Mr. Powderly has been made aware that Catholics and Protestants are a unit on the social equality question.

MONEY SENT TO THE NEEDY

[New York World.]

While the Committee on Credentials were out, the rules were suspended and some important business was transacted. The General Executive Board was authorized to use such amounts of money as it was deemed best to relieve certain members who were in distress in different places. The most important was the Southwest strikers. The locals wanted $12,000 to relieve the men who had been "victimized" by the railroad officials, and the money will be sent at once. A delegate from Massachusetts asked that help be immediately sent to the curriers and tanners of Peabody and Salem, Mass., and the request was complied with.

Then a young woman from Augusta, Ga., explained how a strike, followed by a lockout, occurred in a cotton mill at that place, and requested that the matter be arbitrated. A telegram was at once ordered to be sent to the proprietors of the mill, asking that the hands be put back as they were before the strike and that the trouble be settled immediately on the conclusion of the General Assembly.

[Mr. Powderly said last night that there was no truth at all as to this $12,000. He stated that $100,000 had been raised for the Southwest strike sometime ago; that since that time the membership of the order in District 101 has increased 2,000, and that they have five delegates in the General Assembly here, indicating a present membership of 5,000. He says further that they are not all in need of funds and do not ask for help.]

DISTRICT 49 AND THE COLOR-LINE

[New York Herald.]

It was learned at dinner that District 49 had kept remarkably quiet during the morning session. The "Forty-niners" are well pleased at the rejection of the Brooklyn delegates, as there is no love between them. There is quite a feeling against 49 on account of the excitement caused last night at the Richmond Theatre. T. B. McGuire says he did not intend to take the colored delegate there, but people think he changed his mind when he saw the trouble such action would create. There would have been trouble if 49 had tried to force Ferrell into the Theatre.

The citizens are very indignant over the matter, and the Richmond papers contain letters from various people denouncing 49's action. The delegates of 49 receive daily instructions not to talk to representatives of the press, but a few of them are complaining of the accommodations they receive because they stand by the colored brother. One of them remarked today that he believed in principle, but he could not stand it much longer if principle compelled him to sleep in a room with four men on a bed as hard as a board and inhale the odor at colored receptions. It is unnecessary to say that this gentleman has not communicated his views to Master Workman McGuire, for Thomas loves the colored man.

Richmond Dispatch, October 1886.

21. RICHMOND AND THE CONVENTION HELD UP

The evenings are spent in an everlasting flow of talk, not on the great principles of the order, not on the importance of legislation looking toward bettering the condition of those who toil, but as to which of the two cliques shall control the organization—namely, the Home Club or radical element, or the trades unions of conservative element. As the expenses of the delegates are paid, and in most cases a *per diem* allowed equivalent to their wages by the local assemblies, there is no certainty that another week may not be frittered away before the organization is completed.

Mr. Powderly, if I may judge from what representatives of both the elements say of him, has so trimmed his sails that his election is sure whichever

side comes out uppermost. He patted Assembly 49 on the back in recognizing
the colored delegate Ferrell, and he has soothed the lacerated feelings of
the trade unions by admitting in his address that "some of our organizers
have been so zealous in their way of organizing that they have encroached
upon the prerogatives of other associations." He has won the applause of
the dangerous elements by not denouncing the boycott, and appealed to the
conservatives by his attitude on the eight-hour system and his denunciation
of the Southwestern strike. Finally, in releasing instructed delegates from
obligation to vote for him, he has dramatically announced confidence in his
own election and brought to his side any doubtful members who are likely to
follow the fortunes of the winning candidate.

SECRETARY TURNER'S PROSPECTS

Of Turner, the worthy secretary, there are serious doubts, and if the
representatives of the New York press were doing the voting he would certainly stand no show. He is said to stand in with the Home Club, "to
sympathize with Assembly 49, and to be guilty of other high crimes too numerous to mention." And, moreover, he is charged with being a dull man and a
mere mouthpiece of Powderly. I know but little of Turner personally, but he
strikes me as a plodding man, good at details, not very enthusiastic, and
anxious to make a comfortable living without too much exertion. He certainly
has not the appearance of a man with sufficient snap in him to lead a mob
to destroy factories and workshops, as some try to make him out. It is to
be feared that many of the stories about Turner and the Home Club emanate
from his energetic and breezy opponent, Buchanan, of Colorado. This young
man has sensibly ingratiated himself into the confidence of the represent-
tives of some of the leading journals here and in consequence is much more
popular in the newspapers than Turner, who is a good deal of a slow coach
anyhow, and is often gruff and even rude to reporters. It may be truly said
that Buchanan is working on the outside for the secretaryship and Turner on
the inside. Buchanan says to his faithful corps of reporters that Turner's
success means the Home Club and groans, while his own success means the
triumph of conservative principles, the methods of trades unions, the downfall of Brother Buchanan the--the miniature Powderly"--the elevation of the or
tor and strategist, McNeill, of Massachusetts, and cheers; and from Buchanan's
standpoint I suppose he is more than half right. It will thus be seen that
the scare about the "Home Club" is being used, in all sorts of ways. The
skillful manipulators of the order try to influence public opinion on the
outside that it may indirectly have effect upon the election of officers or
the admission of delegates. Hence the refusal to seat Morrison--particulars
of which will be found in the detailed reports of the Convention telegraphed
from here tonight--is construed into a Home Club victory, and the seating of
some other delegates into a victory for Buchanan and his great conservative
wing. There is nothing in all this except the jealousy of men seeking preferment in the order.

BLOTS UPON THE KNIGHTS' ESCUTCHEON

The most scandalous charges have been made by members, such as these
contained in the "little red book" mentioned in my Tuesdays' dispatch, against
the order, utterly regardless of the fact that the authors criminated themselves in their so-called confessions. That members thus willing to sink
manhood for the sake of controlling the organization should not be drummed
out of the order is indeed a stigma upon the Knights of Labor. For example,
the man who said he was in a conspiracy to blow up an Albany stove factory
and to introduce the small-pox among non-union men. Is a wretch like that
(supposing he is not insane) a fit man for a Knight of Labor? Look at him in
either the light of a conspirator or a liar, and he is equally contemptible.
Drum him out and all others of the same class. It is about time something
was done with these writers of circulars and red books, or else the public
will feel justified in believing some of the infamous stories which these
Knights of Labor themselves get inserted in the public prints are true, or
that wholesale and wicked lying on the part of Knights against Knights is
permitted and endorsed, and it is also about time the Convention began work.

RICHMOND

The only entertainment so far afforded the visiting Knights was the eloquent and impressive speech of Governor Lee. The city of Richmond has not so much as loaned a flag to decorate the hall. The poor hotels of the place, when they did not turn their guests away, have squeezed an extra half-dollar a day out of them whenever it was possible, and the spirit of make-all-you-can-get-out-of-strangers has even extended to the newsboys, who charge visitors five cents right along for a two-cent paper. The only hospitality that has been shown to the Knights was that by their own brethren, and the money subscribed for the purpose by the colored Knights exceeded that subscribed by the whites. Really on the hospitality question honors would seem to be easy. The Knights are certainly paying their way.

A MERCENARY KNIGHT

One of the enterprising and mercenary Knights is selling a *verbatim* report of the secret meetings of the Convention to a prominent journal. General Master Powderly denounced this man today as a traitor to the order, and publicly informed the assembled newspaper-men that he (the Knight) had violated his obligation as such and was liable to be expelled. The whole affair is productive of merriment, for the secret sessions, like the executive sessions of the Senate (which these workingmen oppose so bitterly) are the merest farce. All the newspapers and the Associated Press substantially get what transpires, and the public are simply spared the dry details.

Richmond Dispatch, October 9, 1886.

22. RESOLUTIONS OF THE EQUAL RIGHTS LEAGUE,

COLUMBUS, OHIO

Whereas: The same feelings and damnable traits that actuated the white southerner during the days of slavery seem to exist throughout the south in general and the city of Richmond especially, the hot bed of the late confederacy, which caused the poor slave to shudder with fear and his white sympathiser to stand trembling, and whereas their late action toward the colored delegate to the Knights of Labor Convention is characteristic of their treatment and their abhorrence of the negro.

Be it resolved: That the action of the Knights of Labor in Convention assembled, and their Grand Master Workman Mr. Powderly and of Assembly No. 49 in particular, deserve the plaudits of all mankind who believe in the fatherhood of God and the Brotherhood of Man, and most especially the unstinted praises of the colored Americans of the United States for the manly stand taken in behalf of the fellow-member Mr. Ferrell of Assembly No. 49.

Resolved: That the Equal Rights League of Columbus, Ohio, at their meeting held on the 11th of October send congratulations and best wishes to the Knights of Labor in Convention assembled in the city of Richmond, and wish them success in their labors for the uplifting of humanity.

Resolved: That a copy of these resolutions be engrossed and forwarded to Mr. Powderly at Richmond, Va. and a copy to Assembly No. 49. Also spread upon the minutes of the League.

JAMES POINDEXTER, President,
Equal Rights League

Powderly Papers, Catholic University of America.

23. RESOLUTION ADOPTED BY ALL-BLACK LOCAL ASSEMBLY,

RENDVILLE, OHIO

Whereas, Seeing the position taken by our G.M.W.T.V. Powderly and D.A. 49 of New York, and the whole of the G. A. assembled at Richmond, Va., in the heart of the Southern Confederacy, with reference to our race; and seeing the disposition manifested by our white brethren to elevate us and especially our downtrodden brethren in the South; therefore be it

Resolved, That we, as members of L. A. 1935, K of L, renew our obligations to the Order and pledge ourselves to do all in power to swell the number of our ranks, and declare that we will never relinquish our work until the bulk of our brethren in city, town, County and State are brought within the folds of our noble Order.

Cleveland Gazette, November 13, 1886.

24. A PEACEFUL PARADE

NO TROUBLE ABOUT THE K. OF L. ON RICHMOND'S FESTAL DAY

RICHMOND, October 11.--This has certainly been an off day, so far as the business of the convention is concerned. Nearly every committee that is organized held a meeting, but very little work was accomplished. The feature of the parade was the spectacle of District 49 in the post of honor. Two white and two colored marshals rode in front. Maguire, of the Home Club, officered his men in fine style, and they marched with the care and precision of regulars. Ferrell, the colored delegate, was in the front rank. The citizens accepted the situation quite graciously, considering the excitement of the last few days on the social equality issue.

The colored Knights of Richmond were well represented, and as they marched along the street, constantly cheered for Mullen and District 49.

Pittsburgh Dispatch, October 12, 1886.

25. POWDERLY ON RACE RIGHTS,

THE GENERAL MASTER WORKMAN WRITES AN IMPORTANT LETTER TO THE PUBLIC

RICHMOND, October 11.--In consequence of questions which have been raised by the presence of Ferrell and other colored delegates to the General Assembly, Mr. Powderly has written the following letter:

Richmond, Va. October 11.

Much has been said and written concerning the events which have transpired in the city of Richmond and during the past 10 days. . . . Will my critics stop long enough to tell me why the United States Senate allowed a colored man to introduce before the Vice President of the United States measures for the benefit of the State? Were the laws of social equality outraged when the House of Representatives permitted colored men to take seats in it? Why did not other Southern Representatives leave and return to their homes when that was done? There need be no further cause for alarm; the colored representatives to this convention will not intrude where they are not wanted, and the time-honored laws of social equality will be allowed to slumber along undisturbed. We have not done anything since coming to this city that is not countenanced by the laws and constitution of our country, and, in deference to the wishes of those who regard the laws of social equality

as superior to the laws of God and man, we will not, while here, avail ourselves of all of those rights and privileges which belong to us. The equality of American citizenship is all that we insist on, and that equality must
not be trampled upon.

Now, a word as to hospitality. We are here under no invitation from
any one. We came of our own free will and accord, and are paying our own
way; therefore, such gratuitous insults as those offered by a few mischievous
meddlers are not in order, and do not admit of defense, even though given in
behalf of the laws of social equality. I do not hold the people of Richmond
responsible for the ill action of a few who SAW A MENACE in our every action.
The treatment received at the hands of the citizens generally has been most
cordial. If, during our stay, any representative shall conduct himself in an
unbecoming manner, he alone will be held responsible for his action. To the
convention I say, let no member surrender an iota of intellectual freedom,
because of any clamor. Hold fast to that which is true and right. The
triumph of poise over reason is but transient. Our principles will be better
known, if not to-day, it may be to-morrow. They can bide their time, and
will some day have the world for an audience. In the field of labor, and
American citizenship, we recognize no line of race, creed, politics or color.

The demagogue may distort, for a purpose, the words of others, and, for
a time, the noise of the vocal boss may silence reason; but that which is
right and true will become known when the former has passed to rest and the
ground of the latter's voice has forever died away. Then it will be known
that the intelligent educated man is better qualified to discern the difference between right and privilege, and the unwritten law of social equality
will be more rigidly observed than it is to-day.

T. V. POWDERLY.

Pittsburgh Dispatch, October 12, 1886.

26. THEY WILL FIND OUT FACTS

A BUREAU OF COLORED KNIGHTS FORMED, TO PLAN FOR
THE RIGHTS OF THEIR RACE

RICHMOND, October 14.--Mr. Powderly held a conference at Ford's Hotel last
night with 15 or 16 colored delegates to the General Assembly. They represent the colored assemblies of Knights of Labor of Virginia, Georgia, Florida,
Mississippi and other Southern States. The object of the conference was the
formation of a Bureau of Colored Knights throughout the Southern States, for
the purpose of procuring accurate statistics relative to the condition of
the colored people and their relation to white laborers, whenever they are
employed together. These statistics are to comprise everything in connection
with the hours of labor, the treatment they receive from their employer, their
wages, cost of living, etc. It is purposed to learn whether they receive the
full liberty and rights to which they are legally entitled.

But Mr. Powderly said, in speaking of the conference and its object, the
question of social equality is not one of the objects of the bureau. Its
object is to stimulate the colored people to work for their own elevation.
The delegates he met were bright, intelligent men, who seemed well fitted to
aid in improving the condition of their race. It was decided to elect a
chairman and secretary and have assistants in each of the Southern States.

Pittsburgh Dispatch, October 15, 1886.

27. BANQUET IN HONOR OF DISTRICT ASSEMBLY 49

SUPERIOR TO SCOFFERS

Cultivated Colored People of Richmond Tender a
Banquet to Home Clubbers

RICHMOND, October 14.--The colored people of Richmond gave a complimentary banquet this evening to the delegates of District 49, which was one of
the most interesting episodes of the session. Two tables, stretched the
length of Harris Hall, were crowded with delegates and guests. Whites and
blacks were about even in numbers, and they were seated without reference to
color. Among the white ladies present were three of the cleverest delegates
to the assembly, Misses Henapin and Stirling of Philadelphia, and Miss Lee,
of Minnesota. The master of ceremonies was Dr. Ferguson, a physician of high
reputation, and nearly white. An address of welcome, excellent in compositic
was read by Colonel Wilson, a mulatto; a response was made by J. C. Farley,
a colored photographer, and a really eloquent speech was delivered by a young
attorney named Scott, who is quite black.

All of these speakers disclaimed any desire on the part of the colored
race to compel recognition as social equals. The only social equality that
had ever existed was thrust on them by the whites, and this peculiar feature
of the question was briefly discussed in good set terms by each one of the
colored orators. To illustrate their meaning, take the passage from the
address of Colonel Wilson:

It is with unspeakable regret that I cannot truly welcome you in behalf
of the negro to this festive board. Gathered around you are the remnants of
the offspring of the negro race, which once toiled in the rice, corn, cotton,
and tobacco fields of the South. That race of patient toilers has passed
away. The ruthless hand and the unchecked passions of another race have
destroyed the lineage of our forefathers, supplanting it with the people in
whose behalf I welcome you to-night--a people of all colors and complexions,
of a varied texture of hair and skin, so various that it is with some difficulty race lines are drawn. Do not, I pray you, misinterpret our greeting.
By it we seek no change in the social customs of those who call you the mudsills of society, and call us niggers. Our aim is not to establish a new
social order of things for the people among whom we live. By extending to yo
our hospitality, we mean to convey a recognition of the brotherhood of man,
as you teach it, and have exemplified it during your sojourn in our midst.

Colonel Wilson has been a candidate for Governor, and Attorney Scott is
at present a member of Councils. A leading feature of the evening was the
speech of Victor Drury, who was introduced by Dr. Ferguson as one of the
fathers of District 49. It was only a few minutes in duration, but was one
of the most thrilling and eloquent I have ever heard. He seemed to be inspired by the occasion to a flight of oratory, unusual even in him, though he
is noted as one of the greatest of living orators. Speaking of the aims of
Forty-nine, he said that what Forty-eight was to the oppressed millions of
Europe, it was hoped Forty-nine might be to the struggling masses of America
in this day, and this play upon words and reference to a red letter period of
the revolutionary spirit nearly 40 years ago abroad, were received with cheers
He declared that if it were their fate to die, as three great champions of
the brotherhood of men had died, Socrates by the poisoned hemlock, Christ upon
the cross, and John Brown upon the scaffold, they would go their fate saying
with Christ, "Forgive them, Father, for they know not what they do." [26]

E. W. L.

Pittsburgh Dispatch, October 15, 1886.

28. THE MIXED BANQUET AT HARRIS'S HALL

Some of the Features of That Noted Social Gathering

The special correspondent of the Pittsburgh *Dispatch,* who was present at

the banquet given by some of the colored people of Richmond to District 49
on Thursday night, telegraphs, among other things, the following: The
colored people of Richmond gave a complimentary banquet this evening to the
delegates of District 49, which was one of the most interesting episodes of
the session. Two tables stretched the length of Harris's Hall, were crowded
with delegates and guests.

In addition to what is said by the above quoted correspondent, it is
learned that the banquetting party, consisted of seventy-three whites (three
of them ladies) and thirty colored men. No colored ladies were present; none
were invited.

Richmond Dispatch, October 17, 1886.

29. DISSAFFECTION

There was disaffection among the delegates to the Cleveland Assembly of
last May 6. There is almost open revolt among the delegates to this convention. The situation is due to the arbitrary rulings of the General Master
Workman, to the support given by him to a faction that, if it is asserted,
represents the worst element in the order and to the blunder he made in posing as the instructor of the South on the question of social equality. He
could not have relished today's action of the convention on this very question. In behalf of the Southern white delegates to the convention, W. H.
Barrett, of Philadelphia, introduced the following resolution:

Whereas, Reports have been circulated and impressions been created by
the press of the country regarding the position of the Knights of Labor on
the question of social equality; and

Whereas, We believe the welfare of the order in the South requires that
this General Assembly will take such action as will dispel these wrong impressions; therefore be it

Resolved, That the Order of the Knights of Labor recognize the civil and
political equality of all men and in the broad field of labor recognize no
distinction on account of color, but it has no purpose to interfere with or
disrupt the social relations which may exist between the different races in
various portions of the country.

The Southern white Knights had talked openly of seceding upon the publication of Powderly's letter on the question of social equality. They became
more determined upon being supported by the press of the South, which pil-
loried Powderly unmercifully on the ground that his premises were out of
joint, and that in a general way he didn't know what he was talking about.
The threat of the Southern Knights evidently carried weight, as the resolution introduced for them by Mr. Barrett was adopted by the convention without
debate. This action has had a soothing effect upon the Southern Knights, but
they are still dissatisfied with the extraordinary manner in which the convention has been manipulated, and one of them expressed himself in the
following terms to-day:

New York Times, October 16, 1886.

30. HOW THEIR STAND AGAINST PREJUDICE IS REGARDED BY THE COLORED PRESS

Every colored man ought to treat the order with greater respect and
consideration as it has shown itself courageous enough to face a strong
popular prejudice and honest enough to stand up to one of its cardinal
principles.--Wilmington (N.C.) *Chronicle.*

Whatever may be said in criticism or denunciation of the Knights of Labor, the fact remains that they are doing more to blot out color prejudice and recognize the equality of manhood in all the races than any organization in existence.--Salisbury (N.C.) *Star of Zion*.

If the K. of L. will exterminate class prejudice and color-line, not in form, but in reality, we say colored men this is your chance, but if not it would be leaping from the frying-pan into the fire. We must be made to feel comfortable, as if we had friends at our backs and sides.--Staunton (Va.) *Critic*.

The Knights of Labor justifies the confidence placed in it by the Afro-American people, and its course in Richmond justifies the *Plaindealer* in exhorting the people to combine with it to secure the elevation of the masses and in proclaiming it to be the most potent factor ever yet entered into our American life to secure full justice to the Afro-American.--Detroit (Mich.) *Plaindealer*.

The Knights of Labor have shown themselves to be true to their colored brother, and henceforth colored men will feel that labor begets a fraternity that will in time usurp the power of political and sectional prejudice. The action of the Knights of Labor in Richmond show that they are prepared to sacrifice much for principle, and that they do not intend to build up an aristocracy of caste among those who earn their bread by honest labor.-- Chicago *Observer*.

The last and most heartless difficulty to be dealt with and destroyed in this free land is race caste. Its citadel is in the late slave States. Thus far the poor colored man has been left to combat it almost alone. Reason and religion both show its flagrant inconsistency--in fact, it is at war with every principle of truth and right. God is surely raising allies for its effectual resistance and final overthrow. If the Knights are destined to help us in this contest, then may God bless the Knights and prosper them. -- Philadelphia *Christian Recorder*.

This certainly is a boom for the order among the colored people, because when white men risk so much and deprive themselves of comforts, in order to break down a mean and hellborn prejudice maintained solely on the ground of color, be it assured that the thinking of the race all over the country, no matter what may have been their dispositions towards the Knights of Labor formerly, will surely be convinced of the sincerity of purpose of the order in making no distinctions and protecting the rights and privileges of all its citizens.--Petersburg (Va.) *Lancet*.

The convention of the Knights of Labor of Richmond, Va., afforded but another evidence of the advancement in education and morals that is growing steadily in reference to the position of the Negro of this country. There is further shown a lively appreciation of the relations that bind man to man, and of the fact that when one is affected the other will also be affected. Richmond, the former seat of the confederacy and now the home of race prejudice in its most objectionable form, is having a lesson taught it that while it may not eradicate many of the evils, will still have its influence in demonstrating the futility of withstanding the ordinary customs of civilized communities.--Philadelphia *Sentinel*.

Will the order of the Knights of Labor insist that its component unions accept the Negro to membership? Though the leading spirits of the organization are full of hope and activity, and though they are inspired by the most proper sense of justice, it is doubtful that the rank and file of the order are ready to preach and practice industrial equality. Mr. Powderly and District Assembly 49 have immortalized themselves, so far as the Negro is concerned. We have expressed our doubts about the rank and file of the order being ready to accept the Negro as a man. We hope our doubts are unfounded. For should the whites reach this point, the Knights of Labor will undoubtedly

hold the future government of the United States in the hollow of its hand.
If the Negro has one predominant characteristic it is his gratitude.--
Philadelphia *Tribune*.

New York Freeman, October 16, 1886.

31. MR. POWDERLY AND SOCIAL EQUALITY

It seems to us that Mr. Powderly's statement concerning the race issue
and social equality, which was given to the press last week, is deserving of
more attentive consideration as regards its bearing upon the question of
social equality between the races than it has yet received at the hands of
the Southern press. The proceedings and, as far as possible, the names of
the Knights who are attending the General Assembly at Richmond as delegates
from various portions of the country are kept secret, but it has leaked out
that many of the Southern delegates were instructed by their assemblies to
oppose Mr. Powderly and the Home Club on the social equality question, and
under certain conditions to withdraw from the Order. One of these conditions
was, it is said, that the question of social equality between the races should
be left entirely untouched, or else that the decision of practical questions
arising under it should be left under the control of the principal officers
of the Order in each State. It was apparently in compliance with that demand
that the resolution was passed on Friday declaring that while the Knights of
Labor recognize the civil and political equality of all men, regardless of
color, "it is not our purpose to interfere with or disrupt social relations
which may exist between the different races."
That is very well as far as it goes, but the acts and utterances of the
leading Knights show plainly that the whole organized moral force of the
Order is to be used in breaking down the social barriers that have heretofore
existed between the races in the Southern States. Discovering that the sentiment of the white citizens of Richmond, who had given him such a cordial and
distinguished reception, was against any social commingling of the races,
Mr. Powderly, embracing the first opportunity to defy that sentiment, selected
Francis Ferrell, the colored delegate from New York, to introduce him to the
assembled Knights and spectators on the opening day when Governor Fitzhugh
Lee welcomed them to Richmond. On the day of the great parade Ferrell was
put in the front rank of Assembly 49 at the head of the column, and at the
banquet afterwards given at the Fair Grounds, white and colored delegates and
visitors, of both sexes, sat down indiscriminately to the tables. In fact
everything seems to have been done that could be done to show the determination of the Knights as a body to repudiate and ignore the social distinctions
which they found existing among the people they had come amonst to hold their
General Assembly.
And cautiously as Mr. Powderly's letter is worded, it leaves no doubt
whatever in the mind of the careful reader that the General Master Workman
is in sympathy with the sentiment that inspired that conduct. He attempts
to make it appear that the so-called "prejudice" against the colored man is
a prejudice against his being educated. The truth is, however, as so well-
informed a man as Mr. Powderly ought to know, that the Southern States are,
as a rule, doing just as much for the education of the colored youth of the
country as the Northern States are doing for the education of the white
youth--just as much certainly as they are doing for the education of the
white children of the South. With here and there an exception, the Southern
people realize that the safety of their institutions and their chance to keep
pace with the progress of other civilized States is involved in their educating the colored people to a realization of their responsibility as men
and citizens. The social question as between the races has no relation
whatever to education, and Mr. Powderly knows it, or ought to know it.
The real animus of the letter creeps out in the paragraph where Mr.
Powderly refers to the admission of colored men to the United States Senate
and House of Representatives. He asks "Were the laws of social equality out-

raged when the House of Representatives permitted colored men to take seats in it? Why did not other Southern Representatives leave and return to their homes?"

The plain implication of that is, that if colored men can be permitted to sit in the Senate and House of Representatives, there is no reason why they should not be admitted on equal terms with the whites to cars, hotels, theatres, balls, parties, receptions and the like. He intimates plainly that "the laws of social equality are not superior to the laws of the land."

The fact is, Mr. Powderly's letter makes it plain that the whole influence of the Knights of Labor, as an organization, is to be directed to breaking down the social barriers between the races, and that is a very significant fact indeed. It very greatly increases the difficulties with which the Knights will have to contend in the Southern States, and in the long run it will prevent the Order from attaining the strength in the Southern States that it has attained elsewhere. For the truth is that the white laborer of the South has just as much objection to associating indiscriminately on terms of equality with the colored people as the white employers and professional men have.

The Pittsburgh Dispatch, October 21, 1886.

32. THE KNIGHTS OF LABOR SHOW THE WHITE FEATHER

The following, taken from Friday of last week's proceedings of the Convention of Knights of Labor, in Session at Richmond, Va., is of general interest to the race at large:

Before they took its noon recess Wm. H. Barrett of District Assembly 70, on behalf of the Southern delegates, offered the following, which was adopted without debate:

Whereas, Reports have been circulated and impressions have been created by the press of the country regarding of position of the Knights of Labor on the question of social equality; and

Whereas, We believe the welfare of the order South requires that this General Assembly take such action as will dispel wrong impressions; therefore

Resolved, That the organization of the Knights of Labor recognizes the civil and political equality of all men, and in the broad field of labor recognizes no distinction on account of color; but it has no purpose to interfere with or disrupt the social relations which exist between the different races in the various parts of the country.

The Labor Convention was compelled to do in this matter as the white knight of the South dictated.

Northern sentiment however just has always crawled before and fawned upon the domineering sentiment of the South, however unjust and insolent. The wild goose chase the South led the North on the slavery question is illustrative of the point.

In cold-blooded persistence in the maintenance of an infamous position, --in the subjection of all other matters to the vindication of such position, --the North has never proved itself a match for the South. When the issue is joined the Southern dog always wags his Northern tail.

We are not surprised that the Knights of Labor backed down at the command of the Southern delegates. The whole North knuckled to it in 1856 as voiced by Mr. Justice Taney; every Christian denomination has bowed to it since the war; the Republican party bowed to it in 1876.

The black man constitutes the labor element of the South.

The black man does not ask for social equality--there is no such thing; but he demands and he will have that access to places of amusement and accommodation upon which the Richmond "incident" is based, in the course of time, whatever the Southern high-flyers may say or do to the contrary.

New York *Freeman, October 23, 1886.*

33. AN "IMPRUDENT" POSITION ON SOCIAL EQUALITY

The imprudent attempt of District Assembly 49, Knights of Labor of
New York, to force public opinion at Richmond into acquiescence in its
peculiar and offensive notions of social equality has met with proper rebuke. The white-livered members of that organization entered upon a vain
crusade when they attempted to override recognized social distinctions at
the South, by refusal to board and lodge where a colored member could not
also be entertained. The *State* very pointedly says that while 'the people
of Richmond and of Virginia have kindly feelings for the colored race, and
here the colored man has equal rights with the whites in courts of law and
at the ballot-box and equality of citizenship is unhesitatingly recognized
by the whites, social equality the whites refuse to tolerate in any form.
Sensible and self-respecting colored men do not seek to do violence to these
feelings, nor have they any desire to obtrude themselves where they are not
wanted. Now and then, however, some imprudent fellow is found who is eager
to have at least the appearance of enjoying a social equality that never
can be and never should be his. Whites who have so little sense and so
little decency as to aid and abet him in such offensive capers can hardly
expect to keep the respect of the people of their own race, who are willing
always to do justice to the colored people, but who demand that their own
inherent and ineradicable feelings on the race question shall not be rudely
insulted.'
This language, firm and moderate, reflects the sentiments of all self-
respecting white and colored people in this and other Southern States. We
have heard some worthy people argue that such equality was repulsive simply
by reason of custom. This is a great error, we think. The distinctions
between the two races are fixed, we believe, by a higher law than human
statutes, and will continue for all time, with very little modification, and
with decided advantage to both civilizations.

Norfolk Virginian, October 30, 1886.

34. POWDERLY'S STRADDLING

Mr. Powderly of the Knights of Labor has shown on more occasions than
one that he knows how to put his "foot in it" in haste only to swamp himself in trying to take it out at leisure. The following from the hide-bound
knuckle-close Bourbon Richmond *State* but illustrated Mr. Powderly's latest
"doing it to undo it:"
"Whatever Mr. Powderly himself may think, his friends must confess that
he has made a mistake on the social equality question. His letter of explanation and defence cannot alter that opinion. That he, knowing the dis-
tastefulness of the idea of social equality with the Southerners, should have
departed from the usual method of procedure and had a colored man to introduce
and vouch for him to Richmond people was a mistake. It was calculated to
harm him and the cause he represents."
Mr. Powderly made no mistake in endorsing the position emphasized by the
action of New York District Assembly 49. It was the proper and grand thing
for him to do.
The mistake was made when he subsequently endeavored to soften and gloss
over the matter in craven deference to the yell of the Southern white press
and the demands of white Southern Knights of Labor. And he pandered his honest convictions and his sense of consistency in vain, for no straddling he can
do in the future will appease the implacable indignation of the Southern dog
in the manger and its degraded ally the Southern press.
Mr. Powderly, "be sure you are right and then go ahead," and keep going
ahead.

New York *Freeman, October 30, 1886.*

35. IMPORTANCE OF THE RICHMOND CONVENTION

Undoubtedly the most important subject which this meeting at Richmond has brought prominently before the attention of the nation, is the economic condition of the colored laborers of the South and the bearings of their conditions upon wages and labor throughout the country. If the Knights of Labor can lend a strong hand to lift the colored brother from his industrial degradation, they will be performing a most patriotic and valuable service.

Minneapolis Tribune reprinted in *Public Opinion, October 30, 1886,* p. 42.

36. A FOOTNOTE ON FRANK J. FERRELL

Chief Engineer at the New York Post Office

We present to our many readers in this issue of The Freeman the portrait of Frank J. Ferrell, chief engineer at the Federal building in New York city. The very fact that an Afro-American could receive an office of so much responsibility and honor in New York is an evidence of his worth and integrity. Mr. Ferrell has been before the public for a number of years as the ablest exponent of the race in Knights of Labor circles and it is known to many of the episode at Richmond, Va., a few years ago, when T. V. Powderly took such a decided stand for Mr. Ferrell. We have no elaborate sketch of him, but hope to have at an early date. We clip the following excerpt from the New York Record and Trade Reporter.

The recent appointment of Mr. Frank J. Ferrell, of this city, as Chief Engineer at the New York Post Office is one of the more recent selections from the ranks of faithful and competent men that was at one time identified with the United Labor Party in the Eleventh District. He has already received his commission from the proper authorities and has entered upon the discharge of his responsible duties. He fills the place lately made vacant by the removal of John Kearney, the former incumbent. Mr. Ferrell has a large circle of active personal friends and acquaintances that will be rejoiced at his good fortune of which he is undoubtedly every way deserving. He has for several years been quite influential in politics and his activity and efficiency in business affairs has received the endorsement of many of our leading and best known citizens irrespective of party affiliations.

Mr. Ferrell left the employ of V. B. Matthews estate where he has been filling the place of Chief engineer and master mechanic for the last eleven years.

The Freeman (Indianapolis), February 8, 1890.

V

SUPPRESSION OF THE BLACK KNIGHTS

SUPPRESSION OF THE BLACK KNIGHTS

To defeat the organizational efforts of Northern workers, employers used
the blacklist, the lockout, Pinkertons, "iron-clad" oaths, anti-labor laws,
intimidation, and discharge; Southern employers used all of these and added t
the arsenal sectional weapons of their own: vigilante terrorism, lynchings c
the threat of lynching, the militia, and blatant hysterical appeals to racism
A special fury was reserved for Negro Knights and the men who organized
them, forcing the Knights to work in secret. For example, Hiram F. Hoover,
a white organizer in South Carolina and Georgia, secretly recruited Negroes
into the Co-Operative Workers of America. Its purposes centered around bette
wages and conditions, along with civil and political reforms. The organizati
held its meetings between midnight and daylight to avoid detection, but white
opponents constantly harassed known members. Hoover's experiences graphicall
revealed what treatment organizers of black farm workers might expect to receive. May 1886 was an eventful month for Hoover. In Milledgeville, Georgi
his life was threatened if he refused to leave town. From there he went to
Warrenton, Georgia, where he ignored a similar ultimatum. As Hoover met wit
about 300 blacks in a local church, masked men delivered several shotgun blas
through the window. Near death, the stricken leader was taken to Augusta on
May 20, where physicians removed 150 pieces of buckshot from his face. Hoove
lost the vision in one eye and thereafter his face was a massive scar. En
route to Augusta, he was nearly lynched, but the mob spared him because of hi
condition. After he recovered Hoover moved to New York and returned to obscurity. Documents 1-6 reflect the hostility encountered by union organizers
in South Carolina.
The greatest strike of the decade in which Negro workers were involved,
however, occurred in the sugar districts of Louisiana in November 1887. The
had been several strikes for higher pay in the past, but invariably they were
smashed by the state militia. In 1886, the Knights began to organize black
and white sugar workers, and in November, 1,000 mostly black laborers went or
strike demanding a fifty percent raise which would bring their wage to 75¢ pe
day. In retaliation owners formed the Sugar Planters' Association, drove the
workers from their cabins, and crushed the strike with scabs. But this was
only a rehearsal for the main event. With the average male earning about $13
per month, which he received in tickets redeemable only at the company store,
another stoppage seemed inevitable.
In October 1887, District Assembly 194, representing the sugarmen of fou
parishes, demanded that the planters pay $1.25 per day rendered weekly in leg
tender. When the planters summarily rejected these demands, 9,000 Negroes ar
1,000 other sugar workers walked off the plantations. Immediately the land-
owners called on Governor McEnery to send in the militia. Enraged by the sig
of black and white workers acting in concert, and thus violating the color
line which McEnery declared "God Almighty has himself drawn," the governor
readily complied. When fifty to 100 Negroes refused to disperse, the militia
opened fire, killing four strikers and wounding five others. Throughout the
parishes strikers were arrested or evicted from their cabins.
When the owners agreed to $1.00 per day, but refused to recognize the
Knights of Labor as their bargaining agent, the black strikers flatly rejecte
the offer. As the strike progressed, black leaders were arrested and impriso
while armed white military "clubs" attacked make-shift settlements of evicted
Negro families, reportedly killing twenty inhabitants in one incident. The
terrorism reached its height when a white mob removed two incarcerated blacks
from their jail cells and lynched them. In the face of such viciousness, and
the refusal of the Knights' national organization to become involved, the
strikers' spirits failed, and most of the workers returned to the fields unde
the old terms (Doc. 7-48).
To black workers the sugar strike of 1887 had been a terrible lesson.
Even though 9,000 Negroes had refused to accept a higher wage in order to sec
the recognition of their union, that same organization refused to support the
Once again a white union had demonstrated to black workers that labor solidar
ity was an ideal which did not include Negroes, and in the end this realizati
would help to undermine the Knights of Labor.

OPPOSITION TO THE KNIGHTS OF LABOR IN SOUTH CAROLINA

1. INDUSTRIAL SLAVERY IN THE SOUTH

The present problem in the South is purely industrial. The condition
of things produced by the results of the war is most natural in its every
phase. It should have been the easiest thing in the world to have foreseen
that upon the lines laid down by the moulders of the Reconstruction policy
chattel slavery would certainly be followed by industrial slavery, no less
galling and degrading to the enfranchised class and far more profitable to
the employers of labor. The fetters [of slavery] were no sooner removed
from the limbs of the black slave than the fetters of condition took their
place; so that today it is a painful and a notorious fact that the last condition of the common laborers of the South is, in many respects, much more
degrading and demoralizing than the first.

When the war came to a close the whites owned all the intelligence, all
the capital, all the land. They had been educated as the dominant class.
To rule and tyrannize was bone of their bone and flesh of their flesh. The
war had despoiled them of their property in slaves and largely of their accumulated capital; but it did not despoil them of their superiority of
education and their control of the land. The accumulated increment of labor
had been swept away, but the primal agencies of accumulation had been left
intact. As a consequence, recovery from the exhaustion and prostration of
the war was only a question of time. The black laborer must produce in
order to subsist, and this very necessity redounded to the enrichment of
those who controlled the agencies of production and who in consequence held
a lien upon the surplus earnings of the laborer. In the very effort put
forth by the laborer to subsist he enriched those who controlled those
agencies of production without which labor cannot reproduce.

In nearly every Southern State the white capitalists have managed to
have placed upon the statute books laws intended to protect and enrich the
employer of labor at the expense of the laborer. The legislatures of those
States have not needed any outside influence to pass such laws. They have
passed them to benefit largely those who composed such assemblies--men who had
vaulted into power over majorities contemplation of which staggers the mind.

No state in the South is more completely ruled by the unscrupulous arm
of usurpation than that of South Carolina, because no Southern State has such
a preponderating black majority. Since 1876, when the treachery and cupidity
of the managers of the Republican party gave the State Government over to
the Hamptons and the Butlers, the whole end and aim of the white rulers have
been to make voiceless the black vote of the State and to chain the black
toilers to the car of the capitalists and land owners.

When it became known that the Knights of Labor were going to organize
the black laborers of the South the most serious apprehensions were aroused
throughout that section. The most decided step taken by any Southern State
Legislature to counteract the possible effect of the influence of the Knights
of Labor on the colored laborers of the South has just been taken by the
Senate of South Carolina in the passage of the following law:

"It shall be deemed a conspiracy and shall be a misdemeanor for any
persons united, organized, associated, or banded together to interfere by
threats, force or in any other way with any contract between any employer or
employee, whether such contract be verbal or in writing, or to permit any
person for them or in their name or on behalf of such union, association,
organization, or band to interfere with an employer or employee, whether the
contract between them be verbal or in writing, for wages or for any other
consideration, to prevent the execution of such contract; and each and every
one convicted of the offence shall be punished by imprisonment for not less
than six months, or fined not less than $200, or both fined and imprisoned,

in the discretion of the court. Each one of such contracts interfered with
as above prescribed shall constitute a separate and distinct offence."

Perhaps there stands today in no statute book a law more explicit as
to the inhibition aimed at and more elastic for the purposes of injustice
and cruelty. The law virtually reduces the laborers of South Carolina to the
condition of slaves. The contract need not exist anywhere except in the
imagination of the employer. The mere fact that a man is laboring for
another will be construed as being as binding as a written contract. We
know so well how Southern laws are operated that we see in the wording of
this law the possibility of the most cruel and widespread injustice.

The Charleston *News and Courier* opposes the passage of this law, and
justly says it would be regarded as a firebrand. The committee to which the
measure was referred in the lower branch of the Legislature has already
reported adversely upon it. It will hardly receive further consideration at
the present session of the Legislature.

Speaking on this subject a writer in the December *North American Review*
says:

"New York labor must either give to Southern labor the protection of a
free ballot and fair count, or be prepared to compete with a servitude more
complete than is known in England, Germany, or France. A labor party that
tries to toss this issue into the ash-barrel will go there itself."

In the book *Black and White,* published by the writer hereof in 1885,
the following bearing on the labor question was declared on page 4 of the
preface:

"The labor elements of the whole United States should sympathize with
the same elements in the South, and in some favorable contingency effect
some unity of organization and action which shall subserve the common interest of the common class."

Again, on page 242:

"When the issue is properly joined, the rich, be they black or be they
white, will be found upon the same side; and the poor, be they black or be
they white, will be found upon the same side. Necessity knows no law and
discriminates in favor of no race.

The issue is already properly joined. The time is now when the laboring classes all over the country must take up this question of Southern
labor and the methods by which it is defrauded, pauperized and tyrannized
over before they can hope to accomplish the ends they have in view. The
colored people of the South are gradually, as a class, sinking deeper and
deeper into the cesspool of industrial slavery, and selfishness and greed
are hedging themselves about by statutory enactments of the most unjust and
iron-clad nature. What the end will be no man can safely say, but it is a
comparatively easy matter to predict that the pathway thereto will be honey-
combed with fraud, cruelty, and bloodshed. Capitalists and land owners, in
all times and all countries, from the Helots of Sparta to the Irish tenantry
of today, have been unscrupulous and cruel, yielding no inch to the sentiments of justice or humanity. The capitalists and landowners of the South
of today will be found to be as stubborn and unjust as the ante-bellum
slave-holders. What they yield of justice and fair play will be at the
command of organized and irresistible power; and none but knows just what
this means in the last resort.

New York *Freeman, November 23, 1886.*

2. FIGHTING THE KNIGHTS

THE FARMERS OF SOUTH CAROLINA TAKE PROMPT ACTION

COLUMBIA, S.C., Dec. 17.--The action of some white men in this State who are organizers of the Knights of Labor has caused much bitter feeling against the order among the farmers. Some of the State papers are denouncing in the strongest terms the proposed organization of the negroes in the rural districts. At this date of depression and agricultural poverty it is considered by many as criminal to array the colored people against their white employers. Mr. W. P. Russell, State Organizer of the Knights of Labor, in answering newspaper comments is bitter. He says:

"In your ignorance you may think that mechanics and laborers are not American citizens and that the laborers in the rural districts of South Carolina are to be used as the lazy, intolerant men in these districts choose to dictate; that they are not freemen and shall work for what pay you may choose to allow them for the small time at work upon the 'backbone,' and when that bone is gone beg for bread the rest of the year."

Some papers advise the farmers to "spot" all white men like Russell if they try to organize negro Knights of Labor and to run them from the neighborhood. They advised that the Legislature should appropriate money for the maintenance of the militia, as well-equipped soldiers would be needed if this organization goes on. This the Legislature has done. To further protect the farmers against the organization of the colored people living on their plantations the Senate has passed the following bill by a large majority, and House will doubtless make it a law.

"It shall be deemed a conspiracy and shall be a misdemeanor for any persons united, organized, associated, or banded together to interfere by threats, force, or in any other way with any contract between any employer or employe, whether such contract be verbal or in writing, or to permit any person for them or in their name, or on behalf of such union, association, organization, or band to interfere with any employer or employe, whether contract be verbal or in writing for wages, or for any other consideration, to prevent the execution of such contracts, and each and every one convicted of such offense shall be punished by imprisonment for not less than six months or fined not less than $200, or both fined and imprisoned. Each one of such contracts interfered with as above prescribed shall constitute a separate and distinct offense herein."

The possibility of a strike at cotton picking time, when the whole crop of the State would be lost if not gathered, was the principal argument used, together with the declaration that if a strike occurred among the negroes much more blood would be spilled than last Summer in Chicago and St. Louis.

New York Times, December 18, 1886.

3. "MUCH BITTER FEELING"

Columbia, South Carolina: The efforts of some of the organizers of the Knights of Labor in this State to enroll the colored people in the order has caused much bitter feeling against the order by the farmers. Some papers advised the farmers to "spot" all white men like "Russell" endeavoring to organize colored Knights of Labor, and drive them from the neighborhood. These journals have advised that "the Legislature should appropriate money for the maintenance of the militia, as well-equipped soldiers may be needed if this organization goes on." This the Legislature has done and to further protect the farmers against the organization of the colored people living on their plantations, the Senate passed by a large majority, and the House will doubtless make it a law, a bill making it a conspiracy, punishable by fine and imprisonment, to interfere between employer and employee in any contract, whether written or verbal. The possibility of a strike at cotton picking time when the whole crop of the State would be lost if not properly gathered, was the principal argument used, together with a declaration that if a strike occurred among the colored people, much more blood would be spilled than last summer at Chicago and St. Louis.

Charleston, South Carolina: The bill now before the Legislature to
prevent the organization of colored laborers in the agricultural sections
in Knights of Labor is causing a great commotion among the leaders of the
colored people of this State. Rev. J. Wooford White, one of the most intelligent colored preachers of the State has issued an address in which he
says that this bill has for its aim the grinding down and driving to the
wall of the Negro laborers. In closing his address, Mr. White says: "From
the point of equity considering the circumstances surrounding all laborers,
the Negro is the most excusable in forming organizations of a legal kind to
better his condition. Do the white people imagine that by threats they can
keep away the Negro's agents or organizers and in this way by force keep
them in this State or prevent them from being organized for mutual protection! If so, they reckon without their host. The great drawback to the
Negroes lies in the fact of their being too easily satisfied. The Shylocks
of this State today are the farmers who want the crops made and gathered
without paying a reasonable price for labor. They can reduce wages to the
lowest point, and if they are asked for justice it is refused, and when the
Negroes organize for mutual protection this is to be pronounced illegal and
who dares to resist is to be incarcerated in prison. . . ."

The Cleveland Gazette, December 25, 1886.

4.   THE TROUBLE IN THE SOUTH

The importance of the intelligent organization of the colored workingmen of the south has for some time been recognized by all wide-awake labor
leaders, and by them the action of the General Assembly at Richmond, giving
an impetus to this move, was hailed with joy.
The *Labor Record,* of Louisville, Ky., says:

"The colored laborers can and do exist on an amount that would not pay
for a single meal for a northern white labor. The colored man lives with
his family in a hovel but little better than the quarters of the slaves prior
to the war, and upon food practically the same as was issued to the slaves.
The result of this is that already the cotton mills of the south are fixing
the prices at which the mills of Massachusetts, New York, and Rhode Island,
must sell their products. Injury to one of the meanest laborers in the
United States is an injury to all. Organize, organize, and still organize!
Every laborer, black or white, man or woman, in the United States, should be
a member of some trade or labor union. Thus, and thus only, can we protect
each other and protect ourselves. It is in the interest of all laborers
that the price paid for labor should be a good price; whether the labor be
skilled or unskilled, of the plow, the loom, the forge, or the shop. The
price should be all that the work is worth, due consideration being given to
the different cost of living as far as may be uniform."

This work of southern organization has now met a rebuff by the slave-
drivers of South Carolina. Local papers advise that labor organizers be
driven out of the state of South Carolina. A paper that thirty years ago
said:

"We can assure the Bostonians, one and all who have embarked in the nefarious scheme of abolishing slavery at the south, that lashes will not hereafter be spared. Let them send out their men to Louisiana; they will never
return, but they shall expiate the crime of interfering with our domestic
institutions by being burned at the stake."

This same paper is now advising the people to burn Knights of Labor
organizers at the stake. In the legislature of South Carolina, the senate
has passed the following bill which will possibly be passed by the lower
house:

"It shall be deemed a conspiracy and shall be a misdemeanor for any persons united, organized, associated, or banded together, to interfere by threats

force, or in any other way with any contract between any employer or employe, whether such contract be verbal or in writing, for wages or for any
other consideration, to prevent the execution of such contract, and each
and every one convicted of this offense shall be punished by imprisonment for
not less than six months or fined not less than $200, or both fine and im-
prisonment. Each one of such contracts interfered with, as above prescribed,
shall constitute a separate and distinct offense herein."

The militia is being increased and the papers are demanding that negroes
known to have joined the Knights shall be taken out and shot without trial.
The possibility of a strike at cotton-picking time, when the whole crop of
the state would be lost if not promptly gathered, was the principal argument
used, together with the declaration that if the strike occurred among the
negroes much more blood would be spilled than last summer in Chicago and St.
Louis. Meanwhile the organization of the workingmen of the south is being
rapidly pushed, and as in pre-slavery days the more "nigger-catching" laws
were passed the more negroes escaped, so now the more opposition from the
slave-drivers the more the slaves become convinced of the necessity of
organization; as well try to crowd the eagle back into the egg, as to prevent the man who has tasted of liberty from becoming free.

Knights of Labor, December 23, 1886.

5. HOOVER'S NEGRO DUPES

A Reign of Terror in Laurens County, South Carolina

Charleston, S.C., June 21. Last winter H. F. Hoover, a white man, went
through the upper part of this State organizing lodges of the "Co-operative
Workers of America" among the negroes. He did his best to stir up bad blood
against the whites, and succeeded in forming several lodges. As soon as his
mission was known Hoover was told to move on. He went to Georgia, and
several weeks ago was mobbed near Milledgeville for exciting the negroes to
incendiarism. Hoover has not been back here since, but the seed that he
sowed is beginning to sprout. For the past two weeks a reign of terror has
existed in Youngs Township, Laurens County. As the story goes Hoover's
dupes have been holding midnight meetings with armed sentinels at the doors
of their council chambers, and with pickets on post. Their plan of operation
was to seize the land, kill the men, reduce the boys to slavery, and keep all
the young white women for their wives. It is said that they have only been
waiting for the signal to begin their bloody work. So serious was the situation thought to be, that a cavalry company was organized in the threatened
section and active steps taken so as to be ready for any emergency. The
matter was laid before Gov. Richardson and application was made to Adjt. Gen.
Bonham for arms and ammunition for the purpose of protecting the community.
Gov. Richardson dispatched an aide to the scene of the threatened disturbances and he has prepared his report.
The correspondent of the *News and Courier* telegraphs today:
"There is no doubt that some of the negroes are organized; that they
often hold meetings between midnight and daylight with the greatest precautions at secrecy, sentinels being stationed at convenient distances from the
rendezvous. The various threats that have been so widely circulated cannot
be traced authoritatively to the organization. There will be no outbreak
unless the negro leaders shall act rashly as the whites preserve great caution. The organizations are known as "Co-operative Workers of America," and
are the offspring of the Hoover influence, and many believe they are for
the purpose of extorting money from the ignorant negroes. It costs each
member $1.55 cents to take all the degrees, and $1.50 of that amount is forwarded to Hickory, N.C. Several packages of money have been sent from
Simpsonville, Spring County, and Woodruff, Spartanburg County, to Hickory,
N.C. The objects of the Hoover lodges are to elevate and dignify labor; to
secure to the laborer a just share of the products of his toil; to instruct

him in a knowledge of his rights and his wrongs and his duty to his country
and to his fellow man, and to use all rational means to better his social,
moral, and financial condition. They demand that the abrogation of laws
that do not bear equally upon capital and labor; the enactment of laws to
compel corporations to pay their employes weekly in lawful money; that the
poll tax be repealed and that a free co-operative school system be established. They demand of Congress that the public lands, the heritage of the
people, be reserved for actual settlers, etc.; that a graduated income tax
be levied so that the greater enactment of a graduated forfeiture tax to
be levied on the estates of the rich at their death; that United States
Senators be elected by the people; that the Government establish and maintain a free ballot in every State of the Union, and that the hours of labor
be reduced.

They also declare that they "are opposed to war and consider strikes as
dangerous to society, hurtful to the participants, and contrary to the interest of good government." They promise co-operation with the Knights of Labor
and all similar organizations. It is not expected that there will be any
violent outbreak among the Laurens negroes, and if there should be it is
believed that the people can be protected without any general call to arms.

New York Times, June 22, 1887.

6. FREE SPEECH IN THE SOUTH

We have maintained that free speech is not permitted in the South. We
have maintained that there is one law in the South for the white man, another
for the colored man. During the past week the newspapers have been full of
a so-called "conspiracy" of colored men in Laurens County, South Carolina,
under the inspiration of Knights of Labor, to demand $1.00 and $1.50 for a
day's labor, and if this be denied to kill the white men and old women, take
the young ones as wives, confiscate the land and make the white children work
for them. How preposterous the whole thing sounds to anyone who knows the
real situation of affairs in South Carolina and the general peaceable disposition of colored men!

And, yet, on information furnished by a "private" citizen the Governor
of South Carolina began to put the military machinery of the State in a
posture of war, sent special messengers to Laurens County, and others showed
exasperating symptoms of being all torn up over this tempest in a teapot!

Not long since five colored men were lynched by white ruffians at York,
but the Governor of South Carolina was stone blind to the fact. As Governor
he did not feel called upon to take any action. He was satisfied that the
county authorities would take care of the matter--even to the extent of
shielding, if necessary, the criminals. But a "private" citizen can manufacture a manifest lie and move the Governor to put in motion the military
power of the State to interfere with the secret meeting together of two or
more colored men for purposes obviously unknown to the "private" citizen!
The Governor of South Carolina should brace up, or else he should be braced
out. He is not the right man in the right place. He sees too much difference
in a white face and a black one.

Mr. Henry George says in his paper, the New York *Standard,* commenting
upon this episode: [28]

"It is not many years since the society saviors in certain quarters of
the South entered upon a murderous raid against the blacks for the purpose
of reducing them to political subjection. They were so successful that even
to this day the colored race, which is largely in the majority in the State
of South Carolina, is completely dominated there by the active and vigilant
society saviors of the white race. And now a new enterprise, also murderous
in character, appears to have been inaugurated in some parts of the South
for the purpose of reducing the blacks, who constitute the great body of
workers there, to a state of industrial subjection. The old spirit of
chattel slavery is revived in a new form, but with all its inhuman concomitan

Some weeks ago a man named Hoover was shot in Georgia by a mob. The information we get through the press respecting this murder is very meager. Details of society saving anarchy are not gathered by news distributers with the avidity that characterizes those enterprising individuals when some one in a workingmen's mass meeting, which has been lawlessly dispersed by the police, kills one of the lawless policemen. But the best inference that can be drawn from the associated press dispatches is that Hoover was an organizer of the Knights of Labor engaged in discussing labor questions before an audience of workingmen, which was, naturally enough in Georgia, largely composed of Negroes. For this offense against society he was summarily murdered by saviors of society.

And now we learn that the Governor of South Carolina is organizing troops to break up assemblies of the Knights of Labor in that State. The pretense is that these assemblies are arming themselves to murder white men and ravish white women. That pretense is well understood. It is as absurd as it is stale. It is the manufactured excuse for murdering black men.

The true inwardness of this malicious intimidation of the Negroes under legal forms leaks out in one of the dispatches in a statement to the effect that when the white men have been killed and the white women ravished by the colored Knights of Labor, the colored Knights intend to take possession of the land that belongs to their intended victims. This throws a flood of light on the situation in South Carolina. The fact is, evidently, that the black Knights of Labor are learning, like their white brothers at the North, that the land belongs to all the people--to the worker as well as to the idler, to the black as well as to the white. That they propose to recover their natural right to the land on which they were born and out of which they must live in the same peaceable manner that is proposed by the Knights of Labor everywhere, is clear enough; but they must be accused of contemplated violence as an excuse for using violence against them. Gentlemen of South Carolina--you of the lily hand and azure blood--your tricks are understood by the workingmen of the North and East and West, and if you persist in them--if you persist in thus outraging popular government--you will soon hear with an emphasis that you cannot mistake, from the mudsills whom you despise but a little less than the blacks only on account of the color of their skin.

Your past outrages on the colored race were denounced by the Republican party from partisan motives alone. That party cared no more for the Southern Negro, except as an election perquisite, than it cared for the Northern mechanic. It might raise the Negro outrage cry now if by doing so it could get the Negro vote or then its voting power in the North. But hopeless of such a result it is silent, and it will remain silent about these outrages upon the workingmen of the South. There is a power here, however, that South Carolina society saviors will hear from, and that speedily, if it once comes to be fully understood that free speech and political or industrial organization and agitation are to be prohibited in South Carolina. That power is the spirit of true democracy that now animates the workers of all sections."

It is not necessary that we add anything to what Mr. George has said. It may be that organized rascality in the South may have a tougher time coping with organized labor and Afro-American Leagues in the future than it had with the Republican party of the past. We shall see.

New York Freeman, July 9, 1887.

AN OVERVIEW OF THE KNIGHTS' 1887 SUGAR STRIKE IN LOUISIANA

7. THE KNIGHTS STRIKE SUGAR

Only one labor union ever struck the "Sugar Bowl," as the sugar district

of southern Louisiana is called. That was the Knights of Labor; organization
of the sugar workers began in 1887.

Conditions favored the Knights. It was semi-secret, with passwords and
grips, and was difficult for the planters to judge its strength. They knew
it was there, but that was about all.

At that time there were few large plantations; no giant central refineries owned by corporations dominated the district. The sugar-houses, as
the factories were then called, were rather small affairs strung along the
bayous every two miles or so. Their three-roller crushers seldom exceeded
four feet in length, and a few were still turned by horse power.

Most of the planters were their own general managers, and the majority
were convinced that their "hands," as they called the workers, were too loyal
to ever listen to labor agitators. The situation faced by the Knights was
entirely different from that a union would meet today if it faced the corporation owned refineries and plantations with headquarters in distant cities,
and with workers more or less alien to the field laborers.

Following the Civil War wages had fallen steadily until those of husky
men ranged from 50 to 60 cents for a day lasting from the first grey of dawn
to pitch dark. In addition to these meagre wages the hands were allowed
"rations," which consisted of five pounds of salt shoulder meat and a peck
of cornmeal a week.

Girl and women hoe-hands received from 25 to 40 cents for the long
work-day; blacksmiths and carpenters from $1 to $2, and engineers $2.00.
Overseers (they furnished their own horses and equipment) received from $50
to $75 a month, while from $100 to $150 monthly was considered princely for
the chief overseers and managers. Most of the latter were sons or nephews
of the planters, or if not that then neighbors or more distant kinsmen.

White or Negro, wages and salaries were the same for the same work. As
a whole the district lived on a scant subsistence basis; times were hard,
terribly so, with dispirited farmers and one-hoss not many more jumps ahead
of the wolf than were the workers. Such was the general condition, and it
tended to grow worse as the sugar industry continued depressed. Was it small
wonder that the hands listened eagerly to the message of the Knights when
their organizers appeared in the Sugar Bowl whispering, "In union there is
strength. Organize or starve!"

Discontent was rampant, not only in the Sugar Bowl but throughout the
nation. In addition one of the largest crops on record was in the fields,
with the planters hoping to get enough profit from it "to get from under"
the banks and the New Orleans commission merchants.

Considering this it is not surprising that the sugar workers flocked en
masse into the Knights of Labor when its organizers came into the district
preaching higher wages, better conditions, and "United States money" instead
of "commissary paste-board."

Other factors--in fact the entire set-up in the district, political as
well as economic--aided the Knights in their organization work and propa-
ganda. The great majority of the workers were Negroes, but during the grinding many white men worked both in the sugar-houses and the fields. White
and colored, the men worked side by side--on my uncle's plantation under a
Negro chief-overseer. (White women never worked on the plantations).

And as they worked, the Knights organized them--all, regardless of creed
or color, into one "Assembly," as the sub-divisions were called.

Not only did the K. of L. organize both white and colored together, but
they brought both Confederate and Union Veterans into their fold. We cannot
have the races together today, many assert, without danger of riot or bloodshed. Yet it would seem that what the Knights did in the '80's, barely 15
years after the Civil War, the Unions today might do.

Such was the situation, and such the movement. It was a mass upheaval
against unbearable conditions, as were many other struggles dominated by the
Knights in other sections. It was a movement "of the workers, by the workers,
for the workers!"

No single strong man dominated the struggle in the Sugar District, though
there were many, both colored and white, who deserved to be called heroes.
Jim Brown, a "griffe," (about one-quarter white), was said to have been the
"brains of the Union" in my Parish ("county" in other states) of Terrebonne.

The Knights worked quietly, but long before any demands were made on them the planters were aware of impending trouble. However they comforted themselves with the idea that their hitherto docile hands and hirelings ("hands," permanent workers; "hirelings," those who came in to make the grindings) would not listen to anarchistic agitators, but instead would continue to trust and depend on their "best friends," the planters.

They (the planters) were disillusioned October 24, 1887. That date the New Orleans *Daily Picayune* published a dispatch from Thibedeaux, parish seat of Lafourche Parish, in which Local Assembly 10,499 notified the "Sugar Planters of the Parish of Lafourche" of the action taken by District Assembly 194 of the Knights of Labor, at its district meeting at Morgan City October 19, 1887, in regard to "a scale of wages" it had "unanimously agreed upon for this grinding season, which comprises the parishes of Lafourche, Terrebonne, St. Mary, Iberia and St. Martin."

Local Assembly 10,499 listed the new wages demanded, as follows: "Said rate of wages is $1.25 per day without board, or $1 and board, and 60 cents for watch; watch money to be paid every week, and day money every two weeks: no paste-board to be accepted in compensation for labor."

In conclusion the Assembly requested; "That should this demand be considered exorbitant by the sugar planters, that we ask them to submit such information with reason therewith to this (executive) board not later than Saturday, October 29, inst., or appoint a special committee to confer with this board on said date."

It was a very personal matter to the writer and his family. When the strike was called my uncle "Ami" had died, and our uncle Rodney Woods was in charge of the home place. He gave in to the demands, not because he wished to, but because he had no other option. He would have lost the crop and everything else, including the place, if he had not done so.

Immediately all neighboring planters denounced him as "disloyal to his class," declaring he should be willing to lose everything in defense of his class interests. But he could not see it.

More and more strikers and planters in the five parishes affected began to feel the economic pressure and privation as the strike dragged on. Something had to be done about it, and that "something" began to be evident.

The planters had scorned all petitions or communications (except in one instance) from strikers or Assembly, answering through action at mass meetings.

October 30 the *Picayune* published a dispatch from Thibedeaux emanating from such a meeting, which in part was as follows:

"The following resolutions by a large meeting of the influential people of this parish were adopted today. The meeting was presided over by Judge Taylor Beattie, (a planter, and Republican District judge) and Hon. E. A. Sullivan (Democrat) acting as secretary." The resolutions began: "Our people are quiet, but determined to enforce the law and preserve quiet." Then came a series of resolves in which the Knights of Labor are referred to as a secret organization, conspirital in form, charged with threatening violence and breaking contracts for work at established wages of 75 cents a day with, or $1 per day without board, and 50 cents per watch." ("Watch" was six hours night work.) Such demands could not and would not be considered because "the present depressed condition of the sugar interest of our state forces us to decline to accede to any demand for an increase of wages." To prevent this "We hereby pledge ourselves, one and all, to meet this trouble as good men and law-abiding citizens, and to that end we hereby tender ourselves to the sheriff and other constituted authorities (who) may call upon us in event of necessity for our services;" and

"Resolved, That if any laborers are discharged from the plantations upon which they are now at work, or if any such discharge themselves by refusing to work, we pledge ourselves to give them no employment; that all people discharged for refusal to work be required to leave the plantation within 24 hours, and on refusal to obey that the powers of the law be invoked to assist the owners of property in enjoyment of their rights of property."

(Here it may be stated that the sugar planters, unlike the lumber barons, did not charge employes rent for cabins.)

The closing resolution called upon the governor "to furnish militia to enforce the law, and prevent bloodshed and violence," and he promptly complied. In no instance reported did the unionmen resist orders to leave when eviction notice was served on them by the "constituted authorities."

BLOOD IS SHED

The state militia was called out but had little to do, taking no open or direct part in the suppression of the strike. In Thibodaux, foolishly, the unionists had the delusion that Governor McEnery, one of the most negrophobe of white supremacists, had sent the militia to protect strikers! They were soon disillusioned; the strike was crushed by one of the most ruthless massacres that ever occurred in the United States!

Planters' associations in the other parishes made substantially like replies to the demands, but one, that of St. Mary's addressing its reply directly to the Knights.

The St. Mary Local Assembly, No. 6205, was reported to have passed resolutions protesting the strike, but the District Assembly, No. 194, promptly repudiated the action, declaring that it had been suspended "for non-payment of dues."

On November 2 the *Picayune* had a choice collection of headlines: "The Strike Inaugurated:" "Negro Laborers Quit Work, and are Ordered off the Plantations:" "Planters Determined to Stand Their Ground:" "Beanham's Battery on Duty at Thibodaux--a Possibility of Trouble Today."

The next day it reported 16,000 "intimated" to have answered the strike call in this district; rumors of "trouble expected" and of violence done and threatened as evictions begin, but "peace and quiet maintained as a general thing." "Lafourche . . . the center of the disturbed community," the disturbance being work "of white mischief-makers." Then follows a description of the strikers pouring into Thibodaux or camping on the roadsides with their evicted families:

"They are leaving (the plantations) as fast as they can, and are being brought into town where they are all dumped together. Every vacant room in town tonight is filled with families of penniless and ragged negroes. All day a long stream of black humanity poured in, . . . bringing all their earthly possessions, which never amounted to more than a frontyard full of babies, dogs and ragged bedclothing. . . . On many of the plantations old gray-headed negroes who had been born and lived continually upon them, left today."

There were few evictions in Terrebonne, and little or no violence, but in Lafourche so many were made homeless that 10,000 were reported herded in and around Thibodaux, numbering normally 2,000.

The *Picayune* continued: "J. H. R. Foote and D. Mounier (evidently 'white mischief-makers') are two of the prime movers of this uncalled-for strike. . . . There is some talk of their being ordered to leave town, and it is possible they may get their walking papers before this trouble is over with." So ran headlines and reports day after day, until armed violence finally erupted, the last "riot" breaking in Thibodaux the last week of November.

The strike dragged on, the planters being able to secure but few strikebreakers. One day the report would be that the plantations were working full blast, the next that more and more workers were joining the strike or being evicted. Often these contradictory reports appeared in the same dispatch; and always "trouble expected," yet little occurred until about the last week of the walkout. Four strikebreakers in Terrebonne were variously reported as first wounded and next killed.

This is referred to time and again in the report as indicating a reign of lawlessness on the part of the unionmen; it was at a backwoods settlement called Tigerville. As the "grapevine" brought it, all that happened was that a small gang of canecutters was sprinkled with birdshot.

Here and there reports of sabotage, of roughhousing strike-breakers, and firing on "loyal workingmen" made the front pages, often in the same dispatches saying that unionmen were quietly obeying the law, with little or no resistance to eviction.

The two worst "riots" were in the last weeks of the strike, at Patterson and Thibodaux, that at Thibodaux being by far the worst.

This report of the trouble at Patterson is from the *Times Democrat,* of New Orleans. "Pattersville, La., Nov. 5: . . . An encounter took place to-day between a sheriff's posse, commanded by Hon. Don Caffery, the Attakapas Rangers, under Capt. Cade, and a crowd of negro strikers. Several of the strikers were apprehended and others were ordered to disperse. They re-sisted, and an engagement ensued, in which several of the negroes were killed."

The next day the same paper's account (briefed) said; "Strikers were ordered to disperse; refused; fired upon by posse; four killed, one severely wounded, two boys hit." Singularly, all killed were leaders of the K. of L. Don Caffery, a prominent planter and politician of St. Mary's, (later U.S. senator) denied commanding the posse, saying that it was Col. E. M. Dubroca, another planter. This was verified.[29]

Col. Dubroca withdrew with part of the posse, and Caffery, on his own statement, assumed command, and rounded up "rioters."

The *Times-Democrat* also reported (on the 5th) that "a few planters have resumed work" at old wages, but that "the strikers have insisted upon their demands for increased pay, which the planters are utterly unable to meet; evictions have become a necessary consequence. They were accomplished peaceably and there was no resistance to the proper authorities. The *Pica-yune* had reported to the same effect, and added "No outbreak of any con-sequence since the ambuscade at Tigerville. Troops ready, but not required."

Om the same report it was stated that all trouble was due to "futile work of local anarchists," which term lumped all unionists, socialists, and sympathizers with the strike.

Militia officers steadily denied that any of the troops had fired on the strikers. The "grapevine" account was that 20 strikers had been be-sieged in a building, and refusing to surrender were fired upon, and all killed. Press reports stated that they had assembled in front of a negro saloon, and were fired upon when they refused to disperse. Subsequent re-ports all tended to confirm the "grapevine," and not the press accounts.

THIBODEAUX'S GORY DEBACLE

Headlines from the *Times-Democrat,* November 24 th:-- "Riot at Thibodeaux:" "Pickets Guarding Town Attacked by Negroes:" "Two White Men Seriously Injured--Fire Returned by an Armed Guard and Citi-zens:" "Six Negroes Killed Outright, and Four Dying of Wounds!" The text stated the fighting began at dawn, 5 A.M. Wednesday; but a day later the same paper reported in contradictory terms: "Monday night some unknown persons went to Franklin's coffee-house where there were some negroes playing cards. The negroes made an attack upon the whites, when firing was commenced, resulting in the shooting and killing of two negroes, with one painfully wounded."

This account bears out the grapevine report we received that the shooting began at six o'clock in the evening, and not at dawn. We lived 25 miles below Thibodeaux, and my uncle, noting an uneasy stir among the men, called "Uncle" George Jones, fireman of the kettles, and asked what the trouble was. (This was about 9 P.M.)

"News has come," said Uncle George, "that a terrible riot has broken out in Thibodeaux. The shooting began about six o'clock, and is still going on." Reports the next day confirmed the statement.

It will never be known how many were killed and wounded in this massacre; at the time the number of killed and wounded was estimated at between 500 and 600, including a few women, accidently mistaken for men. All night long the shooting went on, excited planters and their allies losing all control of themselves. It was said that crack shots would take a man they believed a ringleader in the strike to the railroad tracks, place him ten paces ahead of them, give him a chance to "run for your life," and he would be riddled with bullets before he had gone two leaps!

New made graves were reported found in the woods around Thibodeaux for weeks afterwards. Two other uncles of mine lived two miles south of Thibo-deaux, and the following morning they found a dead man in the road near their yard. The heavy casualties given by grapevine are utterly at variance with the press accounts, but the writer has talked with many men at or near the scene, and never met one who questioned its (the grapevine's) accuracy.

In fact, many who took part in the massacre boasted of "putting the black bastards and white anarchists in their place."

So ended, in blood and terror, the first attempt to organize and strike the Sugar Bowl.

(Note: Other than the grapevine, all statements here are from two New Orleans papers, the *Picayune* and the *Times-Democrat*, since merged, and now the *Times-Picayune*.

HIGHLIGHTS, AFTERMATH, AND POLITICS

The bitterness between the embattled forces was intense. The planters had been certain that their childlike and hitherto submissive Negroes would not turn against "Ol' Massa," nor listen to anarchistic outside agitators. Nevertheless, declaring "We will never submit to anyone dictating our business," they prepared for the struggle. When it came the Planters' Association in all parishes was ready and determined to crush the Knights, cost what it might.

At the time the entire country was in turmoil. Miners, railroad workers and many others were striking and being violently resisted, both by employers and government. The "Chicago Anarchists," the first martyrs to the eight-hour day, had been convicted and hanged. The press in Louisiana, as else-where, was filled with pitiless gloating over the execution, and thus reacted not only against the sugar strikers, but the entire labor movement. This was the setting of the strike. It was not strange that violence occurred in the Sugar Bowl, or that the Planters' Associations were more culpable than were the Knights of Labor.

The worst terror was in Lafourche Parish, mainly in and around the parish-seat, Thibodeaux. Judge Taylor Beattie, elected as a Republican, ruthlessly led the forces of "law and order," showing no mercy to strikers, white or colored.

Sanctuary or protection under law was denied those interdicted. The *Picayune* reported that Sol Williams, "a loud-mouthed agitator and leader of the strikers, came to town, sought the sheriff, and wished to surrender. The sheriff told him he could not protect him as there were no charges against him and moreover the jail was not strong enough to protect him. Williams left, swam Bayou Lafourche, and took to the swamps on the other side. It is not probable that he will ever return to Thibodeaux.

Again: "At nine o'clock tonight it was learned by the authorities that an attack was contemplated on the jail in which the Cox brothers, two of the leading strikers, were confined for protection. The two were freed, and made their escape over Bayou Lafourche. The object of the attack was to get possession of the two black men to lynch them."

And then this: "Enoch Adams, also a promoter of the disturbance, who is at large, will be sought and if found will suffer the same penalty."

Day by day came the news of strikers firing on strike-breakers, but dur-ing the whole period only one white man, a picket in Thibodeaux, was reported as seriously wounded. All dead were colored and unionmen though many whites were active members of the Knights.

Far more were killed and wounded than given in press reports. I talked with many who took part in the riots at Thibodeaux, and all had no hesitancy about killing "niggers." In fact they were inclined to boast about it; they had played a part in "teaching the niggers and agitators a lesson they would never forget."

Though the strike had been lost, in 1888 field wages were raised to 75 cents per day for men, though rations were cut. . . .

The defeat of the Knights was utter and complete. Since the debacle of the Knights in 1887 no other labor organization has attempted to unionize the Sugar Bowl. Today (1945) the workers on plantations and in the refineries are still very low priced labor.

Covington Hall, "Labor Struggles in the Deep South," unpublished manuscript, 3 [?] Howard Tilton Library, Tulane University.

8. A PLANTER'S VIEW: EXCERPTS FROM THE WILLIAM PORCHER MILES DIARY

Monday, January 25, 1886

Cld. foggy - Cl. To store with Mr. B. for mail.
Wrote Betsy (in rep.) No. 3.
   Mr. Turcuit of Ar. writes that all his neighbors are paying 75 cts. &
he is losing his hands. Mr. B. wrote him to stick to 65 for the present.
He telephoned to Capt. Murray to stand by him. Murray replies that he fears
they cannot get hands for 65. It seems all planters in St. J. on both sides
of river are paying 75.
   O. G. commenced ploughing for Corn. Cl. also - in afternoon.
Walked on Levee in aft.

Friday, January 29, 1886

Cl - cld - cld. pleasant. Talked with hands at St. J. ab't wages.
Told them there was neither rhyme nor reason for raising wages (from 65 cts
last yr's rate - to 75 ct) & tried to explain to them that at present very
cheap prices of meat, flour &c (lower than for years) & which art's we
furnish them *at cost* - 65 cts. goes further than 80 cts. did a year or two
ago. But made no impression on them. Then talked with hands of F. & B. Ar.
to the same effect & with no better success. Every other planter in the
neighborhood is paying 75 cts. Hence we are in a very tight place. We lose
all of our best hands & will not be able to get *them* back of course, as long
as they can get 75 cts. from others. Those that we may get at 65 cts. will
be the refuse - trifling hands, who will work badly & grudgingly & will
doubtless - most of them - have to [be] sent off in consequence. But Mr.
Beirne seems determined not to pay 75 cts.

Friday, February 5, 1886

Cl - cold - del. 26° - 44°. To N.H. & As. with Sally on 10:30 A.M. boat &
ret'd on 4 P.M. boat.
   N. H. Topping st. with 25 two mule plgs. Commenced planting on 2nd.
Planted about 10 A. Has from Corn Boat 4000 bu. As. Topping st. with 10 four
mule plgs. As Scraping with 8 hoes. As. planted 5 A. on the 2nd. Has from
Corn Boat 4000 bu.
   Surprised on my return to hear from Mr. B. that he had determined to
raise wages on all his places from 56 to 75 cts. Emissaries from Lawless at
Southwood have been drawing away our hands by paying the higher wages than
65 & offering Corn patches besides. We are told Corn patches are allowed
hands at the Ben Tureaud place, Mr. Cofield, the McCall's &c. This is fully
equivalent to 10 cts. additional.

Monday, February 8, 1886

Cl - del - To Riv. Ploughing for Corn & opening furrows & preparing to plant
Cane this afternoon. To Don. Commenced planting Cane (10 hands) Cl. Ploughing for Corn & hauling Corn from boat. To have 5500 bu.
   Managers from As. & N. H. come to say that hands refuse to work - although wages have been raised to 75 cts - unless they continue to be paid
every fortnight - instead of from time to time, whenever a hand has "made
20 dys," as is the custom here. Mr. B. agrees to their terms.
   To Con. in aft. with Mr. B. Topping st. & planting Cane. Con. to have
4000 bu. of Corn. To haul it tomorrow. To O. G. Planting Cane.

Wednesday, July 14, 1886

Cl - 90°. Went to don'ville to meet Gen'l Brent by request.
   The Negroes at Mount Houmas & Southwood are having secret drilling at
night & some apprehension has been felt in consequence. Managers have not
been able to find out what is in the wind. A Major Ramsey in N. O. said to
be at the bottom of it. Radicals organizing for political campaign, no doubt.

Tuesday, November 15, 1887

Fog - cl - del - 46° - 77°. To Lower Places by Miss. V.R.R. with
Hamilton. On arrival there got a dispatch from Jno. Tucker asking me to
come up as the hands on N. H. & As. had all struck. Went to Don'ville on
10:20 A.M. train & drove to N. H. Assembled hands & made them a speech in
which I tried to convince them of the unreasonableness & unfairness of their
demand for $1.25 a day & .50 cts. a watch, & told them we would not increase
the pay agreed upon at the beginning of grinding--viz. $1. a day & .50 cts.
a watch. Called to see Mr. Richard McCall on whose place hands had also
struck. He & Henry McCall & Godchaux & Lemman all bind themselves not to
yield to the demand for increased wages. Ret'd home on 3 P.M. Ferry boat.
Hamilton ret'd from St. J. on 6-i/2 P.M. train.

Wednesday, November 16, 1887

Fog - cl - del - 47°. To Cl. Grinding. All right. Mr. Jim Tucker
thinks there is no danger of a strike on these places - as do Mr. Cochrane -
Booth & Brand - from conversations they have had with negroes.

Thursday, November 17, 1887

Fog - Cl - Cld - R. at n't. To Riv. All right. Bagasse fair -
To Don. All right. Bagasse first rate. To Cl. All right. Bagasse
tolerable. Mr. Branch from Don'ville reports strike over at N. H. & As. &
all hands at work today. The great majority of the hands were opposed to
it, & were forced into it by a few. These latter we will "spot" & get rid
of as soon as convenient.
    Wrote Mr. B. announcing the strike & its termination & what I had done
in the matter. No. 24. Wrote Nancy (in rep.) No. 25.
    Mr. Garnett of Demerara came with a letter of introduction from Mr.
Slack of Washington. He is a very large Sugar Planter in Demerara & is much
interested in "diffusion"--& will go to Gov. Warmoth's to see the experiments
instituted by the U.S. Gov't there. Took him to O. G. & Con. & Cl. in afternoon. On the estate upon which he resides they make 11,000,000 lbs. of Sugar
& have a Vacuum Pan of the capacity of 100,000 lbs. They use fertilizers
freely. They weigh every lg. of Coal that they use & utilize all exhaust
steam. Yet they make little or no money. Their profits last year were only
$15,000 or 3,000.

The William Porcher Miles Diary, Vol. 21, typed copy from manuscript, Souther
Historical Collection, University of North Carolina Library, Chapel Hill,
North Carolina.

9. CONFLICT IN THE LOUISIANA SUGAR FIELDS

The Knights and the Laborers

    BERWICK, La., Oct. 28.--Editor Picayune: In the T.D. of the 27th an
article appears headed: "Strike of Sugar Laborers," and purporting to be an
interview with a planter from the Teche. The article in some respects is
misleading, in that it says no price for work was requested when the present
rate was adopted by the Sugar Planters' Association.
    Please to insert in your paper the two inclosed communications, which
will testify as to whether the Knights of Labor made any attempt to amicably
arrange scale of wages prior to the planters' meeting whereat they fixed the
wages.   B. W. SCOTT
    Communication sent to the St. Mary Branch of the Sugar Planters' Asso-
ciation, Aug. 22, 1887:

    To the St. Mary Branch of the Sugar Planters' Association: Gentlemen--

The executive board of District Assembly No. 194 would be pleased at
any time or place prior to the grinding season to meet with a committee appointed by your association to make some amicable arrangement of a question
in which both planters and laborers are equally interested.

The probability of the coming grinding being the most prosperous of any
experienced for several years by this parish, and any misunderstanding between
employer and employe at such a time would be of incalculable injury to the
prosperity of planters and laborers and the public of the parish in general,
therefore this board in behalf of the labor acknowledging its actions, would
earnestly request that your association appoint a committee of ten with equal
powers as this board to meet as aforesaid.

The executive board of District Assembly 194, K. of L., consists of ten
members, and any arrangements or obligations entered into by said board will
be sustained by four-fifths of the labor in the parish. Most fraternally
submitted,
                                            B. W. SCOTT, Secretary.

Answer from Planters' Association:

FRANKLIN, La., Sept. 2.--Mr. B. W. Scott:
Dear Sir--As secretary of this association I have no reply to make to your
communication of Aug. 22. As a matter of courtesy and politeness, however,
I write to say that your letter was read and discussed in executive session
and by a unanimous vote of the members present it was laid on the table.
     I am very respectfully yours,
                                            JOHN A. O'NEILL

New Orleans Daily Picayune, October 29, 1887.

10. SUGAR LABOR

The Demand of the Negroes for Higher Wages

An Official Communication--A Healthy Opposition to Extreme Measures

The Planters of Terrebonne Refuse to Submit to the Exactions

A General Strike on Tuesday Probable

LAFOURCHE

A prominent lawyer of this city, who is largely interested in planting
in Lafourche, has returned from a visit to his place in that parish, and
reports everything quiet and prosperous. Concerning the recent labor troubles in that section of country the gentleman says that it is impossible for
the negroes to succeed in a strike for the reason that they are dependent on
the planters for their living.

While in Lafourche parish the gentleman was shown a circular letter,
copies of which had been forwarded to all the planters of the parish. The
circular reads as follows:

THIBODEAUX, La., Oct. 24.--To the Sugar Planters, Parish of Lafourche,
La.: Gentlemen--Whereas, District Assembly 194 of Knights of Labor of North
America at their district meeting, held Oct. 19, 1887, at Morgan City, La.,
unanimously agreed upon a scale of wages for this grinding season for its
jurisdiction, which comprises the parishes of Lafourche, Terrebonne, St.
Mary, Iberia and St. Martin:

And whereas, said rate of wages is $1.25 per day without board or $1
and board and 60 cents for watch, board or no board; watch money to be paid
every week and day money every two weeks; no pasteboard to be accepted in compensation for labor;

Therefore, it is resolved by this joint local executive board, representing the Knights of Labor of the parish of Lafourche, That the sugar
planters of said parish are hereby petitioned in behalf of the common laborers

to pay their laborers at the times specified the said rates of hire, and
that it commence from date of agreement.

It is further resolved, That should this demand be considered exorbitant
by the sugar planters, that we ask them to submit such information with
reason therewith to this board not later than Saturday, Oct. 29 inst., or
appoint a special committee to confer with this board on said date.

Respectfully submitted:

J. H. Bailey, president joint local
executive board, K. of L., Joseph A. Clairville, vice president; Gabriel
Edward, secretary. Members: J. R. H. Foot, D. Monnier and J. Dixon delegates to Thibodeaux local Assembly, Thibodeaux, La. J. M. Ricard, 0. Rousseau, Geo. Cox and Jacob Turner, delegates of Excelsior, La., Thibodeaux, La.
Henry Franklin, Nathan Cambridge, Washington Whitby, Gustave Antoine, delegates of Longneville, La. Lockport, Charles August, Lenzy Ingram, Jessie
Ingram and Frank Coleman, delegates of Morning Glory, La., Harangville, La.

A true copy: GABRIEL EDWARD,

Secretary

TERREBONNE

In Terrebonne parish matters were conducted on a somewhat different
plan. The negroes would congregate on the plantations and appoint committees of three, one member of which could read and write, and the committee would notify the planters substantially of the points contained in the
above circular.

The planters, on their side, paid no attention to the circulars and
messages; leaving it optional with the negroes to work or not. On many
places the negroes struck and the plantation continued its operations short-
handed, and it was not long before the negroes returned to work.

Action of the Planters at Houma.

SCHRIEVER, La., Oct. 29.--[Special]--At the request of a committee purporting to represent the laborers of Terrebonne, the sugar planters met in
Houma to try and adjust the trouble. They agreed to make the concession of
60 cents a watch, instead of 50 cents as now paid, day wages of $1 to remain
as before.

They replied that after a careful deliberation of the proposition advanced by the committee they had decided not to depart from the scale of
wages as submitted by the district executive board, which was attached, until
they were authorized to do so by proper authority.

The scale of wages submitted throughout the parishes of Lafourche, Terrebonne, St. Mary, Iberia and St. Martin to take effect at 6 a.m. Tuesday, Nov.
1, 1887, are: $1.25 per day without board, or $1 per day with board, and 60
cents a watch, money to be paid once a week, and day money once every two
weeks, no pasteboard to be accepted as compensation for labor.

It was unanimously resolved to refuse their demand, therefore a strike
is expected on Tuesday, and it is feared trouble will grow out of it.

ST. MARY

FRANKLIN, La., Oct. 29.--[Special]--The rumors which have been rife for
some days that a strike was to be inaugurated by the Knights of Labor in this
and adjacent parishes, are now known to be well founded, and that a general
strike has been ordered for Monday by the executive board of the district,
comprising the parishes of St. Mary, Iberia, St. Martin, Terrebonne and Lafourche.

In view of this action the Sugar Planters Association of this parish has
called a meeting for tomorrow, Sunday, at noon, of all planters of the parish,
to discuss the situation and personally to adopt a course of procedure if a
strike takes place.

It is known that the order of the executive board is opposed by some of
the assemblies to this vicinity, on the ground that such a course is uncalled
for, unjust, ruinous to the planter and to the laborer and demoralizing in its
effect upon both.

A meeting of the assembly of knights of labor of this place it is learned
is also to be held tomorrow, and it is said that an earnest protest will be
made against the strike by the assembly.

NEW IBERIA

NEW IBERIA, La., Oct. 29--[Special]--The news of the labor troubles in Terrebonne parish, as announced in yesterday's papers, was the source of some surprise, and has been the cause of considerable comment. No feeling, however, is manifested in any quarter. Our city has been filled with country people all day, and our tradesmen have been doing a land-office business.

District court adjourned sine die, today, after a busy session. Judge Mouton takes the bench at St. Martinsville on Monday next.

VERMILION

ABBEVILLE, La., Oct. 29.--[Special].--The sugar planters are all or nearly at work rolling and boiling, and all agree in the statement to the effect that the yield is excellent--surprisingly so; no one expected such a large yield.

New Orleans Daily Picayune, October 30, 1887.

11. SUGAR LABOR

THE PLANTERS UNITED AND DETERMINED NOT TO YIELD

Knights of Labor Who Protest Against the Order to Strike

Laborers to Supply the Vacancies

LAFOURCHE

A Mass Meeting of Planters Refuse to Accede to the Demands for an Increase of Wages

THIBODEAUX, La., Oct. 30.--[Special.]--The following resolutions were adopted by a large meeting of influential people of this parish today. The meeting was presided over by Judge Taylor Beattie and Hon. E. A. Sullivan acting as secretary. Our people are quiet, but determined to enforce the law and preserve quiet:

Whereas, a committee of people claiming to represent a secret organization, have called upon the planters of Lafourche to accede to certain demands as to the rate of wages and the manner of payment and whereas, it is publicly asserted that unless these demands are acceded to not only will the members of the secret order refuse to work in accordance with their contracts, but any other people willing to work will be prevented by force and arms by the secret organization from so doing, and the property of the good people of this parish withheld by force from the possession and enjoyment of the same:

Resolved, That we hereby pledge ourselves, one and all, to meet this trouble as good men and law-abiding citizens, and that to that end we hereby tender ourselves to the sheriff and other constituted authorities to obey any and all calls upon us to assist in carrying out the law, and that our names be at once furnished to the sheriff that he may call upon us in the event of necessity for our services.

Resolved, That the present depressed condition of the sugar interest of our state forces us to decline to accede to any demand for an increase of wages, and that we hereby bind ourselves, one and all, to refuse to in any way recognize the body of men who have represented themselves as a committee appointed by a secret organization.

Resolved, That all law-abiding citizens, irrespective of position or occupation, or of race or color, are called upon to join us in carrying out the plain behests of the written law of the land.

Resolved, That if any laborers are discharged from the plantation upon which they are now at work, or if any such discharge themselves by refusing to work, we pledge ourselves to give them no employment; that all people discharged for refusal to work be required to leave the plantation within twenty-four hours, and on refusal to obey that the powers of the law be involved to assist the owners of property in the enjoyment of their rights of property.

Resolved, That it is the sense of this meeting that an emergency has arisen which requires that the governor be called upon to furnish militia to aid in enforcing the law, and to prevent bloodshed and violence, and that the sheriff of the parish be requested to call upon the governor for the aid of some recognized military organization.

ST. MARY

The Local Assembly of Knights of Labor Protest Against a Strike—The Sugar Planters Agree to Resist the Strike

FRANKLIN, La., Oct. 30.--[Special].--The strike ordered for Nov. 1 by authority of the Knights of Labor is the all engrossing topic of conversation, and a large number of planters and others interested in the sugar culture are in town for the purpose of attending the meeting called by the Sugar Planters' Association and also a large number of the Knights of Labor opposed to the order.

A meeting of the Assembly No. 6295 was held this morning and the following protest was adopted by a unanimous vote after a full and free discussion of the situation:

Whereas, a general strike to take effect Nov. 1 has been ordered by the district executive board of District Assembly No. 194, which if carried into effect will operate most disastrously for the interest of both planters and laborers; and, whereas, this action is uncalled for at this time and is equally unjust to the laborer and to the planter in view of the present cordial relations existing between them, and no legal complaints having been made to warrant or justify such steps: therefore, be it

Resolved, That we, the members of Local Assembly No. 6295, Knights of Labor, enter this our earnest protest against the action of the district executive board in ordering a strike at this time, deeming such a course unwise and impolitic, and as tending to the utter destruction of the present crop of sugar, the impoverishment of the laborer and the ruin of the planting interest, and its enforcement will bring only misery and distress upon all laboring classes of the community. We further protest against the order for the reason that this assembly was practically unrepresented in the district board when the order was issued, and we cannot but believe that a majority of the actual laborers composing the membership of the local assemblies of this district will coincide with this assembly in protesting against the order as wholly unjustifiable and uncalled for under the present circumstance

This protest and resolutions were reported by a committee of knights composed of Dr. M. V. Richard, A. G. Frere, B. F. Harris, F. C. Douglas and Fred Marsh.

The planters' meeting assembled at 12 o'clock, Dr. H. J. Sanders presiding and John A. O'Neill secretary.

After a full and exhaustive discussion of the situation a committee consisting of Hon. Don Caffery, L. S. Clarke, J. M. Burguires, O. D. Berwick and T. J. Foster reported the following resolutions, which were unanimously adopted:

Resolved, 1. That the planters and employers of labor in the parish of St. Mary will not recognize nor pay heed or respect to the demands of any organization in respect to the wages they should pay their laborers nor the method of payment.

Second--That the planters of St. Mary hereby solemnly bind themselves each to the other to stand together in this emergency, and under no circumstances to increase the wages they are now paying.

Third--That the strikers on any plantation shall be ordered to leave, and such steps will be taken as will ensure the execution of the order.

Fourth--That in the event of a strike, and other labor is to be introduced, such price will be paid as the planters will among themselves agree to, and a uniformity of price is to be arranged at a period as near as possible.

Fifth--That we each and everyone hereby bind ourselves in case of a strike to carefully note the strikers, a list of whom is to be sent to every other planter, and under no circumstances to employ a striker.

Sixth--That we deny the right of any laborer to violate his contract and to demand more wages than those stipulated to be paid him for sugar-making, and we counsel him to faithfully abide by his contracts for wages which insure a good living while doubtfully yielding the planter a profit, and that after the planters have employed laborers during the whole culti-vation of the crop, it is flagrantly unjust and illegal to demand extortion-ate wages to harvest the same.

A SUPPLY OF LABORERS

In Town Enroute from Vicksburg

Mr. F. M. Welch of Jeanerette, La., arrived in the city last night from Vicksburg, bringing a carload of negroes to take the places of the striking cutters on the sugar farms in the Attakapas country. Mr. Welch was seen by a Picayune reporter, and stated that he found plenty of idle labor in Missis-sippi, and that there would be no trouble in supplying the places of the striking knights with labor from the Mississippi valley country. He goes over to Jeanerette this morning. In speaking of the strike he said that trouble would be had if the strikers interfered with labor. "The planters were determined," he said, "that there should be no interference with men who did not belong to the Knights of Labor lodge, and if any concessions are to be made it must come from the labor side.

New Orleans Daily Picayune, October 31, 1887.

12. SUGAR LABOR

THE STRIKE INAUGURATED

The Negro Laborers Quit Work and Ordered Off the Plantations

The Planters Determined to Stand Their Ground

Beanham's Battery on Duty at Thibodaux--A Possibility of Trouble Today

THIBODAUX, La., Nov. 1.--[Special].--Battery B of the Louisiana Field Artillery, with Capt. W. H. Beanham commanding.

IN OBEDIENCE TO ORDERS

No. 3 from General Glynn, commanding the National Guard of Louisiana, arrived here today at 4 o'clock with the following roster:

Captain W. H. Beanham, First Lieutenant H. B. Thompson, First Junior Lieutenant J. Reynolds, Second Lieutenant F. M. Ziegler, First Sergeant E. Uter, Sergeants M. D. McLaughlin, F. Danzereau, G. B. Hamilton, Corporals J. D. D'Hemecourt, W. Schriver and H. J. Cumpsten, and Privates T. L. Connell, M. Fenlihan, H. M. Nugent, C. J. Fenn, R. Smith, G. Stork, M. Levy, F. Keefe, J. G. Kimble, J. T. Skelly, G. Grandmann and J. Duenas. General Pierce, quartermaster general, accompanied the troops.

On the arrival here they were met by a company of citizens and about 2,000 negroes were on the platforms and around the depot to see what demon-strations they would first make.

Judge Beattie met the company at the depot and they were at once marched to the courthouse where the Clay Knobloch Guards were quartered. Tonight they were detailed to quarters and to guard the town from any insurrection of the negroes.

The town is full of excitement. Today was the day ordered for the strike and a general suspension of all hands on the sugar plantations of Lafourche and Terrebonne took place this morning.

The trouble between the planters and the laborers has been brewing for a month. The knights of Labor demanded more wages paid for all classes of labor than the planters were competent to pay. Their business would not justify the wages ordered by the lodge, and they were notified that no concessions would be made on their part.

Upon this notification the Knights of Labor met on the 24th of October and adopted the following resolutions:

To the Sugar Planters, parish of Lafourche, La., Gentlemen:

Whereas, District Assembly No. 194 of Knights of Labor of North America, at their district meeting held Oct. 19, 1887, at Morgan City, La., unanimously agreed upon a scale of wages for this grinding season for its jurisdiction, which comprises the parishes of Lafourche, Terrebonne, St. Mary, Iberia, and St. Martin; and whereas, said rate of wages is $1.25 per day without board or $1 and board, and 60 cents for watch, board or no board, watch money to be paid every week and day money every two weeks, no pasteboard to be accepted in compensation for labor; therefore it is

Resolved by this joint local executive board, representing the Knights of Labor of the parish of Lafourche, That the sugar planters of said parish are hereby petitioned in behalf of the common laborers to pay their laborers at the times specified the said rates of hire, and that it commence from date of agreement. It is further

Resolved, That should this demand be considered exorbitant by the sugar planters, we ask them to submit such information with reason therewith to this board not later than Saturday, Oct. 29th inst., or appoint a special committee to confer with this board on said date.

Respectfully submitted,
J. H. BAILEY,
President Joint Local Executive Board, K. of L.

JOSEPH A. CLAIRVILLE,
Vice President,
GABRIELL EDWARD,
Secretary.

Members:

J. R. H. Foot, D. Monnier, J. Dixon, Delegates of Thibodaux Local Assembly, Thibodaux, La.

J. M. Ricard, O. Rousseau, Geo. Cox, Jacob Turner, Delegates of Excelsior Local Assembly, Thibodaux, La.

Henry Franklin, Nathan Cambridge, Washington Whitley, Gustave Antoine, Delegates of Louqueville Local Assembly, Lockport.

Charles August, Lenzy Ingram, Jesse Ingram, Frank Coleman, Delegates of Morning Glory Local Assembly, Harrangville, La.

A true copy: GABRIEL EDWARD.

The planters paid no attention to this communication, and as today was the limit all of those belonging to this order went out on a strike.

It is intimated that over 10,000 laborers in this district quit work this morning.

On the E. J. Gay place, three miles from here, about two-thirds of the laborers quit this morning, but a sufficient force was gathered to go on with the cutting and grinding. Colonel Andrew Price, the manager, states that he will have no trouble in gathering a sufficient force by Thursday to resume all operations.

On Major C. Lazard's plantation there is no working at all. Judge Sullivan, a son-in-law of Major Lagarde, left for the plantation at Lockport today to see if he could gather a force to begin work.

It is reported on the street tonight that one of the managers of a plantation was badly beaten by the negro strikers today, and his recovery is doubtful. His name could not be ascertained.

On Trosclaire and Robishaux plantations 75 of the 100 hands stopped work this morning. They were all members of the Knights of Labor and threaten to oppose any demonstration made to oust them from their cabins. Trouble is anticipated there tomorrow.

On Judge E. D. White's place all the hands suspended labor this morning, and upon orders from the manager to leave the place they refused to do so. Charges of trespass were preferred against them and Sheriff Thibodaux and Deputy Frost went out to arrest them. Upon hearing of the sheriff's coming all of them skipped out except John Ballard and Phillip T. Dickson, who were

arrested and brought to jail. They were released on bail of $100 this
evening, their colored friends going on their bond.

The most vicious and unruly set of negroes are at the Allen plantation.
The leader of them said today that no power on earth could remove them unless they were moved as corpses. The time given them for departure expires
tomorrow morning, and if they are still there the militia will be called upon
to expel them.

One of the leaders of the strikers said today that the white people
had never met the negroes united before--that they had been heretofore disorganized when unjust demands had been made them by the whites; now he said
they defied all of the militia of the state; they were right, he thought, in
this movement, and every one of his 400 members would die before they would
concede one point to the planters. There is a meeting of the striking knights
going on in town tonight, but the object of it cannot be understood. A
great deal of whisky-drinking has been going on among them all day, and mad-
dened by drink and defeat, it is feared that they will attempt devilment
before daylight.

The Picayune reporter interviewed L. C. Aubert, master workman of white
Assembly No. 10499. He said that when they received the circular from the
district assembly his lodge met and voted unanimously against the strike. He
was called upon to advise and consult with the colored assembly as to what
course to pursue. They would listen to no suggestion of his and were bent
on a strike at all hazards. When he saw he was opposed and even censured for
his action he immediately resigned from the Knights of Labor lodge. He
thinks that evil-minded persons have instigated the strike.

Henry Cox, a prominent colored Knight of Labor man, was seen late tonight. He declares that the order has been to counsel peace and refrain from
amything that would bring about trouble; that is what he is saying to outsiders, but it is generally believed he is doing more incendiary work then
anyone else.

By tomorrow morning at 8 o'clock every one quartered on the plantations
who refuses to work will be ejected by the militia. Serious trouble is then
expected all over the country, as the negroes generally are stubborn and
disposed to stand their ground.

The planters held a meeting yesterday at the courthouse and adopted resolutions indorsing the governor's action in responding to their call for
troops. They declared that they would never yield to the unjust and exorbitant demands of the colored knights and pledged their aid to the sheriff to
quell all disturbances arising from the strike. Both sides seem determined
and manifestly there is an irreconcilable difference between them.

Battery C is quartered at Frost's Hotel, where they are being royally
treated by the citizens.

Quartermaster General Pierce, who accompanies the artillery, received
orders this evening to assume control of all state troops between Berwick's
Bay and New Orleans.

ST. MARY

Action of the Sugar Planters--They Will
Maintain Their Position at Every Risk

FRANKLIN, La., Oct. 30.--[Special]--The sugar planters and others interested in the plantations in Lafourche, Terrebonne, St. Mary, Iberia and
St. Martin parishes held a meeting today to discuss and take action on the
notices that have lately been served on planters in that section of country.
Dr. Henry J. Sanders presided, and Mr. J. A. O'Neill was the secretary. The
chairman urged all present to adhere to the scale of wages agreed to by the
Sugar Planters' Association which is $1 per day and 50 cents per watch of
6 hours at night.

Mr. Daniel Thompson submitted a notice which he had received on him and
other planters. "It reads: Scale of wages submitted throughout the parishes
of Lafourche, Terrebonne, St. Mary, Iberia and St. Martin, to take effect
at 6 a.m. Tuesday, Nov. 1, 1887--$1.25 per day without board, or $1 per day
with board, and 60 cents for watch; watch money to be paid once a week and
day money once every two weeks. No pasteboard to be accepted as compensation for labor."

Hon. Don Caffery, Mr. Murphy J. Foster and Mr. G. G. Walker addressed
the meeting on the subject. They all claimed that the planters had voluntarily adopted a rate of wages that was conceded to be fair and just to both
planter and laborer, and therefore the strike was not opportune.

A committee composed of Don Caffery, L. S. Clarke, J. M. Burguieres,
O. D. Berwick and T. J. Foster reported the following resolutions, which
were adopted:

Whereas, the laborers of the parish of St. Mary are entirely satisfied
with the price paid them for sugar-making wages and have not directly made
any demand for higher wages: and

Whereas, a large number of planters have been notified, through agents
or representatives of the Knights of Labor, that throughout the parishes of
Lafourche, Terrebonne, St. Mary, Iberia, and St. Martin the scale of wages
will be, on and after Tuesday, 6 a.m. Nov.1, 1887, $1.25 per day and 60 cents
per watch, without board; and $1 per day and 60 cents per watch with board;
and   Whereas, the price now paid to the laborers by the planters is as much
as the business will warrant; therefore, be it

First--Resolved, That the planters and employers of labor in the parish
of St. Mary will not recognize nor pay any heed or respect to the demands of
any organization in respect to the wages they should pay their laborers nor
the methods of their payment.

Second--That the planters of St. Mary hereby solemnly bind themselves
each to the other to stand together in this emergency, and under no circumstances to increase the wages they are now paying.

Third--That the strikers on any plantation shall be ordered to leave,
and such steps will be taken as will insure the execution of the order.

Fourth--That in the event of a strike and other labor is to be introduced, such price will be paid as the planters will, among themselves, agree
to, and a uniformity of price is to be arrived at, as near as possible.

Fifth--That we each and every one, hereby bind ourselves in case of a
strike to carefully note the strikers, a list of whom is to be sent to every
other planter, and under no circumstances to employ a striker.

Sixth--That we deny the right of any laborer to violate his contract,
and to demand more wages than those stipulated to be paid him for sugar-
making, and we counsel him to faithfully abide by contracts for wages which
insure him a good living, while doubtfully yielding the planter a profit,
and that after the planters have employed laborers during the whole cultivation of the crop, it is flagrantly unjust and illegal to demand extortion-
ate wages to harvest the same.

The following planters signed the resolutions: Dr. Henry J. Sanders,
chairman; A. J. Decuir, F. H. Williams, J. N. Pharr, Murphy J. Foster, for
self and as agent; Eugene Bodin, Caaries C. Palfrey, E. M. Dubroes, D. Caffer
Thomas J. Foster, J. D. Capren, E. Scannel, C. S. Palm, S. R. Gay, Boss &
Thompson, Joseph Bing, H. C. Rose, D. R. Calder, Daniel Thompson, for Calumet
plantation and also for Alice plantation; A. Short, R. Habert, Millard Bos-
worth, L. S. Clark & Bro., Rivers & Bidstrup, N. K. Todd, James C. Mahon, F.
Lagemann, J. M. Burguieres, B. F. Queen, W. W. Johnson, Marsh Bros., O. D.
Berwick, W. Schwann, W. P. Kemper, Mrs. E. D. Burguieres, per Viguerle;
Hubert Delhaye; J. B. Chaffe, for John Chaffe; Robert R. Cocke, for Lyon &
Cocke; W. H. Wills, T. Bellissein, Geo. W. Whitworth, G. G. Walker, John B.
Marsh, C. E. Gillis, for Andrew Price; C. P. Bennings, for Des Ligne and
Saule plantations.

The secretary was requested to send copies of the resolutions to Col.
J. H. Oglesby and John Henderson, Jr. of New Orleans, and to the Messrs.
Pecote of Indian Bend, in order to obtain the indorsement and co-operation
of these gentlemen.

On motion of Hon. D. Caffery, the secretary was appointed a committee
of one to provide that a dinner be given to the members of the St. Mary
branch of the Louisiana Sugar Planters' Association, on Dec. 30, 1887, on
which day the officers for the ensuing year will be elected.

The meeting adjourned sine die.

NO TROUBLE SO FAR

MORGAN CITY, La., Nov. 1--[Special]--No developments of importance regarding the labor question in this vicinity. Dr. Darrall and all planters

on Bayou Boeuf have ceased working. The laborers struck at 6 o'clock this
morning and are still out with no apparent probability of an early adjustment.
   One or two plantations between this place and Pattersonville are working
short-handed. There has been no trouble, and it is to be hoped there will
not be any in this place, and but few strange faces are seen on the streets.
   The militia company in our town have orders to hold themselves in readiness for active duty.

IBERIA

Two Companies of Soldiers on Duty

   NEW IBERIA, La., Nov. 1.--[Special]--A call was made for armed forces
by Messrs. Gay, Boss & Thompson, and Colonel Wills, large sugar planters
below here. In their telegram it was stated that laborers who were willing
to work were threatened by the strikers.
   Captain C. T. Cade, of the Attakapas Rangers, received orders to proceed at once with a necessary force to preserve order to Boss & Thompson's
plantation. He left here with a detachment of the Iberia Guards under
Lieutenant H. P. Gates and a detachment of the Attakapas Rangers, numbering
in all thirty-three men.
   Tonight your correspondent learns that orders have been received to
hold the rest of the two companies and the gun detachment in readiness for
a moment's call.

The Strike Inaugurated in the Lower Teche District

   PATTERSONVILLE, La., Nov. 1.--[By Associated Press.]--A general strike
among the sugar-making hands was inaugurated this morning on the lower Teche
in the district between Bartel's station and Morgan City. All places above
Grandwood are still at work, and all places below and including Grandwood
are either idle or working with a few white hands.
   The planters are to unite in resisting the demands of the strikers, and
they have no doubt whatever about the result.
   There is a feeling of intense bitterness throughout the district against
certain prominent leaders who have urged up the strike, and if the matter is
not promptly settled there is no estimating what the final result will be.

New Orleans Daily Picayune, November 2, 1887.

13. PROTECTION FROM RIOT AND VIOLENCE

   The situation in the sugar district has grown more serious in the last
few days. There was, at first, a disposition on the part of some of the
"reform" papers to think that Gov. McEnery had acted hastily in sending the
militia to St. Mary and Terrebonne to suppress, they pretended, a labor movement there.
   As the situation has become threatening there they have changed their
tune, and now that the telegraph brings news of four white men shot down while
peaceably working by negroes they are ready to acknowledge the wisdom of the
Governor in this matter.
   Gov. McEnery has had much experience of the negro character, and was,
therefore, able to appreciate the danger threatened by the condition of affairs
in the Teche country. His experience in North Louisiana had shown him how
dangerous the negro may become when excited, filled with whisky and incited to
deeds of violence by incendiary addresses. He saw this in the political campaign in North Louisiana, in which he was a participant; he saw there violence
of all kinds, outrages on defenseless women, incendiary fires, murder and
rapine, committed by drunken and frenzied negroes, and he determined that there
should be no chance of this in the sugar district, but that peace and order
should be preserved by the troops. There was no question of labor in this

matter. The militia were not ordered to Terrebonne and Lafourche to interfere in any manner with any labor trouble, but simply to prevent violence,
which was threatened, by bad and dangerous negroes left behind as a relic
of Radical days.

The laborers in the sugar district are peaceful and quiet if left to
themselves, and are averse to any deeds of violence, but there are a number
of negro politicians, left stranded high by the failure of the Republican
party, who can make a living only by stirring up trouble and inciting riot.
Gov. McEnery's experience of this class of people was too fresh for him to
hesitate as to the action he ought to take in this matter. He recognized
that promptness was necessary in order to prevent loss of life and property,
and he therefore had the troops ready for that turbulence which his experience had taught him was to be feared from idle and drunken negroes excited
by violent appeals to their passions.

Even the "reformers" admit now that the sending of troops to the Teche
and Lafourche was opportune and fortunate, and see that the militia were
not sent to shoot down people, but to prevent riot, plundering and bloodshed.

New Orleans Times-Democrat, November 3, 1887.

14.   LABOR TROUBLES

ENFORCED IDLENESS IN THE SOUTH LOUISIANA SUGAR FIELDS

THE STRIKERS VACATE THEIR CABINS

Four Laborers Shot From Ambush in Terrebonne

Peace and Quiet Maintained as a General Thing

LAFOURCHE

In the Center of the Disturbed Community--
The Work of White Mischief-Makers

THIBODAUX, Nov. 2.--[Special]--The situation among the strikers remains
unchanged. The sheriff has arrested twelve trespassers today. They offered
no resistance and willingly came to the courthouse where they readily gave
bond.

The negroes remain firm and are not disposed to yield. On all the plant
ations there is a practical suspension of all labor.

The negroes had a meeting last night, and it was understood that they
decided to remain firm. They sent a courier out at daylight this morning
telling all of the strikers to leave the places without resistance. They are
leaving as fast as they can, and are being brought into town where they are
all dumped together. Every vacant room in town tonight is filled with penniless and ragged negroes. All day long a stream of black humanity poured in,
some on foot and others in wagons, bringing all of their earthly possessions
which never amounted to more than a frontyard full of babies, dogs and
ragged bed-clothing.

Some of the planters extended the time until tomorrow morning for their
leaving. On many of the plantations old gray-headed negroes, who were born
and have lived continually upon them, left today.

J. R. H. Foote and D. Mounier are two of the prime movers of this uncall
for strike. Foote's reputation in this community is anything but good--a
common laborer, whose highest ambition and aspiration is to guzzle as much
beer as he possibly can stand--is the instigator of this entire trouble.
There has never been any trouble existing between planter and laborer before
this fellow Foote and Mounier came amongst them. There is some talk of their
being ordered to leave town, and it is possible they may get their walking
papers before this trouble is over with.

Their demands upon the planters are unjust and they might as well understand now that there are to be no concessions made on the part of the planters.

The negroes turned out of house and the most of them penniless will be in a starving condition before many days, then they will want work and in time their places will have been filled with imported labor.

Judge White arrived here this morning and left on the noon train for New Orleans. He states that he has about two-thirds of a force on his place and expects to send to Alabama and Mississippi for the balance of the laborers.

On the Allen place, the largest on Bayou Lafourche, the negroes are leaving. Some few refused to go, but warrants were issued for their arrest and all that could be found were captured.

All work on the Godschaux, Allen, Webb, Ridgefield, Gayoso and Lagarde places has been practically suspended. Captain Jno. R. Teeley states that all of his hands have struck.

There has been no disturbance within the immediate vicinity of Thibodaux.

At Tigerville, in Terrebonne parish four laborers were shot by the strikers. The particulars cannot be ascertained, and whether the wounds were fatal or not is not known.

W. S. Benedict wired Captain Beanham here today of the trouble and asked for militia assistance. The matter was referred to Brigadier General Price who ordered the New Iberia Guards to go to the scene. They arrived there this evening.

Mr. C. S. Matthews and Nicholas Foret from Lockport, in this parish arrived here today with a petition to the sheriff praying for protection from a turbulent and armed mob that menaced the planters of their section. Sheriff Thibodaux swore in a number of deputies tonight and they were at once sent down to the scene of trouble. They state that an unruly set of negroes threaten danger and the people of Lockport are much excited. The names of the trespassers were given to Judge Beattie who issued warrants for their arrest.

The manager of the Chatsworth plantation telegraphs that there are no hands working there, and some of them are resisting the authorities.

Landry Odeson and Naquin Emile are the names of the two white men who were arrested today. They gave bond. D. Mounier, who next to this fellow Foote, is stirring up more mischief among the negroes than any one else, was knocked down by Mr. B. A. Wormald. It was thought then that trouble would result, but nothing has been done about it.

A meeting of the planters is called for tomorrow at 1 o'clock, when the situation will be discussed. The town is well patrolled tonight, for there is no telling when trouble is to commence.

ST. MARTIN

Strike at the Oil Mill, but Not in the Sugar Fields

ST. MARTINSVILLE, La., Nov. 2.--[Special]--The laborers of the oil mills here, comprising eight or ten colored men, Knights of Labor, struck this morning. Their grievance was that they were dissatisfied with the two head press men, who are not knights. They called upon Mr. Rousseau, the proprietor of the works, and asked him to discharge the head press men or they would not work with them. Mr. Rousseau refused to discharge his press men and consequently they struck.

Their places in the oil works were immediately filled by white laborers, and the mills are running as usual, with the exception of the ginnery, which will probably be in operation tomorrow.

These laborers, although they are Knights of Labor, are not acting under order of the knights.

A committee called upon the sugar planters yesterday, and matters were arranged to the satisfaction of all, and no strike was ordered at sugar-houses in this parish.

ST. MARY

The Hands on Many Places Quit Work but No Outbreak as Yet

FRANKLIN, La., Nov. 2.--[Special]--Advices from the lower part of the parish are to the effect that all work has stopped on the plantation from Centreville to Berwick bay, a distance of twenty miles, with the exception of the plantation of Foos & Barnett, near Centreville.

All is quiet at present, the laborers making no demonstration but re-fusing to work unless their demands are complied with. The planters on these places have ordered these laborers to leave the premises by Thursday morning and give place to others.

From the upper portion of the parish it is learned that all are at work in full force with the exception of the Eustis plantation, on which all have resumed with the exception of twenty-five who were discharged. These sought work on other places, but were refused, but at least obtained employment on the Stirling plantation, owned by D. McCann of New Orleans.

In response to the telegraph published in the Picayune of today signed "Bud Scott, secretary, District Assembly 149, Knights of Labor," stating that Local Assembly 6295 was suspended on Oct. 24 for non-payment of dues. Fred C. Marsh, acting secretary of Assembly 6295, says that the dues were paid and the receipt therefore is now in the archives of the assembly.

No Trouble in the Lower End of the Parish, but There May be Today

MORGAN CITY, La., Nov. 2.--[Special]--There is nothing new regarding the strike. I hear that the sheriff went yesterday to evict laborers on the Buckner plantation in the upper end of the parish from this place to Centre-ville. The mills are quiet. Planters claim they will not yield to the de-mand, but the laborer is very quiet and has but little to say. There is some dissatisfaction among leading knights in this place and the same exists at Pattersonville. Developments are looked for Thursday, but no reports are current of anticipated trouble.

The weather is very pleasant and cane is becoming sweeter every day.

IBERIA

Moving the Troops to the Scene of Expected Trouble

NEW IBERIA, La., Nov. 2.--[Special]--The detachment from the Iberia Guards, under Captain H. P. Gates, returned today from the sugar plantations below here in this parish. They report all quiet, but work suspended or nearly so.

Large numbers of idle negroes are collected in all public places. Many of them are willing to work, but are intimidated by threats of the strikers.

The rangers, a cavalry company, under Captain C. T. Cade, will remain until order is restored.

The strikers are told to decide whether they will work or not; if not, they must vacate the plantation cabins and make room for those willing to work. Many are leaving.

Captain Dudley Avery, of the Iberia Guards, has received orders from General Parkerson to sent thirty men to Terrebonne at once. They are ready to leave, and will on the first train unless other orders are received.

By order of Captain Cade some twelve men of the Attakapas Rangers leave for Jeanerette, to take the place of the departing Guards.

The weather is moderate and very dry, no rain having fallen since the storm of two weeks ago.

New Orleans Daily Picayune, November 3, 1887.

15.   LABORERS SHOT DOWN

THE FIRST ACT OF VIOLENCE IN THE SUGAR STRIKE

A Crowd of White Laborers Fired Into by Colored Strikers and Several of Them Wounded--Troops Ordered to Houma

The Strikers Shoot Down Several Men in Terrebonne Parish

Special to The Times-Democrat

TIGERVILLE, Nov. 2.--News reached here this morning of great excitement prevailing on Lacassagne's Greenwood plantation, about seven miles from
this place, up Bayou Black. The strikers interfered with and intimidated
the new laborers brought there on yesterday. The strikers shot at them as
they went out to work. No one was killed, but several were hurt. All is
quiet at this time, the new men having left. No work is doing of consequence.
Troops were sent for, but have not as yet arrived.

Four Men Said to Have Been Killed
Special to The Times-Democrat

BATON ROUGE, Nov. 2.--A telegram was received at the Executive Department today from Mr. W. S. Benedict, at Tigerville, Terrebonne parish, stating
that the negro strikers had attacked the hands on a sugar plantation near
that place and driven them off the place, and also that they had killed four
men who had refused to leave the place. Orders for the proper protection of
life and property have been given.

Considerable Excitement In the City Over the Shooting of Four Men Near Tigerville.

Considerable excitement was occasioned here yesterday morning by a telegram stating that the strike in Terrebonne parish had resulted in the probably fatal shooting of four white men who had been shipped the day previous
from this city to the Lacassagne plantation to supply the places of hands
that had withdrawn from the fields. The telegram referred to, and which was
from Mr. Lacassagne, was sent in duplicate to Messrs. C. E. Black and W. S.
Benedict, and read as follows:
"Strikers shot four of my laborers this morning from an ambush. I have
telegraphed the Governor for troops. Please see that they get off at once.
Answer if they will come today."
It was also stated that further trouble was anticipated, and that considerable anxiety was being felt by the peaceably-inclined people in the
parish over the existing condition of things. Messrs. Black and Benedict,
immediately upon receipt of the above, made known its contents to Gens. Glynn
and Meyer and Col. Richardson, of the Washington Artillery, with a view of
having Capt. Beanham's battery sent to Tigerville, which is about eight miles
from Mr. Lacassagne's plantation. Gov. McEnery was telegraphed to at Shreveport in reference to the above, with the following result, as made known
through a dispatch to Mr. Charles S. Black, received last evening:

SHREVEPORT, La., Nov. 2, 1887

To Charles S. Black, Esq.:
I ordered troops to Tigerville early this morning. See Col. Faries for
information, and telegraph people at Tigerville.
S. D. McENERY, Governor

In connection with the above, Mr. Black stated that he had called at the
offices of Gens. Glynn and Meyer and notified them of the Governor's action.
He also visited that of Col. Faries but found his office closed. At any
rate the troops were ordered to Tigerville last evening, and will have arrived at their destination before these lines meet the reader's eye.
Mr. Benedict, who is largely interested in sugar planting in the vicinity
of Tigerville, has been sending hands in large numbers to Terrebonne parish
since the strike. He says he finds no difficulty in getting as many as he
wants, and especially is this the case if the necessary protection is guaranteed.
The following telegram was received yesterday forenoon by Mr. John T.
Moore, Jr., from Schriever, La.:

SHREVEPORT, La., Nov. 2, 1887

To John T. Moore, Esq.:
"All quiet. No one at work this morning, Mr. George Marshall, manager
of your plantation, has gone to Houma for the sheriff."
The opinion at the Sugar Exchange yesterday was that, while there might
possibly be some bloodshed, the present disturbances would soon blow over

and the crop would be taken from the fields without damage.

Gen. Beauregard returned to the city yesterday, and Col. Faries was in consultation with him during the greater portion of the day. The General read a long dispatch last evening from the Governor, who is at Shreveport, in which the latter told the former to use his discretion in handling troops.

Up to a late hour last night the troops of the Washington Artillery had not received orders to move although momentarily expecting them.

THE EFFECT ON THE LABOR MARKET

Mr. Albert H. Parker, who has for many years been engaged in securing labor for the plantations in neighboring parishes, was asked by a Times-Democrat reporter last evening what effect the present troubles have had upon the local labor market.

Mr. Parker stated that there has been no unusual demand for plantation laborers this season and that there are but few really good men to be had in this city for that kind of work. About sixty men, eighteen of whom were white, were sent out yesterday, but this is not unusual, as the sugar-grinding always necessitates the employment of extra help. Some orders have been given for men, contingent upon the continuance of the strike. Many really reliable men, who are out of employment and are willing to go on the plantations, were deterred yesterday by the report that the blacks had fired on white laborers near Tigerville, and are awaiting further reports. A number of men have recently returned from Camp Levee, reporting that owing to heavy rains they have been unable to work continuously, and have returned with the intention of seeking work on the plantations. There is a disposition among some of the negroes here to hold out for the wages demanded by the strikers. Almost any number of men can be had but they are of a very unreliable class, and probably would not work after their passage had been advanced.

Gen. Meyer received a telegram yesterday afternoon from Capt. W. H. Beanham, at Thibodaux, to the effect that one of the chief disturbers in that vicinity had been captured and jailed during the day.

Mr. J. W. Barnett, owner of the Shady Side plantation, on the Teche, was registered at the St. Charles Hotel last evening. He reports laborers as working harmoniously in his section. All appear satisfied, and there is no apprehension of a strike.

"The truth of the matter is, said Mr. Barnett, "seven-eighths of the laborers on sugar and other plantations, if not interfered with and ill-advised by outsiders, would work to the satisfaction of all concerned and be perfectly contented."

Detachment of Troops Ordered to Houma
Special to The Times-Democrat

JEANERETTE, Nov. 2.--The detachment of Iberia Guards which were here, under command of Lieut. H. P. Gates, were recalled today to New Iberia to join the company, which is ordered to Houma. The Attakapas Rangers will be reinforced tonight, and will continue here on duty under Capt. C. F. Cade.

The Knights of Labor held a meeting this evening and it is reported that they have decided to adhere to their original demands.

The strikers were given until tomorrow to leave the plantations of Lt. Gay and Capt. W. H. Wills, and if they fail to comply with the orders they will be ejected by force. It is not expected that much resistance will be encountered by the officers of the law.

Most of the strikers on the plantation of Boas & Thompson have resumed work.

Strikers Turbulent on a Lafourche Plantation
Special to The Times-Democrat

THIBODAUX, Nov. 2.--The situation in this parish is substantially the same as already reported. On some plantations all hands continued work right through the trouble, but these are the exceptions. In most cases either all or the majority of the laborers are on a strike, but in Lafourche parish no violence has been reported so far. In response to the summons to return to work or quit the place the strikers have as a rule adopted the latter alternative, either flocking into town, where many have arrived today, or making active preparations for a move.

Affidavits were, however, sworn out against some twenty men who refused to adopt either alternative. Twelve of these were arrested, two of
whom, Emile Naquin and Odessa Landry, are white. All the prisoners were
bailed.

It was reported this morning that more serious trouble had occurred
in Terrebonne, and that Capt. Avery's company, from New Iberia, had been
ordered to Houma in consequence. Laborers brought from New Orleans to fill
the places of strikers on the Greenwood plantation were, the report says,
fired upon while at work and two of them wounded.

The hands on the Raceland place of Leon Godchaux, who were at work
yesterday, struck today. This evening Mr. C. S. Matthews, with a deputa-
tion from the neighborhood of Raceland, arrived here, and reported that the
hands on a strike in that quarter are turbulent and threatening and asked
for protection. Judge Beattie directed the sheriff to leave for Raceland
with a posse tonight.

The Garling and twelve-pounder gun, with horses harnessed, stood all
day in front of the courthouse, ready to move at a moment's notice.

Gen. Pierce is the guest of Judge Taylor Beattie, Capt. Beanham's
company is conveniently located in comfortable quarters near the courthouse.
Both officers and men are highly pleased with the arrangements made for their
comfort.

Everything Quiet Around New Iberia

Special to The Times-Democrat.

NEW IBERIA, Nov. 2.--The detachment from the Iberia Guards, under Lieut.
H. Gates, which left here yesterday for plantations below, returned today.
Capt. Avery is in receipt of orders from Gen. Parkerson to send thirty men
at once to Terrebonne. The boys report all quiet in this parish below here,
and that the Rangers under Capt. Cade are equal to any possible emergency.
They also report large numbers of negroes idle. Many are willing to work,
but are intimidated by threats of the strikers. It is thought all will be
working in a day or two.

All Plantations Idle from Centreville to Berwick City

Special to The Times-Democrat.

FRANKLIN, Nov. 2.--Advices from the lower part of the parish are to the
effect that all work has stopped on plantations from Centreville to Berwick
Bay, a distance of twenty miles, with the exception of the plantation of
Foos & Barnett, near Centreville. All quiet at present, the laborers making
no demonstrations, but refusing to work unless their demands are complied
with. The planters on these places have ordered these laborers to leave
the premises by Thursday morning and give place to others.

From the upper portion of the parish it is learned that all are at work
in full force, with the exception of the Eustis plantation, on which all
have resumed with the exception of twenty-five who were discharged. These
sought work on other places, but were refused; but at last obtained employment on the Stirling plantation, owned by D. McCann, of New Orleans.

In response to the telegram published in THE TIMES-DEMOCRAT of today,
signed B. W. Scott, secretary District Assembly 194, K. of L., stating that
Local Assembly 6295 was suspended on Oct. 24 for non-payment of dues, Fred
C. Marsh, acting secretary of Assembly 6295, says that the dues were paid
and the receipt therefore is now in the archives of the assembly.

New Orleans Times-Democrat, November 3, 1887.

16. THE STRICKEN STRIKE

THE BACKBONE OF THE LABOR STRIKE BROKEN

The Negroes Rapidly Returning to Their Work

No Outbreak of Any Consequence Since the Ambuscade Near Tigerville

The Troops Ready but Not Required

THIBODAUX

The Futile Work of the Local Anarchists--The Planters Firm and the Negroes
Returning to Work

THIBODAUX, La., Nov. 3.--[Special]--The backbone of the strike is about
broken. The negroes, when they found the farmers determined, yielded, and
probably one-half of them have returned to work.

A number of mills that suspended operations yesterday blew their
whistles today, and enough hands responded to begin work. There has been
no trouble reported at all.

The negroes are to be complimented on their good behavior. They have
been advised by evil-minded persons but further than leaving their field
of labor no other damage has been done.

The presence of those anarchists, Mounier and Foote, can well be dispensed with from the usual quiet parish of Lafourche, and it is quite likely
they will go.

Twelve negroes have been arrested for trespass today, seven of them being brought in by the sheriff's posse, who went to Raceland this morning.
They will give bond.

The Opelousas military has been ordered to Lockport, but their presence
there will hardly be needed, for a majority of the negroes are returning
to work.

Battery B will likely remain over here until Saturday. The boys are
being handsomely treated by the citizens.

Pursuant to a call from the planters' committee, the planters met here
today and the following resolutions were passed:

Whereas, in spite of the fact that we have lost thousands of dollars
by the strike now prevailing, and in view of the fact that we may still lose
thousands by the same, we hereby reaffirm our determination to stand steadfastly and unyieldingly by the position we have taken, and not to accede to
the demands made upon us by a body of men who have presumed to dictate to
us how we shall manage our private and business affairs.

The planters have adjourned to meet tomorrow, and have resolved to hold
daily meetings until the troubles are settled.

The streets are quiet tonight and no trouble is apprehended. By Monday
it is expected all will be at work.

HOUMA

The Ambuscade--The Law Will Be Enforced

HOUMA, La., Nov. 3.--[Special]--Day before yesterday three men were shot on
Mr. Lacassagne's Greenwood plantation while they were at work by some of the
strikers. Warrants were yesterday issued by Judge Allen for eight persons
supposed to be the guilty parties, and the sheriff went down for them this
morning.

Judge Allen yesterday examined the parties from Captain Shaffer's plantation who were guilty of violence in taking possession of his sugar-house,
and they were all committed for trial before the district court.

Everything is now quiet in this parish. The strikers are evidently
weakening. The strike seems to be under the control of a few young men,
none of whom are laborers, who are ambitious of political preferment. The
planters are firm and will not yield an inch.

Captain Avery of New Iberia arrived here this morning at 11 o'clock
with his company. They are quartered at Durand's Hotel, and will assist the
sheriff of the parish in making arrests when needed.

Judge Allen is determined to uphold the supremacy of the law and all
violence will be suppressed and the guilty punished.

Sugar-houses are going in several parts of the parish, though some of the planters are shorthanded. It is thought that the strike will soon end; unless it does, there will be evictions by the wholesale.

NEW IBERIA

The Disposition of the Troops--Most of the Mills Running

NEW IBERIA, La., Nov. 3.--[Special]--The news of the shooting near Tigersville has been the leading topic here today.

The gun detachment of the Iberia Guards got off this evening under command of Captain E. A. Pharr. Captain Cade with a detachment of the Attakapas Rangers is still at Jeanerette.

This morning was the time fixed for the strikers to choose between returning to work and leaving the plantations. Some returned quietly to work while others left, bag and baggage.

The rangers will remain at Jeanerette a day or two longer, but to save expenses their horses will be sent home.

Every mill in the Fausse Pointe country is running full blast and making good headway. The laborers seem satisfied with a dollar per day and show no disposition to take part in the strike. West of this place in the interior news comes that all is working smoothly; there sugar hands are paid from 75 cents to a dollar per day.

JEANERETTE

Every Prospect of an Early Settlement

JEANERETTE, La., Nov. 3.--[Special]--During several days past talk has been rife about a strike by the hands on the sugar plantations through this parish and predictions of its unhappy results widely spread. The people were feverish on the subject for awhile, but today every indication points to an early settlement of the troubles, planters and workmen alike evincing a laudable desire to come to an amicable arrangement. On the point of such a pleasant settlement the colored women in large numbers trooped into town this evening to join the strikers and Knights of Labor, but it is hoped that their influence may not have any disturbing effect on the community.

Belligerent Strikers on the Dubroca Place Brought to Terms

SORREL, La., Nov. 3.--This morning at 6:00 o'clock the strikers were ordered by Colonel E. M. Dubroca's manager to go to work or leave the plantation and on refusing positively to comply with the orders the deputy sheriff was called in and began at once to eject them.

When they saw that matters were serious many of them wisely concluded to go to work and the others consented to move without any further trouble.

Threats having been made by the strikers, trouble was anticipated and the deputy sheriff called a posse of the following neighboring planters, who answered promptly: Major A. J. Decuir, Messrs. Paul Picot, A. G. Picot, and Millard Bosworth with his home guard, composed of the employes of his refinery, these being well equipped with Winchester carbines.

Everything is quiet now, and the strike is over on the place and work will be resumed in the morning.

BATON ROUGE

Troops Under Arms

BATON ROUGE, La., Nov. 3.--[Special]--The Baton Rouge Fencibles, in obedience to orders received from Assistant Adjutant General Faries, are under arms at their armory, ready to depart for the scene of anticipated troubles on the Teche.

The Deltas of West Baton Rouge are also here.

Notes

The following was received in this city yesterday:

SCHRIEVER, La., Nov. 3.--J. L. Harris, New Orleans: Strike broken here. All hands at work. Commence grinding after dinner.

N. S. WILLIAMS
Ardoyne Plantation

New Orleans Daily Picayune, November 4, 1887.

17. THE TECHE TROUBLES

MANY OF THE STRIKERS RETURNING TO WORK

Moral Effect Exerted by the Militia Companies--Not a Single Case of Violence
in the District Yesterday

Beneficial Effects of Sending Troops to Thibodaux

Special to The Times-Democrat

THIBODAUX, La., Nov. 3.--There is good reason to believe that very many,
if not the majority, of the strikers have gone into the present movement
against their will and judgment, and only in consequence of orders received
from their leaders. A number of the more turbulent among them having been
arrested and placed under bond, several instances have occurred of hands
seeking and readily adopting any possible excuse to return to work. As it
becomes more evident with the lapse of time that there is no prospect of
yielding on the part of the planters, these instances may be expected to
multiply, and it may be hoped that within a few days work will be pretty
generally resumed. Nevertheless, the loss of several days of such splendid
weather as has prevailed all through the present week is to be deeply regretted, and may be irretrievable. Meanwhile, arrangements are being made
by several of the planters to fill the places of the strikers, and hands will
be brought from other States, if necessary.

The hardship and loss involved in present situation falls on others besides the planters and laborers. The loss of time is a serious matter to the
officers and men of the militia organizations. Although everything possible
is done for their comfort and convenience, the fact remains that every day
they are kept under arms represents so much money taken from their pockets.
The men of the local company, the Knobloch Guards, are for the most part
mechanics and artificers, who earn $2.50 to $3.50 a day. These wages are
now lost to them. The Louisiana Field Artillery left New Orleans at the
most inconvenient time possible for themselves and for the merchants and
others in whose employment their members are. Some of them, it is stated,
even run the risk of losing their positions, though it is scarcely credible
that any employer would show such a lack of public spirit as to discharge a
young man for responding to the call of the State. But it will be only
fair to all parties, if the necessity of keeping the troops under arms continues, to allow Battery B to return to New Orleans, relieving them by some
other command.

That the presence of troops in this town has had its effect in preserving the peace can scarcely be doubted and the men themselves realize the
fact, and have consequently borne the loss of time and money in the best
spirit. The strikers driven from the plantations have flocked into town in
large numbers, all more or less excited. But the knowledge of bodies of
armed men, close at hand and in constant readiness to act, has been sufficient
to prevent any approach to disturbance.

The following order was issued by Gen. Pierce this morning:
HEADQUARTERS, THIBODAUX SPECIAL FORCES, Nov. 2, 1887

Order No. 1.
Capts. Beanham and Walsh:
"Under orders from the adjutant general, New Orleans, Nov. 1, I assume
command of all troops between Berwick Bay and New Orleans. Have everything
in readiness to forward orders of civil authorities at a moment's notice.
Have horses harnessed and ready to move at a moment's notice."

The process of arrest, jailing and bailing of strikers who refused to
quit the plantation went on throughout the day. Orders of arrest were issued against twenty-four men, of whom seventeen were taken. All are negroes.
All except five were bailed. The town is absolutely quiet. The planters
held a meeting this afternoon at which it was resolved to hold firm in their
previous attitude, in spite of all losses, past or future.

The planters believe that the worst of the strike is over. This belief
is confirmed by the increasing number of laborers who are returning to work.
There is an impression in some quarters that the labor organization in this
district is an independent body in no wise connected with the regular order

of the Knights of Labor. This, however, is not the case. THE TIMES-DEMOCRAT
correspondent has the clearest evidence to the contrary, having carefully
inspected today the framed charter of the Thibodaux Assembly No.10499,
Knights of Labor. The charter is of the regular pattern, is dated the 8th
of July, 1887, and signed T. V. Powderly, general master workman, and
Chas. H. Litchman, general secretary. Affixed to the charter is the grand
seal of the order with the legend: "That is the most perfect form of
government in which an injury to one is the concern of all."

The Opelousas company, dispatched in response to the request of the
Raceland planters, will arrive at Raceland at 5 a.m. tomorrow by a mixed
train, no earlier train being available, and will be met and cared for by
Mr. C. S. Matthews and others of that neighborhood.

Troops Under Arms at Baton Rouge

Special to The Times-Democrat.

BATON ROUGE, Nov. 3.--Quite a stir was created here this afternoon by
the receipt of orders by the Baton Rouge Fencibles, of this city, and the
Delta Rifles, of West Baton Rouge, to assemble, armed and equipped, and hold
themselves in readiness for marching orders. Capt. Granary is in command of
the Fencibles, and the Delta Rifles will assemble at Port Allen, under command of Capt. Parker.

Opelousas Guards Ordered to Lafourche

Special to The Times-Democrat.

OPELOUSAS, Nov. 3.--The Opelousas Guards, Capt. E. Sumpter Tayor commanding, left for Raceland Station, Lafourche parish, this evening, under
orders from Brig. Gen. Parkerson, commanding this militia district.

All Quiet Around Jeanerette

Special to The Times-Democrat.

JEANERETTE, Nov. 3.--The question of the strike has not yet been settled, but from all appearances a satisfactory understanding between the
planters and their employes will speedily be reached. There has been no
disturbance or violation of law on any of the neighboring plantations, and
all parties interested in the exceptionally fine crops growing evince a
very decided disposition to return to their work with as little delay as
possible. There are a few planters fully supplied with labor, but the great
majority of the hands, including women, are still holding out for higher
wages.

The laborers ordered to leave the plantations of Dr. Gay and Capt. Wills
have all done so.

Capt. Cade was this morning instructed to remain in Jeanerette with a
squad of ten men, and to send the balance of his company to his headquarters.
Tonight he received another order to proceed to Pattersonville at once with
a force of thirty men. The Knights of Labor held a meeting today, and it is
reported that they agreed to assist all who desired to persist in the strike,
but not to molest those desiring to return to work. All is quiet.

The Planters at Schriever Begin Grinding

It was stated yesterday that Mr. Paul Lacassagne, of Terrebonne, had
again telegraphed the State authorities for troops to protect the recently
employed laborers on his place. On inquiry, however, nothing definite could
be obtained with reference to the above, but the belief was generally entertained here that nothing serious had occurred.

Mr. George Marshall, manager of the Waubun plantation at Schriever, La.,
telegraphed Capt. John T. Moore, Jr., to the effect that more troops were
necessary to preserve order and prevent any damage in that locality. He
further stated that, although he had appealed to, he had not received any
assistance whatsoever from Sheriff Budd.

Subsequently, however, the following was received, which would seem to
indicate that peace and good order had been restored:

Schriever, La., Nov. 3, 1887

J. L. Harris, New Orleans:
"Strike broken here. All hands at work. Commence grinding after dinner.

"N. S. Williams, Ardoyne Plantation."

Capt. Moore left for Schriever Station at 12:15 p.m. yesterday by the
Morgan Railroad, where he will remain until matters and things have assumed
a more peaceful aspect.

Up to a late hour last evening nothing had been heard by either Gens.
Glynn or Meyer from the scene of the threatened disturbances.

Work Resumed at Sorrel

SORREL, LA., Nov. 3.--This morning at 6:30 o'clock the strikers were
ordered by Col. E. M. Dubroca, the manager, to go to work or leave the
plantation, and on their refusing positively to comply with the order, the
deputy sheriff was called in and began at once to eject them. When they
saw that matters were serious, many of them wisely concluded to go to work,
and the others consented to move without any further trouble. Threats
having been made by strikers, trouble was anticipated and the deputy sheriff
called a posse of the following neighboring planters, who answered promptly:
Major A. J. Decuir, Messrs. Paul Picot, A. G. Picot and Millard Bosworth
with his Home Guard, composed of the employes of his refinery, these being
well equipped with Winchester carbines. Everything is quiet now, the strike
is over on this place and work will be resumed in the morning.

A COTTON STRIKE THREATENED

A committee composed of four white and four colored members of the
Cotton Yard Men's Benevolent Association waited on their bosses, the cotton
press owners, Wednesday, and presented a new uniform tariff. The committee
were cordially received by some of the press owners, while others ignored
the association.

The workingmen claim that they cannot get along with the wages now being
paid. The press owners would not accept the new tariff presented to them,
stating that on account of the small amount paid them for the storage of
cotton they would not be able to pay the amount asked. Last year the cotton
yard men were receiving ten cents for compressing and eighteen cents for the
yard men.

The Terrell and Atlantic cotton presses are said to be the best-paying
presses in town. They pay eight cents for compressing and fifteen cents for
the yard men. The new uniform tariff requires every press to pay the same
as the two above presses. It was rumored that the cotton men were going to
strike this week.

A TIMES-DEMOCRAT reporter visited a number of presses yesterday. The
men were found working, and stated that they had received no orders to knock
off and go on a strike. A general meeting of both white and colored cotton
yard men will be held next Sunday. A committee will be sent to the press
owners in order to try and settle the trouble by arbitration. If the owners
do not recognize the committee, then there will probably be a strike ordered,
and for the same wages as last year.

New Orleans Times-Democrat, November 4, 1887.

18.   DESERTED CANE FIELDS

Planters Fear That Frost May Swoop Down on Them

Jeanerette Reports Good Prospects for a Resumption of Work There--Two
Military Companies at Baton Rouge Ordered Held in Readiness--No Change at
Morgan City.

NEW ORLEANS, Nov. 3.--H. Zuberbier, of Zuberbier & Bran, owners of several large sugar estates, returned home this morning after a week's absence
spent in inspecting their plantations. He very much laments the occurrence
of the strike as the frost season is at hand and the consequent danger to
this, as fine, if not the finest sugar crop ever grown in Louisiana. Along
the river several planters have conceded the rate of wages demanded, $1.25

per day, where no contracts existed. Mr. Zuberbier says he recognizes the
danger in yielding to this demand for an increase in cases where laborers
have contracted at $1 per day for the season as establishing a precedent of
breaking contracts through the medium of strikers would render the stability
of business estimates, so very necessary to the success of plantation work
impossible.

FEELS BLUE

Judge E. D. White stated this morning that he did not think well at
all of the situation. In Assumption all hands are at work at less rates
than the Judge is paying, and the suspension of labor on his plantation is
undoubtedly the foolish work of some ignorant and unprincipled leaders.
Lafourche planters have always strained every point to pay the highest wages
possible, and until now the parish has had no trouble, and has enjoyed the
best reputation. It is now difficult to say what the end will be.

Savannah Morning News, November 4, 1887.

19.   LABOR TROUBLES IN THE SUGAR DISTRICTS

The labor troubles in the sugar districts are being rapidly settled,
and there is every prospect that the next few days will witness a full resumption of work at all the sugar-houses.

The laborers are returning to their former homes and accepting the
terms offered by the planters, which are the old scale of wages.

The negroes have been led into the strike by a few agitators, who have
been working them for many months past, and did not comprehend the full
significance of their action until the test came.

The past three seasons have been about as disastrous to all connected
with the sugar interests of the State as any in its annals, and if the
laborer has suffered the proprietors of the estates have suffered more. In
fact most of these plantations have been operated at a dead loss.

The prospects are now brighter, and one good crop will go far to put
the industry on a comparatively safe footing. The laborer must share in
that recuperation, but he cannot hope to grasp it precipitately by crippling
the planter in the critical period of taking off the crop.

The cane is represented as being quite rich, and a yield approximating
25,000 hhds. is expected, should grinding operations be pushed with usual
vigor and no disaster in the shape of an early freeze intervene.

New Orleans Daily Picayune, November 4, 1887.

20.   THE SUGAR STRIKE

Advices from the sugar district report the strike as being practically
over. The planters have remained firm and would not listen to the labor demands. The fact is, no demand for an increase of prices was made by the
laborer.

The Knights of Labor organization in the Teche numbers perhaps 5000 men.
They selected as heads of the different lodges men who knew nothing of the
situation and were known as agitators. They could not appreciate the disadvantages under which the planters have labored for three years with short
crops of cane and the low prices of sugar. An increase of the price of labor
under such circumstances meant that every planter would come out further in
debt at the end of the season. The Knights of Labor committee who framed and
signed the circular addressed to the planters evidently did not understand
the situation.

The negroes had no grievances to present other than an increase of wages,
and as that could not be given they have peaceably returned to work, and

with the present favorable weather the crop will be gathered in a few weeks.
The presence of the state militia was in most instances not necessary.
No mischief was attempted except in two cases, the shooting at Tigerville
and Raceland.

The troops, however, did no harm, and it was well perhaps to have been
prepared in case of an emergency.

New Orleans Daily Picayune, November 5, 1887.

21. THE TECHE TROUBLES

A PLANTER SHOT BY A STRIKER NEAR LOCKPORT

Militia Called Upon to Assist in the Arrest of the Assailant--Eviction of a
Number of Strikers Near Raceland

Special to The Times-Democrat

THIBODAUX, La., Nov. 4.--This morning about 10 o'clock a negro striker,
named Moses Pugh, shot and seriously wounded Mr. Richard Foret, a prominent
planter, near Lockport. When a deputy sheriff attempted to arrest him he
was surrounded by about 150 of his friends, who defied the authorities. The
Opelousas Guards, Capt. Taylor commanding, were called upon to assist the
deputy sheriff and succeeded in capturing him without any trouble and bringing him to Thibodaux. He was jailed at 5 o'clock to await the result of the
wound.

Great excitement prevails in that neighborhood, and Gen. Pierce went to
the scene of trouble at once. Affidavits have been made against several of
the party for resisting the officers, and trouble is expected tomorrow, when
the arrests will be made. All is quiet in this vicinity, and many of the
strikers have returned to work.

A secret circular, dated 2d November, has been issued by District Assembly 194, Knights of Labor, from its headquarters at Morgan City, calling upon
the strikers to stand firm in their demands, as any backdown after they have
gone so far would place the laborer in a worse position than ever. The circular goes on to abjure the strikers to refrain from all violence or resistance to the law, so as to prove by their moderate attitude that Gov. McEnery
ordered out the militia without due cause. There is a suspicious flavor of
partisan bias in this. But the necessity of calling upon a militia company
to evict strikers near Raceland today, after the civil authorities had failed
to do so, and the trouble experienced in the arrest of Pugh, prove the Governor's action to have been well advised.

Several more strikers who refused to move from the plantations were arrested and jailed today. The disinclination to move on the part of most of
the others who have expressed their intention of doing so indicates that they
are only waiting for an excuse to return to work. About half the men who
quit work in this neighborhood have resumed it. Most of the plantations are
still short-handed, but the planters say that unless the strikers who are
holding out return pretty soon they will find their places filled by outsiders.
The planters have not shown the least sign of yielding.

It is hoped that the presence of the Louisiana Field Artillery may be
dispensed with tomorrow, but it is more probable that they will be required to
remain here till Monday. Gen. Pierce rode over to Schriever today to view the
situation in that quarter.

Eviction of Tenants at Pattersonville

Special to The Times-Democrat

FRANKLIN, La., Nov. 4.--In order to show the animus of W. Scott in stating that Local Assembly No. 6295, K. of L., was suspended Oct. 24 for non-
payment of dues, and that by reason thereof the protest of the assembly was
of no effect, the following letters and receipt have been exhibited to THE
TIMES-DEMOCRAT correspondent:

BERWICK, La., Oct. 22, 1887
Santa Maria, Franklin Postoffice, La.

To the R.S. 6295,
    Dear Sir and Brother—Inclosed please find receipt for $1.20 paid as
per capita to District Assembly No. 194 for the quarter ending Oct. 1, 1887.
Fraternally,   J. P. McKAY

BERWICK, Oct. 18, 1887

    Received from L. A. No. 6295, K. of L., the sum of $1.20, being ten
cents per member in good standing as per capita for the quarter ending Oct.
1, 1887. $1.20.
                    J. P. McKAY, D.F.S., D.A. No. 194.

    This receipt bears the seal of the assembly. On Oct. 29, 1887, a tele-
gram was received by T. C. Lawless, representing Local Assembly 6295, asking
his attendance at the meeting of the District Executive Board of District
Assembly 194, at which meeting the order for the strike of the laborers was
ordered. This telegram was received too late for Lawless to take the train,
and Local Assembly 6295 was unrepresented at the meeting for this reason,
and not because of the suspension of the assembly, as stated by Scott.
    This morning the sheriff arrested some ten or twelve of the strikers on
D. Thompson's plantation near Pattersonville, who refused to resume labor or
to leave the place, as required, and brought them before Judge R. D. Gill
upon an affidavit for trespass. After a hearing, the judge ordered each to
give bond and security in the sum of $50 for appearance before the District
Court and also in the sum of $250 to keep the peace, and in default to re-
main in jail. They are in the lockup, not having been able to find sureties.
Some of them were accompanied by their wives.
    In this vicinity all is quiet and the laborers are working contentedly.
From the upper part of the parish the report is to the same effect. Conflicting rumors prevail that trouble is anticipated below on the Clarke plantation,
by reason of the refusal of laborers either to resume work or to vacate the
premises and give place to others, but the sheriff says he has received no
notice of such a condition from any authentic source.
    A detachment of militia is under arms at the courthouse, guarding the
lockup in which the laborers now under arrest are confined, as rumors are
afloat that an attempt will be made tonight by parties from below to release
them. Little credence is placed in the rumor, and the present attitude of
the militia is wholly one of precaution.

The Militia to Come Home

    Yesterday Gen. John Glynn, Jr., received a communication from Gen. Beau-
regard, Adjutant General, to the effect that it was his desire to relieve the
State troops now at Tigerville, in Terrebonne parish, as soon as possible.
Gen. Glynn thinks that they will be ordered home today.

New Orleans Times-Democrat, November 5, 1887.

22. GONE TO WORK

The Fizzle Out of the Sugar Laborer's Strike

Nearly All of the Negroes Returned to Their Work

A Few in Jail Charged With Trespass

Feeling Against the Political Labor Leaders

LAFOURCHE

How the Strike Came to an End—Battery B to remain Over Today
THIBODAUX, La., Nov. 4.--[Special]--The strike has practically ended.

The strikers are sick and discouraged, and are returning to work as fast as
they can. In some instances the managers refuse to re-employ the leaders,
but the inoffensive ones are gladly taken back.

A number of mills started today. On the Allen plantation, the place
where trouble was expected, sixty hands were at work this evening. Reports
from adjoining places say there is perfect peace, and the negroes are returning to the fields.

The Iberia Guards, numbering thirty-eight, Captain Taylor commanding,
reached Houma yesterday morning. Seventeen negroes were arrested and jailed
at Houma last night, charged with firing on the Germans who were returning
from work on the Greenwood plantation day before yesterday.

At Raceland, this morning, Moses Pugh, a colored laborer on the Mary
plantation, shot and badly wounded Richard Foret, the manager of the plantation. Before he could be arrested the negro fled, coming to Thibodaux, where
he gave himself up to the sheriff. He claims self-defense, and states that
Foret was beating him over the head, when he was compelled to shoot. Foret,
it is learned, is resting well tonight and will probably recover. The Opelousas military company arrived at Lockport today.

At Schriever and Acadia Everything is Quiet

Captain Beanham's company is still quartered here and will remain until
Saturday or Sunday. While there has been no actual need of their services
their presence has had a most salutary effect on the negroes. A number of
the boys of the company left their business to come and protect the interest
of both merchant and planter.

There is some uneasiness among them for fear that their employers may
supply their places before their return. Surely the merchants of New Orleans
are as much interested in putting down this insurrection as any one else and
should only be glad to render the planters assistance.

TERREBONNE

Most of the Laborers Returned to Their Work--Indignation at the Labor Leaders

HOUMA, La., Nov. 4.--[Special]--Yesterday the leaders of the strikers
asked for a conference with the planters, saying that they would be willing
to take $1 per day and 60 cents a watch. This had been offered by the
planters last Saturday, but it was refused by the strikers. The planters
declined this conference, feeling that the matter had gone too far, and said
they would not treat with them at all. They will give $1 per day and 50 cents
a watch and no more.

Unanimity prevails among the planters and the collapse of the strike is
only a question of time. The hands on Berger's Jolly plantation abandoned
the strikers and went to work yesterday at contract prices; the same thing
at Williams' and the Anodyne plantation. These places are all now in full
blast. Winn's Southdown plantation has been going all the week.

Captain Avery's company went up this morning to Jno. T. Moore's Waubon
plantation, at Schriever, with the sheriff, to evict some of the hands who
declined to vacate their cabins.

McCullum's and W. V. Duffle's places started up today.

Some of the strikers from Berger's "Crescent" plantation were released
from jail yesterday. They said they were done with strikers, and wanted to
go to work. They started in this morning at old contract prices.

The negroes feel here that they have been duped by a few young men, their
self-constituted leaders, who are using them for political effect. They are
candidates for office and care nothing for the laborer, except to use him as
a tool. Much feeling is exhibited against them, and there is some talk of
driving them away from here. It would certainly be a good riddance.

Twelve persons are in jail who did the shooting in Lacampru's place.

ST. MARY

A Few Strikers Arrested for Trespass--Militia Guarding the Jail

FRANKLIN, La., Nov. 4.--[Special]--This morning the sheriff arrested
some ten or twelve of the strikers on D. Thompson's plantation, near Pattersonville, who refused labor or to leave the place as required, and brought
them before Judge R. D. Gill upon an affidavit for trespass. After a hearing

the judge ordered each to give bond and security in the sum of $50 for ap-
pearance before the district court and also in the sum of $250 to keep the
peace and in default to remain in jail. At 6 o'clock this evening they are
in the lockup, not having been able to find sureties. Some of them were
accompanied by their wives.

In this vicinity all is quiet and the laborers are working contented-
ly. From the upper part of the parish the report is to the same effect.

There are conflicting rumors that trouble is anticipated below on the
Clarke plantation by reason of the refusal of laborers either to resume
work or vacate the premises and give place to others, but the sheriff says
he has received no notice of such a condition from any authentic source.

A detachment of militia is under arms at the courthouse guarding the
lockup in which the laborers now under arrest are confined, as rumors are
afloat that an attempt will be made tonight by parties from below to release them. Little credence is placed in the rumor and the present attitude
of the militia is wholly one of precaution.

IBERIA

No More Troops Needed.

NEW IBERIA, La., Nov. 4.--[Special]--The gun detachment of the Iberia
Guards did not get off last night as reported owing to trouble in getting
transportation for their guns and horses. This morning Captain Pharr received other orders making it not necessary to go.

The Rangers are returning, a force of only ten men being left in
Jeanerette.

New Orleans Daily Picayune, November 5, 1887.

23. NINE MEN KILLED

FOUR WHITE MEN SHOT DOWN BY NEGRO STRIKERS

A Sheriff's Posse of Citizens and Militia Sent to the Scene at Patter-
sonville--A Conflict in Which Five of the Strikers Are Killed--Situation in
Terrebonne.

Four Men Killed by Strikers
Special to The Times-Democrat

FRANKLIN, La., Nov. 5.--Reliable information was received here this
morning that four white men were shot by the strikers last night while attending the cane carrier on Capt. John N. Pharr's plantation, near Berwick.
The sheriff, on the receipt of the information, summoned a posse of about
forty men from this vicinity and left for the scene of the shooting, increasing the posse along the line of his route to about eighty substantial
citizens. Capt. Cole's company passed down to Berwick on the train at 12 m.

Rumors are current that the laborers in the Irish Bend will strike on
Monday. Advices from the upper part of the parish and Bayou Cypremont are
that all is quiet and the laborers are at work.

William Price, manager of the plantation of D. McCann, in an interview
today, denies that any of the strikers and ousted hands from the Eustis
plantation are employed on the plantation, and that there is no intention of
employing them or any other strikers.

A telegram from Pattersonville just received, states that a collision
had occurred and five laborers were killed. All is quiet at present, but
further trouble is anticipated tonight.

Battle Between Strikers and a Sheriff's Posse
Special to The Times-Democrat

PATTERSONVILLE, Nov. 5.--An encounter took place today between a sheriff's
posse, commanded by Hon. Don Caffery, the Attakapas Rangers, under Capt. Cade,

and a crowd of negro strikers. Several of the strikers were apprehended and others were ordered to disperse. They resisted, and an engagement ensued, in which several of the negroes were killed.

The companies present, under the command of Capt. C. T. Cade, are the Attakapas Rangers, of Iberia parish; St. Mary Volunteers, of Franklin, commanded by Capt. T. Marsh; Company B, St. Mary Artillery, of Morgan City, under Capt. W. H. P. Wise. Upon arrival of these companies, Capt. Cade, senior officer, took command, W. B. Gray acting as adjutant.

Everything is now quiet, and indications point to no recurrence of this afternoon's work. The militia companies are quartered on the steamer E. W. Cole, subject to the orders of Sheriff Frere. The town is patrolled tonight by squads of militiamen.

Terrebonne Tenants Evicted and New Men Take Their Places

Special to The Times-Democrat

HOUMA, Nov. 5.--With reference to the strike of sugar laborers the situation in this parish is somewhat anomalous. A few plantations have resumed work under the original rates agreed upon at the beginning of the grinding season, viz: One dollar per day and fifty cents per watch on a majority of the plantations. However the strikers have insisted upon their demands for increased pay, which the planters are utterly unable to meet, and evictions have become a necessary sequence. As a rule these have been accomplished peaceably and no resistance has thus far been manifested to the properly constituted authorities that have been evoked on several plantations.

The evicted have taken their departure without waiting for legal process, and thus escaped the penalty that might wait on resistance. Numbers of the evicted have congregated in Houma, and vacant houses for their accommodations are at a premium. In the meantime the places of those removed are rapidly filled by other laborers who are disposed to work for the rates proposed by the planters. The result will inevitably be idleness for a number of home laborers, while those from abroad occupy their places. The authorities are determined to preserve the peace and prevent any interference with those who are disposed to work.

The Laccassagne incident on Bayou Black, where four men were shot and wounded by the strikers, has more than confirmed this determination.

The Iberia Guards, under the command of Capt. Dudley Avery, are stationed in Houma, and their presence has a wholesome influence in restraining any riotous proceedings that may be contemplated by the more obstreperous of the strikers.

Reports have reached town of certain threats directed against managers and laborers disposed to work, warning them of the wrath that awaits them unless they take immediate departure, but these anonymous communications have, as a rule, been ignored and but few are frightened thereby. The strike has been ill advised, and is unjustifiable. The laborers began work at rates mutually agreed upon between employer and employe.

The law-abiding people of Terrebonne are grateful for Gov. McEnery's action in ordering troops here promptly in response to the call of the civil authorities.

Situation Around Tigerville

TIGERVILLE, Nov. 5.--The excitement of a few days since at the Lacassagne plantation has subsided. Thirty-five laborers are at work now. There have been no violent demonstrations on the part of the strikers toward the new men, who arrived yesterday. No militia at all came here. Only private guards are employed.

Resistance to Officers at Lockport

Special to The Times-Democrat

THIBODAUX, La., Nov. 5.--Everything is quiet here. Carts still coming into Thibodaux removing hands from plantations.

The Rienzi has about fifty men at work today. Leighton has a few laborers employed; on Ridgefield twenty-five to forty are expected to fall into line on Monday morning. On Dixie a force were at work yesterday. At Highland the entire force is at work, the strikers having all returned.

Work has never been interrupted on the Caillouet place. On Orange Grove

the few strikers were removed on Thursday, and all remaining continued to
do duty.

There has been some trouble near Lockport. Sheriff Frost has gone down
this morning to make arrests. Report has it that the constables have been
defied in that neighborhood.

Mr. Foret, who was shot on May plantation on Friday, is not thought to
be seriously wounded.

Planters will meet this afternoon and enter into arrangements to import
laborers from elsewhere. In every instance in which strikers have returned
to work it has been at the original prices.

One peculiarity of this strike is that the leaders are all men who never
did a day's work in the field. Some of the white members of the Knights of
Labor have abandoned the organization.

One of the vagaries of the strike occurred in Terrebonne, where about
a dozen men who were cultivating cane on shares struck for higher wages,
leaving their cane at the mercy of the chances. In another instance a man
who was receiving $1.50 a day, 75 cents a watch, struck for $1.25 and 60
cents.

New Orleans Times-Democrat, November 6, 1887.

24.   THE LABOR TROUBLES

Details of the Killing of the Negroes at Pattersonville

More Trouble Anticipated

Movements of Troops in the Disturbed Neighborhood

More Negroes Going to Work Today

ST. MARY

The Particulars of the Affair at Pattersonville

General Frank Morey arrived last evening from his plantation opposite
Pattersonville, and gives the following account of the shooting that occurred
there on Saturday, of which he was an eye-witness:

It appears that on Friday, after a full consultation of the leading
planters of St. Mary, it was decided that there should be unanimous action
in compelling the laborers who refused to work to vacate the houses and
cabins occupied by them, in order that they might be occupied by laborers to
be brought in.

Threats had been freely made by some of the self-constituted leaders of
the negroes that they would not allow other negroes to be brought in to work
in their places, nor would they vacate the houses occupied by them.

It was apparent to the planters that they could not peacefully cope with
the condition of things without co-operation, and they decided upon the
following plan: to have warrents issued for the arrest of the trespassers
who persisted in remaining in the houses or on the premises after they were
ordered to vacate, and to have the sheriff serve the warrants aided by a posse
of sufficient strength to enable him to execute the law.

To this end a posse was organized at Franklin, composed of leading citizens of that end of the parish--lawyers, merchants, planters, etc.--who accompanied Sheriff Frere to Pattersonville on Saturday morning.

Before attempting the execution of the warrants, leading citizens, such
as Hon. Don Caffrey, Henry J. Saunders, George C. Zenor and Frank Williams
stated to the posse that it was of the first importance that nothing should
be done except to aid the sheriff in the performance of his duties and im-
plicitly obey his orders, no matter what the provocation might be.

At first the sheriff was unable to find some of the most flagrant violators of the law, but arrested five in Pattersonville who were put under
strict guard to be conveyed to the boat which was to take them to the jail

at Franklin.   There was considerable excitement in Pattersonville.

There were large numbers of negroes in the streets. On Main street, about midway of the town, a colored man named Jake Norris jostled one of the posse who were assisting the sheriff in that portion of the town. On being remonstrated with and ordered to clear the sidewalk the negro replied with an oath that he had "rather die first." The negro was immediately shot--by whom was not ascertained.

At the first shot, there was great excitement. The prisoners, who were under guard, and were about two squares from the scene of the firing, became alarmed and attempted to escape. They were called upon to halt, and not obeying they were riddled with shots by the posse. Four were killed outright and the fifth made his escape.

Those killed were Alf Anderson and Wash Anderson, brothers. Wm. Cooper, their brother-in-law, and Bob Wrenn. The latter was under indictment at the time and awaiting trial for the murder of another negro man. The justice of the peace held an inquest on the dead negroes, and coffins were provided and they were buried by the parish authorities by the consent of the surviving relatives.

Large numbers of the negroes are satisfied with the schedule and desirous of working, but are deterred by the threats of others who have refused to work. On most of the places in that neighborhood, however, work is going on as usual. The sheriff and posse assured the negroes protection and many of the strikers will, it is thought, go to work in the morning as they have promised to do.

It was reported, however, that a meeting of negroes was held at Berwick Saturday night at which considerable incendiary language was indulged in and threats made of burning the town of Pattersonville.

At Berwick, as the train passed yesterday, negroes with guns in their hands were seen lurking behind the houses.

At Houma there are indications of further trouble. There is less disposition to go to work here than at other points.

Matters About Morgan City

MORGAN CITY, La., Nov. 6.--[Special]--Today has been one of considerable excitement, without demonstration by the laborers. A report was current in Berwick that a crowd from Pattersonville was coming to that place to make arrests, and there was excitement and gathering of arms by some of the people. The report was unfounded and everything is quiet there and in this place up this eve.

The killing of four negroes in Pattersonville Saturday created some excitement here. Their names were A. E. Anderson, Wash Anderson, Bob Wrenn and Cooper. Squire Jefferson escaped. A. E. Anderson has a little store in Pattersonville.

None of the laborers have gone to work in this vicinity. It is rumored they will go to work in the morning, but nothing definite is known.

IBERIA

Movement of Troops

NEW IBERIA, La., Nov. 6.--[Special]--The military company from Opelousas passed down by here today, thirty-two strong.

Captain Pharr with the artillery detailment of the Iberia Guards left on the local train today in response to Captain Cade's call for more men. Ten more of the Iberia Guards leave here tonight to join their command at Pattersonville. All is quiet here.

All the mills in Fausse Point section, as well as in the interior, are at work.

Large numbers of negroes went down on the train today, going to take the places of the strikers.

New Orleans Daily Picayune, November 7, 1887.

25. THE SUGAR STRIKE

PARTICULARS OF THE AFFAIR AT PATTERSONVILLE

A Mob of Negroes Threaten a Sheriff's Posse Guarding Prisoners and Are
Fired Upon--The Louisiana Field Artillery on Duty at Schriever

Special to The Times-Democrat

PATTERSONVILLE, Nov. 6.--The town is profoundly quiet today. Many of
the negroes, who form the majority of the population, have cleared out, in
consequence of the affair of yesterday afternoon. Of that affair everybody
has a different story to tell.
    The following are the conclusions arrived at after some pains and care-
ful consideration:
    Trouble has been threatening in this neighborhood for sometime past.
The negroes have been talking freely of burning the town of Pattersonville.
It is stated that one who is now a prisoner under escort has made a full
confession to the Hon. Don Caffery of a plot to burn the town, which was to
have been carried into effect last night, but the events of yesterday afternoon intervened. Mr. Caffery went to Franklin on the afternoon train, and
has not therefore been interviewed.
    The shooting and wounding of four white men on the Pharr plantation on
Friday decided the authorities here to institute a search for arms in the
town, and at the same time to arrest several men who had made themselves
most conspicuous by the loudness and ferocity of their threats. The troops
were quartered on steamboats lying alongside of Williams' saw-mill, about a
mile from town. From there yesterday afternoon, between 4 and 5 o'clock,
the Attakapas Rangers, under command of Capt. Cade, together with a posse of
citizens partly of this neighborhood and partly from Franklin, moved on the
town. There are several versions of what afterward occurred.
    The correct story is probably this: At the entrance to the town stand
two cottages, the one on the right occupied by a white man named Hibbert,
that on the left by colored people. Here, as the troops approached, they
found a crowd of fifty to 100 excited negroes assembled. This crowd was
ordered to disperse at once, which some proceeded to do, while others stood
fast and assumed a defiant attitude.
    One negro of notorious character threw his hand behind him as if to
draw a pistol; then in a minute the whole affair was over. A regular fusilade was opened upon the negroes by the posse and four men were shot dead
where they stood.
    It is asserted by the militia, and with considerable positiveness by
some of them, that no militiaman fired a shot, and that all the killing was
done by the sheriff's posse. Capt. Cade seems to have had a good deal of
difficulty in restraining his men from firing, but he appears to have succeeded.
    Besides the four negroes killed, one was very severely wounded. Two
boys are also stated to have been hit.
    The sheriff withdrew as soon as the firing began. After the affray the
troops marched through the town, and many of the negroes retired to the woods.
    Capt. Cade, with Capt. Thomson's company, from Opelousas, and a deputy
sheriff went down the bayou this afternoon. For this reason Capt. Cade has
not yet been seen by THE TIMES-DEMOCRAT correspondent.
    The number of shots fired is variously estimated at from thirty to 100,
but the firing was by no means indiscriminate. The four men killed were all
bad characters. Their names are Wash and Dolph Anderson (brothers), Lewis
Cooper, brother-in-law of the Andersons, and Robert Wrenn, a negro saloon
keeper, who killed a man a year ago within a few yards of the place where he
was shot. The dead were buried today by the troops.
    The town is guarded and patrolled tonight by cavalry and infantry. It
is impossible to move in any direction without being challenged.

A Correction from Hon. Don Caffery

Special to The Times-Democrat

FRANKLIN, Nov. 6.--Your special of this date states that "an encounter took place today between a sheriff's posse, commanded by Hon. Don Caffery, the Attakapas Rangers, under Capt. Cade, and a crowd of negro strikers," etc. This is not correct. I did not command the posse, it was commanded by Col. E. M. Dubroca, deputy sheriff, when the encounter took place, Sheriff A. G. Frere being present and making the arrests.

D. CAFFERY

Battery B, Louisiana Field Artillery, at Schriever

Special to The Times-Democrat

PATTERSONVILLE, Nov. 6.--Battery B, Louisiana Field Artillery, under Capt. Beanham, and accompanied by Gen. Pierce, arrived at Schriever from Thibodaux today to afford protection to the laborers who have been employed by surrounding planters to fill the places of the strikers. A twelve-pounder gun was brought to Schriever from Franklin by a detachment of the St. Mary Volunteers, who afterward returned to Franklin. Capt. Avery's company is also at Schreiver.

All Quiet in Lafourche

There were no developments in the strike on the plantations yesterday, as far as could be learned from persons visiting in the city.

Gen. Billiu, of Lafourche, who arrived here last evening, stated to a TIMES-DEMOCRAT reporter that all was quiet in that parish. The General says that the majority of plantations are in full operation, and that the minority of the planters, against whom the strike still continues, are firmly determined not to grant the advance.

Mr. John R. Gheens, of Lafourche, is also in town. He corroborates Gen. Billiu's statement as to the quietness of the situation in that parish.

Mr. Wm. L. Ferris arrived from St. Mary last evening, but could give no further information as to the conflict at Pattersonville on Saturday, the details of which were given in yesterday's TIMES-DEMOCRAT. He stated that all was quiet and no further trouble anticipated when he left there yesterday.

New Orleans Times-Democrat, November 7, 1887.

26. THE SUGAR STRIKE

ADDITIONAL PARTICULARS REGARDING THE PATTERSONVILLE AFFAIR

Interviews with Capt. Cade, Hon. Don Caffery and Sheriff Frere--The Militia Did Not Fire

Special to The Times-Democrat

PATTERSONVILLE, Nov. 7.--Capt. Cade, with Capt. Thompson's company, accompanied by Major A. J. de Cair, who is acting as deputy sheriff and represents the civil authority here, returned last night from their expedition down the bayou. They found all quiet at Berwick, the menacing crowds which were reported as gathered there having dispersed on hearing of the approach of the troops.

Capt. Cade was interviewed this morning, and his version of the Pattersonville affray agreed in the main with the account given in last night's dispatch. It appears, however, that this account contained some minor inaccuracies. The statement that all the whites taking part in or present at the shooting were mounted is incorrect. Only some twelve or fifteen were on horseback, the remainder, including Capt. Cade's men, of whom about a dozen were there, were on foot. According to Capt. Cade's account the whole

affair was a good deal of *melee*, and things were pretty well mixed up for
awhile. He reports hearing some scattering shots a short time after the
general fusilade, but does not know who fired them. He believes that none
of his own men fired, and thinks that if they had fired he must have known
it, as he was with them all the time.

Hon. Don Caffery was appointed deputy by Sheriff Frere immediately after
the affray, but the authority was either withdrawn or resigned, and on the
sheriff's departure for Franklin Mayor de Cuir was left in command.

Some of the negroes are dropping back into town today, but yesterday
the streets were absolutely deserted by the blacks. Previous to the shooting the streets are reported to have been for days crowded with negroes, who
jeered at the troops on their arrival, and said they were a German band and
that their guns would not shoot. In marching up from the depot one of the
companies was compelled to force its way through the crowd. The negroes
outnumber the whites fully ten to one in this neighborhood.

Interviews with Hon. Don Caffery and Sheriff Frere

Special to The Times-Democrat

FRANKLIN, Nov. 7.--Ten men of Capt. Cade's company were sent up to
Jeanerette by the evening train under a subaltern officer, threatened
trouble being reported on one of the neighboring plantations. No details received.

Hon. Don Caffery, on being interviewed here this evening as to the part
taken by him in the Pattersonville trouble of Saturday, made the following
statement to THE TIMES-DEMOCRAT correspondent:

"On the day of the trouble Sheriff Frere, with about seventy men from
Franklin and vicinity, and Capt. Cade's company, moved down on Pattersonville
in response to an appeal from the citizens that the negroes were assembled
there in large forces. Col. Dubroca was appointed deputy sheriff and placed
in command of the whole by general consent. I was one of the posse. The
citizens of Pattersonville stated that a collision with the negroes was inevitable. The troops and posse were formed in column, the militia in rear,
irregular cavalry of posse in front, moved on into the town with two assistants, and made several arrests and turned the prisoners over to the irregulars.
The prisoners were being marched down the road toward the posse when desultory
firing suddenly broke out far ahead in the centre of Pattersonville. It
sounded like the musketry of a skirmish line, and every man in the posse believed that it was a deliberate attack by the negroes. As the firing proceeded a prominent citizen ordered the negroes who were gathered round in
considerable number to disperse to their homes. The prisoners are stated
to have attempted to escape at this juncture. Indiscriminate and rapid fire
instantly began, and the prisoners were shot down apparently for that reason.
The men arrested and shot were ringleaders in the movement against the whites,
and known to be desperate characters.

"After the firing, to prevent which I exercised my best efforts, rushing
out of the ranks and calling aloud to cease fire. Col. Dubroca and Sheriff
Frere retired and said they would have nothing more to do with the matter.
At least half the posse followed them to the steamboat. The confusion being
great and the men without a leader and the town reported full of armed negroes,
I assumed command, put the men in line and marched to points where negroes
were said to be in force. The firing had, however, dispersed them, and after
marching completely through the town, and to all points reported as held by
negroes, Sheriff Frere sent me by an orderly an appointment as deputy sheriff
an hour and a half after the firing occurred. I immediately ordered Capts.
Marsh and Cade with their detachment and began another search for rioters.
I captured only one, whom I protected against the posse. Then after making
provision for the interment of the slain and medical treatment for the
wounded man, I ordered the troops to return to quarters.

"My authority was rescinded by the sheriff soon after it was given by
an order left with Acting Adjutant G. B. Gay. I returned to Franklin the
next day."

Being questioned, Mr. Caffery added: "I saw no negroes fire. I do not
know if any arms were found on the dead negroes, but it was reported to that
effect. Some of our men fired in the air. Seventy-five to one hundred shots

were discharged. Everybody thought the negroes were attacking the posse
when firing was heard in front. I am informed that this firing was really
done by some of the white citizens, who were presumably drunk at the time.
    "The negro arrested stated to me that the negroes had assembled in
their hall for several nights previous and that they had been egged on by
their leaders to attack the whites at the first opportunity. They were
mustered, he said, about 300 strong."

SHERIFF FRERE STATED:

    "At the time the fire from the posse occurred I had gone on into the
town with a warrant of arrest against six negroes on a charge of conspiracy
to commit murder and arson and threatening to burn the town of Pattersonville. The warrant was signed by J. M. Charpentier, justice of the peace.
I arrested three men, and handed them over to Mr. Shelby Sanders to take
back to the posse. As they retired toward the posse the firing suddenly
broke out, and three prisoners and another were shot down. I was about 200
yards from the posse at the time, and could not see who fired on account of
the smoke and dust raised by the mounted men.
    "I returned to Franklin because of a report that trouble was expected
in the immediate vicinity, leaving Col. Dubroca in charge as deputy. The
negroes in this immediate   neighborhood are at work on all the plantations."

The Strike Reaches Plaquemines, La.

Special to The Times-Democrat

    PLAQUEMINES, Nov. 7.--The strike of the laborers on the plantations has
reached this parish. Only one plantation, the Everglades, near this place,
is so far affected. Should the strike spread and continue planters will
suffer to a great extent, as a large amount of the crop is still in the field.

No Chance in the Situation Around Houma

Special to The Times-Democrat

    HOUMA, Nov. 7.--The strike has assumed no new aspect since Saturday.
On several plantations evictions were made this morning without difficulty.
Labor from abroad is pouring in to take the places of the strikers and
planters are confident of resuming operations this week.
    The presence of the Iberia Guards, no doubt, has a most wholesome in-
fluence in preventing any resistance to the civil authorities. A gun detachment of the New Iberia Guards, Lieut. Pharr in command, arrived last
evening to reinforce the company stationed here. Capt. Avery and his men
have met with a most cordial reception from the citizens, and grateful
appreciation of their services is everywhere manifested.
    It is believed that the backbone of the strike is broken. The planta-
tion laborers are not so much to blame for the unfortunate situation as a few
designing men who have made them the victims of their irrational disturbance.

The Morgan City Company Ordered Home

Special to The Times-Democrat

    FRANKLIN, La., Nov. 7.--The Morgan City Company, Capt. Wise in command,
returned home by the noon train today. Most of the plantation between
Pattersonville and Tigerville resumed work today, though, as a rule, with
less than their full force. The men working were in most instances strikers,
who have withdrawn their demands. The Pattersonville negroes are still badly
scared, and many of them remain obstinately out in the woods.

Capt. May's Command Off

    Yesterday at 12:15 Capt. Eugene May's command of the Washington Artillery,
consisting of Battery B and numbering thirty-five men, left for Schriever
Station, with instructions to report to Gen. Wm Pierce, who is in command of
the militia forces there. They will be held ready to reinforce any point
between New Orleans and Berwicks Bay, and will relieve Battery B, L.F.A.,
Capt. Beanham.

One of the Wounded

On Saturday morning twenty-two laborers were sent from this city to work

on the Bay Side plantation, the property of Dr. Gay, near Jeanerette, to
take the place of strikers. Among these men was a young man named Thomas
White. Last evening White returned to the city with a bullet in his left
leg, a little below the knee.

To a TIMES-DEMOCRAT reporter, who met him, Mr. White told the following story:

"We left the city Saturday morning, after having been assured that the
negroes would not interfere with us, and that we would be fully protected
while at work. We reached our destination in the evening. That very night,
while a number of us were eating supper about 8 o'clock one of the men, who
had stepped out of the room, saw a black man stealing up toward the door.
Before he could realize the man's intention and give an alarm the negro
raised a gun to his shoulder, fired and fled into the darkness. The shot
struck me in the leg, as you see. There was no clue to the fellow's identity, nor could we tell whether he was alone or one of a party. The men who
went up with me are all returning."

Interview with Mr. Pierce Butler

The situation in the parishes continues to attract attention. The reports reaching the city yesterday were somewhat conflicting. There were
rumors that the strike had extended to Assumption parish, where the plantation hands have been receiving $1.15 per day, but the report ran, would de-
mand the same wages asked by the laborers in the other parishes.

Among those arriving by last evening's train was Mr. Pierce Butler, a
planter from near Terrebonne. He declared that scarcely any of the plantations were doing anything, both planters and laborers being determined to
hold out.

"Are the strikers being evicted?" asked THE TIMES-DEMOCRAT reporter.

"Yes, sir," replied Mr. Butler, "and are giving no trouble. I told my
men Sunday that they must either go to work or leave the place today. This
morning they all packed up and went. They are quiet now, but what assurance
have we that when the weather changes and these people who are now camped
all along the bayous, without shelter, will remain so? The outlook is very
gloomy in my opinion. The prospects were fine for a large crop, and men who
have been losing money for several years past were looking forward with much
hopefulness a few weeks ago. Now, unless we are favored unusually, we shall
lose a large part of our crops. Nothing has been done on my place for two
weeks and I estimate my losses at one-third of my entire crop. The only
thing that will prevent this loss is the continuance of this fine weather
and the speedy return to work of the strikers."

"No one in your neighborhood has given in to the men?"

"No, sir. One man did grant the advance a few days ago. The men worked
half a day and demanded $1.40, and seventy-five cents for watch. Of course
he could not grant that, and so has declined to pay anything more than the
original wages--$1, and forty cents watch."

Mr. Butler had heard nothing of the rumored strike in Assumption parish.

Hon. E. J. Gay

Hon. E. J. Gay arrived here late last night from Iberville parish. He
reports that there is no danger of any trouble in that vicinity. His plantation has nearly its full complement of hands and the work is going ahead
steadily. The advance has not been granted on his place, nor had he heard
of others yielding. Near Thibodaux, he said, he thought the planters were
firmer than anywhere else. On nearly or quite all the plantations there is
a nucleus of men who have remained at work, and about this nucleus, Mr. Gay
believes others will form until enough to do the work are secured. If a
kindly feeling is manifested by the planters he thinks the strikers will all
go back. Mr. Gay thinks the presence of troops has been of incalculable
value in preserving the peace in the strike districts.

Interview with Mr. Rousseau

Mr. P. O. Rousseau, of Thibodaux, arrived in the city last evening. He
reports that work on nearly every plantation from Raceland to Lockport is at
a standstill. This also applies to Major Lagarde's place. "Below that
point," said Mr. Rousseau, all the planters have given in and the men are
working at the new rates. At Raceland Mr. Godchaux has granted the advance,

as have also the owners of Utopia plantation. Hon. E. J. Gay's plantation
Arcadia, is working nearly a full force at the new rates. The advance has
also been conceded by Whiteland & Kent, of the Eddy plantation, near Thibodaux; Joe Clodet & Bro., a short distance above Thibodaux, and Joe Toupes &
Bro., in the same vicinity.

Mr. Rousseau said that men were being evicted everywhere. None refused
to go, but quietly pack their few movables and move out in the woods or camp
alongside the road. Others make for the towns. Thibodaux is crowded with
these refugees. Every church has become a lodging-house for the homeless
negroes. The cabins are filled to double their capacity and every empty
building is filled.

He believes it was the intention of the negroes in Assumption parish to
strike yesterday. One man who had been working there, and is thought to be
a leader on one of the plantations, was at Mr. Rousseau's place yesterday
morning, and when asked why he did not go to his work answered evasively,
giving Mr. Rousseau the impression that a strike had been ordered.

Mr. Rousseau reports all quiet in his neighborhood.

The Morgan City Rifles returned from Pattersonville to Morgan City, and
a body of militia from Houma were at Schriever Station when the evening train
passed there.

Joseph Lombas, of Lockport, also came in last evening. He says the
situation there is unchanged. The negroes are quiet and the town and vicinity absolutely without excitement.

New Orleans Times-Democrat, November 8, 1887.

27.   LABOR IN THE SOUTH

Some of the Northern papers are sermonizing on the sugar strike in this
State, and seeking to demonstrate that labor is without rights in the South.
Here is one of the *Globe-Democrat's* remarkable and erroneous statements on
this subject:

The strike of the laborers on the Louisiana plantations is to be regretted in so far as it may endanger the finest sugar crop ever grown in the
State; but it has its agreeable side, nevertheless, when considered in a
general way. It shows that the labor element of the South is beginning to
understand that it has certain rights which it may enforce in spite of bad
laws and systematic methods of injustice and oppression. Up to this time,
the employers have practically had things their own way, and the employes
have simply taken what they could get in a tame and forlorn fashion. It is
notorious that the wages paid to working people in all the Southern States
has barely sufficed to prevent starvation. Louisiana has been more liberal
than some of the others, owing to special necessities; but she has been very
careful at the same time to deny her laborers every advantage that she
possibly could. The whole system of labor in the South since the war has
been made as nearly like slavery as the conditions would allow; and the victims have submitted to it mainly from force of habit and want of acquaintance
with the means to assert and protect themselves.

The tribute here paid to Louisiana is a just one, for it has been especially considerate of its labor; but all the other statements in the article
are wide of the mark. It is a vain attempt to work up the question here in
which the Republicans think they see an advantage, for they have undoubtedly
benefited by politico-labor movements in the North.

Judge Kelley and nearly all the prominent Northerners who have been in
this section of late have commented on the infrequency of strikes and the
generally friendly relations existing between labor and capital, and have
counted this among the great advantages this section offered. This relation
extended not to agricultural labor alone, but to that engaged in manufacture;
and while there was no doubt of the fact that the wages paid are smaller here
than in the North and West, the difference is more than offset, those gentlemen showed, by the smaller cost of living, and generally by the fact that the

labor is not as skilled, particularly the factory labor, as in New England.
The cotton-mill hands in Massachusetts get more than those in Georgia; but
at the same time they turn out a larger average production of goods.

But with regard to the agricultural labor, on which the *Globe-Democrat*
principally dwells, it needs only refer to the last report of the Commissioner of Agriculture on agricultural wages, which draws the following comparison between the amounts paid laborers in the different sections:

"Thus, during twenty years past, wages were higher in 1866 than at the
date of any other inquiry, except on the Pacific coast and in the South.
The decline continued to 1879, and amounted to 39 per cent in the Eastern
States, 35 in the Middle States, 30 in the Western States, and 17 in the
Southern States."

Since 1879 there has been an advance all along the line, except on the
Pacific coast--the advance in the South being 7 and in the West 1 per cent.

Relative to the pay of hands in the sugar district during harvest season,
the following is of interest:

Louisiana (pay during harvest) given	$1.50
Louisiana (pay during harvest) asked	1.86
Maine	1.68
New Hampshire	1.66
Pennsylvania	1.65
Maryland	1.74
Ohio	1.75
Kentucky	1.51
Illinois	1.80
Missouri	1.62
Kansas	1.87
Dakota	1.38

There is not much difference here, and the *Globe-Democrat* will find it
difficult to prove that the South is harsh with its labor or pays it ill.
Its manifest purpose is to stir up disturbances; indeed, it does not even
conceal this, but announces that if the laborers strike often enough, even
though their strikes may be mistaken, "they will find the employers more
and more willing to listen to them; and ultimately, if they persevere, the
South will be forced to yield to labor the same consideration given it in
the North."

It will not need a long series of strikes, as the *Globe-Democrat* proposes, to accomplish that result. The South gives labor due consideration
today. There are few fortunes built up in the South by capital; and that
the planters and farmers have paid as high wages as the present prices of
their products would allow is well shown by their bank books.

That the condition of affairs here is not such as the *Globe-Democrat*
represents is well proved by the fact that a great many hands have come down
here from the West to work in the factories, the mines and the sugar district of Louisiana, where white labor is far more abundant than it ever was
before. The number thus seeking employment has increased each year, and it
will be very difficult to demonstrate, as the *Globe-Democrat* pretends, that
they are leaving a region where the laborer receives every consideration
for one where he is ill-treated and tyrannized over and half starved. Its
suggestion that what the South needs is more strikes, is not likely to recommend itself to any intelligent men.

New Orleans *Times-Democrat*, *November 8, 1887.*

28.   THE LOUISIANA STRIKES

In vivid contrast to the idyllic pictures of the laborers' life on the
Louisiana sugar plantations portrayed in the November *Century* are the strikes
reported the past few weeks in the same sections. The daily newspapers gave
alarming apprehensions of violence from the strikers accompanied by destruc-

tion of property, but the following from *Southern Industry*, a labor paper published in New Orleans, places a different face on the matter:

A gentleman who had just returned from the scene of the strikes in the Teche country, informs us that the ordering out of the militia was entirely uncalled for. The men were advised at the meetings of their assemblies to quit work quietly, if the planters refused their demands, and to leave the plantations without making any demonstration. This our informant says, was done, and that at no time was violence comtemplated.

The *Southwestern Christian Advocate* has the following in the same vein:

Fortunately the order of Gov. McEnery to forward troops to the town of Schriever, La., was countermanded. It is not clear why it was ever issued, for there was no disturbance of public order, or no threat of one beyond the ability of ordinary process issued by civil authorities. There was a labor strike by plantation hands, who wanted a slight advance in wages. Providing no contracts are broken, men have a right to work or not.

The *Louisiana Standard* takes issue with the New Orleans *Times-Democrat* for its defence of Governor McEnery's action and says:

There has been no disturbance of the peace by the strikers, nor turbu-lence of any kind. The truth is, the laborers, believing that they had worked long enough at starvation wages, decided to ask for an advance, and this they did in respectful terms.

Later dispatches from Pattersonville, La., apprise us of the shooting of four Negroes in the vicinity of that town last Saturday by a sheriff's posse, who appear to have opened hostilities with murderous haste. It is de-nied that the militia took any part in the slaughter, although they were present guarding the town.

The situation is evidently one requiring cool judgment and discretion to avert the unnecessary spilling of further blood and it is to be feared that these qualities are not to be found among the authorities of the State or parishes.

New York Freeman, November 12, 1887.

29. THE KNIGHTS OF LABOR

SANCTUARY DISTRICT ASSMB'Y
No. 102, Knights of Labor,
New Orleans, Nov. 11, 1887.

At a meeting of District Assembly No. 102, Knights of Labor, held on the above date, the following preamble and resolutions were unanimously adopted and ordered published:

'Whereas, it has come to the knowledge of this District Assembly, offi-cially and through the daily press, that a circular emanating from the Joint Local Executive Board, Knights of Labor, parish of Lafourche, asking an in-crease in wages, in conformity with a scale of wages established by District Assembly No. 194, was presented to the sugar planters; and

Whereas, said circular, couched in respectful and courteous language, was entirely ignored by said planters and treated with contempt; and

Whereas, said planters, in meeting assembled, did agree to earnestly combine and resolve that under no circumstances would they recognize any labor organization or pay the wages, or to the manner of payment, asked for in the circular; and that said planters did further resolve to eject all of their employees who would go on strike, from their plantations and blacklist said employees; and

Whereas, without color of authority or necessity, the Chief Executive of the State of Louisiana ordered out State troops to enforce the aggressive and arbitrary will of said planters; and

Whereas, a sheriff's posse, assisted by detectives or police, did arrest certain of the plantation laborers; and
    Whereas, we are informed that said sheriff's posse, detectives or
police, backed by State troops, killed four or more laborers, without provocation, while said laborers were under arrest; and
    Whereas, we are reliably informed that the laborers were ready to leave,
and did leave the plantations whenever requested; therefore, be it
    Resolved, That it is our belief that said laborers, in the employ of
the aforesaid sugar planters in the parish of Lafourche and adjoining
parishes, had no other recourse to obtain their just demand but to discon-
tinue work until their demands were satisfied or a hearing given them. Be
it further
    Resolved, That we condemn and censure the actions of the chief execu-
tive of the State, Sam'l D. McEnery, in ordering out the State troops to be
uncalled for, and without authority or precedent, and that we admonish the
governor of the State of Louisiana that he shall not override the rights of
her citizens to peaceably assemble and ask a fair conpensation for their
honest labor. And that he must respect the constitution and laws of this
State, and cease the offensive display or use of military force during a
controversy between employer and employee, when no attempt is made or intended to violate law and the peace and dignity of the State. Be it further
    Resolved, That from information in our possession, we believe that the
lawless destruction of human life by the armed force employed was assassination, and we pronounce against it and demand that the legal constituted
authorities, by the process of law, do thoroughly investigate the killing
of the laborers at Pattersonville, and bring the slayers before the bar of
justice for such punishment as they may be found deserving. Be it further
    Resolved, That as District Assembly 102 and the whole order of the
Knights of Labor have pronounced in unmistakable language against Anarchy
and the unlawful taking of human life, we, also pronounce against any armed
force of men, whether sheriff's posse, detectives, police or military troops
taking the life of inoffensive citizens while peacefully exercising their
rights.
    Be it further resolved, That this District Assembly, in unmeasured
terms, deplore the action of the Planters' Association, and in deploring we
give them fair warning that "When Greek meets Greek then comes the tug of
war." And we will at once appeal to our millions of workingmen to ask at
the hands of Congress the repeal of the duties on sugar, which will in the
end bring them to a sense of justice and of the rights of others and benefit
the whole people of these United States.
    Be it further resolved, That this District Assembly appoint a committee
to immediately investigate all matters concerned, herewith expressed in these
resolutions, and see that perfect justice is done. And that this District
Assembly use every endeavor to assist the committee in the furtherance of
this object.
    Be it further resolved, That the Executive Board take such steps as will
materially aid the committee in accomplishing the end sought for, and that
we pledge our entire moral and financial support in the direction.'

The Weekly Pelican, November 19, 1887.

30. SUGAR PLANTATION LABORERS

    NEW IBERIA, La., Nov. 7.--*To the Editor:--The Times-Democrat* of New
Orleans, in discussing an editorial which recently appeared in your paper concerning the present sugar tariff, undertakes to refute your argument, based
partly on the statement of Congressman Scott, in relation to the wages of
sugar plantation hands. The plain facts are that the hands on our sugar
plantations are not much, if any, better paid and cared for than the pauper
labor of Europe. To illustrate: First-class laborers on sugar plantations
are paid from January to grinding season (about the 1st of November) at the

rate of 65 cents per day, subject to deductions for all days or parts of days lost for any cause. They are furnished a cabin or room 12 x 15, in which themselves and families may reside. Out of these wages the laborer has to "feed" and clothe himself and family. I am readily informed by experienced overseers that after all deductions for lost time are made the average laborer makes about twenty days per month, provided he does not fall sick; he therefore receives in pasteboard tickets an average of $13 per month. These tickets are not transferable, and can only be negotiated at the plantation store, where they are exchanged for meat, bread, etc., at the prices fixed by the storekeeper, who generally represents the planter. These prices are usually fixed at about 100 per cent over the wholesale cost of the goods; there fore the planter gets back through his plantation store in profits on his goods about one-half of the wages which he pays the laborer, which makes the actual wages paid by the planter about $6.50 per month.

This rate and mode of payment generally prevail until sugar-making commences, when the wages are increased to 75 cents and $1 per day, and 50 cents for an extra six hours' work at night, which is called "a watch."

The laborer continues to receive his pay in tickets, but continues to buy his meat, bread, and other necessaries at the plantation store. At the end of the year he is as "poor as a church mouse," and the demands of his stomach are such that he is compelled to enter into a new contract for another year.

The strike which is now going on in the Teche and Lafourche sugar district was brought about--as I understand it--by the action of the Knights of Labor, who in the name and in behalf of these poor pauper laborers, composed principally of colored people, demanded $1.25 per day and 60 cents per watch of six hours for first-class laborers, sugh wages to be paid in money instead of tickets. Considering all the circumstances, this demand seems reasonable,--especially so the present year, owing to a fine crop and yield of sugar,--yet the planters have organized themselves, advised and caused the governor to order out the State troops, and refused to pay the wages demanded by the laborers, several of whom were shot and killed at Pattersonville last Saturday. The outlook at present is gloomy for hundreds of the laborers, who have been driven from the cabins and are now without food or shelter other than such as has been given them in the towns by those of their own color, who are poorly able to provide for themselves.

There are some honorable exceptions to the manner of paying laborers, some planters paying in money and allowing their hands to trade wherever they please.

The "I owe you" ticket method has been the largest factor in bringing on the present strike, and as it is in direct violation of section 3583 of the Revised Statutes of the United States, which imposes a penalty of fine and imprisonment for its violation, I trust that the publicity herein given to the matter will reach the department of justice, and that the offenders will be dealt with in such manner as law, justice, fair play, and humanity demand.

I leave the question of "does the tariff on sugar protect the laborer" who, by the sweat of his brow, makes it to gentlemen who are better posted on the subject than I am, leaving them to apply the facts stated, and sustained by the average overseer's time book, to the whole question at issue, and then reach their own conclusions on the subject.

In order that the plantation store profit may be fairly averaged, I suggest the following question to any live country dealer, viz: Suppose you had absolute control of the trade of five hundred men whose credit outside of your store was entirely worthless, and from whom no one could make a cent by process of law, and your trade was to be exclusively with those one hundred people, what rate of profit would you charge them on the goods you sold them, considering their gross trade to be worth $1300 per month?--W. B. Merchant in Chicago Times.

The Weekly Pelican, November 19, 1887.

31. SUGAR PLANTERS' ASSOCIATION OF LOUISIANA

The Sugar Planters' Association of Louisiana is divided into branches, one of which is composed of the parishes of Iberia, Lafourche, St. Mary, St. Martin, and Terrebonne. This district produces one-third of the sugar made in Louisiana. The population is about 110,000 souls, slightly the larger part of these souls encased in black bodies.

The sugar planters in the association number about fifty or sixty persons, and require the labor of several thousand men to cultivate their plantations. The work of sugar making lasts from ten to twelve weeks, commencing generally in the early part of October and ending in the latter part of December.

The work of cutting the cane and making the sugar has to be done in this short period to prevent damage by frosts, and the laborers' work from daylight to dark, and even longer, fourteen and sixteen hours being the usual length of a day's work.

These fifty or sixty sugar planters met and settled the prices they would pay for this kind of labor, and it was the enormous sum of *one dollar per day* and *fifty cents* for watching at night.

All the laborers are negroes, and most of them ignorant and poor. Some one told them of the advantages derived from organization, and they became Knights of Labor. Last month they made a schedule of prices, asking $1.25 a day for labor and 60 cents a night for watching. This was refused and they struck.

Immediately, and without a call from the civil authorities of the parishes, Gov. McEnery troops with a Gatling gun to the "Teche" country, and there men have been forced, at the point of the bayonet and the muzzle of a Gatling gun, to return to work at the wages dictated by the sugar planters, behind whom is the power of the State of Louisiana.

Do the workingmen of the country understand the significance of this movement? The negroes of the "Teche" are practically disfranchised. Their votes are of no value, and for that reason they can be forced to work at starvation wages in the richest spot of land under the American flag.

The servile labor of the south is servile and controlled by bayonets and Gatling guns, because the white voters of the north—the men who labor with their hands—do *not* protect their ignorant fellow-workingmen in the rights which the constitution guarantees them, and allows Democrats to control the country.

The Weekly Pelican, November 19, 1887.

32.   LABOR TROUBLES

A Bad State of Affairs in Lafourche

Several Cases of Attempted Assassination Reported

Action Taken by a Mass Meeting of Citizens Called to Consider

the Situation

A Committee on Law and Order Formed

THIBODAUX, La., Nov. 20.—[Special]—Unfortunately the labor troubles are not over. For several weeks hands working peacefully under can sheds have been fired into. Several were wounded and one has since died. The outlook is very dark. The people of Thibodaux can no longer put up with the strain. The town is full of idle negroes, who each day become more and more audacious.

A number of the citizens of the parish for the past three weeks have been holding daily meetings and have been doing everything in their power to maintain peace and order. This is with the greatest difficulty, for many who attended the meetings are young men, who impatiently wait for the moment to put a stop to this state of affairs.

This morning an alarm of a riot was reported at the back of town, and within a very short space of time over 100 men fully armed marched to the place where the disorder was said to exist. Fortunately there was no appearance of trouble, for it would have gone badly with the participants. This evening a much larger meeting assembled.

The inhabitants of Thibodaux feel a little more secure, for many who for three weeks have been standing by as quiet spectators to the terrible struggle between planters and laborers have come to the conclusion to give help. What is the cause of this sudden change is not as yet known, and planters are glad to see the interest taken in them even at this late date, and are thankful for it.

The town will be patrolled tonight and all the people trust there will be no trouble, but all are so wrought up that at this moment the most trifling incident will bring on a terrible massacre.

PROCEEDINGS OF THE MASS MEETING AT THIBODAUX

THIBODAUX, La., via Schriever, La., Nov. 20.--[Special]--A mass meeting of the citizens of the parish of Lafourche, composed of about 300 of the most prominent residents, was held in the town hall of the town of Thibodaux this afternoon.

The meeting was called to order by Major S. F. Grissmore, who requested Lieutenant Governor Clay Knobloch to preside.

On taking the chair the governor said that he was sorry to say that circumstances required such a meeting. Here were assembled men representing all trades and professions. The good citizens of the community assembled to take counsel together concerning the state of lawlessness in this section. For the past few days would-be assassins were prowling about at night shooting into sugar-houses; on one occasion shooting at a horseman on the public highway. Several persons have already been wounded by those night prowlers. One man died from the effects of the wounds received, and another lost an eye. Such lawless acts must be put down at all hazards.

He hoped the meeting would calmly discuss the situation, not indulge in violent or intemperate language, but take such action as would surely discover the guilty parties and bring them to speedy justice. In this effort he knew that all good citizens would make common cause.

Mr. O. Naquin presented the following resolutions:

"Whereas, certain parties, in violation of law, order and decency, have, from time to time, been firing upon various parties in this parish and wounding others, and have been making threats of violence against other parties; and, whereas, this state of affairs is a disgrace to the parish and a reproach upon its good name for law and order; now, therefore, we, the good and law-abiding citizens of the parish of Lafourche, in mass meeting assembled, do resolve that this state of disorder shall and must cease, and that we all, regardless of calling, avocation or pursuit, do now pledge ourselves and each other to use every means in our power to bring the guilty parties, and those who may have advised such lawlessness, to a speedy detection and punishment.

"Resolved, further, That we now offer a reward of $250 for the detection of the party or parties guilty of those offenses.

"Resolved, That for the better preservation of the peace the sheriff be requested to swear in deputies, and that he shall have a patrol to make vigilant search day and night for the guilty parties.

"Resolved, That a committee on peace and order be now appointed to represent this body, and to co-operate with the law officers in ferreting out the guilty and in preserving the peace, and that full powers be granted said committee."

The resolutions were adopted.

The chairman appointed the following persons on said committee: Judge Beattie, Major Lagarde, Emile Morvant, Andrew Price, L. A. Trosclair, Ozeme Naquin, Ellis Brand, Lawrence Keefe, Dr. Dansereau, Dr. J. H. Fleetwood, Louis Julian, E. G. Curtis, John Seely, H. W. Tabor, Alceste Bourgeois, Taylor Legarde, A. Molaisson, L. D. Moore, Thomas Beary. The name of the chairman was added to the committee.

The meeting was then addressed by Messrs. I. D. Moore, Judge Beattie, Lewis Guion, Andrew Price, J. M. Howell, W. H. Price and S. T. Grissmore, when the committee on peace and order retired for consultation.

In due time the committee reported through Mr. Moore that they had taken action to suppress the prevailing lawlessness, and advised against any individual action--that every person should obey the law and the law officers and aid in preserving good order, but leave all movements to be arranged by the committee.

On motion, the secretary was directed to telegraph these proceedings to the Times-Democrat and New Orleans Picayune for publication tomorrow.

The sheriff then swore in thirty deputies when the meeting adjourned.

New Orleans Daily Picayune, November 21, 1887.

33. RIOT AT THIBODAUX

PICKETS GUARDING THE TOWN ATTACKED BY NEGROES

Two White Men Seriously Wounded--The Fire Returned by an Armed Guard and Citizens---Six Negroes Killed and Five Wounded.

Special to The Times-Democrat.

THIBODAUX, Nov. 23.--The continued threats of the negro strikers in this parish to attack this town culminated this morning in a bloody fight, in which six of the negroes were killed and five wounded, and two young white men seriously hurt.

After the meeting of the sugar planters and other prominent citizens on Sunday, the more violent of the negroes openly made threats to burn the town and commit other depredations. The citizens of Thibodaux, knowing the inflamed condition of the strikers, at once took steps to protect their lives and property. For the past few days white citizens from all parts of the parish have been coming to Thibodaux.

On Sunday night the situation had become so serious that a number of the best young men of the town and parish were sworn in as deputy sheriffs and picketed on the approaches to the place.

Monday afternoon and night alarming reports continued to come in and the excitement increased. Householders, not feeling secure even with the protection of the cordon around the town, stood guard all night or only caught brief snatches of sleep. More timid women were unable to sleep at all, and many have not closed their eyes since they arose Monday morning. The whole town has been under a strain of great uneasiness which was increased from the fact that no one knew when the attack would take place.

Yesterday evening information was received from reliable sources that the negroes were combining and that the attack would be made last night. The cordon of pickets was strengthened, and the coming of the negroes anxiously awaited. The night wore on, however, and there was no sign of trouble. The day dawned, the sun arose, and the men who had stood guard all night over the lives and property of their kindred were preparing to go to their homes, when the sharp crack of rifles, mingled with the rattle of shotguns, awoke the few citizens of the town who were asleep and told the men on guard that the fight had begun.

The outmost picket guarding the town consisted of two of Thibodaux's most respectable young men--Messrs. John J. Gorman and Henry Moiaison. These two were posted considerably in advance of the others, and, the night being chilly, had built a bonfire and were standing near it. About 7 o'clock they were fired upon by a party of negroes in ambush, who had evidently concealed themselves during the night near the bonfire. As the report of the guns rang out both men fell to the ground seriously wounded, Mr. Gorman with a bullet in his head, which entered near the eye, and Mr. Moiaison with a severe wound in the leg.

As already stated, this volley alarmed the rest of the guard and the whole town, and the former immediately rushed to the scene of the firing. Two young men posted near the wounded men soon reached them, and immediately took steps looking to their relief. While they were thus assisting the wounded another volley was fired upon them by the negroes, but fortunately it did no damage.

In a few minutes the entire guard around the town had rushed to the danger point, and other citizens began to assemble with such weapons as they could hurriedly lay their hands on. As they assembled around the wounded men, half of them unconscious of how the wounds had been received, there came a third volley from the negroes in ambush. This volley, like the second, did no damage, but served to unmask the assailants and to indicate to the citizens, who had gathered hastily with the knowledge only that there was danger somewhere, exactly where that danger lay.

There was an instant and prompt reply to the volley, and a general fusilade was poured into the ranks of the negroes. In a few minutes the fight had ended. The negroes replied feebly to the fire of the whites at first, but soon became panic-stricken and fled to the woods.

After the battle the wildest rumors were afloat as to the number killed. At first it was stated that from fifteen to twenty-five negroes had lost their lives and that a large number were wounded. After thorough search by the coroner, assisted by other citizens, however, it was found that only six of the attacking party had been killed and five wounded. The two young men who went down under the first volley were the only white men hurt.

There was a great deal of excitement in town and throughout this section during the day, but tonight all is quiet. As a matter of precaution, however, the town is still guarded by a cordon of armed pickets, and all the white men in town are under arms, acting as deputy sheriffs.

THE THIBODAUX WAR

Interview with a Number of White Residents of the Town Who Fled for Safety, Fearing a Further Attack by Negroes.

The regular Morgan Railroad train, en route to New Orleans, left Thibodaux at 12:45 o'clock. The departure of the train was anxiously awaited by many women and children who were "on pins and needles" to leave the place, fearing that the riotous negroes would carry out their avowed threats of burning the houses and murdering the women and children.

The shooting yesterday morning sent a shock of terror to the hearts of many women and children, hence their fleeing from their homes to the city to seek shelter with friends and relatives.

As soon as the train stopped every available seat was quickly taken. About twenty ladies, accompanied by their children, a number of white men and a large concourse of negroes boarded the train and were soon speeding toward the city. The conductor of the train had his hands full, for but few, if any of the passengers had secured tickets, all having but one purpose to accomplish, and that was to get away from Thibodaux just as fast as the iron horse could carry them off.

The majority of the white people came to the city, but at every station the negroes left the train in squads of five and ten until the city was reached, when but few were left. Among the negroes who came here notably were two of the ringleaders, Marshall Ricar and Christian Banks. When they alighted from the train they were noticed by a Creole gentleman who is well acquainted in Thibodaux, and whose business at the train was to meet some of his relatives. The gentleman, calling the negroes by name, said: "Here you are--you two rascals have been the ringleaders in all the trouble. They ought to have kept both of you in jail and hung you." To this the negroes made no reply, but simply ran out Esplanade street as fast as their feet could carry them.

Among the passengers arriving yesterday was the Hoffman family, consisting of Mrs. Hoffman, Mrs. A. Bouron, three daughters and two sons. At the train they were met by Mr. Bouron, the well-known gun maker, who resides on Chartres, near Jefferson street, where a TIMES-DEMOCRAT reporter called last evening at 7:30 o'clock. All the visitors had retired for the night. Mr. Bouron was interviewed by the writer. He disliked awakening the ladies who were very tired, but if the reporter insisted he said that he would comply.

He said further that the ladies had not had a night's rest for the last
three weeks, being afraid to venture to sleep, fearing that the oft-repeated
threats to kill them and burn their buildings would be carried out.

Mrs. Hoffman's husband keeps a furniture store, and Mr. Bouron keeps a
gun store in Thibodaux. Mr. Bouron's store has been carefully guarded by the
citizens and militia for the last three weeks, it having been reported that
the negroes had decided to set his place on fire, and then plunder the
establishment of all the arms in the place. The ladies stated to Mr. Bouron
that everything was quiet up to 5 o'clock, when two of the guards were fired
at, and the result was that a number of negroes were killed. They heard the
shooting, and momentarily awaited the burning of their homes.

A few families came to the city and everything was quiet when they left.
Mrs. Edgar Rivier, her mother and three sisters, and Mrs. Rivier's children
were among those who came in on the train last evening. Mrs. Rivier was met
at the train by Mr. Lajeau, a merchant residing on Decatur, between Jefferson and Toulouse streets, who is closely related to the ladies and at whose
residence they are staying.

Mrs. Rivier was visited by a reporter of THE TIMES-DEMOCRAT last evening.
She said that there were some fifteen or seventeen negroes killed. She and
a number of other women and children came away from Thibodaux. A large
crowd of negroes left Thibodaux, but at every point they left the train in
squads of five and ten. The train arrived in the city at 5 o'clock, and
Mrs. Rivier was glad to get to New Orleans.

"The reason for killing the negroes was because they shot at the guards,
who had been watching the city, because it was threatened to burn the houses
and kill the women and children. We were afraid that they were going to
burn the houses and murder us when we heard the shooting.

"After the shooting everything was quiet, and by 11 o'clock all the
negroes had fled from the town. The negroes don't want peace; they want to
fight; and when they get into a fight they run away. All the trouble is
caused by several darkies and white leaders. These leaders do no work and
get up disturbances among the field hands and then leave the field hands to
fight it out."

In conclusion, the lady stated that she, as well as other women, were
compelled to leave for fear of the negroes carrying out their threat to burn
the houses and murder the women and children. Her husband, Mr. Edgar Rivier,
and brother-in-law, Mr. A. Bouron, are members of the militia, and they were
on duty yesterday when their families left for the city.

Mr. Lejeau stated to the writter that he learned through the telephone
that two of the negro leaders who had been jailed and were last evening
taken from the jail and shot openly. The gentleman endeavored to obtain
further particulars by telephone about 6 o'clock last evening, but the
telephone office was closed.

A TALK WITH NEGRO REFUGEES

As soon as the news of the fight reached the city a reporter of THE
TIMES-DEMOCRAT was dispatched to meet the incoming train at Gretna.

The train was boarded at the Gretna station by the reporter at 3:30 p.m.
There were several parties in one of the coaches who had come from Thibodaux,
but as they were refugees and had not been in the fight, they did not possess
a very extensive fund of information.

H. Franklin, a colored man, was pointed out as having been one of the
agitators, and he was interviewed.

He said: "So far as I know, two men who constituted the outer patrol of
citizens--J. G. Gorman and Henry Mellaison--were fired into this morning
about daybreak and seriously wounded. A bullet entered Gorman's right eye
and came out of his mouth, while Mellaison received a shot in the knee. The
firing was done by colored people who were out on the strike."

"As soon as this occurred the citizens of the town turned out en masse
and attacked the strikers wherever they met them. I don't know how many were
killed, but heard it estimated at fully twenty-five. The shooting was quite
general. I don't know if the parties who did the firing at the pickets were
caught or not. I don't think there is any doubt about the pickets having
been shot while around their bonfire. I left Thibodaux because I thought I
would be safer away from there."

W. N. Nathaniel, another negro, said the whites had been to his house while he was away and had run his wife off, and he had fled for safety. They had killed his cousin, Willis Wilson.

Mr. Sidney F. Lewis, of the State Board of Engineers, who was also on the train, told the reporter that when he passed through Thibodaux Tuesday night he found the citizens much excited, alarmed and under arms. It looked as if trouble was brewing and they were making preparations to protect themselves against any overt action on the part of the strikers. He did not remain in the town, but his assistant, Bob Smith, did.

Bob Smith, who was also on the train, said he had slept last night in the courthouse and heard random shots during the night. That the strikers were encamped in the town in a big brick house, and the people felt much alarmed over the state of affairs, especially after the shooting into the sugar-houses on Monday night.

"This morning," he continued, "about 5 o'clock, while the outer pickets were around their bonfire, they were fired into by the negroes and two of them badly wounded. The news spread rapidly, and the Clay Knobloch Guards fell in and marched to the front. The citizens hastily collected many of them mounted, and hurried to the scene.

"Shooting soon commenced and in a short while the strikers had disappeared. Several of them were killed, the majority fleeing for parts unknown.

"All of the agitators and strikers have been ordered out of town, and have obeyed without loss of time. There are between 200 and 300 citizens under arms, and do not intend to stand any more trifling, intimidation or threats."

Charles Lussian, a white man, who had been pointed out as an agitator, was next spoken to. He was rolling a cigarette and talking to some negroes. His wife and child were with him. He was a slight-built man of sallow complexion, of about medium height, wearing a small dark mustache. He wore a slouch hat, good clothes, although his shirt collar was wilted, and was minus a cravat.

He said that he had kept a market in Thibodaux, and did a large business with the negroes, but knew nothing of the trouble. He had seen some shooting near his place, in which the colored people were getting the worst of it.

The citizens had warned him to depart from there instantly, and he had taken the train as soon as it came along.

From general conversation with several who had heard of the state of affairs, the reporter learned that the citizens, right after the shooting in the morning, had notified all agitators, irrespective of color or nationality, to quit town within twenty-four hours, and the most of them had availed themselves of the opportunity.

They have also forbidden any of the strikers to enter Thibodaux under any pretext whatever, and it was said that the citizens had declared their intention of putting an end to the labor troubles in that vicinity without more ado.

Everything was quiet when the train left and business had entirely ceased.

THE MILITIA ORDERED OUT

Last night Capt. Adams, of the Louisiana Rifles, stated that he had received orders to start for Thibodaux today on the 12:15 train with his command.

Capt. Adams last night issued the following orders:

QUARTERS COMPANY A, LOUISIANA RIFLES, New Orleans, Nov. 23, 1887.

Pursuant to general orders the members of this command will assemble Thursday, Nov. 24, at 9 a.m. sharp, fully equipped for duty in field.

By order of Capt. C. H. Adams.

L. J. FALLON, First Sergeant.

New Orleans Times-Democrat, November 24, 1887.

34. PEACE RESTORED

ARRIVAL OF THE TROOPS AT THIBODAUX

Re-enforcements from Houma

The Pickets Again Fired Upon

The Wounded Men Doing as Well as Could be Expected

THIBODAUX, La., Nov. 24.--[Special]--Everything is exceedingly quiet in
Lafourche parish today. At 4 o'clock the train from New Orleans brought as
passengers the Louisiana Rifles and a detachment of the Washington Artillery,
the latter having with them a Gatling gun, served by Sergeant Vaughan and
Private Blackman, Rhoderdar, Ashbey, Rube and Kelly. Captain Adams commanded
the rifles with Lieutenant Moer and Oviatt, Sergeants Famou, Duffy and Moses,
Corporals Beyer and Remy and Privates Bonnecaze, Wirth, Bernard, Fallon,
Munroe, Blaise, Calhoun, Barfa, Lazard, Viosa, Marks, Hart, Williams, Hernandez, Talgo, May, Dowler, Mumer, Mayers, Vierre, Reisberg and Reynoir.
    The troops were met at the depot by Judge Taylor Beattie and escorted
to the courthouse, where they were quartered.
    Last night at about 8 o'clock, shortly after the pickets were posted,
and a short distance from where Gorman and Molaison were fired upon the night
previous, the outlaws fired upon the pickets, and rumors of the disturbances
here reached Houma, and Messrs. Winder, Southon, Nelan, Williams, W. F. Gray,
Peter Berger, and other courageous gentlemen taking conveyances, arrived in
town about 9 o'clock. They were about fifteen in all. The contingent greatly
relieved the home guard, for these gentlemen immediately placed themselves
at the dispostion of Judge T. Beattie, and were assigned to their various
posts of duty.
    The hands have returned to work, each one endeavoring to throw the blame
on the other, as is usual under such circumstances. The prime movers of the
shooting into the hands under the canesheds at night time, and several of
the agitators in general have escaped the punishment they so richly deserved,
and left their tools to pay for the folly of their rowdyhood. The people at
large are fully satisfied that the law has in no manner been violated by
these who acted in behalf of peace and order.
    Much credit is due to Judge Taylor Beattie for the admirable manner in
which everything has been conducted. A thorough soldier, having passed his
full time in the confederate army, all the militia of the patrol, picket,
sentinel and other soldierly duties were fully observed and the men well
held in hand, and not one shot unjustifiable or uncalled for was fired from
the beginning to the end of the difficulty. Judge Beattie has impressed
upon the whole people of Lafourche the fact that he is a judge with the power
and innate will to see the laws obeyed to the letter.
    The Picayune's representative called upon J. J. Gorman and Henry Melai-
son, the two wounded white men. They are both doing well. Gorman is the
head of an interesting family--a wife and five little children. He is about
34 years of age and belongs to the firm of Naquin & Gorman, boilermakers.
Melaison, a younger man, clerks for his father, Adrien Melaison, who conducts
a general feed store. Gorman formerly resided in New Orleans, but removed
to Thibodaux about four years ago; he is a brave, courageous and unassuming
gentleman.
    An investigation into the particulars of the shooting of Wednesday
morning has resulted substantially the same as that published in yesterday's
Picayune. Gorman and Melaison were doing picket duty when fired upon by
the negro outlaws. Gorman, who was shot in the right eye, walked away from
the spot, but Melaison, who received a slug in the leg, laid in the ditch.
Frank Zernott, a prominent jeweler of the town, who was on guard, ran to
Melaison's assistance and was fired upon. The general shooting then took
place.
    In conversation with a prominent citizen it was learned that for three
weeks past the negro women of the town have been making threats to the effect
that if the white men resorted to arms they would burn the town and the lives
of the white women and children with their cane knives.

The plantations in the immediate vicinity of Thibodaux, which have been
affected by the troubles, are those of John T. Moore, Jr.'s, Waubun plantation, Logard's Coudet Bros., Tresclair & Robichaux, Lewis Guion and Ernest
Rogers. The few hands on these places who had consented to work were fired
into by the outlaws last week and the result was that not a single hand
would go to work. It was no longer a question of capital against labor,
but one of law-abiding citizens against assassins. The laboring hands here
are not recognized Knights of Labor, but a combination headed as far as their
circular goes by the most worthless of men the parish contains.

A prominent citizen here in an interview stated that the trouble had
been brewing for some weeks among the colored people, resulting from the
labor troubles. Ten days ago T. Boiblis, a sugar boiler, was fired upon by
negroes. Lewis Guion's Ridgefield sugar-house, in which a number of white
men were working, was also subjected to the same ordeal. The overseer on the
Leighton plantation was shot in the face, but not severely injured. The
hands under the cane sheds in numerous places were fired on.

Things changed for the worse, and citizens were afraid to go out upon
the public highway for fear of being shot from ambush.

The Lafourche Sugar Planters' Association sent out a committee of five
to wait upon the leaders of the Knights of Labor, who were the instigators
of the shooting in Lafourche, and notified them that the shooting had to
cease.

On that very same night there was shooting from ambush on five different
places, and on the following night there was shooting on two or three other
places.

The negroes who had left the plantations and taken refuge in the town
of Thibodaux were being put up night and day to do acts of violence. Some
negro women made threats to burn the town down. During the latter part of
last week a person could not go out into the streets without seeing congregations of negroes that wrought no good to the peace and order of the town.

Some of the negroes boasted openly that if a fight was brought about
they were fully prepared for it.

Reports came into town to the effect that the negroes would make an
attack upon it.

A report reached headquarters on Sunday that the negroes had collected
quite a number of arms on St. Charles street. The whites then saw the
necessity of being thoroughly organized to meet the emergency, and the citizens of the whole town, by reason of all these dangers surrounding them, came
together for the purpose of maintaining peace and order in the country.

A mass meeting was held on Sunday evening and a volunteer company was
organized to picket the town and stop the midnight disturbances. The pickets
were placed in position all around town.

The negroes were repeatedly warned by several of the citizens that these
lawless deeds at night had to stop at all hazards, and also the incendiary
talk. A large body of mounted men prepared for any emergency patrolled the
town on Sunday, but abstained from any act of violence until they ascertained
the effects of the mass meeting.

On Monday the negroes became insolent, and sneered at the soldiers and
citizens on the streets. They proclaimed publicly that the white people were
afraid to fire upon them, and that they were prepared.

At night some unknown persons went to Franklin's barroom where there were
some negroes. An attack was made upon the white visitors and in the firing
that ensued two negroes were wounded. Watson, one of the negroes, after running some distance, fell; the other, Page, went to his home and is doing well.

On Tuesday morning following a large number of people came into town
from the surrounding country in order to help preserve the peace. During the
day the two Cox brothers, being leaders of the combination were arrested for
incendiary language and jailed. Towards evening the negroes appeared to have
given up the contest and being entirely subdued they went home and abandoned
the streets.

The night passed off quietly, but at 5 o'clock Wednesday morning the
pickets were fired upon with the result already known.

The organized citizens and the C. K. Guards proceeded to the scene of the
disturbance, when the citizen posse opened fire on the negroes, searched their
homes for arms and ammunition, and in a little more than a quarter of an hour

closed the whole affair.

Nine negroes were buried today, and one more will die probably tonight.

A large number of negroes escaped through the fields and have not returned. The women who had come into the city are returning to the plantations from whence they came.

At 9 o'clock tonight the town is very quiet, the stillness of the night being disturbed only by the patrol of armed citizens and soldiers.

Judge Taylor Beattie, who has made the courthouse his headquarters, is in consultation with the several officers of the military as to how to divide the forces. While this was going on the rumor reached there that a large number of armed negroes were congregating on Terrebonne road, about a mile and a quarter distant from the town. Armed citizens proceeded to the place indicated and their approach dispersed the crowd.

In the event of an attack upon the town, the result will be disastrous to the negroes.

One of the Wounded

Yesterday morning a colored man named Thomas G. Cunio was brought to the city on the Morgan train from Thibodaux, suffering from a gunshot wound of the left hand. The ambulance was called and conveyed him to the hospital, where the wound was examined and pronounced severe, the bullet having passed through the hand.

Cunio stated that about 7 o'clock Wednesday morning as he was getting out of his bed he heard some calling at his front gate to him to come out quick and let them in. As he opened his parlor door he saw a body of men standing there armed with guns. He went to open the gate and found that he had the wrong key, and they threatened to break in if he did not hurry up and let them in. Cunio told them to go around and he would let them in through the rear of his store. Some of them did so, and on entering they informed him that they were looking for arms and fugitives.

They searched the place but failed to find what they were looking for, and then ordered him behind the counter, and as he went there they fired several shots at him, one of which struck hin in the hand and some of the others grazed his feet. He fell, and while lying on the floor in front of his iron safe he says they fired several more shots at him after which they left the place. He claims that he does not know the men, nor would he be able to identify them if he ever saw them again, as he was very much excited at the time.

Cunio's statement, when first seen, was that the men drove him from the house, and then shot him. His house is located in the eastern limits of Thibodaux where he formerly kept a grocery store. He next went to selling furniture on the installment plan, and now he is engaged in buying furs.

He has resided in this town for a long while, and it is strange that he does not know his assailants who belong in Thibodaux.

New Orleans Daily Picayune, November 25, 1887.

35.   THE THIBODAUX RIOT

A Detailed Account of the Fight Wednesday

The Threats and Overt Acts of the Negroes Which Led Up to the Tragedy--
Death of Four of the Wounded Negroes--Further Trouble Expected.

Special to The Times-Democrat.

THIBODAUX, La., Nov. 23.--The Louisiana Rifles, twenty-six in number, in command of Capt. Adams, and a detachment of the Washington Artillery, with a Gatling gun and other necessary equipment, arrived here at 3:30 p.m. today. The trip from New Orleans to this city was devoid of special interest. The effects of the recent riot, however, could be seen all along the line. The depots and stations on the line of the Southern Pacific in Lafourche were crowded with negroes, eager and anxious to get out of the country. Trains bound for the Crescent City were crowded with darkies.

The troops from New Orleans were received at the depot by a large number of the prominent citizens of Thibodaux, including the Clay Knobloch Guards and the volunteers. There was not a negro to be seen in any direction.

The excitement has to a considerable extent subsided, and the leaders of the rioters, it is generally understood, have quit the country. At least they have not been seen since the affair of Wednesday. The citizens are determined to preserve the peace and have organized to that end.

It appears that the trouble leading on to the riot of Wednesday commenced about ten days ago, when negroes fired on a white man named Theodore Baille, passing on the levee. Baille is a sugar boiler, and he was fired upon a mile below town. There was some firing also on Lewis Guion's sugarhouse, in which quite a number of white men were lodged. Several shots were fired at white laborers on the Leighton plantation, and the overseer was struck in the face by small shot, but fortunately not seriously injured. Between Thibodaux and Houma hands under cane sheds were fired upon.

Indeed things had got to such a point that citizens were afraid to go out on the public highway, for fear of being shot at by negroes in ambush. The Sugar Planters' Association of Lafourche appointed a committee of five to wait on the five men who were suspected of being the instigators of the shooting in Lafourche, and notified them that their followers must preserve the peace. On that night shooting occurred at five different sugarhouses in Lafourche, the parties being in ambush, and on the succeeding nights shots were fired at three other sugarhouses.

The colored people, who had been moved away from their respective plantations, and who had taken refuge in the town of Thibodaux, were being harangued day and night for the purpose of inspiring them to deeds of violence. Some of the colored women made open threats against the people and the community, declaring that they would destroy any house in the town. One could hardly go on the streets without seeing clusters of negroes at the different thoroughfares, indulging in conversation that boded no good to the peace and order of the community. Not a few of the negroes boasted that in case a fight was made they were fully prepared for it. Reports were frequent to the effect that the negroes proposed to make an attack upon the town, and on Sunday morning it was reported in the country that the negroes had assembled on St. Charles street and were thoroughly armed.

It was at this time that the whites saw the necessity of organization for the protection of their lives and property, and to meet any emergency that might possibly arise out of the present difficulties. Hence it was that in view of existing dangers the citizens of Thibodaux organized for the purpose of maintaining peace and good order.

On Sunday at 3 p.m., a mass meeting was called and a patrol organized, with a view of stopping lawlessness and crime. A company of volunteers was also organized to picket the town. The pickets were located in every portion of Thibodaux and kept up a nightly watch.

The negroes were repeatedly warned by several of the prominent and influential citizens of the place that lawlessness at night must cease, and that good order must be restored and maintained. During Sunday large bodies of mounted men were in waiting for any emergency. On Monday the negroes were insolent, sneering at the soldiers and citizens alike, and proclaiming publicly the white people were afraid to fire on them, and that, under any circumstances, they were prepared. Monday night some unknown persons sent into Franklin's coffee-house, where there were some negroes playing cards.

The negroes made an attack upon the whites, when firing was commenced, resulting in the shooting of two negroes. Watson, one of the negroes, ran two squares and died, and the other, Morris Page, went to his home, painfully but not fatally wounded.

On Tuesday morning large crowds of white people, planters and others, from the surrounding country came into town armed, and with a determination to maintain peace and order. During the day the two Cox brothers, who were reported to be the leaders of the disturbing element, were arrested and jailed, the people being evidently determined to put an end to future trouble. Toward evening the negroes appeared to have been subdued, and the poor people were led to believe that the trouble was happily ended, and that there would

be no further violence.
    The night passed off quietly, but at 5 a.m. a guard of five men, at
the intersection of St. Charles street and the railroad, at the south end
of the town, was fired upon by a squad of negroes in ambush. The wounded
men were J. J. Gorman and Henry Molaison. Gorman was shot in the left cheek
with a slug, which took a downward tendency and passed out through his mouth.
When seen this evening he was resting easy, but was not permitted to speak.
Mr. Molaison received four shots in the right leg, only two of which have
thus far been abstracted. His coat and pants were perforated in fourteen
different places.

MR. MOLAISON'S STATEMENT

    Relative to the shooting, Mr. Molaison said in an interview with a re-
presentative of THE TIMES-DEMOCRAT this evening: " I was one of the pickets
stationed at the terminus of St. Charles street. My watch was from 12 until
6 a.m. We had quite a fire built, but none of us were near it at the time
of the shooting. Myself, Gorman, Anslett and Gruneburg were fully 250 yards
from the fire, discussing matters and things, when a shot was fired and
Gorman rolled over into the ditch near by. Gorman was shot about 5 a.m. I
thought it was a pistol-shot. Mr. Marouge accompanied Mr. Gorman home.
Both were gone about five minutes, when I told Messrs. Anslett and Gruneburg to take my place, as I wished to assist Mr. Gorman. I had gone about
200 yards from Anslett when I was shot down."
    The shooters were in ambush in a cornfield situated about 100 yards from
the picket lines. Who they were is not known, except that they were negroes.
Mr. Molaison is doing well.
    When the fact of the shooting was made known in Thibodaux the citizens
organized for self-protection a company of volunteers, and the Clay Knobloch
Guards immediately proceeded in the direction of the negroes settlement and
opened fire upon the mob and searched their houses for arms and ammunition,
and in about twenty minutes closed the affair, after having captured a number
of shotguns loaded with slugs and buckshot. Six negroes were killed outright
and four have since died of their wounds.
    The people of the town of Thibodaux and the parish generally regret the
necessity which brought about this bloody affair. Indeed they deeply deplore
it, but nevertheless feel that it was necessary to take immediate and vigorous steps to eradicate an evil which threatened to destroy not only the peace
and good order, but the lives and property of a whole community.
    Lieut. Gov. Clay Knobloch, Judge Taylor Beatty, Sheriff Thibodaux, Col.
I. D. Moore and others who were seen express the deepest regrets at the present condition of things, and hope for an early and satisfactory solution of
existing complications.
    The planters whose places have been made the scene of trouble thus far
are as follows: C. Lagard, Claudet Bros., Ernest Roger, the Guion place,
David Calder's, Orange Grove, Trosclair & Robichaux, John T. Moore, Jr., and
Peter Bergers.
    The members of the Louisiana Rifles, who arrived yesterday, are Capt.
C. H. Adams, First Lieutenant O. T. Maier, Second Lieutenant H. T. Oviatt,
First Sergeant L. J. Fellows, Second Sergeant John Duffy, Third Sergeant
Moses, Corporals Beye and Rolling, and Privates Bonnecaze, Auth, Renaud,
Fallon, Munroe, Blaise, Calhoun, Barba, Longard, Viosea, Marks, Hart, Williams,
Hernandez, Falgo, May, Dowler, Muller, Meyers, Viene, Reinberg and Reynoir.
    The following is that detachment from the Washington Artillery:
Sergeant Vaughan, E. O. Blackmar, H. Rhoderdom, Ashby, Fred A. Rube and Dan
Kelly.
    As previously stated, there was not a single negro to be seen on the
streets of Thibodaux upon the arrival of the troops. Very little business
was being transacted, and the burden of conversation had special bearing on
the riot of yesterday morning. For weeks the negroes had been making every
character of threat, lurking in out-of-the-way places and firing upon innocent and inoffensive citizens. Laborers from abroad were fired upon while in
the fields and driven therefrom, and there was no possible guarantee for the
safety of either life or property under the then existing condition of
things. On some few of the plantations the negroes have already returned to
work, but the great majority of them are still in the woods or have abandoned the country entirely.

Judge E. D. White, of New Orleans, arrived today, and will spend a few days at his plantation, about six miles from this city. He reports all quiet on his place.

Mr. Gorman, one of the victims of yesterday's affair, was formerly a citizen of New Orleans, having moved to this place four years ago. He is the head of an interesting family and runs one of the largest boiler establishments in this section. Mr. Molaison is quite a young man. He is clerking for his father in the general feed business.

Tonight all is quiet. About 8 o'clock last evening there was a rumor to the effect that the negroes were massing on the Terrebonne, about a mile and a half from the city. It was further rumored that they were thoroughly equipped and an attack upon the city was imminent. A squad of citizens immediately repaired to the scene of the threatened danger, but the crowd had dispersed. An attack upon the city is momentarily expected, and citizens and soldiers are alike prepared for any emergency that may arise. A guard placed upon the outskirts of the town was fired upon last night by a negro concealed in a ditch.

THE TROOPS OFF

The following orders were issued from brigade headquarters yesterday:

Nov. 24, 1887

Special Orders No. 10.

I. In obedience to special orders No. 6., headquarters L.S.N.G., First Military District, Capt. C. H. Adams, Louisiana Rifles, will proceed with his company of not less than twenty-six men, armed and equipped for field duty, by the 12:15 p.m. train today to Thibodaux, and will report on his arrival at Thibodaux to Judge Taylor Beattie.

II. Lieut. Col. J. B. Richardson, Washington Artillery, will furnish a detachment of not less than eight men, with Gatling gun and harness, in charge of a competent officer, to move on the same train, to act in conjunction with and report to Capt. Adams.

III. The force is instructed to be used subsidiary to and only in aid of the civil authority, acting in strict conformity to law, as provided in special orders No. 17, A.G.O., dated 23d instant, copy of which is here inclosed.

By command of Brig. Gen. Adolph Meyer.

W. F. PINCKARD, A.A.A.G.

In obedience to the above orders Capt. Adams left on the 12:15 train yesterday, in command of the Louisiana Rifles. A detachment of the Washington Artillery also went to the scene of the trouble.

WHAT A VISITOR THERE SAYS ABOUT THE SITUATION

A TIMES-DEMOCRAT reporter boarded the inward bound Morgan train at Gretna yesterday evening and obtained the following particulars from Md. Louderbough, a gentleman who stopped over in Thibodaux the day of the riot: Everything is quiet today. Hardly any negroes could be seen on the streets. A number of them have decided to go back to work on the plantations, and had furniture wagons to haul their furniture. All business was suspended the day of the riot and the town was wild with excitement. The negroes have scattered and taken to the swamps. The dead negroes were buried by the corporation. A militia company of Thibodaux was called out last night, and, with a number of citizens, quarded the place. The people are determined not to have any more trouble, and will use all means possible to prevent it. The two wounded young men are doing well, and the prospect for their recovery is good. All the stores opened up this morning. Barrooms were ordered to remain closed and not to sell any liquors. The riot is the topic of conversation, and women and children are still very nervous. It is stated that the majority of the negroes killed were rioters.

A few other passengers who passed through Thibodaux yesterday stated that everything was quiet there, but no information regarding the riot could be learned.

ALABAMA NEGROES FOR THE TECHE

Col. Rivers, of the St. Charles Hotel, yesterday sent six negro laborers to his plantation, "Grand Wood," on Bayou Teche. These negroes were
brought from Mobile, having finished cotton picking in Alabama and being
idle. Mr. Rivers declares that he can get any number from the same vicinity, and others may be brought from there if the strike does not end very
soon. Mr. Rivers employs about a hundred men, and as fifteen of the old
hands remained at work, he has now nearly a full complement and will at once
begin windrowing to prevent further loss from frost. He says there has been
no trouble at all on his place, the hands quietly leaving when ordered to
go, and he anticipates no opposition to the new men that he is sending up.

THE SITUATION IN ASCENSION

We had hoped that Ascension was to escape an attack of the "strike
fever" prevalent in other portions of the sugar district, but it was not to
be. Fortunately, however, ours has been so far only a mild case and the
patient seems at this writing to be in a state of convalescence bordering
on total recovery, with little apparent danger of a relapse.
On Tuesday last, hands on Mr. L. Picard's Live Oak plantation, at
Dutchtown, quit work and made a demand for an advance of wages, which was
refused. The laborers thought better of their movement and resumed work
next day at the former rates.
Strikes in quick succession at Mt. Houmas (Messrs. Grossley & Sons'
place), Mr. Adlard Landry's, Mr. J. Emile St. Martin's Pelico, Mr. Oliver
Beirne's Ascension and New Hope, Mr. Richard McCall's McMannor and Mr. Leon
Godchaux's Souvenir plantation, on all of which work was suspended Tuesday
and Wednesday. The demands for higher wages were refused in each case,
and a number of the leading strikers were notified to leave the plantations
on which they had been employed. Five of the most obstreperous--two from
Mt. Houmas, two from McManor and one from Souvenir--were arrested for tre-
pass, threats, incendiary and obscene language, and for bulldozing laborers
who were disposed to keep at work. Judge Durtel accorded the prisoners a
hearing yesterday and fixed their bonds at nominal amounts $25 in three
cases and %15 in the other two--reading them a lecture as to the law bearing
on such conduct as that with which they were charged. The men all expressed
a determination to behave themselves, and three of them readily furnished
bail. The two prisoners from Mt. Houmas were still in jail last evening.
On all the places mentioned excepting Mount Houmas a large majority of
the strikers have returned to work, and many of them expressed regret for
having participated in the movement. Violence was threatened on several
places, but wiser counsels and prompt action of the authorities combined to
prevent any outbreak, a circumstance upon which all concerned are to be congratulated.
Some of the teamsters on Capt. John T. Nolan's St. Elizabeth plantation also struck on Tuesday, but there was no stoppage of work there and the
strikers subsequently asked to be re-employed.
The action of the local authorities of the Knights of Labor, as indicated by the subjoined handbill--issued as soon as the news of the strikes
reached town--entitles them to the thanks of the community, and bears out
their previous declarations that their organization would countenance no
strike in this district during the present grinding:

NOTICE TO KNIGHTS OF LABOR AND WHOM IT MAY CONCERN.

                                      KNIGHTS OF LABOR HALL,
                              Donaldsonville, La., Nov. 15, 1887

Notice is hereby given that the strikes reported to have taken place
on the sugar plantations in this parish have not been ordered by this
organization and will not be countenanced thereby. If any members of this
order have participated in these strikes they are notified to resume work at
once or suffer the penalty provided by the laws of the Knights of Labor.
                                      HENRY SCHAFF,
                              Chairman of Joint Committee

New Orleans Times-Democrat, November 25, 1887 .

36. THE SUGAR DISTRICT TROUBLES

The situation in Lafourche is still somewhat critical and further disturbances may grow out of the excitement prevailing. But it looks as if the
worst had passed, and that with the precautions now taken, order will be
soon restored. The terrible experience of the deluded negro laborers at
Thibodaux will no doubt have its effect upon all the surrounding districts,
and at once suppress the lawlessness which existed.

The negroes have fallen under the leadership of bad men and attempted
to terrorize not only the white planters but their fellow-laborers who desired to work on the plantations. Encouraged by their escape from capture
in their midnight acts of vandalism, such as the firing into sugar-houses
from ambush, they grew bolder and precipitated the contest of Wednesday.

Judge Taylor Beattie, who occupies the bench of that district and is a
Republican, had command of the citizen patrol during the trouble, and sustains their action as necessary to the preservation of the peace and the
protection of property. He is a fair and just man, and would not have
sanctioned any deliberate outrage upon the colored people.

The citizens in the two parishes most affected are thoroughly aroused,
and vigorous measures will no doubt be taken to rid the country of the
leaders who are inciting the negroes to deeds of violence. As soon as that
is accomplished there need be no further apprehensions.

New Orleans Daily Picayune, November 25, 1887 .

37. THE THIBODAUX RIOT

Bodies of Three More Dead Men Found

Negro Women Continue to Make Threats, But No Further Trouble Probable--
The Cox Brothers Released from Jail.

Special to The Times-Democrat

THIBODAUX, Nov. 25.--Today Thibodaux enjoyed a day of comparative quiet,
and a better feeling is existing among all classes. There has been no relax-
ation , however, of the vigilance of citizens and military for the preservation of law and order in this community and parish. Throughout the day
guards were on the watch, and the entire town and its outskirts were thoroughly patrolled. Few negroes are to be seen, although no objection has
been urged against the presence here of those peaceably inclined.

This morning a representative of THE TIMES-DEMOCRAT, with some of the
military, visited a number of the plantations in the vicinity of Thibodaux,
with a view of ascertaining the exact condition of things in these localities.
Mr. R. H. Allen has one of the largest plantations in Lafourche. It is situated immediately in front of the town and employes about 300 laborers. Mr.
Allen said the strike had cost him about one-third of his crop, and that the
demoralization among his negroes was so great that some of those remaining
were rendered totally unfit for duty. He doesn't blame the negroes so much
as the walking delegate, whose chief business for the past few months, he
says, has been to harangue and ill-advise his less intelligent brother.

The splendid plantation of Mr. Andrew Price, about a mile and a half
from the city, was also visited. Mr. Price said that he lost about one-
third of his sugar crop in consequence of the strike, but that there had been
no trouble on his place. The action of the negroes, he said, was a surprise
to him, especially as he had made arrangements with his hands for the grinding
season. For two weeks they had worked with seeming satisfaction and no complaining was made. When he found that the strike had actually been ordered
and the laborers had withdrawn from the fields he endeavored to arrive at
some amicable adjustment of existing difficulties, whatever they might be.
The negroes, nevertheless, left the place.

Within the past day or two the old hands have been returning, and whenever a proposition to return was made in good faith Mr. Price has never failed to accept it. He charges all the recent misunderstandings between the whites and blacks to negro school teachers and barbers in the town of Thibodaux. These people, he says, are really doing nothing but inspiring the ignorant and hard-working negro element to lawlessness and strife.

A negro by the name of Lawless, who was seen by the correspondent, rents several acres of land from Mr. Price, and is working twenty-six hands on his own account. He is not a striker, but, on the contrary, is working faithfully and industriously. He makes $3000 worth of cane every year, which he sells to Mr. Price. He deprecates the present strike, saying that there was no cause whatever for it.

Felix and Mat Brooks, two of the returned strikers on Mr. Price's place, syat that they were urged to a strike by the Knights of Labor of Thibodaux, of which they were members. The Knights insisted on the strike, promising six pounds of meat and a peck of meal to each striker while out of employment. The first week they kept their promise, but after that time confessed their inability to further provide for the strikers.

Mr. B. A. Wormald's Laurel Valley place was also visited. His laborers were quietly returning with the promise of protection. The woods and cane thickets in the immediate vicinity of Thibodaux are filled with fugitive negroes who have abandoned their homes in the town. A number of volunteers out looking for bodies of negroes supposed to be killed in the affair of Wednesday, report the negro women as still threatening the peace of this community.

The bodies of three dead negroes were found this afternoon in a thicket on Mr. Allen's Rienze plantation, on the other side of the bayou. They had evidently been shot in the affray of Wednesday, and taking refuge in the thicket died there without assistance of any kind. The report of the coroner is anxiously awaited, and although promised today had not up to a late hour this evening been forthcoming.

It is, however, understood that fully thirty negroes have sacrificed their lives in the riot of Wednesday, although returns thus far have not equaled that number. Quite a number of darkies are accounted as missing, but whether they have been killed or "skipped the country" is not known.

Yesterday morning Judge Taylor Beattie received an anonymous communication to the effect that his life was in jeopardy. Judge Beattie has incurred the enmity of the negroes by the part he has taken in the present affair. In a conversation with a representative of THE TIMES-DEMOCRAT yesterday, the judge stated that he had several times been warned that the assassin was on the watch for him and that his life was in his own hands.

He further stated that he had exhausted every means within reason to bring the negro to a sense of his real condition; that he had advised him time and again to beware of and avoid those who would plunge him into difficulties with which he was wholly unable to cope; that he would afford him the largest protection with respect both to life and property, but that when the shot of Monday night was fired there was nothing further left for him to do save that of assisting the good citizens in the preservation of law and order. These people, it was stated, had been the means of doing incalculable damage in the parish. Their attack upon the people, he said, was not only unwarranted, but premeditated and malicious, so that question of the supremacy of the whites over the blacks or vice versa became the all-absorbing question.

Capt. Adams, of the Louisiana Rifles, proffered the service of his force to protect the jail in case Williams, one of the agitators, against whom there is much feeling, and who surrendered today, was incarcerated therein, but the sheriff, consideration of the fact that there was no legal justification for his arrest, concluded to avoid the responsibility of holding him.

On all the plantations, as far as heard from, the laborers are returning to the fields, and express themselves as ready and willing to resume work.

At noon yesterday some shooting from ambush by negroes was reported about two miles from town, on the other side of the bayou. The attack, it is stated, was made on recently imported laborers, none of whom were injured. A detachment of the military visited the scene of the shooting, but could ascertain nothing beyond what is stated above.

A rumor was afloat today that there was about to be an uprising of the colored people in Terrebonne parish, brought about by the same causes as those which produced the riot in this place. The white people, however, are fully prepared for any attack that may be made in that parish.

Messrs. Gorman and Molaison, who were injured in the affair of Wednesday, are rapidly on the mend. The Louisiana Rifles and a detachment of the Washington Artillery are stationed at the courthouse, but at night are picketed on the suburbs of the town.

Gov. McEnery, who it was thought, would be here today, was telegraphed by Lieut. Gov. Knobloch that his presence at this time was unnecessary, peace being to a great extent restored. About 8:30 o'clock tonight the notorious Cox brothers were dismissed from the jail and led out to Bayou Lafourche where they swam the stream and made their escape in the thicket. beyond.

A Patrol Established at Houma

Special to The Times-Democrat

HOUMA, Nov. 25.--The Thibodaux riot has created some excitement here, and measures have been taken by the authorities to prevent a similar outbreak in Houma. The town is patroled every night by special guards, and the utmost vigilance is exercised by the citizens. Vague rumors are heard on the streets of threatened violence and incendiarism on the part of the negroes, but these receive only the measure of consideration that they deserve. The prevailing feeling is that no outbreak will occur, but it is thought best to be provided against any contingency that may arise. A negro from the country was reported as trying to purchase a quantity of ammunition this morning, and was immediately notified by Mayor Smith to leave town.

New Orleans Times-Democrat, November 26, 1887.

38.   THIBODAUX

Guarded by Citizens and Soldiers

A Ringleader Whose Surrender Was Not Accepted

A Tour of the Plantations

No Official Knowledge of the Number Killed in the Recent Riot

Judge Beattie's Life Threatened

THIBODAUX, La., Nov. 25.--[Special]--The town was last night strongly guarded by the citizens and military, who prevented any further disturbances. Pickets were placed at points outside the town proper, and sentinels stood at almost every corner, requiring passers-by to give accounts of themselves.

The Louisiana Rifles and the gun detachment of the Washington Artillery were on duty all night and ready for any emergency.

At break of day the same condition of things existed. The negroes who have taken to the swamps have not returned to the town, but many have gone to work again on the several plantations in the immediate vicinity of Thibodaux.

There was a trifle of excitement shortly before noon caused by the coming into town of Sol Williams, one of the most loud-mouthed agitators and leaders of the strikers, who some days ago threatened everything that was white. Williams did not work on any sugar plantation, being a wood cutter by trade, but nevertheless was one of the prime movers in all matters of dissension among the laborers. He came to town, sought the sheriff and wished to surrender. The sheriff told him that he could not protect him for the reason that there was no charge against him, and that, moreover, even the jail could not protect him. Williams then left, swam bayou Lafourche

and took to the swamps on the other side. It is not probable that he will
ever return to Thibodaux, as the feeling against him is very bitter.
     The Picayune correspondent spent the entire day visiting plantations
neighboring the town and conversing with planters and laborers in the field
alike.
     Mr. Andrew Price's Acadia plantation, about two miles from town, was
visited. It was learned that owing to the vigilance and care of Mr. Price
the estate had not suffered as much as others, still it is estimated that
only about two-thirds of the quantity of sugar that should have been up to
date was actually harvested. Since the strike the place has been worked
with a two-thirds force.
     Threats were made to stop the hands on the place from working, but ex-
tra guards with Winchester rifles were placed in position. After Wednesday
morning's riot, and after the citizens of Thibodaux had shown their determination to keep the peace and order of the country many hands, strikers
since three weeks, returned to the Acadia plantation and were reinstated to
their happy satisfaction.
     They regretted the course they had taken, and asserted that they would
no longer be influenced by the leaders of the strike.
     Phil Lawless, a colored man, works the front portion of Acadia on the
tenant system and sells his cane to the plantation owner by the ton. Last
year he sold $3000 worth of cane and cultivated large quantities of corn
and peas. Zach Conner, a driver on the plantation for a number of years,
superintends the cane-cutting gang, about 125 strong. He was spoken to and
said that the negroes though greatly frightened were returning to work.
     Dick Williams, a negro who came from the Teche country with 35 hands,
said everything was working serenely.
     An interview with two negro strikers--Felix Boyd and Matt Brooks--who
have returned to work, was quite interesting. They could not say who had
prompted them to strike. When they did so they came to town where they remained three weeks. During that time their assembly was to have cared for
them. However, only six pounds of meat were given to each of them during
the first five days. On the sixth day the assembly failed to give them any
rations and they were compelled to look out for themselves. They have returned to work in good earnest and will no longer be deceived.
     There were a number of negroes on the place who refused to strike, being
thoroughly satisfied with the treatment they were receiving, and many of them
defied their colored brethren to interfere with them.
     The handsome estate of Mr. R. H. Allen, situated opposite Thibodaux,
was called at. Everything is in operation there, but still the delay caused
by the strike will work some injury to the crops. The hands of the place
are entirely satisfied with the wages they are receiving. On this, as on
all other plantations in this section, laborers are paid $1 a day, given
comforts, quarters and fuel, and 50 cents addition for each watch. Some
hands are boarded and therefore only receive 75 cents a day.
     Judge Taylor Beattie, who has taken a very prominent part in the de-
fense of the town against the blacks, this morning received information that
he would be murdered. The threatening of the judge has had but one effect,
and that is to rally his numerous admirers to his protection. These threats
were recently made against other prominent citizens.
     There was great anxiety expressed during the day as to what would be the
coroner's report. Up to a late hour this evening that official had not been
heard from. It is not positively known how many negroes were killed in the
riot of Wednesday morning. A careful search in the swamps might result in
the discovery of other dead than those already reported.
     Gorman and Molaison, the two wounded pickets, are doing finely, but it
is thought that the former, who was wounded in the right eye, will have to
be taken to New Orleans for treatment.
     Henry Hoffman, cabinet maker, and A. Bouron, gunsmith, did not leave
Thibodaux, but simply sent their families to New Orleans.
     Governor McEnery was expected here today, but did not come, as Lieut-
enant Gov. Knobloch telegraphed him not to do so.
     In conversation tonight with a prominent young gentleman residing here,
who constituted one of a party that during the day searched the thickets and
swamp edges for bodies of negroes in all probability killed on Wednesday

morning, it was learned that three corpses were found on Mr. Allen's Rienzi plantation. It is believed that these negroes were wounded in the riot and escaped to the other side of bayou Lafourche, where they died.

The negroes who were met on the outside of the city continue their threats about burning the place. Many persons who are in a position to know something about the matter say it would not be amazing if more than a score of darkies perished in the last encounter.

Tonight the town is extremely quiet. The Louisiana Rifles, the detachment of Washington Artillery and the C.K. Guards are stationed at the courthouse in readiness for any emergency.

At 9 o'clock tonight it was learned by the authorities that an attack was contemplated upon the jail in which the Cox brothers, two of the leading strikers, were confined for protection.

The two prisoners were let loose and made their escape over bayou Lafourche. The object of the attack was to get possession of the two black men so as to lynch them.

Enoch Adams, also a promoter of the present disturbance, who is at large, will be sought and if found will suffer the same penalty.

HOUMA

The Vigilance of the People

HOUMA, La., Nov. 25.--[Special]--The riot in Thibodaux has awakened the citizens of Houma to the necessity for increased vigilance and the town is now patrolled nightly by a special guard. There is but little apprehension of an outbreak, but preventive measures are thought necessary.

New Orleans Daily Picayune, November 26, 1887 .

39.   THE THIBODAUX TROUBLES

Letter from Judge Taylor Beattie

THIBODAUX, Dec. 1, 1887

Editor of Picayune--In your issue of the 20th ult., under the heading of "Thibodaux," you give a statement of the return to your city of the troops commanded by Captain Adams, and a statement as to certain incidents in our troubles at this place. In this statement are certain inaccuracies which I think best to correct. The Sol Williams incident is incorrectly reported. He was not released by me and I did not see him. There are no charges against him, but he is known to have been one of the principal instigators of the ruffianism lately prevalent in this parish. He came to the courthouse and sought protection, so Captain Adams informed me. He was escorted to the bayou and told to make his escape. It was feared he might be harmed if met upon the streets. I think this was the best that could have been done, for he had outraged the public sentiment of the community and it might have been unsafe for him to be at large. But he did walk through the town that morning, so I am informed, and was not harmed. This speaks volumes for the forbearance of our people.

Until your publication I never heard that any attempt was made to shoot him whilst in the courthouse. No such report was made to me. The Cox brothers did not escape from jail. I released them in the presence of the sheriff, one of his chief deputies and of Captain Adams. We escorted them to the outskirts of the town and bade them shift for themselves. The charge against them was for a minor offense, and they were arrested before the firing upon our guards.   They were strongly suspected of being engaged in the firing upon the sugar-houses in this parish, but at that time we had no proof Had I known as much as I do now, I would not have released them. They were released at night; not from any fear of an attack upon the jail, but to prevent their being attacked upon their release.

No attack was threatened upon the jail while Captain Adams' command
was here. The troops were under my orders and I do not think they would
have fired on anyone without the orders of the civil authorities. I have
too much respect for the discipline of the company to think otherwise.

I will end by saying that no community in the United States would have
stood for three weeks what our people did. These three weeks are a standing
testimony to the law-abiding spirit prevailing in this parish. Whatever has
been done was done after forbearance had utterly ceased to be a virtue and
when force was actually necessary to repel the midnight attack upon the
guards placed over the town to prevent a threatened attack, and to prevent
the attempted murder of peaceful citizens guarding their homes and firesides.

This state of affairs was brought about by a secret, oath-bound association of ignorant and degraded barbarians, who have refused and continually
refuse to obey the laws of their country by testifying as to the lawlessness
prevalent, and who give as a reason that they are bound by their oaths not
to tell.

Our people seek no justification outside of their own consciences, and
are as ready, willing and prepared now as in the past to defend their lives
and firesides whenever the necessity arises, and this whether inside or outside of the mere forms of law.

Very respectfully,   TAYLOR BEATTIE

New Orleans Daily Picayune, December 3, 1887.

40. THE MILITIA IN THIBODAUX

There is now peace and quiet throughout Lafourche, where lately riot and
disturbance prevailed. The negroes have gone to work, and those who have
taken the place of the strikers are now protected from violence and are becoming reassured and confident again. The return of the militia to the parish and the vigorous efforts of the citizens of Thibodaux have brought about
these good results. Had there been no outcry against the sending of troops,
had no attempt been made to drag politics into the strike; and, for partisan
purposes, to attack the wise course of the Governor in taking the precautions
he did, the unfortunate disturbance of Tuesday might have been avoided. But
some of the enemies of Gov. McEnery were short of issues, as they have been
throughout the campaign, and they seized on this just as they did on the
third term and like issues which they took up; and protested to the country
against the use of militia to keep the peace. The supporters of Gen. Nicholis in the Knights of Labor who favored the late manifesto of the District
Assembly denouncing the Governor and the sugar planters, have had nothing to
say about the disturbances that have occurred in Lafourche for more than a
week past, the frequent firing into the sugar houses, the killing of two and
wounding of a dozen hands, because they chose to work instead of striking.
Perhaps in their view these outrages did not warrant the sending troops to
Thibodaux; perhaps they do not think that the militia, should be sent there
even, today. But if they think this, they have not said and are not likely
to say anything to that effect. The people of the State recognize and appreciate the wisdom and foresight of the Governor, whereas some of his reck-
less opponents are partly responsible for the lawlessness in Lafourche since
they insisted on the removal of the militia; and the negro strikers have
flattered themselves with the idea that they had white sympathizers and
backers in New Orleans. It was a great mistake that politics should have
been dragged into this affair, and that some ill-advised supporters of Gen.
Nicholis should have denounced the sending of troops to Thibodaux and demanded their recall, thus leading the ignorant negroes to believe that they had
nothing to fear on account of their lawlessness.

New Orleans Times-Democrat, November 26, 1887.

41. THE SUGAR STRIKE

The negroes of the south found themselves at the close of the war eman-
cipated from chattel slavery only to enter into a condition of competitive
wage slavery, a little more disguised but even more miserable than their
former position. It has often been openly declared by their masters that
they (the masters) prefer the present state of affairs to the old, for now
the negro must keep himself as he can; they are not responsible for his support when they do not want him.
The sugar-planters of Louisiana have been loud in their demands for
protective tariffs--in the interest of their workmen. But as is always the
case, "protection" has enriched the proprietor but has failed in every way
to protect the toilers.
The inevitable result is now being accomplished. A miserable, half-
starved mob of black wretches have undertaken to right the balances by
strikes. They have met force by force and death by death. Their leaders
have been taken to prison, and without a semblance of law from the prison to
the nearest tree. How long will the people be blind?

Labor Enquirer (Chicago), November 26, 1887.

42. A NORTHERN VIEW OF THE THIBODAUX TROUBLES

The St. Louis Republican sees in all violent attempts by striking laborers to settle their differences with employers about wages the self-same
causes and effects as have been made apparent in the outbreaks of anarchism.
Commenting on the recent disturbances in the sugar districts of Louisiana,
it says:
At this distance from Louisiana it is easy to see both sides of the
trouble which may yet cause more. The terrible specter of anarchy is present
before the white people there just as it has been in Chicago. The only difference is that the Louisiana protection is black and not as well educated as
the scientific and transcendental proletarian of Chicago. The African proletarian may in time strive to "realize the ideal" by "improved scientific
methods," but at present he "attacks society" by firing on it from behind a
fence with an old army musket loaded with slugs. Society returns the fire
and with deadly effect.
Unfortunately for the negroes their ignorance makes them the easy victims of bad men. In Chicago the leaders of the anarchists were hunted down
and made to suffer the penalty of their crimes, but it is to be regretted
that just punishment was not visited upon the instigators of the bloody dis-
orders at Thibodaux. The wicked causers of these troubles appear to have
escaped entirely, while the avenging blow fell upon their miserable dupes,
the victims of their own deplorable ignorance and of the criminal ambition
of others.

New Orleans Daily Picayune, November 30, 1887.

43. COLORED PEOPLE

Meet in Mass Meeting to Denounce the Killing of Men of Their Race in the Sugar
Districts

Last evening the hall on Jackson, near Franklin street, held about 300
colored men, assembled to denounce the shooting of the negroes in Thibodaux
and Pattersonville.

A. J. Kemp of the Longshoremen's Association was elected chairman, and
Dr. S. P. Brown, of the same organization, secretary.

Addresses were made by A. J. Kemp, R. Richards, president of the Cotton
Yardman; E. S. Sqan, president of the Longshoremen; Dan Macon, T. W. Wickham,
Hon. T. B. Stamps, R. W. B. Gould and Rev. C. H. Thompson, denouncing the
killing as murder, condemning the action of the administration in not using
proper civil authority before calling out the military, and calling upon
the colored people, by all lawful means, to avenge the killing of the fellow-
blacks by demanding the trial of those who did the killing.

H. H. Blenk, Wm. White, Jeff Green, T. W. Wickham and T. J. Boswell,
the committee on resolutions, reported that as the unjust killing of negroes
at Pattersonville and Thibodaux is deplorable in the extreme, and that this
condition of affairs is not only robbing men of the fruits of their labor,
but tends to disrupt the labor system and the agricultural interests of
Louisiana, therefore the constitutional authorities and the congress of the
United States be petitioned to speedily investigate the trouble and bring
the guilty to punishment; and further, that a committee of five be appointed
to co-operate with citizens and associations to prepare an address setting
forth the outrage against the laboring people of Louisiana.

The resolutions were adopted after much discussion, and the meeting
adjourned.

New Orleans Daily Picayune, December 3, 1887.

44. OUTRAGES IN LOUISIANA

The killing of twelve colored men at Thibodaux last week, also the murder of the two Cox brothers, who were arrested on Tuesday as agitators
charged with making incendiary speeches, and taken from the jail by the
whites and shot to death, are reported as growing out of the Louisiana sugar
strikes. The Coxes were leaders in the strike and prominent in the labor
organizations. Even if the Coxes were leaders in the strike, by what right
were they taken from the custody of the law and riddled with bullets? The
whites who participated in the shooting of the Cox brothers were a more
pronounced gang of law-breakers than were these brothers. They dyed their
hands in innocent blood and stamped upon themselves the brand of cowardice,
because they, a party of supposed law-abiding citizens, overstepped the
bounds of law by taking unarmed men out of the hands of the constituted
authorities, and giving vent to their pent up anger by filling their bodies
with bullets. Such a cowardly act could only be performed by bands of sneaking cutthroats, which permeate nearly every one of the Southern States. The
law holds every one charged with crime innocent until proven guilty; therefore the Cox brothers were innocent until they had been accorded a fair and
impartial trial and adjudged guilty by a jury of their peers. No body of
citizens has any right to constitute themselves into a tribunal of justice,
and especially such a body as this Louisiana rabble proved itself to be.

The most notable feature about this shooting affair is that, as is
usually the case, the majority of the slain, if not all of them, were colored.
This is another example of Mr. Grady's "New South." The usages which oppression have been inflicted upon the inoffensive colored people from
the dawn of their freedom still follow close and fast upon their heels; and
the question may be asked in all seriousness how much longer is this going
to last? Do the whites of the South suppose that colored people are going to
continue to submit without a practical protest against their inhuman treatment? If they do, they are basing their supposition upon a frail foundation.
They may as well make up their minds at once that the colored people will
not in the future continue to be led as lambs to the slaughter. Education is
enabling them to know and appreciate their rights as American citizens, and
in the future they will not be backward in claiming these rights and insisting upon a fair and impartial interpretation of the laws which govern
this country.

Power is a dangerous weapon, especially when it is possessed by unscrupulous men. The oppressed always sooner or later arise and shake off
the galling chains of oppression, and they do this even if they cause rivers
of blood to follow in their wake. Unscrupulous men who possess power which
has been obtained by usurpation and fraud should be careful how they exercise it. The whites of the South should take warning in time, or they may
have to repent when repentance will avail them naught.

New York Age, December 3, 1887.

45. THE SUGAR RIOTS

The attitude of the Knights of Labor of Louisiana regarding the riots
at Thibodaux, substantiates the reports of the kindly feeling existing between the white and the colored members of the Order. The Knights are very
powerful in New Orleans, and they are using their influence to protect the
rights as well as the lives of the colored brethren. They denounce in strong
terms the killing of the negroes at Pattersonville, and will lay the whole
matter before Congress at its coming session. The District Assembly will
also appeal to the Order everywhere to ask for the repeal of duties on sugar
which will have the effect of bringing the planters to a sense of justice as
well as benefiting the people of the country. This resolution has caused
great excitement among the planters and every effort has been made to induce
the Knights to withdraw it, but they steadily refuse to do so. It is a significant fact that the publication of this manifesto by the sugar planters in S�
Mary, in which parish the town of Pattersonville is situated, have generally
granted the increase of wages asked by the negroes, the refusal of which led
to the strike and the killing of the colored Knights. If with so powerful an
organization at their back the colored people are unable to protect their
rights, what must be their condition unorganized and alone to meet the opposition of powerful syndicates and combinations? Let those workingmen who
think they can get along without organization, simply because they have at
the present time no trouble to command good wages, ask themselves what they
would do to protect themselves in case that happy time should cease. It is
then organization proves its worth.

Journal of United Labor, December 3, 1887.

46. W. R. RAMSAY TO T. V. POWDERLY

Star Office
Washington, D.C., December 11, 1887

Hon. T. V. Powderly:

Dear Sir: I know you will pardon the liberty I assume in thus addressing you when I state the motive that prompts me to do so. Although I have
been for nearly thirty years a member of a Trades Union, I am not a member of
the Knights of Labor, but I assume that all labor organizations are striving
to the accomplishment of the same end in the elevation and protection of the
masses.

For the past month or more the press of the country have contained daily
accounts of the shooting down in cold blood (by so-called posses, summoned
by "officers of the law") of colored men in Louisiana, who have had the "auda-
city" to exercise the right of American citizens in protesting against oppression, by striking against what they deem to be injustice and wrong. And
though it is said these men are members of the order over which you have the
honor to preside, and no doubt believe they are but obeying the obligation

they assumed when they became members of your order, not one word of protest,
so far as I am aprized, has gone forth from you or anyone connected with the
order, against the cruel, brutal, unjust and unlawful treatment inflicted
upon these poor creatures. Is a man, because he is not of Caucasian blood,
denied the protection of your order, although he may fulfill every obligation
imposed upon him by your laws? I think not. And, therefore, I believe it
to be your solmn duty to protest against--nay denounce, these outrages in
language that cannot be misunderstood. I believe you have the moral courage
to do this, and that you will. The moral courage you displayed in the position you assume on the liquor question, is sufficient evidence that you are
not lacking in that particular. Although I am not a temperance man in the
true acceptance of that term, there is nothing I so much admire in your
whole course as the decision, firmness, and moral rectitude you have displayed in your position on this question.

Hoping this may be received in the spirit in which it is written, I am
yours in fraternity and justice.

Powderly Papers, Catholic University of America.

47. LABOR'S PAGEANT

The Workingmen of New Orleans on Parade

Sixth Anniversary of the Trades and Labor Assembly Celebrated Yesterday--
The Several Associations Warmly Greeted Along the Line.

Had the clerk of the weather been consulted no more pleasant day could
have been selected by the Trades and Labor Assembly for their annual celebration. The atmosphere was damp; the clouds obscured the sun, which made
it pleasant for walking.

The streets presented an animated appearance and everybody wore a
pleasant smile. The sweet sounds of music, the beating of drums, all showed
that it was an unusual day and an occasion of rare interest.

The occasion yesterday was the celebration of the sixth anniversary of
the combined representatives of the Central Trades and Labor Assembly of
New Orleans, which comprises thousands of STRONG, EARNEST, IRON-SINEWED
SPECIMENS of the laboring element of the Crescent City.

The Trades Assembly of New Orleans is noted the world over as being the
most thoroughly organized and the largest and most influential body of workingmen in the entire South, and merits compliment in that New Orleans has
never been the scene of any of those gatherings and conflicts such as are
frequently witnessed in Northern and Western cities, and this can only be
attributed to the temper of the class of men who belong to the different
organizations who are opposed to strikes, and when they occur are always
quick in having matters amicably settled, always discountenancing demonstrations and advising peace and quiet.

Yesterday many classes of labor were represented in the pageant, which
was a very imposing display.

This is the busy season of the year, and the laborer is afforded but
little opportunity for preparations for the holiday, but still they have
during the past few weeks managed to make ample and complete preparations,
the results of which were witnessed yesterday. Every detail was complete to
the letter, and the day proved to be one of the most pleasant ever spent by
the New Orleans laboring man, and will be remembered in the future as a part
of the history of the labor unions of New Orleans.

The entire parade of yesterday was under charge of John A. McMahon, grand
marshal, who is a member of the Screwmen's Benevolent Association No. 1.

The various organizations represented in the Trades and Labor Assembly,
according to the published order of the day issued by Grand Marshal McMahon,
commenced assembling on Canal street as early as 9 o'clock, where a large
crowd of ladies and children had assembled to get a sight at the hard-fisted
sons of toil.

The grand marshal and his chief aids, W. J. Barrett and Patrick A. Wilson, were stationed at the Grand Opera House, and upon the arrival of an association on Canal street it would pass in review before the grand marshal and chief aids, who would assign them a place, and the aid from that association to the grand marshal would drop out and take his position with the grand marshal. This worked like a machine, and gave those assembled on Canal street a chance to witness each body before it was placed in line.

The various organizations were divided into three divisions, as follows: Screwmen's Benevolent Association No. 1, Cotton Yard Men No. 1 and Cotton Yard Men No. 2 comprised the first division. The second division was composed of the Teamsters and Loaders, Screwmen No. 2 and Typographical Union No. 17.

Third Division--Associations and delegations in carriages in the following order: Pressmen's Union, Retail Dry Goods Clerks, Ship Carpenters and Joiners, and Oyster Dischargers' Union. . . .

As the clock struck the hour of 11, Grand Marshal McMahon gave the signal for starting. Turning to his chief aids, Barrett and Wilson, he asked, "Are they all ready?" The responses were in the affirmative, and the grand marshal said, "Let her go Gallagher." The signal was immediately taken up and passed along the line, and the procession of men, horsemen, carriages with flags and banners flying, and music playing, commenced moving. . . .

All along the route over which the long procession passed, the banquettes, street cars, vehicles and balconies were crowded, and in many sections of the city street cars had to stop to let the parade go by uninterrupted.

The procession was led by Grand Marshal McMahon, who was mounted on a fiery steed. The saddle blanket on the horse was blue silk, trimmed with old gold. The marshal's sash was of blue and gold. Blue is the emblem of labor, and the gold trimming represented gold. Labor makes gold.

To the right of the grand marshal rode Assistant Aid Barrett, and to the left Assistant Aid Wilson. Following the grand marshal and chief aids were the aids from the different organizations. Following the marshals came a brass band and carriages containing Thomas Agnew, president of the Trades Assembly and Messrs. Wm. J. Hammond, J. H. Conners, James Roach, John Delaney, M. E. Brower and Will I. O'Donnell, invited guests of the Trades Assembly. Delegates to the New Cotton Men's Executive Council and Trades Assembly were seated in carriages.

THE TRADES AND LABOR ASSEMBLY

Mr. Agnew has long been connected with the Screwmen's Association, and today, in addition to holding the important trust of president of the Trades and Labor Assembly, is president of the Screwmen's Benevolent Association No. 1, one of the strongest and most wealthy labor organizations, as far as known, in the world.

Under instructions the New Orleans Typographical Union No. 17, in the summer of 1881, appointed a committee to correspond with other unions in New Orleans, with a view to arranging preliminaries to the formation of a central organization for the workingmen of New Orleans. At the regular meeting of the typos, in September of 1881, this committee made a report, in which they recommended the election of two delegates and requested other associations to do the same.

Representatives of nearly all the labor organizations met at Screwmen's Hall on Oct. 16, 1881, and, after appointing W. J. Hammond chairman and J. L. Brown secretary pro tem., appointed a committee on constitution and the adjourned subject to call.

P. A. Graham, the present vice president of the assembly, was for many years president of the Teamsters and Loaders' Association, and has also held other important trusts in the Cotton Council and other labor bodies.

Several meetings were held, and on July 12, 1882, the report of the committee on constitution and by-laws was submitted, the report adopted and a permanent organization was effected. The following officers were elected: President, W. J. Hammond; first vice president, Fendel Horn; second vice president, M. E. Brower; recording secretary, J. L. Brown; financial secretary, A. E. Larouge; treasurer, Thos. H. Hilbert.

The present officers of the Assembly are: Thomas Agnew, president, who is also president of the Screwmen's Benevolent Association No. 1; P. A. Graham, first vice president, who has been president of the Teamsters and Loaders'; James Beggs, of the Typographical Union, is second vice president; John H. Windelkin, employed by the New Orleans Gaslight Company, is recording secretary; D. D. Welthers, financial secretary; J. M. Cressey, treasurer, of the Clerks' Association, and M. Sansovich, sergeant-at-arms.

Mr. J. M. Cressey, employed in the house of D. H. Holmes & Co., is the treasurer of the assembly, and also president of the Retail Dry Goods Clerks' Association. His term of office will expire next month. At the last election he declined a re-election. He is one of the most prominent and hardest workers in the entire body. He is possessed of rare administrative ability, and has frequently been called in to settle differences, which he succeeded in doing in the most pleasant and fair manner--always making friends with both parties.

THE FIRST DIVISION

The Screwmen

For thirty-seven years the Screwmen's Benevolent Association has been in existence, during which time it has managed to bear the enviable reputation of being one of the largest, wealthiest and best organizations of its kind in America, if not in the entire world.

The day was a cold one. It was Nov. 18, 1850, when 150 solid sons of toil hied themselves to the residence of Mr. John Chantil, a stevedore, residing in the Third District, to organize a screwmen's benevolent association, and from this the present organization has sprung, growing stronger every year.

The screwmen were not tardy in completing their organization, for one week later at the same place a meeting was held at which the constitution and by-laws were unanimously adopted and officers were elected. The officers elected were: President, Geo. Hooper; first vice president, James Campbell; second vice president, James Fitzgerald; treasurer, Henry Bier, and secretary, E. A. F. Mitchell.

The Legislature, by act, incorporated the association in April 1851, the act being signed by his Excellency Gov. Joseph Walker, and attested by Hon. Charles Gayaree, Secretary of State.

After holding several meetings at Mr. Chantil's residence, the membership grew so enormously that larger quarters had to be secured, and the association changed its meeting place to Eagle Fire Company No. 7's enginehouse, then situated on Old Levee street, between Bienville and Customhouse streets. From there they removed to the corner of Crossman and Front, where they remained until a few years ago, when they purchased and fitted up the Screwmen's Hall, corner of Exchange alley and Bienville streets, which has become the headquarters of nearly all the labor organizations and many benevolent associations, and frequently social gatherings are given there.

When the war broke out the Screwmen did not remain at home. From the association was organized two companies known as Screwmen Guards, Company A. Capt. Sam J. Risk, and Company B. Capt. Batchellor, and numbering some 350 men. During the entire war twelve members kept the association up, carried on the business and provided for sick members. Since then the membership has been increasing, and now they have over 1,000 active, hard-working men on the rolls.

Prior to the organization, on 4th July, 1850, the Screwmen had a parade, at which time it was suggested that they form an association.

From the date of organization to the present time, the following gentlemen have held the office of president of the association: George H. Hooper, Samuel J. Risk, James Douglas, John Spencer, Henry Houlgrave, Charles Murray, Daniel Murphy, John Delaney, David Lester, E. M. Gannon, Thos. Dennis, James Palmer and Thomas Agnew.

The objects of the association is one principally of benevolence, and annually large sums of money are expended in the relief of their sick and distressed, burial of deceased members and relief for widows and orphans, and for these purposes they have a standing capital of over $100,000.

The screwmen yesterday were divided into four divisions, and as usual made a very fine display.

At the head rode Grand Marshal James Quinn, Sr. He was followed by his aids--John Ellwood, Henry Gilmore, Geo. W. Burgess, Wm. Caldwell, Thos. B. Begg, James J. Savage, M. J. Fitzpatrick, James Quin, Jr., Joseph Quinn, John McGuinn, John M. Livingston , James Eagan.

A band of music followed the aids and a strong screwman bearing a handsome union jack. The officers of the association came next. They are: Thomas Agnew, president; John Breen, first vice president; August Miller, second vice president; John A. Davilla, recording secretary; George J. Burns, financial secretary; Patrick Powell, Jr., assistant financial secretary; John Houlgrave, treasurer. Finance committee--Robert J. Cambias, chairman; Richard A. White, John F. Hureau. Ex-presidents of the association. Exempt members of the association in carriages. Committee of arrangements. Standing and special committees. Banner of the association in carriage.

THE ASSOCIATION BANNER

The banner is of heavy navy blue silk, and is mounted on a magnificent rosewood pole with gold mountings. On the front side of the banner is a beautiful oil painting of a full-rigged ship with all sail set. This picture is surrounded by a double gold cord, handmade, and a border of leaves and cotton bolls just bursting open. Above is a kind of curtain with open cotton bolls, leaves and the buds of cotton plant, and surmounted by a fine gold fringe with acorn pendants. Wrought in white silk, above and below the picture, are the words; "Screwmen's Benevolent Association of New Orleans, La." On the obverse side was a picture representing Charity, containing five figures of a widow and four children. Above are the words: "Organized Nov. 25, 1850," and underneath: "Incorporated April 24, 1850."

The picture is also surrounded with a double gold cord, handmade, and about half an inch wide, and on the side is a spray wrought in silk of a cotton plant, and on the other oak leaves and acorns, all magnificently wrought and designed.

COTTON YARD MEN NO. 1

The Cotton Yard Men's Benevolent Association, or cotton rollers, as they are commonly called, is one of the strongest and most influential bodies in the city. They were organized in December, 1879, at Odd Fellows' Hall, and incorporated in 1880. The first president of the association was Mr. Pat Mealey.

He maintained the position up to 1885, when he declined a re-election and was succeeded by Mr. Will I. O'Donnel, at which time he had the honor conferred upon him by an election to the office of honorary president. To-day he is the presiding officer.

The association numbers about 700 active men in good standing, the major portion of whom were out in parade yesterday.

The association was divided into two divisions, Wm. Sheridan, grand marshal, and his aids. John Carroll, James Ahearn, Richard Kiley, J. Regan, Pat Healey, George Menter, led the cotton rollers. They were followed by Grand Marshal Bat Galvin, of Division No. 1, and William Fritz, William Farrell, W. Ahearn, Pat Carr, his aids. The beautiful and costly banner of the association was guarded by four members in a carriage, after which came the Newsboys' Brass Band, under the leadership of Prof. Fred Kuntz. The finance and governing committee and members of the association were next in line.

The second division was in charge of Marshal Bernard J. Reilly and his aids, W. A. Athens, A. Werlein, John Haggerty and Thomas Owens. A band of music preceded a carriage in which four members held a State flag, and then marched members of the association.

The Cotton Yard Men were very neatly attired in black broadcloth and silk hats, and presented a fine appearance.

Cotton Yard Men No. 2 followed Typographical Union No. 17. The colored cotton rollers do the same class of work as their white brothers. The association was organized through the instrumentality of M. E. Brower, Edward Harrison, John Roach and others of Branch No. 1, on 11th January, 1880, and was incorporated on 5th May, 1880. Today it has a membership of over 500 toilers, the purposes being mainly to mutually aid its members,

mostly cotton rollers, scale hands, etc., both as a benevolent society and
workingman's body.

J. M. Richards is the president of this organization, and he has during
his occupancy of the chair shown himself to be an intelligent presiding
officer.

In the parade yesterday the colored rollers turned out in large numbers.
Just behind the band and in front of the members marched the sons of some of
the members.

Next followed a long line of carriages containing delegates from the
Clerks, Pressmen, Ship Carpenters and Joiners and Oyster Dischargers' unions.

THE DRY GOODS CLERKS

The Retail Dry Goods Clerks' Protective Association was organized the
22d of October, 1882. In 1883 it was incorporated, and today has a membership of nearly 500 male and 300 female members. When sick, members are paid
a weekly benefit of $5.25, a physician and medicines are furnished, and the
association in case of death defrays the entire expense of burial, and in
addition to this a stipulated sum of money is awarded to the family of a
deceased member.

The president of the association is J. M. Cressey, who is also treasurer
of the Trades Assembly. His term of office expires on Dec. 1. His successor
is Mr. F. Leonce Fazande, who has been elected to serve one year, commencing
Dec. 1, 1887, and ending Dec. 1, 1888, and whose likeness is here given. He
has been a member of the association since its organization, and has done
much toward bringing it up to its present standard.

THE PRESSMEN

The object of this union, which is composed of pressmen, is one of
protection and benevolence. They organized this union on the 15th of April,
1884, under the laws of the International Typographical Union, and in May,
1884, they received a charter. The first and present president of the union
is William Russell, who is a first-class workman and a man who was instrumental in organizing the union, which is in a fair condition.

SHIP CARPENTERS AND JOINERS

The domicile of the Ship Carpenters and Joiners' Benevolent Association is in Algiers, where the dry docks are located. The organization is a
representative one, and its members have not been troubled with a strike for
a long time. Every member is a thorough mechanic in the true sense and meaning of the word, and what's more, they are faithful toilers and very popular
with their employers.

The president of the association is Mr. August Kevlin, who has occupied
this position since 1885. In 1881, on the 27th day of July, the association
was organized, and today its membership is somewhere in the two hundreds.
Wm. Jones was president in 1882 and 1882, R. Kammerer in 1884, and since 1885
August Kevlin has presided.

OYSTER DISCHARGERS' ASSOCIATION

The last association on the published programme was the Oyster Dischargers' Association, of which Mr. M. Sansovich is the president. The members being unable to parade in a body sent a delegation to represent them in
the parade. These men discharge oysters from the luggers, and at the present
time their services are in demand on account of the large cargoes continually
arriving.

TYPOGRAPHICAL UNION NO. 17

For the purpose of obtaining a fair and uniform tariff of prices and
of settling differences arising among themselves, in May, 1835, was organized in this city the New Orleans Typographical Society by the printers
employed in the city.

Owing to differences among members in the winter of 1844, by a vote the
society was disbanded, but in the fall of 1845 was reorganized. The object
of reorganization was to try and heal the differences, but to no avail and
another disbandment followed. After various fruitless efforts, in May, 1852,
the present union was organized with Gerald Stith as president, who afterward

was elected Mayor of the city.

In 1853 W. B. Tebo was elected president, and Mr. Stith was appointed to meet delegates from other societies in the United States for the formation of a general organization, and during that year, in the city of Pittsburg, the International Typographical Union was organized. From this body a charter was obtained and the present Union No. 17 was inaugurated.

Delegates were elected in 1881, and, by resolution, requested other labor bodies to do the same, and by this means the present Trades and Labor Assembly commenced its career.

SECOND DIVISION

With flags and banners flying came the second division.

TEAMSTERS AND LOADERS

The members of the Teamsters and Loaders' Union Benevolent Association play an important part in the commerce of this port. Each man, be he a teamster or loader, must be an experienced hand before he can belong to the association, and many years an apprenticeship 'ere being admitted.

The roll of membership contains over 500, with a rapid growth. It has at present over $2000 invested in real estate.

The first president of the association, elected in 1880, was Thomas Redwood, who was re-elected in 1881; Sam Chapman in 1883 and 1884, and D. M. Fee was his successor.

Fully 500 men were in line yesterday and they made a very credible showing. They wore neat black suits and silk hats.

SCREWMEN NO. 2

followed. The colored screwmen are the strongest, largest and most prominent colored organization in the City of New Orleans. They follow their white brothers and never make a move without first consulting them. The association is seven years old, and during its existence has gradually increased in wealth and influence. It affords ample protection to its members and its benevolence and charity has often been the subject of commendation.

J. W. Dickinson, the president, is a very intelligent and educated colored man. He toils in the hold of a ship daily and is counted as one of the hardest workers in the association and in a ship.

The secretary of the association is Mr. Lazarus Thompson, who is truly a representative laboring man. He has served as a delegate in the Cotton Men's Executive Council in the Trades Assembly, and has been a member of several important committees, and is secretary of the new Cotton Men's Council.

THE THIRD DIVISION

This division was made up entirely of carriages containing delegations from the different unions represented in the assembly, and aged members of the various association.

Every association in line halted in front of and serenaded THE TIMES-DEMOCRAT.

It rained in the evening while the procession was returning to Canal street, causing it to disband at Congo Square.

New Orleans Times-Democrat, November 26, 1887.

CONGRESSIONAL REACTION TO THE LOUISIANA SUGAR STRIKE

48. FROM THE CONGRESSIONAL RECORD

Senator William E. Chandler (New Hampshire):[31]
. . . I find in the New Orleans Daily Picayune of Monday morning, September 17, 1888, the following account:

LOUISIANA--BREAUX BRIDGE--CRIME COMMITTED ON NEGRO WOMEN--THE WHITE PEOPLE IN MASS MEETING DECLARE SUCH PROCEEDINGS SHALL STOP.

BREAUX BRIDGE, LA., ST. MARTIN'S PARISH,
September 16.

An awful crime was perpetrated in this vicinity Friday night. A gang supposed to be composed of five thus far unknown parties assaulted a negro cabin, and shooting through the walls mortally wounded a black woman, who died a few hours afterwards. From this place they went to another cabin, outraged a black woman, and then whipped a black man.

The negroes have made no affidavits yet. The white population is very much excited over this matter, and held last night an indignation meeting. About three hundred white men were present. Hon. Charles Delhommer made a stirring speech, in which he denounced such parties and such actions in the most virulent language. He was warmly applauded, and resolutions were immediately and unanimously passed that these negroes will be fully protected, so as to enable them to make the proper affidavits declaring all those whom they may have recognized, so that they may be duly arrested, delivered to the courts, and dealt with to the utmost rigor of the law. . . .

NEW ORLEANS, *September 16.*

A Picayune special from Breaux Bridge, La., says that on Friday night five unknown men attacked a negro cabin, and shooting through the walls, killed a colored woman. At another cabin they outraged a colored woman and whipped a colored man.

A mass meeting of three hundred white men was held Saturday night to express indignation at the outrages. Resolutions were adopted pledging protection to the colored people and punishment to the perpetrators of the crime.

I make the prediction, as I did on a previous occasion, that the indignation will end in resolutions. There will be no indictment and no punishment of the perpetrators of these outrages upon these negroes, the object of which is to affect the approaching Presidential election, when the parish of St. Martin is to be converted from a Republican parish into a Democratic parish. . . .

The Louisiana Standard of September 22 gives the following account of this Breaux Bridge atrocity:

DEMOCRATIC MURDER--AN EPIDEMIC OF ASSASSINATION--ORGANIZED GANGS OF DEMOCRATIC MURDERERS MAKING THE KILLING OF NEGROES A PASTIME--HOW LOUISIANA NEGROES ARE BEING REDUCED TO MEXICAN PEONAGE--ASSASSINATION ITEMS AS TOLD IN DEMOCRATIC SPECIALS--NO POLITICS IN IT, BUT THE MURDERERS ALL GOOD DEMOCRATS.

ST. MARTINSVILLE, LA., *September* 17, 1888

"News reached here this morning of one of the most cowardly crimes that ever was committed in this parish." Friday night, at about 11 o'clock, in the vicinity of Breaux Bridge, a gang of four or five parties, some of them so far "unknown, whipped a black man, criminally assaulted one black woman, and killed another."

The particulars gathered from the mother of the dead woman are about as follows:

On Friday night the gang called at the door of the woman's house and knocked, saying it was the sheriff. She opened the door and recognized one of the parties, Sam Polk. She shut the door on them. They then fired through the door several shots, one of them taking effect in the woman's abdomen and she died next morning.

The coroner's inquest revealed "the fact that she bore seven months' twins, one of them having the ball through the head. The man Polk was recognized as having engaged in the three crimes. His hat was also found at the door of the cabin. He was not found when search was made for him.

"The white people are indignant and very much excited. Warrants have been issued against Polk and three other parties suspected to have participated in the crimes. The white people will see that the colored people are protected and justice done."

This is well enough in its way, in its recounting the damnable crime. All that about the white people being so terribly indignant is so much bosh. The parish has been a hell for the negroes for months. Democratic outlaws, called Regulators, have been and are in control of the parish. The killing and outraging of negroes has been their pastime. The planters have been and are helpless to afford their laborers any protection. The laborers are justly getting generally alarmed.

Those who can are showing the disposition to get away. The grinding season is coming on. The cane has to be gathered, and the sugar to be made. A large increase of laborers is wanted. The parish is getting to be known for the Democratic hell that it is. There is the growing fear that the needed laborers cannot be had, that those now on hand will get out. All this means ruin. These Democratic murders, again, this epidemic of assassination of helpless negroes are reaching the North, may affect the coming election. There is the seeming desire to call a halt, to hold up until the grinding season and the election shall be well over. That is about the measure of the excitement among the whites. It is all fear and gammon. Nobody will be hurt for murdering negroes.

AND YET ANOTHER ITEM

ST. MARTINSVILLE, *September* 18, 1888

"Vilmont Hollier, Decliere Hollier, Detour Hollier, Numa Boudreaux were arrested last night by Sheriff Gardemal and the citizens of Breaux Bridge, for the murder of the negro woman. Sam Polk is still at large and the officers are in pursuit. Vilmont Hollier is an ex-convict, having been pardoned last year."

This closes the present chapter of Democratic specials; maybe something may be done with that "ex-convict." Something evidently must be done, or that sugar crop goes to the demolition bow-wows--there won't be any laborers in the parish to make it.

That "ex-convict" will do to make an example of. There is nothing like an example, you know. The poor devil, as an "ex-convict," is not to be presumed as having any friends. Clean him out. The negroes will be satisfied that they are to be duly protected.

Bah! Why not go for the Democratic chivalry, the sons of the first families, the organized gangs of "regulators?" These are but the later and the smaller crimes. Why not attack that Democratic damnable verdict "parties unknown," covering the assassins of Freetown?

It is no use, gentlemen. Louisiana is overridden with Democratic assassins. You may not wipe out the facts.

The outside world is coming to understand them. You have your Democratic government, installed by force and fraud. Your authorities are in the hands of those who forcibly and fraudulently put them in power. Your bulldozers and ballot-box stuffers are running the State. They are making the State a Democratic hell by murdering and outraging Republican negroes. Your State is virtually damned, is accursed because of an assassin Democracy. The negroes must look out for themselves. They must get out of the State.

The Washington Post of August 27 has the following:

Race troubles in Louisiana--

This case is one of those which the Senator from Louisiana calls the petty grievances with which the Senate of the United States ought not to be troubled. He would score, he says, if any petty grievance of this kind should happen in the State of New Hampshire to unworthyily and in an undignified and unpleasant manner bring it before this lofty body, of which he has the honor to be a member--

RACE TROUBLES IN LOUISIANA

NEW ORLEANS, LA., *August 26.*

A dispatch from St. Martinsville says: "For three or four weeks past wild rumors have been spreading all over the parish that the negroes were arming and that a conflict of races was imminent. These rumors induced whites to organize for protection and safety.

The 1,631 whites of St. Martin are in danger of having the 1,771 colored voters arm themselves and assail and assault, kill and murder these poor, innocent, quiet, well-behaved and peaceful Democrats of that parish; so for protection and safety they decide as follows:

As a measure of preservation, the whites decided to disarm some of the negroes. The whites left yesterday for the Fifth ward, and completed the work of disarming without any resistance, except in one instance, where the whites were fired upon by two negroes, Albert Harris and his son, who were intrenched in a cabin.

The whites of Louisiana, if they hear that two poor negroes have possession of guns in an humble cabin in which they live, forthwith declare that these two negroes are intrenched in their cabin and that the whites are in danger, and thereupon they organize a posse--if there are two negroes, generally of about one hundred and fifty whites--and they go to the cabin and disarm these terrible negroes!

The negroes fired fifteen or twenty shots, which were returned by the whites. After firing for ten minutes the negroes surrendered. One of them was wounded in the arm. They were escorted out of the parish and warned never to return. The work of disarming was continued in a section of the Fifth ward where trouble was anticipated, but the rumor proved to be unfounded. Two bad characters were ordered to leave the parish within a specified time.

I have not the slightest doubt that they were going to vote the Republican ticket if they had stayed there, and according to the modern Louisiana doctrine which the Senator has avowed and attempted to justify upon the floor of this Senate today, if a man wants to vote the Republican ticket he is a bad character, and is to be notified to leave.

The weapons taken from the negroes were mostly old shotguns. A few rifles were found, but there was nothing showing an aggressive armament, except in the case of Albert Harris --one of these two negroes--who had a new Winchester rifle and a good supply of ammunition. All is now quiet.

Undoubtedly all is now quiet, and that kind of quiet will continue until the 6th of November, when the votes for Grover Cleveland in that parish have been counted and the votes for Benjamin Harrison have not been counted, and then the negroes may have some measure of real rest and peace until the approach of another election.

Here is a telegram from Shreveport, La. This is from the Daily Picayune of September 18; no old bones, or time-worn stories, or rotten timber in any of these extracts from the current Southern newspapers. The picayune says:

SHREVEPORT--NEGRO MURDERERS SUE FOR A CHANGE OF VENUE--SHREVEPORT'S DELEGATES FOR BLANCHARD

SHREVEPORT, LA., *September* 17.

The arguments in the case of Henry Brown *et al.* for a change of venue were heard this morning in the district court. A number of witnesses, all summoned by the defendants, testified that a fair trial could not be secured in Shreveport for the accused. The case was continued until tomorrow for further evidence. The accused are held for conspiracy and murder.

They are charged with killing Ed. Scott, a negro Saturday night, September 1, while he was at his home in bed. The crime is one of the darkest and most deliberate ever perpetrated in this community.

The primary election for delegates to the Congressional convention, fixed to convene on September 28, was very quiet. Less than 100 votes were cast throughout the city. All the delegates elected favor BLANCHARD'S return to Congress from this district. He will have no opposition.

[The Daily Picayune, Tuesday morning, September 18, 1888]

TWO MORE NEGROES TAKEN OUT AND SHOT TO DEATH

OPELOUSAS, LA., *September* 17.

Yesterday morning at Villa Platte prairie a crowd of armed men rode to the house of two negroes named Jean Pierre-Salet and Sidairo, and after leading them a short distance riddled them with buckshot, killing both men instantly. This killing is supposed to have been brought about by the incendiary language recently used by these two negroes. The affair created intense excitement in the neighborhood where it occurred.

Doubtless the incendiary language used by these negroes was something like the encendiary language which the Senator from Wisconsin [Mr. Spooner] showed the other day was used by the negroes in Texas, of which complaint was made, which was, I believe, that they argued in favor of a protective tariff.

Since this resolution was before the Senate on a previous occasion I have found one or two accounts in other papers of the Freetown affair, which I desire to incorporate in my remarks at the risk of disturbing the sensibilities of the Senator from Louisiana. This is from the Weekly Messenger at St. Martinsville, La.:

A RIOT--E. PAYSON SMITH KILLED AND ANOTHER MAN SLIGHTLY WOUNDED--TWENTY-FIVE NEGROES KILLED

The news came here yesterday morning of a riot which took place in the parish of Iberia during the evening of Thursday. The particulars we got at the time of going to press are about as follows: It was reported that the negroes were arming and drilling in the section where the riot took place, and Captain Cades, in command of a detachment of his company, went there to quiet and disarm the negroes. The negroes, it appears, were congregated in a cabin, and when Captain Cades informed them of his mission the negroes from within the cabin opened fire on him and his men, killing Mr. E. Payson Smith and slightly wounding another man. Captain Cades then ordered his men to return the fire, and twenty-five negroes fell dead.

The body of Mr. Smith was immediately taken to New Iberia.

At the time we go to press everything is reported quiet.

NEW IBERIA--VERDICT OF THE CORONER'S JURY ON THE NEGROES SLAIN IN THE FREE-TOWN RIOT

[From the Louisiana Standard, New Orleans, August 25, 1888.--Correspondence]

NEW IBERIA, LA., *August* 23.

The coroner's jury reached a verdict yesterday evening in the case of the killing of the ten negroes in the Freetown riot on the 16th instant. Two days were spent in collecting evidence, which resulted in the following verdict:

"We, the jury impaneled to hold an inquest on the body of Tom Simon, deceased, come to the conclusion that he met his death by a gunshot wound inflicted by parties unknown to the jury. From the evidence collected the jury is further led to the conclusion that the following also met their deaths by gunshot wounds inflicted at the same time and place by parties likewise unknown to us: Sam Cahill, Louis Simon, Edw. Simon, Eugene Green, Alex Valere, Edw. Valere, and others. This at Freetown, parish of Iberia, on the 15th day of August, 1888."

Here is the damning outcome. The verdict of the coroner's jury but smoothed over a wholesale massacre. It is a palpable, damning lie. Do the members of this jury realize the position in which this verdict places them? Do they realize that they must stand self-convicted as perjurers before God and man? Where is the honor of a community? Where the honesty of a jury-man's oath? Where is the honor of Governor Nicholls? "Vengeance is mine, saith the Lord."

I also have in the Picayune an account of this "Iberia riot," as it is called, which I desire to insert in the RECORD. The account of the beginning of the affray here given is that the white people of the section began to feel alarmed about the negroes at Freetown, and this is what they did:

The citizens rode into Freetown and found, as rumored, a large number of armed negroes quartered there. They asked its meaning and the negroes were silent. They then demanded a surrender of their arms, with the promise that when they learned to behave themselves--

I judge that means only that when they learned to submit to the policy that has been outlined here today by the Senator from Louisiana of having no ticket in the field except the Democratic ticket--they would be returned, and that the negroes should at once disperse. The great majority of them accepted the terms of the party and surrendered their arms, which were found without exception to be loaded with ball or buckshot.

The negroes took possession, it appears, of Rev. Mr. Nora's house. Then follows the brutal massacre which was described in the Times-Democrat, published with my remarks the other day:

THE IBERIA RIOT--TWENTY NEGROES AND ONE WHITE MAN SLAIN--GLOWING DETAILS OF THE BATTLE--THE NEGROES BARRICADED IN THE PREACHER'S HOUSE--NONE LEFT ALIVE TO TELL THE STORY--SOME INNOCENT MEN WHO SUFFERED WITH THE GUILTY --THE NAMES OF THE SLAIN--THE FUNERAL OF MR. SMITH IN NEW IBERIA--POLITICS NOT A FACTOR IN THE FIGHT.

NEW IBERIA, LA., *August* 17.

Today all is quiet again. This morning a large number of men from various sections of the country and neighboring towns were here, but nearly all of them returned to their homes during the forenoon.

The morning the remains of Mr. E. P. Smith were removed to the Episcopal church. He was forty-two years of age and a native of Ohio, and a bachelor. The funeral services were conducted at the church by Rev. C. C. Kramer. The edifice was crowded to a jam, and the yard and walks in front of the church were also crowded. After the regular service at the church the funeral cortage was formed, as follows: The Iberia Guards, the Attakapas Rangers (of which the deceased was a member), the hearse, the Phoenix Bucket Fire Company (of which the deceased was also a member), Iberia Steam Fire Company, No. 1; American Steam Fire Company, No. 2; followed by many friends and acquaintances on foot and in carriages.

A large number of ladies were in attendance, and their floral offerings were profuse and tasty. Palm leaves figured conspicuously among the evergreens.

At the grave Rev. Kramer finished the services, after which followed a salute of three volleys by a detachment of the Iberia Guards. Thus were the last tributes of respect paid to the departed--a noble spirit, a fast friend, a congenial companion.

The trouble of yesterday grew out of a spirit of revenge on the part of the negroes. The better element of this and neighboring parishes had found it impossible to longer tolerate a certain element of idle and immoral characters. This latter class were ordered away from the various sections and many of them found refuge at Freetown, a small village composed entirely of negro families. There they told their stories to their friends and nursed their growing anger. On Monday last the report reached this place that the negroes were arming and congregating at Freetown. Their number was estimated at from 500 to 600 strong, mounted. Tuesday they had received re-enforcements sufficient to fully double their numbers, and feeling their strength they assumed a threatening attitude, boldly declaring the refugees should not leave the parish and should not be molested.

On Wednesday their numbers were further increased, and the people of the surrounding country began to feel some alarm lest these negroes, overestimating their strength, should attempt some acts of violence.

On Thursday matters had not improved up to noon. By this time the residents and property-owners of this section began to collect at a point a short distance from Freetown, their object to disperse these negroes without violence and to send those who did not belong there to their homes and business.

Rev. H. Nora, a colored minister, left Freetown in the morning to attend a conference of ministers at this place, and during his absence his residence was taken possession of by a number of the armed negroes. This house refused to surrender, returning word that they were not to be taken. The whites then sent a second messenger to the house, saying they would give them twenty minutes in which to lay down their weapons. The negroes again refused.

In this house, situated but a short distance from the main road or street, were quartered some twelve or fifteen negroes, among the number their leaders.

A squad of mounted white citizens were some 150 yards from the house, waiting the expiration of the twenty minutes, and before the given time had expired a door of the house was thrown open and a volley fired at them. One horse was wounded.

This was a surprise to all, and immediately the firing became general. The door of the house was again closed, but a constant fire was kept up from windows and doors partly open for quite an interval. Later the fire was carried on by spurts by both sides, lasting in all for nearly an hour and a half.

At this time Mr. Smith broke from his lines and made for the house. His comrades implored him to return, but, deaf to their entreaties, he went on. The house was reached, the door was forced, and he fell. At his side was a comrade who had followed him on his fatal errand; but when Mr. Smith fell his comrade retreated backwards, keeping up a constant fire from a repeating rifle, and escaped unhurt.

At this stage of the fight the negroes became panic-stricken and attempted to flee from the house, and the deadly work was soon brought to a close.

After the fight closed the bodies of eight negroes were found in the house and five others outside.

Others say three or four more were killed. It is thought by some that a few made their escape, while others who were at the scene deny this.

One of the negroes who shot Mr. Smith was named Smith and was recognized among the dead by Mr. Smith's comrade today.

Coroner J. Wolf called a jury as follows: Mr. William Lamb, Dr. James A. Lee, Messrs. Zenon, Decair, Doud, Laughlin and William R. Burke, and proceeded with them to Freetown to the remains of the negroes.

They returned this evening and have deferred taking testimony until a later date.

From the above statement of facts , it will be clearly seen that politics have played no part; that the negroes brought the trouble on themselves; that they fired the first shot; that they shed the first blood, and that they bore the consequences of their acts.

The negroes who surrendered were not harmed in any way.

FREETOWN--WHERE THE BATTLE WAS FOUGHT--THE FIGHT AND ITS VICTIMS

LAFAYETTE, LA., *August* 17.

The riot briefly reported from this point at a late hour last night as occurring at Cade's Station really occurred about 6 miles southwest of that point, at Freetown, which is located in the corner of Iberia Parish and only a short distance from St. Martin's Lafayette, and Vermillion Parishes. This section is more properly located 4 miles southwest of Burk station on the Morgan Road, and about 10 miles from New Iberia.

Freetown is a little town of negroes, but more of a neighborhood, as it covers about 4 square miles, with fifteen families living in small hut-like houses from 100 to 400 yards apart, with small fields attached, from which they are supposed to make a living, and the houses and fields usually belong to the family using them.

About the center of the settlement is a store kept by a negro, a Baptist church, and a school-house. But a few white families live in the range of this neighborhood. There are but few houses there which could be called comfortable negro houses.

It is understood that for some years back considerable foraging and depredations in stealing of cattle corn, and cotton on the outlying white neighborhood has been carried on, and supposed to have been done by some of those at Freetown. This is said to have been known to be true of Andy Smith and one or two of Tom Simon's sons. Several of these negroes are reported to have been whipped for it, but it was not possible to detect the ringleader,

Andy Smith.
It is said that a few days since the regulators of that neighborhood
sent him word that they were going to whip him. He immediately drew a-
round him sixteen to eighteen negroes of the neighborhood, all of whom
were armed with Winchester rifles, old muskets, and double-barreled shotguns,
numbers of the latter of recent purchase in New Iberia. This was but a few
days since. He then sent word to the white people to come on, that he and
his friends were ready for them, and, it is said, threatened the lives of
four or five white men near by.
Andy Smith, the leader of the blacks in this trouble, has shot two or
three white men in the past four years, and is known to be of desperate
courage and meanness.
The four or five whites receiving this defiant message believed their
lives were in danger, and sent a few messengers to New Iberia and Abbeville,
across the line and into Lafayette, to the effect that they would be killed
and appealed for help.
In response to this call about 150 to 200 men from these three sections
reached Freetown after the dinner hour of yesterday. They found these armed
negroes, about eighteen in number, barricaded in a new four-room frame
house, built by their pastor, Rev. Cleste Noop, who was at the time in New
Iberia, holding a protracted meeting among his people. These negroes had
sent Noop's wife away and were its sole occupants at the time.
The house was surrounded by the whites, and a half hour's delay occurred
in a parley on the part of the whites, who assured Smith and his crowd that
it was peace, if it was desired, and not violence, and if the negroes would
surrender their arms the whites would take them away for the present, but at
a subsequent time, when peace was fully established, they should be returned
to their owners, and guaranteed no violence to any one of the party.
In the interest of this purpose, the whites secured the services of old
man Tom Simmons, father-in-law of Smith, and father of Louis and Edward
Simmons, two of the occupants of the house, and also old man Sam Cohit,
each of whom besought the barricaded negroes to comply with the request to
surrender their arms and prevent any one from being hurt. Surly silence
was the only response. The pacifying efforts were ineffectual. The whites
were about 20 feet from the house. Payson Smith and Alfred Lasalle, of the
whites, approached the house, and as Lasalle opened one of the doors, poor
young Smith stuck his head in and was immediately shot down by Andy Smith.
This was the first signal for a general firing from inside by the
blacks and outside by the whites. The house is new and unceiled and therefore has very thin walls. The doors and windows being closed, the firing
was at and through this thin wall. The blacks standing close up the wall
fired outside, and before it reached the whites the force of the ball was
spent in passing through the wall. The whites at a long range penetrated the
walls easier and only had a few feet to reach those on the inside, and hence
proved more effectual in killing those for whom they shot. There were, it
is estimated, four hundred to five hundred shots fired, and when the battle
was over the walls from 4 inches to 5 feet above the floor were riddled with
bullet-holes. Several of the negroes during the fight escaped and were
shot while running, but most of them fell when they opened battle in the
house.
It is understood when the battle was ended there were over twenty guns
found in the house.
In addition to the killing of Payson Smith, the white forces suffered
a slight wound in the wrist of Mr. Manard, a young creole from New Iberia
Station.
In reference to the results on the side of the negroes, it is not absolutely certain, but from two sources it is made up as follows: A prominent
gentleman who went to the grounds this morning says that he went into the
negro church, when he found there were eight dead negroes who were left there
to await the coroner's inquest. These were Sam Cahil, Earnest Grient, Andy
Smith, Paul Charles, Louis Simmons and three others whom the gentleman did
not know. He was informed that old man Tom Simon had been killed and carried to his own house. He was also informed that an unknown negro was
wounded and died last night, which would make ten killed. He was informed
that four others were missing and unaccounted for--whether absent or dead

was not known.

There was one wounded, Alex Lee, a colored school teacher, who called Dr. B. T. Mosely to attend him. This would make a total of fifteen. Dr. Mosely says Lee is seriously wounded in the jaw and throat, and has a flesh wound in the breast. The other information is denied.

From a negro from Freetown, who was today at Cade's station: He says that there were originally thirteen dead negroes in the church, but that five were carried away, and that Tom Simmons, the unknown negro who died last night, and the school teacher would make sixteen, and the four missing would make a total of twenty.

In addition to the names of the dead first given the negro informant gives those of Edward Simon, son of old man Tom Simon and brother-in-law Andy Smith; Edward Vallier, Jr., Alex Vallier, and T. Pochelle.

Violence is always an important fact in reaching intelligent conclusions, but this case is somewhat independent. Beyond the fact that Andy Smith for his general bad character was threatened with a whipping in retaliation armed himself and friends and defied the white people, and fired the first shot, in the face of the fact that there were ten whites to one, thus manifesting his dare-devil rascality in the last moment of life, as death must have seemed inevitable to him after his killing young Smith.

This information is obtained by a buggy ride of nearly 40 miles today through mud and hot sun and a scarcity of intelligence to furnish it.

LAFAYETTE--THE EXCITEMENT IN A NEIGHBORING PARISH

LAFAYETTE, LA., *August* 17.

Some excitement prevails here today consequent of the agitation in Abbeville and the unfortunate affair at Cade Station, in the lower portion of this parish. There is great uneasiness among the negroes, who fear a repetition of violent acts in this quarter. Many of the whites are supplying themselves with arms and ammunition in case of need, while it is rumored that there is a move to organize a guard for the protection of the town. This trouble seemingly originated in St. Mary and Vermillion Parishes, and to some extent has spread over this parish, but your correspondent has been unable so far to gather definite information in regard to it. Several parties here, so says Dame Rumor, who have been guilty of miscegenation have been waited upon and ordered to leave. It is safe to say, however, that no blood shed need be feared at this place, so the sober judgment of our citizens may be relied on to tide over the present uneasy state of affairs.

The farmers must necessarily suffer under this deplorable state of excitement, as the negroes will not leave their homes for fear of being waylaid. Everything is quiet tonight, and the outlook betokens an early subsidence of the regnant perturbation. . . .

ARTICLES FROM THE LOUISIANA STANDARD, T. B. STAMPS, PROPRIETOR, NEW ORLEANS, AUGUST 25, 1888

If the colored man in this State has a spark of spirit in his body, and desires to be practically free, as is guaranteed by the national Constitution, he must leave here and go at once. Go North, East, or West, where you will be treated at least like a human being born according to God's laws.

We hope to publish next week the fact that the negro has started the immigration from this cut-throat slice of the solid South; that he will demonstrate that he means to be free by leaving a State where he is held now as much a slave as ever before the emancipation proclamation of God's great Christian servant, Abraham Lincoln.

On our front page will be found a letter from Mr. L. A. Martinet, the leading colored Democrat of the South and editor of the Progress, in which he scathingly and manfully denounces the Democratic methods and the cold-blooded butchery of negroes and diabolical outrages on Republicans by the Democrats.

MARTINET ON HAND IN CONDEMNATION OF NEGRO BUTCHERY--HE CANNOT CONDONE DEMOCRATIC METHODS AND DECLINES FURTHER FEALTY WITH THE PARTY OF OPPRESSION.

NEW ORLEANS, LA., *August 23, 1888*

To the *Progress Publishing Company:*

GENTLEMEN: When Saturday I read in the morning papers of the massacre
of the negroes at Freetown, Iberia Parish, I was shocked and horrified. It
was a ruthless and brutal butchery of human beings, without cause, reason,
or sense. Moreover, there exists in the parishes surrounding that section
a reign of terror and lawlessness that is a shame to civilization. Colored
people are unmercifully beaten and whipped for no cause or reason; they
cannot be out at night after 9 o'clock with safety; their property is forcibly taken from them in broad daylight; and old and respectable residents
and families are dirven away from their homes, the latter because the husbands happen to be white.

In view of the fact that every act of violence against negroes in the
South is charged in the North to the Democratic party, and of all that there
is at stake for the Democratic party in the pending national contest, it does
seem as if the perpetrators of these unheard-of outrages, who are said to
be Democrats, have gone mad.

I called on the governor Monday and yesterday again, with a view of
securing some official action for the protection of these injured and outraged people, or for putting a stop to this lawlessness. I explained to
him how critical the situation is, but I regret exceedingly to say that he
does not think that a case has yet arisen where he has the authority to
interfere, and he seems apprehensive that if he does interfere now it might
make matters worse.

Well, if the negroes are to be butchered, flogged, and driven from their
homes under a Democratic administration, without cause or provocation, and
the authorities are not able to speak one word in their behalf for humanity's
sake, or in censure or condemnation of the atrocious deeds, then there is no
reason that I know of why they should change their politics, and thus try to
remove what we believed a bar to relations of amity between their white
fellow-citizens and themselves, especially when it is known that even those
who have voted the Democratic ticket are not exempt from brutal treatment.
Even personal friends of ours of irreproachable character have been molested
and driven away. I mention this to illustrate better the deplorable state
of affairs--not that we would think our friends more sacred than others. If
we favored a Democratic government it was specially for the purpose of assuring protection to our people. This failing, we see no way in which they
are benefited by it.

I confess I am not only disappointed, but pained and grieved beyond
expression. My faith in Governor Nicholls was such that I never could once
believe that such outrages could be committed under his administration without at least immediate rebuke and condemnation. My faith in him is not altogether shaken, and I yet have the hope that he will take some action.

It is all a sad return for our unselfish and disinterested efforts to
establish permanent relations of peace and harmony between the races, an end
for which I have labored long, endured much vexation, and made great personal sacrifices.

A task that forced itself upon the Progress at the outset was to defend
the election of the present State administration against the exaggerated
charges of fraud, of rancorous political opponents. That we have not been
entirely unsuccessful is shown by the readiness with which our articles have
been quoted in the United States Senate and the extensiveness with which
they have been reproduced by the Democratic press.

Thoroughly acquainted with the incapacity of the negro voters in their
present untutored state to govern, and knowing how easy a prey they are to
designing and unprincipled politicians and demagogues, we have labored hard
to convince them that it was best for their interests that the people who
own the property and possessed the intelligence, as I thought, should rule.
Through it all we have been honest and conscientious. We have borne un-
complainingly the ostracism of our people and the odium that, among them,
attaches to the colored man who professes himself a Democrat, and we have
never asked nor expected personal reward in any shape or manner.

Our sole aim and endeavor has been to promote, in our feeble way, the
good and welfare of the whole people. Conscious of having striven to perform
what we considered a public duty, of having, in the interest of what we believed to be the cause of good government, labored to enable these people to
control the mass of illiterate voters in their midst without a resort to
violence or unlawful means, we could rest perfectly satisfied with the little

appreciation our efforts have received from those who were to be first
benefited by them. But I will not, I can not, condone the shedding of innocent blood.

Knowing the worthlessness of professional negro politicians, and how
hurtful they are to their own race, I have been, with your approval, un-
sparing in denouncing them, going to the length of palliating, if not
always justifying the illegal measures taken to rid the community of them,
when no bodily harm or injury was done. But I cannot, I will not silently
countenance the ruthless butchery and cruel whipping of defenseless and innocent people, the despoiling them of their property, and the running away
of others from their homes because they chose to marry or unite according
to their individual tastes.

The right of people to marry to suit themselves is the most sacred that
I know. It is a divine right, and no one has rightfully the authority to
interfere with the contracting parties. I could not say less on this point
without, as it were, submitting to the desecration of the cherished memory
of my dead parents, and condemning their holy union and marriage, of which
I am the product.

No matter what the governor's personal feelings may be concerning these
outrages--he has a strong sense of right and justice, and I know he deplores
and condemns them in his heart--yet it seems to me that his silence will
create on the outside world the false impression that this lawless condition
of affairs is not so extensive, widespread, and critical as it really is,
which would be wrong; or, worse, it may be taken by the "regulators" as
warrant to go on in their nefarious course.

It must be remembered, too, that the Picayune, which may be regarded as
the organ of the administration, has unqualifiedly pronounced itself upon
the question of miscegenation, encouraging the inhuman crusade against it
which is spreading all over the State, and from which spring so many acts of
violence.

The Progress has no circulation outside of the State. It is not a
factor in the Presidential contest--and there is something more sacred than
politics in this matter. A question of humanity is involved. The party that
would use the perpetration of such outrages merely for campaign purposes, as
a steppingstone to power, ought not to succeed; and the party that is too
weak and pusilanimous to denounce them ought not to be intrusted with power.
Also, our efforts to establish and maintain peace and harmony, between the
races have, it seems to me, not only proved futile, but may be, under the
circumstances, considered officious. Therefore, unless the policy of the
paper can be so directed as to deal with this lawlessness as it should be
dealt with, I beg you to accept my resignation as editor.

Very respectfully,

L. A. MARTINET

AN EARNEST PROTEST AGAINST THE WHOLESALE SLAUGHTER OF INNOCENT AND IN-
OFFENSIVE COLORED MEN--MEMORIAL MASS MEETING IN GEDDES HALL--ABLE ADDRESS
OF REV. E. LYON--MATTERS IN DETAIL.

Wednesday night Geddes Hall was filled by a large assemblage of prominent divines and citizens who assembled to enter their protest against the
indiscriminate slaughter of innocent negroes in adjoining parishes. A large
number of ladies were present.

The meeting was called to order by Hon. T. B. Stamps, who announced the
subject of the meeting and read the following list of officers:

Rev. J. W. Hudson, president; Hon. George D. Geddes, honorary president;
vice presidents, Revs. F. T. Chinn, John Marks, A. E. P. Albert, I. H. Nor-
wood, Graham Bell, C. H. Thompson, D.D.; J. W. Hudson, J. T. Newman, M.D.;
Rev. R. Thompson, Messrs. H. C. Nichols, E. Brower, Robert W. B. Gould, Revs.
A. S. Jackson, J. L. Burrell, Maj. C. F. Ladd, Hon. D. F. Diaz, Col. James
Lewis, Rev. T. P. Jackson, Col. R. B. Baquet, Rev. Hon. George Devezin, Hon.
Thomas W. Wickham, Rev. Charles Williams, Rev. M. Dale, Mr. Frank C. Taylor,
Rev. Guy Watson, Hon. L. D. Thompson, Rev. C. H. Claiborne, Mr. Paul Alex-
andria, George Landry, esq., Mr. John B. Williams, Rev. B. Brown, Mr. C. C.
Wilson, Mr. J. W. Hilton, Hon. C. F. Brown, G. W. Wilson, esq., Rev. L. W.
Oldfield, Rev. W. S. Wilson, Mr. Hope Dennis, J. H. Coker, M.D., Drs. Chris.
Graves, Robert J. Estes, Rev. Dick Richard, Mr. W. A. Halston, Mr. J. D.
Brooks, Rev. H. Taylor, Mr. H. Dixon, Mr. H. C. Green, Mr. Ramie Hawkins,

Rev. R. Frazier, Mr. Thomas Wesley, Mr. B. B. Dixon,jr., Rev. C. Monroe, Mr.
H. Powells, Rev. Dave Young, Hon. Henry Demas, E. Duconge, esq., Frank Farr-
er, Capt. N. D. Bush, Capt. D. D. Wethers, Mr. B. Boguille, Mr. L. J.
Joubert, Mr. Walter Cohen, Rev. J. A. Wilson, Mr. Joseph H. Fuller, Mr.
Paul Bruce, Capt. Peter Joseph, Capts. Charles Lewis, D. M. Moor, Hons. W.
S. Posey, Frank Farrell, Messrs. A. L. Chapman, Rev. Henry Davis, Mr. Arthur
W. Woods, Mr. Edward Gaudet, Rev. M. C. Camfield, Mr. John Marshall, Mr.
Alexander Plique, Capt. William Cobb, Capt. J. W. Edwards, Capt. Taylor Mc
Keethen, Capt. Dand Wilson, C. B. Wilson, James F. Thomas; secretary, Rev.
Ernest Lyons; assistants, Paul Green, M. J. Simms, R. C. Cammack.

The meeting was opened by divine services, prayers being offered by
Rev. Henderson, pastor of the Central Congregational Church. The following
committee was appointed to prepare an address: Revs. Ernest Lyon, A. E. P.
Albert, M. C. B. Mason, J. H. Coker, M.D., T. B. Stamps, W. Paul Green,
James D. Kennedy, Charles B. Wilson.

The committee retired, and in a few moments submitted the following
report:

"To the people of the United States:

"We, citizens of New Orleans, as well as of neighboring parishes, from
which we have been driven away without warrant or law, assembled in mass
meeting at New Orleans, La., on Wednesday, August 22, at Geddes Hall, declare
and assert: That a reign of terror exists in many parts of the State; that
the laws are suspended and the officers of the government, from the governor
down, afford no protection to the lives and property of the people against
armed bodies of whites, who shed innocent blood and commit deeds of savagery
unsurpassed in the dark ages of mankind.

"For the past twelve years we have been most effectively disfranchised
and robbed of our political rights. While denied the privilege in many
places of voting for the party and the candidates of our choice, acts of
violence have been committed to compel us to vote against the dictates of
our conscience for the Democratic party, and Republican ballots cast by us
have been counted for the Democratic candidates. The press, the pulpit, the
commercial organizations, and executive authority of the State have given
both open and silent approval of all these crimes. In addition to these
methods, there seems to be a deep laid scheme to reduce the negroes of the
State to a condition of abject serfdom and peonage.

"It is being executed by armed bodies of men, styling themselves regulators, all of whom are white, except when a negro is occasionally forced
to join them to give color to the pretense that they represent the virtue of
their communities in the suppression impartially of vicious and immoral persons. With that pretense as a cloak these lawless bands make night hideous
with their unblushing outrages and murders of inoffensive colored citizens.
They go out on nightly raids, order peaceable citizens away never to return,
whip some, fire into houses of others--endangering the defenseless lives of
women and children--and no attempt is even made to indict them. No virtuous
element in the State is found among the whites to rise up in their might and
sternly repress these outrageous crimes.

"These acts are done in deliberate defiance of the Constitution and laws
of the United States, which are so thoroughly nullified that the negroes who
bore arms in defense of the Union have no protection or shelter from them
within the borders of Louisiana. During the past twelve months our people
have suffered from the lawless regulators as never before since the carnival
of bloodshed conducted by the Democratic party in 1868, and which prompted
the late and lamented General Phillip Sheridan, in an official report, to
style the whites as banditti. Fully aware of their utter helplessness, unarmed and unable to offer resistance to an overpowering force which varies
from a 'band of whites' to 'a sheriff's posse' or the 'militia,' but which in
reality is simply the Democratic party assembled with military precision and
armed with rifles of the latest improved patents, toilers forbidden to follow occupations of their choice, compelled to desist from the discussing of
labor questions, and been whipped and butchered when in a defenseless condition.

"In the instances where negroes have attempted to defend themselves, as
at Pattersonville and Thibodaux, they have been traduced in a spirit of
savage malignity, the governor of the State, with scarce an observance of the

forms of law has hastened his mercenaries or militia to the scene with can-
non and rifles ostensibly to preserve the peace, but actually to re-enforce
the already too well fortified negro murderers falsely assuming to be lawful posses.

A single volume would scarcely afford sufficient space to enumerate
the outrages our people have suffered, and are daily suffering at the hand
of their oppressors. They are flagrantly deprived of every right guaranteed them by the Constitution; in many parts of the State they are free
only in name; they cannot assemble in peace to indicate and discuss an
equitable rate of wages for their labor; they do not feel safe as property-
holders and tax-payers; and are permitted to enjoy but very few public con-
veniences.

"The latest wholesale murder, rivaling the most horrifying brutalities
of the Comanches, took place only a few nights ago near Cade Station, in
the parish of Iberia, in the negro village of Freetown. This place is owned
exclusively by colored people, who were conceded to be industrious and respectable. They were charged with hiding and protecting in their midst
some negroes from other parts of the parish whom the regulators wanted to
whip. When this news was spread abroad a sheriff, fraudulently installed,
with his men, without any warrant or shadow of law, at the hour of midnight
invaded that quiet village, attacked a house wherein a number of negroes
expecting the assault had gathered for self-defense, and deliberately
slaughtered the inmates. No arrests will follow. The civil authorities are
in sympathy with and applaud the crime.

"The governor has shown no disposition to afford our people any protection, because of this and other kindred wrongs, and our sad experience
leads us to expect no redress from that source.

"The papers daily record lynchings, whippings, and murders of people on
various pretenses, such as are not considered sufficient cause for lynch law
for whites under the like circumstances, and tidings pour in upon us like
a flood, of brutalities the record of which is suppressed from the public
print because of the supposed political effect they would have upon the
Presidential and Congressional campaigns in the Northern States.

"We have exhausted all means in our power to have our wrongs redressed
by those whose sworn duty it is to impartially execute the laws, but all in
vain, until now, because of our murdered fellow-citizens, and apprehensive
for our own safety, we appeal to the awakened conscience, the sense of
justice and sympathy of the civilized world, and of the American people in
particular, to assist us with such moral and material support, as to secure
the removal of our people, penniless as many of them are under the feudal
system under which they live, to the public lands and other places of the
Northwest where they can enjoy some security for their persons and property.

"To this end we have organized a bureau of immigration. We have so
done under the following resolution:

"*Be it resolved,* That a bureau of immigration be composed of J. H.
Coker, M.D., president; Rev. Ernest Lyon, A.B. secretary; W. P. Green, esq.,
M. J. Simms, assistant secretaries; Rev. C. B. Mason, A.B., treasurer; Rev.
A. E. P. Albert, D.D., George D. Geddes, esq.; Rev. A. S. Jackson, Hon. T.
B. Stamps, D. D. Wethert, esq.; Rev. J. L. Burrell, C. B. Wilson, esq.   To
our people we advise calmness and a strict regard for law and order. If
your homes are invaded expect no mercy, for none will be shown, and if doomed
to die, then die defending your life and home to the best of your ability.
If convinced that you will not be permitted to live where you are in peace
and perfect security quietly go away. If you are without other means to
travel take to the public roads or through the swamps and walk away.

"Steam-boats and railroads are inventions of recent years; your forefathers dared the bloodhounds, the patrollers, and innumberable obstacles,
lived in the woods on roots and berries in making their way to Canadian
borders.

"Invoking the guiding favor of Almighty God and the sympathy of mankind,
we are your brethren in affliction and the common bond of humanity,

"Rev. M.C.B. MASON.	"Rev. ERNEST LYON,
"Rev. W. Paul Green.	"Rev. A. E. P. Albert
"Rev. J. D. Kennedy,	"Rev. J. H. Coker, M.D.
"Rev. C. B. Wilson	"Rev. T. B. Stamps *"Committee."*

On motion of Rev. A. S. Jackson, which was duly seconded by Rev. M.C.B.
Mason, R.W.B. Gould, and others in appropriate remarks, the address was
unanimously adopted by a rising vote.

The following resolutions, offered by Mr. Marshall J. Simms, were
adopted:

"*Resolved,* That the immigration bureau be, and they are hereby requested
to open immediate communication with the immigration and kindred organizations
in California, Kansas, and the Northwestern States and Territories and to
adopt such other plans as will afford the information and relief for our
oppressed people.

"*Resolved,* That every possible method be utilized to inform our people
and neighboring States of the terrorism which reigns in the disturbed sections of this State, especially in Iberia, St. Martin, Lafourche, St. Mary,
Assumption, Terrebonne, and Vermillion, so that they may be duly warned
against endangering their lives and liberty by going to these places."

Stirring addresses were made by Revs. Ernest Lyon, A. S. Jackson, A.E.P.
Albert, E. S. Swan, J. D. Kennedy, Miss S.A.E. Locket, Rev. M.C.B. Mason,
and others. Meeting then adjourned.

REV. E. LYON'S ADDRESS--THE YOUNG DIVINE HANDLES THE OUTRAGE QUESTION WITH
GREAT SKILL

The following is the able address of Rev. E. Lyon delivered at Geddes
Hall:

When will deliverance come? is the question which is being asked by the
most concerned of our people.

The diabolical system of wholesale and unprovoked murder of our people
in the country parishes continues on the increase. The peaceful and law-
abiding colored citizens of the State thought that after "danger was over"
that affairs would assume their usual tranquility; that after the murder and
giving up of negroes, whose only crime seems to be, from facts obtained, the
attempts on their part to exercise their liberty within the borders of a free
Republic, that innocent and defenseless negroes would be allowed to pursue
their daily avocation in peace, in order that they may provide for the
necessities of their families. But alas! scarcely a wind blows but what it
brings the intelligence of murder and bloodshed--murder and bloodshed confined
invariably within the ranks of a certain class of the people, namely, the
poor and unsuspecting members of the colored race. In all of these engagements the whites have always succeeded in escaping scot-free. This does not
look reasonable. There is foul play somewhere, and the whole world begins
to believe it.

For a decade of years the innocent and unsuspecting negroes have been
made the victims of a cruel fate. The present year dawned upon us, and found
the State rent from center to circumference by perplexing political issues.
Issues which by a strange admixture of political circumstance, assumed the
semblance of labor troubles. Whatever might have been the real causes of
these troubles a bloody massacre was the result. A sham attack was shrewdly
instituted by the whites on paper only, with the negroes as aggressors. This
was only the pretense for the indiscriminate slaughter of men, women, and
children which followed. A mother in Israel, bowed down with many summers,
who remained faithfully at home during the war to watch her master's children
till the battle was over, was mercilessly shot down with impunity within the
very heart of a Christian country.

The intelligent members of the race watched with silence and waited with
patience to hear the secular press and pulpits of the State, either in mild
or in measured terms, denounce the inhuman ravages upon life and property.
But to their disappointment that period has not yet come. Again, we are
startled by the sad intelligence of weeping and mourning, of murder and
bloodshed at Freetown, a village within the very shade of the capitol of the
State. Eleven families in mourning. Eleven wives made widows by a band of
white hoodlums claiming to be regulators. This village is largely inhabited
by colored people who are industrious and law-abiding. The murder marks one
of the bloodiest and most thrilling chapters in the history of crimes.

The offense for which these innocent and helpless people were butchered
was the protection they offered to some of the members of the race who were
flying from the murderous chase of midnight regulators. Confined within
their own premises, they determined to give protection to their fellows in

distress. There was nothing wrong in this. It would be just what the white people would be too glad to do under like circumstances. But of course such manhood on the part of the negroes is exceedingly offensive to the whites, and they must die. These negroes it must be understood were not lawless or clamorous insurrectionists. They were industrious peaceful, and law-abiding citizens armed to defend their rights and property at the sacrifice of their own lives. They were murdered. Nothing less could be expected. The odds were against them. But before they welcomed death and shook hands with immortality they evinced to the cowardly whites courage and heroism worthy the race whose image they so nobly bore.

All honor to the brave men, therefore, who so nobly defended themselves at Freetown. May the hands that were swift in shedding their blood receive speedy retribution, and may the soil which drank their blood, as a fitting evidence of nature's displeasure, be barren forever. We ask, are not the laws enacted by the Legislature, composed of competent men, elected by the people, able to protect the State without the interference of regulators? Who are these regulators, and what are they? Are they acting under the official sanction of the governor of the State?

If they are not, why does he allow without his official protest this uncivilized system of affairs which places the whole people in juxtaposition to the Hottentots of the African reservation. The facts as given to the public by the daily journals and telegraph operator who are white men must be taken for what they are worth. What right has the sheriff posse to compel negroes to give up their arms in the defense of their person and property? Would the white people of the State in like position submit to such a glaring piece of injustice perpetrated on themselves?

If the negroes are to be disarmed, should not the regulators be disarmed also? And if their actions are inharmonious to the constitution of the State, they should be apprehended and punishment inflicted. It is time that the better class of our white friends speak out and clear in the defense of right and justice. There is no protection for the negro. If he attempts to protect himself the riot act is read. His arms are demanded. The militia is called out. A sheriff posse is organized and assisted by regulators, who murder the poor and unfortunate negroes with impunity. An investigation into the cause of the Freetown tragedy should be made; a committee should be appointed by the governor, composed of members of both races, charged with this solemn duty. We would advise the most calm, cool, and prudent of our representative men, both in church and in state, to meet and adopt measures whereby to relieve our people in these suffering districts.

They should wait immediately on his excellency the governor and ask him to appoint a committee of investigation, and if this righteous and godly demand is refused the people who are thus abused should be advised to leave these miserable hells upon earth.

In the days of slavery, when they were surrounded by enemies on every hand, with blood-hounds to hunt their tracks, they ventured to flee for refuge, amid perils indescribable. Guided by the Northern star of liberty, they reached the Canadian shores and Northern asylums.

And now, since freedom has come and every man is supposed to be a man, why not seek homes among those people who will accord to them the common rights of humanity?

If they have to leave with no patrimony but a single potatoe in their pockets, let them take their wives and children by the hand and lead them out of these Sodoms and Gomorrahs. Better die a free man than live a slave.

MEMORIAL MEETING

Geddes Hall was filled on Wednesday night with representatives of our people, including wives and daughters. The meeting was called for the purpose of taking suitable action on the late murders committed on the unfortunate colored people in Lafourche and other parishes.

The meeting was governed by that calm feeling and deliberation which was warranted by the circumstances and which is so necessary to occasions of like serious import. The memorial address, which we print in another column, shows in unmistakable terms the past and present situation of affairs in Louisiana with reference to the colored people.

This was no political meeting, no body of people gotten together for the

purpose of hashing out buncombe for political aspirants, no conclave of
"bloody-shirt" shakers gotten up to fire the Northern heart in the interest
of campaign capital, but a meeting composed of the ministry and representative men and women, who had no other cause at heart than to seek a remedy and
its application in the shape of escape from further murders. The address
of Rev. M. C. B. Mason, Hon. T. B. Stamps, R. W. B. Gould, James D. Kennedy,
and others were splendid efforts, and gave very pointedly the horrible details connected with the late butcheries. The calm reasoning with which they
held the ear of the audience will certainly be fruitful.

We are glad to record the fact that in obedience to resolution offered
a bureau of immigration was organized, which will take immediate steps in
the matter of providing information, etc., regarding homes elsewhere.

A great deal can be said of the possible good, effect of this commence-
ment in behalf of the colored people, but lack of space forbids a further
dissertation on the Geddes Hall meeting; suffice it to say the ball has been
started on a roll and it must be kept rolling until we can place the colored
people out of further harm's way. Emigrate at once. Don't wait for another
butchery.

The colored man is doing himself and his family a great wrong by remaining in this murder-ridden State any longer. We say to you, emigrate to
some other State and risk no longer being slaughtered for being a negro.
You are worse enslaved in Louisiana than you ever were before. Leave and
leave at once.

"KEEP ON WITH IT."

We copy a head-line from the Times-Democrat. Certain Northern journals
are pleased with the conviction of Dennis Kirby for running away with the
keys of a New Orleans ballot-box. The Times-Democrat is happy over the good
work. It advises that we "keep on with it."

We echo the sentiment. The Times-Democrat, however, is content with
small cases. We would advise attention to the far more important. There is
the murder of William Adams, in Monroe, his throat cut from ear to ear, for
peddling Republican tickets. No arrests, no investigations. Would the Times-
Democrat confine itself to the more trivial matters of stealing ballots?

Well, so be it. Take the case of Madison Parish. A return of 3,500
votes for Nicholls--Warmoth without the single vote. Vote, as actually cast;
Nicholls, 588; Warmoth, 2,817--Warmoth with a majority of 2,229; a dead steal,
in effect, of 5,734 votes in the single parish. Will the Times-Democrat take
the case in hand? Dare it challenge the proofs?

What of the present Democratic hell, again, in the Third district? A
white man, killed by whom? Certainly not by the negroes. A dozen negroes
shot down like dogs. No politics in it. Where's the fool that don't know
better? "Why should the prosecution of these criminals be interrupted or
delayed?" We quote the Times-Democrat again. Echo answers, why?

PACK UP AND MOVE

That is our advice to the negroes in the Louisiana bulldozed parishes.
We mean it exactly as we say it. Pack up and move.

There is no other remedy. New Orleans is filling up with refugees. They
are flocking in from the several different parishes and localities. They are
not of the ignorant, or helpless class. They are generally intelligent, are
the owners of their own little homes. They have been driven from home and
family at peril of their lives.

They have been so driven because of their intelligence; because of their
independence. They are not of the old-time class, to be held as servile dogs.
That is why they are driven out. Every negro leader, every negro property-
holder, every negro who can read and write, is branded as dangerous, must be
got rid of. That is the edict openly promulgated and well understood. Take
the situation as it is. You may not return as free men. Free men you must
live and die. You have no protection under the laws. You have no earthly
chance in seeking to protect yourself. There is the one resource. Take it,
and at once. Pack up and move.

We want to be heard and heeded in every bulldozed parish and locality.

We say to the negroes, You have the one and only remedy in your hands.
You are the only producers. You raise the cotton and the sugar. You are the

supporters, in fact, of the men who persecute you. Without your labor they
must themselves go to work or starve. Give them the chance. Let them try
the working or the starving. Let them have the field. Pack up and move.
We don't advise any general exodus. That would entail possible privation and suffering. Let the remedy be gradually applied. Let the young
men and women set the ball in motion. The movement begun makes the certain
better chances for those who stay. There is no single, able-bodied negro
too ignorant to know that his two hands will certainly make him an honest
living.
He knows they will earn it anywhere on the civilized earth. So, too,
with the single, able-bodied woman. She is sure of an honest living anywhere. She has but to work for it. Let the young man and woman get out.
We say it, and we mean it. Pack and move.
Stand not upon the order of going, but go. Don't wait upon any growing
crops, or promises of pay. Steal out through the cane-breaks if you must.
Any way to get out. Don't flock to New Orleans or to any town. Set your
faces toward a free land, a land where an honest life will insure the honest
dues of free men and free women. Go to California, to Arizona, or to any
like place where there is room. You can work your way there if you will.
The will alone is wanted. Pack up and move.
In any other State, North, East, or West, its governor would seek and
demand in person a reason for the atrocious butcheries which have occurred
in this State in the last two or three weeks. But we suppose the governor
of Louisiana knew how the "law was suspended" in his interest and has forgotten that the "danger has passed," or has forgotten his cue and don't know
when to say, "Let up now."
There was a time when some people, were led to believe that the Republican party got up these negro-killing matches for political effect. What say
these people now? Look at the butchery being continued in this wretchedly-
governed State and say whether or not the fact is true that the negro is
being slaughtered for no other reason than that he is a negro by the Southern
banditti, the never-licked and unwhipped Confederate spirit.

LOUISIANA BANDITTI

The history of the colored people in Louisiana, as in other States of
the solid South, has many pages in mourning commemorating the violent deaths
they have suffered at the hands of murderous whelps under one pretext or another. For years the colored citizen of the State of Louisiana has contended
with barbarous inflictions, the like of which we read in history of ancient
eras, when cruel slaughter was rewarded by crown and scepter.
The negro has suffered death or banishment for exercising his rights of
citizenship given him by a nation on whose soil poured the blood of millions
of loyal soldiers and statesmen that this American Union might be saved, and
that all its citizens might be free, as they were created by the Almighty God.
These murders of colored people are the outcome of a lurking feeling of resentment of and refusal to accept of the issues of the late rebellion. A
spirit akin to the animus engendered in behalf of the Confederacy, which,
though subdued on the field of battle, is cowardly resorting to a warfare of
extermination under the cover of civil government.
The pen is again taken up to record another chapter of slaughter and
butchery on the unfortunate colored people of Louisiana, the latest deeds
occurring at Lockport, New Iberia, Freetown, and adjacent localities where
the dastardly idea is rampant that the negro is obnoxious, and they must leave
failing to do which he is to die by the assassin's bullet, the midnight
marauder's bludgeon. What a horrible state of affairs to record against a
government in which crime is suppressed.
On Saturday, August 11 at night time, a hand of white banditti, all
mounted, went out the Bayou road from Raceland to Robert William's house, surrounded it, and concealing themselves in the cane, called for Williams to
come out. Upon coming out, and seeing the state of affairs, attempted to
escape, when he was shot from ambuscade, and died the next morning. After
this piece of butchery, and the same night, they drove up to another colored
man's home, Augustave Antoine, took him off some distance, hung him up to a
tree and riddled his body with bullets, and before doing this they shot and
killed his brother Eugene.

Another case in view is that of a mulatto, who became obnoxious for some reason or another only known to the murderers, who was flogged in regular slave style and given notice to leave the hallowed precincts of New Iberia. He, terror-stricken, left for Freetown, to where some of his friends resided for protection. On learning that he was in Freetown, a leader of the banditti, named Cade, organized an alleged military company for the purpose of slaughtering the colored man's friends, who had collected together in their own defense, and in short order butchered up at least a score of colored people.

We could mention many other instances of like character, but enough is here said, backed by authority, to warrant attention to this deplorable state of affairs.

We say to the colored people that they must leave this State.

The negroes of St. Martin, Iberia, St. Mary, Terrebonne, Vermillion, Lafourche, Assumption Parishes, can never expect anything else than a continuance of this inhuman warfare, and if they have to walk they owe it to themselves and families to leave these parts, for the planter is powerless to protect you as a workman and the governor of the State is apparently indifferent to this condition. We say to you colored people to emigrate to California, Arizona, anywhere else where God's law is respected and man's inhumanity to man in the light of Louisiana methods is unknown and never expected.

Do not wait longer; you have suffered sufficiently long and if you remain you will certainly imperil your own life. Emigrate and leave this infernal hell-hole on earth.

[Extracts from the Louisiana Standard, New Orleans, September 1, 1888.]

THE GOOD WORK GOES BRAVELY ON

Killing and outraging negroes is the order of the day. We ask of the Northern journals that they scan well the certain dispatches as seen in our New Orleans dailies. We mean those purporting to recount the troubles with dangerous and unruly negroes. We mean particularly those as just now appearing from certain sections in the parishes of Terrebonne, Iberia, and St. Martin. Let them read and ponder. The very dispatches of themselves are enough to damn the communities from whence they come.

Here are the armed organizations of whites going about as assumed regulators. Their mission is seen as wholly confined to the negroes. They are themselves outside the pale of all law. They represent no authority whatever save that of organized brute force. They constitute, in fact, nothing more nor less than outlaws; are in honesty to be viewed in no other light.

Here are the armed gangs of outlaws, then, riding roughshod over the country at large hunting negroes to the death. The negroes are largely on their own ground; they appear as living in their own little hard-earned homes.

This was particularly the case in Freetown. The little town was invaded by these armed outlaws. There was the pretense of the sheltering of certain refugees in hiding from the outlaws' threats. A dozen, at least, of negroes were brutally murdered. They were shot down as so many dogs in their kennels. It was the cowardly work of a gang of cowardly murderers. A coroner's jury, as cowardly as the murderers, but serves as the murderers shield. It signs a verdict to the effect that the negroes were killed by parties unknown.

This late hellish work is mainly confined to parishes in the Third Congressional district.

It appears as in effect the beginning of the Democratic Congressional campaign. The three particular parishes are strongly Republican. The latest official registration with returns of the late election may be in order.

Parish	Registration		Election returns	
	White	Negro	Nicholls	Warmoth
Terrebonne...............	2,276	3,035	1,687	2,033
Iberia...................	2,344	3,210	1,262	1,923
St. Martin...............	1,476	2,198	1,107	1,621
Total...............	6,096	8,443	4,056	5,580

The blacks are seen as having the majority vote of 2,347. There is the return of 1,524 majority for the Republican ticket. The voters absent and failing to vote are, for the three parishes, respectively, 1,591, 2,369, and 943, a total of 4,903.

There is here with the free and fair election the large white Republican vote. The 4,903 absentees were unquestionably two-thirds Republican. The three parishes are honestly Republican by fully 3,000 majority.

The bulldozing began previous to election. It was both rampant and fierce on election day. It was by no means confined to the blacks. There were the white Republican leaders coming in for their share. Hon. W. B. Merchant, ex-Republican postmaster in New Orleans, is mentioned for instance by Hon. Senator CHANDLER. Mr. Merchant, as notorious, was outrageously bulldozed; was held a prisoner by an armed body of bulldozers; has since left the State in disgust; is now resident in El Paso, Texas. The election as such was an outrage and a fraud.

The bulldozing broke out afresh immediately following the election in the parish of Terrebonne. Senator INGALLS recounted some of the cases in his famous speech in reply to Senator EUSTIS. An armed band of "regulators" sought to reap their vengeance for being defeated. It appeared, as in evidence, in lead of a brother of Senator GIBSON. The negroes were shot and outraged in every conceivable way. Dozens were driven from their little hard-earned homes in fear of their lives. There are the dozens, so made refugees, in New Orleans today.

Terrebonne, Iberia and St. Martin are virtually in the hands of the outlaws. They have converted these parishes into a veritable hell.

They are riding rough-shod over the country at large. Their path is marked with blood; is strewn with the bodies of a full score of murdered negroes.

These organizations of murderous outlaws are organizations of Louisiana Democrats. They are in effect shielded by the Democratic authorities. Their murders are glossed over and palliated by the Louisiana Democratic press. They are practically a part of the Democratic political methods, murder and outrage for opinion's sake. And still the good work goes bravely on.

MARTINET'S LETTER

We recommend to the colored voters of the country to peruse the letter of Mr. L. A. Martinet, editor of the Progress, published last week in this paper. We address ourselves more particularly to the colored voters of the North, because it matters not how the negroes vote in the South, the result is the same--the South is always solid, through fraud and murder for Democracy--whereas in the North, in several States, they hold the balance of power. The letter presents a mild picture of the fiendish outrages and the condition worse than actual slavery to which our people are subjected in this State, and the colored man who, after reading it, will vote the Democratic ticket is an enemy to his race.

We recommend especially to the colored press, Republican and Democratic, to reproduce this truthful statement from a Democratic source, not with a view of helping one party and injuring the other, but for the sake of humanity and for the purpose of placing the helpless and sorrowful condition of our people in the South before the American people in its true light. It is the more necessary that the colored press should do this as we cannot rely upon the Democratic press to publish the truth about the diabolical outrages perpetrated upon our people. All their accounts are colored so as not to

incur the regulators' displeasure, and they will publish no impartial
statement from any one, colored or white.

There is not a colored man in the State that stood higher in Democratic estimation than Mr. Martinet, yet the Democratic press would not publish
his letter, though couched in moderate language; nor would they publish
the able and considerate address to the American people on the same subject
adopted at the mass meeting of our people held here last week, and which
also appeared in our last Saturday's paper. They even made no mention in
their local columns that such a meeting was held, notwithstanding that
there were reporters present; and yet it was one of the most notable meetings ever held in this city. All our prominent men and ministers were
there and the attendance was exceedingly large. Hence for the dissemination
of the truth about those outrages on our people we must rely especially on
the negro press.

Now, regarding the political bearing the circulation of such facts will
have in the North, it is a matter of secondary consideration with us. As
a Republican, we are sincerely and staunchly in favor of Harrison and Mor-
ton's election, but we will not use the perpetration of such infernal crimes
solely to advance the interests of the party. Our primary object is to make
our helpless and pitiable condition known with the view that the humane
sentiment of the nation will devise means to alleviate the wrongs to which
we are subjected by the Bourbonism of the South.

But we will be frank in saying that the re-election of Grover Cleveland
will be taken by the murderers and destroyers of our people as sanctioning
their deeds, and will encourage them to go on in their career of blood and
extermination, and they will go on with renewed vigor; whereas the success
of the Republican party will show that the healthy public sentiment of the
country condemns those outrages, and will throw a damper and act as a check
on the perpetrators.

This is no surmising. It is clearly shown by the contrast which the
administration of Grover Cleveland and that of President Arthur affords.
Compare the two administrations and see for yourselves. Under the quiet and
peaceable administration of President Arthur, the rough edges of the war
having been smoothed and its wounds almost healed by the long and beneficent
Republican rule, angry passions were gradually cooling down and a better
condition of affairs was quietly taking place in the South. While here and
there at the time of an election some trouble might arise, it was always
local and its effect temporary. Republicanism was undoubtedly fast gaining
ground; prominent white men were continually proclaiming a change of faith
and declaring their adherence to the Republican party, and we confidently
looked to a day not far distant when it would be safe for a colored man to be
a Democrat and when both parties would be composed of whites and blacks
alike.

But the election of Cleveland put a stop to all this. It threw us back
into the seventies. It did not cause a reaction in sentiment, but it effectually put a check on its manifestation, and Bourbonism once more became
rampant and overbearing. His election will give it unlimited sway and will
throw us back in the sixties; while the elction of Harrison will restore
the country for an era of peace, harmony, and prosperity.

Therefore, we say again, colored men, read Mr. Martinet's letter. His
statements cannot be contradicted. The Democrats have everywhere proclaimed
his integrity and veracity, and they cannot today impeach his testimony.
Read his letter and vote the Republican ticket.

OUR MURDERED DEAD--A REQUIEM FOR OUR MURDERED DEAD

Let all join in commemorating the victims of the Freetown massacre.
Let the roll of the murdered dead be held a lasting roll of honor. Let
their names not be forgotten; John Simon, Thomas Simon, Peter Simon, Lewis
Simon, Eugene Green, Edward Valere, Alexander Valere, Antoine Michel, Samuel Kokee, Ransom Livingston, jr. They died, as died the veritable martyrs
of old. They died for daring to assert their rights as free men.

They were murdered for giving shelter and protection to the outraged
and hunted of their race. They gave up their lives in proof of their manhood. They are so many martyrs to Democratic hate. Let them be so held
and revered. "Vengeance is mine, saith the Lord; I will repay."

We assert unhesitatingly that the last Louisiana election was simply

an outrageous wholesale steal; that men were murdered for distributing Republican tickets; that Republican voters were generally bulldozed or defrauded of their ballots; that the officials generally were installed
through fraud; that the State is run practically by bulldozers and ballot-
box stuffers.

We further assert that there exists today in certain sections of the
State a reign of terror; that the country is overrun by gangs of outlaws
known as regulators; that negroes are being hunted as so many animals; that
they are being shot down by dozens, murdered in cold blood for daring to
presume upon their rights as men; that scores again are being driven from
their hard-earned homes, for all of which we challenge the proofs.

We favor emigration in lieu of immigration. We favor, as far as may
be, the general emigration of the negroes.

We don't object to the Northern immigrants. They are of those willing
to concede the negro his rights. We won'd do any lying to induce them to
come. We want the negroes to get out. They have no protection under the
laws. The late outrageous verdict of a coroner's jury over a dozen murdered
negroes at Freetown is abundant proof. We tell them they have no rights the
Louisiana bulldozer is bound to respect. They may be murdered and outraged
at will. They are certain to be murdered and outraged until reduced to a
state of peonage. The only alternative is to pack up and move.

Let the move begin with the young men and women. Let them get out.
Let them stand not upon the order, but go.

THE ASSASSINS LIE

No politics in it; that's the story in connection with the Freetown
massacre. Where's the fool who don't know it to be a lie out of whole cloth.
The assassins are Democrats. The victims are Republicans. That tells the
story. It is the "Old Third." The district is honestly Republican by 8,000
majority. It was carried two years ago by Democrats boodle, and amounted
to say $60,000 in cash. The boodle candidate is now out of the race. There
are no $60,000 this time in the Democratic bag. The want of it must be made
good somehow. There's no other way for it but in killing Republican negroes.
That is the one sure way of keeping Republican voters from the polls. The
Democratic game has begun. A round dozen or so of negroes have been murdered
It is the beginning of the Third district campaign. That's the meaning of
the Freetown massacre.

A CIRCULAR FROM THE BUREAU OF IMMIGRATION

Fellow-citizens and brethren:

After receiving intelligence through the columns of the daily journals
of the terrible outrages and cold-blooded murders of our fellow-citizens at
Freetown and other portions of the State, from time to time, without any
attempt on the part of the executive authorities to bring the murderers to
justice, we felt that patience on our part has ceased to become a virtue,
and that the present dangerous crisis to which matters have been allowed to
reach in the country demanded immediate action on the part of those located
in more favoring districts to adopt measures whereby to relieve those of our
fellow-citizens suffering under a reign of terror and brutalism in the disturbed portions of the State.

Being bound by the ties of duty, as well as of those of race affinities,
memorial meeting was held to contribute honor to those who died in defense
of their lives and property, thus winning for themselves an honorable place
among the number of martyrs who poured out their life-blood as a precious
libation upon the shrine of liberty.

In accordance with this meeting an immigration bureau was organized, wit
authority to communicate with kindred organizations in California and New
Mexico, in order to remove our suffering brethren to regions equally favored
in fertile resources, and among a people who are willing to accord to us the
common rights of humanity.

It was therefore agreed at a meeting of the board that before such a
step is taken a pioneer be sent to the above-mentioned places, whose duty it
shall be in surveying the country and make arrangements with the planters of
that region so that our people instead of moving on a wild goose chase, will
have something definite and sure before them.

It was also agreed by a series of resolutions, both at this board meeting and at the memorial meeting, that an appeal be made to every church organization, secret society, and benevolent association, and every friend of the race to contribute little or much towards defraying the expenses of such an individual upon so important a mission. The board promises to use care and discretion in the choice of such a man.

In accordance, therefore, with those resolutions, we issue this circular, calling upon you in the name of God and the name of common humanity to come to the help of the Lord against the mighty. We need not say to you that the uncivilized methods of regulators are creeping all over the State, like a cancer creeps all over the human body, and that this now peaceful region may soon be disturbed by the hideous yells and the murderous fires of lawless regulators, and you likewise may be found on your way to some safe region where you and your family can dwell together in peace.

Send contributions to J. H. Coker, M.D., president, or Rev. Ernest Lyon, secretary. Office Geddes Hall, No. 220 Erato street.

All contributions will be acknowledged in the S.W.C.A., the Standard and Pelican.

We are your brethren in distress.

> J. H. COKER, *President,*
> ERNEST LYON, *Secretary,*
> M. J. SIMMS,
> PAUL GREEN,
> *Assistant Secretaries.*

Remember Iberia. Let negro laborers give the parish of Iberia a wide berth. Let the Democratic bulldozers go to work. Leave them to gather the cane and make the sugar. You can have no protection for your lives. Avoid Iberia as you would avoid a pestilence. Go somewhere else for work. Let those already there get out. Let everyone who can, pack up and move.

At Opelousas last week another negro was riddled with bullets by white assassins for the reason that it was thought he had purchased buckshot. The mayor of the city gave them the right of way and a *carte blanche.* And so the cruel work goes on. Colored people, you must emigrate. The respectable white people of this State deplore the condition of affairs, but they are powerless to stop this murdering. It is in order for Mr. Nicholls to petition Congress for more power to carry out the laws of this State.

Boycott Terrebonne. Let the colored laborers boycott the parish of Terrebonne. That's the word that with the Irish means the next thing to anathema. It fills the bill. Terrebonne is overrun with Democratic bulldozers. They are hunting and killing Republican negroes. Don't give them a chance at you. Keep away. Get your work elsewhere. Let the bulldozers make their own sugar. Let those who are there get out. Every man who can, take the cane-breaks, if need be, and get away.

Shun St. Martin. Don't go there for work. Leave the cane and the sugar to the bulldozers. Let them go to work, or starve. They propose to reduce you to the status of the Mexican peons. Let them have the field to themselves. Go to California, to Arizona, anywhere outside of bulldozed Louisiana.

[Extracts from the Louisiana Standard, New Orleans, September 22, 1888.]

WHAT ARE THEY GOING TO DO?

What are they going to do about it? That is the question for our Louisiana negroes to decide. They are citizens and men in the eyes of the law. There is even the special clause in both national and State constitutions pledging them their rights. The law, in so far as they are concerned, is but a cheat and a lie. The national and State constitutions, as applicable to them, amount to naught. There is for the negro absolutely no protection for life or property in Louisiana. He is shot down with as little compunction as is the veriest mangy cur. No one ever hears of his murderer being punished for the crime. He is even hunted down as is the wild beast and shot at sight for no earthly offense but daring to presume upon his lawful rights. He is open to every outrage and contumely; his wife, sisters, and children to every insult and abuse. He has in point of fact not even the protection accorded him in the days when held a slave. He had then his lawful masters at least interested in seeing him free from the abuse of others.

The situation withal is growing worse and worse. The negroes are being gradually cowed into abject submission.

A goodly proportion of Louisiana today is for the Louisiana negroes a veritable hell. In the parishes of Terrebonne, St. Martin, Iberia and portions of Lafayette, in particular, there exists a reign of terror. All of law is here practically suspended. Gangs of outlaws, known as regulators, are the law unto themselves. Negroes have been wantonly massacred by the wholesale in broad light of day, as evidenced in the shooting down in cold blood of no less than ten in the massacre at Freetown.

Negroes are being hunted as so many wild beasts, are being as mercilessly murdered. Negroes everywhere are being driven from their little, hardearned homes, are everywhere being wantonly outraged and abused. The infection of lawlessness is spreading, is heard of daily in some new locality.

Governor Nichols has so far done nothing. He cannot plead ignorance of the facts. They are being daily reported in the press. They are matters of common notoriety. His attention, again, has been specially invited, and that, too, by prominent citizens and friends. He was talked to and plead with by Hon. L. A. Martinet.

We have it on good authority, too, that no less a man than Hon. Mr. Breaux, elected with Governor Nicholls as State superintendent of education, has specially interested himself in the matter. We have it that he talked with Governor Nicholls, and plainly enough told him of the terrible massacres, of the outrageous and general lawlessness, of the serious injury it was doing, of the disgrace it was certain to entail, and besought the governor to interfere in behalf of law and order.

Governor Nicholls sits with folded hands while the murders, the whippings and the outrages against Louisiana negro citizens are being daily carried on. He overlooks both the Constitution of the United States and the constitution of Louisiana.

He appears as giving no heed to enforcement of the laws, as ignoring all obligation as a man, as forgetting his registered oath.

These massacres, these daily murders and outrages, are crying aloud to Heaven. They are being registered beside the oath pledging the law's protection to life and property. Governor Nicholls the while joins in the devotions of the faithful, chanting the anthems ascending before the same High Throne. Is that registered oath to count as nothing? Is there no responsibility for these continued murders? Are these church professions and communions to be measured as sacrilege? Is Francis T. Nicholls to command respect as governor of Louisiana? Is he governor only in name?

PROFOUND IMPRESSION

By reference to the columns of the Northern and Western press it has been seen that the Geddes Hall address made a profound impression whereever read. Editors who heretofore have received intelligence of Southern crimes with a feeling of incredulity accept the vigorous protest of a large and respectable mass meeting as conclusive evidence of their perpetration.

From the country parishes it is learned that in at least two places the whites, after reading the address, came together and resolved to assure colored laborers that bulldozing should be stopped and they would guarantee protection of life and property. But so great is the mistrust of the people that little reliance is placed upon those pledges.

It has been felt for many months that the colored people of the State should organize in some manner for common defense, precisely as the Irish do, who suffer in many respects under similar conditions of oppression.

The organization of a bureau of emigration is approved in the country parishes as a practical measure of redress; and many inquiries have been made as to means at hand to convey out of the State the hundreds of laborers who are willing to go. A question has arisen in the minds of some whether to go at once or wait until after the crops are gathered; but the good sense of the people tells them that to await the gathering of the crops is largely to defeat the primary object of an exodus of labor, namely, the embarrassment of those planters who aid and direct the marauders against their lives and homes.

It having been demonstrated that the whites are without tender consciences on the Thibodaux and Freetown massacres and other numerous outrages, the idea now is to touch them sorely in their pocket-books and bank accounts

by depriving them of sufficient labor to gather their crops. Let this purpose be openly avowed and energetically carried out.

Timid counselors have said that the plan will fail, because other
laborers will rush to take the places of those who go. Our advices show
that such is not the experience of several planters who are already in distress. They offer high wages, but liberty of citizenship is not being sold
by the negroes to undergo experiences of the kind visited upon the departed
laborers, a very little will probably satisfy them, while those who enjoy
their freedom in Northern States will extend them their sympathy.

A letter has been received from a United States Senator, in which
inquiry is made in regard to the operations of the bureau of emigration.
When it opens up communication with leading Republicans and capitalists,
the way for effective work will be made clear. Let the bureau be sustained
by words of cheer and liberal contributions.

[Extract from the Telegraph, Monroe, La., August 18, 1888.]

It would be a mistake to confound the principle of white primaries with
that of representation in Democratic conventions.

We do not hesitate to concede that under normal social and political
conditions, the Democratic vote is the fairest basis.

But have we normal social and political conditions in the Fifth Congressional district?

On the contrary, are these conditions not emphatically and pre-eminent-
ly abnormal?

We have white parishes and we have black parishes, each class widely
and notoriously different with respect to these conditions.

The purpose of this discussion do not require that we analyze, re-
iterate, and enumerate these differences. They are well known and well
understood throughout the district.

These two classes of parishes are not dissimilar in one important
feature--they all return safe Democratic majorities.

For political purposes they are all Democratic parishes.

[Extract from the Post, Washington, September 20, 1888.]

It is an undoubted fact that in a number of the Southern States the
negroes have been practically disfranchised. The honest men of the South
admit this. * * * It is an undeniable fact that in the disfranchisement of
the blacks in the South the effect is not confined to local government,
but extends to national affairs, and thus becomes a matter of serious
interest to the people of all the States. The people of Oregon are as
directly interested in the election of Congressmen and Presidential electors
in Mississippi as in similar elections in their own States.

If the political complexion of the Federal Government is changed by
suppression of the ballot, to just the extent of that change the Federal
Government is wrested from its constitutional basis.

We have stated these facts because they are facts, the facts of a very
ugly situation viewed from any possible standpoint. If it be true, as we
think it is, that black rule is intolerable to the whites of this country,
if it be true also that in eliminating that which is locally intolerable
the National Government is necessarily vitiated by fraud, what is to be the
outcome? It strikes us that this is one of the most serious problems ever
presented to the statesmen of the Republic. It ought to be discussed without malice and with a recognition not of a part but of all the facts we
have cited. It is a two-sided question, apparently as far from a solution
today as it was a dozen years ago.

*Congressional Record, 50th Congress, 1st Session, September 27, 1888,
XIX, Appendix, pp. 8989-97.*

VI

GRAND MASTER WORKMAN TERENCE V. POWDERLY AND THE BLACK WORKER

TERENCE V. POWDERLY AND THE BLACK WORKER

The *Noble Order of the Knights of Labor* national leadership espoused
racial views which were considerably more progressive than those held by most
Americans, especially in the South. Both of the Order's most influential
spokesmen had been strongly influenced by the ante-bellum reform movements,
including abolition. Uriah Stevens (1821-1882), who served as the first Grand
Master Workman between 1869 and 1879, approved of segregated locals, although
he believed that both black and white locals should be treated equally.
Stevens' successor, Terence V. Powderly, held even more advanced racial atti-
tudes. For him the goal of organized labor—"Freedom of the man who worked"—
applied to all workers black or white.

In his second official decision as Grand Master Workman, he declared
that the color of a man's skin had no relationship to his admission to the
Order. In his memoirs, Powderly observed that in the field of work, blacks
and whites were economic equals. Those poor whites who hated blacks, he
concluded, did so because they were ensnared by the bondage of prejudice as
well as poverty, and suggested that there was a direct relationship between
the two conditions. He reminded southerners that however subconsciously,
they had long ago recognized the absurdity of their own racial taboos by
sexually levelling any meaningful distinction between the races. During the
hullaballoo created by the Ferrell case at the 1886 convention, Powderly with-
stood considerable denunciation for supporting Ferrell's direct challenge to
racial customs of Richmond. Although Powderly did not permit Ferrell to
introduce Governor Lee, as District 49 desired, Ferrell was allowed to introduce the Grand Master Workman, whom, in this charged atmosphere, Ferrell described as a man "above the superstitions which are involved in these distinctions" of race. Powderly further revealed his equalitarian bent when he revoked
the credentials of white organizers in Alabama and Georgia who had exploited
newly formed black locals by failing to turn over the dues collected from
these locals. The official organ of the Knights of Labor, the Journal of
United Labor, demanded their expulsion for injuring the Order's cause among
blacks.

Nevertheless, the Grand Master Workman's racial views were not so ideal-
istic as to prevent him from attempting to soothe the ruffled nerves of white
southerners. Although he did not oppose integrated locals, and there were
many, he accommodated himself to the strategy that segregated local assemblies were the only "practical" manner by which the South could be organized.
To Powderly, the issue of "social equality" obscured the primarily economic
goals of the labor movement. In his memoirs he wrote that he did not seek
"to interfere with the social relations of the races in the South, for it is
the industrial, not the race question we endeavor to solve ." Moreover, he
was willing to curtail work among Negroes when it conflicted with organizing
southern whites. Although Powderly appointed black organizers in the South,
excellent opportunities to expand the Negro membership were neglected even
after 1886 when interest in the Order was so high among Afro-Americans. In
his correspondence are letters from black leaders requesting an audience, and
correspondence from others desiring to organize local assemblies, many bearing
Powderly's stamp, "No Answer Required."

Although a clear inconsistency existed between Powderly's racial views
and some of his actions, ambivalence was a relatively progressive position in
the 1880s. As the leader of a national organization which depended upon the
support of anti-Negro white workers for its national existence, Powderly was
confronted with the complex problem of organizing blacks to prevent employers
from using them as tools against organized labor. Resolution of the dilemma
required the education of all workers to their class interests. Consequently,
Powderly attempted to circumvent the potentially destructive racial issue by
maintaining that the goal of the Order was economic redress, not the solution
of racial discrimination. Aware of the problem which racism presented to
organized labor, however, Powderly tried to steer a middle course. The result was bifurcation of equality, a modified segregation within the organization. The documents presented in Part VI reveal a union leader caught between long-run ideals and short-run realities.

CORRESPONDENCE RELATING TO THE BLACK WORKER IN THE POWDERLY PAPERS

1. T. V. POWDERLY TO WM. J. STEWART OF RICHMOND, MO.

Scranton, Pa.
October 8, 1879

Dear Sir and Bro.:
Our organization makes no difference with the outside color of the man,
if he is white on the inside it is all we ask.
There is an assembly in this District composed exclusively of colored
men and it ranks among the best in the D. A. . . . .

Powderly Papers, Catholic University of America.

2. T. V. POWDERLY TO BROTHER WRIGHT

Scranton, Pa.
September 19, 1880

Brother Wright,
As your name indicates you are *right*. I am of the opinion that the
brothers who oppose the black man the most in the L. A. would not object to
his assistance in any struggle against grasping capital. But under the laws
of our order a brother no matter what his color is can visit any local in
the order if he is clear and in good standing. I think that the cheapest
method for these colored brothers to adopt would be to enter L. A. 1,100
untill they are strong enough to form a new colored assembly.
If there are enough to form a new local of colored brothers at Warrior
it can be done if they are so anxious to come within the folds it is too
bad to deny their admission. I see no good reason why the D.A. should not
grant them permission to locate in Warrior. Whichever is most convenient
for the brothers to do under the law should be done to keep them in the order.
Brothers remember that when capital strikes a blow at us it does not
strike at the white working man, or the black working man, but it strikes at
Labor. Can the wisest of us tell what color *labor is?* I doubt it.
In Heaven's name let not our foolish prejudice keep us apart where our
enemies are so closely allied against us.
Does any man suppose that the universal Father will question our right
to Heaven because of our color? If the color of the heart is right no matter
about the color of the skin.
Do the best thing possible under the laws for the brothers and for the
unity of the order.

Powderly Papers, Catholic University of America.

3. ROBERT D. DAYTON AND GILBERT ROCKWOOD TO T. V. POWDERLY

Pittsburgh, Pa.
May 10, 1883

My Dear Terry,
The writer of the enclosed letter is in error in supposing that Sect.
2 of Article XVI. Local Constitution, gives them the power to adopt Local
By-Laws excluding anyone from membership on account of color, for that
Section says an A. shall have power to adopt By-Laws, etc., *provided* they
do not conflict with the Constitution, and such a By-Law conflicts with
Section 2. of Article 1, Local Constitution, also with Decision of G.M.W.
on page 90, which is Constitutional law, having been approved by the G.A.
It is a somewhat delicate question to handle in the South, because we
can never force a *social* equality, and it would be better for the colored
men to form Assemblies by themselves, at the same time a By-Law excluding
them on account of color is illegal. Will you give him the benefit of your
logical reasoning on the subject?

Powderly Papers, Catholic University of America.

4. JOE B. KEWLEY TO T. V. POWDERLY

Richmond, Ind.
"News Office"
May 14, 1883

Dear Sir and Bro.
I write you for advice in regard to a matter that is likely to cause
considerable discussion in our assembly. Briefly the case is as follows:
Unfortunately the charter members were enthusiastic and without discretion
extended a general and special invitation to colored men to join the
assembly. To make the matter clear to you is scarcely within the scope of
a letter, especially the strong color line that is drawn by those outside
the assembly, whom it is possibly to induce to join us if it were not for
that element. Almost immediately after the founding of the assembly the
colored men began to flock in, indeed so rapidly that they now number one-
fourth of the membership. This of itself would at this time have been no
cause of trouble, but it was understood at the founding that as soon as the
colored element should become numerically strong enough they would form an
assembly by themselves. This they will not do, and they at this writing
will not even consider the advisability of so doing. This refusal on their
part has been one cause of disagreement; another is their action--almost as
a body--politically at the recent municipal election. There was placed at
the head of the ticket for Mayor a shyster lawyer--an aristocrat in every
sense of the word, as well as an attorney for railroads and corporations--
and a plain business man. It was the sense of the assembly that our support
should be given to the latter, but the colored men thought or at least acted
otherwise, and not only voted for but their leaders openly electioneered for
the lawyer. This was another sore point for the white element. It has been
our policy to bear with them through it all, but the breach has become so
open that the battle will either have to be fought now or in the very near
future, as we are now and have for some time been initiating two colored men
to one white, and consequently they now have one-quarter of the assembly,
and at the same ratio of increase they will soon have a most decided majority,
and either they or the whites will have form a new organization. The feeling
has become so strong that the whites have commenced to black ball the blacks,
without regard to character, and the colored men have threatened to retaliate
by doing the same hereafter, and so you see we are in a very bad predicament.
I wish your advice as to what course it would be best to pursue. It would be
plain sailing if we could induce the colored faction to form another assembly,

but they will not,--at least they show no disposition so to do, for as one of them observed at a recent meeting: "This is the only organization in which we stand on an equal footing with the whites, and it is a big thing, and unless we can work here we will work nowhere." This equality is what seems to be sticking in their craw. If a separation could possibly be amicably made it would be of great benefit to the cause in this city, as a large number of the workingmen can not or will not affiliate with the colored element.

From a notice we received from District Assembly No.---, I see you are announced to appear there (at Brazil) on the 12th of June. As you probably will pass through our city on your way there could you not make it convenient to meet with us. Your presence would have a very conciliatory effect, and you could probably settle the matter at once. We could probably heal the breach until that time if there was any likelihood of your meeting Us. Of course the assembly would pay all expense you would be put to in a chance of your arrangements. Pardon me for occupying so much of your time, and hoping to receive an early answer.

Powderly Papers, Catholic University of America.

5. T. V. POWDERLY TO M. W. PATTELL OF CHATTANOOGA, TENN.

Scranton, Pa. May 15, 1883.

Dear Sir and Bro.
I am powlerless in the matter of changing or amending the constitution. You will see on examining the constitution Article I Sect. 2, that the law is explicit. Again you will find a decision on page 90 which also permits the colored man to join.

The best plan to adopt now is to organize a colored assembly in your city and turn all applicants of that kind over to them. Then your by-laws will be binding.

I quote from your letter "It will not answer now to tell us that the ballot is the place to settle it." The ballot is really the only means of settling who shall or shall not be members and if enough members cannot be found in an assembly to vote against a colored man why its a pretty healthy sign that they don't object to his being a member.

Powderly Papers, Catholic University of America.

6. GILBERT ROCKWOOD ("GIL") TO T. V. POWDERLY

Pittsburgh, Pa. May 17, 1883.

My dear Terry,
Yours just received. Your answers are good, and right to the point. I do not see any need of trouble in the South on account of color, as long as the colored man and brother can form Assemblies of their own. A white Assembly cannot adopt a By-Law excluding colored men, because it would conflict with the Constitution, but if a majority of the A. are opposed to having colored members they could quietly black-ball them without any violation of the *letter* of the law.

The Executive Board notify us of a meeting here soon, probably next week, but have not set the date yet. . . .

Powderly Papers, Catholic University of America.

7. T. V. POWDERLY TO S. T. NEILSON OF NASHVILLE, TENN.

Scranton, Pa.
October 1, 1883

Dear Sir and Bro.
I have nothing to say on organizing the colored race only "organize them as fast as you can." I think it the most prominent plan to organize them in assemblies of their own. . . .

Powderly Papers, Catholic University of America.

8. JOHN R. RAY TO T. V. POWDERLY

Raleigh, N.C.
January 19, 1885

Dear Bro. Powderly,
I was truly glad, as you know, to receive assurances that you would soon visit us, but I regret to say the outlook for a successful meeting is gloomy. Race prejudices, engendered by politicians, has greatly injured us here, but I believe if you can get the white mechanics interested enough to organize an assembly entirely of whites the order will yet flourish. . . .

Powderly Papers, Catholic University of America.

9. AN OPEN LETTER ON RACE BY T. V. POWDERLY

Notes By The Way

RALEIGH, N. C., Feb. 4.--Raleigh has made no progress since the war. The streets are covered with a six-inch coat of bright red mud. It is very gaudy and makes quite a display, but it has a stick-fast-to-your-boots kind of a way about it that I cannot approve of. The only thing that can be said in favor of it is that it is preferable to the pavement on Lackawanna avenue. The color will wash better. Raleigh is the capital of North Carolina. Remove the capital to another part of the state and Raleigh finds "a long farewell to all her greatness." Three lines of railway diverge from this point and each one vies with the other in charging exorbitant rates of fare and killing time, for they never run fast enough to kill anything else. Four cents a mile for the privilege of riding in a coach, the seats of which are half-soled with a different material from the original. I cannot describe it. I never experienced anything like it outside of a glue factory. If the cholera ever visits this country on business or pleasure it will demolish every passenger coach on the North Carolina Railroad, and it ought to. I would do it if I was the cholera, and yet Raleigh is nicely situated and has nice people in it. I looked in upon the North Carolina Legislature and saw five colored Representatives, and two Senators of the came complexion. Just fancy a colored man in the Pennsylvania Legislature. We may talk as we please about the rights of the colored man, but he enjoys more privileges in the South to-day than in the North. Here he has his schools. In Raleigh there are three colored schools; the population is under ten thousand. The colored people here are intelligent, respectable, law-abiding citizens. A great many of them own their own homes and keep them nicely. On my arrival in the city I was invited to visit a colored man and brother and in company with a friend of mine, Mr. Ray, I made the visit. The old gentleman had invited some eight other colored men to assist him in receiving me. On being ushered into their presence they all stood up until the introductory ceremonies were performed then the nine sat

down in a row. Each man lifted his right leg and deposited it on top of his
left knee, then the business of the hour was transacted. Among the important
questions discussed was, "Do you think the inauguration of Mr. Cleveland will
deprive us of our liberties in whole or part?" I assured them that such a
thing was preposterous. It is a fact that speakers on the stump during the
last campaign solemnly assured the poor simple colored men that they would
be remanded to slavery should Cleveland become president. These poor people
follow naturally the lead of the white man and the idea of doubting his word
never entered their heads. You can imagine the feelings of the black man
when the news of Democratic success reached his ears. The colored man will
from this time forth have more confidence in himself, and will work with
more of a will to build himself a home and accumulate property. Heretofore
he felt that, no matter how well directed his efforts might be in this direction, he and his property would be brought to the auctioneer's block if
the Democratic party gained the ascendancy. This idea will now be dispelled,
and the blacks can look to the future with more of hope than heretofore.
One of the old gentlemen, a white haired, venerable man, who had been a slave
for nearly half a century, informed me that political agitators had terrified
his neighbors by exhibiting to them a picture of the old auction block on
which men of their flesh and blood had been sold over a score of years ago.

A Large Labor Meeting

The meeting which I addressed was held in the city hall and opera house,
the seating capacity is twelve hundred, every seat was taken. The standing
room was occupied and many could not gain admittance. Over half the audience
was colored. A more attentive, appreciative audience I never addressed. The
meeting was presided over by one of the wealthiest manufacturers in Raleigh.
Col. McClure, who spoke in this city before I came, did not have near as
large an audience. I visited the United States National Cemetery and looked
over the long rows of white stones which mark the resting place of a portion
of the eternal army. This cemetery was established in 1866. There were
1161 interments made, 648 of them are known, the remaining 513 are unknown.
The cemetery is kept very neatly and is dotted here and there with magnolia
and cedar trees. On my way back to the city, for the cemetery is outside of
the city limits, I saw a cotton field for the first time. Of course the
cotton had long since been picked, but I saw enough to give me a good idea of
it. To the east of the state house stands a large cedar tree which has a
history. When Raleigh was evacuated by the Confederates and the Union forces
entered the city, Gen. Kilpatrick was fired at by a rebel who stood within a
few feet of him on the road side. The rebel was captured, and without any
unnecessary ceremony or fuss was hanged from the lower limb of this cedar.
Mr. Ray, who was a resident of the city at that time related the story just
as I have told it.

I left Raleigh at 4:45 p.m. and spent five hours in riding eighty-four
miles. Our train stopped for two hours during the night at Charlotte, N.C.,
waiting for another train. At Seneca S.C., the engine ran into a land slide
delaying us two hours more. We were due in Atlanta at one o'clock, but did
not reach there until five in the evening.

The Scranton Truth, February 7, 1885.

10. THE SOUTH OF TO-DAY.

By T. V. Powderly

What is the condition of the Southern people? What do they stand most
in need of? What manner of people are they? How do they feel toward the
North? and how do they receive a Northern man when he goes among them? These
are among the questions asked of every man who travels through the South and
they are the questions I will attempt to answer in this paper. If I were a
stranger to both North and South and had never heard of the late war I would
leave the South and be none the wiser on that point unless I accidentally met

something in the way of a cemetery, a monument or the ruins of an old forti-
fication to tell me of the past. The evidence of the struggle must be
gathered from the face of the country which still bears the scars of battle;
but from the speech of the people, you learn absolutely nothing. They never
even refer to it unless questioned on that point. But I did not travel South
in the capacity of a stranger and as a consequence asked questions of every
person that I thought would give me an answer. I visited not only the homes
of the well to-do workingmen but the homes of the poor and lowly as well as
those of the rich and influential, and from the information gathered from
all quarters I feel that I can answer some of these questions.

The condition of the Southern people is not so prosperous as I would like
to see it, but on the whole it will compare favorably with a great many places
in our Northern and Eastern States. It is a common thing to hear Northern
man say, 'The South is poor because her people are not energetic; they are
slow to act, in fact they are lazy." This is unjust, and by way of answer
let me ask this question: If the late war had been fought right here among
our own hills and valleys; if our coal breakers, machine shops, blast fur-
naces and rolling mills had been burned down; if the farmers surrounding us
had lost every cow, horse, mule and agricultural implement just twenty years
ago, and if the help which the farmers had on the farms would crowd into
the cities, what would be the condition of the farmer after twenty years of
struggle who alone and unaided had to replace everything from the fence
surrounding his farm to the dwelling itself? What would be the condition of
our manufacturers who found themselves without factories, without material
or money to start up again? How could they hope to hold the market which
they could not supply? Would not our people present a poverty-stricken aspect
to the Southern visitor? Without capital after the war they were helpless.
Carpet-baggers in quest of cheap bargains in lands and property swooped down
upon them. The Shylock of Europe as well as America loaned money at the
highest possible rate of interest to those of the South who had anything to
give as security, and to-day after twenty years you will meet men in the
South who are contributing the pound of flesh to the Northern man who sitting
in his cosy parlor over his wine will accuse the people of the South of being
lazy because they didn't pick up like the North did after the war.

The people of the South are poor but there is a more equal distribution
of both poverty and wealth than in the North, and between the ex-slave and
his old master though the relations existing between them have been changed,
the old feeling of dependence still exists and if trouble darkens the door
of former he goes to his old owner for assistance and he never goes in vain.
The colored men will to-day be received with more of welcome and with a kinder
word in the home of his old master in the South than in the home of the
Northern man who preaches friendship for the negro. That slavery was wrong
no man, North or South will deny that many a slave-owner regarded it as a
curse in Ante-bellum days is true, but the money of the planter was invested
in the slave. Every slave represented so much capital and how to remove the
evil without entailing heavy losses was a question which would have puzzled
a Northern man as well as a Southern slave-owner. But no matter what plan
we would now propose, it is recorded in history that four years of civil war
have solved that part of the question. Before the war the slave-owner did
no work and labor in the South was degraded in the extreme. No matter what
the color of the worker might be he was looked upon as an inferior being because he labored for a living.

There were poor white men in the South who felt that because the black
slave worked while his master did nothing they would be lowering themselves
to the status of the negro if they worked. This class of miserable beings
eked out on existence after a fashion but they were despised by all others
and regarded with supreme contempt by the black men who applied to them that
peculiarly fitting appellation, "The low white trash." The remnants of that
army of idlers can be found in the South to-day, they have no ambition, no
pride, nor have they any more intelligence than the poor slave who deprived
of the protection which his master gave him had to shift for himself at the
close of the war. Although this class is now very small in this South yet
when added to the number of Freedmen who are too shiftless and lazy to work
it assumes formidable proportions. Education among the children of the low
white trash was as much neglected as among the children of the colored people,

and until recently the school room was a novelty in parts of the South. Today all men are anxious to establish the school as a permanent institution
in the hope that with the aid of education the children may be better enabled
to take care of themselves than their fathers were. The man who goes South
with no capital and no trade can make but little headway. It makes no difference how much Northern energy or push he brings with him he will find
that as a laborer he soon sinks to the level of the low white trash and the
lazy, shiftless blacks who infest the cities and towns. I do not charge
that all the colored men are lazy and shiftless or that those who are lazy
will not work at times; but they are unsteady and will rather sit in the sun
than work at any time, and no matter how ambitious a laboring man may be he
soons finds that this element is the club which beats back every effort to
improve his condition.

I believe that the man who talks of going to the West to invest in land
or manufacture, can find good lands in the South and that he can invest as
profitably as in the West. He can live cheaper, the climate is not so rigor-
ous, he is nearer to his market. The railway facilities of the South are
improving wonderfully and the seaboard advantages are unsurpassed. The
South does not lack for energy and push. It has any quantity of these qualities.

What the South requires is capital to develop her resources, for she
is rich in minerals of all kinds. She extends a warm welcome to the man who
goes there with a view to improving his condition as well as those who surround him. The people of the South are honest and truthful. Go to any door
in the South after bed time and you will find it unbarred and unlocked. The
reports of such horrible outrages as we read of during election times are
not true. When we are told that droves of men are led to the polls in the
South and compelled to vote as their bosses tell them, I can say that the
ballot is regarded as a merchantable commodity by a great many Southern
people who have been entrusted with it, and who will say that the same system does not prevail in the North? Who will say that men have not sold themselves on election day here in Lackawanna county? The Southern people are
not only honest, but they are generous and hospitable as well. It is true
that they have but little to give but they give with a free heart.

As regards the hostility of the people of the South toward those of the
North I could find but little trace of it and I believe it exists principally
on paper. It must be borne in mind that aside from those who made up the
rank and file of the Confederate army, fully two-thirds of the present population of the present South were children when the war closed or else they
have removed there since then, and as a consequence have no quarrel with the
North. The young men of the South to-day are a generation removed from the
influence of slavery, and if they entertain any feelings toward the North it
is because they have been misrepresented. So far as the ex-Confederate
soldiers are concerned I am satisfied that no feelings of ill will are rank-
ling in their hearts. I met with scores of mén who were in the Southern
army and asked of them in various places whether they would extend as warm
a welcome to me if it were true that I had been a Union soldier during the
war, and the answer was the same everywhere. The words of Lieut. Col. Hammond
voice the sentiments of all of them that I met and spoke to on the subject.
In answer to the question, "What kind of a reception would you give to an old
Union soldier?" he said, "If you could send your entire Northern army down
here we would give them a warmer reception than we gave them from '61 to '65,
but of an entirely different character. There is nothing in the South too
good for us to give them. When I laid aside my sword after the surrender of
Appomattox, I also laid aside every feeling of resentment with it, and I am
to-day ready to take any Northern man by the hand and say as I say to you,
welcome." It must not be supposed that because editors of papers and members
of Congress express hostility toward the North that they are representing
their constituencies in so doing. Suppose Mr. Connolly had in the last
session, or Mr. Scranton would in the next, say hard and bitter things calculated to keep alive the bitterness of the past between North and South, would
they not misrepresent rather than represent the Twelfth Congressional District? When I spoke to a meeting of over sixteen hundred citizens in the
city of Richmond I made use of these words: "You stand face to face with a
stern living reality, a responsibility which cannot be avoided or shirked.

The negro question is as prominent today as it ever was. The first proposition that stares us in the face is this: The negro is free; he is here,
and he is here to stay; he is a citizen and must learn to manage his own
affairs. His labor and that of the white man will be thrown upon the market
side by side, and no human eye can detect a difference between the article
manufactured by the hand of the black mechanic and that manufactured by the
hand of the white mechanic. Both claim an equal share of the protection
afforded to American labor and both mechanics must sink their differences
or else fall a prey to the slave labor now being imported to this country.
Our people have had their differences and it is the sincere wish of my heart
that nothing shall ever divide us again, and if we must fight again, let it
be as a united people battling against a common enemy. I repeated that
sentiment in nearly every place that I spoke and it was everywhere received
with unbounded enthusiasm.

I wish that every Northern man could make at least one visit to the
South and that every Southern man could return the compliment. We would
then learn that the South is really "in the saddle," but only with a view
to riding side by side with the North in the onward march of progress.

The vast majority of the men who fought in the Confederate army were
not battling to uphold slavery. They did not like the work they were engaged
in, but they went with the State and when I in taking a man to task for
fighting against the old flag was asked this question,"Suppose that the old
Keystone State went out tomorrow would you stand by the flag that belongs
to all of the States as well as your own or would you go with Pennsylvania?"
it sent my thoughts back to the mountains, the valleys and hills of Pennsylvania, and I could make but one answer: "I am afraid that I would forget my
allegiance to the flag and stand by my native State."

Yesterday I saw it stated in a New York paper that "they have been
selling pictures of Jeff Davis right along from the car on which the old
liberty bell is stationed." Those who have been to the New Orleans Exposition will know that that cannot be done. It may surprise the people of the
North to know that Jefferson Davis is not so popular in the South as he is
said to be. I have seen pictures of Gen. R. E. Lee in private and public
houses, in bar rooms and billiard halls. Side by side with Lee's picture I
have seen that of Stonewall Jackson, but in only one place did I see a portrait of Davis, and that was in a restaurant in Mobile. I saw the old gentleman himself at the St. Charles Hotel in New Orleans, and no one seemed to be
aware of his presence. He created no more of a sensation than I did, and
if the people who thronged the corn area and rotunda of the St. Charles Hotel
that day made anything of a demonstration over me they never told me about it.

It is fashionable to growl about everything in the South. I met men on
the cars who condemned the management of the road we were traveling over and
blamed the South for it. A look at the printed list of officers of the road
would have shown that president, directors and managers of the road were
Northern men. Reflection would have shown them that where travel is not so
heavy the roads cannot be expected to pay as well as in the North. I saw a
man sit down to dinner at a railway eating house. He eyed the piece of meat
on his plate for a moment, and then asked what kind of meat it was. The man
who sat next to him sententiously remarked, "Dog," and that man began to
abuse the South and left the table, while the man who said "dog" took the
piece of meat and ate it. If it rains in the South while some of our Northern
cranks are there they blame the country for it. If they have the dyspepsia or
suffer from a disordered liver until everything looks blue they charge it up
to the depravity of the South, it is fashionable to do this and then come
home and say that not only is the South behind the age, but she will never
catch up. I think the time has come to stop this system of warfare both
North and South and clasp hands over the grave of by-gone animosities. If
we must differ let it be upon such questions as relate to the future well-
being of the country, leaving the dead past to bury its dead.

The Scranton Truth, March 17, 1885.

11. JOHN R. RAY TO T. V. POWDERLY

Office of United States Attorney
Eastern District of North Carolina
Raleigh, N. C.
May 19, 1885

Dear Bro. Powderly:
Why is it that I have not heard from you in so long? Is it because you have forgotten me, or because you have become disgusted with Southern people generally and Southern working people in particular? Probably a little of both.
The cause is making some progress here especially among the blacks, 3282 is increasing its membership rapidly with the best of the colored people, but the whites still stand aloof.
I have one or two questions I would be glad if you would answer right away. The *colored* women (washerwomen and domestics) wish to organize an Assembly. Do you think it would be advisable to organize them? You know they are very ignorant and illerate as a rule. . . .
Can you not come or send some one else down here to deliver a lecture or to get the people enthused in some way? I am working all the time among the colored people, but can't do much with the white and have ceased to try much. . . .

Powderly Papers, Catholic University of America.

12. T. V. POWDERLY TO J. M. BROUGHTON OF RALEIGH, N.C.

Scranton, Pa.
June 12, 1885

Dear Sir and Bro.
Sometimes it is not prudent to initiate certain men or women at certain places and this may be such a time in the history of the order in Raleigh. Go to Bro. Ray and consult him on the matter, and if deemed advisable, postpone the organization of the colored women until the men (of both colors) are more thoroughly enlisted in the movement. Get the men so well organized that everyone will know that they are in earnest in the work when they do come in. I think it better to postpone the work, at least for a time under the circumstances.
Give my kindest regards to Bro. Ray and all other members of the order you may meet.

Powderly Papers, Catholic University of America.

13. JOHN R. RAY TO T. V. POWDERLY

Office of Master Workman
Raleigh, N. C.
June 22, 1885

Dear Bro. Powderly:
You have no idea of what I have to contend with in the way of prejudice down here. There is a continual cry of *"nigger! nigger!"* in politics, society, labor organizations, and everywhere. I believe that *our* order is intended to protect all people who work, the poor ignorant underpaid and over-

worked cook as well as the skilled mechanic, and have tried to act upon that principle. And from this alone I have incurred the abuse and social ostracism of those who claim to be the friends of labor and have made *enemies* of those who should be my friends and my brethren. Oh how I would like to live in a country of freedom where industrial and moral worth, not prejudices and birth, are the controlling influences!

In regard to those women, I do not think , myself that it would be expedient just now to give the enire work, and should not have done so if nothing had been said against it, but they need organization in some way to protect them from the avericiousness of some of the bretheren (?) and *they shall have it,* if I am forced to remain here long enough to accomplish it.

Both locals here promise well now as to numbers, and I hope that 3282 will begin the new year out of debt.

I am willing--yea, anxious to move North if I can get work, and I hope you will do what you can for me in that direction. Hope to hear from you at your earliest convenience.

Powderly Papers, Catholic University of America.

14. P. M. MC NEAL TO T. V. POWDERLY

Palestine, Tenn.
October 12, 1885

Dear Sir:

As I see the great need of organization among the colored people of the South and it takes the full time of an organizer to travel among them and lecture and organize them I apply for Commission as Organizer (Traveling) for the Southern District.

Hoping that you will dispose of the communication according to your own judgment.

Powderly Papers, Catholic University of America.

15. T. V. POWDERLY TO THOMAS CURLEY OF GLEN COVE, N. Y.

Scranton, Pa.
January 14, 1886

Dear Sir and Bro.

The objections presented were not sufficient to reject the candidate.

If he is in other respect qualified to become a member his color cannot debar him.

The employer of labor in reducing wages does so regardless of color. Th men who work with colored men dare not find fault, they take their wages and *abuse* side by side and our Order will not recognize the right of any man to blackball another on account of his race or religion.

Permission is hereby granted to reconsider that ballot by which the colored man was rejected.

Powderly Papers, Catholic University of America.

16. TOM O'REILLY TO T. V. POWDERLY

Macon, Ga.
March 4, 1886

My dear Brother Powderly,
    The order is making wonderful headway in the South, but the colored
assemblies are the most perfectly disciplined. You possess, in a marked
manner, the fealty--the very hearts of the Southern people. The very mention
of your name sets them wild with enthusiasm. The poor Niggers believe that
"massa Powderly" is a man born to lead them out of the house of bondage. . . .

Powderly Papers, Catholic University of America.

17. T. V. POWDERLY TO W. H. LYNCH OF MAYSVILLE, KY.

Scranton, Pa.
April 13, 1886

Dear Sir and Brother:
    That which has become law through usage and is not in conflict with the
law of the order cannot be declared null and void by the M. W. without the
consent of the Assembly.
    That which is acted on in committee of the whole, voted on and approved
by Assembly at subsequent meeting cannot be declared null and void by the
M. W. if the same is not in violation of law of the order.
    The M. W. of an Assembly has no more right to say what is or is not law
than any other member, it is his duty to act as M. W. under the law, and not
to make the law, or the wishes of the Assembly subordinate to his notions.
    Decision 173 has nothing to say about members at all, it refers to
clergymen seeking admission. You must have made a mistake in the number of
the decision.
    Members of the order in the same D.A. need no travelling cards in order
to visit the Assemblies in the same D.A. and if there is a D.A. and an Assembly that does not belong to a D.A. in the one locality the members can visit
the different Assemblies without travelling cards by having a special pass-
word made for their use by the G.M.W.
    I want it understood that this order recognizes no color or creed, no
nationality or religion, no politics, or party, and the M.W. who denies the
right of admission to a brother member on account of his color is false to
the vow he took on becoming a member and false to the obligation he took on
being installed. And I will go farther, the M.W. who does as you say your
M.W. does is not the kind of man to preside over an Assembly of KNIGHTS.
Your duty is to ask of him to resign and allow the Assembly to select a member who is willing to act as the instrument of the Assembly, and not to make
an instrument of the Assembly to carve out his own notions.
    There must be no trifling in our Assemblies for the future, I tell you
that you cannot tell by looking at the finished piece of work whether it was
a white man or a colored man who did it, capital makes no difference in op-
pressing labor whether it is white or black and we *must* know no differences
if we would win as a unit on the question of HUMAN RIGHTS.

Powderly Papers, Catholic University of America

18.   ALEXANDER WALKER TO T. V. POWDERLY

Whistler, Ala.
May 18, 1886

Dear Mr. Powderly:
    I take it upon myself to ask you is it wright that a colored member
cannot speak in the white assembly. Last meeting the whites they was dis-
cussioning labor. One of the colored members ask the Master Workman could
he speak a word or to on labor. He told him he could not speak in this
assembly and when they come to our meeting they speak as long as they please
in the meeting. I have no more to say at this time present. Please send me
anser as soon as you can i like to have it by the next meeting night.

Powderly Papers, Catholic University of America.

19. D. B. ALLISON AND EDWARD GALLAGHER TO T. V. POWDERLY

Morgan City, La.
July 7, 1886

Dear Sir and Bro.
    At a meeting of the above Assembly held July 3, 1886. I was directed to
communicate with you and try to get an "organizer" appointed for the purpose
of organizing the colored laborers in this place and vicinity.
    It will be of great benefit to this Assembly to have them organized at
an early a date as possible, and of mutual interest. The colored laborers
desire to be organized into a separate Assembly. In fact they have already
two or three bodies that meet every week and are in every way prepared to be
organized and admitted into our noble order--From the Statement of our Statistician, Bro. Ed. Gallagher hereto attached. It appears that there is nearly
150 that has already paid in funds and signed lists to be organized. As he
states, they are daily asking for information in regard to their speedy organization.. It will be of great benefit to us to have them organized.
    Hoping this will meet with your favor

I remain yours fraternally,
D. B. Allison
Recording Secretary

P.O. Address: Daniel B. Allison
Lock Box 110. Morgan City, Louisiana

    Having been instructed by our Assembly to inquire into and ascertain the
number of colored laborers desirious of joining and being admitted into our
order. I will report that there is about 150 men now on lists and attending
meetings and are very desirious of being covered with our shield.
    In fact they are enquiring every day when can they be organized and ob-
tain a charter. I am confident it will be of great and mutual advantage to
both white and colored labor for them to be speedily organized, which I hope
will be done at an early date.

Yours Fraternally,
Edward Gallagher
Statistician

Powderly Papers, Catholic University of America.

                    20. R. W. KRUSE TO T. V. POWDERLY

                                          Petersburg, Va.
                                          August 3, 1886

Dear Sir and Bro.
    I am requested by the Knights of Labor of Petersburg to correspond with
you in reference to my Commission as Organizer. I have forwarded my Commission to the Gen'l. Sec. Treas. and have not heard anything in regard to
it. We have no Organizer now in this part of Va. now and I have notices from
three (3) Counties to organize White Assemblies. I understand Lee A. Nelson
Colored of Petersburg has been commissioned as Organizer. I hope you do not
expect these white assemblies to be organized by a Colored Organizer. I hope
you will answer this without delay by that means I can act accordingly.

Powderly Papers, Catholic University of America.

                    21. H. G. ELLIS TO T. V. POWDERLY

                                          Durham, N. C.
                                          August 17, 1886

Dear Sir and Brother,
    An M.W. of the "senior assembly" in this locality "in date of organi-
zation," I feel it incumbent upon me to transmit for the consideration of the
Executive Board, any and all matters of importance involving the good of our
Noble Order in this section of the State. The most urgent necessity of the
order now, especially in this manufacturing centre is the appointment of a
white organizer. We must deal with matters as we find them, trusting to time
and education, and especially a better understanding of the principles of our
order, for the correction and obliteration of all errors. The colored people
have an organizer, and a very worthy and efficient one, in the person of the
Rev. W. G. H. Woodward, colored. There is a race prejudice, natural, instructive, and while brother Woodward will be an useful worker among the
colored people, he is utterly useless to us among the whites. The appointment
of a *white* organizer is therefore a necessity. I suppose you are aware of the
fact that brother Jno. R. Ray has left the State, and that we now have no
white organizer in the state.
    Clubs from every part of the State are appealing to us to be covered by
the shield of our noble order, while, under present circumstances we are helpless. We feel that to send a *colored* man among the large number of *white*
farmers and mechanics and factory operators who are appealing to us, would be
to jeopardize the interests of the order in creating a prejudice against us,
and thereby greatly retard the progress of the labor movement in this State.
    Brother Charles C. King, having been recommended by the late convention
which convened in Raleigh on the 10th and 11th inst. for the purpose of electing
Representatives to the Gen. Assembly which convenes in Richmond in October,
and to organize a State Assembly, and having also been warmly endorsed by
each of the Assemblies in this city, I am instructed to request that his
credentials (commisions) be forwarded at the earliest practical moment. Inclosed find endorsement of each of our L.A.

                                          Yours fraternally,
                                          H. G. Ellis, M.W.
                                          L. A. No. 4105, K of L

Powderly Papers, Catholic University of America.

22.   R. W. KRUSE TO T. V. POWDERLY

Petersburg, Va.
September 23, 1886

Dear Sir and Bro.
    I forwarded to you two (2) months ago my application for an Organizer's
Commission and have not heard anything in regard to it.   There are now three
White Assemblies waiting to be organized.   We have a colored organizer in
Petersburg but they will not be organized by him.   Let me hear from you so I
will know what to depend on.

Powderly Papers, Catholic University of America.

23.   J. A. BELTON TO T. V. POWDERLY

Copiah County, Miss.
November 15, 1886

Esteemed Sir:
    My application for the position of Organizer will be mailed you today.
I feel authorized to write that in some respects no state in the Union needs
organization, and the promulgation and inculcation of the principles of
Knighthood, more than Mississippi.   In many instances political and industrial liberty is a mere farce.
    Out of little more than a million of inhabitants we have more than two
hundred thousand majority of the colored population.   I have no doubt much
opposition will have to be confronted in the attempt to organize them.
Without their organization the Order can effect next to nothing in any department of industry, nor need we hope to accomplish anything by legislation
till the masses of laborers of all colors and nationalities understand one
another better, and more fully comprehend the mutual duties and reciprocal
obligations between themselves and employers.   Unless by means of organization we can be brought to cooperate, our case is lamentable, and will be
perpetuated by the gross ignorance that pervades every nook and corner of our
state.   The old Bourbon element so long used to its almost unopposed labor,
political, and pernicious system, will not remain passive and indifferent,
while the masses are seeking to ameliorate their condition educationally,
politically, morally, and financially.   Some of them are already imputing to
us the purpose of inaugurating the social equality principles, knowing that
said principle deters from the Order. . . .

Powderly Papers, Catholic University of America.

24.   C. V. MEUSTIN TO T. V. POWDERLY

Seddon, Ala.
January 17, 1887

Dear Sir and Brother,
    I write you in regard to an assembly of colored men that were organized
at Riverside about the 24th of Oct. 1886.
    J. W. Robertson was one of the charter members of Seddon Assembly.   He
was appointed U.S. by W. J. Winters, Master Workman and immediately afterward
was recommended to the General Assembly for an Organizer.   After having had
due time to receive a commission I asked him if he had received his commission
he said he had but had left at his home in Birmingham.   So I made no objection

to his organizing the assembly. But it afterward turned out that he had no
commission. The (colored) assembly numbered about 34 members. He had them
to elect and installed their officers. They are in possession of the secret
work of the Order as far as Robertson had it.[33]
    Can you or the General Assembly do anything for them? I have held
them together promising them that we would do all we could to get them a
charter. They paid Robertson all dues of an Organizer and I think it would
be to the best interest of the Order to grant them a charter. If the General
Assembly cannot grant them a charter please let me know so that they may know
what to do.

Powderly Papers, Catholic University of America.

25. V. E. ST. CLOUD TO T. V. POWDERLY

                                                    Savannah, Ga.
                                                    January 23, 1887

Dear Sir,
    At the last regular session of DA#139 held this a.m. I was instructed
to communicate with you, & ask for a reply, to the communication of Dec. 10,
1886 in regard to the orgztion of a Colored Female Assembly, in this City.
The communication referred to enclosed the Protests, forwarded to the DA
by Several locals in the City, & asked you for a final decision in the case.
We have received no reply up to date. Please favor us with your decision in
the matter.

Powderly Papers, Catholic University of America.

26. W. H. SIMS, M.D. TO T. V. POWDERLY

                                                    Texarkana, Texas
                                                    January 26, 1887

Dar Sir:
    We, the colored people are greatly in need of an organizer. Down in
this country the wt. people have set a decoy & fooled the colored people so
much it is simply impossible for a wt. organizer to orgze them to any good.
In view of this fact DA 145 elected me as orgzer for the colored people but
before I sent my commission to you: the Secty of DA 145 said he got a letter
from you stating that you would not appoint a man who has not been in the
Order over 18 mos. Now is:--I've been in the Order only 14 mos., M.W. 12 &
believe it to be very necessary to have a colored orgzer. I write you thinking
you do not really know the true situation of things in this section of the
country.

Powderly Papers, Catholic University of America.

27. J. M. BROUGHTON TO T. V. POWDERLY

                                                    Raleigh, N. C.
                                                    February 8, 1887

Dear Sir & Bro.

I write you at the instance of Bro. Frank Johnson of this city. He was an Organizer, and as such gave satisfaction so far as I have ever heard. Recently his commission has been cancelled and called in. This occasioned him no surprise as I had previously informed him that you would cancel all commissions in this State as soon as the State Assembly met and was put into working trim. (So per your letter of instructions to me of Dec.--.) But up to this date the commission of Bro. Johnson is the only one that has been cancelled. And naturally he begins to feel that there must be some other reason for your recalling his commission. Will you do me the favor to let me know the facts in the case. He is a good man--a colored man you know is somewhat sensitive about honors--and I don't like to see him under a cloud like this.

Powderly Papers, Catholic University of America.

28.   FRANK JOHNSON TO T. V. POWDERLY

Raleigh, N. C.
February 14, 1887

Dear Sir & Brother,
Pleas do me the favor to read these few lines. I received an order from you revoking my commission as organizer & waited to hear the cause of the revokcation & was inform it was becaus that my name apeared in the public press as organizer. I say here I did not directly autherize any one to publish my name as organizer of the K of L. it was don at the suggestion and the enstence of Bro. John R. Ray the former organizer becaus he received so meney letters of inquiry who the organizer was. He did it to let the people who desired to organiz know who to apply to. neither he nor myself thought it any harm when all the other organizer did the same thing. every organizer in this state publish him self in the paper. I think it hard that I should be condemned for doing that which others hav done & I am to be punish & they are not. I greatly regret that should hav accurred just at this time for many reasons. The order promis much to my people while it has as yet done little or nothing and they are wavering in their confidence. the revokcation of my commission for no other caus than you give will arous the suspicsion of the colored people that all is not right--and especially so when others who are equally with my self are not molested. I know my race of people & the leas sign of difference they think that it is all for white man & none for the Negro I have tryed to do my duty honestly for the up building of the order & the greatess truble I hav had whith my race was to make them believ that the order was not a white man trick to get their money.

Powderly Papers, Catholic University of America.

29.   S. F. S. SWEET TO T. V. POWDERLY

Florence, S.C.

Mr. Powderly Sir.
I tender you these few lines to ask you could not let us have let us have an orgzer, but the great trouble is that color line. Our white Brothers down South is not eager to orgze the Negro race, that's why we appeal to you for a colored orgzer & if you apply favorably much good will be done in the State of South Carolina.
So I would be pleased to hear from you as early as possible.

Powderly Papers, Catholic University of America.

30. GEORGE H. WILLIAMS TO T. V. POWDERLY

Moss Point, Miss.
March 21, 1887

Dear Sir & Brother,
I drop you a few lines steing our presand condishion we are in a condishion so far dear brother we the brothers of Walkes Assembly do kindly ask of all of our brothers to assist us in building a hall the one we meet in now is so small that not more than half of our members can meet at once. We want to build us one at the earliest opportunity, we have the majority of labors in our mills now & dear brother I tell you the honest thruth I do beleave that we are treated worse than any humans on earth, and to call our selfs free men we have to leave home to go to work before daylight & it is black dar when we get home again, we have to work from daylight to twelve o'clock & we only get a half of an hour for dinner & then we go towork at half past twelve & work till dark & we only get from 90 cts. to $1.25 per day & dear brother I think it too hard, I kindly wait for a favorable reply from you.

Powderly Papers, Catholic University of America.

31. PETITION TO T. V. POWDERLY

Montgomery, Ala.
April 1, 1887

Sir & Bro.
We the undersigned, officers of the above named L.A., petition your favor of getting on in the field as Organisers. Jno. D. Brookes for reasons herein after stated to wit. As a general thing the Colorded people of the South do not understand the white, and the white organizer cannot do just what is necessary for the upbuilding of the Order.

Signed: A. J. Leaveless, M.W.
C. Williams, W.F.
Jno. D. Brookes, R.S.

Powderly Papers, Catholic University of America.

32. FOURTH OF JULY CELEBRATION ANNOUNCEMENT

KNIGHTS OF LABOR

FOURTH OF JULY CELEBRATION

GREETINGS:

To...................................Assembly, No. ....
In pursuance to the request of our General Master Workman, the White Assemblies of this city will celebrate the Fourth of July at Powderly, Ala.
All white members of the Order, and their friends are cordially invited to attend. Please notify the Secretary as soon as possible if your Assembly will participate and the probable number that will attend. Also, what arrangement you can make for transportation.
By order of General Committee.

Powderly Papers, Catholic University of America.

33.   T. V. POWDERLY TO J. M. BANNAN OF CHETOPA, KA.

Scranton, Pa.
July 8, 1887

Dear Sir and Bro.
    I scarcely know how to advise you on so delicate a question. The color line cannot be rubbed out, nor can the prejudice against the colored man be overcome in a day.
    I believe that for the present it would be better to organize colored men by themselves. In the present instance you must act in strict accord with the law bearing on organization, act as though you were in no way interested in the matter. I leave the matter in your own hands.

Powderly Papers, Catholic University of America.

34.   T. V. POWDERLY TO J. O. PARSONS OF WHARTON, TEXAS

Scranton, Pa.
July 19, 1887

Dear Sir and Bro.
    Our Order does not recognize any difference in the rights and privileges of the races of mankind. Colored men are regarded as entitled to the same treatment as whites, they may be admitted to Assemblies having white members, but the best way is to organize them in Assemblies of their own and allow the work of education to do away with the prejudice now existing against them.

Powderly Papers, Catholic University of America.

35.   T. V. POWDERLY TO C. A. TEAGLE OF WACO, TEXAS

Scranton, Pa.
September 8, 1887

Dear Sir and Bro.
    Enclosed you will find the letter from L.A. 6141, I think you took the proper course in recommending that this man be proposed and balloted for, after the organization of the Assembly.
    Had the delegates, who got together to arrange for a Fourth of July demonstration, represented Assemblies of the Knights of Labor and then refused to allow the colored men to parade with them, they would have acted in violation of the letter and spirit of our laws but in representing other Orders, they were in duty bound to carry out the instructions of the other organizations. The matter having gone so far it is best to let it drop. . . .

Powderly Papers, Catholic University of America.

36. ANDREW MC CORMACK TO T. V. POWDERLY

Louisville, Ky.
December 4, 1887

Bro Powd.
The greatest difficulties to be met all over the South are the old party leanings and color prejudice. These two are so mixed up & played upon by unscrupulous self-seekers of every kind, some so-called knights,--that a harmonious coming together of the divided elements will be little short of a modern miracle.

Powderly Papers, Catholic University of America.

37. B. W. SCOTT TO T. V. POWDERLY

Berwick, Ga.
December 8, 1887

Dear Sir & Bro.
I am requested by LA 4738 to get your decision on the following. Said LA is about 250 members & there has about 20 joined the State Militia which the LA does not approve of, and have by a large majority vote requested the said militia to accept withdrawal cards, or be expelled from the Assembly. You will understand that the Militia in this State is not used for the pur- pose for which it is intended but for pol. purposes & to intimidate Labor as has just been demonstrated in the late Strike here on Sugar Plants, when K of L were shot down. It is supposed by the militia or at least while they were present & never made an effort to prevent the killing so long as nothing but K of L were shot consequently LA 4738 does not want members who are sub- ject to orders such as the militia of this State are & unless the LA can get rid of them it will cause it to break up as they are determined not to asso- ciate with them now the question you are requested to decide is. Is our As- sembly of 250 compelled to retain as members 20 persons whom they do not want to associate with. In other words is there any way in which they can get rid of them & save the Assembly from breaking up.

Powderly Papers, Catholic University of America.

38. T. V. POWDERLY TO B. W. SCOTT OF BERWICK, GA.

Scranton, Pa.
January 6, 1888

Dear Sir & Bro.
If your Assembly, with full knowledge of the facts & circumstances sur- rounding the case of our members who joined the Militia, are of the opinion that it is unwise for them to remain members of the Militia, they may request their withdrawal from the same, on the ground that there is no just cause why a member of the K. of L should belong to an org. that is based upon violence.
The K of L is an org. of peace, militia means war at some time or another. I think the matter can be adjusted by your own Assembly for since there is no law upon the matter the best judgment of the M.W. officers & members of the Assembly should be called into play & the case decided upon its merits.
I think it would be a, safe plan for all workingmen to attend to their own peaceful occupations & not join any mil. co.; in case of invasion rebel- lion or war of any kind in the state or our country at leage, why our members,

I believe, could do volunteer service as well as though they were members of a mil. co. I therefore leave the matter with your assembly for decision.

Powderly Papers, Catholic University of America.

39.   B. STOCK TO T. V. POWDERLY

Birmingham, Ala.
February 17, 1888

Dear Sir & Brother.
Accept my sincere thanks for your photo. I assure you that whenever I have occasion to look at it, it will be with pride.
Now then to business. I have told my people that you are coming to Ala. rejoicing & renewed hope is on every lip, the diff. in our cond. is, in 68, only the black man was a Slave, in 88 the wt. & black man are in Slavery. The majority of our members are unable to pay the State & General tax 13, every 3 mos. their suffering is beyond your comprehension. These people look upon you as the coming Savior & for their Sake I beg you not to disappoint them. It would be worse than useless to attempt to have your lecture under a roof there is no bldg. in the State of Sufficient Capacity to accommodate a 5th of your audience and I would not think of asking you to visit us until your health is restored & the weather is pleasant. The 30th of May is our annual labor day. We hold our picnic in a beautiful park here in the City. If you will give us yourself on that day 10 or 12 thousand people will Surround you within its gates. As I said we are in a critical condition financially, the State Assembly is balanced between life and death, "but we will not down." Last year we charged an admission fee of 25¢. This year we intend to do the same. The proceeds are used for the best interests of the order.
The contents of this letter is confidential & I ask you as a Special favor not to think that I want you to come to Ala. on Speculation of any kind. If you come on the 30th of May though we will be able to bear your Expense in a way you deserve. I am done. You have heard my appeal. Give it your Earnest consideration & let me know the result at your leisure.

Powderly Papers, Catholic University of America.

40.   HILLARD J. MC NAIR TO T. V. POWDERLY

Battleboro, N.C.
March, 2, 1888

Bro. Powderly Sir,
It is with much complacency that I write you a few lines stating my troubles to you in behalf of my poor downtrodden race. We the under signed members have made a partial bargain with a very rich man to buy a six horse farm from his so that we can build us a hall on it. As we are here in a county where we have to be secretly about what we are doing we have to meet in school houses and churches and we have to run from place to place to keep the landholders from finding out what we are doing. And after I made this arrangement our Master Workman sliped to the man of whom I expected to buy the land of and told he wanted an acre of said land. and then he was told that I was going to buy the plantation he then said that I did not want all of the land that was there. and told the assembly that he wanted $50 dollars to pay for that acre to build a hall on it and if he does that in this county every white man in the county find it out and we can not get any land for

nothing that is why write to you to let you know our objects whether or not
it is expedient to buy the plantation and build us a hall on it so we meet
there all the time or let him go ahead buy one acre so that we will have to
quit meeting entirely. I am satisfied if we let him go the way he is going
every assembly in this county will be ruined. let us know whether or not
to buy the plantation. let me know what we must do because we are awaiting
your decision.

Your most obedient Servant
Hillard J. McNair, R.S. [34]

Powell Battle, Stat. he told the man something untrue. he said he wanted to
a dwelling house on it. and if you say buy one acre and build on it after
saying he was going to build a dwelling on it he will forfit the bargain
and the land and hall will be taking from us. then there goes us and the
money to.
Direct your letter to Bro No. 18.

Powderly Papers, Catholic University of America.

41. J. A. BODENHAMER TO T. V. POWDERLY

Jacksonville, Fla.
April 10, 1889

T V Powd.
        The Order in the South must of necessity be composed largely of the
Negro race. The great bulk of the labor in this country is performed by
colored hands, against whom a cultivated prejudice (akin to hate) is most
intense. Ridiculous as it may appear to men of broader intelligence there
are toilers with wt. skins, whose lot is in no sense superior to that of the
black slave's, who will not join the Order because of the prejudice that has
been instilled into them against the Negro. They have not yet learned the
great lesson that greed makes no distinction in the color of the victims of
its robbery.
        Again, there are shrewd, calculating politicians who act solely with a
view to personal gain, or to endeavor to control the colored vote. The
greatest difficulties, so far, the Order has had to contend with have come
from the contentions raised by this class of men in their struggles for
leadership. In some localities the effect has tended largely to injure the
Order, but it will grow upon the ruin of all such characters. It is a most
encouraging fact that the colored people make good knights--they are exceedingly watchful of their liberty--and a strong and powerful org. of them is
only a question of time.
        Our State Master Workman, Bro. G. Y. Mott, works faithfully and earnestly,
and with good results, though at times strongly antagonized. He is a mechanic
--a worker with his paint brush--and a good one. Yet I am told that a few
days ago he was "relieved" of a job on a banker's property, with no reason
assigned, other than his "insurrectionary movements among the Negroes."
This, I consider, the best indorsement he could get, in the estimation of
working people.
        In Bro. J. J. Holland, I am persuaded you will find an able and effi-
cient Lieutenant, especially for work in the South.

Powderly Papers, Catholic University of America.

42. C. C. MEHURIN TO T. V. POWDERLY

Jacksonville, Fla.
April 15, 1889

Dear Sir:

I am mngr of this business--have been such for about 20 mos. When I
first took charge there were branches in Columbus, Miss. Decatur, Ala.
Chattanooga, Tenn, as well as here. During the past 5 yrs. I have
traveled over much of 9 So. Sts, & Been in a position to note the lamentable
condition of labor; so I feel able to address you on this very vital sub-
ject--labor in the South. Of course, the great distracting source is negro
competition. The negro is forced to accept 50 to 75 cents per day & that
forces the wt man to take about the same. These wages will not enable a wt
or black to ed. his children or feed them such food as will nourish body &
brain properly. The poorer classes are becoming grosser every day because
of their diet of corn meal and "sow-belly" from the beginning to the end of
the years. In the name of charity for poor man, can not something be done
to right this terrible wrong before oppressed labor endeavors to right it
with force & thus increase the evil? I have evolved a partial remdy; but you
may have done more in the way of thinking on this line than I & more to the
purpose. Standing at the head of a frt. org as you do, can you do, can you
not start some reform? This dreadful competition of cheap labor in the so.
must sooner or later very seriously effect the prices of wages in the north,
and almost chivalize our great masses. I will be glad to aid in any movem,
to better the condition of labor in the so. but not in any open way unless
it be in connection with an orgzed effort; for to move in the matter is to
stir up the most intense prejudices of the wts. & to combat with the dense
ignorance of the blacks & "poor wt. trash," & which of the 3 would be most
to overcome is hard to say. In self defense the Knights ought to move in the
matter at once.

That you may be assured that you are not being imposed upon I wish to
say that I am originally from Ohio; am a marble workman, but for years past
have been in the newspaper work--In inclose one of my old business cards.
Allow me to also refer to ex-Lieut. Gov. Lyon of Ohio as fo my identity.

Can I be of service to you in bringing about some greatly to be desired
reforms?

P.S. I am corresp. of some city dailies, & may use them to a *little*
purpose. CCM.

Powderly Papers, Catholic University of America.

43. C. E. YARBORO TO T. V. POWDERLY

Editor
The Southern Appeal
Atlanta, Ga.
November 18, 1889

Sir:

I have endeavored repeatedly to gain a conference with you but have
always found you engrossed in other matters.

I send with letter copies of my paper. If you deem that it can prove
beneficial to the Order and can get the Negroes in Georgia, I would be glad
to have it made the official organ for the Knights of Labor for this state.

If further explanation is desired I shall be pleased to call at whatever
time you suggest.

Powderly Papers, Catholic University of America.

44. JOHN DERBIN TO T. V. POWDERLY

Jacksonville, Fla.
November 2, 1890

My Dear Powderly,
You are a bad man. You have got me into a hot box by sending me to Fla.
You wanted me to prevent Holland from making any more mistakes. But the
mistakes or rather blunders, they may possibly be worse, were all made before
I got here. I am rather inclined to think worse. I find that the Bro. (Taylor) who it was alledged was an expelled member was not an expelled member
at all. He never was tried by the court of his A. or any other A. There is
no record of trial on the books of his A. up to the evening that the committee of the State A. assisted the Assembly. I attended the A. at its last
meeting heard the minutes of that meeting read (the one which the investigation committee was present at). The record shows that the Bro was expelled by *motion* in the A. The notice to the State Secty states that he
was expelled Aug. 29th. The books has no second of it untill the meeting
mentioned in October. The charge against him was for taking $57.00 in cash
against the will or consent of the A. and unlawfully holding books, key of
desk, and Seal of the A. The bro puts another face upon the charges made
against him. But you will see that if it were true as charged, he should
have been tried by the court and given an opportunity to defend himself.
Such was not the case, and Holland knew it, or could have known it if he
wanted to. But that is not all, I find that when the State A. met in September that the regularly accredited delegates who had not up to that time
been covered by the exclusion decree and they constituted all but about four
were not admitted to the meeting untill after the ex-delegates had settled
the question of Taylor's right to sit. They were then admitted and initiated.
So that I find that it was not the regularly accredited delegates that decided against the ruling of the S.M.W. but a lot of ex-delegates who have as
I believe no right to decide anything, in fact the matter was never brought
before the S. Assembly after the regular delegates were admitted. Rather a
strange way of doing business these people have in Florida. I might say that
L.A. 9686, Bro. Taylor's A., is a colored A. and when I attended their meeting and Bro. H. was with me I received a rather *HOT* reception because I asked
a few questions. O such a storm. The M.W. and R.S. told me flatly that they
would not give me any information and when I insisted upon the R.S. answering
my questions a big burly Negro threw of his coat and I began to think I might
find the pavement without going down the stairs. All this time Bro H. set
there and never opened his mouth so far as to check the disturbance. The
officers would not answer any question only that Bro. H. told them to answer
and they were very few. So you see you have got me into hot water with my
Bro. H. He has paid me but little attention since I began investigating and
when I talk to him about the matter he gets very hot under the collar. The
brothers here who have been thrown out of office are going to protest against
his being admitted and request an opening of the case as to the legality of
the called session. . . .

Powderly Papers, Catholic University of America.

45. T. V. POWDERLY TO REV. P. H. KENNEDY OF HENDERSON, KY.

Scranton, Pa.
December 2, 1890

Dear Sir:
I am written to by John H. Adams, of Empire, Ky., to drop you a line
concerning the attitude of the Knights of Labor toward the colored race, and,
as my time is limited, I must be brief.
We organize neither race, creed or color in our membership and make no

distinctions whatever, believing that moral worth should be standard. We
do not load the colored man with fulsome flattery or praise him for qualities which he does not possess, we simply place him side by side with his
white brother on the same plane.

One thing I realize and that is that long years of thraldom have denied
the colored man the same opportunities that the white man possesses, and
because of that the colored man should receive more encouragement in order
that he may win what was kept back from him for centuries.

The education of the colored man on the political, social and economic
questions of the day is as essential as can be the education of the white
man on these same lines and its intense desire to bring about such results
that the Knights of Labor have earned the enmity of all who would make slaves
of the white and black who toil for bread.

Wherever you find a true Knight of Labor there will you find one who
stands side by side with all true men on the basis of equality.

Powderly Papers, Catholic University of America.

47.   SAMUEL G. SEARING TO T. V. POWDERLY

                                        Jacksonville, Fla.
                                        June 15th, 1892

Mr. T. V. Powderly G.W.M.
    Just before my appointment expired as organizer I consolidated all the
white assemblies here in one #3578 that being the oldest assembly, & had not
my commission expired I would have consolidated all the Blacks in one that
would have put the order here in such shape that our enemies could not have
got in and caused dissentions we could have had a committee from the white
assembly to go there and assist in enlightening and learning the blacks and
they could send a delegation to see how the whites got along and each could
assist in advancing the interests--This is the way it is done in St. Augus-
tine and the order there is in good condition and a power there *locally*.
We want it a power all over the state and I believe that large assemblies
and fewer of them much preferable to so many small and weak ones. . . .

Powderly Papers, Catholic University of America.

48.   POWDERLY'S OPEN LETTER TO SECRETARY FOSTER [35]

The Latter a Mere Artificer in Political Trickery.

To the Hon. Charles Foster, Secretary of the United States Treasury:
    DEAR SIR:--On the 24th of last December I opened up a correspondence
with your predecessor, the late Mr. Windom, on the subject of the discharge
of Knights of Labor from the Bureau of Engraving and Printing. Your recent
public statements, as made through the medium of newspaper interviews and
conversations with public men, strengthen the impression made upon my mind
at our first and only interview--that you knew little or nothing about the
merits of the controversy. [36]
    You have given out the impression that the primary cause of the diffi-
culty lay in the demand of a Knight of Labor for the discharge of a colored
girl with whom he refused to work. In answer to a question put to you by
Mr. Cavanaugh as to what led to the trouble, you said: "I'm damned if I
know."
    If you spoke truly to Mr. Cavanaugh you could have had no faith in your
statements to the public as made through the press. If you believed what you

published you must have told to Mr. Cavanaugh that which you intended to be
untrue. Within the last three days you have given out garbled extracts from
a letter written by to you. You have stated that the contention is between rival organizations. You have charged that we threatened the defeat
of Mr. McKinley in Ohio. You have congratulated yourself on having tricked
the General Officers of the Knights of Labor. I say that you have done these
things, and they must have originated with you, for it has been our purpose
since the beginning to make nothing public except that which was unavoidable.
Your exalted position as a Cabinet Officer, the Minister of Finance of our
country, and adviser of the Chief Magistrate of a nation of 62,000,000
people, is indeed a responsible one. Next to the Presidency, it is the most
responsible office in the Republic. You very aptly said to Mr. Devlin on
June 30: "This is a big place." A place that was made great by a Hamilton
and a Windom is indeed a big place, but it becomes only a vacuum when an
artificer in political trickery attempts to fill it.[37]
    The public press, even the most bitter opponents of the Order I repre-
sent, in commenting on the various lights in which this controversy has been
shown by you, has not failed to penetrate the thin guise of statesmanship in
which you have veiled yourself, and, while many condemn us on the strength
of your misrepresentations, not one word of approval has been spoken or
written of the course pursued by a statesman who did not feel too small to
squeeze through the narrow crevice of deception and treachery when the broad
pathway of truth and manliness lay open before him.
    Before this trouble began a plate printer, and a Knight of Labor too,
complained to his Local Assembly that a colored girl had been appointed as
his assistant. The Local Assembly placed the facts before the General
Executive Board. I was present at the meeting, and the decision of the
Board was that the remedy lay with the plate printer himself. If he did not
wish to work with her he could quit, unless he could prove that she was unfit
to perform the duties of the position. In any event, her race, creed or
color could not enter into the controversy. That decision of the General
Executive Board was accepted by all concerned. It settled the matter. The
plate printer who remonstrated was not and is not one of the men whose discharge is now in dispute, and, furthermore, he is still at work in the Bureau
of Engraving and Printing. The girl is not there now. Mr. Meredith can tell
you where she is and why she left. That episode cuts no figure in the argument, and the demagogic appeals, to race prejudice which emanate from you,
and which furnish the meat for misleading editorials in many papers, are
based on nothing more tangible than your hope to deceive the public.
    So much for the race question.
    Members of L. A. 3837 at work in the Bureau of Engraving and Printing
discovered that the Chief of the Bureau was not conducting himself as a
gentleman or a watchful guardian of public interests. They charged him with
immorality, with obscene and profane language in the Bureau, with drunkenness,
and with making a beastly exhibition of his depraved nature. When a workman
applied for leave of absence on account of sickness he was asked by the Chief
of the Bureau if he were not afflicted with a vile disease which those who
travels the paths of virtue are not likely to contract. The Chief of the
Bureau was informed that certain employes were unclean and that vermin was
communicated to others by them while at work. The answer of Mr. Meredith as
contained in the affidavit before me is too filthy for publication.
    It was charged that inferior inks of foreign make were being used, and
it was intimated that some one was receiving a commission on the purchase of
these inks. American ink of a superior quality could be purchased for less
money than the foreign ink which was being used. The Treasury notes printed
before we forced a partial investigation were printed with ink that did not
stand the test. If you doubt my word, you have only to rub the back of one
of these Treasury notes on a piece of white paper and you will discover that
the colors are not fast, for they will rub off and discolor the paper with
which the bill comes in contact. If it was proper to so protect American tin
as to cause the people of the United States to use it in preference to foreign made tin, it was eminently so on the part of the plate printers when
they demonstrated that the government should practice what it preached. You
evidently fell in with that idea when you ordered a change of inks, but you
did not follow up the investigation to ascertain what percentage of the

profits on the sale of the foreign inks went into the pockets of heads of departments and bureaus.

A United States Senator recommended a plate printer for employment in the Bureau under Chief Meredith. The officers of the Knights of Labor entered a protest against his employment on the ground that he was incompetent, dishonest, and that he ill-treated his wife. The Chief reported the matter to the Senator, but did not say a word about the man's character. The Senator naturally became angry and insisted that no labor organization should interfere with government affairs. He met the officers of L.A. 3837; they proved to his satisfaction that the man he recommended was a worthless character; he thanked them for their vigilance and withdrew his recommendation.

I have before me the sworn statements of plate printers on the irregularities of the Bureau; but what has been detailed will show that we have a cause for complaint--if not as Knights of Labor, then as American citizens and tax-payers interested in the discipline and honest administration of public affairs.

Away back of all of these things stand the patentees of the steam presses, on which a former official of the government received a royalty, and who naturally felt angry at the Local Assembly that exposed the steal and deposed the stealer. The steam presses cannot do the work as it should be done--in the highest style of the art; but a percentage of the profits, if given to Mr. Meredith, would no doubt reconcile him to the use of the steam presses. The officers of L.A. 3837 stood between the government of the United States and inferior workmanship that could easily be counterfeited. They also stood between the Chief of the Bureau and a share of the profits. If these things were not known to the Secretary of the Treasury they should be made known to him and not to the public, for they reflected not alone on officials, but on every American citizen.

With these ideas in view I wrote the following letter:
SCRANTON, PA., December 24, 1890.

Hon. Wm. Windom, Secretary of the Treasury, Washington, D.C.:

DEAR SIR:--I am encouraged to again address you on a subject which is of great importance to the Order of which I am the responsible head. The fact that you have special attention to and investigated the protest against the appointment of Thomas Furlong at our request causes me to hope that you will again use your great influence in our behalf, and thus undo a wrong which has been perpetrated upon members of our Order. I have been requested to take official notice of the discharge of members of Plate Printers' Assembly, No. 3837, from the Bureau of Engraving and Printing, on the order of Mr. Meredith; but, before doing so, I beg to ask you to give the matter some attention, and, if possible, have the trouble adjusted without any interference from our General Executive Board. If what I have been told is true, Mr. Meredith has denied to Mr. Jordan and others the right to be heard in their own behalf. It is also alleged that others who preferred charges against Mr. Meredith have not been given a fair opportunity to present testimony. As to the nature of the charges against Mr. Meredith I know nothing, for I did not consider it necessary to listen to them until after the court of last resort had been appealed to. I believe that such matters are best settled through the heads of departments and the avoidance of any publicity, for scandals reflecting upon the character of public officials injure us as a nation in the eyes of other people, and for that reason I would rather not make public the charges preferred against Mr. Meredith. Mr. Jordan asserts that although he had nothing to do with the charges against the Chief of the Bureau of Engraving and Printing, he is held responsible for the same. May I ask you to cause an investigation to be made into the controversy now progressing between members of L.A. 3837 and the Chief of the Bureau of Engraving and Printing? When in Washington the other day, I was requested to call upon you, but, knowing the harassing details and perplexities consequent upon the present financial situation, which demanded attention at your hands, I refrained from troubling you, preferring to ask you through the medium of a communication to take official notice of the matter which I now bring to your attention.

Very respectfully yours,
T. V. POWDERLY
General Master Workman.

That letter was answered by the Assistant Secretary, Mr. Nettleton, who, in closing his communication, used these words:

I do not need to say that, if it can be shown that injustice has been practiced toward any employe of the Bureau, the wrong will be promptly righted, and I will add, in conclusion, that if any one inside or outside of the Bureau of Engraving and Printing has knowledge of any misconduct on the part of the Chief or any other officer or employe of the Bureau, and will prefer charges to that effect, such charges shall be promptly and impartially investigated.

On receipt of that letter I instructed the officers of Plate Printers' Assembly to reduce to writing such facts as they possessed, and they did as directed.

In company with Mr. Hayes, the General Secretary-Treasurer of the Knights of Labor, I called on Mr. Windom, the Saturday before his untimely death, and made arrangements to present these charges. They were intrusted to Mr. Hayes for presentation. Mr. Windom's death caused a delay, and then you became Secretary of the Treasury. When the matter was presented to you and an investigation asked for you declared it unnecessary, inasmuch as it would be easier to reinstate the men and have no investigation. When the time arrived to put that plan into execution you shifted the responsibility to the shoulders of the president, asserting that Mr. Meredith was his special appointee, and that His Excellency had interfered in his behalf. You were informed that, no matter though the discharged men were restored to their places, the charges against Mr. Meredith must be subjected to investigation, and from that position we have not receded one jot or tittle.

After every meeting held between you and members of our Board malicious and garbled accounts of what occurred appeared in the Washington papers, these false statements came from your desk in the Treasury Department. Though they were extremely aggravating, we held our peace. Even after the termination of the interview which you held with Messrs. Devlin and Hayes early in June, we remained silent, and when our Board met in Columbus, Ohio, the newspapers that friendly to you were the first to charge us with making threats to defeat Major McKinley. We made no threats then; we make none now. Actions speak more eloquently than words sometimes.

Previous to the meeting of our Board at Columbus and the meeting held between Senator Sherman, Major McKinley and yourself at Mansfield, you discussed the settlement of this matter with Mr. Cavanaugh, the General Worthy Foreman of this Order, and told him you would bring it up at the Mansfield meeting. The following letter will bear out that statement: [38]

Fostoria, Ohio, June 22, 1891

Hon. Wm. McKinley, Jr., Canton, Ohio:
DEAR SIR:--I called upon Senator Sherman to-day and was advised by that gentleman to come here and have a talk with Secretary Foster which I have done. I cannot say that my visit has resulted in a settlement of our trouble, but it looks, however, as though it would lead to that. Mr. Foster informs me that he is to meet you at Mansfield on the 24th, upon which occasion this subject may be referred to. Feeling assured that we can depend upon your assistance in the matter, I hope the opportunity will present itself during the meeting to advise a settlement in our behalf.
Yours respectfully,
HUGH CAVANAUGH.

Mr. McKinley answered that letter on the 25th at the close of the Mansfield meeting, and stated that the matter had been discussed.

On June 26 you sent this telegram to Mr. Cavanaugh:

WASHINGTON, D.C., June 26, 1891

Hugh Cavanaugh, Cincinnati, Ohio:
Think matter can be arranged on the basis of talk. You had better be here on Monday.
CHARLES FOSTER.

In response to that telegram Mr. Cavanaugh came on to Washington, and, in company with Mr. Devlin, had an interview with you on the afternoon of June 30 . At that meeting you wrote a letter to Mr. Jordan, signed it, and handed it to Mr. Devlin. You did not ask him for it again; and as he was directed to get an acknowledgment of some kind from you, over your signature, of the injustice done the plate printers, he did right in retaining it.

You have stated that the letter was stolen from you. That is either an error of speech or judgment on your part. But let the letter speak for itself. It is as follows:

TREASURY DEPARTMENT
WASHINGTON

June 30, 1891

Mr. Jordan
   Sir:
   In accordance with an understanding arrived at with Mr. Devlin and Mr. Cavanaugh it was agreed that the seven men discharged by the Bureau of Engraving and Printing of which you are one are to be re-employed in the places held by them when discharged.

Will you please advise whether you desire to be so re-employed.

Yours truly,
CHAS. FOSTER

Journal of the Knights of Labor, July 16, 1891.

VII

RACE RELATIONS WITHIN THE KNIGHTS OF LABOR

RACE RELATIONS WITHIN THE KNIGHTS OF LABOR

The Knights of Labor attempted to circumvent the racial issue by argu-
ing that it had no relationship to the economic goals of the Order without
at the same time betraying its own constitutional principles on racial equality. In this the Knights failed. Opponents of "social equality" successfully undermined the Order's effectiveness in the South, and fractured the
working class along racial lines. Racial liberalism among many leading
southern unionists only served to heighten the tensions among rank-and-file
workers within the Order, and displayed the fundamental weakness in the
Knight's strategy of accepting blacks as economic equals while accommodating
southern views on social inferiority. This ambivalence manifested itself in
the structure of the organization in the South where the vast majority of
local assemblies were segregated.

On the other hand, district assemblies were generally integrated, but
pressures for segregation often came from blacks themselves. Those black
locals which favored the establishment of racially separate districts did so
in order to expand the number of Negro delegates sent to the state and general
assemblies. State assemblies in the South also were integrated, with blacks
participating fully, including election to state office. In short, the Knights
compromised with segregation at the local level, but maintained integrated
assemblies at the higher levels of organization. The leadership realized
that in the South it had to court blacks, for to organize only white workers
would be self-defeating. Racial mores in the region, however, militated
against working-class unity. Often, white Knights steadfastly opposed the
organization of Negroes if it meant that they would attend the meetings of
white locals. After the Ferrell incident at the 1886 convention, criticism
of the Knights' racial posture reached a crescendo. The public association
of the Knights with "social equality" took a heavy toll in white membership,
and by 1887 the Order was under attack from every quarter in the South. The
charges against the Knights of Labor seemed to be confirmed by the heavy in-
flux of blacks until, as one Negro Knight remarked: "Nigger and Knight have
become synonymous terms" (Doc. 4).

Ultimately, most white Knights failed to accept the notion that black
and white economic problems bound them together in a common cause. Whites
refused to break away from the standard racial etiquette of the region, and
resented the growing influence of Negroes within the Order. They had no intention of seeing black workers elevated from a servile position. As one
authority has noted: "In the contest between economic interest and racial
prejudice, prejudice won, as usual."

As the somewhat opportunistic strategy of the national leadership became
more and more apparent, interest among black workers began to fade, until by
1890, it ceased to exist at all. By then the Order had abandoned the black
worker, as many Negroes suspected it would all along, and refused to take a
stand even in general terms against the rising tide of racial segregation.
In 1894 the Knights announced that the only solution to the "Negro Problem"
in the United States was to raise federal funds for the deportation of blacks
to Africa. A poll of white locals revealed overwhelming sentiment in favor
of the idea, and James R. Sovereign, the Iowa editor who succeeded Powderly
as Grand Master Workman that same year, was instructed by the Executive Board
to mobilize support for the African colonization of American blacks. Pre-
dictably, Negro workers were outraged, and the black press was filled with
angry protests denouncing the Noble Order in the most ignoble of terms.

By 1893 the Knights' membership rolls had dropped to 200,000. Two years
later it stood at 20,000, and after 1895 it ceased to exist as a viable labor
organization. Documents 1-14 reveal the conflicting tendencies within the
Order, while Documents 15-20 demonstrate how far the Knights had fallen from
their original ideals, finally to succumb to colonization, that most still-
born of American solutions to the "Negro question."

1. RELATIONS BETWEEN BLACK AND WHITE KNIGHTS FROM THE
1886 RICHMOND CONVENTION TO 1889

NO COLOR LINE WANTED

A national convention of colored men is to be held soon, for the advancement of the colored race. The propositions at present advanced point
to the marshalling of the colored vote in every State through a general
executive committee, whose duty it shall be to advise voters.

This is a great scheme--for party politicians--if it will only work.
But how it can effect any advancement of the general body of colored men remains to be seen. The disabilities from which they suffer are social and
economic, and cannot be remedied by laws or by being used as a stepping
stone for office seekers.

The only way by which the colored men can benefit themselves is to affiliate with the white races wherever possible in trades unions and K. of L.
assemblies, and prove by practical work that their aims and objects are the
same--the advancement of the material welfare of the whole race, without
drawing any color line.

The Labor Leaf (Detroit), December 22, 1886.

2. IDA B. WELLS DESCRIBES A KNIGHTS OF LABOR MEETING IN MEMPHIS [40]

I was fortunate enough to attend a meeting of the Knights of Labor.
. . . I noticed that everyone who came was welcomed and every woman from
black to white was seated with courtesy usually extended to white ladies
alone in this town. It was the first assembly of the sort in this town where
color was not the criterion to recognition as ladies and gentlemen. Seeing
this I could listen to their enunciation of the principles of truth and
accept them with a better grace than all the sounding brass and tinkling
cymbal of a Moody or Sam Jones, even expounded in a consecrative house and
over the word of God.

New York Freeman, January 15, 1887; Cleveland Gazette, January 22, 1887.

3. A FLORIDA STRIKE

Colored and White Workmen Unite Against
Oppression--A Laughable Incident

PENSACOLA, Feb. 5--On Tuesday, 1st inst., the bay men (or the men that
work in the bay) struck on account of some wrong doing of a certain stevedore. The scene on Palafox's wharf was not a pleasant one, owing to the rage
the major part of the men were in. Some of the offending parties were badly
used, getting several severe blows, and having to leap into the bay or seek
refuge in the boat houses. On the 2d the "guano men" (or the men that work
in guano) all quit work and marched to Sunday's Hall, held a meeting,
elected officers and formed a society to be known as the Guano Association.
They wanted better wages, $2.50, $2, and $1.50 per day. Some of the leading
spirits called on their employers (the officials of the L. & N. R. R.) and

expressed their desire in a polite manner, only to be told that they would
not get it. On the 3d they called to get the pay due them. Their employers
paid them, but refused to agree to give the wages they asked. Tuesday was
a laughable day indeed. The Escambia Rifles (white) marched out with
glittering muskets and bayonets to make the poor and oppressed colored and
white men fall in submission; but they were badly mistaken, for as soon as
they got as far as the workmen cared to have them come, they were surrounded.
The workmen politely pointed out the way and they willingly went back to
their armory. Wednesday at 12 o'clock the stevedore in fault gave satisfaction. Yesterday the officials of the railroad brought in from along their
line about 160 men to take the places of the guano strikers. They were met
on the wharf by the strikers, who told them what would be the consequences
if they went to work. After hearing the awful wrath that would befall them,
they told the officials that they would not risk their lives. Hon. P. H.
Davidson, Assembly-elect, is one of Florida's most prominent Knights of
Labor. Rev. Thos. Darly, pastor of the A. M. E. Zion Church, is having his
commodious church repaired and plastered, preparatory to the convening of
the annual conference of the connection some time this month.

New York Freeman, February 12, 1887.

4. "PERSECUTION"

Oxford, N.C., May 20, 1887

Editor:
    The Assemblies of this place and vicinity wish me to make known to the
Order at large the unenviable position of the Knights of Labor here. As
soon as it became generally known that we had an Assembly here persecution
followed, and no stone was left unturned to create ill-feeling against us.
The Chicago anarchist riot was used to our prejudice. The disregard of the
"color-line" by the Richmond General Assembly and the partial success of the
Republican party in our State last November were also used against us. They
pointed at us with scorn, and kept crying "Nigger! Nigger!" until the two
words "Nigger" and "Knights" became synomous terms.

R.J.C.M.W., L.A. 7478, *Journal of United Labor, June 11, 1887.*

5. "KNIGHTSVILLE IS SOLID"

Calera, Ala., June 4, 1887.

Editor:
    Knightsville is a village composed of nothing but colored people, who
now number thirty-three. They own about two hundred and eighty acres of land.
Knightsville is solid for the Knights of Labor. The Anderson Local Assembly
now numbers forty-four, and applications are coming in weekly. Steps are
being taken to start a co-operative store in Knightsville.

                              Fraternally,
                              H. D. and R. S., L.A. 9867.

Journal of United Labor, July 2, 1887.

6. "GLORIOUS 4TH"

Pensacola, Fla.,

The colored Knights of Labor will go to the park and the whites to Magnolia Bluff. They could not possibly all go to the same place and whoop off the "glorious 4th" together. That would be too much like social equality for our Southern brethren.

New York Freeman, July 9, 1887.

7. "HE IS ON OUR SIDE"

Graniteville, S. C.
July 20, 1887

Editor:
I guess you would like to hear from this part of the Sunny South. We are about to have some trouble here with the trustees of the Masonic hall, owned by the Masons and Odd Fellows. The trustees said we could not have the hall any more if we permitted negroes to meet there with us. That is their excuse, but I know better. I see through their little game--they want to break up the Knights of Labor here, but we intend to have the Knights of Labor in spite of all opposition, for we know our noble Order is right, and when we are right God is on our side, and when He is on our side I don't care a straw who is against us. You will see what kind of people we have here. We are going to carry on our work without the fear or favor of any one.

Yours Fraternally,
L.A. 8413.

Journal of United Labor, August 6, 1887.

8. A CRUEL NEGRO

"Charley White was arraigned before Esquire Gavin yesterday on the charge of cruelly beating an eleven year old boy. At the trial it was proven that he knocked the boy down and kicked him until his nose bled. He was fined $15.00 and cost. The victim is bruised from foot to crown and is in a critical condition."
You will notice that this outrage is palmed off to the outside world as having been perpetrated by "a cruel negro." You will also notice that this "capitalistic news-rag" is as silent as the grave as to the place where this diabolical crime was committed. The allegation that any negro was directly or even remotely connected with this outrage is as black and false as the heart and brain which concocted the subterfuge, which was invented for no other purpose than to shield the pious rascals [White is a teacher in the Duke M. E. Church], who are robbing the blacks and stomachs of the laboring people in order to build five churches and fill their souls with a spurious modern article, as so-called salvation. Through the machinations and blandishments of the pious (?) leaders of the M. E. Church, many of our former brothers and sisters have been weaned from their feality and allegiance to our noble Order. They have been made to understand that their situations in the factory depended upon their attendance or membership in the above farcical synagogue.

The Recorder finding public indignation so stormy was reluctantly compelled to make at least a show of noticing the affair. Hence the above
item, White, the maltreater, is a human (?) thing with a white skin, is one
of the Duke bosses, and a sanctified--God save the mark!--saint and a member
of the Church. The boy beaten is also white, and of a highly respected white
family. The item above quoted is a specimen of some of the tricks resorted
to by the subsidized press to hide the flagrant rascality of those who are
attempting to crush out our noble Order in the town.

Durham, N.C.

Journal of United Labor, August 6, 1887.

9. A PITTSBURG STRIKE

Why the Colored Workmen Take Little Part In It

To the Editor:
     As a strike is now in progress at the Black Diamond Steel Works, where
many of our race are employed, the colored people hereabouts feel a deep
interest in its final outcome. As yet few colored men have taken part in it,
it having been thus far thought unwise to do so. It is true our white
brothers, who joined the Knights of Labor and organized the strike without
conferring with, or in any way consulting us, now invite us to join with
them and help them to obtain the desired increase in wages and control by
the Knights of Labor of the works. But as we were not taken into their
schemes at its inception, and as it was thought by them that no trouble would
be experienced in obtaining what they wanted without our assistance, we question very much the sincerity and honesty of this invitation. Our experience
as a race with these organizations has, on the whole, not been such as to
give us either great satisfaction or confidence in white men's fidelity. For
so often after we have joined them, and the desired object has been attained,
we have discovered that sinister and selfish motives were the whole and only
cause that led them to seek us as members.
     A few years ago a number of colored men working at this mill were in-
duced to join the Amalgamated Association, thereby relinquishing the positions which they held at these works. They were sent to Beaver Falls, Pa.,
to work in a mill there controlled by said Association, and the men there,
brothers too, mark you, refused to work with them because they were black.
It is true Mr. Jaret, then chairman of that Association, sat down upon those
skunks, but when that mill closed down, and those men went out from there to
seek employment in other mills governed by the Amalgamated, while the men
did not openly refuse to work with them, they managed always to find some
pretext or excuse to keep from employing them.[41]
     Now, Mr. Editor, I am not opposed to organized labor. God forbid that
I should be when its members are honest, just and' true! But when I join any
society, I want to have pretty strong assurance that I will be treated fairly.
I do not want to join any organization the members of which will refuse to
work by my side because the color of my skin happens to be of a darker hue
than their own. Now what the white men in these organizations should and
must do, if they want colored men to join with and confide in them, is to
give them a square deal--give them a genuine white man's chance--and my word
for it they will flock into them like bees into a hive. If they will take Mr.
B. F. Stewart's advice! "take the colored man by the hand and convince him
by actual fact that you will be true to him and not a traitor to your pledge,
he will be found with them ever and always; for there are not under heaven
men in whose breasts beat truer hearts than in the breast of the Negro.

JOHN LUCUS DENNIS
Colored Puddler at Black Diamond
Steel Works, Pittsburg, Pa., Aug. 8.

New York Freeman, August 13, 1887.

10. LETTER FROM A COLORED KNIGHT

Franklinton, N.C.

Editor:
Shady Grove Assembly is booming. Since October 10 we have initiated
82 members. Although we are living under many difficulties and oppressions,
we intend using every means at our command to advance the interests of the
Order. Knighthood is moving right along among the colored people of this
State. We believe that one of the ends for which man was created is labor;
he is constituted for this mentally, morally and physically. Labor is a
fixed law of man's nature and is necessary to his happiness; and, being a
primeval law of his nature, it is honorable and dignified, and to disregard
this law is to set the all-wise Creator at defiance. Heretofore agricultural
labor and learning have been widely separated, and this is one cause why
such labor has, by certain classes, been deemed degrading. Nothing can be
more injurious to progress in agriculture than this baneful hallucination.
Here in the South this mistaken sentiment must be got rid of. Our necessities, our prosperity demands it. Young men must be educated to honor and
dignify labor in its actual performance, and to accomplish this there must
be a change in our educational system.
The man who does not honor labor is an enemy to his own and his country's welfare. I think that discussing the benefits of a people in secret
is the best method of all; when we reap those benefits we shall see them
openly. For a long time the secrets of Knighthood were hidden from public
gaze, but at last we see the light breaking forth and illuminating the mind
of every thinking man in America. Its principles have aroused men to think
for themselves, and has added one of the brightest pages to the history of
the toilers. It has proved that the concentration of wealth in the hands of
the few means death to labor. May the good work still continue until the
rights of labor are acknowledged and accorded.

Fraternally,

J.W.M.R.S.
L.A. 10471

Journal of United Labor, December 10, 1887.

11. "MUSTERING UP COURAGE"

Woodland, N.C.

Editor:
When the condition of the people of our county is considered, I think it
will be admitted that our increase in membership is very encouraging. Although many are led to believe by some of the white people that no good will
come of their connection with the Order, and that if they join they will
give them employment no longer, they are mustering up courage and will eventually become members. Men on the farms get .50, women .25 to .30, and
lumber-getters .80 cents a day; section hands $18.20 and school teachers
$15 to $25 a month. Meat sells for .10, flour .03-1/2, and coffee .25 cents
a pound.

J.B.L., L.A. 816

Journal of United Labor, May 10, 1888.

12. "AN ACTIVE PART"

Bay Minetta, Ala.
May 21, 1888

Editor:
    We have two assemblies in our vicinity--one colored and one white--
both in good working order. They were organized last September by our State
Master Workman. The larger portion of the members of our assembly (No.
10853) are residing upon the premises of their employers, causing them to
suffer oppressions of various kinds, which could be avoided if they had
homes of their own. We have started a small co-operative grocery store.
The prospects for success are very promising. The majority of our members
are employed on turpentine farms. The Knights in this county are taking an
active part in the interest of the United Labor Party, and held a nominating
convention on May 5.[42]

S. J. B.

Journal of United Labor, June 9, 1888.

13. LIVELY SOUTHERN KNIGHTS

Editor:
    It may be of interest to the rest of the Knights of Labor world to learn
some of the happiness in the Bluff City of the South. The Order here is
composed of L.A.'s 5075 and 7944 with a membership of 500 of the very best
material in the community of both races. Our members are all employed.
Wages for unskilled laborers, however, are not as high as in other portions
of the country, though mechanics and artisans are paid well. The industries
of the place are two cotton mills, two oils, a foundry, and machine shop,
cotton compress, lumber yards, and a small number of minor industries. On
the 13th inst. Brother W. H. Bailey, of the General Executive Board paid a
visit to our city, and a meeting of the two locals was hastily called, at
which he delivered an address that was very instructive and attentively
listened to by the 300 or so who were present, who went away much impressed
with what they heard. One of the great needs of the South is lecturers to
instruct not only the public, but the members in the true principles of the
Order. . . .

R. V. S.
Natchez, Miss.

Journal of United Labor, June 9, 1888.

14. KNIGHTS OF LABOR

A Speech Delivered by Hon. Jas. J. Sullivan on June 28,
at Donaldsville, La.

    At a meeting of Knights of Labor, held Sunday, June 28, 1889, in the
hall belonging to that order, and situated on Claiborne street, in the town
of Donaldsonville--the object of the meeting being to devise ways and means
for raising funds to extinguish the mortgage bearing on the said property.
Mr. J. J. Sullivan, responsive to an invitation, made the following address:
    Friends and fellow citizens, and brother Knights: I congratulate you
upon the spirit shown on so important an occasion as that of raising money

to save your property, which is right and proper, and I gracefully acknowledge the compliment implied in calling upon me to assist in expressing
the thoughts and sentiments natural to this and other occasions. "One like
many other good causes it has its ebbs and flows, successes and failures,
joyous hopes and saddening tears." In the days gone by, we gratefully and
lovingly repeated the names of our great men and their works. We shouted the
praises of these great men as God inspired benefactors. At that time, too,
it was well enough and easy to blow aloud our trumpets and call out the
crowd through the streets with gay processions, for since the great exodus
of the Hebrews from Egyptian bondage, no people had had greater cause for
such joyous demonstration. But the time for such demonstration is over. It
is not the past but the present and the future that most concerns us to-day;
our past was slavery. We cannot recur to it with any sense of composure.
The history of it is a record of stripes, a revelation of agony. It is
written in characters of blood; its breath is a sigh its voice a groan, and
we turn from it with a shudder. The duty of to-day is to meet the questions
that confront us with intelligence and courage, without the least desire to
awaken undue alarm. I declare to you that no home since the abolition of
slavery in these Southern States of the Union, have the moral, social and
political surroundings of the colored people of this country been more
solemn and foreboding than they are this day. If this statement is startling
it is only because the facts are startling. I speak only of the things I
do know, and testify of the things I have seen. Nature has given me a buoy-
ant disposition. I like to look upon the bright and hopeful side of affairs.
No man can see the silver lining of a black cloud more joyfully than I but
he is a more hopeful man than I am who will tell you that the rights and
liberties of the colored people in this country have passed beyond the danger
line. Mark, if you please, the fact, for it is a fact, an ominous fact, that
no time in the history of the conflict between slavery and freedom has the
character of the Negro as a man been made the subject of a freer and more
serious discussion in all the avenues of debate than during the past and
present year. Against him have been marshalled the whole artillery of science,
philosophy and history. We are not only confronted by open foes, but we are
assailed in the guise of sympathy and friendship, and presented as objects
of pity.

The strong point made against the Negro and his cause, is the statement
widely circulated and greatly relied upon, that no two people so different
in race and color can live together in the same country on a level of equal
civil and political rights and powers; that nature herself has ordained that
the relations of two such races must be that of domination and subjugation.
This old slave-holding Calhoun and McDuffy doctrine, which we long ago thought
dead and buried, is revived in unexpected quarters, and confronts us to-day
as sternly as it did forty years ago. Then it was employed as the sure defence of slavery, now it is employed as a justification for later and greater
wrongs visited on us.[43]

To those who are assuming that there is no cause of apprehension; that
we are secure in the possession of all that has been gained by the war and
reconstruction, I ask what means the universal and palpable concern manifested through all the avenues of debate as to the future of the Negro in
this country? for this question meets us now at every town. The brain of
every statesman in this country is taxed with this question. Whence this
solicitude or apparent solicitude? To me, the question has a sinister
meaning. It is prompted not so much by concern for the welfare of the Negro
as by considerations of how his relation to the American government may effect the welfare and happiness of the American people. The Negro is a member
of the body politic. This talk about him implies that he is regarded as a
diseased member. It is wisely said by physicians that any member of the
human body is in a healthy condition when it gives no occasion to think of it.
The fact that the American people of the Caucasian race are continually
thinking of the Negro and never cease to call attention to him, shows that
his relation to them is felt to be abnormal and unhealthy. Justice and
magnaminity are elements of American character. They may do much for us but
we are in no condition to depend upon these qualities exclusively.

History repeats itself. The black man fought for American independence;
the Negro's blood mingled with the white man's blood at Bunker Hill, but this

sacrifice on his part won for him only temporary applause. He was returned to his former condition. He fought bravely with General Jackson at
New Orleans, but his reward was only slavery and chains. These facts speak
trumpet tongued of the kind of people with whom we have to deal, and through
them we may contemplate the sternest. [44]

I have said that at no time has the character of the Negro been so
generally and seriously discussed as now. I do not regard discussion as an
evil in itself. I regard it not as an enemy, but as a friend. It has
served us well at other times in our history, and I hope it may serve us
well at this time.

Controversy, whether of words or blows, whether in the forum or on the
battlefield, may help us if we make the right use of it. We are not to be
like dumb driven cattle in this discussion, in this war of words and conflicting theories; our business is to answer back wisely, modestly and yet
grandly.

While I do not regard discussion as an enemy, I cannot but deem it in
this instance as out of place and unfortunate. It comes to us as a surprise
and a bitter disappointment; it implies a deplorable unrest and unsoundness
in the public mind; it shows that the reconstruction of our national institutions upon a basis of liberty, justice and equality is not yet accepted
as a final and irrevocable settlement of the Negro's relation to the government and of his membership in the body politic.

I deny and utterly scout the idea that there is now, properly speaking,
any such thing as a Negro problem before the American people. It is not the
Negro, educated or illiterate, intelligent or ignorant, who is on trial or
whose qualities are giving trouble to the nation. The real problem lies in
the other direction. It is not so much what the Negro is, what he has been,
or what he may be, that constitutes the problem. Here, as elsewhere, the
lesser is included in the greater; the Negro's significance is dwarfed by a
factor vastly larger than himself. The real question, the all-commanding
question, is, whether American justice, American liberty, American civilization, American laws and American christianity, can be made to include and
protect alike and forever all American citizens in the rights which, in a
generous moment in the nation's life, have been guaranteed to them by the
organic and fundamental law of the land; it is whether this great nation
shall conquer its prejudices, rise to the dignity of its professions and
proceed in the sublime course of truth and liberty marked out for itself
since the late war, or swing back to its ancient moorings of slavery and
barbarism. The Negro is of inferior activity and power in the solution of
this problem; he is the clay, the nation is the potter; he is the subject,
the Nation is the sovereign. It is not what he shall be or do, but what the
Nation shall be and do, which is to solve this great national problem. The
real problem lies in the other direction. It is not so much what the Negro
is, what he has been, or what he may be, that constitutes the problem. Here,
as elsewhere, the lesser is included in the greater; the Negro's significance is dwarfed by a factor vastly larger than himself.

The difference between colored and white here is, that the one by reason
of color needs legal protection, and the other by reason of color does not
need protection. It is nevertheless true that manhood is insulted in both
cases. No man can put a chain about the ankle of his fellow-man without at
last finding the other end of it fastened about his own neck. The lesson of
all the ages on this point is, that a wrong done to one man is a wrong done
to all men. It may not be felt at the moment, and the evil day may be long
delayed, but so sure as there is a moral government of the universe, so sure
will the harvest of evil come. Color prejudice is not the only prejudice
against which a republic like ours should guard. The spirit of caste is dangerous everywhere. There is the prejudice of the rich against the poor, the
pride and prejudice of the idle dandy against the hard-handed workingman.
There is, worst of all, religious prejudice; a prejudice which has stained a
whole continent with blood. It is in fact a spirit infernal, against which
every enlightened man should wage perpetual war. Perhaps no class of our
fellow-citizens has carried this prejudice against color to a point more extreme and dangerous than our Catholic Irish fellow-citizens, and yet no people
on the face of the earth have been more relentlessly persecuted and oppressed
on account of race and religion than the Irish people; but in Ireland perse-

cution at last reached a point where it reacts terribly upon her perse-
cutors. England to-day is reaping the bitter consequence of her injustice
and oppression. Ask any man of intelligence to-day "What is the chief source
of England's weakness? What has reduced her to the rank of a second-class
power?" and the answer will be "Ireland." Poor, ragged, hungry and oppressed
as she is, she is strong enough to be a standing menace to the power and
glory of England. Let me say right here to our Caucasian brother, you need
no black Ireland in America, you need no aggrieved class in America, strong
as you are without the Negro, you are stronger with him, the power and
friendship of seven millions of people scattered all over the country,
however humble, are not to be despised. We do not ask for revenge, we simply ask for justice; we are willing to forget the past, willing to hide our
scars, anxious to bury the broken chains, and to forget miseries and hardships, the tears and agonies of two hundred years.
      Another opportunity is given for the people of this country to take
sides. According to my belief the supreme thing for every man to do is to
be absolutely true to himself, all consequences, whether rewards or punishment, whether honor and power or disgrace and poverty, are as dreams un-
dreamt. I have made my choice; I have taken my stand. Where my brain and
heart go there I will publicly and openly walk; doing this is my highest
conception of duty. Being allowed to do this is liberty. If this is not a
free government, if citizens cannot now be protected, regardless of race or
color, if the three sacred amendments have been undermined by the supreme
court we must have another, and if that fails then another, and we must
neither stop nor pause until the Constitution shall become a perfect shield
for every human being beneath our flag.

New Orleans Weekly Pelican, July 27, 1889.

DEPORTATION: THE KNIGHTS' SOLUTION TO THE
PROBLEMS OF THE BLACK WORKER

15. "SPEAK OUT"

      On behalf of the Afro-American members of the Order in Chicago, we ap-
peal to the General Assembly to speak out in thundering tones against the
discriminations against our race throughout this country, against Jim Crow[45]
cars, race prejudice from every section and source, also Judge Lynch; and
we further request the General Assembly to appoint or elect as a member of
the General Executive Board an Afro-American as a lecturer throughout the
United States, so as to educate the race in the advantages of our noble
Order, there being no color line in the Order, and our watch word being "an
injury to one is the concern of all." We send happy greetings and the
Seventeenth session will be productive of such good in the cause of the
Fatherhood of God and the brotherhood of man.
                              J. B. Bubbins, Master Workman
                              J. W. Coble, Recording Secretary

Proceedings, General Assembly, Knights of Labor, 1893, p. 34.

16. A BLACK WORKER TO GRAND MASTER WORKMAN, JAMES R. SOVEREIGN[46]

      I take exception to your proposition to deport the Negro back to Africa
(as being the best way to solve the Negro question) as being contrary to all
international law. There was a day when you preached the universal brotherhood of man. . . . Now, I will suggest an easy solution to the whole trouble,

that is, for Mr. Sovereign to accept Negroes into the order in the South.
. . . but in case you attempt to force the Negro from the country to make
it easy for the K. of L. to continue the inculcation of prejudice and inhumanity, you may run against a greater force than the one you bring to bear
upon the Negro.

Chicago Inter-Ocean, March 12, 1894.

17.   OPINION OF THE CHICAGO COLORED WOMEN'S CLUB

Negroes have been residents of this country for two hundred and fifty
years and are as much American citizens as anybody. If this country is too
small for the Knights of Labor and the Negro, then let the Knights leave.

Chicago Inter-Ocean, March 13, 1894.

18.   OUR LABOR PROBLEM

The propriety of its claim to the title of "City of Brotherly Love"
was most creditably exemplified by the city council of Philadelphia last
week. A resolution limiting contracts for and engagements in the public
works of the city to none but American citizens was promptly voted down.
Hereafter, as formerly, public work and contracts may be secured without
regard to race or nationality. Of course, a different verdict would not have
materially affected Afro-Americans, as they have never been discriminated
against in the public work of the city.

In connection with the action of the City Fathers of Philadelphia, there
are two reflections as important to members of the colored population in
other places, as to those in this great city of progress and fraternity.

Everywhere the Negro is identified as a laborer and everywhere he de-
preciates his power and prerogatives as such. Especially is this shortcoming
true of him here in the North and East. He is a recognized laborer universally, but one apparently satisfied to operate in common ruts and along
the lower planes. He appears plentifully enough as a common workman, but
seldom as a boss or contractor in any department of the enterprises of the
leading and more liberal cities of the country. Like Italians, Irishmen and
other nationalities, when he begins to organize, control, and apply his kind
to the best advantage, he will cut a much greater figure than that which out-
lines his shape at present.

Because he will eventually make his labor thus tell in more directions
than one, is a probable reason why an opposition should be started against
him in certain industrial high circles in this country. Because he may
speedily open his eyes and elbow some less energetic competitor out of his
way may account for the desire on the part of the Knights of Labor to have
him out of the country. If so, it were to be hoped that their most painful
fears may be realized.

Let the Negro remain in the kitchen, carry the hod or stay in the field,
and he will meet no resistance. Let him but attempt to surpass himself in
these respects, and so-called Knights of Labor with drawn swords in bumptious,
quixotic, windy valorousness, would challenge his movements. But as the
Negro himself has established his claim as the only true Knight of Labor in
the past, he will not so easily give way to the false claims of others to
such, now or hereafter. He will remain here, attend to his business and invite others to do the same.

The Christian Recorder, March 15, 1894.

19. ON DEPORTATION

The Knights of Labor propose to "deport the negro to central Africa" probably to relieve labor competition. That plan comes within one of deportation of the knights by the negro. Why not deport the American capitalist? Importation of laborers under contract is illegal, because it practically imports foreign labor prices. Wholesale deportation of nearly eight millions of colored people would affect the labor market considerably. The knights hope to induce the government to pay for the deportation. That is a thrifty consideration, even if it is not knightly Americanism. Who came to this country first, the negro or the knight?

The Cristian Recorder, March 15, 1894.

20. EPITAPH

As between the black and white races, there is no community of interest in labor organization. For a short time some Negro laborers were connected with the Knights of Labor.

Virginia Bureau of Labor, *Annual Report* (Richmond, 1899), Vol. I, 366.

VIII

BLACK FARMERS ORGANIZE SOUTHERN ALLIANCES

BLACK FARMERS ORGANIZE SOUTHERN ALLIANCES

The Knights of Labor had never really served the economic interests of agrarians who, by the 1880s, were suffering from a long list of economic maladies. The most significant organization created by Southern farmers to express their grievances in the 1880s was the Farmers' Alliance, the forerunner of the Populist, or People's Party. While the Populists created a third party movement, the Alliances preferred to remain within the Democratic Party. [47]

Founded in Lampasas County, Texas, in 1874 or 1875, as a cooperative for purchasing farm supplies, the organization expanded, quickly spreading eastward and merging with similar groups. By 1887 the National Farmers' Alliance, usually known as the Southern Alliance, had become a major agrarian force in the South.

The Southern Alliance did not admit blacks, but with three-quarters of the Negro population engaged in agriculture, it was imperative that a parallel black organization be created. Thus, the Colored Alliance was founded December 11, 1886, in Houston County, Texas. It had a magnetic attraction for poverty-stricken black farmers. In 1888 movement leaders decided, for legal purposes, to regard the Colored Alliance as a trade union, and the Colored Farmers' National Alliance and Cooperative Union officially was born (Doc. 1, 14-15). The Colored Alliance recognized that while whites refused to admit them into the same organization, blacks themselves had little desire to integrate at this time. In fact, one of the key reasons for the separate Colored Alliance was the increasing emphasis of blacks upon self-help as an uplift strategy. Separate racial organization was a short-term tactic to attain wealth and power which, it was believed, would earn the respect of whites and eventually lead to equality. The two Alliances worked together closely, however, especially in the recruitment and organization of Negro farmers. Nevertheless, social imperatives in the South required that whites control a subordinate black population, and this significantly hampered the development of Negro self-sufficiency. The conditions of life and labor, and the major concerns of the Colored Alliance are partially demonstrated in Documents 2-5, 17-19, 25. The cooperation and strains in race relations between the black and white Alliances are shown in Documents 16, 20-21, 24-32.

The downfall of the Colored Alliance resulted from a combination of factors, but disunity constituted a major problem. As late as 1889 there were two Colored Alliances until a compromise was finally achieved in 1890. Moreover, after dedicating itself to economic uplift, the organization had to produce some tangible results in the fight to arrest the economic erosion of poverty-ridden black farmers. Therefore, in 1891 the Colored Alliance unwisely became involved in an abortive strike which led to the eventual demise of the union. In the fall of that year, numerous merchants and planters, especially in Tennessee and South Carolina, formed an organization to cut the already demoralizingly low wages of cotton pickers (Doc. 33-35). Even though the Alliance had no chance to win a strike against the powerful planter-merchant coalition, pressures from the membership forced the union to become involved. Plans were initiated for a general strike on a scale unprecedented in the history of black labor. Strike plans were maintained in a shroud of secrecy; not even the white Alliance was informed. In the end, however, the massive work stoppage never materialized, primarily because of poor organization, disunity, and inadequate finances. Small sporadic strikes actually occurred only in Arkansas and South Carolina, and there they were viciously suppressed (Doc. 50-65). After the 1891 strike most of the approximately one million black members became disillusioned with the Colored Alliance and drifted away to be absorbed into the Populist protest.

1. THE COLORED FARMERS' NATIONAL ALLIANCE AND
    COOPERATIVE UNION, 1890-1891

HISTORY OF THE COLORED FARMERS' NATIONAL ALLIANCE AND
CO-OPERATIVE UNION

By General R. M. Humphrey, Superintendent of the Colored Farmers' [48]
National Alliance and Co-operative Union

The Colored Farmers' Alliance had its origin in Texas. The first subordinate Colored Alliance was organized in Houston County, in that State,
on the eleventh day of December, 1886. Immediately following this, a number
of others were organized in Houston and adjoining counties. The necessity
for general organization soon became apparent. Accordingly these several
Alliances chose delegates to a central convention, which assembled in the
Good Hope Baptist Church, at Weldon, on the twenty-ninth day of the same
month. After some discussion and earnest prayer, it was unanimously agreed
that union and organization had become necessary to the earthly salvation
of the colored race.
     The convention then proceeded to adopt the following declaration of
principles:--
     "1. To create a body corporate and politic, to be known as 'The
Alliance of Colored Farmers of Texas.''
     "2. The objects of this corporation shall be: (a) To promote agri-
culture and horticulture; (b) To educate the agricultural classes in the
science of economic government, in a strictly non-partisan spirit, and to
bring about a more perfect union of said classes; (c) To develop a better
state mentally, morally, socially, and financially; (d) To create a better
understanding for sustaining our civil officers in maintaining law and order;
(e) To constantly strive to secure entire harmony and good will to all mankind, and brotherly love among ourselves; (f) To suppress personal, local,
sectional, and national prejudices, and all unhealthful rivalry and selfish
ambition; (g) To aid its members to become more skillful and efficient
workers, promote their general intelligence, elevate their character, protect their individual rights; the raising of funds for the benefit of sick
or disabled members, or their distressed families; the forming a closer union
among all colored people who may be eligible to membership in this association."
     This declaration was promptly signed by the following colored men, being
all the delegates present: H. J. Spencer, William Armistead, R. M. Saddler,
Anthony Turner, T. Jones, N. C. Crawley, J. W. Peters, Israel McGilbra, G.
W. Coffey, Green Lee, J. J. Shuffer, Willis Nichols, Jacob Fairfax, Abe
Fisher, S. M. Montgomery, John Marshall.
     J. J. Shuffer was elected President, and H. J. Spencer, Secretary.
Suitable committees were appointed to draft a constitution and by-laws a
ritual, and a form of charter. After receiving the reports of these committees, it was agreed that the Colored Farmers' Alliance should be a secret
association.
     R. M. Humphrey of Lovelady was elected General Superintendent, and to
him was committed the work of organization. The new order had no money, no
credit, few friends, and was expected to reform and regenerate a race which,
from long endurance of oppression and chattel slavery, had become exceedingly besotted and ignorant.
     On the 28th of February, 1887, a charter was obtained under the laws of
Texas, and the organization assumed definite shape as The Alliance of Colored
Farmers. The work now spread with great rapidity over the State of Texas,
and was soon introduced into several of the neighboring States. The colored
people everywhere welcomed the organizers with great delight, and received
the Alliance as a sort of second emancipation

On the 14th of March, 1888, a meeting of the States convened at Lovelady, Texas, and after some discussion, agreed to charter as a trades-union, in accordance with the laws of the United States. The new association adopted the Texas State work, with only such changes as were necessary to give it national character. The new charter was duly filed in the office of the Recorder of Deeds for the District of Columbia, in compliance with the laws of Congress, and will be found recorded in Book IV., at page 354, Acts of Incorporation, United States of America. Under this new arangement, the alliance continued to thrive.

About this time, leading minds among the colored people in the South began to realize the importance of a better system of co-operation. They were desirous, too, of utilizing and, as far as possible, extending the benefits of their organization. The national trustees addressed the following communication to the general superintendent:--

> "Lovelady, Texas,
> July 20, 1888

"To the General Superintendent of the Colored Farmers' National Alliance

"Sir: Upon receipt of this order you will at your earliest convenience proceed to establish such trading post, or posts, or exchanges, for the use and benefit of our order in the several States, as in your judgment will be most conducive to the interests of the people. We leave you to adopt such plans as in your opinion will be most effective.

> "With much respect yours,
> "J. J. Shuffer, *President*

"H. J. Spencer,
*"Secretary Colored Farmers' National Alliance
and Co-operative Union."*

In compliance with this order, exchanges were established in Houston, Texas; New Orleans, Louisiana; Mobile, Alabama; Charleston, South Carolina; and Norfolk, Virginia. These institutions, with varying success, are still in existence, and have accomplished great things for the elevation of the colored race. Occupying as these posts do, the great centres of the country's commerce, we are not without hope that they will be, in the future as in the past, well supported by the people . Our method in their establishment is this: An assessment of $2.00 is levied upon each male member of the order, within prescribed boundaries, for the benefit of the exchange within his territory. These small amounts paid by each member become a cash capital for the basis of our business operations. The money may be used to buy a stock of bacon, or to pay off a mortgage, and being at once replaced, is ready the next week for some similar investment. Being thus often turned over, it will, in a year, save many times its value as against the speculator, who always reckons the term of a credit at twelve months, and *t*he rate of interest at fifty to one hundred per cent, though the actual time of such credit may be only from August till September.

Again, this kind of cash basis is not exhausted nor exhaustible; fifty or a hundred years hence it may be still present to do the same work it is now doing; or should the Colored Alliance cease or become extinct, the funds on hand might be turned to the endowment of schools or colleges for colored youths, and so render a perpetual service during all time.

With the beginning of 1889 the Alliance established a weekly newspaper, called *The National Alliance*. They designed it for the practical education of their members. It has been reasonably well supported, and is still published weekly, at Houston, Texas, each of its editions reaching many thousand colored families.

At this writing, Texas, Louisiana, Mississippi, Alabama, Florida, Georgia, South Carolina, North Carolina, Virginia, and Tennessee have State Colored Alliances, working under State charters. Several other States expect to be chartered at an early day, while organizations of greater or less extent in more than twenty States. The total membership is nearly 1,200,000, of whom 300,000 are females, and 150,000 males under twenty-one years of age, leaving 750,000 adult males.

It is freely admitted by all that the colored people have made great strides forward in intelligence, morals, and financial standing during these

years of organization. Thousands of their public free schools have been
wonderfully improved in character of teaching, and the duration of their
sessions much extended by the combining of the people, and the payment by
each member of the Alliance of a small sum in the form of tuition. Very
many Alliance academies and high schools have been opened in various sections
of the country. In not a few communities the people, impelled by the higher
cultivation of their social instincts, have built new places of worship, while
the intellectual and moral grade of their pastors and teachers has been im-
measurably advanced.

The relation of the colored people in the South to their white neighbors had been long a question of the last importance to both races. There
were not wanting those who believed in race conflict, race war, and even
race extermination. These beliefs and opinions were shared by some of the
best people on both sides, as, perhaps, painfully inevitable results which
must follow from existing conditions; but there were others who were in apparent haste to put their views into practical operation, and who, if judged
by their own testimony, were ready to baptize their prejudices in the blood
of their fellow-beings, and dishonor themselves by the destruction of their
country. The Alliances, both colored and white, were organized from the
first largely with a view to the suppression of all prejudices, whether
national, local, sectional, or race, and to create conditions of peace and
good will among all the inhabitants of our great nation. On this account
the "race question" was from the beginning a matter of profoundest interest
to the order. At first practicable moment steps were taken looking to the
peaceful solution of that much-vexed and intricate problem.

December 3, 1889, the representatives of the Colored Farmers' National
Alliance convened in the city of St. Louis. During this session they were
visited by committees of fraternal regard from the Farmers and Laborers'
Union, the Farmers' Mutual Benefit Association, and the National Farmers'
Alliance. These visits were acknowledged with the utmost good will, so that
the messengers from the several brotherhoods were looked upon rather as ministers of light and salvation. Like committees were appointed from our body
to visit and bear our good will and fraternal greetings to these several
organizations.

Again, in Ocala, Florida, at which place their National Council was
held in December, 1890, they were visited by committees from the Farmers and
Laborers' Union, and by officers of the Knights of Labor, and by members of
other labor associations. They appointed committees to each of these bodies,
as bearers of their good will and fraternal regard. They further proposed
the holding of a joint meeting by these committees to form an association or
confederation of the several orders represented, for purposes of mutual
protection, co-operation, and assistance. The committees, in their joint
session, found themselves able to agree, and the matter of their agreement
being reported back to their several orders, was heartily indorsed by all
concerned. It recognizes common citizenship, assures commercial equality
and legal justice, and pledges each of the several organizations for the
common protection of all. This agreement will be known in future ages as
the burial of race conflict, and finally of race prejudice. Its announcement
has fired many hearts with renewed hope, has given a new impetus to progress
among the people, and will exert tremendous influences in the healing of
sectional and national misconceptions and prejudices throughout the entire
country.

"Declaration of Purposes of the Colored Farmers' National Alliance and Co-
Operative Union of the United States

"The seventh section of the charter declares the object of this corporation shall be to elevate the colored people of the United States, by
teaching them to love their country and their homes; to care more for their
helpless and sick and destitute; to labor more earnestly for the education
of themselves and their children, especially in agricultural pursuits.

"To become better farmers and laborers, and less wasteful in their
methods of living.

"To be more obedient to the civil law, and withdraw their attention
from political partisanship.
"To become better citizens, and truer husbands and wives."

N. A. Dunning (ed.), *The Farmers' Alliance History and Agricultural Digest*
(Washington, D.C., 1891), pp. 288-92.

2. THE ORDER SYSTEM

No more crafty and effective device for defrauding the Southern laborer
could be adopted than the one that substitutes orders upon shop-keepers of
currency in payment of wages. It has the merit of a show of honesty, and
it puts the laborer completely at the mercy of the land-owner and the shop-
keeper. He is between the upper and the nether millstones and is thus ground
to dust. It gives the shop-keeper a customer who can trade with another
storekeeper, and thus leaves the latter no motive for fair trade except his
own moral sense, which is never too strong. While the laborer holding the
orders is tempted by their worthlessness as a circulating medium to get rid
of them at any sacrifice, and hence is led into extravagancy and consequent
destitution.

The merchant puts him off with his poorest commodities at highest prices,
and can say to him take those or nothing. Worse still. By this means the
laborer is brought into debt, and hence is kept always in the power of the
land-owner. When this system is not pursued and land is rented to the freedman, he is charged more for the use of an acre of land for a single year
than the land would bring in the market if offered for sale. On such a system of fraud and wrong one might well invoke a bolt from heaven--red with
uncommon wrath.

It is said if the colored people do not like the conditions upon which
their labor is demanded and secured, let them leave and go elsewhere. A
more heartless suggestion never emanated from an oppressor. Having for years
paid them in shop orders, utterly worthless outside the shop to which they
are directed, without a dollar in their pockets, brought by this crafty
process into bondage to the land-owners, who can and would arrest them if they
should attempt to leave them when they are told to go.

We commend the whole subject to the Senate Committee of Labor and Education, and urge upon that Committee the duty to call before it not only the
land-owners, but the landless laborers of the South, and thus get at the
whole truth concerning the labor question of that section. . . .

Treatment of Convicts

Another sore grievance that calls for the consideration of this Convention is the treatment of convicts, a large proportion of whom are colored.
It is inhuman and cruel in the extreme. We do not refer to those that are
here within the walls. They are under the immediate care and supervision of
the management, and we believe considerately treated. But most of the convicts are scattered over the State on farms, having no one to administer to
their physical, moral or spiritual needs but a host of inhuman, brutal convict guards. When a fresh convict is carried to the farms, he is taken down
by the other convicts and beaten, at the command of the guard, and that, too,
with a large piece of cowhide. The guard takes this method of taming the
newcomer. Of course this lays him up, but in a few days he is hauled out of
his sick quarters and put to work, whether he is physically able to do it or
not. The law provides that a convict physically unable to work shall not be
required to do so, such inability to be ascertained by the examination of
the penintentiary physician. But, convicts on farms, who are mostly colored,
have no physician to determine such inability, and even when sick and dying
have none, unless the hiring planter, who has no particular interest in saving his life, sees fit to employ one. In many cases sick convicts are made
to toil until they drop dead in their tracks. Many again, driven to desperation by inhuman treatment, seek to relieve themselves by attempting to

escape when the chances are against them, thus inducing the guards to shoot
them, which they are ready to do on the slightest pretext. Others are maltreated by being placed in the pillory or stocks until they are dead or
nearly so.

When convicts are brutally murdered, nothing is done with their slayers
unless the indignant citizens are prompt in insisting upon their punishment.
In nine cases out of ten, parties sent to investigate these occurrences report the killing justifiable, because guards and their friends find it convenient to make it appear so. When legislative committees visit one of these
convict camps, they always find the convicts ready to report that they are
well treated, because all of them, both white and black, are previously
warned by their guards to report thus or accept the consequences which will
surely follow. Again we will state, although the law justifies the killing
of a convict escaping from the penitentiary, when his escape can be prevented in no other way, still we fail to see wherein it can be justified
when the convict is carried on a farm, away from the penitentiary, and given
a chance to escape only to be deliberately shot down in attempting to do so.
We believe such to be deliberate murder, and should be punished as such.

Believing that most of the evils can be remedied by the appointment of
a colored inspecor who is a humane man, having power to investigate the affairs of convict camps and the management of convict labor on private farms,
therefore, we recommend to the Governor and Board such an appointment at the
earliest possible moment. We recommend also, that as most of the State convicts are colored, that there be appointed at least one colored commissioner
of penitentiaries. Though our men and youths are sent to the penitentiary
to be reformed, in most cases they are made worse by the inhumanities and
immoral habits of their guards, who, in many cases, are worse morally than
the convicts themselves. We think that this Convention should pass a resolution condemning, in strongest terms, the practice of yoking or chaining
male and female convicts together. This is an act of officials done only
for the purpose of further demoralizing those persons, especially so where
they are only county convicts.

*Proceedings. National Convention of Colored Men, Louisville, Kentucky,
September 24, 1883* (Louisville, 1883).

3. SOUTHERN GRANGERS [49]

By Le Duke

To show the base uses to which respectable names and titles can be applied, I desire to call your attention to some of the practices of *Southern*
Grangers. As I understand the object of the society of Grangers, it is the
protection of farmers against unjust railroad freight charges and the en-
croachments of stock-jobbers in grain—in fact, it is a society formed for
the purpose of seeing to it that the labor, so essential in this country by
reason of its indispensability, is properly compensated. These are the objects of the Northern Grangers. But the Southern Grangers seem to have objects far different in view. The organization, known as the Grangers, which
has grown to alarming proportions at the South, seems to have and *really* has
for its object the pauperization of the colored farmers, the filching of all
their hard-earned money, and the propagation of a vicious sentiment which
tends to reduce the colored people in the estimation of the whites at the
South. And so artful are the designing *scoundrels* (that's the term) that
even the judges of courts and ministers of the Gospel have been induced to
join in the wholesale fraud. This organization, or at least the one operating in Tennessee, (and it is fair to presume that those in States farther
South are still worse) has made a history, for knavery and dishonor, which
should so shock the respectable Grangers at the North as to cause them to
give a new name to their organization. The *modus operandi* of the Tennessee
Grangers is something like this: A colored farm-hand or small farmer is

hired by one of the Grangers to cultivate said Granger's farm, say of 75 acres. The laborer is furnished with the stock and utensils necessary, together with a sufficient quantity of provisions to run him from seed-time to harvest, *provided* said laborer will agree to give said Granger two-thirds of the entire yield. In the case of the small farmer, who has the necessary utensils and stock, it is agreed to give him three-fifths of the entire crop. And should he need provisions, they will be charged against his share of the crop on settlement. The colored laborer or farm-hand sets about the performance of his part of the contract right earnestly. In the meantime the Granger in his turn sets about devising ways in which to cheat the laborer of his hire. The laborer is supplied with provisions, but he is informed by the Granger that he, the Granger, is forced to pay fifteen per cent, in advance of the usual cost, on account of the great length of time between purchase and settlement. In addition to this the colored laborer is informed that the Granger *ought* to have some little *consideration* for his zealous friendship in securing the above provisions at such a reasonable advance-- *only* 15 per cent. The consideration he claims for this, is all the way from 15 to 25 per cent, which will amount to an advance of between 30 and 40 per cent on provisions. Besides this, the Granger does all the figuring. He keeps the books and superintends the disposition of the crop. The crop must be sent to St. Louis or New Orleans for sale.

This is done through a commission merchant who charges for his commission, about 10 per cent and puts a tariff on that of 10 per cent more, for the Granger, and in his bill and remittance such deductions are duly recorded. The extra "tariff" which the merchant charges is kept subject to the draft of the Granger and the regular 10 per cent commission charge must be shared by Granger and colored man equally. Thus Granger pockets the little difference. Upon settlement Granger opens his books, runs over the articles claimed to have been furnished, does all the adding and substracting and after a vigorous and eloquent speech on the infallibility of figures, presents laborer with a statement. And the statement is a faithful verification of the old doctrine, "Naught's a naught, figure's a figure, all for the white man and none for the nigger;" for it turns out almost invariably that Granger is still creditor. And thus the colored man is cheated. He leaves the last place to try his luck with another farmer, but it turns out that the farmers are generally Grangers and that the treatment is uniform.

The colored man is charged with everything and credited with nothing. If a pig dies or the wind blows a barn down and kills a sheep, the colored man must pay for it, and if he dare question the farmers of the charge he is ordered off the farm, and the Justice of the Peace says that he has violated the contract and cannot have his share of the crop.

What can be done to change this high-handed robbery? Would it not well for us to leave the place and let the Grangers set about cheating themselves, just to see how it works? Let us go West!

People's Advocate (Washington, D.C.), December 1, 1883.

4.   WHY HAS THE NEGRO OF THE PLANTATION MADE SO LITTLE PROGRESS?

Do you ask a more particular answer to the question, why the Negro of the plantation has made so little progress, why his cupboard is empty, why he flutters in rags, why his children run naked, and his wife is bare-footed and hides herself behind the hut when a stranger is passing? I will tell you. It is because the husband and father is systematically and almost universally cheated out of his hard earnings. The same class that once extorted his labor under the lash, now extorts his labor by a mean, sneaking, and fraudulent device, which is more effective than the lash. That device is the trucking system, a system which never permits him to see or save a dollar of his hard earnings. He struggles, from year to year, but like a man in a morass, the more he struggles, the deeper he sinks. The highest wages paid him are eight dollars a month, and this he receives only in orders on a

store, which in many cases is owned by his employer. This scrip has a
purchasing power on that one store, and that one store only. A blind man
can see that by this arrangement the laborer is bound hand and foot, and
he is completely in the power of his employer. He can charge the poor
fellow just what he pleases and give what kind of goods he pleases, and he
does both. His victim cannot go to another store and buy, and this the
storekeeper knows. The only security the wretched Negro has under this
arrangement is the conscience of the storekeeper--a conscience educated in
the school of slavery, where the idea prevailed in theory and practice that
the Negro had no rights which the white men were bound to respect, an arrangement in which everything in the way of food or clothing, whether tainted
meat or damaged cloth, is deemed good enough for the Negro. For these he
is often made to pay a double price. But this is not all, or the worst
result of the system. It puts out of the power of the Negro to save anything of what he earns. If a man gets an honest dollar for his day's work,
he has a motive for laying it by and saving it for future emergency. It will
be as good for use in the future, and perhaps better a year hence than now;
but this miserable scrip has in no sense the quality of a dollar. It is
only good at one store and for a limited period. Thus the man who has it is
tempted to get rid of it as soon as possible. It may be out of date before
he knows it, or the storekeeper may move away and it may be left worthless
on his hands. . . .
    I ask again, in view of it all, how in the name of human reason could
the Negro be expected to make progress, or rise higher in the scale of morals,
manners, religion, and civilization than he has done during the twenty years
of his so-called freedom? Shame! Eternal shame on those writers and speakers who taunt, denounce, and disparage the Negro, because he is today found
in poverty, rags and wretchedness!

Emancipation Address, 1888 in Philip S. Foner (ed.), *Frederick Douglass:
Selections From His Writings* (New York, 1945), pp. 84-85.

5. LAYING OUT THE WORK

    The *Caucasian,* an electrified old mummy, resurrected from the Shreveport
pyramids, in which so many worthless Democratic papers have shriveled up
into forgetfulness, has been laying down the law that is to govern the inter-
course between the two races wherever the curse of Bourbonism is allowed to
blight this fair land of ours. The editors of that poor one idea, narrow
groove sheet, probably never did a useful day's work in all the years of
their wasted lives. They know nothing of the dignity of labor, having always
succeeded in living off the earnings of others, and yet they have the impu-
dence to dictate to those who do work how their tasks shall be apportioned to
them. The Negroes are to be sent to the fields and to other descriptions of
hard, grinding labor exclusively. They are to be driven from the compari-
tively easier positions of porters, barbers, waiters, clerks, the mechanic
arts, watchmen, teachers, professors, etc., and these places given only to
white men. Under the ukase of the *Caucasian,* which launched ex-cathedra
as purely a Southern idea, no white man, whatever may be his own views or
his interests, is to be permitted to employ a colored man to black his boots,
drive his carriage, attend to his office, or in any other manner than at the
hardest and most degrading tasks.[50]
    This superlative nonsense, which violates the rights of every freeman
in the State, is swallowed as straight-out, dyed-in-the-wool Democratic
doctrine by the benighted sand-hillers of Caddo parish. It is a pity the
idea, unimpaired by trimming, unsoftened by plausable and gracious words,
could not be incorporated in all its original ugliness and meanness into the
next Democratic platform. "The South" would be "solid" for it, as it is to
any monstrosity that ministers to white indolence and greed at the expense
of the colored race. Doubtless the Northern copperheads would approve it,
as they have so long been led by their Southern associates that it is doubtful

whether they have yet any manhood remaining. The trouble is, that to adopt the Shreveport plan in any convention of responsible beings would make the North irretrievably solid; while to attempt to enforce it by law (either statute or shotgun), would precipitate a second national uprising greater and fiercer than that which was stirred up by danger to the Union. There is no danger, however. The pernicious idea must be limited to the mean locality in which it had its origin. It would not live in a more generous soil; and there are few places in this wide world so sterile in noble sentiments as that which immediately surrounds the publication office of the *Caucasian*. The proposition is only usefulness as showing the depths to which uncurbed selfishness will drag the thoughts of a man who is too impotent for vigorous action.

New Orleans Weekly Pelican, July 27, 1889.

6.   FARMERS OF WEST FLORIDA

I gained some information about the colored Farmers' Alliance in the Western part of the state while there. I am indebted for this information to Mr. R. B. Martin who says he was one of the victims of this now very little appreciated organization in that section. It is said that an agent came there from Texas for the purpose of organizing branch organizations and that he proceeded to do so and also establish an exchange store. To establish this store each farmer was taxed so much. The store was started with a capital of one thousand two hundred dollars. The object of the store was that the colored farmers might exchange their produce there for groceries and when buying for cash obtain groceries cheaper than at other stores. The store was established by the agent sent out and run more in the line of a personal affair than for what it was intended. Colored farmers were charged as high prices for goods at this store as at others, and in some cases where produce was left to be disposed of no returns were ever made of it. The store is now closed and the Alliance is said to owe the store $161 and the firm or store although said to be run on a cash basis is $600 in debt. . . .

                                                                    T. T.Fortune

New York *Age, November 2, 1889.*

7.   H. H. PERRY TO ELIAS CARR, PRESIDENT, COLORED ALLIANCE OF NORTH CAROLINA

Dear Sir & Bro.
        I drop you these few lines to ask your views in regard to the organization known as the Colored National Alliance, do you think it adviceble to incourage their organization in our state there are now over 300 colored alliance in the state.
        I think it would do good to incourage their organization they are here among us & we must make the best of them we can it know doubt would stop the tide of emergration from the cotton countys of our state the knights of labor are organizing them in every county.
        The Colored National Alliance has no connection with the Farmers Alliance it belongs to the colored people. please let me hear from you at once.

Elias Carr Papers, East Carolina University.

8. THE NATIONAL ALLIANCE (HOUSTON, TEX.,) ORGAN
OF THE COLORED ALLIANCE, ADVISES:

Vote for principles, not for parties. It can make no difference with
us whether a man is a Democrat, a Republican, or any other partisan, so long
as our wives are barefoot, our children naked and our homes mere hovels. We
want a man who will work for the sub-treasury, who will see to it that the
people have money at one per cent interest, just as the bankers have it.

National Economist, June 21, 1890.

9. GEN. R. M. HUMPHREY WRITES FROM PULASKI, TENN.,
August 12, as follows:

The Colored Farmers State Alliance of Tennessee, in session at this
place, to-day adopted resolutions declaring in favor of the sub-treasury
plan, complimenting those who have worked so faithfully for its adoption,
and declaring that they will co-operate with the white people of the State
of Tennessee for the promotion and election of such public servants as will
give us the sub-treasury or some equivalent measure. This is the second of
Colored State Alliances (Louisiana being first) to declare boldly in favor
of more money for the people and for sovereign home rule. I was glad to
find these people thoroughly informed in Treasury matters, and that, like
their white neighbors, they are watching our Congress.
It is with a sense of thankfulness THE ECONOMIST is able to lay this
action before the people of the country at large. There is no doubt that
as the annual meetings of the State Alliances of the Colored Farmers Alliance
and Industrial Union are held in other States, similar action will be taken.
Under the wise counsels of their grand old leader, the colored farmers are
laying a basis for the final adjustment of the race question as it appears
among the people.

National Economist, August 23, 1890.

10. THE NATIONAL ALLIANCE (HOUSTON, TEX.) ORGAN OF THE COLORED ALLIANCE:

The party papers are beginning to fight THE NATIONAL ECONOMIST for its
bold exposure of party frauds in Congress. THE ECONOMIST has and deserves
the confidence of the toiling masses. Would that every farmer in the United
States was a subscriber to THE ECONOMIST.
Thanks! The Alliance also says:
The Louisiana Farmers Alliance expelled nine members, who were also
members of the legislature, because they had voted in favor of the lottery
bill. The Farmers Alliance means business, if it isn't political, and the
future lawmakers may as well take notice and not vote to injure the people
unless they want to be retired from public service. The colored Alliances
are working in perfect harmony with the white Alliances, and are helping to
settle the race question by united effort along lines where all can agree.

National Economist, October 11, 1890.

11. THE ALABAMA MIRROR (SELMA) NOTES A GRATIFYING FACT

The canvass for the Democratic nominations in South Carolina and Georgia
has developed the fact that the Alliance is a power, and has put on the stump
speakers who are astonishingly well versed on all public questions, and who
can ably compete with any of the speakers of the opposition.
What is true of the Alliance in those States is also true in this State.
All that is needed is for the Alliance to assert itself.
The Mirror is in error in the following in that the admission of colored
members and not colored organizations was provided for. This met a condition
thought necessary by the brethren from the Northwest. There are colored Alliances in all the Southern States, having separate autonomy, and in harmony
with the Alliance, indorsing the provision made:
The National Farmers Alliance and Industrial Union permits the organization of colored Alliances, but at the same time denies to them representation in the National Alliance and in the Supreme Council. The Mirror is
in favor of equal and exact justice to all men, regardless of race, color
or previous condition, but it wants all colored organizations to have their
own State and national organizations, as well as their own schools and
churches and separate hotels and railroad accommodations.

National Economist, September 6, 1890.

12. THE NATIONAL ALLIANCE (HOUSTON, TEX.).

The National Alliance (Houston, Tex.) talks sensibly and firmly to the
million members of the Colored Farmers Alliance and Industrial Union, of
which it is the organ, General Superintendent Humphrey being the editor:
The general superintendent is expected to be in Louisiana, Tennessee,
Alabama, Georgia, Virginia, North Carolina, Florida, Mississippi, Texas and
other States. He will visit all the State Alliances in his reach. Let the
brethren come up prepared to help in the great work. Let the exchanges be
the first consideration. They are our own, and we know now that by supporting them we can free ourselves and our children from the grasp of the dreadful speculator. Let all see to it that our paper the National Alliance is
circulated and the people taught; for remember our hope is in education.
Finally do not forget the sub-treasury bill now before Congress. Our
government lends hundreds of millions of dollars every year to the rich
bankers and railroads without any interest. Then why not lend to the farmers
the same way? Farm supplies are much cheaper on cash at 1 per cent, than
on credit at 50 to 100 per cent. Let no man forget this. And when the
election comes vote for no man who is not in favor of the sub-treasury.
Don't let men deceive you about interest and the value of money. It costs
no more to print money than to print newspapers. The trouble is that a pack
of thieves are allowed to print the money and pretend that it costs. Stop
this extortion. Your votes can stop it. Vote neither Republican nor Democrat. Vote for yourselves and your families.

National Economist, September 6, 1890.

13. ELECTION BILL[51]

The White Folks Farmers Alliance at Ocala, Fla., adopted a resolution
condemning the Election Bill, and the Colored Folks Farmers Alliance at once
adopted a resolution condemning this political action. It was discovered
that the resolution against the Election Bill was dictated by the Democratic
Senator at Washington.

The Appeal (St. Paul), December 20, 1890.

14. THE COLORED ALLIANCE

Annual Address of the National Superintendent

The General Superintendent of the National Colored Alliance and Co-operative Union, R. M. Humphrey, delivered the following address at the Ocala convention of that body:

In the goodness of God you and I have been spared to meet again in an-nual convocation. Since our meeting a year ago a number of our leading mem-bers have been called from the ranks of the Alliance on earth to the fold of the great Alliance in heaven. With the mutual congratulations we extend to the living we cherish the names and memories of our dead and mourn the loss we have sustained in their death. Our order has enjoyed a year of great prosperity. We have made a forward step along the lines of our work.

Organization has been pushed into new States, and in all the organized States we have made a marked progress. In gathering together and organizing our people we must not lose sight of the fact that our work is chiefly edu-cational. The farmers and laborers of the United States lack nothing else as they lack education. Let memory recall your condition a few years ago. You had, as you, well remember, given very little thought to the science of government. To be sure you knew that all was not well. You told yourselves and believed that a return into abject slavery seemed to be inevitable. But a great change has come about since then. You and your neighbors are now able to meet in your Alliance halls and intelligently discuss the cause of all your troubles. You can now realize that the millions of acres your gov-ernment has given to a few men were taken from you, and that billions of dollars wrung from you by unjust and cruel taxation for the enrichment of your fellow citizens have impoverished and degraded you and your families. You have thus discovered the root of the disease that affects you. . . . To further the educational work of the Order one of our first cares was the establishment of an Alliance newspaper, which should have for its aim the furtherance of our principles, and the gradual enlightenment and education of the people. This enterprise drew upon us a considerable share of public attention, and several causes have operated to retard its progress.

1. Many of the white people, looking upon themselves as special favor-ites of Heaven, were violently opposed to the education of the colored race in any form.

2. The newspapers of the country, being wholly in the employ of mono-polies, and of the exploiting classes of our citizens, including speculators, landlords and stock gamblers, were radically opposed to the Alliance in all its phases, but their horror and resentment culminated at the thought of its proposing to educate and elevate a race of down-trodden slaves and serfs.

3. The colored people themselves, acting on the advice they received from these, their most bitter enemies, have shown remarkably small interest in enterprise involving so immediately their own welfare and the future destiny of their families.

We continue to hope that these conditions will yet be dissipated, and the National Alliance received, as it has ever deserved, the hearty support of the colored race.

One of the most cruel wrongs inflicted by the government upon the farmers is the power given the national bankers by, and with, the aid of certain speculators to withdraw the money from circulation, and so to contract or diminish the currency of the country that there shall not be enough left in circulation to buy our crops. It is doubtful if there is in circulation this year money enough to pay for the cotton crop at 4 cents a pound, and the wheat at 30 cents a bushel. And but for the influence of the Alliance and its Exchanges and its watchfulness there is no probability that your cotton would now sell above 4 cents a pound.

In view of this pressure brought to bear upon the farmer, we support an act to be known as the sub-treasury bill; therein providing that certain warehouses shall be conveniently established to our necessities in which we may store our crops, receiving from the government 80 per cent of their value to enable us to pay our debts and hold the crops for that sure advance in price which never fails to come with the opening of the spring season, or, rather, with the increase of money in circulation.[52]

Under this sub-tresury system speculation in the products of our farms would at once cease, because each farmer could hold his own produce, and when prices were reasonably good he could sell and repay to the government the money advanced. Identically the same arrangement asked for having been made by our government years ago in favor of the distillers of the country, and Congress having the sole power to issue money without paying interest or premium therefore, it was hope that no difficulty would be interposed in the way of a proposition so simple, and withal so important and so natural. But the money powers were awake. Speculators saw that they could not, if this wise and just measure became a law, any more buy up our crops at half price. National bankers saw that they could not any more lend us money at exorbitant rates of interest. And so all of these combined together to oppose us, and it now remains to be seen whether the farmers of the country will be true to themselves and may offer, choose only such men to represent them in Congress and in our State legislatures as will work for equal rights to all, and special privileges to none. Should such a course of action be adopted by all our labor organizations results may be slow, but in no way will they be uncertain. Prosperity will inevitably follow the enactment of just and equal laws.

At the request of thousands of the best and most influential colored people of this country, both within and outside the Alliance, it becomes my duty to call your attention to the necessity that exists for independence in political action. During this year no less than five representative bodies of colored men, assembled in Chicago, Washington, Raleigh, Richmond and Philadelphia, have declared their disaffection and unaffiliation with existing political parties. None of these, great conventions have appealed willing to formulate a platform that they considered would be satisfactory to their race. It remains, therefore, that you should give your earnest attention to this all-absorbing question, and if by a spirit of mutual compromise and conciliation you may be able to secure such pledges from the great labor organizations now represented in this city as will warrant reciprocal and hearty co-operation, doubtless great good will result to both the white and colored races.

You must remember that you are a race of farmers, seven-eighths of the colored people being engaged in agriculture, and these organizations now assembled in Ocala being chiefly farmers, your interests are theirs and theirs are yours. . . . [illegible] of the reformation of either of the existing political parties, or of inaugurating any considerable practical reform under their auspices. Those who hope to equalize the burdens of taxation, to relieve the depression of agriculture, or restore the government to the service of the people on whom it now tramples, must join together and stick together; and they must have as well a platform of principles distinctly their own. To this name and platform they must invite their fellow citizens of the United States as to a refuge and a fortress.

In the recent elections the influence of the Alliance was felt and every man realizes what tremendous power it is destined in the near future to exert. But it must be remembered that in this case the Alliance was fettered by party names which it could not bear, and in many of the States refused to vote at all. Among others we here mention that in Mississippi 40 per cent of the white and 70 per cent of the colored people absolutely refused to vote, or even attend the polls. In Texas and many other States the elections went rather by default than otherwise. The people were not satisfied with the standard bearers and rather than be considered Democrats or Republicans they remained at their homes and refused to take any part in electing men in whom they could feel no interest.

Our order is sadly in want of a national lecturer. It is a well-known truth in human nature that no cause can succeed for any great length of time without the presence of the living orator. Our difficulty heretofore has been that we were unable to pay for a suitable man to fill this important station. But if this body should select and indorse a suitable person for national lecturer, is it not probable, to say the least, that our sub-Alliances would second and support the work by paying him out of their home or subordinate treasuries? In our last annual message we congratulated your order on its independence. You have your own national charter, and your own peculiar forms of organization. You are independent of all other organizations, and thereby you are in a position to co-operate with any other whenever it may appear profitable to do so. We recommend that you persevere in this liberty; friendly to all, dependent upon none. This principle will in no way interfere with necessary co-operation and confederation. We feel that all of your surroundings call upon you to be at all times the confederates and helpers of those brave Alliance men who, alike in Kansas and Georgia, as Republicans and Democrats have carried Alliance banners over fields of confusion and battle to scenes of victory and peace. Finally, homes for the families of the colored people of the United States should be, by pre-eminence, the business of our Order. Whatever else we may do or fail to do, our work will be wholly unfinished and incomplete so long as three-fourths of our families are homeless. . . . [illegible]

But we have still a multitude of homeless renters. Perhaps the system of renting a home for our wives and daughters must in some sort continue to the end of time. But it is certain that we can greatly abridge, if not cure an evil, so monstrous. God has given this earth in usufruct to all the living. Men have as much right to monopolize the air we breathe and the sunshine that warms us as the land that by God's ordination feeds our families. We take this occasion to distinctly affirm that land is not property; can never be made property; holds no allegiance but to the man who lives on it. His improvements are his. The lands belongs to the sovereign people. In view of these indisputable truths we recommend to our people the principles of the single tax party, and that we should remove the burdens of taxation from all property, because the value of all property is decreased by taxation; but on the contrary land, if carrying all the taxes necessary to support the government, would not be held by speculators as it is now and would soon become abundant and cheap.[53]

There are already millions of our people, colored and white, who favor this single tax plan, and we recommend it to you as its enactment into law would place homes within the reach of all the people.

We rejoice that individual effort, with the assistance of diligence and economy, has been able to supply homes for so many, and we again call your attention to the importance and necessity of forming land and trust companies among yourselves with a view of furnishing homes to the unfortunate homeless of your race. This recommendation may appear superfluous in a view of our earnest exhortation a year since upon the same subject. But you did take our advice. You people did lay hold of this great work. You yourselves are now witnessing what great things have been accomplished in this direction; how many families now have homes? We therefore to-day rather congratulate you, and again send up to the front the watchword "Forward."

Again we acknowledge the wisdom and goodness of that God Almighty who has guided and defended us thus far, and laying all our hopes before Him and casting all our trophies at His feet we pledge ourselves to follow where He leads, until every chain of slavery is broken, every dungeon's door is thrown open, every captive is set at liberty, and the human family lifted to that high plane to which infinite love and mercy call them.

The National Economist, December 27, 1890.

15. UNSAVORY SENATOR [54]

The Farmer's Alliance, of Kansas, has ninety-one votes, and there is a determination to defeat Senator Ingall's for re-election, who is unsavory to the farmer element. They claim that Ingalls is not in sympathy with the measures which are for the relief of the farmers who are struggling under mortgages, railroad magnates and combines. A desperate struggle in politics is on, and the prospects are that Ingalls will be returned to private life. This, should it occur, will be unfortunate for the Negro race, as in many instances has his voice been quick to the race's defense.

The Freeman (Indianapolis), January 24, 1891.

16. THE RACE PROBLEM

By J. H. Turner, National Secretary-Treasury of the National[55]
Farmers' Alliance and Industrial Union

Since President Lincoln issued his emancipation proclamation, January
1, 1863, no question has provoked more discussion and serious consideration
that this one, and after twenty-eight years of discussion and legislation,
until recently the question seemed no nearer solution than it did when the
famous proclamation was issued. Writers of every character, both white and
black, have taken a turn at its discussion, and have widely differed as to
the means to be employed in its solution.

In writing this short article, I fully realize the gravity of the subject I have in hand, and will therefore remain near the shore. It is not
my purpose to solve this question, but simply to give my experience with
the negro in the South, coupled with such facts and suggestions as will
enable those who know but very little of the real conditions that exist in
the South, to form correct ideas in regard to the true conditions that exist
between the great masses of the white and colored people of the South. I
shall be perfectly satisfied with my effort, if I am able to elicit one
thought, word, or deed that will help to bring about a better understanding
all over this country, that will bring peace and prosperity to the great
common people, both white and black.

I hope the reader will pardon me for alluding to myself in this connection just enough to state that I was born on a farm in middle Georgia.
At the time I was born my father was a slave-owner. I have been intimately
associated with the negro on the farm, all my life, and know something of
the relation of the two races from actual experience. What I have to say on
this subject shall be entirely free from all party spirit, and solely in the
interest of truth.

After the war, when the negro found himself a citizen of the United
States, he was besieged by a class of pretended friends (I allude to the
carpet-baggers from the North) who have proven to be his worst enemies. To
control them politically, these same carpet-baggers promised each head of a
family forty acres of land and a mule, if he would vote right; that is, for
the carpet-baggers. The poor negro was not only promised this, but social
equality with the whites, and a great many other things which, since he has
found out better, he neither needs nor wants. The negro at that time followed willingly the lead of these fellows, because he had no one else to
follow, politically. The white people of the South ignored him politically,
and hated him, because he followed those whom they knew to be enemies of
good government. Under such circumstances, the negro was easily led to believe that his old master was his worst enemy, and would again enslave him
if he could, though when he would get into trouble or business complications
of any kind, the first man to whom he would apply for advice and counsel
would be his old master, who would almost invariably give him the best advice, and very often protect and defend him in his business affairs.

Thus the two races lived for several years after the war. As years
passed on, the negro found that the promises of the politician were made only
to be broken. When this dawned upon him, he at once began to rely upon himself, and from that day he began to make progress. He realized the fact that
if he was ever independent and happy, he would have to educate himself and
acquire property.

All the Southern States have public school systems. The whites and
blacks are required to attend separate schools, though the black child receives the same amount of public school fund that the white child does. In
my own State--Georgia--the colored children receive more money, in the way
of public school funds, than the whole colored population in that State pays
taxes of every kind; therefore they do not contribute anything toward supporting the State government. This statement will doubtless appear strange
to those who are unacquainted with the facts, and have only heard the demagogue's side of the question. However, an honest investigation among the
white and colored farmers (and they constitute a large majority of the population) will reveal many such facts.

The negroes are making a heroic effort to educate the rising generation,
and will send their children to school, when the public schools are opened,
whether they have anything to eat and wear or not. They will make any kind
of sacrifice to send their children to school.

A great mistake has been made, and doubtless thousands of honest people
have formed erroneous opinions in regard to the relations of the great
masses of the two races in the South, basing their opinions upon the reports
of riots and other disturbances in the towns and cities, in which, nine
times out of ten, no one took any part except a few worthless negroes, who
generally work by the day at some public work, and a few drunken white men,
who lounge around the saloons and street corners, and whittle goods boxes.
I have never heard of a race riot or disturbance of any kind in the rural
districts of the South, except two or three instances that occurred soon
after the war, in what is called the Black Belt of South Carolina, Mississippi, and Louisiana.

For partisan political purposes, these riots among the worthless whites
and blacks about the towns have been paraded in the partisan press of the
country for the purpose of keeping the old fire of sectional hate fanned
into a flame. Such things have been used in the North by the politician, in
the press and on the stump, to continue a solid Republican North, pretendly
that the Southern brigadier might be kept under; while the same class of
politicians in the South has used the same thing to keep a solid Democratic
South, pretendedly that negro supremacy might be kept down. The people of
the North and South have listened to these politicians, while plutocracy has
done its perfect work in robbing both.

The politician in the South has seemingly been in mortal fear of the
negro in politics, all the while, but has so managed as to keep the negro
in a solid political phalanx. If the negro was such a menace to good government, and the inferior race mentally, morally, socially, and naturally, why
have such tactics always been used as would keep them in one solid political
party?

The true answer to this question will perhaps shed more light upon this
subject than a great many are willing to admit is true. It is admitting a
thing that the evidence will not sustain, if we should claim that a superior
race, that has enjoyed the blessings of civilization, education, and culture
for ages, is unable to persuade an inferior race; and if persuasion were not
the thing to use, there were various other expedients to which easy access
could have been had, to divide their vote so that negro supremacy would have
forever been out of the question.

To convince the reader that the negro vote could have been divided long
ago, and will be divided in the near future, I will make a short quotation
from a newspaper article, written last February, by Rev. J. L. Moore, a
colored Methodist minister of Crescent City, Florida, who was a delegate to
the meeting of the Colored National Farmers' Alliance and Co-operative Union,
which met at Ocala, Florida, at the same time the National Farmers' Alliance
and Industrial Union met there. The article quoted from was written in reply
to an editorial that appeared in one of the partisan newspapers of Jacksonville, Florida, on the race question. It is as follows:--

"According to our privileges, I think we have helped the white men all
they could expect under our condition; and we are not clamoring for social
relations with the whites either. We do not want to eat at their tables,
sleep in their beds, neither ride in the cars with them; but we do want as
good fare as the whites receive for the same consideration. As to the Alliance, in the language of Hon. R. M. Hawley of Missouri, we believe this to
be its mission:--

"'No protection to party favorites; no force bills to keep up party and
sectional prejudices; no secret caucuses by members of Congress or members
of the legislatures, to consider matters of legislation. Let these be abbol-
ished by law. Also abolish all party primary elections and party conventions
for nominating candidates, and provide for a people's primary election, where
every voter can write on his ticket the name of any person he prefers for any
office, from President down to constable. Let the proper county, State, and
national officers, who shall be designated by law, receive the returns, count
up and authorize the result, which shall be that the candidate receiving the
highest number of votes, and the one receiving the next highest number for

each office shall be declared the contending candidates for final election.
This would empty politics of party strife and all its concomitant evils, and
lead to the representation of the leading industry of each district in Congress, and county in the State legislatures. Party blindness would be removed, and let in the clear light of the science of economical government.
I believe that non-partisanism will not reach its full and natural results
till these things are accomplished; and this I believe to be the mission of
the Alliance.'

"But, Mr. Editor, can we do anything while the present parties have control of the ballot-box, and we (the Alliance) have no protection? The greatest mistake, I see, the farmers are now making, is this: The wily politicians
see and know that they have to do something, therefore they are slipping into
the Alliance, and the farmers, in many instances, are accepting them as leaders; and if we are to have the same leaders, we need not expect anything else
but the same results. The action of the Alliance in this reminds me of the
man who first put his hand in the lion's mouth, and the lion finally bit it
off; and then he changed, to make the matter better, and put his head in the
lion's mouth, and therefore lost his head. Now, the farmers and laboring
men know in what manner they were standing before they organized; they lost
their hands, so to speak; now, organized in one body or head, if they give
themselves over to the same power that took their hand, it will likewise take
their head.

"Now, Mr. Editor, I wish to say, if the laboring men of the United States
will lay down party issues and combine to enact laws for the benefit of the
laboring man, I, as County Superintendent of Putnam County Colored Farmers'
Alliance, and member of the National Colored Farmers, know I voice the sentiment of that body, representing, as we did, 750,000 votes, when I say we are
willing and ready to lay down the past, take hold with them irrespective of
party, race, or creed, until the cry shall be heard from the Heights of
Abraham of the North to the Everglades of Florida, and from the rock-bound
coast of the East to the golden Eldorado of the West, that we can heartily
indorse the motto, 'Equal rights to all, and special privileges to none.'"

It is a pretty general custom with the Democratic party in the South,
that when the county executive committee meets to arrange for and call a
primary election, to nominate candidates for any office, it passes a resolution setting forth that no one except *white* Democrats will be allowed to vote
in that election. This county executive committee is generally made up of
the political bosses of the county,--the ones who are looking forward to the
loaves and fishes. Why not let colored Democrats vote in a primary election?
The politician says to himself: "That would never do; for then we would soon
have the negro vote divided, and the bugaboo of negro supremacy would vanish
like the mist before the sunshine, and my occupation, like Othello's would be
forever gone."

Judging from the signs of the times, the professional partisan politicians
both South and North, have had their day, and honest, good men will soon rise
up and administer the affairs of this nation in the interest of right and
justice. Henry W. Grady uttered the true sentiments of the great mass of
the Southern people, especially the farmers, when, in his speech before the
New England Society of New York, he gave utterance to the following eloquent
extract taken from that speech:-- [56]

"But what of the negro? Have we solved the problem he presents, or progressed in honor and equity toward solution? Let the record speak to the
point. No section shows a more prosperous laboring population than the
negroes of the South; none in fuller sympathy with the employing and land-
owning class. He shares our school fund, has the fullest protection of our
laws and the friendship of our people. Self-interest, as well as honor, demands that he should have this. Our future, our very existence, depends upon
our working out this problem in full and exact justice. We understand that,
when Lincoln signed the emancipation proclamation, your victory was assured,
for he then committed you to the cause of human liberty, against which the
arms of man cannot prevail [applause]--while those of our statesmen who
trusted to make slavery the corner-stone of the Confederacy doomed us to defeat as far as they could, committing us to a cause that reason could not
defend or the sword maintain in the sight of advancing civilization. [Renewed
applause.]

"Had Mr. Toombs said, which he did not say, 'that he would call the roll
of his slaves at the foot of Bunker Hill,' he would have been foolish, for
he might have known that whenever slavery became entangled in war it must
perish, and that the chattel in human flesh ended forever in New England
when your fathers--not to be blamed for parting with what didn't pay--sold
their slaves to our fathers--not to be praised for knowing a paying thing
when they saw it. [Laughter.] The relations of the Southern people with
the negro are close and cordial. We remember with what fidelity for four
years he guarded our defenceless women and children, whose husbands and fathers were fighting against his freedom. To his eternal credit be it said
that, whenever he struck a blow for his own liberty he fought in open battle, and when at last he raised his black and humble hands that the shackles
might be struck off, those hands were innocent of wrong against his helpless
charges, and worthy to be taken in loving grasp by every man who honors loyalty and devotion. [Applause.] Ruffians have maltreated him, rascals have
misled him, philanthropists established a bank for him, but the South with
the North, protests against injustice to this simple and sincere people. To
liberty and enfranchisement is as far as law can carry the negro. The rest
must be left to conscience and common sense. It must be left to those
among whom his lot is cast, with whom he is indossolubly connected, and whose
prosperity depends upon their possessing his intelligent sympathy and confidence. Faith has been kept with him in spite of calumnious assertions to
the contrary, by those who assume to speak for us, or by frank opponents.
Faith will be kept with him in the future, if the South holds her reason and
integrity. [Applause.]" [57]

The above was delivered before a Northern audience; and to show that
Mr. Grady was perfectly sincere in every word he said on this subject, I will
now give an extract from a speech delivered by him at the Augusta, Georgia,
Exposition, in 1889, which is as follows:--

As for the negro, let us impress upon him what he already knows, that
his best friends are the people among whom he lives, whose interests are one
with his, and whose prosperity depends on his perfect contentment. Let us
give him his uttermost rights, and measure out justice to him in that fulness
the strong should always give to the weak. Let us educate him that he may be
a better, a broader, and more enlightened man. Let us lead him in steadfast
ways of citizenship, that he may not longer be the sport of the thoughtless,
and the prey of the unscrupulous. Let us inspire him to follow the example
of the worthy and upright of his race, who may be found in every community,
and who increase steadily in numbers and influence. Let us strike hands with
him as friends--and as in slavery we led him to heights which his race in
Africa had never reached, so in freedom let us lead him to a prosperity of
which his friends in the North have not dreamed. Let us make him know that
he, depending more than any other on the protection and bounty of government,
shall find in alliance with the best elements of the whites, the pledge of
safe and impartial administration. And let us remember this--that whatever
wrong we put on him shall return to punish us. Whatever we take from him in
violence, that is unworthy and shall not endure. What we steal from hin in
fraud, that is worse. But what we win from him in sympathy and affection,
what we gain in his confiding alliance, and confirm in his awakening judgment,
that is precious and shall endure--and out of it shall come healing and
peace. [Applause.]"

Every time the partisan politician speaks on this subject he purposely
complicates and makes it worse; but thanks to an all-wise Providence for the
power that now rests in the hands of the Farmers' Alliance, which has taken
up this great question where the noble Grady laid it down. Until the advent
of the Farmers' Alliance, and Industrial Union and the Colored Farmers, the
negroes, as a class, have taken but very little interest in politics for
several years. They lost their former faith in politics and politicians,
which was very natural to one acquainted with the fact that they had always
been loyal partisans, and for their devotion and zeal they had been paid off
with a few appointments as postmasters in, most generally, third or fourth-
class postoffices.

Since the negroes have been organized into the Farmers' Alliance, they
have made considerable progress in the study of economic questions, and,

judging from the utterances of their leaders, they are willing and anxious
to sever all past party affiliations, and join hands with the white farmers
of the South and West in any movement looking to a betterment of their condition. The white farmers of the South, while they are more reluctant to
cut loose from party, are perfectly willing and ready to take the negro by
the hand and say to him: We are citizens of the same great country; we have
the same foes to face, the same ills to bear; therefore our interests as
agriculturists are one, and we will co-operate with you, and defend and protect you in all your rights.

In proof of the above, I will simply submit the agreement entered into
by the National Farmers' Alliance and Industrial Union and the Colored
National Farmers' Alliance and Co-operative Union, at their meetings in the
city of Ocala, Florida, on the second day of December, 1890, which is as
follows:--

"Your committee on above beg leave to report that we visited the Colored
Farmers' National Alliance and Co-operative Union Committee, and were received
with the utmost cordiality, and after careful consultation it was mutually
and unanimously agreed to unite our orders upon the basis adopted December 5,
1890, a basis between the National Farmers' Alliance and Industrial Union
and the Farmers' Mutual Benefit Association; to adopt the St. Louis platform
as a common basis, and pledge our orders to work faithfully and earnestly for
the election of legislators, State and national, who will enact the laws to
carry out the demands of said platform; and to more effectually carry it into
effect recommend the selection of five men from each national body, two of
whom shall be the president and secretary, respectively, who shall, with
similar committees from other labor organizations, form a Supreme Executive
Board, who shall meet as often as may be deemed necessary, and upon the joint
call of a majority of the presidents of the bodies joining the confederation;
and when so assembled, after electing a chairman and secretary, shall be empowered to do such things for the mutual benefit of the various orders they
represent as shall be deemed expedient; and shall, when officially promulgated
to the national officers, be binding upon their bodies until reversed by the
action of the national assemblies themselves--political, educational, and
commercial; and hereby pledge ourselves to stand faithfully by each other in
the great battle for the enfranchisement of labor and the laborers from the
control of corporate and political rings; each order to bear its own members'
expense on the Supreme Council, and be entitled to as many votes as they have
legal voters in their organization. We recommend and urge that equal facilities, educational, commercial, and political, be demanded for colored and
white Alliance men alike, competency considered, and that a free ballot and
a fair count will be insisted upon and had, for colored and white alike, by
every true Alliance man in America. We further recommend that a plan of district Alliances, to conform to district Alliances provided for in this body,
be adopted by every order in confederation, with a district lecturer, and
county Alliances organized in every county possible, and that the lecturers
and officers of said district and counties co-operate with each other in con-
ventional, business, educational, commercial, and political matters."

After the above agreement was entered into, the following communication
was received from the Colored National Farmers' Alliance and Co-operative
Union:--

"*To the National Farmers' Alliance and Industrial Union,* convened at
Ocala December 3, 1890: Alliance and Co-operative Union recognizes your fraternal greeting; gladly do we accept your right hand, and pledge ourselves
to the fullest co-operation and confederation in all essential things."

To one who feels a deep interest in this matter, this looks more like a
step in the direction of settling this question in the South than anything
that has ever been done since the question existed.

"God moves in a mysterious way, his wonders to perform," and who knows
but that he has raised up a Moses, in the person of these farmers' organizations, to lead us out of these our troubles? So mot it be.

N. A. Dunning (ed.), *The Farmers' Alliance History and Agricultural Digest*
(Washington, D.C., 1891), pp. 273-80.

17.

J. J. ROGERS, VIRGINIA STATE SUPERINTENDENT, COLORED FARMERS ALLIANCE,
    TO ELIAS CARR, PRESIDENT, COLORED ALLIANCE OF NORTH CAROLINA

Norfolk, Virginia
April 30, 1891

Dear Sir & Bro.
    A letter from Bro. R. M. Humphrey informs me that you want an organi-
zer for The Col. Alliance in your county. I recommend Rev. W. A. Pattillo,
who is State Lect. & Organizer, he has been in the work for a long time,
is perfectly reliable.

Elias Carr Papers, Eastern Carolina University

18. W. A. PATTILLO, NORTH CAROLINA ORGANIZER, COLORED ALLIANCE, TO
     ELIAS CARR, PRESIDENT, COLORED ALLIANCE OF NORTH CAROLINA

Granville County, North Carolina
April 30, 1891

Dear Sir,
    Please report progress if any for your part of the state. I have been
in the Southern & Western parts of the state with very good success. But
very hard work. I was assisted by Col. & White Alliance men which was great
help. I would like to know when you think would be a good time for me to
come down East? Let me hear from you.

Elias Carr Papers, East Carolina University

19. J. J. ROGERS, VIRGINIA STATE SUPERINTENDENT, COLORED FARMERS ALLIANCE,
    TO ELIAS CARR, PRESIDENT, COLORED ALLIANCE OF NORTH CAROLINA

Norfolk, Virginia
May 17, 1891

Dear Sir & Bro.
    Yours received & noted--Rev. Pattillo knows how to manage his people
better than anyone I know. He has been true to the best interest of the
Alliance from beginning. I will give as my experience with the Col. Alliance
that you need not expect to organize the Negro to-day & expect him to vote
with us to-morrow. But first organize them because their interest & ours as
farmers & laborers are the same, and teach them--they will then if called on
vote with us for our good & theirs--You understand all this--Excuse haste
for I am pushed with work. Would it not be to the interest of your County
to join this Exchange? If you think so & will let us know when & where your
next County meeting is to be held Mr. West or myself will try to visit and
explain its workings, etc.

Elias Carr Papers, East Carolina University

20. PEOPLE'S PARTY CONVENTION

    At the People's Party convention in Cincinnati, Mr. Powderly said:
"And to the South let me say, when you recognize the 'nigger' as a man, we of

the North will join with you hand in hand for reform."
    Some Southern representatives might have replied, that politically, in
giving offices to the Colored man, in business, by giving him employment
and in some other respects, the South does recognize him as a man to a greater
extent than the North. Socially, the South draws a broader line of demarkation than the North, but otherwise it gives the Colored man far better
opportunities than the South.

The Appeal (St. Paul), June 20, 1891.

21.   A GREAT ABSURDITY

    The idea of conflict of interest between the whites and blacks of the
South is a great absurdity. The fact is, that they are to a great extent
mutually dependent upon each other, and therefore that the most perfect harmony and unity of interest must exist. The Southern farmer knows and feels
it is his duty to protect and assist the poor colored people who are his
neighbors. No one realizes better than he, if he allows sharpers to swindle
the colored man by paying him excessively low prices for his cotton, by
taking advantage of his necessity for money, that the flooding of the market
with cotton at such low prices will tend to keep prices low until others
whose necessity for money was less at the beginning of the season are also
compelled to sell at the same low prices, and their sales will tend to perpetuate the low prices until all the crop is sacrificed on the same rock.
The fact is, that the law of self-preservation compels the Southern white
farmer to take the Southern black farmer by the hand and hold him out of the
clutches of the exploiter who every year manipulates the volume of moneys as
to develop the "power of money to oppress."

National Economist, July 4, 1891.

22.   COLORED FARMERS ALLIANCE MEETS

An Interesting Meeting--Officers Elected--The Speech of President
Williams of the Va. I.M.& B. Association

    The meeting of the Colored Farmers Alliances of the State of Virginia
held its second annual meeting August 8th and 10th, '91, Richmond, Va.,
10:30 A.M. Hon. R. M. Humphrey of Houston, Texas called the convention to
order. As J. J. Rogers, State Superintendent failed by some means to put in
his appearance, M. F. Jones of Lynchburg, Va., was made Secretary. Brother
Humphrey gave a good talk and able instruction to the meeting.
    The examination of credentials of delegates was the next business taken
up.
    This being done W. H. Warwick, State Lecturer and Organizer of Virginia,
requested the general Superintendent to explain fully to the convention how
the exchange should be conducted, as there existed grave doubts as to its
proper management, which was done with no hesitance. By motion of E. D.
Howell, a committee of (5) five was appointed to go to Norfolk and have an
examination of the books and report its condition. W. H. Warwick, E. Austin,
Jr., M. F. Jones, R. A. Manson and A. J. Doswell. The question of subscrib-
ing to the "National Alliance," a paper published for the benefit of the
organization was discussed with the hope of getting all the members to sub-
scribe for it.
    By motion of R. S. Hukless a committee of (7) seven was appointed on
permanent organization--committee: W. Williamson, R. A. Manson, R. S.
Hukless, S. H. Mayo, Jr., J. B. Riddle, E. Austin, Jr., and E. D. Howell.
    By motion of M. F. Jones, the President of the Va. Industrial, Mercan-
tile and Building Association was extended an invitation to address the
convention and that a committee of three be appointed--J. B. Riddle, John Smith

and M. F. Jones. Hon. R. M. Humphrey left on Sunday the 9th inst.

By motion of M. F. Jones a committee of (3) three was appointed to draw up a circular letter getting forth paramount work of the convention and the change of officers, etc. H. C. Green, F. R. Ivy, and M. F. Jones.

Promptly at 2 P.M. on the 2nd day the chair declared that order of the hour was the election officers.

Report of Committee on permanent organization. For Superintendent of State, W. H. Warwick vs. J. J. Rogers, Trustees: R. A. Manson vs. D. C. Beazley, M. F. Jones vs. H. C. Green, A. J. Doswell vs. J. T. Kinney. Tellers: J. A. Lee and F. B. Ivy. The officers were ballotted for and the votes resulted as follows:

For State Superintendent W. H. Warwick, for Trustees: R. A. Manson, M. F. Jones and A. J. Doswell. The Supt. elect came forward with gratitude to the convention for the honor conferred upon him, in like manner followed the Trustees.

By motion of J. B. Riddle the convention proceeded to elect a Board of Directors consistinf 11 members.

> W. H. Warwick,
> M. F. Jones
> A. J. Doswell
> R. A. Manson
> A. B. Goins
> R. S. Hukless ⎬ Board
> Y. E. Hines
> H. C. Green
> E. Austin, Jr.
> J. B. Riddle
> J. T. Kinney

By motion of W. H. Warwick, the "Midland Express," was adopted as the State organ of the Colored Farmers Alliance.

By motion of A. J. Doswell a committee of (7) seven was appointed on legislation--A. J. Doswell, H. C. Green, J. W. Cary, F. B. Ivy, W. H. War- wick, B. Ellis, and J. B. Riddle.

By motion of A. J. Doswell a committee of (5) five was appointed on resolutions. H. H. Jenkins, A. B. Goins, E. Austin, Jr., J. T. Kinney and D. C. Beasley

The hour having arrived to hear an address by the president of Virginia Industrial, Mercantile and Building Association,

Mr. Chairman and members of the Colored Farmers National Alliance of Virginia:

It is with no small degree of pleasure that I accept the invitation extended to me to address you on this occasion. I will say however, that you may congratulate yourselves upon the opportunity offered you to meet here in this our city, under the dome of the Capitol of our honored old State, distinguished for her statesmen, her orators, and her liberal and intelligent citizens. I take the liberty to welcome you in our midst, to our homes and to the common pleasures we enjoy.

We do not hesitate to acknowledge our allegiance to the farmers, and to confess our dependence upon them for our food, clothes, and to some extent our fuel. We are extremely dependent upon you for the privileges of going to your farms where we enjoy the refreshing country air, inhale the odor of the fresh mown hay,--a relish that cannot be enjoyed in the crowded and noisy city.

In coming before you, I do not come in the capacity of a politician nor do I have any political aspiration other than the position we may be placed in, will demand, but I come before you as one interested in a dependent, and to some extent an oppressed people. I come to you as one who views the condition of the colored people of this country similar to that of the sinner from a Biblical standpoint. Wherein it was said, "First seek ye the kingdom of Heaven and all things shall be added unto you, so also, I say to the colored people first seek religion, and acquire the possession of wealth, and other things will be added.

I would have you be cognizant of the above fact, irresponsible, dependent, thriftless people cannot demand anything, politically, materially, and but a very little intellectually, regardless of their number.

Many of us are aware of the fact, that ten years after the war was lost in looking for "My young mule" and "My forty acres of land," that we expected from some one else.

Next came the Freemen's Bank, that was managed by some one else; ever since that, some of us have been thinking that our "Salvation" was hanging upon politics, but careful study and experience have proven that we lose more such than we gain, since we have had so many faulty leaders to contend with.

The right to vote, we do not deny, but we do say that there is but little to be gained by any people with nothing in hand except a bare ticket, without something to back it. This is not the age for us to be a slave to any political party, but on the contrary we should launch our boats out into the seas of industry and trust God to steer them aright.

When we have our own houses, not only for the use of ourselves, but rented, out to others; when we can shake hands with skill and industry in every department with our own capital, bosses and clerks, then and not until then, will we receive that recognition for which we are each day struggling. It has been said by one "That he who would be free must himself strike the blow." If we would be free, independent and progressive and grow to an intelligent race, we must ourselves, make the effort, and our friends (the better element of the white race), will assist us. When we do this we will only do what the better classes of white people have advised us to do. They have said don't take up all of your time with politics, but buy homes, build houses, run business, and educate your children and we will help you.

I feel it due the best element of white people to say, that the colored man has but little to fear from the old-fashioned aristocratic Southern gentlemen, those who know the real character and disposition of the colored people, and who were to some extent brought up around the colored mamma's knees.

We, having come up out of the wilderness of slavery have a double duty to perform, by struggling to get our cattle upon a thousand hills; our manufactories, our stores and commission houses. When we will have done these things, we will have access to the legislative halls and after getting there we will have something to represent.

We must acknowledge our heartfelt thanks and gratitude to the white people for the good they have done us, and are still doing, yet we are not forgetting of the fact, they claim to like Negroes in their places, and will assist them.

Now, if being courteous and polite means staying in our places, we do that. But they claim we get out of our places when we run for public office to dominate or rule over them. This they claim we shall not do, North as well as South, but they say if we want office, start up business among ourselves, buy homes, build houses, run manufactories, stores, and commission houses, and they will help us, thus making offices for our young men and women when they come out from the schools and colleges with a classical edu-

It is, gentlemen, for this reason I address you, with the full assurance of support from our good white friends from all over the land. We are in a good position to make a break for the buiness world. We have our farmers to supply, our commission houses and our wood yeards, and we have purchasers for our goods, clerks for our stores, and renters for our houses and capital to carry on these things if we would only put it together.

We have in the cities our Mechanics, our Lawyers, our Doctors, our Bank and our young ladies whose voices can warble like birds, and render such melodious music that one is lulled in the noon day, at its sound.

Thus we see the importance of uniting our forces,—the forces of the colored people in the country and those of the city, co-operating together in one gigantic business institution.

I am glad to know you all are so well organized because in union there is strength, there is power, a power that can be used either for a good or bad purpose. It is for you all, as colored Farmers Alliance to say whether you are receiving any benefit from your order or not, it is for you to say whether you have any of your people at the great chief-head in the big office where the money goes.

I know the deputies face the cold winter's wind and are scorched by the hot burning summer's sun, traveling to and fro to organize these sub-branches,

also I know many of your members are guided to their humble homes by nothing
but the mid-night star, traveling weariedly and slowly from your lodge or
hall rooms where you meet from time to time paying your dues and discussing
subjects tending to your advancement. Whether you accrue any benefits, I am
unable to say, if you do not, however, then we say it is time to call a halt
in that direction and co-operate and associate yourselves with the Va. I.M.
& B.A., an organization run by your people, where the clerks in the main office are your people, and where the profits will go to your people. If you
do these things we will be on the road to success.

There is a lack of confidence we have in ourselves, that must be re-
legated to the rear. If you find a dishonest person in charge of your affairs, don't break up the concern, but throw him over the battlement, as did
God when "Lucifer the Great" became unruly, and let the good work go on.

Let us be inspired and confide in each other and we will be better
citizens; we can pay more to support the government, and will be more respected by our white brother.

Fear not to step out into the free air of independence, be not content
to bear others fruits. We inhale the common air, and bask in the universal
sunshine. We glory in the grass, the passing clouds and the flowers. And
we must unite our forces for good.

The Association of which I have been honored with the Presidency, proposes to raise a capital from the colored people and establish stores and
other business enterprises in the several counties and cities in this and
other States, that we might get a portion of the millions of dollars that
are spent in purchasing the various commodities for the support of ourselves
and families.

This Association when successfully put into operation will spread its
wing over our common country and give employment to thousands of our young
men and women who are to-day crowding the doors of our school houses and
institutions, and being graduated yearly, going forth into the world empty
handed and seeking employment where it cannot be found. We must join hands
for the purpose of opening up the avenues of industry, and put in motion the
wheel of industry so our children can seek employment at our hands. Our
present condition and mode of procedure relative to this matter, demands our
immediate attention. Unless something is done to better the condition, we
will never tread the paths of progress which leads to highest peaks of independence.

Our capital stock is $100,000--divided into shares of $5.00 each. And
in order to keep down monopoly, no one will be allowed to buy more than one-
twentieth of the Capital Stock. The shares of stock are transferable and
will give a perpetual income to the widows and orphans after the death of the
holder or holders. The only after payment is a semi-annual fee of twenty-
five cents.

A dividend of the net earnings of the Association will be declared
annually, State Fairs will be given annually under the auspices of the
Association and each share-holder will receive an equal proportion of the
profits accruing therefrom.

Will this not help to ameliorate our condition and give us some standing
in the business world, and receive that recognition we are so unjustly denied
--"Get hold of the strings of the purses of gold and the doors of the palaces
will swing wide to bid you welcome."

Thanking you for the honored invitation and courteous attention I conclude, hoping that I have at least started you to thinking, and the thoughts
arising, will cause you to exclaim with one accord. We are you, we are with
you.

Mr. Williams gave an excellent address touching on what the Negro should
do to become a nation. He said many things to inspire on the one hand and
to be desired on the other, after which the chair and E. Austin, Jr., responded in behalf of the convention. M. F. Jones offered a resolution showing
how important it is to have our people united upon the two bodies co-operate
as far as practicable.

National delegates and alternates: W. H. Warwick and M. F. Jones; E.
Austin Jr., and R. A. Manson, Alternates.

Mr. Chairman--I have a resolution to offer in connection with the address
just delivered.

WHEREAS, George Williams, Jr., Esq., president of the Virginia, Industrial,

Mercantile and Building Association has met us, the C.F.A. in the State
meeting now convened and delivered a speech setting forth the aims and objects of the aforesaid institution, and

WHEREAS, we are made glad to know that out of its growth, the Negro is
to be blessed and by its influence, "Ethiopia shall soon stretch out her
hands unto God;" and,

WHEREAS, we view on every hand that which promises to us as a race a
brighter future in business, trade, art and education, it is not for us to
hesitate when for us to succeed we must focolize our aims, energies and
business tact on one united effort and must concentrate our powers, geniuses
and means on that business principle which elevates us to the topmost platform of the business world, by bridging over every chasm of discord by the
sweet fragrance of a hearty co-operation by tearing down every mountain of
opposition by "gordian knot" of a solid union. And,

WHEREAS he who would be free from the lethargy, or ugly monster of
Independence must strike the first blow; Therefore be it,

RESOLVED that we do now co-operate with the Virginia Industrial Mercantile and Building Association when such terms of co-operation can be agreed
upon for the following reasons:

1st. Because our objects and declaration of purposes are one, and have
entwined themselves as a net work.

2nd. Because, it is impossible for either to be what it should be in
strength and efficacy both competitors with the same prize in view.

3rd. Because our means are small and our needs can only be appeased by
unity and city and country alike, must come to the redemption of the race.

4th. Because the State Fair cannot be a success unless we clasp our
hands into a firm co-operation and unite the Negro in-to-to.

5th. Because two organizations with aims and objects so closely related as these two can't successfully move along in their present attitude
without jealousy of one encroaching upon the rights of the other, to some
extent from which a friction would set in--detrimental to each.

WHEREAS, our sojourn here has been so pleasant and interesting, and
since we have been so cordially received by the citizens of this city,

RESOLVED, that we tender our sincere thanks to the citizens and friends
of this city for their kind hospitality; and also to the judge of Henrico
county for his kindness in giving us the use of the Court House. Also be it

RESOLVED, That we extend our thanks to the reporters of the city
papers who have so carefully published our work.

Respectfully submitted,
E. AUSTIN, Jr.

Richmond Planet, August 15, 1891.

23. THE CONVICT LEASE SYSTEM [58]

The country has recently been considerably agitated over the convict
troubles in Tennessee. This is no new thing. The same question has been the
cause of more or less agitation for a number of years. Every labor platform
of modern times has announced against the competition of convict labor with
free labor. It has been an issue to a greater or less extent in nearly
every State election of modern times. A candidate who desired popularity with
the masses has simply announced against it, to secure his election, and still
the tendency has been for the Legislatures to perpetuate the system, apparently in order to lessen the expenses of conducting the penitentiaries.

There are some fundamental principles involved in the question that it
is well at this time to consider. First, the government has a duty to perform. Second, the people have rights which should be respected. Third, the
convicts themselves have rights which should be respected.

The duties of the government in regard to criminal offense, and criminals
who commit them are indicated by its duty to society in general. In the
exercise of its plain and evident duty to protect the individual in the

pursuit of happiness and the peaceable enjoyment of the fruits of his own labor, it is evidently its duty to restrain those who would violate this pursuit and this enjoyment. If, in order to secure that end, it becomes necessary to deprive some citizen of his liberty, even that is considered justifiable, as a matter of absolute right. No one in this day and time will for a moment contend that the government has a right to inflict any punishment as a matter of retribution. Retribution, revenge, or even chastisement is entirely beyond the province of government as now understood. The only theory on which it is pretended to justify the government in depriving a citizen of his liberty is, that he exercises his liberty so as to be a menace to the freedom and happiness of the public and in such a manner that the public good requires he should be restrained. True, restraint is practically a punishment to him or a condition which is disagreeable to him; which fact being generally known will deter others from engaging in like unlawful passages. The plain duty of the government, while such person is under confinement or restraint from his liberty, is to reform, instead of punish him, if possible. The duty of the government is then to restrain from liberty those persons whose course when at large seems to threaten the peace of society or the safety of property. In doing this, it should conduct the restraint in such a manner as to be at the least expense to society at large, and to interfere in the least possible way with the individual rights of the person so confined or restrained from liberty. This points out a rational way of diminishing crime. It can never be diminished by retribution, revenge and punishment. It can only be diminished by education and proper restraints.

The rights of the public are largely foreshadowed in the above description of the duties of the government. The public has the right to insist that the government shall protect each citizen in the pursuit of happiness and in the peaceable enjoyment of the fruits of his labor, and that for this purpose the government shall deprive such persons of their liberty as would violate these plain rights. That in depriving such persons of their liberty for the benefit of the general good, the government shall incur as little expense as possible in maintaining the institutions necessary to secure their confinement. The other rights of the public will be better shown by consideration of the rights of the criminal.

The rights of the criminal are all the rights of the citizen except that of liberty or personal freedom. He is under a restraint imposed for the good of society. One of his rights has been taken from him by due process of law for the benefit of the whole community, and that one alone is the only one that either the community or the government has a right to deprive him of. But in doing that, the rights of others may be invaded. For example, take a criminal who has an innocent wife and children, with no means of support except his labors; when the government deprives him of his liberty and confines him in prison, it makes paupers of his wife and children. They may be innocent and pure. He may in spite of his crimes love them as sincerely as is possible for man to love and be desirous of the chance to labor for their support; evidently the government or society has no right to deny him that privilege if he can do it. And this brings out the point that while society and the government has a right to deny him his liberty, they have no right to appropriate the fruits of his labor. There are many convicts who would work diligently and pay all the expenses of their own support and guarding, as they are supported and guarded, and make enough money besides to support their families, if they only had a chance. Of course there are many who would not, but there are some who would, and hence many believe no government has a right to sell the labor of the convicts to contractors at all. All condemn the evil of selling such labor at a nominal price, so that it brings nothing to the convict or the government; but go to the contractor, and they enable him to cut prices on the product and interfere with the labor market of the country outside. This system, is introducing a species of slavery to compete with the free labor of the country, in violation of a fixed principle of justice. Every single article that is a product of the labor or a convict should be sold by the government at the highest market price for like commodities anywhere in the United States and the proceeds set apart for the use of the convict or his family as may be best for him in the long run. Under such a system of administration based on right and

justice, the products of convict labor would not demoralize prices and come
into any unfair competition with the products of labor on the outside, consequently it would tend toward preserving the rights of the public in this
particular as well as those of the convicts. It would stop an iniquitous
system of jobbing whereby a few men were enabled to appropriate the labor
of thousands of slaves and use it to demoralize the prices of honest labor.
Again, such a condition or such a system would be a great incentive to the
convicts to labor and reform, because those who had loved ones to support
would find that in their own exertion they had the ability to do so, and
those who had not but had been impelled to crime by sloth, would find that
they could lay up a snug sum during their confinement, which upon liberation
would enable them to have a start in life which might prevent them from
ever again being exposed to like temptation. It would tend to make the
prison self-sustaining, because those who work of their own volition will do
more, and turn out more, and be more easily managed, than those who are
forced to work by whip and punishment with no signs of reward ahead. The
public need fear no competition from convict made goods where the labor was
not jobbed off by contract, but where everything was done under government
supervision and the products sold at the highest market price for like commodities. As long as prices are not demoralized by the competition of convict made commodities there is no injustice. They would work the same outside. It is not a question, however, for solution in a single day. It has
been a long time growing up, and it has been for some time creating more or
less dissatisfaction which seems certainly to foretend the speedy termination of the convict lease system.
    Many other potent reasons might be given for its termination, but in
this article the effort has been simply to strike at some of the fundamental
principles involved, and show that the abuses all depend on evils in principles that underlie the system.

The National Economist, August 15, 1891.

24. CAMP MEETINGS

    National Alliance (Houston,Tex.) says: We have notice from many of the
white Alliance lecturers and leaders that the Colored Alliance members will
be welcome at the camp meetings, and will receive all possible attention and
instruction. We hope that a great many of our people will avail themselves
of these opportunities. Applications come to us daily from the Alliance
who want lecturers. In most of the States our lecturers complain to us
that they have not been supported and cannot continue to work without better
pay. We therefore rejoice at the invitations extended our members to attend
the white people's camp meetings and hear them. We beg you to attend. It
will do you good.

National Economist, August 22, 1891.

25. NOTICE

*To the Presidents of State Alliances, State Unions, State Agricultural
Societies and other Agricultural Associations of the Cotton States:*

    In pursuance of resolutions adopted by the State Alliances of South
Carolina, Georgia and other cotton States, a convention of delegates from
all State organizations interested in the cultivation of cotton, its manufacture or sale, are hereby called to meet in Atlanta on Tuesday, September
14.
    We expect every agricultural State organization of the cotton States to
send delegates, colored as well as white. Every question connected with

the cotton crop of the South will be under discussion.   Come one, come all.

National Economist, September 12, 1891.

26. AFRO-AMERICANS AND THE PEOPLE'S PARTY

At the convention of the Farmers' Alliance, or Peoples party, in Texas,
there were a few Afro-American delegates. Upon the attitude that the Alliance should bear to the Afro-American in that State, there was considerable discussion, and greater freedom of speech was permitted to the delegates than they have ever had in any political convention outside of the
Republican party, and as a result two of them were put on the committee
representing the State at large, but whose special work should be among
Afro-Americans.

The Plaindealer has always welcomed these side issues in the South,
since for a time it sets faction against faction among the bourbons, and
opens a wedge for free speech and greater political liberty, and enables the
race to make a step forward. Some impression, too, is made by these issues,
toward dividing the whites on political subjects, impels all to enlist the
support of the Afro-American, causing them also to divide on issues, unres-
trained by a unity of purpose growing out of their condition.

Free speech in Texas in the ordinary assembly, unless used in glorifying
the lost cause and eulogizing its dead and living leaders, and abusing Washington and Lincoln, has not been tolerated, and they who used it otherwise
than according to Texas thought, did so at their peril, hence it is that the
position assumed by Afro-American delegates seems all the more encouraging
from the sturdy independence manifested. The Plaindealer gives a part of the
debate to show its nature.[59]

The speaker having referred to the claims of the colored man, the following colloquy followed.

Melvin Ward, colored,--I would like to know what you mean by considering
the colored men's claims in contradistinction to the claims of any other
citizen of the United States?

The chair disclaimed drawing distinctions. He had been asked who were
entitled to work in the organization. The committee would proclaim the answer to the world.

Captain Evans--Every colored citizen in these United States has the same
privileges that any white citizen has, and that is what is meant.

Melvin Ward--When it comes down to practice, such is not the fact. If
we are equal why does not the Sheriff summon Negroes on juries? And why hang
up the sign "Negro" in passenger cars? I want to tell my people what the
People's party is going to do. I want to tell them that it is going to work
a black and a white horse in the same field.

The Chair--That is what I mean in bringing it before the committee, so
that they should know our action.

Dr. Harris suggested that there be white and colored clubs, and let them
confer together.

Mr. Johnson--Resolved that each Congressional district, through its
chairman, appoint one colored man to co-operate with those already appointed
in the organization of the People's party.

A delegate--This will not do. The colored people are a part of the
people and they must be recognized as such.

Colored Delegate Hayes--If you cannot take us and elect us in this convention we will not thank you. We do not propose to be appointed by chairman. You must appoint us by the convention and make us feel that we are men.
You will lose in spite of the devil and high water if you do not treat the
Negro squarely.

Captain Evans--We have no disposition to ostracize the colored people,
but they are poorly represented here. The only thing we can do in the absence of their representation is to elect a representative for the State at
large, and I recommend that Mr. Hayes be elected, and let him organize the
colored people in harmony with the People's party.

A delegate offered an amendment placing two colored men upon the committee from the State at large. Adopted.

Detroit Plaindealer, September 18, 1891.

27. SPLIT AMONG WHITES

The Times Democrat of New Orleans professes to be much disturbed over the growth of the Farmers' Alliance in that State, because it seems to augur a split among the whites. The Plaindealer most earnestly wishes that such a condition as is described below may come, for out of it something better might come to the Afro-American in that State.

"What we have fought against--a split among the whites, a white movement against the Democratic party--has come at last, and we do not think the danger can be over-estimated. The new party has in its platform a plank that is extremely popular with the farmers, and is winning converts among them throughout the Union; it has a National organization behind it, very strong in some of the States, and very active and ambitious; it has a good backing of white voters in North Louisiana; and it has some tens of thousands of Negro voters already organized in its interest, and pledged to carry out its aims and purposes. Here is the nucleus of a new party, and what is worse, there is division in the ranks of the whites among the Democrats who have fought side by side in former battles.

We have laid the facts before the people because we think the Democrats should make every possible effort to meet the new party at the very beginning, and do all in their power to crush it out before it becomes too dangerous, and because we believe that every effort should be made to show the men who are embarking in this movement how dangerous it is to peace and the political future of Louisiana.

There is no State in the South that can stand a third party just now. A movement of this kind turned over Virginia to the Republicans, and Arkansas made a very narrow escape. Louisiana is threatened with the danger to-day, and will escape only by antagonizing and opposing in every way possible this third party movement, which has been presented to the voters by leading lights in the Farmers' Alliance.

Detroit Plaindealer, October 2, 1891.

28. THE RANKEST BOURBON

The Farmers' Alliance, which is now a thorn in the flesh of the old-line bourbon, is protesting that every man must have a fair chance to vote, and have his vote counted. It occurs to the Plaindealer that Governor Tillman of South Carolina made similar promises when he needed the Afro-American vote to place him where he is. After election he imitated Andrew Johnson in catering to the rankest bourbon ideas in trying to edge himself into the society of the bloods. He has been snubbed at every attempt, and will no doubt join with other Alliance men again in crying for a free ballot and a fair count.[60]

Detroit Plaindealer, October 9, 1891.

29. WHEN THINE ENEMY SPEAKS WELL OF YOU

The *New Orleans Picayune,* of a recent date, has an editorial on "The Negro Alliance in the Cotton Field," the tone of which, coming from the source it does, is a compliment to the Negro's perspicuity and general business sagacity, that is quite worthy of notice.

Speaking of the two organizations, the Negro and the white Alliance,

The *Picayune* expatiates as follows:

"When the white farm proprietors formed their Alliance, the Negro farm laborers imitated the example and also organized an Alliance. The white agriculturists encouraged their colored brothers in establishing these secret organizations, fully expecting to use them in forwarding their own special schemes. But the Negroes, recognizing their opportunity to do something for their own advantage, lost no time in learning the lesson taught them by the whites. If the farm proprietors can use a secret, oathbound order to further their interests there is no sort of reason why the Negro farm laborers should not use a secret organization for the own ends, and to remove all doubts on the subject the Negroes have consumated just such an undertaking. While the white Alliance has been working away at its Sub-treasury scheme the Negroes appear to have busied themselves with something decidely more practical. They have not troubled themselves about converting the National Government into a money-lending concern, nor do they seem to care whether or not the Government shall ever control the railways and all other private corporations. What is of vastly more importance to the black brothers of the Alliance is that there shall be an increase in the wages of the laborers who gather the cotton crop.

While the white farmers are figuring on great questions of State policy the black brothers, in the secrecy of their fraternal order, have decreed that the wages of cotton pickers shall be doubled. That is enough to knock all the brotherhood out of the bosoms of the white membership. It may be ten or one hundred years before the sub-treasury business can be put in operation, but this cotton-picking business takes effect at once. In view of the extreme low price of cotton this doubling of the price gathering the crop is a stunning blow."

But while *The Picayune,* unconsciously perhaps, compliments the Negro, true to its bourbon instincts, it scents danger and commercial evil in this secret organization, and the union of the Negroes, and is disposed, as the following language implies to place the blame where, in its judgment, it belongs:

"The farmers (the white) will have only to thank themselves for this new trouble, but recrimination and criticism can no good to relieve the evil. It is to be hoped that the disease has not spread extensively."

Per contrary to *The Picayune,* let us hope that the "disease," if so it is, will continue to spread until the great principle of racial union and co-operation is understood by all the race, and being understood, will, upon all occasions, and for all purposes, be acted upon.

In union there is indeed strength, force and directness, and without it, little, if anything can ever be accomplished for good in the multipled interest of a people. It is for this reason that this move on the part of the Negro farmers is a significant one, full of hopeful signs.

When the Negro race, as a whole, learns to observe and guard their racial interests, in labor marts, by uniting in demands for a just and fair equivalent for physical strength expended, it may also learn to demand a just and fair equivalent for influence and aid extended through the avenue of the ballot.

The only difference between the tyrants of labor and the tyrants of political parties, is this: the former grows rich and arrogant from the profits of labor expended in their service, frequently ill paid, while the latter grows famous, sometimes very rich, and generally arrogant, from the political fealty of voters, that in the case of Negro voters, especially, has never been appreciated at their just valuation.

The Freeman (Indianapolis,) October 10, 1891.

30. THE SOUTHERN ALLIANCE--LET THE NEGRO TAKE A THOUGHT

The Farmer's Alliance has been strong in the South, and at the recent meeting in this city many of the delegates hailed from that section.

Their plea has been and is justice for the farmers, and in pursuance thereof they make many complaints, and claim a good many things. Especially do they murmur at unjust laws and their discrimination against them as a class, all of which reminds us of the old saw, "that it makes a great difference whose ox gets gored."

Among a great many accusations, they make 'plaint that the halls of legislation are closed against them, their burden of taxation is too much, that they are not fairly represented in the national halls of legislation, and while the manufacture's and corporate interests engage the attention of the Solons, their's are completely ignored and avoided.

For all of these reasons they are sick and disgusted with both the old parties, and in the name of a suffering class demand a new deal that will comprehend within its broad embrace, the abolition of the national banking system, a recreation of the currency, the free coinage of silver, more paper money, and a series of Government loans for the especial delectation and benefit of farmers, and in accordance with the white man's nature when in distress, they are shouting "good nigger," and inviting him to help them out of their supposed dillema.

Should the colored man help them, and are their demands consistent with the kind of treatment that for over a quarter of a century they have stood by in silence and saw meted out to him?

Most of the southern delegates came from States, that since the war have never known such a thing as honest elections.

Within twenty-five years, scores of men have been sent to Congress, who secured their seats through fraud intimidation and murder.

These Southern Alliance delegates, who were present with us last week in Indianapolis, know this to be true, and in many instances, no doubt have been active procurators of such crimes.

Thousands of colored voters and farmers have been made the victims of these machinations and outrages, and these self-same, white farmers, who are shouting now, "Help me Casius or I sink,"--have either assisted to make them victims, or have stood placidly by chewing the cud of indirrerence, while it was being done.

"Those who seek equity must first do equity" is a principle of chancery jurisprudence, older than most of the thrones of the world.

Strange how this class of American citizens, who have been so long blind to the injustice meted out to their black fellow-citizens, are so suddenly and violently moved, to demand it in pugnacious tones, for themselves.

They would appear in a much more consistent plight, did they first commence by demanding that the rights and opportunities that for nearly twenty years, the Negro has been robbed of in the southland, be restored and given back to him.

They hold their hands up for succor and relief, but those hands are dripping with blood, and are marked with "damn'd spots that will not out."

They desire free silver. Let them first guarantee to their brother in black, a free ballot, and an honest count. If government should control railroads, why, by the same course of reasoning should not government control elections, for we say to these ex-Negro haters, masquerading in the guise of "friendly farmers" that that principle that demands for the humblest black man of the South, full and perfect protection, in his constitutional rights as an American citizen, is a million times more vital, to the future of this huge misruled commonwealth than every one of the prayed for reforms demanded by the Farmer's Convention.

Let the southern farmers first remove the mote from their own eye, before they point with leering gaze to the beam contained in others eyes.

They have worked iniquity for many years against the Negro of the South, and until they shall show some signs of purging themselves of these habits, and the stain they have left upon their souls, let the Negro look to himself, and "beware of the Greek's bearing gifts."

The Freeman (Indianapolis), November 28, 1891.

31.   SOCIAL EQUALITY

Is It Favored by Ex-President Cleveland?

When Grover Cleveland was inducted into office, Frederick Douglas
(colored), an appointee of President Arthur, was Recorder of Deeds for the
District of Columbia. This office is an exceedingly desirable one as the
estimated fees run up the income of the incumbent from twenty to thirty
thousand dollars per year. Making it a salaried office at $6,000 per annum
has been agitated, but politics forbid, and the old custom of collecting
fees still predominates. The activity in the real estate market of the
District for the last few years has been great, and the consequent income of
the recorder much enhanced thereby. [61]
      Mr. Douglas was retained in office by Mr. Cleveland, as he himself
states, almost a year; was allowed to then resign, and a colored man from
Albany, N. Y., by the name of Matthews, named by the President. This nomination, strange to relate, was received with such disfavor by a Republican
Senate, that in executive (secret) session it absolutely refused to confirm
it. Mr. Cleveland, entire unabashed, energetically applied himself to
scouring the country for another man of the same race, and finally supplied
his desire by the appointment of one Trotter, from Boston, Mass., also a
negro, whom the Senate, it is claimed reluctantly confirmed to get the matter
out of its way. Recorder Trotter, during his administration of office, fell
seriously ill. A wag of Washington, knowing the temper of its people, which
was in no wise friendly to the colored incumbent and his force of dusky
assistants, male and female, who aggravated the business men during their
visits to the office by stern admonitions to "heed the rules and remove their
hats in the presence of ladies," etc., went about the streets asking people:

"Did you know Cleveland's black Trotter was sick?" which greatly amused the
citizens and passed into a standing joke.[62]
      Feeling ran so high over this appointment that a resident of the Capitol
hired a band to parade the streets one night playing only one air--"There's
a New Coon in Town"--and round and round the White House reverberated these
strains as the band marched, according to orders, back and forth past it.
      The city was ablaze with comment next day, and dozens of witnesses can
be produced to testify to the occurrence.
      Mr. Trotter was succeeded by the appointee of Mr. Harrison, ex-Senator
Bruce (colored), of Mississippi, who to-day fills the office.[63]
      The deductions to be drawn from these facts are: First. The Recorder-
ship of Deeds in the District of Columbia is a spoil of office pledged to the
colored vote. Second. The people of the District, having no suffrage recognition, are despised by the President in their claim to fill the office
with some man of known ability and local popularity. Third. Mr. Cleveland
proved his complete subserviency to either prejudice in favor of a colored
office holder or some existing deal with dictating powers.
      Touching the slight, put publicly upon Miss Winnie Davis, by President
Cleveland and wife, nothing more need be said than that it was the sensation
of the day in press and social circles, and occurred at Richmond, Va., when
Mr. and Mrs. Cleveland were the guests of the city and invited by its citizens to meet Miss Davis at a grand reception. Mrs. Cleveland declined, ex-
plaining as reason for doing so, that they considered it highly impolite to
fraternize with the daughter of Ex-President Davis of confederate record.
Col. R. Q. Washington, the nestor of the Washington Press, during the Chicago
convention, published over his signature in the Fort Worth Gazette, (Texas),
a letter from which some extracts are made. Col. Washington, let it remembered
is responsible for the following utterances:

      Time passed. Mr. Cleveland was sworn into office and recited his inau-
gural. It was very hard pulling on the part of Southern Congressmen to get
him to remove the Republican officeholders in the South, and it was not done
finally on the ground that they were Republicans, but on a side issue of alleged misconduct in office and pernicious activity in politics. But one thing
seemed very queer. Fred Douglas held the most lucrative office in Washington,
that of Recorder of Deeds, and he was not removed. Douglas had systemically

slandered the South and the Democratic party, but despite all this it was given out that the President did not propose to turn him out at all, but accept his resignation at some distant day that would suit his convenience. And this proved to be strictly true. Douglas staid in office about a year after Mr. Cleveland became President. Meantime winter came, and with winter the fashionable season. The President gave three grand receptions, one to the Diplomatic Corps., one to the House of Congress and a third to the officers of the army and navy. The receptions were regarded as grand and select affairs. Out of some 65,000,000 of the American people, only 1200 or 1500 persons in all were invited. There appeared at the White House, at the very first reception, Fred Douglas with his white wife on his arm, and, also, a colored daughter by his former wife. Here you have social equality and miscegenation both condoned and patronized by a Democratic President of the United States.[64]

Douglas did not get there by any precedent or intrusion; he did not invite himself. He was at home there, and as much at home as any guest of the evening. Mr. Cleveland treated him and the white woman he married with fully as much respect as he accorded the wives and daughters of the Southerners who were present. The publication of this fact in the papers caused considerable surprise and comment, many supposing there had been some mistake about Douglas getting in that reception, but all doubt on this point was put to rest when, at the second reception, Douglas and his family again appeared to meet a most cordial greeting from Mr. Cleveland. There was more comment in the press, and there was a third reception of specially invited guests, the public being excluded. Again Fred Douglas was there with his family, placed by the President on the highest plane of social equality to which he, in his wildest dreams, had ever aspired.

It was now summertime, in leafy June, and all the fashion and magnates of the federal city were assembled at Mr. and Mrs. Cleveland's wedding reception. Douglas was no longer in office. He had resigned, sometime before, and the President not being able to find a white man to suit him, had appointed another negro to the office, one imported from Albany for this very purpose. Douglas was not now in office, and, indeed, was not even in Washington. If he came at all to the reception it must be by reason of an invitation to him as a private citizen, but he did come. He came on from New York, figured prominently at the wedding reception and stated freely that he would not have come at all save to attend the reception, once again the favored guest. The Southern whites present had whatever doubtful honor might be gathered from the opportunity accorded them by the President.

It was a grand achievement, truly, for Mr. Cleveland to thus blend the races, and we may presume that he was both happy and proud of it. Where were the voices of the honored and usually outspoken men in public life condemning this attempt to commit the Democratic party by the highest example it could offer to the doctrine of negro equality?

Colonel Washington next quoates Fred Douglas upon the subject of President Cleveland's treatment of him as follows:

I am a Republican and did all I could to defeat Mr. Cleveland. He was under no political obligation to me whatever. Yet I held the office of recorder nearly a whole year under his administration, an office by law held not for a term, but solely at the pleasure of the President. He could have removed me at his pleasure at any time after his inauguration. When he asked for my resignation he simply asked me to set a time when it would be agreeable for me to tender it. I did set the time, and when that time arrived I sent in my resignation. His manner to me was very courteous, and I have nothing whatever to complain of. While in office President Cleveland treated me as he treated other office-holders in the district. He was brave enough to invite Mrs. Douglas and myself to all his grand receptions, thus rebuking the timidity, I will not say cowardice or prejudices, of his predecessors."

Colonel Washington comments on this as follows:

The predessor above referred to who had the too honorable instincts of the white race and would not invite them to the White House, was ex-President Arthur. He is now dead. I differed from him widely in politics, but he has my cordial respect for the precedent he has set, and which the man who came after him lacked the decency to follow. I give Mr. Cleveland all the benefit of Fred Douglas' encomium upon him for his bravery in espousing the theory of

social equality, but I shall always adhere to the old-fashioned doctrine of
gentlemen in the South, that there is no surer touchstone in this country
of a low and base man than his readiness to associate with negroes.

On June 25, 1892, the Forth Worth Gazette, a leading Democratic daily
says in a lengthy editorial that Colonel Washington's letter is true.

This matter, THE ECONOMIST desires to say, has been prepared and published in response to numerous requests. It partakes of a personal character
and appeals to the prejudice of race. It has been the policy of this paper
to deprecate sectionalism and passion, and Mr. Cleveland's record, in so
far as related above, would have to flow from other sources was it not that
the people demand the information.

National Economist, September 17, 1892.

32. INDORSED BY THE COLORED FARMERS

Supt. R. M. Humphrey Before the Senate Committee
on Agriculture and Forestry.

MR. CHAIRMAN AND GENTLEMEN OF THE COMMITTEE: I appear before you as
the representative of the Colored Farmers National Alliance and Co-operative
Union, an organization extending over thirty States and having an enrolled
membership of more than a million. I am not here to teach Senators wisdom,
nor to go over these facts, and statistics, and arguments which have been
presented to the committee by others, my associates. I appear before the
committee simply as the representative of a great people--a people, however,
who are devoted entirely to agriculture. The colored people are either farmers or farm laborers. As a matter of course we have a few exceptions, but
the great masses of them are interested in agricultural pursuits, and are
affected by their surroundings just as are other agriculturalists. I come
to present their interests; and before I begin it is probably important that
you should know, and you have an interest in knowing, who speaks. It is not
I, of course. I am the representative of about one million citizens of the
United States. If I plead before Southern men or before Northern men, it is
simply indifferent; they are our fellow citizens.

Some twenty-five years ago the shackels were broken from the limbs of
some four millions of slaves. That four million, or four million and a half,
number to-day about eight millions. With matters of that sort you are just
as familiar and just as well informed as I am, and I do not propose to waste
time in questions which are already published to the world.

Now these people, when first released from slavery, were as ignorant, as
degraded, as penniless as you can well imagine, friendless and without a dollar, barefoot, ragged, homeless. Now, from that condition they have advanced
to a very high position as a civilized people. I know of what I speak. I
have traveled through the whole country, and am acquainted with their position
and their situation. Thousands of them own their own homes; some of them
have accumulated property. But the thing that I am here to show is not what
they have accomplished, but what they ought to accomplish under more favorable
conditions. These people are not idlers, as sometimes published. When I
first commenced farming twenty-five years ago men told me to get a lot of
Germans, that they were the good workers. I got them and found them a failure
so far as cotton was concerned. Then they said "get Chinese," and I got them;
and they worshiped their little josses, and the cotton did not grow. I then
threw all that aside and followed my own inclinations. I got a lot of negroes,
good colored people, and cotton and corn grew over my premises; and I did not
have to say "go to work." They went to work. I know that if we were to judge
by newspaper statements, and by the statements of some people, we would say
the negro is a sort of lazy, worthless creature, who ought to be beneath the
contempt of Government. I want to say, honored Senators, that is not true;
that the negro is as faithful and as diligent as any other human being in
existence. I remember to have ridden up to a fence and found a little girl of
seven summers, with a thin calico dress on, and no hat on her head, cutting

away with her little hoe in the cotton. I said "what are you doing there, little girl?" "Why, I am helping papa to make a living." That is the general way of the men, and the women, and the children; they all work, and they work diligently.

Senator George. What part of the country is that in?[65]

Mr. Humphrey. In Texas, in Mississippi, in Alabama, Georgia, South Carolina. I can not speak for Ohio, as I never saw much of the negroes of that State. I can speak for North Carolina, for Virginia. I can speak for any of the Southern States. I say that wherever these people are scattered they work as well as any other race. That is all that I affirm. I do not affirm that they are demi-gods at all, but that they work just as diligently as any race under heaven. Now, the next thing is that not simply do they work, but they are not extravagant. When men charge that they spend too much in useless clothing, and food, and the like, you may receive the statement with a good many grains of allowance. Certainly there are great diversities among them, but the great majority are not extravagant. You can take the great majority of the colored farmers of the South and you will find that their women spend the season in the cotton fields, with a single thin garment, without shoes, and they live upon the coarsest, commonest food, upon which you cannot subsist other laborers. I desire to make the statement here, that these people are a necessity with us in the South, and that we cannot substitute their labor. I could demonstrate that fact if it were necessary. I do not think it is necessary. So much I have said about the people I came here to represent. The next thing would be the special bill I came to advocate before the Senate, known as the sub-treasury plan. The Chairman and gentlemen who are present I suppose are acquainted with the bill sufficiently, so that it is unnecessary for me to read it. In connection, however, with the introduction of that bill before the honorable committee, I will say this, that the trustees of this great national organization, the Colored Farmers Alliance, met on the 29th of April last in the city of Birmingham, in Alabama, and instructed me to proceed here and present before you, as far as possible, the necessity, the deep necessity, with them of the passage of this or some kindred measure, either the sub-treasury bill or some kindred measure, "for," said they--I want to use their own words as far as possible--"the proposition to lend money on lands can be of little avail to us. We have no lands to mortgage. The proposition to increase the amount of currency can be of very little avail to us, for we have nothing to buy the money with. Our muscle is our stock in trade, and what we must beg the Government to do is to recognize that muscle, recognize the principle that labor is the basis of all wealth, and if the Government will aid us to take care of the product of our labor that will be all that we demand."

Now, gentlemen, know that the bill provides that certain warehouses shall be built in certain counties producing five hundred thousand dollars worth of certain lines of production, and that in those warehouses the cotton, the surplus of corn, oats, or tobacco, may be stored, and eighty per cent of its value paid to the party who stores it there, the remaining twenty per cent to stand as surety against risk, danger and the like, and to be eventually paid to the owner, if found worthy. What would be the effect upon this special class of people I represent? That is the point I want to get at. Not what it would be to other people, but to these colored people. I put it in this shape. During the twenty-five years which are passed the fluctuation in farm products has not been less than twenty per cent; that is, at some period during each season, farm products of every variety would average twenty per cent higher than at some other period. Take for instance, cotton. We know that there is not money enough in circulation in the United States to pay for a cotton crop; all the money is drawn from New York, all the money is drawn from the banks of the country everywhere; the supply is exhausted, and still the cotton crop is not paid for. Well, now, what would be the consequence if I should bring ten bales of cotton to the city of Washington for sale and there was just a hundred dollars in the city? It must be apparent to all of you that I can get but ten dollars a bale for that cotton. The cotton of the colored people which sold last September and October at seven cents is now selling at eleven and a half cents. The only question is, are these people entitled to the protection of the government in common with the white farmers of the land?

In regard to the fluctuation in prices, some other solution may be

presented to you, but, Mr. Chairman, I think all will agree that the only
genuine, the only real cause of fluctuation is, as I have stated, the lack
of currency in the country. I do not look upon every man as being dishonest.
I do not consider every man a thief because he deals in futures. That is
not my style. I simply believe that man buys on the very best terms he can,
and when money becomes scarce, and scarcer still, the prices tend downward,
and downward still. By and by, when further supplies of money have been
gathered into the country, prices tend upward again. That is perfectly
natural. This sub-treasury plan would tend to relieve this thing by allowing
the farmer, white or colored, to store his cotton and receive 80 per cent on
the value of it, and pay his debts. The cotton would lie there and dry out.
Some of you have handled cotton. It dries out about 3 per cent in the cotton.
    Senator George. In how long a period?
    Mr. Humphrey. From three to six months; depending on the atmosphere it
is kept in.
    Senator George. Do you know how long it is after cotton is baled and
stored before the lessening of weight ceases?
    Mr. Humphrey. About six months.
    Senator George. It last six months?
    Mr. Humphrey. Under similar circumstances. If you changed the circum-
stances it would lose again or gain.
    Senator George. In making the answers you have already made, do you
speak of a dry or a humid climate in which the cotton is stored?
    Mr. Humphrey. In a humid climate the cotton will gain weight.
    Senator George. In an ordinary climate it loses?
    Mr. Humphrey. Yes, sir.
    Senator Jones. How about the drying out process? I understand your
theory to be that cotton dries out about 3 per cent in six months? [66]
    Mr. Humphrey. Yes, sir.
    Senator Jones. In a humid climate it gains instead of loses?
    Mr. Humphrey. Yes, sir. It must be given an absolutely dry warehouse.
    Senator Jones. How do you arrive at that conclusion? On what do you
base your opinion in relation to the drying out of cotton?
    Mr. Humphrey. Actual experiment.
    Senator Jones. I wish you would tell us in a short way about those ex-
periments, how extensive they were and how great they have been.
    Mr. Humphrey. Well, I am somewhat of a cotton dealer. My hands have
been in cotton for twenty-five years, and I have watched this process. I
suppose it is very generally understood that when we bale cotton it is damp
to a certain extent, and in process of three to six months it will dry out
or lose about 3 per cent of its weight; from 3 to 5 per cent.
    The Chairman. Under average climatic conditions?
    Mr. Humphrey. Average conditions.
    Senator Jones. A bale will lose from fifteen to twenty pounds?
    Mr. Humphrey. Yes, sir; no less, and sometimes more.
    The Chairman. With the average atmospheric conditions which prevail?
    Mr. Humphrey. Yes, sir. If we compress a bale and then remove it to
the Gulf, it will increase in weight on account of the humidity of the atmosphere.
    Senator George. Are you sure you are right about that?
    Mr. Humphrey. Yes, sir.
    Senator Jones. You have tested that?
    Mr. Humphrey. Yes, sir.
    Now, Mr. Chairman, and gentlemen of the committee, I want to call your
attention to this, that where alcohol, whisky, or brandy is manufactured, it
must have time to season or dry out--ripen (is not that the word, or something
of the sort). Gentlemen will understand distinctly what I mean. Consequently the Government has kindly provided for the distiller a place where he may
store his liquor until it is worth $3 for $1 it was worth when he made it.
We poor farmers ask you in God's name to help us, and add just 25 per cent
to our cotton crops. You can do it very easily. Have we not the same right
to ask for this 25 per cent to be added to our cotton crops that the distiller
has to ask that 250 percent be added to his distilled spirits? That this
argument is just, Mr. Chairman, will not be questioned, and I would rather
answer questions than make a speech.

Senator George. If that is the case I will ask you a question. The increase in the value of whisky, as I understand it, comes from an increase, or an improvement rather, in the character of the liquor resulting from age?

Mr. Humphrey. Yes, sir; that is right.

Senator George. Does that improvement come to cotton, or corn, or wheat, or oats?

Mr. Humphrey. It comes to cotton very materially.

Senator George. I mean as respects quality?

Mr. Humphrey. I will explain again. We all know that cotton last September sold for 7 cents; now it is 11-1/2 cents.

Senator Jones. The same grades?

Mr. Humphrey. Yes, sir.

Senator Jones. The same markets?

Mr. Humphrey. Yes, sir; everything the same.

Senator George. I will ask you if the increase in the price of cotton did not come in the increase of the general price of some given quality of cotton, and not, as in the case of whisky, from an increase or an improvement in the value of the thing itself; in its intrinsic value?

Mr. Humphrey. Now, Senator, that allows me to answer your question, and I can answer it definitely. By getting the cotton together in bulk, so that we can furnish the spinner a thousand bales of the class he wants, and by having it dried out and ready for his machinery, the price of it in every sense is absolutely improved, like the whisky, as much as 20 to 25 per cent.

Senator George. Do you mean the actual quality of the cotton is improved, or simply the market price?

Mr. Humphrey. I mean the actual quality, for when we put together a thousand bales of any special class of cotton the buyer pays a higher price for it; and the warehouse would allow us to put it together. In regard to this warehouse custom, the warehouse plan for distilled spirits, which I know is fully understood, I will only stop for one moment. Of course the improvement comes from age. That is not questioned. But the Government allows the distiller to place the whisky in a bonded warehouse and gives him a certificate of deposit, which certificate can be taken to a bank and made into money; and that money can be put into circulation and used every hour of the time until the whisky is worth three dollars for one. It is very kind of the Government to do that. I am not finding fault with that; but I am asking in the name of mercy that you grant us farmers the privilege of adding 25 per cent to our crops where you can do it just as easily as you do with the distiller. There can be no possible loss in a cotton crop. There is no chance for a loss in the case. I want in this connection to call your attention to the fact that a tariff reduction can be of very little benefit to the people I represent, because they do not buy a great amount of the goods which are taxed. As a matter of course a tariff reduction might affect the thing we have to buy one way or the other. It might help; I do not say it would not. And so an increase in the volume of money might help; I do not say it would not. I do say this, that however large you may make the volume of money, it will not meet the demands of the case, because, suppose we had in circulation six dollars for one now, what then? Six will be worth one, and six dollars' worth of goods will be worth about one dollar's worth now. You preserve in that way a sort of evenness of the scales, and that is all. An increase in the volume of currency cannot materially affect any one except the debtor class. Certainly, if you will double the volume of money I can pay a debt of $200 just as easily as I can now pay a debt of $100. If you will destroy half the volume of money, giving us $100 where we now have $200, then it will be as hard for me to pay a debt of $50 as to now pay a debt of $100. All of us understand these principles so fully that I feel ashamed of myself for stopping to repeat them, but they seem to be a necessary part of the business on which I was sent here. There was another feature in the argument sent up by these colored people which they begged me not to forget to say to you, that the mere repeal of existing laws which might be considered as of a paternal character cannot meet the demand in this case.

Senator George. What laws?

Mr. Humphrey. The national bank law. I also refer to the warehouse for distilled spirits, the bonded warehouse law. I need hardly illustrate further than just to say, we see the national banks.

The Chairman. You mean to say that the colored people engaged in agriculture are not a debtor class; that is, that they have not mortgages outstanding?

Mr. Humphrey. They have, indeed, mortgages outstanding.

The Chairman. I understood you some time since to say that they were
necessarily a debtor class, because they do not own the land?

Senator George. Is there any class in any community that you may go
into who use their credit more--they are necessarily bound to do so--than the
colored farmer?

Mr. Humphrey. He uses it pretty freely.

The Chairman. Then they really belong to the debtor class?

Mr. Humphrey: Yes, sir; and certainly an increase of money would be
profitable to them in that particular. An increase of the volume of currency would be immensely profitable to them in that particular view of the
case.

Senator George. You are very familiar with the colored farmers. I
have some knowledge of them, too. Is it not true that nineteen out of twenty,
if not more, of the colored farmers of the country, raise their crops upon
credit, based upon the crop when it is sold to be paid?

Mr. Humphrey. I think that a few years ago, perhaps, that number would
be correct; but the Alliance has taught them much better principles. There
would not be anything like that number to-day. I imagine, perhaps, not more
than one-half of them; perhaps one-half raise their crop this year on credit.

The Chairman. How as to the white farmers, do they get an advance before the crops are raised?

Mr. Humphrey. Yes, sir. The white farmers have drawn more largely on
their credit this year than the colored farmers.

Senator Jones. What have you taught them which has brought about that
condition of affairs?

Mr. Humphrey. We have taught them to starve. That is what. We have
taught them to work and get out of debt.

Senator Jones. To live without money; to just starve, and get out of
debt.

The Chairman. In speaking of the indebtedness of the colored people,
do you mean to say real estate mortgage indebtedness or chattel mortgage
indebtedness?

Mr. Humphrey. Not real estate, but chattel. A great many of them have
homes.

The Chairman. As a rule they do not own their own farms.

Mr. Humphrey. No, sir. Not as a rule.

The Chairman. And their indebtedness is in the nature of chattel mortgages?

Mr. Humphrey. Yes, sir.

Senator George. Have you ever run through your mind--I have done it--
the proportion of adult colored males who own their own land? Is it one-
tenth?

The Chairman. What percentage?

Mr. Humphrey. No, I cannot give a definite answer to that question.
I may say this, that in the State of Alabama 13,000 colored farmers filed
their names as owning their homes and being out of debt, and with a resolution to stay out of debt; to keep out of debt; to starve through and get out
of debt.

Senator George. Have you an idea of the number of colored made adults
in Alabama, say voters? We could get it through the Census.

Mr. Humphrey. Yes, sir, and better than through my poor memory. I
think it is about ninety-eight thousand. But do not hold me responsible for
that.

Senator George. Suppose there were a hundred thousand of them. Then
if thirteen thousand of them were land owners it would be about--

Senator Jones. Thirteen per cent.

Mr. Humphrey. It would be about one-seventh.

The Chairman. Did the colored people who made this agreement to get out
of debt and try to be economical, represent the agricultural class of the
colored people?

The Chairman. Not those living in towns?

Mr. Humphrey. No, sir. They help one another. I should reply a little more definitely to that question. If one has five dollars, he who is in most need can get it. They aid one another powerfully to get out of debt. I give them credit for doing just about all that human beings could do in that direction.

The Chairman. Has there been much increase in their acquisition of lands during the past ten years?

Mr. Humphrey. There has been a considerable increase; an increase, I tell you, Senator, I am proud of, because notwithstanding I am a white man, a southern man, and have not been very friendly always toward the colored people, I am proud to see them succeed. I want them to have justice, right.

The Chairman. They are making decided progress?

Mr. Humphrey. Decided progress, grand progress. It would be a good place to stop right here and to say that in my state, Texas, for fifty miles up and down the Trinity, they own their own rich river bottom and have turned it into farms. The Alliance did that much for them, and they feel proud of the Alliance and work diligently together to uphold their organizations.

Senator George. So far as those on the Trinity are concerned, they are in a prosperous condition, are they not?

Mr. Humphrey. Well, now, Senator, that has to be answered again. They would be prosperous, if they just could have held their cotton until now. Every man would have had plenty of money if they could have held their cotton until now.

Senator Jones. Why could they not hold it?

Mr. Humphrey. Because they were dreadfully pinched with hunger.

Senator Jones. They did not eat up the entire cotton crop at once?

Mr. Humphrey. No; but they were compelled to pay their taxes. Their taxes had to be paid; shoes must be had. But when I say out of debt I mean out of mortgage debt. Many of them owe little debts to their negro neighbors.

Senator Jones. Would it not have been easy for them to have postponed those debts for a few months if there was an absolute certainty of a rise of 50 per cent in the cotton?

Mr. Humphrey. No sir; they could not do it. The sheriffs would have sold them out for taxes, for one thing, and for another thing. They would have suffered with winter cold, and such winter cold as no human being can stand before when he has it in his power to do otherwise. So they sacrificed their crops rather than see their families deprived of the necessaries of life and go barefooted in the ice. That is what you or I would do if reduced to their extremities.

Senator George. I want to call your attention to this. How many white men are there in Texas who are out of debt?

Mr. Humphrey. Senator, you must not call upon me about that, because these negroes have had me employed.

Senator George. I will ask you whether the men who had cotton, whether bought or raised, did not foresee the great rise in cotton which has come recently, and whether a great many did not sell who were not compelled to sell?

Mr. Humphrey. We know that for twenty-five years this fluctuation of 25 per cent has been the average. We know that it is bound to go up.

Senator George. Do you mean to say that for twenty-five years the price of cotton about the month of May has been 20 per cent higher than in October?

Mr. Humphrey. I would not undertake to say that that was the case in every year. It is simply the case at the same season in the year.

Senator Jones. Is that uniform?

Mr. Humphrey. It is not uniform.

Senator Jones. Can you tell beforehand when these fluctuations are to occur?

Mr. Humphrey. We might if we were permitted to know exactly the bank statements of Wall street. Whenever there is no money to pay for cotton it is bound to go down.

The Chairman. As a rule, does the price of cotton average lower immediately after the harvesting of cotton than later on?

Mr. Humphrey. It never fails.

Senator George. What never fails?

Mr. Humphrey. The price of cotton to be lower immediately after harvesting.

Senator George. What do you call "after harvesting?" I want to know what you mean, because the harvest commences in September and ends the first of January, sometimes February.

Mr. Humphrey. With us it commences in July. Now, Mr. Chairman, if you will let me answer that question.

The Chairman. You spoke of the necessity of having stores for a time in order that the cotton might be dried out and be in condition to work. I believe that is what you said.

Mr. Humphrey. Yes, sir.

The Chairman. Now what length of time is that?

Mr. Humphrey. I was in favor of storing for as long as three months, if possible.

The Chairman. Is the cotton not marketable before it goes through that process?

Mr. Humphrey. Oh, yes.

The Chairman. But at lower prices?

Mr. Humphrey. Yes, sir.

The Chairman. Is that the reason it averages lower immediately after it is ready for market?

Mr. Humphrey. Yes, sir. Here is a feature that I must take time to illustrate for a moment. During the summer season, right now, some of our leading cotton speculators are in Europe. They have sold thousands of bales of cotton, which is to be delivered in October and November and later. Now they will come home about August, and they may happen to have sold so much cotton that they will put prices pretty high to get that cotton. As soon as those orders are filled cotton will touch bottom, sometime about November, right when the poor negro get his cotton in, and the man who has credited and trusted him and who has fed his family, says: "Sam, you must pay." Sam is honest as the days are long. Do not tell me the negro will steal. Sam is honest. "I will pay," he says. "Well, Sam, you must go and sell that cotton to-day." "Well, sir, I can do it." Sam telegraphs to me. Now I will relate an occurrence. It was last week. A telegram came: "To Colonel Humphrey: I have one bale of cotton left, and I can get clear of the mortgage. The gentleman will give me the forty-five dollars mortgage for the bale of cotton. Shall I take it, or can you do better? I telegraphed, "Send me that cotton." I sold that bale of cotton for $61.93, and the difference between the $61.93 and the $45 is how much Greenbury saved on his one bale of cotton. You say, "Then can not you furnish universal relief in that way? " No, I am not able to do it; it would take the Government to do it. One man can not do it. Mr. Gould can not do that thing. Mr. Vanderbilt and Mr. Gould united can not do that thing. The Government must furnish the relief, or that relief can not be had in anything like a perfect condition. But I have slighted your question, Senator.

Senator George. You said some time ago that cotton was lower immediately after harvest than it was at any other time. I want you to explain to this committee, many of whom are familiar with cotton, when harvest is. My idea is it commences about the first of September, in my country, at least, and ends about the first of January or February.

Mr. Humphrey. It is not much harvest with you. With us it is a grand harvest. It commences in July and ends in November generally. When you get to a country where they do not harvest cotton until September, we consider it too far North for a good crop.

Senator George. In your answers you wish to be understood as referring to the harvest as from the 1st of July to the 1st of November.

Mr. Humphrey. Well, put it from the 1st of August; three months.

Senator McMillan. Do these colored men own their own lands?

Mr. Humphrey. Some of them do. [67]

Senator McMillan. It is rich land?

Mr. Humphrey. Yes, sir.

Senator McMillan. And those who do not own the lands, how do they get their cotton?

Mr. Humphrey. There is a variety of ways. If they do not own land,
perhaps they own stock, and can rent land by giving one-fourth of what they
make in cotton; and if they have neither stock nor land, then they go to some
white neighbor and propose to work for half. He gives half of what they can
make.

Senator McMillan. And Furnishes stock and land?

Senator George. And agricultural implements?

Mr. Humphrey. Yes, sir. In this case, and in every case, Senator, take
notice that this negro is necessarily just like the poor white man, exactly
on the same terms as the poor white man. He is forced to go in debt while
he makes that crop. There is a necessity, a sort of force, to go in debt
while he makes that crop.

Senator George. I want to see if your experience agrees with mine.
They go in debt under a mortgage or lien to a country merchant. Is it not
almost universally a country merchant? And he charges them very extravagant
prices for that credit?

Mr. Humphrey. Two hundred and fifty percent is considered reasonable.

Senator Jones. By whom?

Mr. Humphrey. By the country merchant.

Senator George. Is it not also true that the country merchant always
allows those who are in debt to him two or three cents more for his cotton
that he could get for cash?

Mr. Humphrey. Never. He tells them that he is allowing them a half a
cent or so more. But that is not true. I never knew such a case. I have
known as many transactions of that kind as I have hairs on my head. I never
knew a country merchant to pay a man for his cotton because he held a mortgage on that cotton. He comes down to his collection in this fashion. He
says: "Pay me that thow owest me." If I do not pay, he sends for the justice
of the peace and make me pay. That is what. Now I want to call attention
to this fact. Mr. Chairman and gentlemen of the committee, I am a Southern
man. My name is known over the entire South. I could not stand before you
and tell a falsehood. That would be impossible. I say to you, candidly,
that race prejudice and race problems have not hurt the colored man in the
South any more than they have hurt men in the North or anywhere else in the
world. The one thing which has perplexed, which has troubled, which has
starved and killed the colored race in the South is the fact that the Government, by the constant fluctuation of money has held the colored man by the
shoulder every November while a Southern sharper flayed him. That has been
the trouble. Give us now the warehouses, and let the colored man deposit
his cotton there and get his 80 per cent and pay the little that he owes.
You will see him step proudly around, and he will be a home-owner quick, because I tell you the colored people are as honest a people as the sun shines
on. I have worked in the field with them day after day; I have ploughed by
their side; I have known them ever since I was born, and a more honest, true,
more faithful set does not exist. I know the truth of what I speak, when I
say to you that if I, by some accident, should be injured or killed in the
city of Washington to-night, there are thousands of colored men who would
sell their last blanket or shirt to come to Washington to look after my remains. What is the reason? Because I have befriended them, and they never
forget a friend; they never lose sight of a kindness. Now, gentlemen, so
far as making a speech is concerned, I am not here for that purpose, but I
should like to answer reasonable questions in regard to the sub-treasury bill
as far as I possibly can. I am honest when I tell you that the bill is the
very thing we farmers can make, possibly, the best we can do. You can do
better. We know you can. You have legal talent among you. You have all the
advantages, and what we ask is not that you give us the sub-treasury bill as
we have framed it, but give us that or a better bill. We know that you can
better the bill. We do not doubt that. We only ask that you give us this
sub-treasury bill or some better bill. Now there are some other questions
gentlemen may want to ask, and I do not want to leave the floor hurriedly.
I do not want to occupy your time too much, either.

Senator Blair. Let me ask you one question. You get eighty per cent
when you deposit the cotton? 68

Mr. Humphrey. Yes, sir.

Senator Blair. And you get some certificate that entitles you to the other twenty per cent in money.

Mr. Humphrey. I suppose that would be just the way. Received of G. H.
one bale of cotton weighing 480 pounds valued as so and so; class so and so;
paid him so many dollars on that. Then as a matter of course he would see
how much remained due.

Senator Blair. You would get a certificate for the balance, payable at
what time, at the end of the year?

Mr. Humphrey. No, sir; when this cotton was sold, if there was a remainder after paying back the debt due, the owner would get it.

The Chairman. The certificate would be for eighty per cent.

Senator Blair. On what?

Mr. Humphrey. The value of the cotton.

Senator Blair. How would the value of the cotton be determined?

Mr. Humphrey. Would be classified just like it is now and listed. The
price of it would be listed then just as it is now.

Senator Blair. You would go by the prices prevailing at that time!

Mr. Humphrey. By the quotations of that day. The warehouses would
stop the fluctuation any further. The price of cotton one season, say the
first of May, would be the same as at another. The farmer when he planted
his crop would know what he was working for, just as a salared man. It would
absolutely evaporate the business of fluctuation and dealing in futures higher
than "High Eden." It would be blown away.

Senator Blair. Do you think the colored man would keep the certificate
for this balance, or the white man for that matter, as a rule, or would he
sell that for what he could get at the time? Would not that go into the hands
of the speculators? The law might prescribe that these certificates shall not
be transferable.

Senator George. But this bill prescribes that these certificates shall
be negotiable.

Mr. Humphrey. My understanding of that part of the merit of the bill is
that I would certainly move to amend.

Senator George. And make them non-assignable?

Mr. Humphrey. Yes, sir; and non-negotiable, that would be my idea. I
am only one member of this thing.

Senator Blair. You would not have then assignable at all?

Mr. Humphrey. No, sir.

Senator Blair. So that nobody could collect them but the man who deposited the cotton?

Mr. Humphrey. That is it; yes, sir; such a paper not negotiable or
assignable, might be deposited in bank.

Senator George. Oh, no, it could not. Banks only deal in negotiable
paper.

Mr. Humphrey. But it could be deposited in banks.

The Chairman. If you should deposit a collateral of any kind at the
bank, and upon that should receive an advance or loan, you would have to
make a blank assignment or an assignment in full of the collateral you deposited. Otherwise the bank would not have it.

Mr. Humphrey. I do not think it is necessary to make that certificate
for twenty per cent assignable or negotiable at all. I think the man who
sells the cotton had better hold that certificate. Just the same transactions
have been occurring in my State every day in the year. A. B. sends me or a
merchant ten bales of cotton and receives an advance of $35 a bale on that
cotton, or whatever per cent you may name. Very well, C. D., the merchant,
receives the cotton and instructions, and steps over to the bank and has the
bill of lading filed away and sends this man so many dollars.

Senator Blair. Would you make this law so that every man who raises
cotton must put it into deposit, or would you allow everybody to trade as he
wants?

Mr. Humphrey. I would make it so that he would be free to deposit his
cotton or not as he chose.

Senator Blair. Would not that leave you subject to fluctuation and
perhaps an increased fluctuation?

Mr. Humphrey. No, sir.

Senator Blair. You could not eliminate this speculative element in human nature. There would be some effort to get this cotton.

Mr. Humphrey. We might not absolutely eliminate it, but we would do this. We have to draw on New York and draw every dollar now to pay for the cotton crop and—

Senator Blair. And you would have to draw on the Government?

Mr. Humphrey. The Government is naturally more able to bear the burden.

Senator Blair. What would the Government have to advance?

Mr. Humphrey. As much as fifty millions in a year. It might be called on to advance fifty millions.

Senator Blair. As for other crops in the same year; have you ever calculated what the wheat crop and the corn crop would require?

Mr. Humphrey. No, sir; I cannot answer for the wheat crop. The things I am interested in are the negro and his cotton crop. Somebody else must answer for the wheat crop.

Senator Blair. The committee or whoever makes the law has to answer for all the crops?

Mr. Humphrey. I will produce you a gentleman who will answer for the wheat crop.

Senator Blair. Here is the scheme and those who advance it ought to be able to answer questions, if they are natural and sensible questions for which the men who makes the laws have to be responsible.

Mr. Humphrey. I am trying to answer. I will answer any question I am able, but when I get to a question I am not able to answer I will frankly tell you so. We shall probably call on the Government in September, October and November for $50,000,000 of money to handle the cotton crop. When the cotton is sold it will be repaid to the Government in time.

Senator Blair. Do you think $50,000,000 will be enough?

Mr. Humphrey. I am satisfied we shall never use that.

Senator Blair. There are 7,000,000 bales of cotton. About how much is it worh a bale?

Mr. Humphrey. About $40 a bale probably. Do not count that all into the warehouse.

Senator Jones. What becomes of the balance?

Mr. Humphrey. It will be sold at once. Men would lose sight of their intent to speculate. Down in our country, where they used to skin us with speculation, we have, without the aid of law, stopped all that. We have stopped all the minor speculations that were brought against us. We have in this case, however, a speculation so heavy that we cannot handle it. It is impossible. This fluctuation in prices never can be handled, I say, except by the power that issues money to the country.

The Chairman. Is it your idea that this system should be inaugurated that it would do away with dealing in futures?

Mr. Humphrey. Yes, sir. It will kill the bucket shops.

The Chairman. The whole speculative element in the market would be eliminated?

Mr. Humphrey. Yes, sir; at once.

Senator George. Mr. Humphrey is representing a class of persons I have some knowledge of myself. You of course know that there is a very great difference in the classification of cotton. It runs from what I believe is called inferior to what they call fair. There are inferior, low ordinary, good ordinary, low middling, and middling.

Mr. Humphrey. Strict low middling.

Senator George. That is not in the classification. Then there is good middling and then we have fair, I believe, or middling fair, and fair. There are nine different classes of cotton. There are some half grades besides.

Mr. Humphrey. Yes, sir.

Senator George. All these classifications bring different prices. The prices are graded according to that. Now, is not the classification of cotton except as between very low grades and high grades, where there are three or four grades difference, is it not a very difficult thing to do to distinguish between them? Does it not require an expert?

Mr. Humphrey. Yes, sir; but it is the easiest thing in the world, gentlemen, when a man is accustomed to it.

Senator George. How many colored men do you know who are capable of classing cotton as between the three grades of low middling, middling and good middling?

Mr. Humphrey. I doubt if I am acquainted with colored cotton classer who cannot make the assignment.

Senator George. Do you think that is true of the white people?

Mr. Humphrey. No, sir; they do not learn that sort of thing as fast as the negro.

Senator George. You think all colored farmers can assign and sample cotton?

Mr. Humphrey. In a general way.

Senator George. As to the classification between the grades I have mentioned.

Mr. Humphrey. I will not undertake to say that they can assign it to put it into the newspaper.

Senator George. But for all practical purposes?

Mr. Humphrey. Yes, sir; they can do that.

Senator George. The most of them can.

Mr. Humphrey. Yes, sir.

Senator George. And that is not true of the white farmers?

Mr. Humphrey. No, sir. That is my observation. The white farmers know nothing about it. The negro always knows.

Senator Jones. Do you attribute that to superior intelligence on the part of the negro?

Mr. Humphrey. No, sir; I do not consider it superior intelligence in the dog that he smells better than a human being.

Senator Jones. Do they classify cotton by smell?

Mr. Humphrey. No, sir. It is instinct. I do not consider that they can do it on account of being bright or of superior intellect, or anything of that sort.

Senator Jones. What does the classification of cotton depend on?

Mr. Humphrey. Touch, handling, and sight.

Senator Jones. The cotton cannot either see or feel?

Mr. Humphrey. It must be touched or seen.

Senator George. Then you think the colored men would be amply able to protect themselves at these warehouses against an improper classification by the manager?

Mr. Humphrey. I think so. I think they would be better protected than they are now, when they must deal with sharpers all over the country.

The Chairman. You mean the middlemen?

Senator George. You think they would be amply protected?

Mr. Humphrey. I do think they would be. I am sure that no arrangement would be made in which they would not be protected.

Senator George. Do you think that the white farmers would be protected in the classification of cotton by this Government manager?

Senator Blair. Put a colored man in as manager. Then they would be protected.

Mr. Humphrey. I think so. I think that the whites would be protected, too. I do not know a white man who would intentionally cheat a colored man in the sampling of cotton, or a colored who would intentionally cheat a white man.

Senator George. You think, then, that the manager of the warehouse would give a fair classification?

Mr. Humphrey. I believe he would.

Senator Bate. Does not the classification of cotton depend upon how it is gathered and how it is put up? Does all the cotton grown in the same neighborhood come up to the same standard?

Mr. Humphrey. No, sir.

Senator Bate. A negro can see whether the cotton is clean or not, just as well as a white man.

Mr. Humphrey. I would go further on this evidence, because I think he knows.

Senator Bate. You think because the negroes as a class handle the cotton, pick it, and bale it, they know more about it than the white men.

Mr. Humphrey. I will whisper to you that I have a negro to select for me, because he knows more about it than I ever could learn.

I thank the committee for their courtesy.

The National Economist, June 7, 1894

THE 1891 COTTON PICKERS' STRIKE

33.   THE COTTON PICKERS

Reports of a Formidable Organization

Simultaneously All Pickers in the South are to Strike Against
Organized Planters--A secret Circular

GALVESTON, Texas, September 5.--A gentleman well and favorably known
throughout the State arrived in the city tonight, and was seen by the press
representative, to whom he made the following statement: A startling rumor,
he said, had gained currency among the planters that an immense organization
of cotton pickers throughout all the States had been effected within the
past six weeks or two months, pledged not to pick any cotton for less than
$1 per hundred pounds and board; that this organization had been effected
through the colored alliance, and now numbers more than a half million names
on the rolls, with thousands being added every day. Knowing that this, of
course, means that no cotton will be picked, as planters cannot afford to
pay that sum for picking at the present prices for the staple, I determined
to investigate the matter. I have interviewed R. M. Humphreys, general
superintendent of the colored alliance, with headquarters at Houston, but
could not get any definite information from him. Humphreys admitted that
some organization of the kind had been effected, induced by counter organizations of planters and merchants in certain sections, notably at Memphis
and Charleston, to reduce the prices for picking to a very low standard, but
declined to enter into particulars. Humphreys, however, stated that the
colored pickers had combined to protect themselves from this dictation and he
thought they would be able to do so; that he (Humphreys) had recently returned
from a tour of all the Southern States in the interests of the colored alliance
and found matters moving smoothly and the membership rapidly increasing, and
he thought the move for the advance in wages for picking would be made very
soon.
     Unable to get any more definite information from Humphreys, I pushed my
investigation further and found that a secret circular was being printed in
Houston, which will be sent out to all the colored suballiances throughout
the Southern States tonight, outlining that plan and fixing the date whem
simultaneous action by the pickers for higher wages throughout the cotton
States shall take place. I tried to secure one of those circulars, but was
unsuccessful. This is a most serious matter with the planters, for they are
almost entirely dependent upon this class of labor for gathering their crops,
and if the organization is as extensive as it now seems to be the delay in
picking necessarily resulting there from will cause a material loss if bad
weather sets in.

Houston Daily Post, September 6, 1891.

34. NEGROES FORM A COMBINE

They Want $1 Per Hundred and Board for Picking Cotton

The Combine Numbers Over a Half Million Paid Members and Will Immediately
Make Itself Felt

GALVESTON, Tex., Sept. 5--It has been learned that an organization of
colored cotton pickers exist, who have agreed not to pick cotton after
September 12 for less than $1 per 100 pounds and board. This organization
has been perfected through the colored Alliance, and now numbers more than
half a million, with thousands being added every day throughout the Southern
States. Col. R. M. Humphreys, general superintendent of the Colored Alliance,
with headquarters in Houston, admitted the existence of this organization,
saying: "It had been induced by organizations some time ago of planters and
merchants in certain sections, notably Memphis and Charleston, to reduce the
prices for picking to a very low standard, and that the colored pickers had
combined to protect themselves from this dictation," and he thought they
would be able to do so.
        It is learned that a secret circular has been mailed at Houston to every
colored sub-Alliance throughout the cotton belt, fixing the date when the
strike of pickers will be simultaneously inaugurated and how it shall be
conducted.

Memphis Appeal-Avalanche, September 6, 1891.

35. COLORED COTTON PICKERS

Organizing for the Enforcement of Their Demand

PARIS, Tex.,--If reports be true the colored Alliance men are calling
the turn on the white brethren in a way that they will despise. The following
was made public today:
        HEADQUARTERS COLORED ALLIANCE.
HOUSTON, Tex., Sept. 6.--WHEREAS, The planters and spectators are firm in
their demand that you pick at starvation wages as offered by them, and
        Whereas, above 600,000 pickers have already bound themselves together to
pick no cotton except their own, before November 1, at less than $1 per hun-
dred pounds, with board, and
        Whereas, Your success depends upon depends upon your united action.
        Now therefore, I, R. M. Humphrey by virtue of authority vested in me,
do issue this my solemn proclamation, fixing the twelfth day of September,
1891, it being Saturday, as the day upon which all our people shall cease
from and absolute stop picking cotton, except their own, until November 1,
unless their just demands for wages shall be acceded to. For the furtherance
of these objects let all leagues and unions unite more closely and stand
firmly together. Use all peaceable and lawful means to secure the sympathy
and hearty co-operation of all pickers in every section. If any are so mean
as to continue to pick and thereby defraud their brethren and injure their
race, mark such and have no communication with them. Avoid all public
gathering in public places and insolent display. Show yourselves to be men
who seek peace and desire justice. Further steps will be taken about October
20, unless recognition of your just demands shall be made.
                                                        R. M. HUMPHREY,
General Superintendent Colored Farmer's Alliance and Cotton-Pickers' League.
        Humphrey declares the league is now 800,000 strong and is growing at
the rate of 40,000 a day and expects a membership of 1,200,000 by the date
fixed for the strike. Farmers are paying 50 cents per hundred, and cannot
pay more, and will make a stubborn resistance to this attempt by the laborers
for higher wages.

If there is a struggle much cotton will probably be left ungathered
in the fields. The organizations, so says Humphrey, cover all the cotton
States.

American Citizen (Kansas City, Kansas), September 11, 1891.

36. NOT A BIT ALARMED

Victoria County Not Uneasy About Getting Cotton Pickers
Plenty of Mexican Labor, and Besides Pickers Cannot
Live Without Money

VICTORIA, Texas, September 7.--The reported organization of the negroes
for the purpose of exacting $1 per 100 pounds for picking cotton does not
cause much uneasiness among the farmers of this section with whom your correspondent has conversed. Such a movement if successfully carried out might
cause the planters to lose some cotton, but there would be great distress
and poverty among the strikers this winter if they lost the wages for cotton
picking. Besides, Mexican labor is too easily obtainable for Texas farmers
to worry about the matter.

Houston Daily Post, September 8, 1891.

37. THE COTTON PICKERS' LEAGUE

If the proposed strike of the cotton pickers, mentioned in our special
from Houston, Tex., yesterday, comes off it is not likely to amount to anything.
The movement is in no sense the outcome of the alliance reform crusade.
It was organized by General Superintendent Humphrey, of the Colored Farmers'
Alliance, who, working through the lodges of the order, has succeeded in
getting up a cotton pickers' league. This man, Humphrey, when he recently
visited Georgia, was not very cordially received by our alliancemen. Our
Georgia farmers in the alliance thoroughly understand the negro. They know
how to deal with him, and they have not encouraged him in any movement that
would probably be inconvenient and injurious to both races.
This strike of the cotton pickers, if it materializes, will be the work
of Humphrey and his associates. It will not receive the endorsement of genuine alliancemen, whether white or colored.
Perhaps it is unnecessary to treat the matter seriously. The demands
of the league, as stated by Humphrey, are absurdly extravagant. Cotton picking was never worth, and never will be worth, $1 per hundred.
If an organized effort is made by the colored cotton pickers to take advantage of the planters by this sudden movement, they will find all the employing, land-owning and business classes of the south so solidly arrayed
against them that there will be nothing before them but starvation or emigration. The negroes very generally understand the situation, and it will
take something more than Humphrey's order to plunge them into a strike which
promises so little and threatens so much of evil to themselves.
The farmers are not responsible for this rash break, and will not be
hurt by it.

Atlanta Constitution, September 8, 1891.

38. WON'T HURT GEORGIA

The Proposed Strike of the Negro Alliancemen
Will Have Little Effect

Will the negro alliance go out on a strike and refuse to pick any cotton for less than $1 per hundred?

Maybe they will, and maybe they will not.

But if they do it will probably not injure the Georgia farmer to the
extent of one dollar.

That's the opinion of several of the most prominent farmers in the
state.

The special in yesterday's CONSTITUTION from Dallas, Tex., telling about
this movement of the negro alliancemen, was much discussed in Atlanta yesterday.

By most people the story was given credence, but some said they did not
believe there was such a movement among the colored alliances throughout the
south.

What President Livingston Thinks

Colonel Livingston was seen and asked for his opinion about it.

"It may be true," said he, "and then again it may not. But what if it
is true? It would be rather a benefit than an injury to the Georgia farmers.
They will not lose a cent by it, but it might have the effect of raising the
price of cotton. I would not be surprised if there was something in it."

Many prominent members of the legislature express the same opinion.

Most of these gentlemen are among Georgia's most prominent farmers and
their views are, therefore, of peculiar value upon this subject. They speak
from a close observation and a thorough knowledge of the true status of
affairs.

What They Say

Senator Zachry was present when President Livingston expressed his views.

"I think it will help the Georgia farmers, but it will hurt the large
planters in Mississippi and other places in the southwest. Now in my county
--Henry--four-fifths of the farmers are not dependent upon the negro alliance
men or any other negroes to pick their cotton, and it may be taken as an
average county. They pick it themselves, or it is picked by their tenants.
I believe it would go a long way to raise the price of cotton if they were
to do it. There is no negro alliance in my county and I have no opportunity
of knowing whether such a movement is being worked in Georgia or not."

Mr. Calvin, of Richmond, saw a silver lining to the cloud: "Providence,"
says he, "works in a mysterious way. I believe that all these troubles are
settled by adjustment, and I believe that this will in some way be to the
good of the farmers of Georgia. But I can hardly believe that there is anything in the story. It is so unlike Humphrey. And it is unlike the former
actions of the negro alliance. They have, heretofore, been co-operating
with the white alliance, and working along harmoniously together, and I can
hardly believe that there is such a movement among the colored alliance."

Mr. Barrett, of Pike, is very confident in regard to the cotton crop
and the labor connected with it. He says:

"This attempt to raise the price to $1 is all buncombe. They will never
do it in the world. Why, they ought to be glad enough to pick it at any
price. The cotton crop will be short this year in the state, and in my opinion there will be more pickers than there will be cotton. In middle Georgia
the negro alliance is not well enough organized to affect a single farmer.
At the low price at which cotton is selling now the farmers would let it stay
in the patch before they would pay such exhorbitant prices to have it picked.
I do not fear any edict of the negro alliance, and I think the farmers may
rest assured that no serious harm will be done."

Mr. Reid of Putnam: "If this plan is carried out the farmers just can't
afford to have their cotton picked. It would amount to 3 cents on the pound
for lint cotton, which is far more than it is worth. I can very readily see
that the object of these resolutions is to have the land rented or worked on
shares. If they are well organized they may be able to carry out their object,

but I hardly think they will be able to do so in Georgia. This is my only
hope for the farmers of the state, and I would not be surprised if the
organization did some damage in other sections.

Mr. Payne of Upson: "There is no order of the colored alliance in my
county that I know of, but I have some fears that this strike may interfere
with the farmers in other sections. If they have to pay $1 per 100 pounds,
it would be ruinous. Why, at the rate of 50 cents per hundred it costs
just one bale in six for picking, and at the proposed price it would amount
to one-third of the cotton picked. The result would be to leave much of the
cotton in the field."

Mr. Mobley of Harris: "The colored alliance in my part of the country
don't amount to much, and I don't think the strike will or can affect us to
any extent. They will hardly attempt to raise the price to any such figure
in my section, and if they did it would affect very few, as nearly all the
hands are either croppers, and have to give the land owner one-half the
crop, or they rent the land at a certain sum and raise their own crop. So
it will be hard to affect our section to any great extent."

Mr. Faust of Oglethorpe: "In our section the hands that grow the cotton
pick it, so it is necessary for us to hire very little picking. So I think
it likely we have all our cotton picked. Such a price, however, if rigidly
adhered to, would cause the destruction of much cotton, simply from the fact
that the farmers would not be able to pay that amount, and the cotton would
remain in the fields."

Mr. McAfee of Crawford: "I believe that the very situation of the
negroes themselves will prevent the price from going much above the ordinary
standard. It's a matter of meat and bread with them. I am familiar with
the whole section about where I live, and I don't think this threatened
strike will do us much damage. The farmers will pay no such price and I
don't think it can be forced on them. Over one-half of the farmers in my
section rent out portions of their farm to the negroes who run them. I
hardly think this alliance has the power to do what it threatens, at least
not in Georgia. What damage it may do in the west and in Texas where the
cotton crop is so large, and they rely entirely upon the negroes, is another
matter, and probably a very serious one."

Mr. Swain of Gordon: "I don't think there is any branch of the colored
alliance in my county. A negro came there and tried to form one, but the
negroes there were afraid of it, so I think we will have very little trouble,
even though such a strike should go into effect in the alliance. Most of
the people in my county who raise cotton have hands on their places and those
who don't can get all the help they want at 50 cents per hundred. They will
never pay a cent more. No, threats of a strike give us no fear.

Mr. Hill of Cherokee: "I live in north Georgia and there are very few
negroes in that section. I don't think they have any organization of this
order there. Our people will never pay such an exorbitant price, and I don't
think the hands will dare to ask it. Its effect will hardly be felt up our
way."

Mr. Traylor of Troup: "My opinion is that this raise in the price of
picking cotton won't hurt us much. We have an order of the colored alliance
in my county, but it is not of sufficient strength to warrant much fear on
the part of the farmers. If, however, $1 per hundred is charged, I think the
farmers will be obliged to pay it, or they will have to let their cotton rot
in the fields."

Mr. Meriwether of Wilkes: "We have some might bad negroes in our part
of the state, but if there is any colored alliance there I don't know it.
The farmers would be unable to pay such an exhorbitant price, and as the
negroes have to live, I think they would very easily come to terms. This is
the view I take of it, and I am perfectly satisfied that the farmers in
Georgia won't suffer to any material extent by this threatened strike."

Mr. Oattes of Muscogee: "If the pickers carry out this strike the cotton
will simply rot in the fields. The price of cotton is too low, and the
farmers cannot afford to pay $1 and rations for picking it. The organization
may be strong enough in some parts of the state, but my impression is that
the negroes will have a sweet time while on their strike, as they are entirely
dependent upon the farmers for what they eat. After paying such prices for
picking cotton the farmers would have absolutely nothing left, and they cannot

and will not stand it."

Mr. Pope of Oglethorpe: "In my section the colored alliancemen will be
the ones who will have to hire the pickers and pay the price. They rent the
land, raise the cotton, and then either have to have it picked or pick it
themselves. The strike won't amount to much over my way, but it looks as
if it might be a serious matter in the west, out through Texas and Mississippi."

Mr. LeConte of Bartow: "I don't believe the strike will affect the
people at all in our section. We have very little cotton, and so hire very
little labor. The strike can't affect us much, because what little cotton
that is raised is generally picked by the farm hands, and by the families
of those raising it."

Mr. Graves of Newton: "I think this strike will embarrass the farmer
very much, but not so much in middle Georgia as in other sections, as that
is the cropping portion of the state. I believe the strike will affect
Georgia less than any other state, however, as there are such a large number
of croppers and colored alliancemen who merely rent the land on which they
plant. One harm it will do, however, if this one-dollar-a-hundred rate is
paid to any extent, and that is, the negroes will abandon their crops,
which are generally covered up by mortgages, and will go to work to make the
wages. But I think there are enough laborers outside the alliance to do
Georgia's cotton picking, and to do it at the same old rates."

Mr. Everett of Stewart: "We would let the cotton rot in the fields in
our section before we would pay such prices for picking it. We can't afford
it, and won't pay it. If enforced, this strike would be ruinous to the whole
cotton crop; but in my opinion Georgia is safe from any evils which the
colored alliance may inflict, as there is plenty of outside labor we can get
at any time."

Mr. Harris of Quitman: "It has been my experience that most of the intelligent negroes admit that they get more for picking cotton than it is
worth. I am of the opinion that the strike will not affect us at all. Most
of my cotton is picked by croppers who get half of what they make. I don't
think they can or will raise the price of picking it, for it would not do
the least good. The croppers are compelled to gather their own crops, or
they get nothing."

Mr. Wheeler of Walker: "The strike won't affect us much as there are
not many niggers in our section. The colored alliance does not amount to
much up there, but before I pay R1 a hundred for picking, I'll hire white
laborers at $18 per month, and can get plenty of them at that. The strike
won't work."

Mr. Twitty of Jackson: "This strike may have a serious effect out in
the west and through Texas, as the cotton crop is so extensive out that way.
But it will scarcely touch us here in Georgia because the conditions are
different. We have a shorter crop in the first place, then there are
numbers of croppers throughout the state besides others who rent land. These
will be compelled to gather their cotton, and I think it will be a matter of
starvation or not starvation with a good many others. I scarcely think we
will pay $1 per hundred."

Mr. Brodnax of Walton: "This strike is not going to amount to anything,
whatever, simply because the alliance hasn't the strength here in Georgia
to carry out the plan proposed. The farmers will not pay any exorbitant
prices, and the negroes are obliged to live; so, between them both, I think
the cotton will go to market as it usually does."

Atlanta Constitution, September 8, 1891.

39. THIS STATE IS SAFE

From the Proposed Cotton Pickers' Strike

President E. S. Richardson Speaks

MARSHALLSVILLE, Ga., September 8.--[Special.]--There will be no strike among the cotton pickers of Georgia.

That is what the people say who know most about the colored alliances of the state, and who are responsible for their government.

The Letter from President Richardson

The following letter, from President Edward S. Richardson, is furnished THE CONSTITUTION as the best answer to the rumors floating around:

"MARSHALLSVILLE, Ga., September 8.--Editor Constitution: I have just read your special from Houston, Tex., regarding the colored alliance.

"I cannot speak for Mr. Humphrey, but I must say that the report is false, so far as it relates to the colored alliancemen of Georgia.

"We have not obligated ourselves to do anything of the kind, and I am glad that a few of those you interviewed had sense enough to discredit the story.

Not Organized to Injure

"We are not organized to injure farmers of any color or condition, but to further and improve the system of agriculture among the race. The only burden or hindrance with which the colored alliance has had to contend has been two or three white men that have tried to shape its policy.

The Work of White Men

"I do not doubt that the circular mentioned in your dispatch has been sent out to the different colored alliances, but the instigators of the movement are white men, working for personal gains.

"We hope to co-operate with the white alliance in an agricultural way. We are here together, and peace must reign supreme.

Causes For Suspicion

"The colored alliance has been suspicious of the white alliance of late, owing to two or three bills championed by them in the legislature, but that, of itself, was not sufficient to warrant a retaliation of the kind mentioned.

A Hope For Rest

"We hope some day that this negro question will be settled. We are tired of being tools and dupes of men who have no interest in the race. The negro must call a halt and support those who will support him. We have borne this treatment for twenty-five years. We cannot and will not stand it longer. We voted men into office only to be discarded by them. Let the white men who intend to ignore the negro or get him into trouble swap seats.

There Must be Peace

"I am sorry to be continually denying reports about our order, and I will say once for all that peace and friendship must exist between the races.
                    Respectfully,
                    "EDWARD S. RICHARDSON."

State Lecturer Carter Talks

THOMASVILLE, Ga., September 8.--[Special.]--J. W. Carter, state Lecturer of the Colored Farmers' Alliance of Georgia, has a card which will appear in tomorrow's Time-Enterprise. He is strongly opposed to the advance of price in cotton picking, as proposed by the cotton pickers' league. Among the many things he has discussed in his card, Jack says:

"As a member of the state board of trustees, and a mouthpiece of the colored alliance of Georgia, by virtue of my office of state lecturer, I condemn the members no only as being foreign to the constitution, but perfectly dangerous in every sense of the word. It is dangerous for a thousand

reasons. There are a great many colored farmers who have to hire cotton
picked, and the new order would be equally as hard on them."
    Carter strikes hard truth in the following sentence:
    "I am opposed to strikes. They have never done poor people any good,
only those who order and lead them are benefited."
    In conclusion, Carter gives the following advice to the colored farmers
of Georgia:
    "Have nothing to do with the strike. Thousands of you have made debts
to be paid by picking cotton, and you know better than any one else, what
you can pick cotton for. We don't intend to interfere with your local affairs, but would advise you to arrange your matters as best suits your circumstances. Strikes may do for the alliance of Texas. It will not be the
case in Georgia."

Atlanta Constitution, September 9, 1891.

40. GATHERING COTTON

The New York Times Speaking of the Pronunciamento of
President Humphrey, of the Colored Alliance

    The prospects of the strike which the general superintendent is insti-
gating seem to be especially gloomy. If it were possible to induce all the
cotton pickers to quit work at once, the question how are they to be sustained throughout the strike would at once arise. They cannot resist each
other, and such is the improvidence of the race that very few of them will
be able to support themselves. What are known in Caucasian unions as "assessments" will be likely in an African union to take the form of raids on the
chickens and on the hogs and hominy of the oppressor. These means of sustaining life have been regretfully recognized by the colored cotton picker
as rather a supplement to industry than as a substitute for it. If it were
an adequate and trustworthy substitute they would not work at all. For the
same reason it is not likely that the strike proclaimed will even be attempted. The colored laborer, according to the testimony of those who know him,
works only that he may eat, and strikes work as soon as his immediate wants
are supplied. That is to say, when he has provisions to sustain him during
even a short strike he will strike of his own accord. When he has not such
provision he will not strike even at the bidding of a proclamation by the
general superintendent of the Colored Farmers' Alliance and Cotton Pickers'
League.
    The Times does not understand the situation. In the cotton regions the
cultivation of cotton is a partnership between the white land owners and the
negro laborers. Most generally the partnership specifies that the negroes
shall furnish the labor and get one-third of the crop. It is the duty of
the negroes in almost every contract with the land owner to supply the labor
for chopping and picking. If they strike the burden of the strike will fall
on the negro tenant.
    When the period of chopping and picking occurs it is necessary to call
in the women and children of the colored tenants. Of course the negroes
who are interested in the crop will want to keep their price down. The
negroes who are interested in keeping up the prices of chopping and picking
are the negroes who are not bound to the landowners--the surplus negroes
who are engaged spasmodically in railroad work, turpentine orchards and saw
mills. These surplus hands are the men ready to strike at any time for
higher chopping and picking wages. There is no way to control these men.
The Farmers' Alliance have organized them into a solid phalanx, and have extended to them their sympathy and support. The tramp negroes from the railroads, the turpentine orchards, the steamboats and the saw mills will organize
to strike for higher wages for chopping and picking whenever they wish.
    Just here we are brought face to face with the situation. Must we sur-
render to the negro tramps? It is easy for the negroes to organize into

secret societies. They like that sort of business. They will have no
difficulty, now that Adams' Farmers' Alliance coalesces with them, to demand anything they may wish and to enforce their wishes through their secret
society.

There is nothing more dangerous to liberty than secret political societies, and there is nothing more dangerous to the white land-owners of the
South than the secret political societies of negroes which can dictate wages.

Mobile Daily Register, September 12, 1891.

41.   THE GEORGIA PICKERS

The President of the State Colored Alliance Speaks

He Repudiates the Humphrey Scheme and Says the Georgia
Negroes are Not in it at All.

"MARSHALLSVILLE, Ga., September 9.--Editor Constitution: I have just
read your special from Houston, Texas, regarding the colored alliance. I
cannot speak for Mr. Humphrey, but I must say that the report is false, so
far as it relates to the colored alliancemen of Georgia. We have not obligated ourselves to do anything of the kind, and I am glad that a few of
these you interviewed had sense enough to discredit the story. We are not
organized to injure farmers of any color or condition, but to further and
improve the system of agriculture among the race. The only burden or hindrance with which the colored alliance has had to contend has been two or
three white men that have tried to shape its policy.

The Work of White Men

"I do not doubt that the circular mentioned in your dispatch has been
sent out to the different colored alliances, but the instigators of the
movement are white men, working for personal gains.

"We hope to co-operate with the white alliance in an agricultural way.
We are here together, and peace must reign supreme.

"The colored alliance has been suspicious of the white alliance of late,
owing to two or three bills championed by them in the legislature, but that
of itself, was not sufficient to warrant a retaliation of the kind mentioned.

A Hope For Best

"We hope some day that this negro question will be settled. We are
tired of being tools and dupes of men who have no interest in the race. The
negro must call a halt and support those who will support him. We have borne
this treatment for twenty-five years. We cannot and will not stand it longer
We voted men into office only to be discarded by them. Let the white men
who intend to ignore the negro or get him into trouble swap seats.

"I am sorry to be continually denying reports about our order, and I
will say once for all that peace and friendship must exist between the races.
Respectfully,
                "EDWARD S. RICHARDSON."

State Lecturer Carter Talks

THOMASVILLE, Ga., September 9--J. W. Carter, State lecturer of the
Colored Farmers' alliance of Georgia, has a card which will appear in tomorrow's Time-Enterprise. He is strongly opposed to the advance of price of
cotton-picking, as proposed by the Cotton Pickers' league. Among the many
things he has discussed in his card, Jack says:

"As a member of the State board of trustees, and a mouthpiece of the
colored alliance of Georgia, by virtue of my office of State lecturer, I
condemn the measure not only as being foreign to the constitution, but perfectly dangerous for a thousand reasons. There are a great many colored
farmers who have to hire cotton picked, and the new order would be equally
as hard on them."

Carter strikes hard truth in the following sentence:
"I am opposed to strikes. They have never done poor people any good,
only those who order and lead them are benefited."
In conclusion, Carter gives the following advice to the colored farmers
of Georgia:
"Have nothing to do with the strike. Thousands of you have made debts
to be paid by cotton picking, and you know better than any one else what you
can pick cotton for. We don't intend to interfere with your local affairs,
but would advise you to arrange your matters as best suits your circumstances.
Strikes may do for the alliance of Texas, it will not be the case in Georgia.

Houston Daily Post, September 12, 1891.

42. PRESIDENT POLK'S MENACE

Here in the South a great trouble has arisen between the cotton pickers
and the planters. It would seem that the Alliance could be of service in
such a juncture. Indeed, it was said to have been organized for just such
business. But Messrs. Polk and Macune and the rest of the officers have no
time to give to such things, but must spend the money of the order in stump-
ing tour for political purposes all over the Union. Peffer and Polk are
birds of a feather and they seem to have a thorough understanding. Peffer's
position, however, is more honest. He is an Alliance man and the head of the
Third Party. He regards the latter as the offspring of the farmer. He favors
throwing the whole Alliance vote to the Third Party. He goes about the country openly and emphatically urging this course. Polk, being in entire sympathy with Peffer, secretly tries to achieve by indirection the same end.
Peffer must, therefore, command more respect than Polk. The Democrats of the
South cannot afford to palter with either. [69]

Memphis Appeal-Avalanche, September 13, 1891.

43. STILL SNATCHING COTTON

Czar Humphrey's Million of Negro Strikers All A Myth

Reports From All Over the South Show the Negroes Picking Cotton for Dear Life
--Reports Also Indicate That the Negroes Have Never Heard of Humphrey.

Alabama Negroes at Work

BIRMINGHAM, Ala., Sept. 12.--The threatened cotton pickers' strike in
Alabama has not materialized. Reports have been received here from all over
the State, and the men are working everywhere. No strike was feared in Alabama, however. Sixty per cent, of the colored Alliance men of this State
rent land or work on the lease or shares system. Hence, a strike would be
impracticable.

Still Picking in North Carolina

WILMINGTON, N.C., Sept. 12.--Thus far there are no indications of a strike
of cotton pickers in North Carolina, and if inaugurated it is believed it will
prove a dismal failure. The white Alliance men cannot afford to countenance
such a movement, and will use their best efforts to prevent it. . . .

No Strike in Mississippi

Special Dispatch to the Appeal-Avalanche
VICKSBURG, MISS., Sept. 12.--No trouble with the cotton pickers, as
threatened by Humphrey, their Texas leader, has occurred in this territory.

Hands are in plentiful supply at the usual rates.

A Myth in Georgia

ATLANTA, Ga., Sept. 12--The reported strike of cotton pickers in Georgia proved to be a myth. The negroes are all at work, except in such portions of the State where it is raining.

Memphis Appeal-Avalanche, September 13, 1891.

44. IT DID NOT DEVELOP

The Cotton Was Picked on Yesterday Just as Usual

A Talk With Manager Humphrey

NEW ORLEANS, September 12.--A Picayune's Houston, Tex., special says today is set for the big cotton pickers' strike which is to embrace every state in the cotton belt. Colonel Humphrey, the white man who has engineered the scheme, and who expects to reap the benefit, said last night to your correspondent:

"I have the names of 1,100,000 pickers in all portions of the south who stopped picking last night until they get a $1 a hundred and board. These men are all under oath to pick no man's cotton but their own until the 1st of November."

In reply to the question as to where the movement was strongest, he replied: In Louisiana, Mississippi and Alabama nearly every colored picker has joined the league, and that in the Atlantic states the membership is large. As to how the pickers will exist through the fall and winter, he says they have been advised to seek other employment at any price, all of which is utterly impracticable, as cottonfield negroes could not make much headway in the cities and towns, and if they should strike it would mean just so many petty thieves turned loose upon the communities, colored cotton pickers, as a rule, being the most impoverished and thriftless class of men on the plantation.

Reports from different sections of south Texas show that no trouble is anticipated though there is some dissatisfaction among the darkies of the black belt, but, of what nature he did not know.

North Carolinians Not Afraid

CHARLOTTE, N. C., September 12.--Cotton picking has not fairly begun in this section as yet. Consequently nothing is heard of the cotton pickers' strike. A special to The Chronicle from Raleigh gives the following correspondent, Butler of the white Farmers' Alliance of this state. President Butler said:

"A strike is not yet ordered for North Carolina. I read today the organ of the colored alliance. It is Humphrey's paper, and is published in Texas. It orders a strike for Texas and South Carolina. The reason why a strike is not ordered for this state is that the strength of the alliance is not so great here as in the states above referred to. I do not think the figures giving 35,000 as the strength of the colored alliance in North Carolina are correct. I think that the alliance is exaggerating its strength. Today we had a sort of conference here in regard to this matter of strike. No definite action was agreed upon.

The Colored Men's Mistake

"We await the order for a strike in this state. We hope it will not come. Next week The Reform Press will lecture colored alliancemen and will take a decided stand in disapproval of their course. The Progressive Farmer will have an editorial on the matter, and so will my paper, The Clinton Caucasian. The fact is, the negro alliance is kicking at things in sight instead of joining the white alliance in getting at the cause of the troubles. The negroes have made a mistake. Some years ago the white alliance struck

and made a failure of it. This strike is aimed directly at the cotton
planter, who is a friend and supporter of the negro. We will try to induce
the colored alliance to reconsider its hasty, ill-timed and improper action.
If persuasion is of no use, and the strike is called to North Carolina, then
we will crush it out. We have the strength in the white alliance here to do
it."

No Signs in South Carolina

CHARLESTON, S.C., September 12.--Specials to The News and Courier from
all parts of South Carolina state that there are no signs of a strike in the
cotton fields. Nobody seems to know anything about the alleged strike of
cotton pickers. Farmers are paying from thirty to forty cents per hundred.

No Strike in Florida

JACKSONVILLE, Fla., September 12.--Inquiry in all sections of the cotton
belt in Florida fails to discover any locality where the negro cotton pickers
have joined the strike announced for today. A large portion of the cotton
lands are cultivated on the lease and share system.

All Quiet in Alabama

MONTGOMERY, Ala., September 1w.--There is no development of the cotton
pickers' strike in Alabama. As far as known no such movement was ever intended here.

Florence Has Not Heard of It

FLORENCE, S.C., September 12.--[Special.]--The reported cotton pickers'
strike has not been heard of by the alliance in this section. No circulars
were received from Humphrey. Neither farmers nor cotton pickers could afford
it.

New York Times, September 13, 1891.

45. A FLASH IN THE PAN

That's What the Cotton Strike Amounted To

The Negroes Not So Foolish as to be Gulled Into Engaging in a Hopeless Contest

Mr. R. M. Humphrey, superintendent of the Cotton Pickers' league, was
found in bed at 10 o'clock last night when a Post reporter called at his
residence on Magnolia street to learn if he had any news from the cotton
pickers' strike.

Several heavy knocks on the big walnut door aroused Mr. Humphrey from
his slumbers, and a moment later he put in appearance.

Mr. Humphrey's home is in a secluded spot a hundred yards back from the
street. When he appeared at the opened door and asked who was there, it was
necessary for the reporter to make known his identity.

"Anything from the league, Mr. Humphrey?" asked the reporter after
apologizing for the abrupt intrusion.

"Not a word," came the reply instantly.

"Have you received nothing from the outside country showing to what extent the strike has grown?"

"Not a word, sir."

"Did you receive any further memberships today?"

"A few came in, but not many."

It was evident that the leader of the Cotton Pickers' league did not
want to talk, and the interview was brought to a close.

In Other Counties

Walker County

HUNTSVILLE, Texas, September 12.--From a general inquiry it is evident
that the Walker county negro population is hardly aware that such a thing as

a general strike of cotton pickers is expected to take place today. They
are not "in it." The majority of them are tenanted anyway, and pick their
own cotton. It is hardly thought the average cotton picker can afford to
strike, as the little money he makes the next month or so is very essential
to his existence during that time. The only strike noticeable here this
evening was the "strike" the pickers were all making for town, to get a
chance to spend the money they have made the past week. A few of the largest
cotton raisers interviewed, laughed at the idea of a strike and said if such
a thing should happen they would let the cotton rot in the field before they
would pay $1 per 100 and board, especially during the present low prices for
the staple.

WALLER COUNTY

HEMPSTEAD, Texas, September 12.--The 12th of September has come and gone
and with it Humphrey's cotton pickers' strike. The demand for $1 per 100
pounds has not even been mentioned by the colored pickers and Monday morning
hundreds of pickers will leave this place for different parts of the county
at the usual rate, 50 cents per 100 and board. No county in the State would
have been more seriously affected by such a strike than would Waller county.
We are right in the negro belt and depend upon negro labor entirely. But
the best of feeling prevails between the whites and blacks and Humphrey's
scheme, had it been successful, would have been a curse to the very people
he pretends to wish to benefit.

WASHINGTON COUNTY

BRENHAM, Texas, September 12.--The Cotton Pickers' league has no following in this county. The cotton pickers all worked till noon today with
no thought of striking, quitting then for their usual Saturday half holiday.
The POST correspondent has interviewed a number of them and they are all
unanimous in the opinion that the scheme could not have been carried out here
for the reason that all the members of the colored alliance in this county
are farmers and it would be against their interest to encourage a raise in
the price of picking, as they would have to pay it. As far as Washington
county is concerned the league is a failure and no strike has or will take
place.

WHARTON COUNTY

WHARTON, Texas, September 12.--It suddenly developed here today that
there were five colored alliances in this county. As this is the day set for
the strike. The POST reporter learns that delegates from the different alliances in the county are in secret session discussing what action to take.
From leading negroes in the alliance it is learned that no strike is probable.
Only one of the lodges hold out for a strike, while four are against it. The
dissension comes from tramp cotton pickers. Leading colored men in the
county are against the strike to a man.

VICTORIA COUNTY

VICTORIA, Texas, September 12.--The threatened cotton pickers' strike
did not alarm nor affect Victoria county farmers. The city was crowded with
colored people today, but not one of them could be found who had complied with
Czar Humphrey's mandate or who intended to do so. There was no strike in any
part of the county. The colored people of this county are sensible and
generally prosperous and have wisely decided to let well enough alone.

BURLESON COUNTY

CALDWELL, Texas, September 12.--After diligent inquiry we fail to find
any materialization of the great cotton pickers' strike. The negroes constitute the bulk of the cotton pickers in this county, and as the darkey is
not a bright and shining example of a secret keeper, and as we have heard
nothing of the strike here, we conclude that the pickers of this county are
not "in it" to any very considerable extent.

TRINITY COUNTY

TRINITY, Texas, September 12.--After interviewing the business men of
the city and several of the colored leaders, THE POST representative is
authorized to state that there will be no strike of the cotton pickers

in this section.

BRAZORIA COUNTY

VELASCO, Texas, September 12.--The representative has not heard of any
league among the negro cotton pickers to strike for $1 per 100 pounds, though
it may exist and crop out later. As a class the plantation hands in Brazoria
county are probably better paid and housed than in any other part of the
South, as proves by recent census statistics and the appearance of their
cabins and surroundings.

AUSTIN COUNTY

BELLVILLE, Texas, September 12.--There is no organized strike of the
cotton pickers here, although a gentleman of color was in town yesterday,
who, it was said, was using his influence in that direction. From what can
be learned, the movement will amount to nothing in this county.

SEALY, Texas, September 12.--If there is now or going to be a strike
among the cotton pickers in this locality, there is at this time no evidence
of it.

CALDWELL COUNTY

LULING, Texas, September 12.--A number of farmers were seen this morning,
none of whom anticipate any trouble with the cotton pickers. None have had
any intimation of a strike. One or two prominent negroes were seen and they
think their people are very well satisfied with prices. One very sensible
negro said that he thought the pickers were making more money than the producer, and that at the present prices the farmer is paying all that he can
afford.

RAYS COUNTY

SAN MARCOS, Texas, September 12.--Our planters and dealers unite in
saying that the proclamation under the auspices of the Colored Farmers'
alliance of a Cotton Pickers' league for the advancement of the wages of
pickers has fallen still-born here. A large part of the crop is gathered.
There are a sufficiency of Mexicans to complete the work and the negroes
themselves are taking little or no interest in the movement.

ROBERTSON COUNTY

FRANKLIN, Texas, September 12.--Our town has been quiet today as regards
the cotton pickers' strike. Negroes here seem to know nothing of the organization and are wholly indifferent on the subject where interviewed. The prevailing opinion here is that Humphrey is panting for a little notoriety and
fell upon this plan to obtain it. The cotton crop is falling 25 per cent
short.

ANDERSON COUNTY

PALESTINE, Texas, September 12.--The cotton pickers' strike met with
little attention here and was scarcely agitated upon the streets. Most of
the negroes here deem it to their interest not to make such a demand. Two
worthless white colored men electioneered the apprehended strike without
success. One farmer reports an attempt. He discharged them and matters
immediately settled.

FORT BEND COUNTY

RICHMOND, Texas, September 12.--The cotton pickers in this section of
the county seem to be taking very little interest in the proposed general
strike to take place tonight for $1 per hundred. Your reporter has inter-
viewed many of the largest cotton planters and they anticipate no trouble
whatever in getting enough labor to pick the growing crop at reasonable
wages.

LEON COUNTY

JEWETT, Texas, September 12.--No strikers in Jewett. THE POST correspondent has interviewed several of Jewett's leading men on the sensible results should the negroes succeed in their effort, and the popular opinion
seems to be that it would not affect the cotton crop much but would cause
the farmers to cultivate other staples which would be far more profitable
than cotton.

DE WITT COUNTY

CUERO, Texas, September 12.--The question of the negro strike is not known here among the darkies. After dilligent inquiry from whites and blacks from all sections of the county, nothing can be learned of any intended strike. The alliance has several lodges in the county, but none are going into the strike. In fact, all darkies interviewed were opposed to the movement.

GUADALUPE COUNTY

SEGUIN, Texas, September 12.--There is no strike here by cotton pickers. There is no talk among pickers of undertaking a strike. Two-thirds of the pickers don't know anything about the agitation. No interest is taken in it. Cotton is being rapidly harvested and in thirty days more the work will be over. Some are finishing now.

WILSON COUNTY

FLORESVILLE, Texas, September 12.--The negroes of this county as far as can be learned have paid no attention to the strike proposed for today. Very few negroes are employed in picking cotton in this county anyway, most of it being done by Mexicans and by the families of the men who raise it.

POLK COUNTY

LIVINGSTON, Texas, September 12.--THE POST representative has made inquiry of planters and pickers as to the proposed strike, and all concur in the opinion that it will not affect the cotton interest here in the least; that there will in a word not be any strike in this section of country.

LEE COUNTY

GIDDINGS, Texas, September 12.--No uneasiness here about the alleged strike of cotton pickers. As a rule negroes are working on shares and only have their own cotton to pick. Others get 60 cents per 100 pounds and board.

WILLIAMSON COUNTY

TAYLOR, Texas, September 12.--Can't find anyone here that knows anything about Humphrey, his organization or the proposed strike. About two-thirds of the cotton crop is gathered.

COLORADO COUNTY

ALLEYTON, Texas, September 12.--Up to 1 o'clock no demonstrations of a strike among cotton pickers, and farmers entertain no fears that there will be any in this immediate vicinity.

MONTGOMERY COUNTY

WILLIS, Texas, September 12.--The cotton pickers at this point do not seem to know anything about Mr. Humphrey's manifesto, hence there is no indication of a strike.

FAYETTE COUNTY

FLATONIA, Texas, September 12.--Cotton pickers in and near Flatonia are not among strikers. At Moulton, eight miles south of here, thirty-three have struck.

NAVARRO COUNTY

CORSICANA, Texas, September 12.--No strike among the cotton pickers announced here today. The farmers are not anticipating a strike.

HAYS COUNTY

KYLE, Texas, September 12.--No strike here. Pickers know nothing about it.

KARNES COUNTY

RUNGE, Texas, September 12.--There was no cotton pickers' strike in this neighborhood today, as was expected. Several farmers were in town and report that no trouble is feared. Quite a number of cotton pickers were hired today for 60 and 65 cents per 100.

BRAZOS COUNTY

BRYANT, Texas, September 12.--There are no demonstrations of any strike

here among the cotton pickers. Our darkies are either owners of land or
renters, and do not pay any attention to set days for something they know
they can't get. A few of the town bums and loafers are grouped about the
corners, but to no effect. Monday is the day cotton pickers' contracts are
made.

GRIMES COUNTY

NAVASOTA, Texas, September 12.--No importance is attached to the contemplated strike of cotton pickers in this section today. Everybody has
heard of it and talked about it, and even the colored people are averse to
it, as most of them have cotton to be gathered and are unwilling to pay the
prices of the demand. Don't think it will materialize.

Houston Daily Post, September 13, 1891.

46. PRESIDENT L. L. POLK

The National Farmers' Alliance Leader Speaking in Kansas

Partial Approval of Humphrey's Plan
The Probability of a Third Party, and the Part It is
Likely to Play

TOPEKA, Kans., September 13.--[Special.]--President Polk, of the national alliance, has made three addresses in Kansas. President Polk's opening
has been devoted principally to himself. After giving his boyhood history,
he reached the war period.

Was Forced Into the War

He states that he did not go into the rebel wing from choice. He upheld
the union until the wave of secession swept over the south, when he did as
many others did who were forced to shoulder their muskets. He had been
offered the command of a company, but refused it, as acceptance would have
been construed into an endorsement of the cause whose arms he carried.
He afterwards accepted the office he held because by doing so he could
indirectly aid those who were fighting for the preservation of the union and
in a degree mitigate the sufferings of those who, like himself, had been
forced to bear arms against their country.

Upholds the Strikes

While not speaking directly about the contemplated strike of the cotton
pickers in the south, he said the oppressed agricultural laborers should and
shall demand the right of naming the compensation for their services, and
until these demands are acceded to let every field in the land contain rotted
produce, north or south.
"You here are fortunate in being your own laborers, but the plutocrats
of other states must be compelled to acknowledge the God-given rights of
laborers, whether they be white or black.
Some of our brethren have already made their demands, and they will be
granted or entire regions will contain only families ruined by their own
greed."
In an interview today, Colonel Polk stated that the alliance movement was
gaining thousands of converts throughout the south daily, and the great mass
of farmers, planters and laboring men had deserted the democratic party and
were standing squarely on the Ocala platform. "I believe the third party
will sweep every state in the south in 1892. The old bosses down there have
tried to bulldoze and force the people to take their democratic medicine,
but without result. Within the past six months I could have had any office
in the gifts of the democratic party, but I would not sell my principles for
pottage."
Mr. Polk uttered these words with feeling, and declared eternal warfare

on both the old parties. The bloody shirt, he said, will be wrapped around
the old sectional agitators, and they will be buried too deep for resurrec-
tion.

There Will Be a Third Party

"Will the alliance conference at Washington in February declare for a
third party?"
"I cannot say; but there will be a third party. It might have been
prevented four months ago, but now it is too late. Our people in the south
have been abused and sneered by the democratic bosses and the democratic
press, and we will stand it no longer. The negro domination cry won't prevent a break of the solid democracy. We will take care of the negroes and
see that they are allowed to vote. They are largely in this movement and
will be an important factor in the campaign next year."
"How about the pension question?"
"The alliance has nothing to say against the pensioning of soldiers who
fought for the union. When we were defeated, we accepted the result as final
and acquiesced. We shall never raise our voice against the legitimate pensioning of union soldiers. It is the result of warfare and we can shake
hands with our northern brothers who wore the blue and feel that they are
receiving only justice from a government whom they helped to preserve."

Confident of Victory

Mr. Polk said the people's party would, in his opinion, carry every
southern state next year. The alliance was for the Ocala demands and would
have nothing else.

Atlanta Constitution, September 14, 1891.

47. THE EXODUS OF NEGROES

It Occurred Yesterday, But Was Not Alarming in Extent

Cotton Picking Hereabouts Will Not Be Affected by It--Factors and Planters Want the Idle and Vagrant Negroes Driven From the Towns

The city ticket offices of the Kansas City, Fort Scott & Memphis and
the St. Louis, Iron Mountain & Southern Railroads in Memphis were yesterday
besieged during business hours by swarms of colored people in quest of the
cheap transportation to Oklahoma that had been advertised by the roads mentioned.
Every negro who went to inquire about the excursions did not buy a ticket. Many of them went for display, and many more because they had heard the
matter talked about so much that they could not forbear investigating an
excursion that they could not afford to participate in. About 150 tickets
represent the entire sales of the two roads, and these were about equally
divided between them. Most of them were sold to negroes who do not live in
Memphis, but work small farms in the adjacent territory. They came in early
in the morning with their families, and by midday had made Oklahoma the subject of conversation all over the city wherever there was a group of colored
people.
One rather aged negro, who got a ticket for himself and wife, was asked,
as he shoved the pasteboard into his pocket, where he was from.
"A couple of miles beyon' Bartlett."
"Have you a farm out there?"
"Yes; I've got some cotton planted."
"Isn't it pretty nearly ready to pick?"
"Yes, but I guess it'll stand for a month or so. Anyhow, I ain't goin'
to miss dis yer chance to see Oklahomy. If I like the country I will come
back and sell out."
All the tickets sold are for return trips, so that the exodus has but

little significance at the present time, except as it may influence other
negroes to go in the same direction to stay at a future time. Early in the
summer a good many negroes went to Oklahoma on a trip, and upon their return
were extravagant in their praise of the country and bold in predicting that
thousands of negroes would move there to stay this fall. But so far very
few of them have moved, although the outlook for such action was very favorable a week ago, when a protracted meeting in Chelsea was suspended, to be
resumed in Oklahoma when the participants all met in that promised land.
Those who went yesterday said that if they brought back a favorable report
the hegira would be taken up by thousands, but that threat will probably fall
as harmless as did its predecessor.

In any event the picking of cotton in this territory is not going to be
seriously interferred with. 'Squire Hughey, who operates a plantation near
the city, said yesterday that cotton in this vicinity will be ready for picking at the beginning of next week, and the work will be entered upon at once.
He said he did not think the combined action of either planters or pickers
would cut any figure in the prices paid the negroes, neither combination
being strong or general enough to interfere much, and prices this year will
be fixed as in former years, by the conditions in each case.

"I am not surprised," he said, "to learn that many of the negroes who
raise cotton have gone to Oklahoma and left their crop to suffer. That is
not contrary to their usual mode of procedure. They are very slovenly in the
management of their affairs. They are always in debt and always expect to
be. It is a curious fact that if one of them finds himself in debt at the
end of the year he estimates his profits at that much. If he can't get ahead
of his merchant he considers that he is losing money."

In view of the near approach of the cotton picking season the police
officials of Memphis have been requested by planters and factors, in an individual capacity, to drive from the city all the idle and vagrant negroes
that they may go to the country and help harvest the crop. The police say
they would be glad to do this as it would reduce the amount of crime in the
city, and the suburban robbery would be suspended for a time. Yet they do
not do it. Probably they are waiting for orders from the commissioners.

Memphis Appeal-Avalanche, September 16, 1891.

48. NEGRO COTTON PICKERS THREATENING

COFFYVILLE, Miss., Sept. 25.--The white people all along the line of the
Illinois Central railroad and in every county of the delta are actively preparing for an anticipated general attack by the blacks. Prominent men with
whom interviews have been had are seriously considering the outbreak and arms
are being bought on both sides. At Water Valley, ten miles north of here,
200 men have organized for protection. At Grenada, ten miles south of here
it is supposed that negro cotton hands have organized and will demand an
increase in their wages or guard the fields with shotguns and prevent others
from gathering crops. The present price for picking is 50¢ per hundred.

Leavenworth (La.) Advocate, September 28, 1889.

49. DELTA TROUBLES

GLENWOOD, Miss.--Louis Nelson and John Coleman were killed at Winter
City yesterday evening and Wilson Porter was hung at Sunnyside this morning.
. . . This swells the total number killed in the Delta troubles to 25. The
latest reports from Winter City say that 13 white men had surrounded Geo.
Allen the Negro leader a few miles from there. He has only one follower and
both are well armed. They will never surrender alone. A majority of the

women and children from up the river who ran away from their homes and came here for protection have returned home as they were assured that the trouble had about ended.

It has been discovered that the Durant Commercial Co. of Farmers' Alliance store at Durant, Miss. has been furnishing the money to Negroes by which they procured their guns. They of course did this as a regular commercial transaction, but they have been resolved upon. The Valden Negro newspaper has been ordered discontinued.

The number of guns captured amount to 220. They are improved Winchester and Spencer rifles. The plan of the Negroes becomes more diabolical as each tale is unfolded. Last Sunday four Negro excursion trains from Greenville, Jackson, Durant and Winona were to have arrived here early in the morning. The alarm given on last Saturday caused the railroads to cancel the excursion trains. It is estimated that 1,000 Negroes were to come.

The planters met at Sunnyside this morning and unanimously adopted the following resolutions:

WHEREAS, It is the sense of this meeting that the organization known here as the Colored Farmers' Alliance is being diverted from its original or supposed purpose and is being used by designing and corrupt Negroes to further their intentions and selfish motive. . . .

Washington Bee, September 27, 1889.

50.   A BLOODY RIOT

Fatal Fight Between Negro Cotton Pickers in Arkansas

The Culmination of a Strike For Higher Wages

MARIANNA, Ark., Sept. 26.--The trouble between the cotton pickers in St. Francis Township culminated in a riot. Forty armed negroes appeared in the township and drove all the pickers from the field and burned Planter Bond's gin-house. Subsequently the pickers and the armed invaders met and engaged in a fierce struggle, resulting in several negroes being killed and a number wounded. The Sheriff of the county quelled the disturbance and has the leaders in custody. The riot grew out of a strike inaugurated by a number of pickers who demanded 75 cents per 100 pounds, an increase of 25 cents. The planters refused their demands. The dissatisfied negroes at once struck and their places were immediately filled by others. The strikers became annoyed at these proceedings and tried to persuade the working negroes to quit. Being refused, a great fight ensued, women, men and children participating, armed with hoes, sticks, knives and revolvers. It is reported that two men were killed outright.

St. Louis Post Dispatch, September 27, 1891.

51.   BLOOD AND TERROR

Negro Uprising in Lee County, Ark.

Death and Destruction Threatened to the Planters

White People Organize to Resist the Black Mob

An armed band of 100 negroes, bent on death and devastation, is carrying terror over Lee County, Ark.

One well-known planter, Tom Miller, agent for J. F. Frank, has been

killed, so report has it, several ginhouses have been burned, and the black
mob is still at large with a posse of white men in pursuit.

This information was brought to the city yesterday by gentlemen from
Lee and Crittenden Counties, and confirms reports that have already come to
this paper by wire. The apprehensions of those who predicted bloodshed as
the result of the strike of negro cotton pickers in Lee County have been
realized, and the end is not yet.

The strike has been on in Lee County for four or five days. The planters offer 50 cents per 100 for picking cotton, and the negroes have refused
to work for these figures. Hence work has been at a standstill, and the
mutterings of the idle, hungry and dissatisfied blacks have taken definite
form. On Saturday the cloudburst. An armed gang of about 100 negroes, all
mounted, appeared along the road leading to J. F. Frank's plantation, near
Dr. Peters' mound. Tom Miller, the agent of Mr. Frank, met the marauders
and tried to parley with them, but they shot him down in a manner unknown to
those who brought the story to Memphis.

The negroes proceeded on their way, uttering dire threats against the
planters who had not acceded to their demands and denouncing and reviling all
white persons they met. They next appeared in the Park place, where Bond &
Terrell's ginhouse was fired, and burned to the ground with all its contents.
Other ginhouses they treated in the same way. In the afternoon Mr. Frank
Bond, of the firm of Bond & Terrell, learning of the fate of his ginhouse,
set out on horseback to meet the rioters.

"Come on, men! I'm one of you!" he shouted when he came up with them.
They followed him, not knowing who he was. He proposed that they proceed to Raggio's village and loot the hamlet. This fell in with their inclinations, and they permitted him to guide them. He went on ahead, to re-
connoiter the place he said. But instead he rode into the village, gave the
alarm, and soon had a large posse armed to resist and exterminate the mob.
But the negroes got wind of the preparations that had been made to meet them.
A negro preacher at Raggio's village rode out and warned them. They turned
back, and thus saved themselves for other deeds of vandalism.

By this time the entire county had been aroused. The sheriff had been
called out by Mr. Bond, and these two soon organized a posse of 50 men to go
in pursuit of the blacks, who fled toward Scanlan's Landing. Yesterday morning the chase was resumed, and Sheriff Werner, of Crittendon County, was
called upon for aid and responded.

Up to a late hour yesterday the negroes had not been captured, but a
report was current in the city that two of them had been killed.

Memphis Appeal-Avalanche, September 28, 1891.

52.   THE COTTON PICKERS' STRIKE

The law officers of Lee County, Ark., will probably be able to deal with
the riotous negroes who have set out to burn houses and gins and to kill all
who oppose them. If not, the Governor of the State should promptly assist
in restoring order. The cause of the trouble is said to be the dissatisfaction of the negroes over the reduction in the price of cotton picking, neces-
sitated by the low price of cotton this fall. It is more than probable that
some mischief-makers, whose identity is not yet known, have been stirring
the negroes to bloody revolt. That question can be investigated afterward.
The present business in hand is to capture the black devils who have been
disturbing the peace of Lee County and destroying property. One man is reported to have been killed. There is no telling what further troubles may
ensue, unless the Lee County sheriff succeeds in extinguishing the flame that
has been started. The negroes should be made to understand that they cannot
commit these outrages with impunity, and that the penalty is very severe.
The APPEAL-AVALANCE gives a full account this morning of what happened in Lee
County Saturday, and it is gratifying to find that the officers of the law

have been so prompt in taking hold of the case.

Memphis Appeal-Avalanche, September 28, 1891.

53. BLACKS IN BRAKES

Details of the Lee County Riots

The Riotous Negroes Have Taken to the Canebrakes

MARIANNA, Ark., Sept. 28.--The search continues for the negroes who on last Friday began a strike, on Friday night burned a ginhouse, and on Saturday afternoon waylaid and assasinated Thomas Miller, overseer on J. F. Frank's plantation, in the eastern or bottom part of the county. The negroes are hiding in a dense canebrake covering some 20,000 acres, and it is impossible for the officers to reach them. At noon today a few of the sheriff's posse, who left Saturday, returned and reported the true condition of things. The scene of the trouble is in the Mississippi and St. Francis river bottoms, and it is almost impossible to get accurate information promptly. There is no telegraph, telephone or railroad connection between here and there, and horseback is the only means of travel, as the roads will not permit the use of a buggy or wagon.

The Trouble Had Its Origin
on Sunday night, September 20, when about 25 negroes, under the leadership of two men whose names could not be learned, assembled at Col. H. P. Rodger's place and agreed to strike if the price for cotton picking, which was recently fixed by a convention of farmers of Arkansas, Tennessee and Mississippi at 50 cents a 100 pounds, was not raised. Col. Rodgers heard of the occurrence the next morning, and compelled the ringleaders to leave his at once. It was supposed that this was the end of the matter, as all the pickers worked steadily and quietly in all the fields for several days, but Friday morning about 20 of the negroes refused to go to work and in a short time began to visit the cotton field and compel all pickers who were working for 50 cents to quit work. This became monotonous, and the planters applied to the officers to put a stop to it. A local deputy sheriff summoned a small posse and attempted to arrest the intimidators, but they eluded him. He then sent word to Sheriff Derrick at Marianos, and Friday night the sheriff and five deputies left here for the scene of the trouble. The next morning a second posse of 15 men followed them. The negroes seemed to have a particular spite against Frank Bond, one of the largest planters. During the day on Friday, while returning to his store at Raggio City from Possum Ridge, he was met by a body of armed men, who compelled him to turn back, when he took a circuitous route and reached his store. That night his fine new gin and nine bales of cotton, valued at $4,000, were burned by incendiaries, supposed to be the strikers. Deputies continued the chase all Friday night, but without result, and began anew upon the arrival Saturday of reinforcements. Shortly after noon the sheriff, at the head of a posse of about 75 men, about 25 of whom were negroes, who were with the planters and against the strikers, started out again in search of the rascals. Thomas Miller, overseer on the J. F. Frank place, was one of the posse, but from some cause lingered behind and was finally lost to sight. Several miles had been traversed, when the posse heard firing some distance behind them. They at once began a return journey and soon came upon the dead body of Thomas Miller, lying by the side of the road. In his body were 14 buckshot, while his head and face was torn to pieces by hundreds of squirrel-shot. He had been waylaid and assassinated. The assassins had cut his watch off and stolen it, and robbed the dead body of some money and a pistol. This occurrence added fuel to the flame, and the search was begun with increased zeal, but all to no avail. The impenetrable canebrake hid the murders in its mysterious depths, and they were safe in that immense swamp of 20,000 acres. It is thought that the posse passed the hiding place of the fugitives without seeing them, and they, thinking the entire party had passed,

ventured out. Mr. Miller came upon them and they first murdered him and then
robbed him. The coroner was notified and left for the scene with a posse
of men to hold an inquest. All night long the search for the fugitives was
continued, and Sunday, too, was spent in the fruitless effort to bring the
murders within the reach of the law. Sunday morning Robert Fuller, a negro
man, who was at first identified with the strikers, was seen at O'Connor's
store at the Peters' Mound place and said he had deserted the marauders.
He gave no difinite information, however, and soon disappeared. When officers arrived soon after, Fuller was not to be found. They searched diligently in all the fields houses, but he had mysteriously disappeared. It is
thought the trouble is ended and that the strike is over with. About 50
officers are still in pursuit of the fugitives, but there is little prospect
of a capture so long as they use the canebrake for a hiding place. It was
reported yesterday that a negro had been killed by the strikers, but the
report is false. The report that the Governor will be appealed to for
assistance is also without foundation. The sheriff is amply able to take
care of the matter. It is expected that the sheriff and those of the posse
who reside here will return tomorrow.

Memphis Appeal-Avalanche, September 29, 1891.

54. RACE RIOT IN ARKANSAS

Special Dispatch to the Glove-Democrat.
    "MARIANNA, Ark., Sept., 28.--The search continues for the negroes who
on last Friday began a strike, on Friday night burned a gin-house, and on
Saturday afternoon waylaid and assassinated Thomas Miller, overseer on J. F.
Frank's plantation in the eastern or bottom part of the county. The negroes
are hiding in a dense cane-brake covering some 20,000 acres, and it is impossible for officers to reach them. At noon today, a few of the sheriff's
posse, who left Saturday, returned here and reported the true condition of
things.
    The scene of the trouble is in the Mississippi and St. Francis river
bottoms, and it is almost impossible to get accurate information promptly.
There is no telegraph, telephone or railroad connection between here and
there, horseback is the only means of travel, as the roads will not permit
the use of a buggy or wagon. The trouble had its origin on Sunday night,
September 20th, when about twenty-five negroes under the leadership of two
men whose names could not be learned, assembled at Col. H. P. Rodgers' place
and agreed to strike if the price for cotton picking which was recently fixed
by a convention of the farmers of Arkansas, Tennessee and Mississippi at 50¢
per hundred pounds, was not raised. Col. Rodgers heard of the occurrence
the next morning, and compelled the ringleaders to leave his place at once.
Friday morning about twenty of the negroes refused to go to work and in a
short while began to visit the cotton-field and compel all pickers who were
working for 50¢ to quit work. This became monotonous and the Planters
applied to the officers to put a stop to it.
    A local deputy sheriff summoned a small posse and attempted to arrest
the intimidators but they eluded him. He then sent word to Sheriff Derrick
at Marianna, and Friday night the Sheriff and five deputies left here for
the scene of the trouble. The next morning a second posse of fifteen men
followed. The negroes seemed to have a particular spite against Frank Bond,
one of the largest planters. During the day on Friday, while returning to
his store at Raggio City, from 'Possum Ridge, he was met by a body of armed
men and compelled to turn back, when he took a circuitous route and reached
his store. That night his fine new gin and nine bales of cotton valued at
$4,000, were burned by incendiaries, supposed to be the strikers.
    Deputies continued the chase all of Friday night, but without result,
and began new upon the arrival of Saturday's reinforcements. Shortly after
noon, the Sheriff at the head of about seventy-five men, about twenty-five
of whom were negroes who were with the planters and against the strikers,

started out again in search of the rascals.

Thomas Miller, overseer on the J. F. Frank place, was one of the posse but from some cause lingered behind, and was finally lost to sight. Several miles had been traveled when the posse heard firing some distance behind. They at once began a return journey, and soon came upon the dead body of Thos. Miller lying by the side of the road. In his body were fourteen buckshot while his head and face were torn to pieces by hundreds of squirrel shot. He had been waylaid and assassiniated. The assassins had cut his watch off and stolen it, and robbed the dead body of some money and a pistol. This occurrence lent fresh fuel to the flames, and the search was begun with increased zeal, but all to no avail. The impenetrable cane-brake hid the murders in its mysterious depths, and they were safe in that immense swamp of 20,000 acres. It is thought that the posse passed the hiding place of the fugitives without seeing them, and they, thinking the entire party had vanished, ventured out. Mr. Miller came upon them, and they robbed and murdered him. The coroner was notified, and left with a posse of men to hold an inquest.

All night long the search for the fugitives was continued, and Sunday too, was spent in the chase. It is thought that the trouble is ended and that the strike is over with. It was reported yesterday that a negro had been killed by the strikers, but the report is false. The report that the Governor will be appealed to for assistance is also without foundation.

Richmond Planet, October 17, 1891.

55. NINE NEGROES LYNCHED

The Lee County Trouble Settled With Rope
Nine Negroes Taken From the Deputies and Hanged

HELENA, ARK., October 1.--It is learned that Sheriff Derrick, of Marianna, Ark., left Cat Island Last night, having in charge nine of the thirteen cotton picker rioters who killed Inspector Miller in Arkansas last Friday. The Sheriff was on his way to Marianna where he was going to put his prisoners in jail, but the party was overtaken late last night by an armed posse, who took the prisoners after a sharp struggle, and hanged the entire party. Further particulars are expected tonight.

THE REPORT CONFIRMED

HELENA, ARK., October 1.--There has been considerable excitement in this city today over the rumors concerning the warfare in the county caused by a body of imported cotton pickers inciting the negroes to a general strike for higher wages for cotton picking. This trouble would not have been very bad, but when the lawless rascals who are nearly all supposed to be from the crap dens of Memphis and other cities went so far as to forcibly prevent all the negroes from picking cotton at all till their demands were acceded to, and armed themselves for that purpose, and finally waylaid and shot to death Mr. Thos. Miller, the manager of J. F. Frank's plantation and followed up this dastardly deed by burning the gin house of Messrs. Terrell & Boyd, the situation became a very serious one. Sheriff W. B. Derrick, of Lee County, went over to the district several days ago with a small number of deputies, which was increased the next day by several more, making a large posse. The ringleaders of the mob were traced to a swamp, where they were surrounded. This was the status of the situation when the steamer Jas. Lee landed here this morning. From a passenger on board the boat and from her officers it was learned that a negro badly wounded in the thigh, came on board the boat at Cat Island. About midnight he was taken to the barber shop and confessed that he was one of the crowd which assassinated Mr. Miller on Tuesday last; that he and his companions had been hiding in the swamp; that they had made a break for liberty and had been fired on and some of them, he didn't know how many, killed, and the balance captured. He had escaped and made his way through the darkness to the landing. The same man was taken off the boat at

Hackle's Landing by a crowd of masked men and carried on shore. They were
cool, orderly and heavily and brooked no opposition, making the officers and
passengers stand back until they had carried the wounded negro up the bank.

As the boat moved away from the landing a number of shots were heard,
and the presumption is that he was killed. It is thought that the negro was
the notorious Ben Patterson, who organized the riot, and led the crowd that
assassinated Mr. Miller. The locality is an isolated one and communication
is entirely by the river, consequently full particulars are slow in reaching
here.

Later, Deputy Sheriffs Frank Mills and Jessie Hodges, who have been
with Sheriff Derrick the last three days, have just arrived in this city and
report as follows: Yesterday afternoon they succeeded in locating thirteen
of the worst of the rioting negroes in a cane break near Cat Island. . . .
When ordered to surrender and give up their arms. The negroes answered by
a volley of shots, and made a dash to escape. Two were killed, two escaped,
and nine were captured. These nine were discovered and given in charge of
Deputies Mills and Hodges, who started with them to Marianna, the county
seat, a few miles back of Hackley's Landing. The Deputies found themselves
and prisoners surrounded by a crowd of masked men mounted and armed. They
demanded the prisoners at the hands of the deputies, who expostulated with
them and begged that they be not deferred from the peaceful discharge of
their duty, which was to land the prisoners in jail, to be dealt with by the
law of the land.

The masked party were determined, however, and, as they outnumbered the
Deputy Sheriffs twenty-five to one, took charge of the nine prisoners,
marched them into a thicket and hung them until they were dead. The same
party must have met the steamer Jas. Lee at Hackley's Landing, and captured
the wounded man referred to. From these accidents it appears that the only
man escaped out of the thirteen was the one who had taken refuge in the brake,
two being killed by the Sheriff's posse and ten by the masked mob.

The negroes were mostly, it is thought, from Memphis, though several
were killed who lived in the vicinity of Cat Island. Ben Patterson, who is
known as a crap shooter, and all-round negro gambler, organized the strike
in behalf of the crowds of cotton pickers, who annually go from Memphis to
the bottoms. The negro Alliance had nothing to do with the disturbance
whatever. Patterson had enough influence with his crowd to organize and
then by force of threats and by violence forced the resident negroes to support them.

They swore they would never pick a lock of cotton for less than $1 per
hundred, nor allow anybody else to pick it. After they had gone so far as
to kill Miller and burn the gin-house of Terrell and Bond, it became a matter
to be dealt with whether the trouble is over although the general impression
is that it is. The death of Patterson settles it.

THE RING-LEADER SHOT

HELENA, ARK., October 1.--The labor troubles in Lee County are probably
over for the present. A passenger on the James Lee this morning says that
the leaders of the negroes have either been killed or captured. At Star
Landing a negro got on board the Lee who was pretty badly wounded in the
thigh. He was carried to the barber shop and acknowledged that he was with
the crowd that shot Miller a few days ago. He also states that the party of
fifteen negroes who had been hiding in a swamp surrounded by the Sheriff's
posse had made a break for liberty, and that five or six of them had been
killed or wounded and one of them captured a few miles below Star Landing.
While at the landing a crowd of masked men came board the boat and took the
wounded negro on shore with them. As the boat backed out a number of shots
were heard, but it is not known whether the prisoner was shot. It is thought
the man was Ben Patterson, the leader of the rioters. With the dispersion
of the mob it is thought the troubles will soon be forgotten.

Arkansas Gazette, October 2, 1891.

56. PRISONERS LYNCHED

Ten Negroes Taken from Officers and Hanged or Shot

Masked White Men the Avengers

Story of the Riot Precipitated by the Cotton Pickers' Strike in Arkansas-- A Terrible Reckoning

HELENA, ARK., October 2.--There has been considerable excitement here over the warfare in the country caused by the imported cotton pickers inciting the negroes to a general strike for higher wages, which has culminated in a riot. Yesterday Deputies Frank Mills and Jesse Hodges, who have been with Sheriff Derrick for the last few days, arrived in the city and report as follows:

Wednesday afternoon they succeeded in locating the worst of the rioting negroes in a canebrake near Cat Island. The negroes had been trying to work their way toward President's Island and thence to Memphis. The sheriff's posse called upon them to surrender and give up their arms. The negroes answered by a volley shots and made a dash to escape. Two were killed, two escaped and nine captured. These negroes were disarmed and given in charge of Deputies Mills and Hodges, who started with them to Marianna, the county seat. A few miles back of Hackley's Landing the deputies found themselves and their prisoners surrounded by a crowd of masked men, mounted and armed. They demanded the prisoners at the hands of the deputies, and as they outnumbered the deputies two to one, took charge of the prisoners, marched them into the thicket and hanged them.

It is believed that most of the negroes were from Memphis. Among the killed is Ben Patterson, who is known as a crap shooter and all around gambler, and who organized the strike on behalf of the cotton pickers, who annually go from Memphis to the bottoms. The other eight negroes had nothing to do with the disturbance whatever. It remains to be seen whether the trouble is entirely over, although the general impression is that it is--that the death of Patterson settles it.

Coroner F. M. Mills, one of the sheriff's posse, who has been out since last Saturday hunting the riotous negroes, gives the particulars of the strike as related to him by the leaders of the strikers, Patterson. Mit Jones came to him last Thursday and told him a white man in the bottoms told him (Jones) that the negroes were fools to pick cotton at 50 cents a hundred and if they would strike they would be backed by himself and other responsible white men. They therefore concluded to call a meeting to take some action in the premises. It was held at the house of a negro named McDonald on the Peters Mound place last Thursday night. This was attended by twenty-five or thirty, and was engineered by Mit Jones and his father, Peter Jones. They decided to strike and nineteen of them armed themselves, and on Friday morning started out to stop picking at the rate named, moral suasion to be used if it would do, but force if necessary.

They commenced at J. F. Frank's farm, intending to visit every farm from there to Cat Island. They hoped to strengthen their forces as they went. All those arrested, nine in number, so far as information which is supposed to be reliable goes, claimed to know nothing of the burning of Bond's ginhouse. After his gin was burned, Bond came to Marianna after the sheriff and posse, and old man Peter Jones came to the strikers and told them that Bond had gone for the sheriff and they had better look out. Mit Jones, when he heard it, said: "He will never get there. We will head him off and kill him."

MURDER OF MILLS

The rioters then went up toward Bledsoe's landing. Sheriff Derrick and posse started out and, passing Mr. Frank's farm, summoned Mr. Miller, a member. Miller was not ready, but promised to follow later. The gang saw the sheriff and posse pass and started to fire into them, but concluded that the woods were not thick enough to make their escape, and let them pass. They had gone a mile or two when Miller came along. Mit Jones halted him and Miller stopped. Miller asked what he wanted. Mit Jones said with an insulting

oath: "We are going to kill you." Miller parleyed, gave up his pistol,
watch and money at the demand of one Daney Fields, a member of the mob.
They commanded him to come into the woods and he gathered up his reins as
if to comply, and striking spurs to his horse started to run, whereupon all
hands shot him save three. He fell off his horse and after he was down they
shot him through the head and dragged him into the bushes. The mob took to
the cane where they stayed during the day and that night all went to their
homes. The sheriff's posse having passed them and being unable to take them
turned back and finding the body of Miller took him home and had him buried.
The posse stopped at Alligator haven that night and next morning where reinforced by about twenty-five negroes of the neighborhood who came armed and
equipped and tendered their services to the sheriff. These stayed with the
posse all the time afterward as long as needed.

At Peters Mound place they divided into squads of fifteen or twenty,
the squads being commanded by J. H. Hackney, of Council Bend, and James E.
Wood and Lon Slaughter, of Marianna. Mr. Mills was detailed to go into the
squad commanded by Hackney. They searched the canebrakes between there and
Bledsoe, where the posse met.

It was reported that about fifteen negroes had been seen going on foot
toward Horseshoe Bend, on the Mississippi river. Citizens there had captured
one of them who was turned over to the sheriff. That evening the prisoners
who were landed in the jail yesterday were caught. Next day Hackney's squad
struck their trail, and toward evening, when riding down a road between impenetrable cane thickets, they saw where some of them had crossed the road.
The posse dismounted and crawled on hands and knees about two hundred yards,
where they came upon Patterson, the leader, Ed. Priton and two who are unknown.

BATTLE IN THE CANEBRAKE

Patterson and Priton were together and when within about twenty yards
Patterson shouted "hold on, boys, I will stop them;" and fired two shots
into the posse. The fire was returned and Patterson was seen to fall forward on his face. Priton then received the bulk of their attention and
received about forty shots, the fingers of one hand being shot off. Patterson had been shot three times. Mr. Cobb, one of the posse, went to him and
rolled him over to see if he was dead and he opened one eye. Patterson
said: "I'm not dead." The crowd started to kill him, but Captain Hackney
interfered and saved his life. They left Priton where he fell and took
Patterson to the Dr. Peters place to guard him until he could be sent to
jail next day.

Two more were caught who were put under guard at the same place. Mills
accidently shot the mule he was riding and was detailed by the sheriff to
bring Patterson, who was so badly wounded, to jail by river via Helena. Mills
went to Cat Island with his prisoner to take a boat, and when he started to
get on board a man came to him and asked if he had Patterson. His reply
being affirmative, he was informed that he would not be troubled with the
scoundrel long, as he would be relieved of him before he got far. No sign
of trouble appeared until the boat was passing Hackler's landing, where it
was hailed.

As soon as it landed fifteen men wearing white masks came on board, and
at the point of Winchesters and pistols took Patterson away from him. A
part of the Whitecaps stayed on the bank where they had two of the negroes
whom Mills did not know. Patterson was clear grit and never uttered a word
as four men took hold of the quilt which he was laying and carried him off
the boat. At the end of the stage plank the hold of the men who were
carying Patterson's head slipped and he fell. Then they caught him by the
heels and dragged him up the bank. When he fell Patterson said: "For God's
sake be easy, gentlemen." to which one replied, "You will be easy directly."
The Whitecaps told Mr. Mills: "We not only want to take this -- --, but we
are going to have everyone of them". As the boat bounded out ten or fifteen
shots were heard from the bank and it is supposed that Patterson and his two
partners were killed.

Two or three landings below there a white man came on board the boat
and told the captain and Mr. Mills that this crowd had overpowered the
sheriff's posse and taken every man he had, except one, and killed them.
Still later below Peter's landing another man came on board and said they

had also captured Mit and Early Jones, the men whom Howe in his confession yesterday said had shot Miller and killed him. These, according to Mills' account, were Patterson, Priton, Early Jones, Mit Johnson, whom the White-caps had captured at Hackler's Landing, and four which it was reported had been taken from Sheriff Derrick.

FIFTEEN NEGROES KILLED

NEW ORLEANS, La., October 2.--The Picayune's Helena, Ar., special says: It now appears that no less than fifteen negroes were killed of the gang of nineteen who commenced the trouble. Of the remaining four, three are in jail at Marianna and one in jail at Forest City. To the millionnaire mer-chant, J. F. Frank, of Memphis, is laid the charge of having incited trouble by saying in the presence of a hundred negroes at his store that he would not have his cotton picked if he had to pay a dollar per hundred for the work.

Mobile Daily Register, October 3, 1891.

57.   THE ARKANSAS MAN HUNT

The negro rioting in Lee and Crittenden counties, Ark., has undoubtedly been effectually squelched.

Two of the negroes were shot and killed, three are now in the Lee County jail, and five more who were captured have not been heard from in a couple of days, and it is presumed that their corpses are now dangling from limbs somewhere between Peters' Island and Marianna.

The uprising was one of the most serious that has occurred in these parts in several years, and the story of how it was subdued by the white people bristles with incidents of an interesting character. Yesterday morn-ing the steamer James Lee brought to Memphis a half dozen of the deputy sheriffs who were sent out by Sheriff Werner to protect the marches of Crittenden County. They left for Marion, Ark., later in the day. They were headed by Deputy Sheriff N. M. Gibson, a nephew of Sheriff Werner, who com-manded the Crittenden County contingent. He told all he knew about the affair thus:

"Last Sunday Sheriff Werner got information that the Lee County negro rioters were heading toward the line of Crittenden County, and he at once organized a posse of 40 of us, who left Marion that evening, going toward Horseshoe lake, to which point we understood the negroes were flying. When we reached that vicinity we learned that we were in the neighborhood of the rioters, and a message was sent to Sheriff Derrick, of Lee County, to close in on their rear with his posse of 60 men. We had the country covered with scouts for miles around, and though we did not close in upon the fugitives we kept them guessing where to go. They had had a long run, were short of food and what with hunger, weariness and natural cussedness they were a dangerous party to encounter. We had no definite idea how many was in their party, but we aimed to find out. Monday morning our party, after riding all night, arrived at the Peters' place, between Horseshoe Lake and the river. We were informed that a squad of some 15 negroes had rode by the house of a farmer named Bogan, near there, and at the muzzle of their guns forced Mrs. Bogan to prepare breakfast for them all. They ate ravenously and struck off toward the lake. They were all armed and mounted, some on horses and others on mules. Our party spread out for scouting, and followed after the negroes. We came upon their trail at different places, but it was not until we reached the Holloway place, that one of our men came upon 13 of the bucks. They order him to halt, but instead of that he put spurs to his horse and flew to notify the rest of the posse. We were then only half a mile behind the fugitives and might have corralled the whole gang in the open, only the course was so short, for the swamp was near at hand, and into it the negroes disappeared. It was toward night when we reached the Kittrell place, where we had just arrived when we heard heavy firing not far off. Hastening to the spot I found that a portion of my posse had surrounded the negroes in an old

disused ginhouse and had captured two of them and three guns, while the remainder were in flight, running and sneaking toward the canebrake, which
was only a few hundred yards distant. The Lee County posse was close upon
our heels at this time, and at nightfall some of that party ventured into
the brake and then the shooting of Peyton and Ben Patterson occurred. Next
day six live negroes, including Patterson, who was wounded, and the dead
negro Peyton were given into the hands of Sheriff Derrick. A coroner who
was with Sheriff Derrick's party held an inquest on Peyton, and a verdict of
justifiable homicide was returned. There were half a dozen negroes still in
the canebrake when I came away, but the Lee County posse was around them and
they cannot escape, but must come out and surrender soon or die of hunger.
All the prisoners turned over to the Lee County officers were taken across
the country to Marianna except Patterson, who was too badly wounded to be
moved in that way. He pretended to be much worse wounded than he really was.
He was put on board the James Lee to be brought up this way, but I understand
that when the steamer pulled into Hackley's landing in obedience to a signal
a party of masked men went aboard and took Patterson from his bunk in the
barber shop, carried him on the boat, and--. That's all I know. They say
that shots were heard as the party went up the bank of the river, and it is
supposed that the leader of the mob met his death there, but I know nothing
of that. I don't know anything about the lynching reported in this morning's
papers. Such a thing may have occurred, in fact, it is very probable that
it did.

The party with Mr. Gibson had evidently seen some hard service. They
had been sleeping out since Sunday and their rations were irregular and
scant very often.

ALL LYNCHED, SAYS HELENA

But Marianna Sticks to it That only Two Were Lynched.
Special Dispatch to the Appeal-Avalanche.

HELENA, ARK., Oct. 2.--There seems to be considerable excitement yet in
Lee County growing out of the assassination of Miller and the burning of ginhouses by negro rioters, and the lynching of the negro rioters by mobs composed of white and negro citizens of the county. The following additional
facts are learned from a gentleman who came from Lee County this evening:

There are now in jail at Marianna three negroes named Ed Howe, Bob White
and Jim Sims, who were part of the mob that assassinated the overseer named
Miller. Howe, who was put in jail yesterday, fearing that he would be lynched,
confessed that there were

TWENTY-THREE NEGROES

in the crowd that burned the gins and killed Miller, and that they intended
to fall upon the sheriff's posse as it passed and kill them, but they lost
courage, as the posse was too strong Of the 23, 15 of them are in jail at
Marianna, two of them fatally wounded. One of them is in jail at Forrest
City, and the others are missing. The missing ones are supposed to have been
wounded and died in the canebrakes. Howe declares that he, with several
others, were forced into the demonstrations by the leaders of the riotous
strikers. It is not probable that those who are in jail will escape the
vengeance of the mob. It seems that as the rioters were arrested by the posse
they were locked up in places under guard of the mob, and as the posse left
the mob took charge of the prisoners and made short work of them.

MARIANNA DENIES IT ALL

Special Dispatch to the Appeal.

MARIANNA, Ark., Oct. 2.--Sheriff Derrick reached town this noon with
three prisoners, Charles Harris, Sam Murphy and Eli Patterson, who were placed
in jail, charged with complicity in the murder of Tom Miller last Saturday.
In an interview Harris said: "There is no truth in the report that the Jones
brothers, who were most active in murdering Miller, have been captured." He
was with them just before his capture, and they told him they were going a-
cross the river and stay there. Members of the posse who returned today say
the whereabouts of the Jones boys was known yesterday, but when Messrs.
Slaughter, Blount and Dupuy, of the Marianna crowd, tried to find three more
men to go with them and capture the fugitives they were unsuccessful. The

men were completely worn out by their long journey. Will Murphy and Charlie
Lloyd, the latter of whom is said by the prisoner Harris to be the man with
a red hat who was active with the Jones boys in killing Miller, were captured yesterday and placed in charge of Deputies Duncan Brown and Andrew
Bickerstaff, of Marianna. It is thought by those who returned today that
Murphy and Lloyd were killed last night, as there was a very bitter feeling
against them and threats were made. As was thought here yesterday, the
reports sent out from Helena that nine were taken from Sheriff Derrick and
lynched were absolutely false. There was no foundation for them whatever.
So far as known Peyton, who was shot by officers while in the canebrake,
and Patterson, who was taken from Deputy Mills and lynched, are the only
ones killed. Ten men have been captured so far. Of these six, Ed Howe,
Bob White, Jim Sims, Charles Harris, Sam Murphy and Eli Patterson, are in
jail here; two, Ed Peyton and Ben Patterson, were killed, and the remaining
two, Will Murphy and Charles Lloyd, are in charge of officers on their way
to Marianna, that is, provided they have not been lynched.

Deputy Frank Mills, who was interviewed at Helena, and whose name was
used yesterday in connection with the very sensational statement sent out
from there, called on the APPEAL-AVALANCHE correspondent today and declared
that most of the statements were never uttered by him. He is very indignant,
and says the reports sent out from here are incorrect in every particular.
Every report sent from here was a correct repetition of the substance of
his words.

Memphis Appeal-Avalanche, October 3, 1891.

58.   FORCE AGAINST FORCE

The deplorable events in Lee County which culminated in the lynching of
several negroes by a masked mob, while under arrest, grew out of an attempt
to solve a labor problem by brute force. The cotton planters deemed 50 cents
a hundred pounds as much as they were able to pay for picking cotton. Many
negroes went to the fields, and were quietly laboring under contracts made
on that basis.

This action was resented by the more turbulent negro element, whose
leaders in their brutish ignorance resolved to use force, if necessary, to
compel the peaceful laborers to quit the fields.

Force was necessary, and force was used. Those ruffians drove the cotton pickers into idleness. They would neither work themselves nor permit
others to work. The fields, white with cotton, were abandoned to ruin, if
needs be; for the fiat went forth that no cotton should be picked below the
rate these ignorant, though temporarily all-powerful, dictators had established.

The spark igniting the powder magazine had been thrown. The blood of
the white planters, whom ruin stared in the face, whose homes and vital interest were at the mercy of the brutal mob, began running, hissing hot,
through their veins. The inevitable followed. It was mob against mob; force
against force. The vengeance was quick and terrible.

It is the old story told over and over again since time began. It is
useless to moralize. Denunciation of the lawless mob will avail nothing
unless human nature can be changed, and that meekness which commands turning
the unsmitten cheek when its fellow has been scourged shall become the rule
and guide of mankind.

Arkansas Gazette, October 3, 1891.

The Arkansas white toughs in taking nine colored men and lynching them, because said colored men desired higher wages; were as brave as the mob of cowards in Indiana who whipped severely a woman because her morals did not agree with their code. The ordinary fire and brimstone hell will not be hot enough for these white devils.

American Citizen, (Kansas City, Kansas), October 9, 1891.

59. WHOLESALE LYNCHING

Nine Negroes Reported to have been Hung in Arkansas

The Men were of the Party of Riotous Cotton Pickers that Killed Miller Last Friday, and Were Under Arrest When Seized by Their Slayers

HELENA, ARK., Oct. 1.--It is learned that Sheriff Derrick of Marianna, Ark., left Cat Island last night, having in custody nine of the thirteen colored cotton picker rioters who killed Inspector Miller in Arkansas, last Friday. The sheriff was on his way to Marianna, where he was going to put his prisoners in jail, but was overtaken late last night by an armed posse who took the prisoners after a sharp struggle, and hanged the entire party.

ANOTHER KILLING REPORTED

ST. LOUIS, Oct. 1.--A dispatch to the Republic from Helena, Ark., says: "The labor troubles in Lee county are probably over for the present. A passenger on the James Lee this morning says that in that neighborhood most of the negroes have been either killed or captured. At Star Landing, a negro got on board the Lee who was probably wounded in the thigh. He acknowledged that he was with the crowd that shot Miller a few days ago. He also stated that a party of fifteen negroes who had been hiding in the swamps, surrounded by the sheriff's posse, had made a break for liberty, and that five or six of them had been killed or wounded, had then captured a few miles below Star Landing. While at the landing, a crowd of masked men came on board, and took the wounded negro on shore with them. As the boat backed out a number of shots were heard, but it is not known whether the prisoner was shot. It is thought that the man was Ben Patterson, the leader of the rioters.

Richmond Planet, October 17, 1891.

60. THE ARKANSAS BUTCHERY

A Dozen or More of Striking Cotton Pickers Lynched

HELENA, ARK., Oct. 2.--Riot and bloodshed have been the order in the neighborhood of Frank's and Terrell & Boyd's plantations for several days. Information received late last night and early this morning shows that the situation is indeed serious. Thus far a dozen of the rioting cotton pickers have been shot and lynched. Planter Miller has been assassinated and the guard houses on the Terrell-Boyd plantations have been destroyed. The trouble, it appears, was caused by the negro cotton-pickers from Memphis. They went on a strike for $1 a 100 and swore they would permit nobody else to pick cotton at a lesser rate. The strike was led by Ben Patterson, who led the mob to Miller's house Tuesday night. A few days since Sheriff Derrick organized a posse and started out to quell the rioters. The strikers were driven into a swamp and shots were exchanged before the negroes surrendered. Two were killed and nine captured. The prisoners were put in charge of a couple of deputies, who undertook to take them to the County jail. On the way they were surrounded by about fifty masked men and compelled to give up the prisoners. The negroes were taken into the woods by the mounted men and lynched. One of the negroes who escaped from the swamp with a bullet in his leg sought refuge on the steamer James Lee, but at Hackley's Landing the boat was boarded and the injured man taken off and killed. He was no other than Patterson, the leader of the strikers.

There is danger that more blood will flow before quiet is restored.

St. Louis Post Dispatch, October 2, 1891.

61. FRIGHTFUL BARBARITIES

The striking and riotous cotton pickers of Arkansas have been far from successful. Last week a gang was surprised and routed by the sheriff, two of them were killed, two more escaped and nine of them were taken prisoners. These prisoners were sent to the nearest jail by the sheriff with a guard, and on the way were mete by a company of masked men and lynched.

These men had not been guilty of any offense that warranted capital punishment, and this crime but adds to the list of the horrible and frightful barbarities of the South. Another instance of Southern injustice and intolerance, and a crime of the Nation. The country at large is just as responsible for this outrage as they who committed it. The silence of the whole country when other barbarities just as frightful were committed but lends encouragement for the committal of others; just as the outrage has met with no general condemnation, as those who committed it will not suffer because of it, so will this example result in encouraging other and perhaps more frightful crimes.

How long are these crimes to continue? Have the people of the Republic no conscience, no compassion for the poor unfortunates of the South? Do not these almost daily crimes against humanity have any effect upon their christian training? The great moral leaders, where are they that their voices are not heard in loud protest, clamoring for justice? The great Republic is dotted with churches. Christian truths are dealt out weekly to listening millions. Does the seed fall on stony ground that such terrible things are permitted to go on unrebuked? To the Afro-American, christian civilization seems a most cruel farce; the church a pharisaical hypocrite, that has departed from the teachings of the blessed Master. But the history of the world is a history of retributive justice. This has been strikingly exemplified in the history of the Republic. Slavery was a crime against humanity and christianity. At its altar thousands were offered up to insatiate greed. Retributive justice came upon both in the shape of the civil war, and thousands upon thousands of the North and South lost their lives before it was extinguished, and this question for a time settled. So these outrages, this denial of justice and prostitution of the courts, this silent acquiescence in crime, will meet a retributive justice, and the punishment will be in kind and the North as well as the South suffer because of them.

Detroit Plaindealer, October 9, 1891.

62. THOSE WHOLESALE MURDERS

The wholesale lynching in Arkansas, an account of which we published in our last issue tells with striking force the relentless barbarity resorted to in that benighted section of this country.

Simply because the cotton pickers of Mississippi and the adjoining states saw fit to strike, they had to be butchered.

No talk is indulged in relative to bringing their murderers to justice.

The announcement is made that nearly all of the Negroes have been either killed or captured.

When we read these terrible accounts we are led to wonder how long God
will tolerate such crimes. How long will these murderers be allowed to go
"unwhips of justice?" What would we do under the circumstances? Why, we
would take the white man's plan--sell our lives as dearly as possible, and
tread the chilly waters of death with our assailants for company.

It is the only way out. We do not advocate retaliation. That would be
the killing of a white man for the murder of a colored one. We advocate
self-defense. We mean the killing of the responsible party--our would-be
murderers. We believe this is the proper course. This belief is intensified
by the fact that it has been the white man's policy and under it he enjoys
immunity from outlaws and has none to molest him or make him afraid.

We want more stalwart, brave hearted men, who have the vital interests
of the race at stake. When we get them--lynch-law will go! and the lynchers
with it.

Richmond Planet, October 24, 1891.

63. PEACE PREVAILS

An attempt may be made to lynch the three Negroes therein confined. Fifteen
out of the Nineteen Leading Strikers Killed--J. F. Frank, of Memphis, said to
be Indirectly the Cause of the Strike.

Special to The Arkansas Gazette

HELENA, ARK., October 2.--The Lee County troubles are probably at an
end, unless the mob hangs the three negroes in the Marianna jail. Some fears
are entertained that such an attempt will be made tonight. It now appears
that no less than fifteen negroes were killed out of the gang of nineteen
who commenced the trouble. Of the remaining four, three are in jail at Marianna and one in jail at Forrest City. Sheriff Derrick, of Lee County, had a
well organized squad of about fifty deputies. It is to his credit that only
one or two negroes were killed in the attempt to capture them, and after the
negroes had fired upon his men. He had a list of the names of the nineteen
offenders and as fast as they were captured he left them in charge of guards,
with instructions to land them in jail at Marianna. Special Deputy Sheriff
J. E. Woods, who is the editor of the Lee County Courier, was the only man
who succeeded in getting his prisoners to jail. The mob which took the
negroes from the different squads of guards, numbered nearly 800, and were
from the town and from Crittenden, St. Francis and Lee Counties. At the door
of the millionaire merchant J. F. Frank, of Memphis, it is laid the charge
of inciting the trouble. Two weeks ago Mr. Frank visited his plantation,
known as the Hope Place.

He was dissatisfied because his cotton was not being picked out fast
enough. His manager, Mr. J. F. Miller, explained to him that he was getting
along as fast as possible with the number of hands he had, and that he had
agreed not to pay over 50 cents per hundred. Mr. Frank, in the presence of
nearly a hundred negroes who were congregated at his store, remarked in a
loud tone that was an old man and had been in business many years, and that
the only way to get a thing was to pay for it. He said he wanted his cotton
picked out, and proposed to have it done even if it cost $1 per hundred.
The next day his manager offered 60 cents, but the negroes did not go to
work. Then it was that Ben Patterson, Joe Peyton, Met and Early Jones
started out to the adjoining plantations to notify the negroes that they could
get $1 per hundred, and that they were fools to work for less. The majority
of them quit work, and finding themselves successful, they began to forcibly
prevent others from working. Plantation owners expostulated with the ringleaders, but to no effect. A day or two afterward Miller was killed by a
crowd of nineteen negroes, headed by the four named above. Then followed the
burning of the fine gin houses of Frank and Terrell and Bond. The balance
of the story has been told in these dispatches.

An angry mob killed fifteen of the ringleaders and are muttering threats against Mr. J. F. Frank.

They say he had a right to say what he pleased, but that he went too far when he said he knew only his own interest, and did not care for the interests of his neighbors. The seed sowed by his remarks has yielded bloody fruit and all good people hope the end has been reached.

The Marianna jail will be doubly guarded tonight, for Sheriff Derrick has determined that no more lives shall be sacrificed.

Arkansas Gazette, October 3, 1891.

64. ALL SERENE NOW

The Cotton-Pickers' Trouble in Lee County, Ark., Ended

CONFLICTING REPORTS REGARDING THE LYNCHING OF RIOTERS

The Number Variously Estimated at From Two to Twelve--What the Officers Say --Ringleaders Killed--Eight of the Rioters Now in the Jail at Marianna-- Cause of the Outbreak

HELENA, ARK., Oct. 3.--The latest reports from the scene of the cotton pickers' riot, in Lee County, state that the trouble is ended, and that all is calm and serene. There are different accounts of the outcome of the affair, and it cannot yet be definitely stated how many men were lynched, if any. There were undoubtedly a number of the rioters, probably ten or twelve, killed, but it is alleged that they were killed while resisting arrest and were not lynched by a mob as first reported. While the excitement has fully died away, the exact facts with reference to this matter cannot be ascertained. Nothing is known definitely regarding the lynching. Your correspondent had an interview yesterday with Deputy Sheriff Frank Mills, who was with the officers during the entire time they were in pursuit of the rioters. This is the officer who was carrying the negro leader, Patterson, to Helena on the steamer James Lee. An armed crowd took the man from him at Hackley Landing, and it is presumed he was shot to death. Mr. Mills stated that the previous evening Sheriff Derrick had started to Marianna with nine prisoners, whose arrest had been effected, and that the crowd who took the man from him at Hackley told him that Derrick's prisoners had been taken from him and shot or hung. This report is contradicted at Marianna.

Sheriff Derrick reached that place yesterday afternoon with three prisoners, Sam Murphy, Charles Harris and Eli Patterson, who were placed in jail. These men are charged with the killing of Mr. Miller, the manager of J. F. Frank's plantation, where the trouble originated. It is claimed by the Marianna people, that, as far as is now known, only two men have been killed. Peyton, who was killed in the canebrakes and Patterson, who was taken from Officer Mills. Ten men have been arrested so far, six of whom, Ed. Howe, Bob White, Jim Siles, Chas. Hains, Sam Murphy and Ben Patterson, are reported as in jail at Marianna. Peyton and Patterson have been killed, and Murphy and Lloyd werw started to Marianna in charge of officers and may probably reach there, though they had not shown up at last accounts from that place.

In some of the dispatches sent out from here it is made to appear that Officer Mills stated that nine of the men had been lynched. This is not the case, as the gentleman only gave it as the report that had reached him. The trouble was a very serious one, more so, in fact, than any that had occurred in this section in many years. The negroes determined that they would not pick cotton for the price offered them by the planters. Not content with this they also resolved that no one else should do any picking and and they said they would have $1 per 100 pounds or they would devastate the Arkansas side river front from Raggio City to Memphis. Their first act of violence was the killing of Miller. The burning of several valuable houses followed. Realizing what they had done, and knowing the whites would soon be after them to call them to account, they took to the swamps and canebrake. Parties of

men were soon in pursuit of them with the result above given. It is a fact
worthy of mention that when the officers reached Raggio City, in pursuit of
the murderous black demons, a large number of the better element of the
negro farmers of that section armed themselves and volunteered their services
in helping to run down the rioters. The trouble may be regarded as settled.

TWO MORE BROUGHT IN

Six Rioters Now Incarcerated in the Jail at Marianna

MARIANNA, ARK., Oct. 3.--Deputy Sheriff Duncan Brown, the last of the
squad, came in this evening, bringing two more of the prisoners, making six
guilty of murder and two accessories after the fact, now in jail. One of
the six is the man that fired first upon Miller, shooting him in the face
with small shot. The Sheriff informs your correspondent that only two men
were killed and ten escaped among them the Jones brothers, who first started
the trouble. The whole riot may be directly traced to the curse of alien
ownership of lands, especially to the selfishness of one J. F. Frank of
Memphis, Tenn. Tuesday has been set for the preliminary examination, after
which particulars will be given.

St. Louis Post Dispatch, October 4, 1891.

65. THERE WAS NO LYNCHING

The Arkansas People React With Moderation Toward Rioters

The History of the Affair Brought in by People From the Neighborhood in Which
It Occurred--The Last Seen of Capt. Ben Patterson

The sensational reports of lynching of negro rioters in Lee and Crittenden Counties, Ark., have been without foundation.

The true history of the episode known as the cotton pickers' riots was
brought in yesterday evening by parties direct from the scene, and it appears
that the white people acted with extreme moderation toward the black des-
peradoes. The party comprised Messrs. Monroe D. Cartwright, Tom O'Connor,
J. P. Hackler, Press Walker and Dick Morgan, Squire S. P. Williford, Attorney
General Peters, of Memphis, and several others.

The troubles have all been settled now. Cotton picking has been resumed,
the whites and blacks are living in peace again, and all things are moving
along as though no such difficulties had arisen. Only two negroes were killed.
Peyton was shot while firing at close quarters upon the deputy sheriffs in
the discharge of their duty, and Ben Patterson, the leader of the rioters,
was taken from the James Lee and has not since been heard from. Three others,
the two Jones boys and their father, escaped, and the other eight negroes are
now in jail. Thus are all the negroes that laid in the canebrake at Cat
Island accounted for, and it is apparent that the reported wholesale lynchings
had no other foundation than a vivid imagination.

The gentlemen who reached Memphis yesterday say that the riot was discussed and planned for three or four weeks before it broke out. The ringleaders were the Jones boys and Ben Patterson. Patterson commanded the gang
and was called captain. He was 30 years old and a native of Georgia and was
brought to this section by the late Dr. Peters. He was working on the Mound
place. The rioters calculated that the rising would be general and that some
50 negroes would join the forces, and such might have been the case, but that
the killing of Tom Miller showed the seriousness of the undertaking and
dampened the insurrectionary ardour of the better disposed negroes. The details of that killing have been divulged by the captured negroes. Miller
became separated from the squad of white men with whom he was associated in
the pursuit of the rioters and while riding along, found himself covered by
the guns of the negroes who had been concealed in the brush, and called him
to halt.

He would not do it, and several surrounded his horse, whereupon he
spurred up and attempted to ride away from them. But the two Jones boys had

a grudge against him, though the other negroes were not disposed to harm him.

"You drove my father off your plantation," said one of the Jones and they both fired. It is not known how many times Miller was shot, but one load of buckshot went through his back, another scattered all over his face and another lodged in his shoulder. There was a big dent in the back of his head, as though he had been struck with the butt of a gun. His watch and pistol were taken, and probably thrown into a bayou hard by. The negroes pushed on toward the canebrakes at Horseshoe lake by a course that showed they had studied the route long beforehand. A little negro boy, under compulsion, pointed out their hiding place to the officers. Two deputy sheriffs crawled in under the brush while the remainder of the squad surrounded the place. Presently those who were crawling in heard a rough voice within eight feet of them say:

"I'll just kill them right now!"

And bang! the revolvers cracked. The officers on every side fired. Then the brake was searched. Peyton was found riddled with bullets and already dead. Ben Patterson was also apparently dead, but when one of the officers threatened to fire another shot into him to make sure of him he jumped up and was very much alive. There were 13 negroes in that brake. The three Joneses, father and two sons, escaped, and the remaining eight were captured and are now in jail at Marianna. Deputy Sheriff Mills placed Ben Patterson on the James Lee to carry him down the river. It was about 1 o'clock in the morning when the boat reached Hackler's a regular mail landing. As soon as the gang plank was down some 15 masked men ran aboard and demanded Ben Patterson. Deputy Sheriff Mills acted to protect him but he was soon surrounded and rendered helpless. Patterson was not suffering then. He had only received a flesh wound, and was staying up so that he had to be tied up to prevent him from jumping overboard to escape. The masked men soon seized him and [hustled him up]. He did not flinch, but was heard to say:

"I suppose you are going to kill me, but I don't care if you do."

He has never been heard from since.

Steamboats arriving at the Memphis levee from down river points are bringing hundreds of bales of cotton per day from the neighborhood in which the riot occurred, and everybody in the community is busy gathering crops.

The whites and blacks are on good terms, nor has any spirit of race intolerance displayed in the treatment of the benighted creatures who took part in the strife. The people have behaved with rare good judgment.

Memphis Appeal-Avalanche, October 5, 1891.

IX

OTHER EXPRESSIONS OF BLACK LABOR MILITANCY

OTHER EXPRESSIONS OF BLACK LABOR MILITANCY

Black labor militancy was not confined to destitute southern farmers. On September 28, 1891, about 1,500 black longshoremen walked off their jobs at the docks in Savannah, Georgia. Their demands included an increase in wages, a guarantee that the employers would cease cheating them of their overtime pay, and union recognition. The strike was exceptionally well planned and orderly. A war chest of $5,000 had been accumulated, fliers were circulated asking other blacks not to become scabs, and Negro preachers appealed for solidarity from the pulpit. The black community held balls, the proceeds of which were designated for the support of the strikers' families. Although several other groups of workers joined them, the strike was confined primarily to the wharf laborers who handled the transfer of freight between ships and the railroad cars (Doc. 1-6).

Immediately after the men quit work, the railroad companies sent out agents along the line to hire replacements, promising them free transportation and permanent employment. The first contingent of strikebreakers consisted of poor Negroes from the hinterland who arrived on the same day the strike began. Many of the new hands soon quit, however, claiming they were hired under false pretenses. The companies had not informed them that they were to be scabs. Thus, when 150 black recruits arrived in Savannah on October 1, they refused to go to work and joined the strikers. Others rejected employment because they feared retaliation. The stoppage was so well organized in fact, that city officials conceded the improbability that replacements could readily be found. By October 1, the strikers' numbers had increased to about 2,500 and business along the wharfs ground to a standstill. As the economy of the port city began to feel the strain of idleness, a committee of the Savannah commercial leaders organized to pressure the companies to end the strike by any means available. Since a sufficient number of blacks could not be recruited to break the strike, company officials decided to hire white replacements. Most of the recruits were poor white section hands employed as extras by the railroad companies. The new men were kept on the job by hearty meals served at long tables on the wharfs (Doc. 7-10).

On October 3, five days after the walk-out began, morale of the striking longshoremen sagged, and most were ready to resume work at a compromise rate of pay. But when the black workers discovered that union recognition was not forthcoming, they voted to continue the strike. In retaliation the companies announced that the strikers would not be reemployed as a body. On receipt of this news the black wharfmen panicked and began individually to reapply for their old jobs. Under these circumstances, the collective determination required to continue the struggle evaporated, and leaders reluctantly called off the walk-out. Even though the strike had failed, the Savannah strike demonstrated a pervasive unity destroyed not by black workers, but by whites (Doc. 11-18).

While race could be used to divide the working class, the Chicago Culinary Alliance reflected the potential for solidarity when desired. In Chicago where black waiters had been an important element in the Knights of Labor, and where they, together with white waiters, had won a strike for higher wages in 1887, the Culinary Alliance was a powerful organization. Most of the black waiters left the Knights in 1890 and affiliated with the independent Culinary Alliance, an interracial union of waiters and hotel employees. Founded in January 1889, the absence of racial and ethnic prejudice in the organization stimulated the growth of the Alliance until, with a membership of 30,000, it quickly developed into the strongest union of its kind in the United States. In 1890 the Alliance struck for higher wages. Typically, Chicago employers attempted to pit black and white waiters against each other, but Negro waiters refused to go to work as scabs. The union had several black leaders and, together with whites, they forged one of the few labor associations during the era to reject racial prejudice, both in principle and practice (Doc. 20-24).

THE SAVANNAH WHARF WORKERS' STRIKE, 1891

1. THEY STRIKE TODAY

Negro Wharf Laborers in Savannah Want More Pay--Trouble Feared

SAVANNAH, Ga., Sept., 27.--The wharf laborers of the Central Railroad and
the Savannah, Florida & Western Railroad will strike tomorrow for an advance
of 5 cents an hour in wages. The Laborers' Union and Protective Association
decided on a strike today and the men were ordered not to resume work tomorrow morning. The strikers number 1,500 and are all colored. They have
been paid 15 cents an hour for time worked. Saturday a demand for 20 cents
was refused. As a precaution against trouble the military has been ordered
to be in readiness. Five thousand rounds of ammunition have been furnished
by the Governor from the State arsenal for the military and it arrived today.

Memphis Appeal-Avalanche, September 28, 1891.

2. TO PATROL UNDER ARMS

Trouble Threatened by the Colored Longshoremen

Five thousand ball cartridges are on their way to Savannah for the military of the city for use in case of an emergency arising out of the threatened strike of the colored longshoremen.
    The cartridges left Atlanta last night and will arive here this morning,
and will be distributed among the armories. They were ordered yesterday by
telegraph by Col. Peter Reilly of the First regiment, after a conference with
Mayor McDonough and Col. Garrard.
    The walking delegates of the longshoremen's organization waited on the
officials at the Ocean steamship and Savannah, Florida and Western railway
wharves yesterday and notified them that the longshoremen wanted 20 cents an
hour for their services hereafter, instead of 15 cents.
    The demand was refused. The delegates then threatened trouble. They
said the men they represented would not work after last night for less than
20 cents an hour, nor would they allow any others to take their places except by walking over their bodies.

A CONFERENCE WITH THE MILITARY

    The kind of talk alarmed the officials and they at once reported to
Mayor McDonough. He immediately sent for Lieut. Col. Peter Reilly, commanding
the First Georgia regiment, and Col. William Garrard of the Guards battalion
and laid the state of affairs before them. After a lengthy conference, in
which, it is understood, the military authorities pledged themselves to compel obedience to the law, and prevent any riotous disturbance. Mayor Mc
Donough requested Col. Reilly to telegraph Gov. Northen for 5,000 ball cartridges, to be ready to meet any demonstration in the nature of a riot.
    The telegram was sent at once, and the requisition was honored by the
governor.
    Mayor McDonough doesn't think anything serious will occur, but he called
the military into the conference for the purpose of being ready for any emergency that may possibly arise. He proposes to have the law recognized and
obeyed, and will take precautions to have any outbreak promptly and summarily
suppressed.

20,000 BALL CARTRIDGES ON HAND

Including the 5,000 cartridges which will arrive this morning, there are about 20,000 in possession of the military and police, and it wouldn't be well for either the longshoremen or any one else to start a riot at the present time.

A reserve force of police was kept in the barracks yesterday afternoon by Chief Green but there was no demand made for their services.

The colored hands quit work at the Ocean Steamship wharves at the usual hour last night without any demonstration, but many ugly threats were heard about what would be done if the company adhered to its refusal of the increase of wages demanded.

GUNS TAKEN TO THE WHARVES

At midnight Sergt. Muse of the Central railroad force carried all the rifles belonging to his department from the barracks to the wharf, together with a quantity of ammunition. This was done as a precautionary measure. A wagon was used to convey the firearms to the wharf.

The corporations refuse positively to accede to the demands of the men. They say that sufficient labor can be found to work at the present rate of wages, and if the old hands don't want to remain new ones will be placed in the positions and protected at all hazards.

There may be trouble today or tomorrow, although the authorities hope that wiser counsels will prevail upon the dissatisfied workmen to make their issue in a peaceable and orderly manner.

Savannah Morning News, September 27, 1891.

3.   ONE THOUSAND MEN OUT

The Colored Wharf Laborers' Strike Inaugurated

The wharf laborers' strike went into effect yesterday morning. Over 1,000 men are out. There is a complete tie-up at the Central railroad wharves. Between 800 and 900 men are out there. At the Merchants and Miners' wharves over 100 men are out. The strike did not extend to the Savannah, Florida and Western wharves and the 800 laborers there were working as usual yesterday.

The strikers are quiet and orderly. The only disturbance that occurred was at the Baltimore wharves. As the non-union hands who had been unloading the steamship Allegheny left the yard at 6 o'clock last night they were met by a crowd of strikers who began cursing and abusing them. They started to run and all of them managed to escape but four. These were collared and beaten with stones and clubs by Isaac Polite, Wadley Screven and Jim Scott. A telephone message was sent to the barracks for officers, but before they were ready to start for the scene of the trouble another message was received that the row was over and the assailants had escaped. One of the men was badly injured. All were new hands.

KEPT AWAY FROM THE WHARVES

The strikers did not go near the wharves yesterday morning, but held a meeting instead at Odd Fellows' hall, on Duffy street. The hall was well filled with the strikers. The speeches were of a temperature tone, and the leaders cautioned the men to avoid any violence, saying that if they adopted a dignified course they would have the sympathy of the community behind them, and would probably carry their point. The hasty action at the Baltimore wharf indicates that all the strikers are not in accord with their leaders.

The strike has been systematically conducted. The laying of the plans has been going on for weeks and a determination was arrived at to head off the corporations from securing help in the country. The union has in its treasury, it is said, over $5,000, and circulars announcing the intention to strike, together with its grievances and a plea to the colored people to remain away from the city, were printed and scattered broadcast through the country districts by agents. The pulpit was also appealed to, and the agents managed to get the preachers to talk of the intended strike and beg their people to remain at home and not be induced by any promises of the railroad companies to take the places of the strikers.

THE POLICE IN READINESS

Chief Green kept the entire police force, with the exception of the street patrol, in the barracks until nearly midday ready to respond in case of necessity, but no demand was made for their services. . . .

Mayor McDonough was asked by this *Morning News* reporter if he had anything to say in reply to the card of the Labor Union and Protective Association published yesterday, asking him if he would be a friend of the strikers if they didn't disturb the peace of the city.

"As long as the Labor Union and the Protective Association obeys the laws," said Mr. McDonough, "the members will be granted fully as much protection as any other class or corporation. They must respect good order and conduct themselves accordingly, otherwise they must expect to be dealt with as the law directs. I have no feeling in the matter one way or the other except to see that the laws are obeyed."

"As long as the strikers do this," continued Mayor McDonough, "they will find me as friendly toward them as anyone else. I am acting in the matter according to my sense of public duty, and the precautionary steps taken already by the city authorities were because of the rash statements made by some of the laborers. I therefore urgently request all connected with the strike in progress to be peaceable and keep within the law, and I will guarantee them ample protection."

THE STRIKERS' MEETINGS

The strikers have held daily meetings for several days at the Odd Fellows' hall at Duffy and Cuyler streets, attended by immense crowds. Their meeting there Sunday lasted almost all the forenoon, and people living in the vicinity say that the whole neighborhood was black with colored people. They have been holding meetings there at nights for some time in preparation for the strike and the colored military companies have been doing a great deal of drilling there. Balls are held frequently, and one was held last night, the proceeds of which, it is said, go into the fund of the strikers.

One of the party of excursionists that came in yesterday afternoon from among the Central said that a large number of them would remain in the city, and work for the steamship company or anybody else that wanted them.

Everything was quiet on the wharves last night. The strikers kept away, and there was no effort to interfere with the new workers that were brought in from the country.

John Youngblood, vice president of the Labor Union and Protective Association, said that the union will adhere to its demand for an advance in wages, but it will not countenance any disturbance or interference with men outside of the union who went to work. The union men, he said will stand together, and none of them will be allowed to resume work until the union's demands have been acceded to.

THE POLICE HAVE A QUIET TIME

The police detail which guarded the Ocean Steamship bridge with rifles in the early morning to see that none except those who were willing to work should trespass on the company's property, had little to do except to admire each other. It was the same story during the remainder of the day. Not a striker appeared and not the slightest intimidation was attempted on the few hands which the Central managed to secure.

In the afternoon the wharves were almost deserted. Everything south of the river front had a funeral air. No loungers were hanging around the bridge, as is usually the case, and but a few trucks were seen hauling goods. The hand cotton trucks were standing where they were left Saturday night by the strikers, and the policemen walked around with their Springfields as if guarding a tomb.

The City of Macon of the Boston line which arrived yesterday morning was lying in the first slip diagonally across from the bridge, with eight

colored men and a couple of white men trying to unload her. They were
making little progress, however, and were only taking off the light goods.
The cotton and rosin yards presented the same deserted appearance as the
rest of the wharf.

CLERKS TAKING IT EASY

On the river front wharves the clerks were lounging in the offices
chatting and discussing the situation. They had nothing else to do. The
Chattahoochee, which also came in yesterday morning, was lying alongside of
the dock with her hatch doors open, but no one working on her. Four white
men and five colored men were unloading rosin and other goods from freight
cars just opposite in a listless manner.

The Kansas City, which was practically loaded Saturday night, was preparing to sail, and things were a little more lively at her dock than anywhere else. A gang of men had just completed the storing of 200 barrels of
rosin and spirits and some other small freight, and were busy getting in the
trunks of passengers. As soon as the Kansas City sailed things once more
assumed the forlorn condition at other points, and the clerks gathered in
groups and discussed the outlook. Not over fifty hands were at work on the
wharves.

PICKING UP HANDS

The Central sent out agents along the line of the road to get hands,
and shortly after 4 o'clock about forty country negroes arrived and were taken
to the wharves and put to work with the other hands that had been secured in
the city unloading the two steamships. The work progressed rather slowly,
however, because of the men being green at the business.

The entire Central railroad police force has been on duty at the wharves
since night before last at 6 o'clock. The officers are not allowed to leave.
Their meals are sent to them and they sleep on their arms in a sleeping coach
on a switch just west of the bridge. The arms consist of Springfield rifles
and bayonets, besides clubs and pistols. The cartridge boxes are filled with
ammunition and the force is in position to do thorough military duty and
deadly service should the necessity arise.

Agent Wilkinson took a cheerful view of the situation last night.
"Everything is quiet and has been so all day," said he. "We have between
fifty and sixty hands at work and by tomorrow afternoon I expect to have 600
at work."

"Where will you get the men?"

HELP FROM THE INTERIOR TOWNS

"From the interior. Men are being picked up at every station on the
roads and we will have ample force in a day or two. The steamships will not
be delayed, because we will put extra force loading and unloading them."

Agent Anderson of the Ocean Steamship Company took the same view. He
said the business of the line will not at all be interfered with by the
strike, as the force which arrived last night and is expected today will be
ample to get the vessels off on their sailing days. The Chattahoochee is to
sail tomorrow, and the City of Macon Thursday. The City of Augusta will
arrive today.

The freights at this season are very heavy, and a great deal of labor
is necessary to properly handle it.

ALL QUIET ON THE LOWER WHARVES

Things were very different on the lower wharves than was anticipated.
There was very little evidence of a strike. In fact, the strike did not go
into effect on the Savannah, Florida and Western wharves at all, nor any of
the wharves east of the city except at the Baltimore Steamship wharves.
There it was plainly evident that something was wrong. Two or three clerks
and a few green hands were found at work making feeble efforts at unloading
the steamship Allegheny, which arrived up yesterday morning. The Allegheny
is scheduled to leave tomorrow night, but unless the company gets more men
the vessel will not be unloaded by that time. The force of from 80 to 100
men failed to put in an appearance yesterday morning. Half a dozen green men
were picked up and started to work.

Agent J. J. Carolan of the Merchants and Miners' Company said that
unless he can get a full force together the sailing of the Allegheny may be
interfered with for a day. He received a notice of the demands of the
Labor Union and Protective Association Friday, but paid no attention to it,
thinking it had been sent as much as a matter of form as anything else. The
men had all the work they wanted with his company, and he was a little surprised to find that the strike had extended to his line. The situation of
affairs was telegraphed to the traffic manager and Mr. Carolan received a
reply to do the best he could and keep the company advised. He said that the
Merchants and Miners' will be guided entirely by the action of the other
corporations interested in the strike. There are plenty of men in the city,
Mr. Carolan said, who are willing to work, but they are afraid of the strikers.

AT THE PRESSES

At the lower presses work was going on as usual. On account of the
small sales of cotton Friday and Saturday one of the presses was shut down
for a day or two, making it necessary to drop about 110 men; but there is
no strike among the employes, and none is anticipated.

A number of men asking work were turned away during the day, and if
necessary to start up the other press enough could be found in a few hours.
The men are paid 12-1/2 to 15 cents an hour at the presses, averaging $7 to
$8 a week, and are well satisfied.

Alderman R. F. Harmon was pushing work on the Gordon wharf, and with no
wrinkles on his brow because of strikers. He said all of his men reported
promptly for work, and he expected them back again this morning. None of
them had intimated any intention of striking.

"They make $1.50 a day," said Mr. Harmon, "and get their pay every week
and are satisfied. I have some men here that have been with me four years.
I don't think the strike will amount to anything on these wharves."

ON THE S., F. AND W. WHARVES

All down the line of the Savannah, Florida and Western wharves, the
spirits wharf, the rosin wharf and the long lumber wharves the men were
working as usual. Some of them were spoken to about the strike. They said
they hadn't quit work because they were satisfied to stay where they were.
They said, however, that pretty nearly all the laborers on the wharves belonged to the union.

One man who was sitting astride a cotton bale and who might have been
a walking delegate, as he said he was not working, responded in reply to an
inquiry:

"Yes, sir. They's all going to strike. There won't be nobody down here
tomorrow. They's all going to quit."

The cotton workers said they had no intention of quitting work. The
report put in circulation yesterday that there would be no longshoremen loading cotton in ships today is without foundation.

THE OFFICIALS NOT NOTIFIED

General Superintendent Fleming of the Savannah, Florida and Western
railroad was seen yesterday afternoon and was asked why it was that the men
had not struck on the Savannah, Florida and Western wharves. He replied
that he did not know. They went to work yesterday morning without saying
anything to the officials of the road. He did not know himself whether the
men would go to work yesterday morning and could not tell whether they will
go to work this morning. The men at the Savannah, Florida and Western wharves
are paid 12-1/2 to 15 cents an hour and they get their pay every Saturday.

The police had a light day of it, notwithstanding anticipations of
trouble with the strikers. Chief Green does not anticipate any trouble. The
police will be held in readiness, however, in case trouble should arise. The
whole force is sixty men, including officers, besides the Central railroad
police force of twenty-two men, and the Savannah, Florida and Western railway
police force of twenty-five men, a total available force of over 100 officers
and men.

LUMBER HANDLERS STRIKE

Another strike has cropped out as a result of the Labor Union and Protective Association trouble. It is that of the Lumbermen and Timber Workers' Mutual Union. The only firm affected so far is Dale, Dixon & Co. The reason the lumber hands struck there, it is said, was because one of the members of the association was discharged for being unable to do the work required of him. Yesterday morning his co-laborers demanded his reinstatement, and when it was refused they quit work. Forty men were employed by Dale, Dixon & Co.

The other lumber concerns engaged in loading vessels will most likely be affected today, judging from a note sent by the secretary of the lumbermen's organization to the meeting of the labor union. It reads: "We are glad to announce that the L. and T.W.M.U. has stopped work. Those who didn't want to stop had to stop, anyhow."

It is not known what the lumbermen's grievances are.

Mr. Stillwell, of Stillwell, Miller & Co., said that the men employed by his firm were perfectly satisfied, and he expects no trouble. They are not paid by the hour, but get $1.50 a day.

A COUNTRY STRIKE

William and Harry Hudkins, contractors at Statesboro, were in town last night and said to a MORNING NEWS reporter that the strike idea prevails all throughout the country around Statesboro. The cotton pickers have not struck yet, but some trouble is expected. Messrs. Hudkins' laborers, whom they were paying $1 a day, struck for $1.25, and their brickmasons whom they were paying $3 a day struck for $3.25. They refused to give the increase demanded and their men left them.

THE CENTRAL'S NOTICE

The following notice was posted at the cotton exchange yesterday; "Supt. McBee notified the members of the cotton exchange that the Central railroad will give guarantees of delivery of cotton to vessels in ten days from date of transfer."

The above is a rule which has been in force heretofore and applies to f.o.b. cotton in transit. The order, it is understood, will not apply to the cotton already here.

TOOK THEM FOR LABORERS

A big colored excursion from Milledgeville arrived in the city by the Central railroad last night at 6 o'clock. There were fourteen coaches on the excursion train and the crowd numbered over 500 people. The general impression of everybody that saw the big crowd pouring out of the Central railroad depot was that they were laborers brought down by the Central to take the places of the strikers on the Ocean Steamship wharves. Any of the excursionists that want to work on the wharves will be readily received by the steamship company, however.

Savannah Morning News, September 29, 1891.

4. THE STRIKE ORDERED ON

The Wharf Laborers To Go Out This Morning

The Central and Savannah, Florida and Western Authorities Refuse to Accede to the Laborers' Demands for an Increase in Wages and the Strike Ordered --Fifteen Hundred Men Involved--The Strikers' Demands--Precautions by the Police and Military to Prevent an Outbreak--None But Workers to be Allowed on the Wharves.

The strike of the wharf laborers at the Central railroad and Savannah, Florida and Western wharves for an advance of 5 cents an hour in wages was ordered yesterday by the Labor Union and Protective Association to go into effect this morning. The strikers number about 1,500.

Both the Central and Savannah, Florida and Western people say there will be no increase of wages.

"The first intimation I received of the action of the hands," said Agent Wilkinson of the Central railroad, "was Friday afternoon when a committee waited upon me and said the association had decided to ask for 5 cents an hour increase. I told the committee that I would present the matter to Supt. Dill as soon as he returned to the city and asked that further action be deferred. The chairman of the committee answered that the Central would find an answer in the MORNING NEWS next day. The Central is willing to be just and reasonable in the matter of wages, but it will not be intimidated. It considers 15 cents an hour ample wages, and can get plenty of men to work at $1.25 per day. Between 800 and 900 men are employed at the wharves and their places can be filled rapidly should they quit. There was never any kick on the wages until the laborers found out they had to work for their money, and then they decided they must have an increase.

OPPOSED TO A STRIKE

"I understand," said Agent Wilkinson, "that many of the men are opposed to the strike and will return to work if not intimidated. Any who wish to return to work will be protected. The Central has taken every precaution to protect its property and employes, and should there be any attempt at disorder it will be speedily quelled."

A force of police is stationed at the bridge this morning and no one will be allowed to cross except they intend to work. All others will be excluded. The following card is published by Agent Wilkinson:

The authorities of the Central railroad, having understood that it was the intention of their wharf labor to quit work, pending decision as to increase of pay demanded, have conferred with the municipal authorities, and wish to assure all concerned that a delay to freight being very detrimental to the interests of the public as well as to the company, desire to publish, for the information of those who wish to continue their services as heretofore, the following notice, as the demands made are inconsistent with reasonable justice or equity in the employment of labor.

Any laborers in the employ of the company who wish to continue at work will be protected to the fullest extent of the law. Therefore, do not be misled by those who wish to create trouble, but who have not the power to protect you should trouble ensue; and further, those not intending to work must not trespass upon the company's property.

AT THE LOWER WHARVES

About 600 men are employed at the Savannah, Florida and Western wharves and are involved in the strike. General Superintendent Fleming said yesterday that no increase in pay will be granted, as the present rate of wages is considered sufficient for the work. Plenty of hands can be found to do the work at the present rate. Fleming thinks, and they will be gotten at once. No trouble is expected by the Savannah, Florida and Western people. Supt. Fleming said that the company is prepared to protect its labor and property at all hazards. No more precautionary measures have been taken at the wharves, but several policemen will be out there to-day to see that no disorder occurs.

It was understood around town that the order to close work went into effect at 6 o'clock Saturday night and no work was to be done after that time at present prices. However there was a large gang at work all day yesterday at the Central wharves loading the Kansas City. The men worked with their usual vigor, and nothing was said about any intended strike or any intention of not resuming work today.

THE POLICE IN READINESS

Chief Green does not expect any trouble, but still he will hold the police force in readiness to respond at once should any outbreak occur.

Sergt. Muse of the Central railroad police force reported everything quiet yesterday and said that he had no reason to anticipate any trouble. Precautionary measures have been taken on the principle that an ounce of

prevention is worth a pound of cure. It is on the same principle that the
military have been notified to be in readiness to answer the alarm. Notices
were posted in the armories yesterday ordering the men to hold themselves
in readiness.

That the threatened strike is by the longshoremen and stevedores is
denied. Several longshoremen and stevedores said yesterday that they had
nothing to do with the strike and knew nothing about it. They say they are
satisfied with present prices and want nothing but plenty of work.

THE STRIKERS' ORGANIZATION

The Labor Union and Protective Association is entirely composed of
wharf laborers and railroad hands. They claim a membership of from 1,500 to
2,000, though whether they can control all their members is doubted. They
have been organizing for some time in preparation for a demand for higher
wages. The laborers are paid 12-1/2 cents to 15 cents an hour for the time
they work. They do not consider this pay sufficient as frequently they do
not put in more than half a day and are paid accordingly.

A well-known stevedore said yesterday that about $1.10 a day is what
he understood the average earnings of a wharf laborers to be. This, he
said was less than the railroad have paid in previous years.

While the strike appears imminent, it is believed the precautions already taken will have the effect of preventing trouble.

FOR PEACEABLE METHODS

It was reported on the streets last night that at the meeting of the
strikers held at Odd Fellows' hall yesterday afternoon, it was resolved that
none should cross the Ocean Steamship Company's bridge and that they would
make no offensive demonstration.

William Crutcher, one of the strikers' committee, said yesterday that
there will be no trouble so far as the strikers are concerned.

The prices demanded by the laborers are 20 cents an hour for all men in
shipshold and 30 cents an hour for heads of gangs, and to be paid weekly and
not every two weeks. The price demanded is an advance of about 5 cents per
hour on present prices.

The following card is published by the laborers' organization this
morning, and indicating that the association is for peaceable methods and
discountenance violence.

The Labor Union and Protective Association is not prepared for war, but
is prepared for labor. We ask the mayor if he will be our friend if we
didn't break the peace of the city. The members of the Labor Union and
Protective Association are all law-abiding citizens.

THE RAILROAD LABORERS' STRIKE

The strike of the laborers employed by the Central railroad yards and
on the wharves of the Ocean Steamship Company and Merchants and Miners' Transportation Company which occurred yesterday was not unexpected. It was thought
it would include the laborers in the yards and on the wharves of the Savannah,
Florida and Western Railway Company. This class of laborers formed a protective union several weeks ago with the view of having alleged grievances
remedied and of securing an increase of wages.

While the public cannot help taking a certain amount of interest in the
relations between the foregoing companies and their employes, and is certain
to express its sympathy with one side or the other in the issue which the
strike has raised, it has virtually no concern with these relations. But if
the companies fail to carry out their contracts, and thus disturb and embarrass the business of the community, the public has a right to demand the
reason, and will not be slow to do so.

Whether or not the strikers have a reasonable basis for their grievances
and demand is a question to which there are doubtless two sides. They think
they have. All strikes are based upon a genuine or fancied grievance and
they are occurring all the time in different parts of the country. In some
instances, having the power or being in the right, their demands are granted
or a compromise is effected. In most instances, however, strikes fail, and
the failures are due to various causes, the main one being that they are
ordered without a careful consideration of all the attendant circumstances.

The strike of yesterday is based upon a demand for higher wages. Other
demands have cropped out since the strike was inaugurated, but they are
rather in the nature of grievances, which, if properly presented, would
probably be adjusted. The companies themselves must, of course, be the
judges as to whether they can afford an increase of wages. It is not probable that they will grant an increase if they can get all the labor they
want at the wages they are now paying. If they are dependent upon the
strikers they will have to grant the strikers' demands. The fact that they
have refused to grant them is pretty good evidence that an ample supply of
labor can be obtained at the wages they are paying.

There is no doubt of the right of the laborers to strike, though it
may turn out that they were not wise in doing so. If the companies succeed
in getting along without them the unpleasant fact will be forced upon them
that they made a mistake. It is always a mistake for a laboring man having
no means of support to give up the work he has before he sees a chance of
bettering his condition.

The strikers seem to understand that they have no right to prevent
others from taking the places they have abandoned. To attempt to bring the
business of the companies to a standstill in order to enforce their demand
would produce a condition of affairs that would array the public against
them, and call for the interference of the authorities. And they would gain
nothing by such a course. Strikers who resort to violence seldom or never
gain their ends. They are the losers. If the strikers here are wise they
will rely wholly upon peaceful means to accomplish their object, and from
the published reports they do not appear to have exhausted these means,
particularly in respect to what may be called their grievances.

Savannah Morning News, September 29, 1891.

5. THE STRIKE SPREADING

The Warehouse and Rosin Yard Hands Quit Work

The wharf laborers' strike has extended to the Savannah, Florida and
Western hands, the naval stores, warehouse, and cotton press hands and the
draymen. In all there will be in the neighborhood of 2,000 men out this
morning.

The warehouse hands to the number of about 100 struck yesterday afternoon, 150 Savannah, Florida and Western hands went out last night, and the
400 naval store hands, between 200 and 300 draymen, the cotton press hands,
numbering about fifty and about fifty warehouse hands gave notice last night
that they will quit work this morning.

The naval stores hands notified the inspectors of their intention to
strike in communications written in red ink. The cotton press hands informed
Supt. Wade of the Cotton Press Association last night that there would be no
necessity to start the fires this morning, because they would not be on hand
to work. The demands of the strikers for wages are the same--20 cents an
hour.

The cotton business is seriously affected, and work on the wharves was
almost at a standstill yesterday. The obstruction of freights is causing
businessmen a great deal of embarrassment and is creating considerable uneasiness.

A CONFERENCE WITH THE STRIKERS

A three-hours' conference between committees from the cotton exchange,
board of trade and the strikers was held at the cotton exchange yesterday
afternoon. The strikers' committee, after detailing their grievances and
demands, agreed to leave the matter with the commercial bodies as a sort of
arbitration committee between themselves and the railroads.

Col. J. L. Warren, president of the cotton exchange; J. F. Minis, Col.
W. W. Gordon, Capt. John Flannery, H. M. Comer, Edward Karow and Alderman

W. G. Cann, composed the cotton exchange committee and John R. Young, W. B.
Stillwell and George P. Walker represented the board of trade.

These committees met General Superintendent McBee and Agent Wilkinson
of the Central, General Superintendent Fleming and Assistant Freight Agent
Papy of the Savannah, Florida and Western. Agent Carolan of the Merchants
and Miners' Transportation Company, and Agent Anderson of the Ocean Steamship Company, in the gentleman's parlor of the De Soto last night for a
conference.

LEFT WITH THE COMMITTEE

The representatives of the cotton exchange and board of trade asked
the strikers' committee to leave the matter in their hands and an effort
would be made to bring about a settlement. If they could get a proposition
which they discerned fair from the railroads they would report to the strikers' committee at 10 o'clock this morning. They advised the strikers that
if their statements regarding overtime were correct they would insist on a
remedy. . . .

The meeting lasted 24 hours, and it is understood that a conclusion was
reached to offer a compromise proposition to the strikers this morning.

THE COTTON EXCHANGE ACTS

The first action on the strike by the commercial men was taken at noon
yesterday, when the cotton exchange held a meeting to consider the situation
and see if anything could be done to remove the strike. A resolution was
passed appointing a committee to confer with the Central, and Savannah,
Florida and Western officials with a view to arriving at a settlement of the
strike. Mayor McDonough and the board of trade were requested to co-operate.

In accordance with the action of the cotton exchange Clerk of Council
Rebarer forwarded the following letter to the strikers:

Savannah, Ga., Sept. 29, 1891

H. S. Lowrey, Chairman Committee L. U. and P. A.

Dear Sir--His honor the mayor requests that you will appoint a committee representing your organization to meet with committees from Savannah
Cotton Exchange and Board of Trade at the cotton exchange building this
afternoon at 5 o'clock, for the purpose of endeavoring to adjust the differences at present existing between your association and the railroad systems,
your committee to have power to act. Very respectfully,

FRANK E. REBARER,

Clerk of Council

THE AFTERNOON CONFERENCE

The committees from the commercial bodies and the strikers were promptly
on hand at the appointed hour, but the railroad officials could not attend
on account of the press of business. Mayor McDonough was made chairman of
the conference. A reporter of the MORNING NEWS sent up his card, but received a polite notice that it was the sense of the meeting that reporters
were not wanted.

The members of the strikers' committee presented their grievances in a
lengthy and detailed manner. They said, in substance that the men were not
paid enough for their labor, and were defrauded of their overtime. They said
that lately it had been the custom to start gangs to work at the Central
wharves unloading cars a short while before the quitting hour, and compel the
men to continue the work until all the freight was out. Sometimes they would
run over fifteen minutes, and sometimes half an hour. When they demanded
overtime for the work, they were told it was Agent Wilkinson's orders that
wherever the unloading of a car was begun during regular hours and was not
completed at the usual quitting time the work must be finished and no overtime was to be allowed.

A CONFERENCE WITH THE OFFICIALS

The conference between committees of the commercial bodies and railroad
and steamship men began in the De Soto at 9:30 o'clock and it was midnight
before an adjournment was reached. At the conclusion of the conference the
MORNING NEWS reporter was furnished the information that an agreement had

been reached and a proposition would be made to the strikers today. The committee declined to state the nature of the proposition.

It is understood, however, that it is a compromise on the basis of something like 8 cents an hour and the allowing of all overtime. The temper of the railroad authorities, it is said, was against granting any concessions. They denied the complaints of the strikers and argued that the pay was sufficient.

The business men, on the other hand, pointed out the necessity for a prompt settlement of the difficulty, and the damage which has already resulted to the city's business, and insisted that some arrangement be arrived at.

Whether the strikers will accept the recommendation of the committee is a matter of conjecture.

BUT FEW HANDS AT WORK

There was little change in affairs at the Central railroad wharves yesterday. The officials secured between fifty and seventy-five men, and together with the fifty men secured the day before, managed to unload the Chattahoochee, which was finished at 9 o'clock last night. The work was rather slow on account of the hands being green. The work of loading the vessel was begun at once by the same force and she will sail on schedule time this afternoon, though probably with not half a cargo. The work of unloading the City of Macon was also begun last night and the taking out of the cargo of the Nacoochee will begin this morning. The same deserted air prevailed at the wharves on the preceding day, and the policemen walked around with their guns as if the stillness pervading everywhere made them weary.

Agent Wilkinson was asked last night about the situation. He said everything was quiet, and work was progressing rather slowly. He expected to get the steamers out on schedule time, but he wasn't willing to say that they would go with full cargoes. He said there are 200 men at work. Others in position to know say there are not over 125 to 150.

Agent Wilkinson said he expects to have 600 hands by this afternoon. A number of the new hands which came the day before yesterday quit work yesterday, claiming that they had been brought to the city under misrepresentations. Agent Wilkinson believed that the leaders of the gangs who remained at work did so with an object in view, and that they are working under cover in the interest of the strikers for the purpose of running off the new hands.

AFRAID OF THE STRIKERS

The attack on the non-union hands of the Merchants and Miners' Transportation Company had the effect of frightening the new hands off altogether. Not one of them showed up yesterday morning. Agent Carolan managed, however, to secure the services of a dozen white men and got the Allegheny unloaded last night. She will be loaded today and tonight, and will sail tomorrow morning, about eighteen hours behind schedule time. The men employed by the Baltimore line told Agent Carolan that they would like to return to work, but the union wouldn't allow it. On account of the previous day's disturbance a detail of police was at the Baltimore wharf last night at 6 o'clock to protect the men working there, but their services were not needed, as no attempt was made to molest them. The strikers disclaim any connection with the assailants of the non-union men. They say they are not members of the organization, and that it shouldn't be held accountable for the acts of irresponsible outside parties.

THE WAREHOUSE HANDS' STRIKE

The strike of the warehouse hands was rather a surprise to their employers, as no grievances had been heard. When asked for a statement of grievances, they said that all they want is 20 cents an hour, which would bring their wages up to $2 per day, they having been paid at the rate of $1.50 for ten hours work with permanent employment.

If the demands of the naval stores hands, cotton press hands and draymen are acceded to their wages will be brought up to the same standard, the men having been paid $1.50 a day of ten hours. It is understood that the naval stores inspectors have the demands of their men under consideration. The following is the notice of the striking draymen:

We are the Draymen's Labor Union Association, and are not disposed to make any disturbance whatever. All that we ask is 20 cents an hour. We do not want any more than what we ask for. We simply ask the boss draymen for more wages. We have to work very hard in all kinds of weather, night and day, and think our demands reasonable.

It is rumored that the strikers will demand the removal of Agent Wilkinson of the Central railroad. They blame him for the condition of affairs which caused the strike.

HEADING OFF NEW MEN

The strikers are so thoroughly organized and are working in such a systematic manner that the railroads will have a hard time getting men to take their places. Yesterday morning the Central brought in forty-three new hands from along the line of the road, but among the forty-three were two delegates from the strikers' association who had gone out in the country to head off the railroads' endeavors to secure men. The delegates mingled with the country negroes in a quiet way without attracting any special notice, explained the situation of affairs and appealed to their brotherly instincts not to go to work. The strikers' representatives promised to take charge of others in the city, feed and lodge them and return them to where they came from. They were taken to the Duffy street hall and given breakfast. They said the agents of the road had said nothing to them about a strike, but had told them that there was more work in Savannah than the home workmen could attend to, and that they needed extra hands. . . .

THE STRIKERS' MEETINGS

The strikers are quiet and orderly, and no trouble occurred. They held meetings at Odd Fellows' hall on Duffy street yesterday morning and afternoon. The morning meeting opened with prayer and singing "Stay in the Field Till the War is Ended." The strikers announced that they will not interfere with the Central or the men it may employ. They declared that they intended to conduct themselves peaceably.

The employers of labor on the wharves east of the city felt last night that they had badly fooled themselves. Work went on during the day as it did the day before on the eastern wharves, except at the lumber wharves, where the laborers failed to put in an appearance.

At the Baltimore Steamship Company's wharf about a dozen white men were unloading the Allegheny. Further down, the Savannah, Florida and Western employes were at work. A number of the old hands failed to put in their appearance, but others were found to take their places. Later in the afternoon, however, the entire force went out.

ANXIETY AT THE PRESSES

At the cotton presses everything seemed to be running smoothly. It was evident, however, that the strike was progressing. The employers and clerks said they expected no trouble and they did not believe the strike would prevent their getting all the men they needed, but it was evident they were anxious. The walking delegates were circulating around, telling the men they must quit work. A number of men were persuaded to quit. The new men were the readiest to quit and the men who had been longest in the employ of the companies were the least inclined to go out. Some of the old employes said they had been threatened and they were afraid to go to and from their work.

QUIT WORK QUIETLY

What was generally noted and commented upon with regard to the strikers was that when they got ready to quit they had nothing to say and made no demands, but left their work without a word.

Hundred of laborers who will fail to show up at the wharves this morning said nothing whatever of their intentions on leaving work last night. It was noticed that the men who were at work went about it in a listless sort of way, as if they were not interested in what they were doing.

Disaffection was evident among the draymen and warehousemen as well as the wharf laborers, and there was evidently a movement on foot to bring all classes of labor connected with the shipping business into the strike.

EFFECTS OF THE STRIKE

The strike was about all that was talked of among the cotton men on the Bay. Its effects are already severely felt. It is plain that if it continues even for a short time, it will lessen the cotton receipts of Savannah by many thousand bales, which will go to other ports, and will interfere with the arrangements between consignors and factors, causing serious loss.

Another effect will be to block up the Central railroad yards and wharves in such a manner that it will be very difficult to clear them again, and that too at a time when it is hard work to handle the daily receipts as they come in. The unanimous opinion was that if the strike only continued a few days it will seriously affect the cotton interests.

WILL CORNER MONEY

Instead of hurrying home as usual as soon as business was over the cotton men gathered in front of the cotton exchange from 5:30 to 6 o'clock and discussed the strike.

STANDING IN THEIR OWN LIGHT

The strike of the draymen and warehouse hands is the worst feature of the situation. "The laborers' union," said one cotton man, "is standing in its own light and is aiding the corporations against which it is fighting by keeping these men out. It gives an excuse to the roads to say to the merchants who want their cotton, 'Where are your trucks to remove it!' The strikers should think this over. The keeping away from work of the draymen and warehouse hands is not helping the strike one iota but is rather injuring the strikers' chances." . . .

"It will have a very serious effect in exhausting Savannah financially," said one of the largest cotton factors on the Bay to a MORNING NEWS reporter. "All the money that can be raised from the banks will soon be wrapped up in the cotton coming in, and the cotton men will be unable to raise money, because they will not be able to transport their cotton. The factors will hold the railroads responsible for all losses by reason of failure to deliver cotton consigned to them. If the railroads undertake to transport the cotton and are unable to carry out their contract that is their lookout."

ONE OF THE STRIKERS

John Williams, one of the vice presidents of the Labor Union and Protective Association, came up to the exchange with the strikers' conference committee. He said the men were striking for a small advance of 5 cents an hour, and they would have to have that before returning to work. He declared it was untrue that they had endeavored to intimidate new hands, and that nothing of the kind would be allowed. The whole trouble, he said, began on the Central railroad wharf where the men were pushed and hustled all the time, and with a policeman over them to "hunch" them in the side with a club if they did not move fast enough.

Williams intimated that the strikers had very little use for Agent Wilkinson.

The effect of the strike upon the receipts was plainly seen. The receipts yesterday were only 2,861 bales, against 6,606 the corresponding day last year. The railroads are said to be holding cotton back along their lines on account of their inability to handle it here. Very little of the heavy cotton receipts of Monday have been unloaded and delivered yet. Almost all of it is still in the cars.

Savannah Morning News, September 30, 1891.

6. TO THE PUBLIC

We, the Lumber and Timber Workingmen's Union Association take pleasure in stating that we have never refused to work for anybody that pays our wages

and complies with our laws. It has been reported that we had struck on
Messrs. Dale, Dixon & Co.'s work, but it is everything except truth, and we
hope that said company will not hold us responsible for such conduct. It
was all done through Mr. Jones and his foreman, Tom Jones because they
wanted to discharge Joe Thomas, a man that stands 6 feet in height and 24
inches across the breast, and in good health, and subject to inspection,
and was one of the "right hand" men there, until he found some mistake in
his time and held a little contention for his money. It was just then they
found out that he was insufficient for the work if he did refuse duty. Mr.
Jones had a right to knock him off; but to discharge him without a legal
cause would be a violation to Section 22 of By-Laws; and because three did
not break this section of law Mr. Jones refused to give the Lumber and Timber
Workingmen's Union Association any more work. Isaac Roberson was appointed
a committee to wait on Mr. Jones all day and get such men as would suit Mr.
Jones, and nothing could be done to satisfy him but to discharge all of the
union men. The grand reason for making this section of law is that we have
often found our money short, and when we contend for our money we gain a
discharge. And we, the Lumber and Timber Workingmen's Union Association
also take pleasure in saying that we will guarantee that we can do as good
and as much work as any other men in America.

ADAM COLLINS, President.

W. D. JENKINS, Secretary.

Savannah Morning News, October 1, 1891.

7. PROGRESS OF THE STRIKERS

The committee, representing the cotton exchange board of trade and the
city, interceded to adjust the differences between the strikers and the
transportation companies failed to accomplish its object, and will so report
to the trade bodies this morning. The transportation companies, although
confident of their ability to secure an amount of labor within a short time
sufficient to answer their purposes, consented to make concessions rather
than have the business of the port interrupted, but the strikers were obstinate and insisted upon their original demands.

The wages which the transportation companies consented to pay are as
high as those paid at any other southern port for the same class of labor.
To pay higher wages than are paid at other ports would drive business away
from our port. This fact was pointed out to the strikers, and they were
assured also that every grievance of which they had complained would be remedied. Neither argument nor concessions had any influence with them. They
spoke as if they felt they had the power to compel compliance with their demands and intended to use it.

At the beginning of the strike there was a quite general feeling that
their demand was entitled to consideration, but their refusal to accept the
compromise, which the committee is unanimous in thinking is fair and just,
has caused whatever sympathy they had to be withdrawn. By demanding more
than they are entitled to, and more than the business of the port will stand
and remain prosperous, they indicate very clearly that they care very little
about the business interests of the city.

The only thing that remains to be done is for the transportation companies to get labor elsewhere. That they are doing and are confident of their
ability to handle their freights within the next day or two.

Savannah Morning News, October 1, 1891.

8. STRIKERS WON'T GIVE IN

THEY REFUSE AN ADVANCE OF TWO AND A HALF CENTS AN HOUR

The Strike Spreading

The Conference Committee's Proposition to the Labor Union and the Strikers' Reply--They Adhere to Their Original Demands--The Tie-up Stops the Loading of Foreign Vessels, and Longshoremen Idle--Business Crippled and Serious Financial Embarrassment Threatened--The Situation on the Bay and Along the Wharves--Vessels Going Out Half Loaded--White Hands Filling the Strikers' Places.

The wharf laborers' strike is as far from adjustment now as at its in-auguration. The railroads have offered a compromise, but the strikers refuse to listen to anything short of a concession to their original demand of 20, 25 and 30 cents an hour. "We want nothing more nor less than what we have asked for" is their motto.

The proposition agreed upon at the conference of the railroad and steam-ship officials and the committee of the commercial bodies was an increase of 2-1/2 cents all around.

Yesterday morning the strikers' committee met the cotton exchange and board of trade committees at the cotton exchange and listened to the report, together with a recommendation that the Labor Union and Protective Associa-tion adopt the scale. The strikers' committee declined to recommend the scale, but said the proposition would be submitted to its organization.

THE COMMITTEE'S PROPOSITION

The proposition was given to the committee, and is as follows:

Savannah, Ga., Sept. 30, 1891

To the Committee of the Labor Union and Protective Association,
The joint committee from the cotton exchange and board of trade, with the mayor as chairman, have conferred with the officers of the railroad and steamship companies in your behalf.

The Central railroad officers state that they have already given notice that after Oct. 1 wages would be paid weekly. The steamship companies al-ready pay weekly.

This committee recommended that the companies advance your wages to the following figures, viz:

	Regular	Overtime
Railroad handlers, per hour...........................	15¢	20¢
Wharf truck hands, per hour..........................	17-1/2¢	23-1/2¢
Men in hold, per hour................................	20¢	21¢
Headers, per hour....................................	25¢	30¢

This will give about 25 cents per day additional to each laborer.

The committee recommended your association to accept this advance and resume work.

The committee request you to submit this proposition to your association and report to this committee the decision of your association. . . .

THE STRIKERS' REPLY

The strikers' committee went at once to the meeting of the union at the Duffy street Odd Fellows' hall and laid the proposal before it. It didn't meet with their approval and the strikers almost unanomously rejected it. They remained in session discussing the situation until after 1 o'clock. The committee had promised to report back to the commercial bodies at 4 o'-clock the result, but it was nearly 5 o'clock when the reply was received. It is as followes:

Savannah, Ga., Sept. 30, 1891

To the Board of Trade:
Dear Sirs:--The proposition your honorable board submitted to us this morning was submitted to the Labor Union and Protective Association since, and they request us to report to you that after mature deliberation and

after many days considering the justness of our demands, they wish us to report that they cannot, under any circumstances whatsoever, deviate from their
first proposition, viz: 20 cents for common labor, 25 cents for men in ships
hold and 30 cents for headers of gangs. Respectfully yours,

H. S. LOWERY,

Chairman of Committee, 90 Montgomery Street.

A 2-1/2 CENTS INCREASE

It will be seen from the above that the joint committee of the cotton
exchange and board of trade, with Mayor McDonough acting as chairman, succeeded in getting the railroad and steamship lines to consent to an advance
of 2-1/2 cents per hour to all their laborers, which the committee thought
to be fair and just compensation for the classes of labor performed.

When the joint committee found that it had failed in its efforts to
bring about an adjustment, owing to the laborers failing to accept the proposition made by the joint committee, it concluded that nothing further could
be done in the matter.

There will be a general meeting of the cotton exchange and board of
trade this morning at 10 o'clock and the arbitrating committee will make a
report. The railroad and steamship companies were notified of the failure
to arrive at a settlement.

THE STRIKE EXTENDING

The strike is assuming rather alarming proportions. It has got beyond
the original lines. The porters and truckmen of several hardware establishments quit work yesterday, and when asked for a grievance said they had none,
but being members of the union were compelled to go out. Several negroes
employed at Taggart's and Dixon's coal yards also struck. They said they
wanted $2 a day. The dry culture hands of the city quit work yesterday morn-
ing, and the drivers of the scavenger department threaten to strike this
morning. They are paid $10.50 a week, but want $2 per day. This state of
affairs will involve the city. The colored cotton samplers have also given
notice that they will strike this morning. In all about 2,500 men are out
so far.

The tie-up is seriously interfering with the white and colored longshoremen loading foreign vessels. They can't get cotton to load, and many
of them have had to quit work. If the strike lasts a day or two longer, all
the longshoremen will have to stop. This will bring a big loss to hundreds
of men.

LIKE SUNDAY ON THE BAY

The strike has brought about almost a complete paralysis of trade.
Yesterday had the appearance of Sunday along Bay street, with the exception
of the offices being open. The factors, commission merchants and shippers
stood around in front of the cotton exchange in groups, discussing the situation, listening to and offering suggestions as to how the trouble might be
brought to an end. They had nothing else to do, because there was no business of any consequence to be transacted. Their cotton is tied up at the
wharves, and can't be moved. Some of the railroad authorities are coming in
for a share of disapprobation from the business men to as great an extent
as the strikers.

They won't compromise. "The strikers have become entirely too head-
strong," said a well-known cotton man. "The committee from the commercial
bodies endeavored to get them to agree to take compensation by the day at
$1.50, at the rate of 15 cents an hour for ten hours work, to be paid weekly
and engaged monthly, but they rejected this proposition. They said they
wanted to work by the hour and get 20 cents, because they might get tired
sometime and want to stop, while if they were working by the day they would
have to keep on. Their disposition is to concede nothing at all. The
strikers said in substance, they have the business of the city within their
grasp and will hold it tight, and will remain on strike till Christmas if
necessary. They said they can starve as well as the next one, and will starve
out business while the corporations are trying to starve them.

THE STRIKERS WELL ORGANIZED

"The strikers intimated to the committee that they hadn't begun this fight unprepared, but had been thoroughly organizing and laying aside money for months. They even claim that their organization is in a condition to tie up the greatest portion of the ports of the South Atlantic, and will do so unless their demands are acceded to.

"The committee promised the strikers," continued the cotton man, "that if they would accept the proposition, which in the opinion of the committee was a fair and just one, it would guarantee that all their other grievances would be adjusted, but this had no effect. Up to the refusal of the compromise the strikers had the sympathy of a large portion of the business community in the struggle, but their arbitrary attitude has turned this sympathy from them. They are compelling the innocent to suffer for the guilty and damaging the commerce of the city. By their present course they will array the business community against them to their own injury."

CRAMPING BUSINESS MEN

The cotton and naval stores men are inclined to believe that the railroad officials here do not sufficiently realize the gravity of the situation so far as they are concerned. One of the factors said to a MORNING NEWS reporter that a financial crisis is threatened if the strike is prolonged any length of time. Large amounts of money have been advanced by the cotton and naval stores men to the producers. Under a normal state of affairs cotton would be coming in now at the rate of 7,000 bales a day, or to the value of $2,000,000 a week, and the factors would be able to realize on it all that they needed to meet their obligations. The same is true of those in the naval stores business. Money is at present difficult to secure, and if the strike continues there will be serious embarrassment.

CONFERENCE WITH HIGHER OFFICIALS

Some prominent cotton men suggested yesterday that if a satisfactory agreement is not reached with the strikers today that President John H. Inman, Pat Calhoun and General Manager Green be asked by telegraph to come here and assist in bringing the trouble to an end. This was generally received with favor and may be acted upon this morning if the outlook is not more promising than it was last night. . . .

THE MEN HAVEN'T SHOWN UP

The hands which Agent Wilkinson had been expecting every day since Monday have not arrived, and only about 150 are at work on the wharves. The steamship City of Macon was in practically the same loaded condition she was in Monday, and a white man and negro were trying to relieve her of small freight, but their movements were rather slow. In the cotton yard sixteen gawky-looking country negroes were trucking the fleecy staple as if the bales were as big as a house.

The largest force was at work loading the Chattahoochee. The vessel sailed about 5:30 o'clock with something like half a cargo. She carried only 3,034 packages altogether, including 1,310 bales of cotton.

AMUSING SCENES ON THE WHARVES

The loading of the vessel by the green hands afforded the passengers and crew and a number of spectators on the wharf as much amusement as a minstrel show. The hands rushed in and out of the Chattahoochee on the inclined gangplank as if shot from a circus catapult. The scenes were ludicrous in the extreme. The men looked as if they were frightened, from the way in which they kept their mouths open and the manner in which their eyes bulged out as they ran with the trucks. They handled the trucks as if they were plows and coming out of the hold after unloading their freight many of them got such headway down and up the gangway and slip that they ran nearly to the middle of the wharf before coming to a halt. It was dangerous to be within several feet of them, and the spectators had to look sharp to keep from being jammed. Collision after collision occurred on the gangway, and it was surprising that none of the negroes fell overboard. Several pieces of freight got a dip.

BAGGAGE DUMPED OVERBOARD

While the baggage was being put in the vessel two truckmen had a collision and a trunk was sent flying into the river. It was secured only after a good deal of hard work and a thorough soaking.

Agent Anderson said last night that he expects to get the Boston steamship City of Macon off on schedule time today. The gangs which loaded the Chattahoochee were put to work last night unloading the City of Macon. If she sails today it will only be with a light cargo.

The Nacoochee, which arrived day before yesterday, hadn't been touched in the way of unloading up to last night. She is booked to sail tomorrow afternoon.

The Central brought in about twenty-five hands yesterday morning, and another small lot last night. The great trouble experienced with the new hands is that many of them quit after working a day, the association men working at the wharf under cover using their influence to make them join the strikers.

AT THE BALTIMORE WHARF

The Baltimore steamship Allegheny, which was to have sailed yesterday afternoon, is still at her wharf loading. She will get out this afternoon with a fair cargo, about twenty-four hours late. The strike has interfered to a much greater extent with the Merchants and Miners' company than the other corporations. Agent Carolan is taking the situation as cheerful as possible, however, and is working hard to secure a new force. He managed to get thirteen white men yesterday and these with the twelve he had previously gave him a force of twenty-five men. As all are white they learn the way of loading and unloading a vessel much quicker than the negro hands. The Wm. Lawrence will be in tomorrow.

The Savannah, Florida and Western railway brought in forty white men from along the line of road yesterday to take the places of the strikers. Supt. Fleming expected to get another force of white hands today.

The strikers still maintain their orderly demeanor, and no disturbance of any kind occurred yesterday. There is considerable complaint however, among the business men about the walking delegates calling on their colored employes and urging them to join the strike in sympathy with the labor union.

TO ARREST WALKING DELEGATES

The thing became so annoying that Mayor McDonough determined to find out what the law is on the subject. He asked City Attorney Adams for an opinion and received the following reply:

Savannah, Sept. 30, 1891

Hon. J. J. McDonough, Mayor:
DEAR SIR--Answering your verbal inquiry I beg to say that by an act, approved Oct. 20, 1887, the legislature has made it an offense against the laws of the state for any person or persons by threats, violence, intimidation or other unlawful means to prevent or attempt to prevent any person or persons in this state from engaging in, remaining in, or performing the business, labor or duties of any lawful employment or occupation. The act also punishes any combination or conspiracy to prevent or attempt to prevent any person or persons by threats, violence or intimidation from engaging in the business, or labor or duties of any lawful employment or occupation. There are other provisions in it which are broad and sweeping, and are designed to meet the state of facts mentioned by you to me today. There is no city ordinance on the subject, and a party violating the state law would be amenable to the state courts if prosecuted for the offense. Yours very truly,
SAMUEL B. ADAMS,
City Attorney.

In accordance with this opinion Mayor McDonough has instructed the police officers to arrest any person found endeavoring to interfere with parties at work on the wharves or elsewhere. He will then turn over the offender to the state courts.

THE STRIKERS' MEETINGS

There was another big meeting of the strikers last night at the Duffy

Street Odd Fellows' hall, and speeches were made by leading members of the union. The proposition of the commercial committee which was rejected in the morning was brought up again for consideration and was promptly rejected.

"Our demand is very plain," said one of the strikers after the meeting, "and the railroad might as well understand at once that we want nothing more nor will we accept anything less. We will carry on the struggle quietly and peaceably and rely upon God for our rights."

At midnight everything was quiet on the wharves. The police were patrolling with their rifles at shoulder arms, and most of them said they were tired of that sort of duty.

Supt. Wade of the Cotton Press Association called at the barracks last night and told the officer in charge that the hands employed at the presses had informed him that they would not go to work this morning unless they were given protection. Supt. Wade asked that two officers be placed at the entrance to the presses and his request will be granted. Two mounted men will be stationed just below the gas house this morning to see that the laborers are not interfered with by the strikers.

Savannah Morning News, October 1, 1891.

9.   BRINGING IN LABOR

THE STRIKERS' PLACES BEING FILLED

No Signs of a Compromise

The strikers endeavoring to Force a General Tie-up of All Branches of Labor--The Cotton Exchange and Board of Trade Measures to Bring About a Termination of the Strike Unsussessful--The Mayor Takes Steps to Protect Laborers Who are Willing to Work--The Situation on the Wharves.

The fourth day of the wharf laborers' strike ended without any disorder. The situation is practically unchanged, except that the strikers are adding to their ranks from various lines of business. They refuse to compromise, and announce that they will accept nothing less than their original demands.

The Labor and Protective Association is taking in all classes of labor. A number of the city scavenger department drivers struck yesterday morning without giving any explanation of their conduct. It is inferred that membership in the union with the wharf hands is at the bottom of the trouble, and intimidation is suspected. They were paid $1.50 per day and had permanent employment. Their places are being filled by new men and the service will be in full running order again in a few days. The crematory hands also struck only five out of the nineteen hands working.

The twenty hands employed by the dry culture department failed to show up for work yesterday morning, and are supposed to have joined the strikers. The white engineer and colored fireman on the city tug Theckla also walked off without a word of explanation.

THE WALKING DELEGATES

The walking delegates of the strikers are going through the city interfering with and intimidating colored men employed in various kinds of business. These delegates are shrewd enough to keep out of the way of the police, but, nevertheless, get in their work. Yesterday afternoon they visited the stables of the horse car companies and endeavored to get the car drivers and stablemen to quit work. Policemen were telephoned for, but when they arrived the delegates had disappeared. The drivers and stablemen intimated last night that they wouldn't show up this morning, but in such an event the street car companies will utilize the conductors until they can secure white labor and the schedules will not be interfered with.

It is thought that the back of the strike will be broken by tommorrow, as the railroad and steamship companies are getting in considerably white and colored labor from the country.

The police force will be augmented today by about 200 special officers, and, if necessary, the number will be increased to 500, to protect the new labor.

THE COTTON EXCHANGE MEETING

A joint meeting of the cotton exchange and board of trade was held on the floor of the exchange yesterday morning at 10 o'clock. President J. L. Warren presided, and there was an unusually large attendance. By invitation of President Warren, Mayor McDonough and H. A. Crane, acting president of the board of trade, took oath with the chairman.

President Warren said that the joint committee of the cotton exchange and board of trade, with the mayor as chairman, having in charge the adjustment of the differences between the railroads, steamship companies and the Labor Union and Protective Association, had called the meeting to report that the committee had utterly failed in discharging the duty imposed upon it.

The chairman complimented the gentlemen composing the committee upon the deep interest every member had taken in the matter, neglecting their own work to meet with the labor union, hearing the grievances and undertaking to redress the laborers' wrongs, if any, and after consulting with them for three hours had spent the balance of the night with the railroad people differing the situation. After hearing both sides, the committee conferred with the union the next morning and discussed with its members the situation from beginning to end, and could only report failure to accomplish a settlement of the trouble.

Secretary Merrihew read the letters which passed between the Labor Union and Protective Association and the joint committee.

AN ADVISORY COMMITTEE PROVIDED FOR

J. F. Minis moved that a joint committee from the cotton exchange and the board of trade, consisting of seven members, to be known as the advisory committee be appointed to take general charge of the business interests of the city effected by the strike, and to preserve the interests as far as possible, the committee to have authority, if necessary, to call the joint bodies together again. The motion received a second, but action was delayed in order that the meeting might hear from the representatives of the railroad and steamship companies.

Supt. Fleming of the Savannah, Florida and Western railway said he did not agree with the mayor as to the seriousness of the situation. The trouble with the Savannah, Florida and Western hands, he said, commenced Sunday. The force decreased Monday and Tuesday, and Wednesday the men were intimidated and drawn off by the strikers. White and colored laborers were imported Wednesday, but the colored laborers joined the strikers.

Yesterday, Supt. Fleming brought in a lot of colored men from the country, but the train was depopulated before reaching the city. He said he had no difficulty in getting all the laborers he wanted, but they struck upon their arrival and only helped to fill the town with idle men. He could not say what he would do, but he had about concluded to abandon colored labor if he could get protection from the authorities for whites. He said he would probably meet the situation today if protection were granted to the men he brings here.

READY TO BRING LABORERS

General Manager Sorrel, of the Ocean Steamship Company, stated that he had only just reached the city, but was fully impressed with the gravity of the situation. He agreed with Capt. Fleming as to the intimidation of the men, but believed they would be able to stamp out the trouble if protection were guaranteed. He was ready to bring from New York a force of 200 or 300 or even more, white men to handle the work. If the situation demanded it he could have the force here by Monday, but they must be guaranteed protection. The Ocean Steamship Company, he said, will do all that is necessary regardless of expense.

The following resolution by Mr. Comer was adopted:

Resolved. That it is the sentiment of this meeting that the recommendation made by the joint committee is a fair one, and that we give the people fighting the strike our cordial and hearty support.

Mr. Minis' motion was then unanimously adopted, and the chair appointed the following committee:.. J. F. Minis, H. M. Comer, W. W. Gordon, John Flannery, J. R. Young, George P. Walker and W. B. Stillwell.

The following resolution by Mr. Stillwell was adopted:

Resolved, That the mayor be requested to appoint a committee from the board of aldermen, to confer and act with the advisory committee in all matters they may consider in reference to the present trouble, and that this committee recommend to the mayor that he give all the protection in his power to men willing to work.

EVERY PRECAUTION TAKEN

Mayor McDonough at this point stated that everything had been done that could be done, and he was willing and ready to do anything in his power. The report of the joint committee was received and adopted, and the committee was discharged.

Mr. Comer suggested that all possible forbearance should be exercised toward the strikers, as they undoubtedly have some moving spirits upholding them.

Supt. McBee of the Central railroad expressed his thanks for the manner in which the committee had striven to adjust the trouble. The company, he said, had not anticipated the trouble, having received no notice from the men of their intention to strike. It had practically placed itself in the hands of the joint committee and would stand by any recommendation made by it. The Central will bring men here from this and other states and will soon be in a condition to handle the work as well as before the strike. Supt. McBee said he will not only bring enough men to handle the work of the Ocean Steamship Company, but enough free of charge to handle all work deserted by the strikers.

THE ADVISORY COMMITTEE MEETS

Mayor McDonough called a special meeting of council at 12 o'clock, to meet the advisory committees of the commercial bodies, railroad and steamship officials and citizens. The meeting was held at the mayor's office. The situation and the result of the conference between the commercial bodies and the strikers was discussed at length.

A member of the committee from the cotton exchange explained in a concise way the result of the endeavors to bring about a settlement. He said after the grievances of the colored laborers had been attentively listened to, it was proposed to them that instead of working by the hour they accept a permanent scale of wages at so much per day, week or month, to be settled monthly. This proposition was rejected by the strikers. They said they wanted to work by the hour and would work no other way, even though the committee guaranteed them that the other grievances complained of would be adjusted. The striking laborers displayed anything but a conciliatory feeling in the matter, acting as if they felt they had the business community by the throat and proposed to squeeze if their demands were not acceded to.

IN THE COMMITTEE'S HANDS

Supt. McBee and Supt. Fleming stated that so far as they were concerned the matter had been put in the hands of the committee, with the understanding that the railroads would abide by its decision. They still stand ready to agree to the scale of wages proposed by the conference, and have already put it in force with the hands now employed at the wharves. All the roads ask of the city is that they be protected the same as any other class or corporation in the lawful transaction of business.

Supt. McBee showed by his remarks that the railroad and steamship companies are willing and anxious to do everything fair and just to bring about a settlement.

The council authorized Mayor McDonough, after hearing the situation discussed decided to augment the police to any number necessary to protect the men at work and to preserve the peace and good order of the city and to also issue a proclamation.

THE MAYOR'S PROCLAMATION

After the meeting adjourned Mayor McDonough issued a proclamation as follows:

PROCLAMATION

CITY OF SAVANNAH
MAYOR'S OFFICE

In view of the present unusual state of affairs growing out of a discontinuance of labor by a large number of workmen and their consequent idleness, and the importance of special and immediate attention to the preservation of the public peace, I, John J. McDonough, mayor of the city of Savannah, hereby issue this, my public proclamation, urging upon the citizens of Savannah its prompt and complete observance.

1. The intimidation or interference in any way with men desiring or willing to work is contrary to the laws of the land, to the rights of the individuals, and the public safety.

This cannot, and will not, be tolerated. Absolute protection against such interference is guaranteed. To secure this protection I have largely increased the regular police force, and I will invoke all the powers vested in me as chief magistrate of this city. Among these powers are those given with reference to the military of the city by the act of the legislature of Georgia approved Oct. 13, 1885, the ninth section of which follows this proclamation, and is now published for the information of the people.

2. In this emergency it becomes particularly important that all causes of excitement be removed as far as possible, and to this end citizens are hereby prohibited from obstructing the streets, sidewalks, wharves and other public places, and from gathering together in groups on the same. Policemen are strictly ordered to disperse such groups and prevent such obstruction.

3. The co-operation of all good citizens white and colored, is expected in the maintenance of the public peace and tranquility. While the right of individuals to elect whether they shall work or not, and all individual rights, shall be fully respected, violators of the law and of the public peace will be quickly apprehended and severely punished.

Witness my official signature as mayor of the city of Savannah and the seal of the city this first day of October, A.D. 1891.

JOHN J. MCDONOUGH, Mayor

Attest: FRANK E. REBARER, Clerk of Council

INCREASING THE POLICE FORCE

The swearing in of the special policemen began last night and nearly 100 were secured. As many more will be sworn in this morning and will patrol the wharves and streets and see that the law is obeyed. In dispersing gatherings on the streets Mayor McDonough has given the officers rigid instructions to act kindly and patiently and not to precipitate trouble. In acting in this manner, however, they must at the same time be determined.

The sympathy the strikers had among the merchants has turned. The sentiment of business men is that the strike no longer means a question of an increase of wages, but whether the commercial people will allow themselves in the legitimate transaction of their business to be dictated to by organizations.

Cotton is coming in slowly because on account of the strike, the merchants having telegraphed to the interior to stop shipments.

In connection with the question of wages it will be interesting to know the rate at other southern ports. The following is the scale:

	Per hour
Brunswick..	15¢
Charleston..	15¢
Wilmington..	10 and 15¢
Portsmouth..	15¢
Mobile..	15¢

ON THE CENTRAL WHARVES

The appearance of things in the Central railroad yards and on the wharves

of the Ocean Steamship Company was much more cheerful yesterday than on any
day since the strike was inaugurated. Several hundred men were at work,
and they are working very earnestly. Four hundred more men were expected in
last night, and today the movement of freight will be much more lively.
     The Birmingham got in between 5 o'clock and 6 o'clock yesterday morning,
and by 10 o'clock all of her perishable freight was unloaded. The unloading
of the City of Macon has been completed, and she will be loaded and got off
this morning. The Nacoochee was being discharged yesterday, and there is a
fair prospect that she will be loaded and started on her trip to New York
this evening.
     Additions to the working force of the Ocean Steamship Company and
Central railroad are being made all the time, and the officers of the two
companies are feeling much more cheerful. Ample protection is guaranteed
to all who return to work.
     The report has gained currency that some of the headers in the employ-
ment of the Ocean Steamship Company are not true to the company; that they
are emissaries of the strikers and try to make the men dissatisfied. This
report they indignantly deny. Yesterday they united in making a statement
that they are loyal to the company, and are faithfully doing all they can to
promote the company's interest. Their names are as follows:
     Ret Enguine, Ed. Bailey, Ed. Wallace, Tom Hayes, Oscar Floynold, York
Jackson, Mackey Jackson, William Chisholm, Jim Brown, Adam Smyley.
     The head stevedore says that the headers speak the truth, and that they
are giving entire satisfaction in every respect.
     The Merchants and Miners' company secured fifteen more white men yester-
day, making a total force of forty. The Allegheny will sail at 5 o'clock
this morning, thirty-six hours late, with a good cargo. Agent Carolan is
paying his hands the scale agreed upon at Tuesday night's conference, and the
men are well satisfied. They are learning the knack of handling freight
rapidly and will make excellent workmen in a few days. Agent Carolan expects
a large addition of white men today, and by Sunday will have an ample white
force for all the requirements of his company.
     Agent Wilkinson is sick in bed. He had two chills yesterday and was
unable to attend to his duties.

BRIGHTER OUTLOOK BELOW THE CITY

     Things had a much better appearance on the lower wharves yesterday than
on any day since Monday. About forty white men were at work loading the
Allegheny at the Baltimore steamship wharf. The loading of the vessel was
completed yesterday afternoon and she will sail this morning at 5 o'clock.
     A number of men, white and black, were at work at the warehouses, though
that section presented no such busy appearance as is natural at this season.
     Work went on at the lower presses as usual. The lower presses have not
shut down an hour since the beginning of the strike, and do not expect to so.
They had about sixty men at work yesterday, including a number of white men
and green hands. The "green hands" are catching on, and many of the strikers
will find that they are not wanted when they make up their minds to return.

ALL RIGHT AT HARMON'S WHARF

     Alderman Harmon was working his usual force at his cotton wharf, and
informed a MORNING NEWS reporter, who was taking a trip on foot along the
wharves, that he had a much better force than the day before. The force of
laborers at the Savannah, Florida and Western wharves was largely increased
yesterday. About seventy negroes were brought in from Thomasville and along
the line of the road early yesterday morning. If they had all stuck the road
would have had nearly enough men to transact its usual business, but the agents
of the strikers got in their work. A number of the strikers got with the
gangs, as is their manner of doing, and went to work with them. It was impossible to distinguish them from the workmen, and they soon began to get in
their work with threats and persuasion, and it was not long before gangs of
six and seven at a time began to quit work and walk off without saying anything
to anybody. However, enough of the old men were got together with the new men
that remained to give the Savannah, Florida and Western wharves a livelier
appearance than for the last three or four days. Supt. Fleming expects to
have a much larger force at work today.

NOT LIKELY TO LAST LONG

The opinion was expressed by several employers along the wharves that the strike is beginning to weaken and that in a day or two they would have all the men they wanted. They said that in several instances men who had quit work three or four days ago returned yesterday and want to work as usual.

The Savannah Lighterage and Transfer Company was at work as usual yesterday with about fifty men. The company has kept up its work regularly since the beginning the strike.

The original strikers are very obstinate in their demands and will have the pound of flesh or nothing. In fact, they do not seem to want to work for individuals and small employers at all unless the railroads will grant to their fellow strikers all their demands.

A number of cases have occurred where work was almost imperative where employers offered 20 cents an hour and even more. The men refused to work at all unless they were guaranteed a full day's work. In several instances draymen offered their former employes as high as 30 cents an hour to move cotton that was billed to the outgoing steamships, but the men refused even this unless guaranteed a whole day's work. Work on any condition until all their demands are granted is not desired.

SUPT. FLEMING'S PLANS

Capt. Fleming, superintendent of the Savannah, Florida and Western railroad, was seen at his office by a MORNING NEWS reporter as to the situation and was asked what he was doing to mend it. Capt. Fleming said:

"The Savannah, Florida and Western is arranging to bing in a number of white men to take the places of the negroes who are being intimidated. A number are expected to arrive tomorrow [this] morning. There is no danger of them being intimidated, and they will not have to guarded. Our forces of negro laborers will probably be increased today also.

"Proper steps are being taken to protect the laborers on the Savannah, Florida and Western and Baltimore steamship wharves and warehouses and to allow all hands to work that wish to do so.

"The Savannah, Florida and Western railroad notified their employes yesterday that the scale of wages offered the strikers by the joint committee of the cotton exchange and the board of trade will go into effect with all hands that were at work or would come to work from the time that the committee made the proposition Wednesday morning."

Capt. Fleming said that it was his understanding that a large amount of white labor would be put on the wharves by the different companies.

CAUGHT JUST IN TIME
Charlie Davis in the Barracks for Trying to Shoot Officer Dwyer

Charles Davis, one of the colored strikers, while under the influence of liquor at West Broad and Waldourg streets, last night at 9:30 o'clock, amused himself by cursing people generally.

Mounted Officer Dwyer rode up and ordered Davis to desist, but the negro promptly threw his hand to his hip pocket and drew a revolver. He had reckoned without his host, however, and before he could raise the weapon to shoot, Officer Dwyer gave him a blow on the wrist which almost broke it and sent the pistol flying across the sidewalk from the negro's hand. Then the officer arrested his would-be murderer, secured the pistol and carried him to the barracks, where he was locked up on a charge of carrying concealed weapons and disorderly conduct.

Savannah Morning News, October 2, 1891.

10.   THE MISTAKE OF THE STRIKERS

The strikers made a mistake in not accepting the advance in wages which the transportation companies offered them. The advance was liberal, and, in the opinion of the committee of business men who secured it, all that the transportation companies could reasonably be accepted to grant. And the strikers should have borne in mind that the committee acted as their friend and did for them all that it was possible to do.

The leaders of the strikers are proving themselves to be bad advisors. Instead of obstinately insisting upon their original demand they should have accepted the offer that was made them, because they had the best of reasons for thinking that they would not get all they asked for, or even a better offer. The committee told them as much, and that committee was composed of men in whom they had every reason to have confidence.

They have crystallized against themselves the sentiment of the whole business community. The business men are now united in sustaining the transportation companies. The strikers may continue for several days to cause some embarrassment in the city's business, but there is not the least probability that they will succeed in their purpose. The transportation companies are obtaining laborers all the time, and will soon be able to get along without the strikers. The strikers will then realize how great a mistake they made in refusing the very fair offer that was made them.

The intimidation of laborers is about ended. The authorities will not tolerate that any longer. The law is clear with respect to intimidation, and it will be enforced. It is right that it should be. If there are men who want to work they should be protected in doing so.

Some of the strikers may be disposed to be ugly as their prospects of success become less promising, but they should remember that a fair settlement was offered them and that they refused it. And they should bear in mind that no exhibition of bad feeling would assist them in the least. They would be the sufferers. If they are wise they will repress all tendency to violence among their members. They began the strike with the avowed determination not to break the peace. They will stand better with the community if they continue to abide by that determination. And they should remember that the offer of the transportation companies is still open to them, though it may not be very long.

Savannah Morning News, October 2, 1891.

11.   THE STRIKE IS SETTLED

The strike is settled and everybody is glad of it. Business will again move along in its accustomed channels, and its volume promises to be such that at the end of the season there will be nothing to show that it suffered an interruption of several days.

The more intelligent of the colored men of the community and of the strikers became convinced yesterday that the MORNING NEWS was right in telling the strikers that they had made a mistake in rejecting the offer made them by the transportation companies through the committee of the trade bodies, and they set to work to bring the more obstinate of the leaders of the strike to reason. Their efforts were crowned with success and the strikers will return to work today in a much more cheerful frame of mind than they were before the strike was inaugurated.

It is a source of satisfaction that the strike was not marked by violence of any kind. It is not often that a strike on so large a scale is brought to an end without exhibitions of bad feeling. Some irritation was caused by the efforts to intimidate laborers, and by the apparently unreasonable desertion of their employers by those who had no grievances and made no complaints, but

such things, to a greater or less extent, are features of every strike, and
are to be expected. Now that the trouble is ended there should be an effort
and general willingness to make up for lost time.

Savannah Morning News, October 3, 1891.

12. STRIKERS TO RESUME WORK THIS MORNING

THE COMPROMISE AGREED TO

The Union's Committee of Eleven Advises the Acceptance of the New Scales
of Wages--The Central to Employ its Old Hands as Fast as There are Places
for Them. But Not as Union Men--The Tieup Broken by the Employment of New
Labor--The Situation on the Wharves Greatly Improved Yesterday--A General
Return to Work Today.

The wharf laborers' strike is virtually at an end. After holding out
for five days the strikers have agreed to accept the compromise offered by
the conference committee, and by 10 o'clock this morning all the strikers
who can get back will be working.

This decision was reached last night by the strikers' committee of
eleven after a conference with several well-known disinterested colored men.
The fact of the railroad and steamship companies securing all the hands
necessary to carry on the work was what caused the strikers to reconsider
their action and accept the compromise. When they saw their places being
rapidly filled by new men they saw that unless they promptly came to terms
their bread and butter would be put in jeopardy.

ADVISED TO RESUME WORK

The day opened up with the strikers fully as determined to hold out for
20 cents an hour or nothing as they had been the first day. The better and
more intelligent class of disinterested colored citizens, seeing that the
sympathy of the community was turning against the strikers because of their
arbitrary course, decided that something must be done at once to bring matters
to a termination. With this end in view R. W. White, L. M. Pleasants, W. A.
Pledger of Athens, Rev. Alexander Harris and Rev. E. K. Love, Prof. James
Ross and C. C. Christopher held a conference with a view to urging the
strikers to accept the compromise and go back to work.

The men were disinclined at first to listen to the committee, but the
majority finally decided that they wanted to go back to work upon the terms
and at the scale of wages offered by the conference committee.

WILLING TO GO BACK

The mediators, together with John H. Kinckle, Esq., the colored attorney
called on Mr. H. M. Comer and discussed the situation with him. He expressed
a willingness to do whatever was right and just toward helping the strikers
get back, but told the committee he could only act as an individual, because
the commercial committees had been dissolved.

The committee waited on 'the strikers' committee of eleven and fully explained the situation, advising that the union accept the terms if it didn't
want to do the members and city at large irreparable damage. It was shown
to the strikers that they had the sympathy of the community in their fighting
until they rejected the proposition giving them half of the advance asked for.
They were told that unless they accepted the ultimatum they need expect
neither sympathy nor support from the white people in the future.

TO BE DECLARED OFF

Ten members of the committee agreed at once to give in, but one was
stubborn and wanted to continue the fight. But wiser counsel prevailed,
however, and the committee told the mediators that the strike would be declared off this morning and the strikers to make application for their old
places.

R. W. White and W. A. Pledger then called upon Supt. McBee of the
Central, and had a conference with him. He said he had secured a sufficient
number of men from Georgia and North and South Carolina to carry on the work
on the wharves without any further delay to business and is now in position
to furnish hands to the warehouse men and other lines of business interfered
with by the strike.

PLENTY OF WORK

A great many of the new laborers, Supt. McBee said, are railroad section
hands brought here temporarily until a settlement of the troubles. He says
he has no ill feeling against the strikers, because he believes they were
misled by bad advisers, and as far as it is in his power he will see that
the strikers are not discriminated against in accepting workmen. Supt. McBee
said that the scale of wages adopted by the conference committee will be
strictly adhered to.

The Central railroad brought in 500 men yesterday, and 400 more are on
their way and will arrive today. These hands are mostly from South and North
Carolina. No doubt all the strikers will be taken back, because an immense
force will be required to relieve the blockade at the wharves and warehouses.
The declaring off of the strike means that the draymen and others who have
struck will resume work today.

THE FEELING ON THE BAY

The condition of things along the Bay yesterday presented a much more
animated and improved appearance. It was evident by 10 o'clock that the
backbone of the strike had been broken, and it was only a question of a few
hours when the strikers would surrender. This made the merchants more cheerful, and men who have carried serious countenances since Monday were smiling
and shaking hands.

700 MEN AT WORK

The scenes at the Ocean Steamship wharves yesterday to a person not acquainted with the situation would never indicate that there had been a strike.
Over 700 hands, white and black, were at work moving freight, unloading cars
and loading the Nacoochee and City of Macon, and three big lighters with cotton for the tramp steamships.

The Macon got out at 6:30 o'clock with a fairly good cargo, and the
Nacoochee will sail this morning. The unloading of the Birmingham was commenced at 4 o'clock and progressed fairly well with the green hands. The
new men are a little slow in their movements yet, but it won't take them long
to learn the knack of handling freight.

The Central brought in about 500 men during the day from along the line
of road. The most of them are roadway hands brought temporarily until the
settlement of the trouble.

Agent Wilkinson was in excellent humor when seen by a MORNING NEWS reporter, he felt so good over the turn affairs had taken that he really didn't
know exactly how many men he had at work.

THE TIRED POLICE

The policemen had a more jaunty air about them, and carried their rifles
in a more soldierly fashion. The removal of the Sunday appearance from the
wharves seemed to loosen their joints, and they moved around with a better
step than at any day since the inauguration of the strike.

The only work they had to do besides walking around and feeling like
soldiers was to make two arrests, one of the walking delegates who by some
means had got on the wharves and was trying to induce the new men to quit
work, and the other a header who threatened to shoot one of the country contingent. A white man who had been employed on the wharves for several months
was discharged on suspicion of being in league with the strikers and helping
to run the new men off.

The Central adopted a new scheme to hold the men. Long tables are spread
and when the meal bell is sounded the scene is of an amusing character. The
hands drop the trucks in every direction and rush pell mell over each other
to get to the tables, and eat as if they never before had a square meal.

THE LOWER WHARVES

The Merchants and Miners' company added to its force yesterday thirty-two white men and three colored men bringing up its total to seventy-five. The Allegheny sailed yesterday morning and the Wm. Lawrence arrived shortly afterward. The work of unloading her was begun at once. Last night she was pretty well relieved of freight and she will be reloaded and got off some time tonight.

The majority of the hands brought here by the Savannah, Florida and Western railroad are white.

The swearing in of special policemen was stopped last night by Mayor McDonough, because the necessity for them having practically passed. Between 75 and 100 specials were on duty yesterday and last night along the wharves and through the eastern and western portions of the city. They were armed with Winchester rifles and pistols. The larger portion of them will be dismissed today.

There was great improvement in the situation on all the wharves below the city. About fifty white men and a few negroes were at work at the Baltimore steamship wharf unloading the Wm. Lawrence. The lower press was running as usual with all the men needed. A large number of men were at work in the warehouses which were not there the day before.

THE DRAYS RUNNING

A number of drays were hauling in cotton. All of Ryals' drays were running and a large number of the drays of the other firms in the business in the city. Some of the drays were manned by white men, but most of them were manned by negroes.

Alderman Harmon had a large and better force at work than the day before. On the Savannah, Florida and Western wharves nearly the full force was at work. Nearly 100 white men were among the workers. The Savannah, Florida and Western brought in sixty or seventy white men from along its line yesterday morning and put them to work.

"De railroad is bringing all dem white folks down from Jesup," said a colored striker eyeing the crowd suspiciously as it embarked from the train. Jesup is a kind of Georgia Edgefield to the mind of the average South Georgia negro.

The white men were doing good work, despite their inexperience. They receive the same pay that was offered the colored hands. Supt. Fleming said that the men would be retained as long as they cared to work, whether the strike ended or not.

COST OF THE STRIKE

Now that the strike is at an end, the losses to the railroads, steamship companies and business of the city will be begun to be footed up. It will run into the hundreds of thousands of dollars, and maybe higher. The steamships have been kept twenty-four and thirty-six hours later than their sailing time, and their schedules have been broken into so that it may take weeks to straighten them out. The railroads have had every switch within 200 miles of Savannah filled with loaded freight cars, and the losses to shippers and others by delay will be no small item. Taken from any point of view, the strike has been a disastrous one all around, and has entailed the city with an enormous loss.

ADVISING THE STRIKERS

The early settlement of the strike is largely due to the efforts of the more conservative and intelligent of the colored people. A number of them have been at work using their influence with the strikers to have them return to work at the wages offered, telling them they were injuring themselves by holding out and the city as well.

D. B. Morris, a colored carpenter served as foreman of the carpenters at work upon Dr. R. G. Norton's house, at Barnard and Anderson streets, called at the MORNING NEWS office last night. Morris said he had just had a very lively discussion with a member of the strikers in front of their hall on Duffy street. He has been telling them ever since they refused the offer of the joint committee that they had committed a great mistake, and were rapidly losing the sympathy of the community by their obstinacy.

NOT A UNION MAN

Morris is not a member of the Labor Union and Protective Association, but he is president of the Archery Club and also of the Mystic Tie of Arabs, of which societies a number of the strikers are members. He is well-known and has some influence among his people. He said a number of threats were made against him because of his action, but he paid no attention to them. The more intelligent portion of the strikers were willing to listen to reason, he said, but the ignorant element seemed to be in control.

Last night as Morris was passing by the Odd Fellows' hall on his way home from his work he was approached by a number of the strikers who make the hall their headquarters and the discussion about accepting the offer of the committee was renewed.

BETTER GO BACK TO WORK

Morris told them they were making fools of themselves by their conduct, that they were injuring themselves by staying away from work and at the same time injuring the city, and that it was impossible for them to force the railroads to terms. Some of the strikers replied that they would "starve the railroads out." Morris told them that they would starve themselves out first. Some replied that they would stay out till Christmas or get their demands. Morris told them that while they were staying away from work the railroads were filling up with hands from other places, and would soon have no use for them and the city would be full of idle negroes with the prospect of starvation or the chain-gan before them. He told them they had taken large numbers of strange negroes, who had come here to work, away from their work and were keeping them idle on the town. He thought if they had persuaded them away from their work they ought to spend some of the money in the treasury to send them back to their homes.

A CARD TO THE STRIKERS

Morris came to the MORNING NEWS office with a card addressed to the strikers which he submitted for publication. The card is as follows:

My Dear Friends of Color:
    I hope you will all look before it is too late or I am afraid you will do yourselves a great injury. Remember, if we do anything against the interests of this city we do it against ourselves. We should not think that this is the only shipping port in the country, because the companies that we are at war with, continue the shipping to other ports, and then we will have worse times to contend with than when we were getting 12-1/2 cents to 25 cents an hour. The company that we are contending with, has already carried a great deal of capital from amongst us by removing their head offices to Atlanta.
    All of these people we are stopping here will make it harder for all of us, and our streets will be filled with idlers that will go to swell the chain-gangs. What injures this city injures us, so let us concede to this offer at present and try to cultivate a more perfect peace among our home people. It will be better for us to restore peace now, or it will be too late.

Morris told all that wanted to go to work to meet him at Barnard and Anderson streets this morning, and go with him to the railroad. He expects about 300.

Savannah Morning News, October 3, 1891.

13. BADLY ADVISED

The strikers are being badly advised. The understanding on Friday night was that they had decided to accept the wages offered by the transportation companies and return to work yesterday morning. They did not return to work, however, because they learned that the transportation companies would not recognize their union and allow them to dictate who should be employed. The transportation companies can get along without them. They have a sufficient number of men to handle their freights and can get more if they need them. And all the other places which have been deserted will soon be filled, because the labor to fill them is obtainable. The desire to favor the old hands is the chief reason why new ones have not been sought.

If the strikers persist in their obstinate course they will soon find themselves without a chance to obtain work. Their first great mistake after the strike was inaugurated was in refusing the liberal and very fair offer of an increase of wages. They would have acted wisely had they accepted it promptly.

Their second great mistake was in not going to work when they had finally decided to accept the wages offered. All of them might not have found places at once, but the most of them would, and eventually all of them would have obtained employment.

Every day they remain idle increases the difficulties of their position, because of the new men who are all the time coming in to fill the deserted places many are likely to remain permanently.

The rank and file of the strikers should think for themselves. They should look at the situation as it is. If they should do that they would see that their leaders are not safe advisers, and that there is no possible chance for gaining anything more than has been already willingly conceded to them. If they listen to reason, they will seek employment on Monday morning and take the places that are still open to them. That is better advice than they are now acting upon.

Savannah Morning News, October 4, 1891.

14. STRIKERS SPLITTING UP

THE UNION DEMANDS TO BE RECOGNIZED

The Railroads Refuse

A part of the Strikers Ready to Go Back, but the Union Will Not Come to Terms--It wants the Railroads to Sign an Agreement Guaranteeing the Schedule of Wages Recommended by the Conference Committee--the Railroads Getting all the Hands They Want and are Independent of the Strikers--Everything Going Smoothly on the Wharves.

The wharf laborers strike is still on.

It was understood might before last that it was virtually at an end, and that the men would return to work yesterday morning. This information was furnished by the disinterested colored mediators, whose advice the strikers had agreed to follow. They said the strikers' committee had agreed to declare the strike off, and would urge the men to go back to work on the basis of the proposition offered by the conference committee. It transpired yesterday morning that the strikers would not resume work unless the transportation companies would agree to take them back as members of the Labor Union and Protective Association. It is understood they also insist on the signing of a contract guaranteeing the scale of wages agreed upon by the conference, the agreement to be witnessed by the members of the cotton exchange and the board of trade committees, who had been instrumental in getting the concessions.

WILL NOT RECOGNIZE THE UNION

The railroad and steamship companies will not agree to recognize the union. They hire the men as individuals, and not as members of any organization. If they want to go back to work they must do so as when employed before the strike. The strikers are not asked to sever their connection with the union, but will not be recognized as union men in being taken back. Neither will the signing of any contract be agreed to. The commercial bodies will not recognize the union in the matter or agree to witness any contracts.

A committee of the strikers called upon a prominent cotton man to see
what the prospects were for the recognition of the union. It was promptly
informed that recognition of the organization was out of the question entirely. There was no use, he said, in discussing such a matter. The strikers must resume work as individuals or not at all. A fair proposition for
settlement had been made and it had been rejected. That proposition was
still open without any entailments about recognition of the union or anything
else. The cotton men advised the committee to go back and urge the strikers
to declare the strike off.

ADVISED A RETURN TO WORK

Attorney John H. Kinckle and Walking Delegate John Williams were members of the committee, and they went at once to the Duffy street hall, where
the strikers were meeting and began to urging an acceptance of the transportation companies' terms. The strikers refused to listen to them, and said
they wanted nothing now, more or less, than 20 cents an hour.

Samuel Connolly, James Williams, Newton Oliver, Isaac Brown and Joe
Collier, who were members of the strikers committee which conferred with the
commercial bodies, announced last night they they had cut them from the strike
and will return to work tomorrow morning if they can get it. They also said
that they will endeavor to get the strikers to do likewise.

NO MORE HANDS NEEDED

The Central has brought to the city over 1,000 hands and yesterday
stopped a crowd on the way there because a sufficient number had been secured.
Up to night before last carloads of extra hands continued coming in to take
the places of the strikers.

Friday night in the neighborhood of seventy-five able bodied negroes
came to Macon from along the Georgia Southern and other roads bound for
Savannah, and fifty more were brought in on the Southwestern train.

The train from Atlanta brought in a tremendous body, numbering over 200.
This makes a total of nearly 500 who have passed through Macon.

WORK ON THE WHARVES

The work at the Ocean Steamship wharves was moving nicely, and things
were getting along almost as well as before the strike. Over 100 cars were
sent out loaded, and nearly as many unloaded. Supt. McBee said last night
that he will never agree to take back the strikers as members of a union.
The idea that because a considerable number of the new hands are roadway men
their stay here is only temporary, Supt. McBee said, is wrong.

The portion of the men who are roadway hands are extra gangs and can
easily be spared from the roadway. Even after the settlement of the strike
as many as feel so disposed can remain. The strikers will not be taken back
in a body, nor will the new men be discharged to make room for them. They
will be re-employed as they are needed. Supt. McBee thinks that the reason
the strike didn't end yesterday was that some white adviser told the strikers
that the roadway hands would have to be returned to their work in a few days,
and if they held out for awhile longer they would be bound to win. If this
is the theory they are working on, he said, they will find temselves badly
mistaken.

DON'T NEED THE STRIKERS

There is now a sufficient number of men in the city to do all the work,
and it makes little difference whether the strikers agree to go back to work
or not. The backbone is broken, and by day after tomorrow the strike will be
a part of the history of the past, as far as the transportation companies
are concerned.

Supt. McBee furnished all the warehousemen with hands yesterday and sent
fifty to Agent Carolan of the Merchants and Miners' company.

ALL THE HELP IT NEEDS

Supt. Fleming of the Savannah, Florida and Western said that his road
had all the men needed at work on the wharves, about half white and half black,
and besides was able to furnish several white to the Merchants and Miners'
Transportation Company. The Savannah, Florida and Western brought in about a

dozen white men yesterday morning from along its line and put them to work.
Supt. Fleming said he could have brought a great many more, but they were
not needed. He says the Savannah, Florida and Western now has all the men
it needs and is not worrying about the strikers. They are hampered somewhat by the merchants and others, who are not able to take their freight as
delivered, but Supt. Fleming said he expects to see everything in shipshape
by tomorrow. There was a general increase in forces all along the lower
wharves yesterday.

Supt. Fleming said he will refuse to recognize any union in taking men
back. In fact he isn't paying any further attention to either the strikers
or their demands because he has all the laborers required by the Savannah,
Florida and Western. He furnished the Merchants and Miners' with thirty-
five men.

BUSINESS ON THE BAY

Business is lightening up, and yesterday things were moving along the
Bay in a spirited manner. The draymen secured quite a number of drivers,
and the delivery of cotton was quite large. The longshoremen are all back
to work, because cotton is being lightered to the tramps from the Ocean
Steamship wharves in large quantities. In the neighborhood of 1,000 bales
were transferred in this way yesterday.

The men employed at McDonough & Co.'s mill have also joined the strike.
There were about fifteen, and some of them had been in the firm's employ for
over ten years. Mayor McDonough received a communication from the men reading: "Wese want enuff muney to pay our honest debts. Wese all the mill hands
and wese all belong the union." They didn't stipulate what rate of increase
they desired and never waited for an answer, but quit work. Their places
were promptly filled, and Mayor McDonough said he will never take the strikers
back under any circumstances.

STRIKE OF THE CITY HANDS

The scavenger, dry culture and board of health departments of the city
have secured all the hands necessary to fill the strikers' places, and things
are moving as if no trouble ever existed. It is the same story in all lines
of business where the colored laborers struck. Their places have been filled
and now they are not wanted.

The report was current on Bay street yesterday that if the strike is not
declared off tomorrow a general meeting of the business men of the city will
be held and resolutions adopted agreeing that hereafter no members of the
Labor Union and Protective Association will be employed by them. The business
community's patience is about exhausted. Every fair means were resorted to
for a settlement of the troubles, but as the strikers refuse to listen to
reason, or the merchants are getting tired, and will adopt a boycott to protect themselves in the future.

SHIPS SAILING ON TIME

General Manager Sorrell announces that the Ocean Steamship Company's
vessels are sailing on their regular schedules without delay, and that freight
is being promptly handled. The company, the officials say, is not being
interfered with in the sailing of vessels either from Savannah or New York.

Attorney Kinckle and Walking Delegate John Williams are in a bad fix,
judging from their stories. They say that they have been charged by some
people with instigating the strike, and now the strikers claim that they have
been trying to sell them out to the corporations.

Williams said that Wednesday he spoke at the Duffy street hall, urging
the strikers to accept the compromise. They refused, and said they wanted 20
cents an hour or nothing. He went back Thursday and again endeavored to persuade the men to go to work. They promptly branded him as a traitor and
Williams claims that they fired him out of the hall. He tried to talk to
them yesterday and was charged with having Central railroad money his pocket
for talking compromise. He said he has resigned from the committee and the
organization and will go back to work tomorrow.

NOT BACKING THE STRIKERS

Lawyer Kinckle said he heard it rumored that he was at the bottom of the

strike, but there is not a word of truth in the report. He is not so blinded
to the interests of the colored people or the interests of the city to do
such a thing. He said he has done everything in his power to bring about a
settlement of the difficulty without avail. The only recompense be received
for his trouble was to be charged with treachery and trying to sell out the
labor union. Lawyer Kinckle said last night that he had washed his hands
entirely of the matter and would let the strikers settle matters to suit
themselves. He had tried to reason with them and show them that they are
blind to their own interests in remaining on strike, but they have displayed
a high degree of obstinacy and will listen to no argument.

COL. PLEDGER'S EXPLANATION

W. A. Pledger, one of the mediators who thought that the strike was
settled night before last, was seen yesterday by a MORNING NEWS reporter and
asked for an explanation of the statement that the strikers would give up.

"Yesterday, said he, "a number of colored men met individual members
of the strikers' committee, as well as the attorney and president, and discussed the situation. I know that assurance was given that the committee,
except Lowry, was in favor, and so were the attorney and president of declaring the strike off and permitting the men to go to work. These leaders
led myself and others to believe (and we now believe) that they had the
power to declare the strike off, since they represented the real intelligence
of the organization. Today they are attempting to deny that they were in
favor of declaring the strike off. In the presence of Mr. H. M. Comer,
Lowry and other members indicated their desire to declare the strike off and
to accept the propositions of the committes appointed by the board of trade
and cotton exchange.

"It seems to me," continued Pledger, "that there is some one powerful
for evil behind these men, and it may be that he is not a colored man. The
little that I have done is due to the fact that I hated to see hundreds of
women and children breadless and without homes. To have accepted the proposed proposition was to win and cover themselves with the glory that would
naturally grow out of the universal sympathy extended by all classes of all
colors. As it is, those that can must hustle to find a place in the ranks
of laborers. To gain the applause of the ill-advised striking populace is
nothing when we think of the suffering that will follow this folly. The
strike is, of course off, yet the folly of the deceptive leader will haunt
the few who could have aided the rank and file in joining thd merchants on
Wednesday in a peaceable solution of the matter."

NO STOPPAGE OF NAVAL STORES

The strike on the Savannah, Florida and Western wharf did not impair the
working of the naval stores department in the least during last week, which
was due, in a great measure, to the admirable management of Wharfinger Harris.
There was not a single delay in the deliveries to vessels except that caused
by the wet weather. As a matter of fact, the outward movement of rosin was
the heaviest had in several weeks. Stevedore Frank Bergman, who loaded the
bulk of the foreign vessels clearing last week, says he had no difficulty
whatever with his labor, and that he worked all of his men on full time.
The vessels were dispatched without any delay or demurrage according to
charter. He says that there was no exhibition on the part of his men of discontent or a desire to strike, but seemingly worked right along cheerfully,
they being apparently satisfied with the wages paid them.

The new hands will be worked at the wharves today for the purpose of
catching up and getting business in thorough shape.

The scenes around the colored Odd Fellows' hall, where the strikers hold
their meetings, resemble those of a political convention. The streets in
the vicinity are filled with the strikers.

Savannah Morning News, October 4, 1891.

15. STRIKERS ARE STILL OUT

THE UNION INSISTS ON BEING RECOGNIZED

The Railroads Provided With All the Hands They Need Now and are Ind-
dependent of the Strikers--The Work On the Wharves Going On Without Interruption or Delay--The Strikers' Card--What Some of Them Say

The strike has not yet been declared off, though there are evidences
of dissatisfaction in the ranks of the strikers.

The strikers held a big meeting yesterday afternoon at the longshoremens' hall, at East Broad and Anderson streets, and discussed the situation.

Chairman H. M. Lowery and Isaac Brown of the strikers' committee urged
the men to give up the fight and seek employment this morning.

A. L. Coleman, president of the union, told the men, it is said, to
remain firm. This advice was accepted by the majority of the strikers, who
announced their intention to stand firm.

It is not likely that the transportation companies will trouble themselves as to the course the strikers may pursue. They have all the hands
they need, and their freights are being handled expeditiously.

THE MEN DOING WELL

The new men are rapidly catching on to the handling of freight, and are
rapidly becoming as proficient as the strikers were. Work was carried on
all day yesterday at the Ocean Steamship wharves and Merchants' and Miners'
wharf. The City of Birmingham sailed yesterday fully loaded at 6:30 o'clock.
The Wm. Lawrence went out between 5 and 6 o'clock with a big cargo. The City
of Augusta will sail today on schedule time. By tomorrow all traces of the
strike will have about disappeared from the wharves, and the dray men expect
to get sufficient drivers today to run all the cotton trucks and drays.

A meeting of the merchants to pass resolutions refusing hereafter to
employ any one connected with the Labor Union and Protective Association
will, it is expected to be held today if the strike is not declared off by
noon. This will mean that the strikers will be out in the cold entirely.

Dissatisfaction has broken out in the ranks of the union and a number of
the members have announced their intention of applying for work today at the
wharves. If this is done the strike will most likely die a natural death
without the necessity of any declaration of its being off.

A CARD FROM THE STRIKERS

A. J. Coleman, M. J. Christopher, A. O. Pierrieaeu, G. W. Shaw, E. D.
Lynch, R. Jones and J. Youngblood sent a communication to the MORNING NEWS
last night giving official information that the strike has not been declared
off. "It is not because we have not the interest of the city at heart, nor
because of stubbornness," says the communication, "that it has not been declared off. The association promptly accepted the recommendation of its committee, and agreed to return to work for the advance named. But before doing
so, the association wanted to know if its members would be given their places
in a reasonable time, and not discharged because of membership in the union.
Our committee has not been able to get this informationand it is for this
reason that the strike has not been declared off. We make this announcement
because the public has been led to believe that we have no grievance, and as
it was erroneously stated that we did not accept the advance offered."

A LATE ANNOUNCEMENT

It is rather a late day that the association determined to make such an
announcement. It is a matter of record that at first the proposition of the
conference was rejected without any question about the union. The strikers
then thought they had things their own way and intended to dictate everything
to suit themselves. Since they awakened to the fact that they made a griev-
ous mistake they have raised the question about the union. The transportation
companies knew nothing about the union before the strike was inaugurated, and
they are not taking it into account now. All they say is that their laborers
left them and new men have been obtained to fill their places. They are

willing to employ other men as they need them, whether they belong to the
union or not. They are not asking questions about the union, as that organization does not appear to be one with which they have anything to do.
And the committee of the trade bodies through whose efforts the advance in
wages was secured, having been dissolved when the increase in wages was rejected, there doesn't appear to be anybody authorized to give any guarantee
about matters relating to the union. The thing for the strikers to do is to
apply for work and if they are needed they will be employed. The longer
they hold off the worse their chances for getting work will be.

THE MEDIATORS DONE

Those who have acted as mediators have washed their hands altogether
of the affair, and say it is now a matter of as little difference to them
as to the transportation companies whether or not the strike is declared off.
They reasoned with the strikers until they were tired, endeavoring to show
them that they are injuring themselves and families more than anyone else
in remaining away from work. Obstinacy, however, held a higher hand than
intelligence and reason, and their efforts to bring about a settlement were
put down as sure evidence of treachery and an attempt to sell the strikers
out to the corporations.
The men brought here to take the strikers' places are delighted with
their treatment. A dollar a day was about all they averaged in the country,
and now they are averaging $1.75 per day.

WANTED TO OBSERVE SUNDAY

Nearly all the white men and quite a number of the negroes brought here
during the week objected to working yesterday because of its being Sunday.
The transportation companies didn't insist and the religiously inclined
individuals spent a quiet day.
What good it is doing the strikers to hold out now no one can understand,
as the backbone of it has been broken by the bringing in of new hands.

Savannah Morning News, October 5, 1891.

16. THE STRIKE AT AN END

THE PRESIDENT OF THE UNION DECLARES IT OFF

The Strikers Returning to Work as Fast as They Can Get Places--The
Railroads Have All the Hands They Want and Business Moving With Renewed
Activity--The Strikers to Be Taken Back Whenever There Are Vacancies

The wharf laborers' strike was declared off last night by the president
and chairman of the Labor Union and Protective Association.
Dissatisfaction arose in the ranks of the union, and hundreds broke
away yesterday morning and applied to the transportation companies to be reinstated. About fifty were taken back by the Central railroad.
When the ex-strikers started to cross the bridge to apply for work they
were stopped by the police. The police had no instructions to allow them
to cross even if they asked for work, and they were kept waiting a short time.
Then as many as there were places for were taken back. The others were told
to apply from day to day, and as they are needed they will be reinstated.
The Savannah, Florida and Western railway and Merchants and Miners' company
also took back what old hands they had places for.
The drivers of trucks and drays applied for their old positions, and as
many as were needed were taken back. Quite a number of the places had been
filled.

THE STRIKE DECLARED OFF

The futility of the strike became apparent to the leaders and after a
prolonged meeting last night the strike was declared off.

Bay street presented an animated appearance yesterday. Trucks and
drays were moving in every direction with cotton and merchandise.

The new hands didn't take long to get onto the knack of handling freight
and are now as proficient at the work almost, as the men who had quit work.
The majority of those brought here have come to stay. Some of the roadway
hands will be sent back and the strikers will be given work in their places,
but it won't do for them to count on too heavy an exodus, because the most
of them belonged to extra gangs, and if they want to stay the railroads will
keep them.

EVERYTHING MOVING ON TIME

The steamship City of Augusta sailed last night on schedule time with
a full cargo. Several hundred bales of cotton were lightered and freight
cars were loaded and unloaded as before the strike. Everything on the Ocean
steamship wharves is moving briskly. The Deshong arrived yesterday and the
work of discharging her cargo was begun at once. She will sail tomorrow.

The Berkshire, of the Merchants and Miners' company, also arrived
yesterday and a full force of over 150 hands began unloading her. She will
be reloaded and will sail tomorrow on time.

A strike of rather small proportions took place yesterday at Dale, Dixon
& Co.'s lumber wharf. The laborers employed there demanded the discharge
of the fireman, a colored man named Jones, for some imaginary grievances.
The firm refused and the men said unless their demand was granted they would
quit work. Mr. Merritt Dixon promptly ran the men off the wharf and secured
others to replace them.

Alderman Wm. F. Reid and Mrs. Reid celebrated the 10th anniversary of
their marriage last night with a tin-wedding at their home at South Broad
and East Broad streets. A large party of friends were invited and several
hours were spent in singing, dancing, etc. An elegant supper was partaken
of at midnight. Alderman and Mrs. Reid were the recipients of numerous presents in the tin line.

ON THE LOWER WHARVES

The effects of the break in the ranks of the strikers was plainly per-
sceptible on the lower wharves. A long procession of drays, loaded and unloaded, moved continously up and down the east end of Bay street leading
to the warehouses. The warehousemen seemed to have all the men they could
use and cotton was moving in and out rapidly.

At the lower press about 140 hands were at work. About half of these
were strikers, who returned to work in the morning. They worked with a vim
and seemed be anxious to make up for lost time. The clerks said the men were
glad to get back to work, and that some of them were extremely penitent on
account of their part in the strike.

All of the strikers who returned to work yesterday morning, were taken
back without question and no mention was made of the strike.

THE PRESS HANDS GO BACK

The press laborers made no demands when they went out and asked for no
increase when they went back. Only one of the lower presses was running
yesterday but both could have been run as easily as one. Both the presses
will probably be running tomorrow.

Full forces were found at work on the Savannah, Florida and Western and
on all the other lower wharves. The stevedores all had full gangs, composed
almost entirely of the strikers. The naval stores inspectors also had full
gangs and were at work as usual for the first time since the inauguration of
the strike.

Supt. Fleming said last night that the Savannah, Florida and Western has
all the men at work that are wanted. A number of the strikers were taken
back yesterday, and a number more were refused because they were not needed.
Supt. Fleming said that the white men now at work on the wharves will be retained as long as they care to work and will not be displaced to make room
for the strikers.

Master Mechanic Antz of the Central railroad said last night that a number of the men who struck from the Central railroad round house applied for work yesterday, but their positions had been filled.

Savannah Morning News, October 6, 1891.

17. THE STRIKE ENDED

The wharf laborers' strike is over. It virtually ended Saturday, but those who saw the mistake they had made did not then dare antagonize the leaders of the movement. Yesterday morning hundreds of laborers returned to work and many more would have done so could they have obtained employment. The leaders, however, were unwilling to give in and fought against the inevitable until last night, when the president and chairman of the labor union officially declared the strike off.

The ill-advised movement has made a break between the business men and their colored laborers which it will take time to mend. It will be difficult to forget that men who had for years been faithful to their trusts deserted their posts at the dictates of those of whose very names even they were ignorant. Those who were true to the best interests of the community, however, will not be forgotten.

Were it not for the strong commercial position which Savannah has established for itself the strike would have done much injury to the city's business interests. Yesterday business resumed its former activity, and today every trace of the recent troubles caused by the derangement of labor will doubtless disappear.

While the MORNING NEWS, as usual, has kept abreast of the news every day, its conservatism in handling the grave issue did much to allay the antagonism which the strike engendered. A single indiscreet paragraph would have inflamed the minds of either side, and might have brought about a collision. In the interest of law and order much that was talked about by the strikers and the thousands of wild rumors, was suppressed. The trouble is over, and it is hoped that such a state of affairs will never again be known in Savannah.

Savannah Morning News, October 6, 1891.

18. LOOKING OVER THINGS

General Manager Green on the Strike and Other Matters

General Manager Green of the Richmond and Danville is on a general tour of inspection of the system. He spent yesterday in looking over the Central's properties here and will leave this morning for Columbia, S.C. He reports everything in fine condition. He said the wharves here will be extended and improved after the busy season.

While the Central's terminals are now of an extended character, General Manager Green said they are not large enough to accommodate the business of the great railway system. Freights are increasing rapidly and things will be rather crowded at the wharves this season.

In speaking of the strike, General Manager Green said the strikers didn't seem to take into consideration the fact that the Richmond and Danville system controlled over 5,000 miles of road and has many states to draw from.

"We could have put 10,000 men here as easily as 1,000," said the general manager. "There are hundreds of negroes in South Carolina, North Carolina and Virginia waiting now for the Savannah trains anxious to come here for

work, and the company's representatives have hard work telling them that
the strike is at an end and their services are not wanted.

"If we had acceded to the demands of the strikers," continued General
Manager Green, "the situation would have been made worse. In less than a
year they would have been demanding higher wages. It would have caused
trouble at all the southern ports. The men at these points would have demanded an increase of wages to the Savannah standard and as soon as it was
granted the laborers here would have wanted to go higher. The strike never
worried us. We knew we could get all the labor we wanted to take the places
of the strikers, and all the aid we asked from Savannah was the protection
of our properties."

Mr. Green spoke in highly complimentary terms of the manner in which
General Superintendent McBee has handled the strike, and said he was glad
that no violence had occurred.

"Have you many more office changes in view here?" was asked.

"Well, don't you think we've changed about all that could be changed.
No there's none in view now."

The general manager was asked what he proposed to do about the change
of the Augusta schedule, which is causing so much dissatisfaction.

"I was speaking to Supt. McBee about the matter today," he said, "and
the trouble will be remedied. A schedule of close connections at Millen
will be arranged at an early day. I know it's pretty hard on travelers to
have to lay over at Millen for several hours."

General Manager Green, General Superintendent McBee, General Manager
Sorrel of the Ocean Steamship Company, General Superintendent Fleming of the
Savannah, Florida and Western, and Mayor McDonough spent about three-quarters
of an hour in the sun parlor of the De Soto last night discussing the events
of the past week.

Savannah Morning News, October 7, 1891.

19.   THE ALLIANCE IN LINE

THE NATIONAL ORGANIZATION TO AID SAVANNAH IN GETTING DEEP WATER

Deep water has been given a great boom. The National Farmers' Alliance
has wheeled into line and the powerful influence of that organization will
be exerted to secure from Congress, sufficient appropriation to deepen the
Savannah river and make this port one of the greatest of the Atlantic.

Capt. D. D. Purse, who returned from Atlanta yesterday brought the news.
It was mainly through his efforts that the alliance took up the fight. He
first got the state alliance interested, and through it the national body.

The following is a copy of the official document sent out by the national
alliance on the subject:

WASHINGTON, D.C., Oct. 3, 1891.

To Whom it May Concern:

Believing that unity of interest begets unity of sentiment, and that by
the establishment of close commercial relations between the south and west
we can more thoroughly establish that sense of mutual and more effectually
eradicate the lines of sectional prejudice, we deem it but right that everything looking to these great ends should be encouraged.

And, since the state of Georgia by her legislature and through her state
alliance is appealing to congress for a sufficient appropriation to deepen
the channel to the city of Savannah; and, since this port is one of the natural outlets for the produce of the south and what to the trade of the world,
and will establish for our people direct trade with foreign ports and furnish
a competitive market for all our products as against markets of the northeast,
which now monopolize our commerce, we earnestly recommend that our alliance
brethren of the western and southern states examine into the question thoroughly and see how greatly they will be benefited by shorter routes to the
sea and competitive seaports; and, when convinced of all these facts, that

they make their wishes known to their congressmen, by petitions urging them
to do all in their power to secure for the port of Savannah ample appropri-
ations to meet the desired ends.

J. H. TURNER, N.F.A. AND I.V.
J. F. TILLMAN, Sec. Natl. Ex. Board of N.F.A. AND I.V.
C. W. MACUNE, Chairman Executive Board.

Harry C. Brown, who has been engaged to speak before the alliance of
the country on the deep water scheme, has begun his work. He has letters of
introduction from President Polk, C. W. Macune and N. A. Dunning. President
Polk's letter reads:

WASHINGTON, D.C., Oct. 1, 1891

This introduces Brother H. C. Brown of Atlanta, Ga. (formerly editor of
the *Southern Alliance Farmers,* who visits your section in the interest of
improved water facilities at the city of Savannah, Ga.

In view of the growth and development of the south and west, whose
interests demand the cheapest and most accessible outlets to the world for
their products, and in view of the superior advantages, geographical and
otherwise, offered by the port of Savannah, I heartily commend Brother
Brown and the worthy enterprise he represents to your most favorable consideration.

Fraternally,
L. L. POLK,
President National F.A. and I.U.

Dr. Macune's letter is as follows: WASHINGTON, D.C., Oct. 3, 1891

To the Brethren:
This is to introduce Brother H. C. Brown of Atlanta, Ga., who has for
several years been editor of the *Southern Alliance Farmer,* the official organ
of the Georgia state alliance. Brother Brown is a perfect gentleman, in whom
I have great confidence. He is a thoroughly devoted allianceman and worthy
of the confidence and esteem of the brotherhood . Any courtesies extended
him are worthily bestowed.

C. W. MACUNE

N. A. Dunning's letter reads: WASHINGTON, D.C., Oct. 3, 1891

To the Brotherhood:
I am personally and well acquainted with the bearer of this, Brother H.
C. Brown of Atlanta, Ga., and know him to be a man of honor and integrity.
I have examined to some extent that project in which he is interested and
believe it would aid materially in the equitable distribution of the fruits
of labor.

Sincerely and fraternally,
N. A. DUNNING

Savannah Morning News, October 7, 1891.

BLACK AND WHITE UNITY: THE CHICAGO CULLINARY ALLIANCE[70]

20. LIMITED OPTIONS

The limited sphere in which the Afro-American has been compelled to work,
has confined him almost exclusively to the choice of being a waiter or a
barber, unless he has had the advantage of a collegiate education, in which
case he becomes a minister or a lawyer. This limited sphere of action in the
avenues of employment had compelled the Afro-American to work for wages not
near as good as the "white brother" gets. Since the [Chicago Cullinary]
Alliance, the way points fair to an adjustment of all differences and it is

said that the scales will be brought to an equilibrium.

Cleveland Gazette, May 31, 1890.

21.   THE LABOR MOVEMENT

On May 1st, 30,000 toilers representing nearly every association of
organized labor in the city turned out. This was one of the largest and
most orderly demonstrations ever held in Chicago. Their object is the
eight-hour movement with ten-hours pay, and extra pay for overtime. There
are many men idle, and if their demands are not acceded to their will, undoubtedly be much suffering. The waiters were to have walked out Saturday
last at noon. Their main grievance was that the union should be recognized,
and that the leading large restaurants here employing white waiters should
work nothing but union men, recommended by the unions. The bosses acceded
to their demand and a general strike was averted among the white waiters.

The Freeman (Indianapolis), May 31, 1890 .

22.   THE CHICAGO WAITERS' STRIKE

Table-waiting has grown to be an art, and is recognized as a legitimate
business. As long as people can afford to take life easy, they must have
this kind of service, and somebody must follow it. It is to the interest of
the professional waiter to do all he can to elevate his business, and bring
to it all the respect that its importances entitles it. The waiters of
Chicago have caught the idea very thoroughly, as indicated in their manly
conduct in the strike for right. In accord with the spirit of the times,
they have organized a union, and by so doing have made themselves a power in
the hotel world. Every man in Chicago who must support himself and family
by this calling, should ally himself with the union, and aid the struggle
for fair play. Strikes are always a last resort, but when other means fail,
they are justified in defending their interest in anyway that promises
victory. In union there is strength, and by joining hands and dignifying
their labor, the waiters of Chicago will be the pioneers of a great reform.

The Freeman (Indianapolis), May 31, 1890 .

23. HISTORY OF THE UNION WAITERS' STRIKE

The *Freeman* takes pleasure in presenting to its many thousands of
readers a brief history of the Union Waiters' strike in Chicago. It is the
largest and most important movement ever inaugurated among waiters. As the
results will depend much upon any future movement here by waiters, the object is one well worth long and due consideration.
    The Chicago Cullinary Alliance is one of the largest and strongest
organizations of the kind in existence, having many branch unions, and controlling many hundreds of waiters in many sections of the country. It was
organized January 3, 1889, with a membership of only sixteen and was composed of German waiters, meat and pastry cooks and bartenders. It was
organized for the mutual protection in all the trades followed by its members.
No prejudice as to color or nationality existed, and its books and doors
were thrown open.

Among the organizations in Chicago, it controls Chicago Waiters'
Assembly, No. 7475, E. J. Parker secretary; German Bartenders and Waiter's
Assembly, Otto Stritter secretary; Chicago Waiter's Union No. 1, E. J.
Wheeler, secretary; Chicago Waiter's League Branch, No. 100, B. of U.L.,
E. B. Maurice, secretary; Meat and Pastry Cook's Union, Jas. J. Gilligan,
secretary; Columbus waiters and bartender's association, Ben Rosenbaum,
secretary. Colored: Wm. Lloyd Garrison Assembly, 8286, K. of L., J. W.
Cable, secretary; Chas. Summer Waiter's Union, J. B. Hart, president.
Officers of the Cullinary Alliance: Thos. M. Lambs, president; Wm. C.
Pomeroy, secretary; Theo. Birr, treasurer. Directors: J. J. Gilligan, E.
J. Wheeler, Wm. C. Pomeroy, John Estein, Wm. Langhenry.

The strike was first inaugurated by the white brother waiters. For the
following universal scale of wages, shorter hours, and better treatment in
many of the places where they were exclusively employed.

SCALE OF WAGES OF FIRST-CLASS OYSTER HOUSES AND RESTAURANTS

Steady men per week, $10; dinner men, over three hours work, per week,
$5; dinner men, three hours work or less per day, 75¢; extra men evenings,
$1.25; overtime, per hour or less, 25¢.

RESTAURANT AND LUNCH COUNTERS

Six and one-half days to constitute a week's work, the half day to be
worked on Sunday. Steady men all night, per week, $10; steady men, day time
per week $9; extra men Sundays, $2; special dinner men, $1; overtime per
hour or less, 25¢; dinner men, same scale as Oyster Houses; hotels, per
month, $30.

BEER GARDENS

Sunday work, waiters, per day, $3; evenings, week day, $1.50; concert
halls, 7 to 12 p.m., per week, $8; extra men per week, $8; extra men Sundays,
$3.

BALLS, BANQUETS, EXCURSIONS AND PICNICS

Bartenders, lunch and $5; waiters. lunch and $3.50; waiters on commission, 24 checks for $1.

RESTAURANTS WHICH ARE CLOSED SUNDAYS

No scale is made for steady or night men. Dinner and extra men, same
as Oyster Houses.

SUPPERS FOR CATERERS

The halls or club houses: Waiters, with dress coats, $3; weddings and
banquets, $2.50.

ORDINARY SUPPERS

Public halls: 50¢ suppers, waiters, 75¢ and $1 suppers, waiters, $3.50.

PRIVATE PARTIES

Waiters, $5; waiters for caterers $4.

The employers asked for time to consider their request and demands. It
is a little scheme of their own and while in the pretense of considering,
rather than accede to their demands, they endeavored to secure and employ
other help or substitute Afro-Americans. But this was anticipated and communicated to No. 8286, K. of L. The officers and leaders, Messrs. R. B.
Cabel, R. S. Bryan, B. A. Lewis, Dr. Bubbins, and J. B. Hart proceeded at
once to overcome any such outrage on a brother knight, and was successful,
even though large salaries were offered some of the colored head-waiters to
take charge of some of the places with colored crews.

WHY THE STRIKE WAS SO VIGOROUS AND SUCCESSFUL

The loyalty and manhood of the colored head-waiters at once, aroused the
anxiety of the Cullinary Alliance and the advisability of consolidating all
the waiter's unions and make war for the demands, was discussed and adopted,
the contracts to last one year, and in that time a proprietor cannot change
a white crew for a colored crew, or a colored crew for a white crew, even if

they have gone out on a strike, and should sign the Union contract, they are duty bound and can only have back the old crew. While the strike is and may be prolonged, they will take anything in the shape of a man from the streets to assist through a meal, and for bums and mimic men who will do anything for two bits, a drink, a meal, or a place to sleep. Second consideration, Chicago can challenge any city. There is an ignorant class of men that can only be reasoned with by the proprietor. Some even go so far as to refuse to join the Union, when the house has signed the scale, but when he understands that he must join or get, he will send his name and tuition.

Many of the leading hotel and dining hall proprietors have formed an association as they term it, to protect themselves against the dictations of the Union or any set of men, or Negroes led by white men, and ask for police protection which is laughed at. In no instance have there been any demonstration on the part of a single waiter. Everything has been conducted quietly, successfully and creditably to any set of men or race. Some of the proprietors say their men are well enough paid, especially those who only pay their men $6 and $7 per week, and expect just as much of them and if not more, than the men getting $9 and $10. As they are colored, they must look as neat, work as long, and be fed worse. Let every man fare alike--get the same wages--have the same hours and pay and many other necessary advantages in the demands of the Union.

OFFICIAL

We solicit the consideration of the general public. Among us are many men of families, whom much responsibility rests upon, and any financial assistance will be thankfully received, and given credit for, by sending the same with amount and address, they will be published from week to week in THE FREEMAN.

ORGANIZATION

We are ready to receive into our association, or organized Unions and for any information of the same, address Wm. C. Pomeroy, 127 La Salle Street, Chicago, Ill.

Letters and communications appertaining to the Union and for publication, will be answered through THE FREEMAN. Address such to R. B. Cabell, 127 La Salle Street, Chicago, Ill. Representatives of THE FREEMAN, 166 Wells Street, or 2443 State Street.

The Freeman (Indianapolis), May 31, 1890.

24.   LEADERS OF THE CULLINARY ALLIANCE

WILLIAM C. POMEROY

William C. Pomeroy, the Secretary of the Cullinary Alliance, is the Central figure in the strike. He is the recognized leader in the movement and the entire membership relies upon his prudence, ability and energy to help them win.

Mr. Pomeroy is quite a young man hailing from the good state of Kentucky, where he was born in 1862. His early years were spent in school at St. Mary's Institution in Dayton, O., where he received a liberal education. Having the misfortune to lose both parents, he was early compelled to leave the city and hunt for work. Thus he visited New Orleans, Wheeling, W. Va., St. Louis and Chicago, arriving in the latter city in 1883.

While in St. Louis, Mr. Pomeroy began the agitation which has since gained for him a national reputation. He found the waiters there poorly treated, subjected to numerous impositions and miserably paid for their work. He organized a flourishing Union, secured its recognition, secured comfortable accommodations, and a raise of forty per cent in salary. . . .

E. E. BYRAM

E. E. Byram was born in New York City of German parents, has been a resident of Chicago six years and is a member of Chicago Waiters' League, head secretary of the Labor Bearn and one of the hardest workers in the interest of the present cause.

B. A. LEWIS

B. A. Lewis, the colored leader was born in Oglethorp, Macon Co., Ga., and is the youngest of four children of Berry and Martha Lewis, who gave him the benefit of the best district schools in those days. His father died in 1871, leaving his mother, one sister and two elder brothers with a small farm. The entire family with the exception of Mr. Lewis are still remaining on the old farm. Mr. Lewis remained at home about eighteen months after the father's death as he had to leave to accept a position as clerk in a grocery in Albany, Ga. After a short experience in the business the successively held positions as coachman, barber, brakeman, newsboy and waiter, in which last vocation he was engaged for five years in Exchange.

He first organized the white waiters and put their Union upon substantial basis. Having secured contracts and recognition with advance in pay he turned his attention to the colored waiters.

In this movement he has been fair and honorable. He was in favor of good men receiving good pay, and contended that proprietors should treat their men fairly. He maintained that the interests of colored waiters and white waiters were common and that both classes of workers should join in a common contest. He declared in giving colored waiters the same wages as white waiters, and in fact abolishing all odious discriminations against the colored men. His energy, tact and fairness enabled him to win his way and the result was the splendid success of the Alliance. His work has won him great prestige and he well deserves the reputation he enjoys.

R. B. CABBELL

R. B. Cabbell, the well-known newspaper correspondent, is the colored representative in the Cullinary Alliance, being one of the secretaries. He has shown active and intelligent interest in the strike, faithfully serving the Alliance, but at the same time prudent and conservative in his dealings with employers. To him much credit is due for securing to the colored waiter the co-operation from the white members. He is very popular with the Alliance also among the Knights of Labor, in which order he is a prominent member. He is one of the most enterprising young men in Chicago, a thorough businessman. He was once connected with the Chicago staff of THE FREEMAN but is now city editor of the Methodist Advocate, a weekly paper, and is also secretary of the Charles Sumner Waiter's Union. He is considered one of the shrewdest engineers of the strike and is agent for one of the largest jewelry establishments in Chicago.

W. B. WARWICK

W. B. Warwick was born at Richmond, Virginia, Oct. 12th 1867. At the age of eight years he, with his parents moved to Baltimore where he was educated in the public school. At the age of fifteen he went to work in the dry goods business serving two years and came to Chicago on July 11th 1876, engaged in the waiter business a month later and has followed it ever since, joined the Knights of Labor June 6, 1886, was elected two terms as Master Workman, together with Wm. C. Pomeroy drew up the first scale of wages ever written up for waiters and was successfully adopted by the restaurant proprietors of Chicago. Seeing the necessity of having the colored waiters combined with us to benefit our line of business they organized them together and fought the only successful fight of its kind ever known.

R. S. BRYAN

R. S. Bryan, has done much to make the strike successful. He is well-known in the Knights of Labor and very highly esteemed. He was the Knight of Labor candidate for the Legislature two years ago, and received a large vote. Mr. Bryan is proprietor of the Estella Cafe and is a successful

business man.   President of the R. S. Bryan Association of the First Ward,
representative union man. He has been elected a delegate to the Labor District of Knights of Labor for a term of three years, also a delegate to the
Labor Councils for one year. Mr. Lewis is never better satisfied than when
he is at work in the Councils of his Labor organization, grappling with the
various economic and social problems of the days. He is a good, practical,
forcible speaker, uses apt illustrations and has a fund of humor at hand to
make his talks enjoyable. He is a power in the Alliance, and well deserves
the prominence he has attained.

HENRY JOHN

Henry John was born in Germany and came to this country in May, 1880,
had followed the business in the old country and so resumed it here. He
first associated with the K. of L. 9620, but severed his connection some two
years ago and joined the German Waiters and Bartenders Benefit Association,
a part of the Cullinary Alliance, and has been twice elected a delegate to
the Alliance and was appointed as one of the Executive Committee, and has
been one of the most efficient and hard working members of that body, both
in clerical and manual work in the successful movement almost finished.

J. B. HART

He was born at Charlottesville, Va., where he received his early training at the Jefferson school. He left home in 1880, and lived in Washington,
D.C., a short while, from whence he went to New York, Pittsburg, Memphis,
St. Louis, and Louisville, stopping only a short time in each of the cities
mentioned. He came to Chicago, December 1885, following various pursuits in
business. He was a member of Wm. Lloyd Garrison, L.A., No. 8286, K. of L.,
and was its Worthy Foreman. He was delegate to District 24, K. of L., also
delegate to the Central Council K. of L. Mr. Hart was a representative at
the Labor Men's Worlds Fair Committee. He was one of the nine proxy holders
elected by that committee, and was the only colored delegate present. He
was temporary president of the Chas. Sumner Waiters Union, and also delegate to the C.C.A. from No. 8286, K. of L.

DR. J. B. BUBBINS

Dr. Bubbins was born at College Point, La., but his home was in New
Orleans. He began life upon a sugar plantation, but at the age of 14 he
went to steam boating, serving from deckhand to steward. He has navigated
the principle rivers, lakes, gulfs, and oceans and visited many parts of the
world. He came to Chicago in 1884. Returning to New Orleans for a brief
stay to finish his profession, he returned to Chicago and opened up his
office and laboratory at 1471 State St., and enjoys a large white and
colored practice. He is well known throughout the country as a Knight, being
a Past Grand Master Workingman. He is also compounder of an original French
oil for internal and external use for all chronic pains and rheumatism,
also a special kidney and bladder remedy, all of which have effected permanent cures. Dr. Bubbins is also a French scholar and speaks that language
fluently, and is one of the financial backers of 8286 K. of L.

The Freeman (Indianapolis), May 31, 1890.

NOTES

1   See for example, Melton Alonza McLaurin, *The Knights of Labor in the South* (Westport, Conn.: Greenwood Press, Inc., 1978). For an overview, see Philip S. Foner, *Organized Labor and the Black Worker, 1619-1973* (New York: International Publishers, 1976), Chapter 4.

2   The Exodus is discussed in Vol. II, pp. 305-52.

3   For a discussion of the Freedman's Bank and its demise, see Vol. II, note 3.

4   James L. Pugh (1820-1907) had been a prominent secessionist and a member of the Confederate Congress before entering the Senate in 1880. Born in Georgia, he moved to Alabama with his parents, where he attended school, and studied law. Admitted to the bar in 1841, he began to practice in Eufaula and became involved in politics. In 1858 he was elected to Congress where he served until January 1861, when he withdrew to join a Confederate military unit. He then served in the Confederate Congress from 1861 to 1865. Pugh became President of the Democratic State Convention in 1874, and a member of the state constitutional convention in 1875. Elected as a Democrat to the U.S. Senate, he served in that body from 1880 to 1897, when he retired from public life.

5   The Civil Rights Act of 1875 was the last major piece of civil rights legislation to be passed by Congress until 1957. The 1875 bill declared it illegal to deny blacks equal access to public "accommodations, advantages, facilities, and privileges of inns, public conveyances on land or water, theaters, and other places of public amusement." In 1883, however, in a strict construction of the constitutional authority of the states to regulate themselves, the U.S. Supreme Court declared the act unconstitutional.

6   The reference to Negroes as a "Hamitic Race" stems from the Biblical story of Ham (Cham). The original story in Genesis 9 and 10 was that after the Flood, Ham had looked upon his father Noah's nakedness as he lay drunk in his tent. Noah's other two sons, Shem and Japheth, had covered their father without looking upon him. When Noah awakened, he cursed Ham's son, Canaan, saying that he would forever be a "servant of servants." Over the ages, this simple allusion to slavery became associated with Africans because it was believed that Africans were descended from at least one of Ham's sons. When this alleged connection became widely accepted in western thought during the seventeenth century, it was normally used to explain blackness rather than slavery. Gradually it took on the added burden of rationalizing slavery.

7   George Washington Williams (1849-1891) joined the military at the age of fourteen, and even though discharged because of his youth, he promptly reenlisted and served as a sergeant-major in General N. P. Jackson's staff. He was wounded in Texas, then joined the Mexican Army for a year, and later enlisted in the U.S. Cavalry. Passed over for promotion, Williams resigned at the age of twenty. He attended Newton Theological Institution and in 1874 graduated, the first Afro-American ever to do so. Thereafter he served as a pastor in Boston, Editor of the *Commoner* in Washington, D.C., and then as a minister in Cincinnati. He read law in the office of Alphonso Taft, was admitted to the Ohio bar in 1879, and that same year was elected to the Ohio legislature. Between 1876 and 1883 Williams researched and published his two-volume *History of the*

Negro Race in America from 1619 to 1880, which was immediately recognized as the best book on Negro history published in the nineteenth
century. It has since become a classic. He later published a less
well-known volume on the *History of the Negro Troops in the War of
Rebellion.* Subsequently, Williams visited the Congo, and served as
U.S. Minister-Resident to Haiti from 1885 to 1886.

8   For a biographical sketch of Frederick Douglass, see Vol. I, note 8.

9   John P. Green, a black Ohio state senator, was founder of Labor Day
in Ohio.

10   The *Freeman* was a weekly edited by T. Thomas Fortune, the author of
an influential book, *Black and White: Land, Labor, and Politics in the
South,* published in 1884. In his book Fortune advanced the single tax
idea of Henry George (see Vol. III, note 16), that at the root of most
economic misery lay "land monopoly," or control of the land by a select
few. Fortune argued that since blacks were primarily laborers, it was
natural that they should side with other workers in a revolt against
the monopolists for a "juster distribution of the results of labor."
The future struggle in the South, he was convinced, would not be between
the races, but between labor and capital. Thus workers black and white
must unite. Fortune shrank from the direction his own analysis led
him, however. In fact, coupled with his clarion calls for class solidarity for the impending struggle was a plea for accommodation to the
very society he condemned. That society, he argued, was governed by
immutable laws of competition to which the Negro must adjust in order
to survive.

11   From the outset the Knights of Labor did not exclude male workers
because of color or race, political or religious belief, or place of
birth--unless they were Chinese. When efforts were made to organize
local assemblies of Chinese in New York and Philadelphia, the General
Executive Board of the Knights refused to grant them charters. Black
workers were prominent in the fight to admit the Chinese. Frank J.
Ferrell (see Vol. III, Introduction and p. 134), an outstanding black
leader of the Knights, made a special effort to get the GEB to reverse
its stand.

12   John Roy Lynch (1847-1939) was born in Vidalia, Louisiana, to a
white father and a black slave mother. His father left provisions that
Catherine Lynch and their children were to be freed should anything
happen to him, but his wishes were not carried out. His mother and her
children were sold and carried to Natchez. After the Union troops
occupied that city, Lynch attended night school, but received most of
a good classical education from private instructors. Lynch also worked
as a photographer until 1869, when he was appointed justice of the
peace by the Republican governor. Active in the Republican Party, he
was elected to the state legislature that year for two terms, the second term as Speaker of the House of Representatives. Lynch was then
elected to two terms in the U.S. House of Representatives between 1872
and 1876. At twenty-six Mississippi's first black representative was
the second youngest man ever to sit in that body. Lynch remained
active in Republican politics in his state, and later served as an
officer during the Spanish-American War. After the war he moved to
Chicago and became a member of the Illinois bar. In 1913 he published
a now well-known account of Reconstruction, *The Facts of Reconstruction,* and later an autbiography, *Reminiscences of an Active Life.*

13   George Washington Cable (1844-1925) served with the Confederate cav-
alry, and after the war became a reporter for the New Orleans *Picayune*.
As a free-lance writer he began to publish stories about Louisiana life.
His essays criticizing the rising system of segregation within the post-
Reconstruction South infuriated native whites, and in 1885 Cable moved
to Massachusetts. His books include *The Silent South* (1885), *Strange
True Stories of Louisiana* (1889), and *The Negro Question* (1890).

14   For a biographical sketch of Isaac Myers, see the Introduction and
Document 7 in Vol. I, Part XI.

15   Cornelius Vanderbilt (1794-1877) was born on Staten Island, New York.
He emerged into the world of high finance after gaining control over
most of the ferry lines running between New York and New Jersey, expanded his holdings to the Hudson River, and opened several overseas
shipping lines. Vanderbilt invested in railroads during this period as
well. After acquiring the New York Central, he parlayed the line into
a major railroad system. When he died Vanderbilt left a $100,000,000
fortune to his son, William Henry (1821-1885), who in turn doubled the
family fortune.
        Jay Gould (1836-1892) was another New York financier who, along with
James Fisk and Daniel Drew, acquired the Erie Railroad in 1868. Noted
for his ruthless entrepreneurial tactics, he and Fisk attempted to
corner the gold market in 1869. In the 1870s and 1880s Gould built a
group of railroad lines in the trans-Mississippi West. The "Gould system," as it was known, became one of the six largest railroad systems
in the nation (see Vol. III, note 23).

16   "Saint-Simonianism" referred to the social theories of Claude-Henri
de Rouvray, Count de Saint-Simon (1760-1825). The French social scient-
ist and philosopher was convinced that society needed to be reorganized
along the new philosophical guidelines of "positivism." In this new
system, leadership would be entrusted to a scientific elite which alone
was capable of ordering the world and taming nature for the welfare of
mankind. The author of many works, most of them outlined the contours
of the new technocratic order.
        "Henry Georgism" referred to the ideas of the American reformer, Henry
George (1839-1897). His theories regarding the causes of poverty and
inequality distinguish him as one of the few original American economic
theorists. His book *Progress and Poverty* (1879) sold over two million
copies before 1900, and made him an international figure. According to
George, poverty was attributed to rent. He proposed a single tax on land
as the appropriate remedy. The single tax theory called for the elimina-
tion of unearned income (speculative gain), and by insuring equal access
to natural resources, would prevent monopoly and promote equality for
all social classes.

17   Peter M. Arthur (1831-1903), associated with the Brotherhood of Locomotive Engineers from its inception in 1863, was elected Grand Chief
Engineer of the Brotherhood in 1874 and held that office until his death.

18   The Labor Bureau, now the Federal Bureau of Labor Statistics, was
established in 1884 to gather data on wages, working conditions, un-
employment, the cost of living, and related data, to facilitate a more
intelligent understanding of economic conditions. The Bureau was the
only significant result of a series of hearings conducted by the Senate
Committee on Education and Labor in 1883 to examine the relations between
labor and capital. See the Introduction to Vol. III, Part I.

19   "A Douglass" was an obvious reference to the major black American spokesman of his time, Frederick Douglass (see Vol. I, note 8).
        "Senator Bruce" was a reference to Blanch Kelso Bruce (1841-1898), the first Negro to serve a full six-year term in the United States Senate. Born a slave in Farmville, Virginia, he spent the Civil War years teaching school in Missouri, and worked as a printer, and a porter on a steamboat. After the Civil War he established himself as a successful planter in Mississippi. Bruce rose quickly in Mississippi Republican politics, holding numerous state offices before being elected to the U. S. Senate in 1874. Bruce remained a powerful influence in the Republican Party after leaving the Senate in 1880. He was reportedly the most wealthy black individual in the land. During the 1890s Bruce served as Recorder of Deeds in Washington, D.C., and as Register of the Treasury.

20   Terence Vincent Powderly (1849-1924) was born in Carbondale, Pennsylvania. At seventeen he was apprenticed to learn the machinist trade, joined the Machinists' and Blacksmiths' Union in 1871, and soon became a prominent figure in that organization. In 1874 Powderly was initiated into the Knights of Labor, rising to become Grand Master Workman in 1879. He held this post until 1893, during which time the Order was the most powerful labor organization in the United States. In 1878 Powderly was elected to the first of three consecutive terms as Mayor of Scranton on the Greenback-Labor ticket.
        As a labor leader, Powderly showed himself an idealistic reformer, but inadequate to the task of achieving immediate economic gains for workers. This stemmed in part from his view of the Knights as an educational mechanism. It would reform society by demanding that the government regulate all utilities, trust, and monopolies, and abolish various social evils such as child labor. He opposed the craft union method of organization because he believed that the skilled laborer should assist the unskilled worker. Also, he opposed strikes and placed little importance upon demands for better pay, hours, and conditions as an end in themselves. Powderly perceived these as short-term solutions which ultimately would come to pass anyway as society was reformed.
        A ready intelligence assisted Powderly in acquiring a sound classical education on his own. He had begun to study law before his retirement from the Knights of Labor and in 1894 he was admitted to the bar in Pennsylvania. Having assisted William McKinley in his pursuit of the Presidency, in 1897 Powderly was rewarded with an appointment as United States Commissioner-General of Immigration. He wrote numerous essays on labor, but is best remembered for his personalized history of the labor movement, *Thirty Years of Labor, 1859 to 1889* (1889).
        Charles H. Litcheman (1849-1902) was the National Secretary of the Knights of St. Crispin (see Vol. II, note 25), and General Secretary of the Knights of Labor in 1882.

21   For an explanation of these events, see Vol. III, pp. 91-101.

22   Boycotts were not mentioned in the Knights of Labor's Constitution and seldom employed during the first years of the organization's existence. But by 1885 the Order had become the most successful boycotting agency in the history of the American labor movement. The term "boycott" became so common that it was frequently used interchangeably with strike. *Bradstreets'* (Dec. 19, 1885) listed 196 boycotts as having taken place throughout the country in 1885, of which 59 ended successfully, 23 were failures and 114 were still pending at year's end.

23   In spite of the Knights' hostility to the strike as a weapon, the Order attained its greatest membership when it became involved in strikes. The walkout against the Missouri Pacific Railroad, the backbone of Jay Gould's southwestern system, was no exception (also see Vol. III, notes 15 and 24).

In October 1884, Gould slashed wages ten percent, and by March 9, 1885, the walkout became general along all points of the southwestern railroad system involving 10,000 miles of track and 4,500 workers in Missouri and Texas. Local assemblies leaped to the support of the strikers. Aware that popular sympathy was on the side of the workers, the Gould management ordered the wage cut rescinded. The company also agreed that no worker would be dismissed for participating in the strike. The prestige of the Knights soared, but Gould had no intention of co-existing with the union. The Gould management decided to destroy the local assemblies by discharging the leaders and their most militant followers. By June 16 the company had locked the men out, and the Knights reciprocated by ordering a strike against Gould. But Gould retreated temporarily by suggesting a conference of the interested parties, and headed off the strike. The Knights demanded the dismissal of all scabs, and the reinstatement of all discharged men. They also demanded as-surance that no future discrimination would be shown to members of the Order. Gould agreed to the terms presented by the Knights.

It soon became clear after the settlement in 1885, however, that Gould had no intention of permitting a union to exist within his system. In violation of the agreement, Knights were fired, overtime work went unpaid, and wages were not restored to pre-strike levels. The showdown came on the Texas and Pacific Railroad early in 1886, and soon spread throughout the southwestern system. Unfortunately for the railroad workers, many of the engineers, firemen, brakemen, and conductors re-mained at work because they had received preferential treatment. Thus the workers were divided and conquered. Also, this time Powderly and the Knights of Labor gave only lip-service to the workers' effort, and the Gould management refused to negotiate with him. Meanwhile, the attack upon the workers reached new heights of fury. Yet, with strikers being shot and arrested, Powderly confined himself to lecturing Gould on his responsibilities as a leading industrial spokesman.

On April 12, 1886, the House of Representatives ordered an investi-gation of the strike, and three days later, a committee of seven Con-gressmen left for a tour of the strike area. Long hearings were held after which the committee wrote a report finding many of the strikers' grievances justified. Nevertheless, the committee did an about-face and declared that the real cause of the strike was the fault of "Martin Irons, chairman of the executive board of District Assembly 101" (see Vol. III, note 24).

The workers saw things differently, and recognized that they had been sold out by Powderly. By the end of April 1886, it was clear the strike was lost. On May 4 the walkout officially ended with an unconditional surrender. The first Gould strike marked the peak of the Knights' mem-bership--the second Gould strike marked the beginning of the end for the Order. See Philip S. Foner, *History of the Labor Movement in the United States,* Vol. II (New York, 1955), pp. 50-53, 83-86.

24   Martin Irons, Socialist Chairman of D. A. 101's executive board, directed the initial stages of the Knights of Labor strike against Jay Gould's southwestern railroad system (see Vol. III, note 23). His mili-tant strategy and tactics frightened the top leadership of the Order, however, and by March 1886, Powderly decided to intervene. The Grand Master Workman immediately informed top management officials that Irons' policies did not reflect those of the Order. When Powderly sought a conference with the Gould management, he was told that a conference could take place only when the workmen were on the job. Thus Powderly ordered Irons to yield to these terms and send the men back to work. But Irons refused to surrender to such a crushing defeat after his followers had suffered so much already, and instead called on the workers to prepare for a last-ditch battle. The positive response of the strikers forced Powderly to agree to a continuation of the walkout.

When the Congressional investigating committee studying the strike released its report, the committee charged that Irons was the real cause of the strike, for had he not refused to follow Powderly's orders, the strike would have ended. The committee failed to explain why the strikers

felt betrayed. Irons himself was, like other strike leaders, black-
listed in every industry, and deprived of any opportunity to earn a
living as a worker.

Misfortune hounded Irons. His wife died during the strike and his
furniture was seized to pay his debts. Forced out of every subsequent
job he attempted to lecture but failed, and during his last years was
reduced to keeping a small saloon lunch counter in Missouri. He died
in 1900, but his memory was venerated in 1910, when under the auspices
of the Missouri State Federation of Labor, a monument was placed above
his grave paying tribute to Irons as a "Fearless Champion of Industrial
Freedom". See Philip S. Foner, *History of the Labor Movement in the
United States,* Vol. II (New York, 1955), pp. 84-86.

25   Fitzhugh Lee (1835-1905) was born in Fairfax County, Virginia. His
father was an elder brother of General Robert E. Lee, and his mother was
a granddaughter of the Revolutionary philosopher George Mason, and a
sister of Senator James M. Mason. Lee graduated from West Point in
1856, and after receiving a dangerous wound fighting Indians in Texas,
he was named Assistant Instructor of Tactics at West Point. When the
Civil War came, Lee joined the Confederate cavalry. After compiling a
distinguished battle record, he received a commission of major-general.
His family name and personal popularity won Lee the governorship of
Virginia in 1885. His four-year term was undistinguished, but he did
solidify the Democratic hold over the state.

26   Little is known about Victor Drury except that he was a leader in
District 49 of the Knights of Labor, and formerly had been an important
figure in the French sections of the First International in the United
States. Also, Drury was among the few members of the Knights' General
Executive Board to favor the admission of two Chinese local assemblies
in New York, both organized by Timothy Quinn, District Master Workman of
49, and Frank J. Ferrell, the most famous Negro in the Order.

John Brown (1800-1859) grew up in Ohio, and after several moves,
settled in North Elba, New York. Violently anti-slavery, Brown raised
his sons to hate the institution as well. Five of his sons moved to
Kansas in 1854 to participate in the anti-slavery agitation, and the
father joined them in 1855. Brown believed himself to be the Lord's
instrument chosen by God to destroy slavery. In Kansas the Browns were
involved in the heavy border warfare between the pro and anti-slavery
forces. He led a party which killed five innocent pro-slavery men and
he became notorious for this "Pottawatomie Massacre." Returning East,
on October 16, 1859, Brown and about twenty anti-slavery radicals captured the federal arsenal at Harpers Ferry in western Virginia, to assist fugitive slaves and to establish a base for a slave insurrection.
Captured two days later, Brown was convicted of treason and hanged.
Radical abolitionists mourned the loss of a martyr, while southerners
condemned him as an insane fanatic.

27   An authoritative source on Hiram F. Hoover is Thomas W. Kremm and
Diane Neal, "Clandestine Black Labor Societies and White Fear: Hiram
F. Hoover and the 'Cooperative Workers of America' in the South,"
Labor History 19 (Spring 1978): 226-37.

28   For a brief biographical sketch, see Vol. III, note 16.

29   Donelson Caffery (1835-1906) was born on his father's sugar plantation near Franklin, St. Mary's Parish, Louisiana. Caffery attended a
private school in Baltimore, Maryland, read law in an office in Franklin,
Louisiana, and then attended Louisiana University. Upon graduation he
became a sugar planter. Although he did not favor secession, when it
came he joined a military unit, serving as a lieutenant on the staff

of Brigadier-General W. W. Walker. After the Civil War, Caffery engaged in the practice of law and in sugar planting, and worked energetically to rid the state of carpetbaggers. In 1879 he was elected delegate to the state constitutional convention. Caffery was elected to the state senate in 1892, and later that year he was appointed to fill an unexpired term in the U.S. Senate. In 1894 he was reelected and served in the Senate until 1901. During his public career Caffery was known as a man true to his principles even when it ran counter to his own economic interest. Thus he incurred the wrath of his fellow sugar planters when he opposed a bounty on sugar.

30   Beginning in 1910, the International Workers of the World made a determined effort to recruit black members. A massive educational campaign was launched to convince blacks that they had no real chance in white unions; only the IWW would organize them on a completely equal basis, skilled or unskilled. All IWW journals participated in this educational campaign, including *Voice of the People,* the southern organ of the IWW, published in New Orleans. The editor of this journal was Covington Hall. Mississippi-born and a one-time adjutant general in the United Sons of Confederate Veterans, Hall became a radical, a Socialist, and an active organizer for the IWW, especially among Negroes in the South. He regularly featured appeals in the *Voice* urging white workers in the South to remember how racism had always been used by the ruling class to divide black and white to the injury of both. He predicted that no real progress in the conditions of life could be realized until the workers of both races united. In issue after issue, Hall drove home the message: "The workers, when they organize, must be color blind. . . . We must aim for solidarity first, and revolutionary action afterwards."

31   William E. Chandler (1835-1917) was born and died in Concord, New Hampshire. After graduation from Harvard Law School in 1854, he served a few years as court reporter, then turned to politics. In 1863 he was elected to the New Hampshire legislature, and was reelected twice more. During the Civil War he vigorously supported Lincoln, and was rewarded with an appointment as Solicitor and Judge-Advocate General of the Navy Department. President Johnson appointed Chandler as Assistant Secretary of the Treasury. In 1867 he returned to the practice of law, and became an important figure in the Republican Party organization. Although he played a significant role in the final election of Rutherford B. Hayes to the Presidency, he was disgusted with the President's friendliness toward the South, and later issued a manifesto which charged Hayes and the Democrats with a corrupt bargain, whereby Hayes won the election in return for a withdrawal of federal troops from the South. When Chester Arthur became President, Chandler was appointed Secretary of the Navy, in which capacity he began a policy of transforming the naval fleet from wood to steel-constructed ships. In 1887 Chandler was elected to the Senate to fill a vacant seat, and won reelection in 1889, and again in 1895.

32   For a biographical sketch of Jefferson Davis, see Vol. I, note 53.
        Robert Edward Lee (1807-1870), was Commanding General of the Confederate armies during the Civil War. Born in Westmoreland County, Virginia, the son of "Light Horse Harry" Lee of Revolutionary War fame, Robert graduated from the U.S. Military Academy (Class of 1829) and joined the Corps of Engineers. He married Mary Curtis in 1831 and lived in Arlington House a Curtis family estate near Washington, D.C., until the Civil War. Lee's career included service in the Mexican War, Superintendent of West Point, and Regimental Commander in Texas. Lee had no sympathy for secession, but when it came he assumed command of the Army of Northern Virginia, and in 1865 finally became Commander-in-Chief. He surrendered at Appomattox in April 1865, then served as President of Washington College until his death. One year later it was renamed Washington and Lee University.

Thomas Jonathan ("Stonewall") Jackson (1824-1863), was born in West Virginia and graduated from the U.S. Military Academy in 1846. After service during the Mexican War, he taught mathematics at Virginia Military Institute. When the Civil War began he served as an officer in the Confederate Army. At the first battle of Bull Run, Jackson stood as firm as a "stone wall," according to a fellow officer, and thereafter was referred to by that sobriquet. Considered a brilliant military tactition, he won acclaim in the Shenandoah campaigns, at the second battle of Bull Run, and at Antietam. Jackson was at the peak of his powers in 1863 when he was mortally wounded by one of his own sharpshooters while reconnoitering.

33   "U. S." is an abbreviation for "union statistician," an office in the local assembly which was the equivalent of treasurer.

34   "R. S." is an abbreviation for "recording secretary."

35   Charles Foster (1828-1904) was born in Fostoria, Ohio, a name which commemorates his father. His formal education was scanty and Charles worked for many years as an assistant, then partner in the family business. Foster expanded his business interests and amassed a fortune, much of which he lost in the 1890s. Although an ardent Republican, Foster did not enter politics himself until the 1870s when he served three consecutive terms in the U.S. House of Representatives. In 1879 he was elected Governor of Ohio. President Harrison named Foster Secretary of the Treasury in 1891, in which post he favored sound money and high tariffs. Upon the expiration of Harrison's term, Foster returned to private business in Ohio.

36   William Windom (1827-1891) was born to Quaker parents in Ohio. He graduated from Martinsburg Academy and then read law in the offices of Judge R. C. Hurd of Mount Vernon. Admitted to the bar at twenty-three, Windom began his practice and entered politics as a Whig. In 1835 he moved to Winona in the Minnesota Territory. There he practiced law and was elected to Congress as a Republican in 1858 when Minnesota became a state. Windom served in the House until 1869, and allied himself with the Radical wing of the party. In 1870 he was elected to the U.S. Senate and was then reelected for a second term, but resigned in 1881 to become Secretary of the Treasury in the administration of James Garfield. After the President's death, Windom was selected to complete his own term in the Senate. In the Senate Windom served on several powerful committees, and was particularly aggressive about internal improvements. He lost the election of 1883, moved east, and never again returned to Minnesota. In 1889 Windom was once again called upon to be Secretary of the Treasury. He held that office until his sudden death in 1891.

37   William McKinley (1843-1901) was born in Niles, Ohio. During the Civil War he served in the Union Army, then returned to Canton, Ohio, where he practiced law. Elected to Congress in 1876 as a Republican, McKinley served in that body until 1891, with the exception of one term. His position on high tariffs gained the attention of powerful industrialists, especially Mark Hanna of Ohio, who engineered McKinley's campaign for the governorship (1892-1896), and secured for him the Presidential nomination in 1896. On domestic issues McKinley was hardly distinguishable from other Presidents of his day, but in the field of foreign affairs, he is noted for his imperialistic ventures in Cuba and the Far East. McKinley was shot and killed on September 6, 1901, by the anarchist, Czolgosz, while attending the Pan-American Exposition at Buffalo, New York.

38   John Sherman (1823-1900), the younger brother of the renowned Civil
War general, William Tecumseh Sherman, was an Ohioan who practiced law
in Cleveland. He helped to organize the Republican Party in Ohio, and
thereafter entered upon a long career in public service. Sherman was
elected to several terms in the House of Representatives between 1855
and 1861, and then to the U.S. Senate from 1861 to 1877. A fiscal
conservative, Sherman acted as a moderate during Reconstruction. When
Rutherford B. Hayes became President in 1877, Sherman was appointed
Secretary of the Treasury until 1881 when he returned to the Senate.
Sherman remained in the Senate until President McKinley appointed him
Secretary of State, an office he was forced to resign that same year
because of ill health.

39   McLaurin, *The Knights of Labor in the South,* p. 148.

40   Ida B. Wells (1869-1931), born in Holly Springs, Mississippi, was
left to support four siblings when only fourteen. Still, she managed
a formal education, studying at Rust College and Fisk University. Miss
Wells became one of the leading anti-lynching crusaders, beginning her
career in Memphis as a journalist for the *Living Word,* a black weekly.
As editor and co-owner of the Memphis *Free Speech,* in 1892 she wrote a
startling expose of white lynchers for which she was forced to flee
Memphis. In New York Miss Wells found employment for another black
weekly, the *New York Age,* and in 1895 married another journalist, Ferdi-
nand L. Barnett. Three years later she led a delegation to the White House
to protest the continuance of black lynchings in the South.

41   John Jarrett (the correct spelling), born in England in 1843, emigrated to the United States where he became Vice President of the Sons
of Vulcan in 1873. He served as President of the Amalgamated Association of Iron and Steel Workers from 1879 to 1883.

42   The Union Labor Party was organized in Cincinnati in 1887. It attempted to unite the remnants of the Greenback-Labor Party with discon-
tented industrial workers during a period of extreme conflict between
capital and labor. Although the party was short-lived, it ran Alson J.
Streeter for President of the United States, but polled only 147,000
votes.

43   The "Calhoun" and "McDuffy" referred to are John Caldwell Calhoun
(1782-1850), and George McDuffie (1790-1851), both of whom were senators
from South Carolina.
        Calhoun practiced law in South Carolina after graduation from Yale
and, through marriage, became a wealthy planter. Most of his adult life
was spent in public service at the highest levels of government, serving
in Congress from 1811 to 1817, as Secretary of War from 1817-1825, and
as Vice President from 1825 to 1832. Calhoun resigned the office for a
seat in the U.S. Senate from 1832-1844. In 1844 he became Secretary of
State, then returned to the Senate from 1845-1850.
        McDuffie was also a South Carolinian. Born to very poor parents, he
was educated at South Carolina College under the sponsorship of an interested employer. After graduation in 1813, he was admitted to the bar,
commenced practice in Edgefield, and entered politics. McDuffie was soon
elected to the U.S. House of Representatives, served two terms, and returned from 1821 to 1834 to become Governor of South Carolina. In 1842
McDuffie was elected to the U.S. Senate, but resigned to return to private
life in 1846. Although he was born in poverty, McDuffie eventually merged
into the very upper levels of Carolina society.
        Both Calhoun and McDuffie became champions of "states rights," as it
came to be called. McDuffie followed Calhoun's lead in challenging the
federal government's power to regulate tariffs during the Nullification

Crisis of the early 1830s. Also, both men attempted to defend the
South from the charges of the abolitionists, and devised the pro-slavery
argument that is referred to in this passage. The cornerstone of the
"Calhoun and McDuffie Doctrine" was that, since blacks and whites were
so different, it was "natural" for one to subjugate the other--especially
since whites allegedly were the superior race. This line of reasoning
sprang from a pseudo-anthropological premise which had been present in
racial thought before Calhoun and McDuffie, and continued for over half
a century afterward. In the late nineteenth century it was resuscitated
to justify the system of *de jure* segregation.

44   Andrew Jackson (1767-1845) was born on the South Carolina frontier,
fought in the Revolution at thirteen, and was orphaned at fourteen.
After reading law he was admitted to the bar and moved to Nashville,
Tennessee, where he built his estate, The Hermitage. In a long and
illustrious political career, Jackson served as the state's first representative in Congress, was elected to the Senate, but resigned to
become a judge on the Tennessee Supreme Court. Also a major general in
the state militia, Jackson was a noted Indian fighter. He was commissioned Major General in the U.S. Army, and at the Battle of New
Orleans (1815) decisively defeated the British during the War of 1812.
Although the treaty had already been signed, his exploits earned him
national acclaim as the "Hero of New Orleans." Jackson became the
Democratic Presidential candidate in 1824, and although he won the
popular vote, the electoral majority was lost to John Q. Adams. Four
years later "Old Hickory" was swept into the White House by a decisive
electoral vote. During a stormy two terms as President, Jackson virtually revolutionized that office, making it a strong and independent
branch of the government.

45   The term "Jim Crow" originated in the ante-bellum minstrel show, but
came to be applied to laws passed by southern states during the late
nineteenth century which created a racial caste system. This system of
racial segregation remained intact until the civil rights movement swept
the American South between 1955 and 1965.
         "Judge Lynch" refers to the extra-legal execution of an alleged
criminal by a mob, which in effect becomes the "judge and jury." The
word itself is believed to have originated with a Virginian named Lynch
who led a small band of vigilantes during the Revolutionary Era which
meted out punishment to loyalists and outlaws. In the South, lynching
became a form of social control over blacks who lived under the threat
of "Judge Lynch" for breaking racial taboos. From 1882 to 1936 there
were 4,672 persons lynched in the United States, 3,383 of whom were
black.

46   James R. Sovereign of Iowa was a newspaper editor who supplanted
Terence V. Powderly as Grand Master Workman of the Knights of Labor in
1894.

47   The Populist Party first met in national convention at Omaha, Neb-
raska, in 1892 to find a remedy for the economic ills of debt-ridden
farmers in the South and West. The platform was drawn up by the veteran
reformer, Ignatius Donnelly, and called for a flexible currency system,
a graduated income tax, postal savings banks, public ownership of the
railroads, an eight-hour work day, the direct election of senators, the
secret ballot, and the unlimited coinage of silver to expand the money
supply. The party's Presidential candidate, James B. Weaver, polled
over one million votes. In 1896, William Jennings Bryan, the Democratic
candidate, succeeded in gaining the support of the Populists, but failed
to win the election. When the two major parties incorporated the Populist Party's platform in the late 1890s, it ceased to exist.

48   Historians know very little about R. M. Humphrey, who became the General Superintendent of the Colored Alliance. An obscure itinerant white minister from Lovelady, Texas, Humphrey was virtually unknown before assuming this post, and with the demise of the Colored Alliance, he sank back into obscurity. Humphrey was described as "an Elderly man . . . with plain speech and a free blunt manner," who reportedly was popular among Negroes because of his many years of Baptist missionary work among them, and for his fair dealings with blacks who worked on his plantation. His selection probably was tempered by the fact that, as a white spokesman, he could openly express a militance that would be denied to blacks. To Humphrey goes much of the credit for spreading the organization among southern blacks.

49   For an explanatory discussion of the Grangers, see Vol. II, note 66.

50   The *Caucasion* was a white racist newspaper published in Shreveport, Louisiana.

51   The Federal Elections bill, which had been recommended by President Benjamin Harrison (see Vol. III, note 63) in his annual message of 1889, came to the floor of Congress in 1890. The bill was designed to give more protection to blacks in the exercise of their right to vote. In his message, Harrison noted that the bill had encountered heavy resistance from the southern bloc, which intended to eliminate the black vote in the South. To the end of his term, Harrison pushed for passage of the Elections bill, but was unable to gain its passage because southern congressmen were solidly against it. Southern politicians who were busy installing segregation were uninterested in protecting the black franchise.

52   The main ideas behind the sub-treasury plan are most succinctly stated in the so-called Ocala Demands of December 1890, adopted by the Southern Alliance: "We demand that the government shall establish sub-treasuries or depositories in the several states, which shall loan money direct to the people at a low rate of interest, not to exceed two percent per annum, on non-perishable farm products, and also upon real estate, with proper limitations upon the quantity of land and amount of money." From the *Proceedings of the Supreme Council of the National Farmers' Alliance and Industrial Union* (1890), p. 32.

53   In this context, the "single tax party," and the advisability of Southern Alliancemen to support it, refers to the followers of Henry George (see Vol. III, note 16).

54   John James Ingalls (1833-1900), was born in Middleton, Massachusetts. Ingalls graduated from Williams College, read law for two years, and was admitted to the bar in 1857. The following year Ingalls moved to Kansas, and settled in Atchison where he entered political life. During the Civil War Ingalls served as a judge advocate in Kansas, and as Editor of the Atchison *Freedom's Champion*. Beginning in 1872 Ingalls served three terms in the Senate and, after losing his bid for reelection in 1890, devoted his time to lecturing and writing magazine articles.

55   J. H. Turner was National Secretary of the National Farmers' Alliance and Industrial Union. As a leader in the agrarian reform movement, he founded the *Record Review*, one of several newspapers which interpreted the movement from a socialist perspective, a view emphatically rejected by pragmatic populist politicians. Also, Turner was a leading proponent of single-plank populism, which advocated the free coinage of silver as

a cure-all for the farmers' ills. Populist politicians charged that Turner intended to move the agrarians into the Democratic Party, a charge that rings of truth, since Turner immediately announced his support for William Jennings Bryan in 1892 and intimated that the People's Party now had no reason to exist. Critics charged that he sold out to the Democrats for patronage.

56   Henry Woodfin Grady (1850-1889), was a graduate of the University of Georgia. As the Editor of the *Atlanta Constitution* from 1879 to 1889, he became a major spokesman for the "New South," which accepted the doctrines of northern capitalism and made a strong case for the industrialization of the South. The machine would save the poverty-stricken region, if only northern financiers would invest their capital in the South and leave the racial problems to southerners.

57   Robert Toombs (1810-1885) graduated from Union College in 1828, and returned to his home in Georgia to practice law. As a member of the planter class, he found quick entry to political life, serving in the U.S. House of Representatives from 1845 to 1853, and then in the Senate from 1853 to 1861. Although he stood firmly for the Union, he resigned from his Senate seat in 1861 when Lincoln was elected, and helped to organize the Georgia secessionists. During the Civil War he commanded a brigade, and after the fighting, played an instrumental role in the struggle to overthrow Radical Reconstruction.

58   The convict lease system was used primarily in the southern states during the late nineteenth century. Under this system, prison convicts were leased to a contractor for a specified sum and for a fixed period of time. Normally, the leasees lodged, clothed, fed, controlled, and disciplined the convicts which they leased. The system was frought with abuse, with blacks vastly overrepresented in the prison populations. Negroes were arrested for trivial reasons, or for no reason at all, and sentenced to work out their fines. The contract usually gave the leasing company cheap labor, while the state eliminated the expense of prison maintenance. Convicts worked at a wide variety of jobs. For example, in Georgia they supplied cheap labor for the construction of railroads, while in Alabama and Tennessee thousands of black convicts labored in the coal mines. The barbarity associated with the system caused periodic public outcries, until, by 1910, most states had outlawed the leasing of prisoners to private entrepreneurs.

59   "Washington and Lincoln" is an obvious reference to Presidents George Washington (1732-1799), and Abraham Lincoln (1809-1865).

60   Benjamin Ryan Tillman (1847-1918), a farmer-politician, became a "radical" leader of the poor upcountry South Carolinians who won the governorship from 1890-1894. Although Tillman's rhetoric usually was couched in terms of class warfare, he distinctively excluded Negroes from the struggle. As Governor he initiated progressive reforms, but his ideas about racial supremacy, the stock-in-trade of southern demagogues, helped install *de jure* segregation in South Carolina. His anti-Negro attacks were so crude that "Pitchfork Ben" made most sensitive people wince.
Andrew Johnson (1808-1875) succeeded Abraham Lincoln when the latter was assassinated in 1865. Johnson's opinions regarding Reconstruction collided with those held by the Radicals, and led to Johnson's impeachment in 1868. Critics charged that he catered "to the rankest bourbon ideas." meaning that he was conservative on racial issues, and refused to grant equal civil rights to blacks. He therefore vetoed most Radical legislation that came before him.

61   Grover Stephen Cleveland (1837-1908) was born in New Jersey, the son
of a Presbyterian minister. When his father died, Cleveland apprenticed
himself to a law office, and was admitted to the bar in 1859. He entered
Democratic politics in Buffalo, New York, where he had moved, and was
elected Mayor. As a reformer, Cleveland attracted sufficient acclaim to
win him the governorship of New York in 1882, where he furthered his
reputation by opposing the corrupt Tammany machine. Running as a "good
government" candidate, Cleveland defeated James G. Blaine for the Presidency in 1884. He lost his bid for reelection in 1888, but won the office again in 1892. As President he supported civil service reform, opposed the spoils system, and favored lower tariffs. His effort to preserve the gold standard alienated the more radical elements in the
Democratic Party, and the rift became irreparable when Cleveland used
federal troops in the Pullman Strike of 1894.
        Chester Alan Arthur (1830-1886) graduated from Union College in 1848
and practiced law in New York City. An ardent Republican, President
U. S. Grant rewarded his loyalty with an appointment as Collector of
Customs for the port of New York. The customs house had always been
scandalously corrupt, but Arthur transformed it into such a machine
that President Rutherford Hayes removed him from office in 1878. Arthur
was a close ally of Senator Roscoe Conklin of New York, a leader of
the "Stalwart" wing of the party. So, when James Garfield was nominated
as the Republican standard-bearer in 1880, the convention nominated Arthur
as the vice presidential candidate to appease the Conklin group. Garfield
won the election, but when he was assassinated in 1881, Arthur moved
into the White House. To everybody's surprise, Arthur demonstrated a
capacity for reform, and opposed the more obnoxious abuses of the spoils
system. He lost his bid for renomination, however, whereupon Arthur
returned to New York City and died a few years later.
        Frederick "Douglas" is a misspelling of Douglass. See Vol. I, note
8.

62   "Trotter" is a reference to James Monroe Trotter (1844-1912), a prominent nineteenth-century Negro. Trotter was born in Mississippi, but grew
up in Ohio where he received a modest education. During the Civil War,
he served as a lieutenant in the Fifty-fourth Massachusetts, a black
regiment. Active in Boston politics, he was appointed Assistant Superintendent in the city post office, but resigned the position because of
racial discrimation. Trotter was then nominated for Recorder of Deeds
in Washington, D.C., a traditionally Negro appointment. Approval was
delayed by political opponents, but finally the Senate approved Trotter's
appointment on March 4, 1887, to succeed Frederick Douglass. His son,
William Monroe Trotter (1872-1934), became a well-known black activist
during the late nineteenth and early twentieth centuries.

63   Benjamin Harrison (1833-1901) of Ohio was the grandson of President
William Henry Harrison, ninth President of the United States. Benjamin
graduated from Miami University (Oxford) in 1852, and practiced law in
Indianapolis, where he became a well-established corporation lawyer. He
served in the U.S. Senate from 1881 to 1887, and in 1888 was chosen by
the Republicans to run for the Presidency against Grover Cleveland. Even
though Cleveland won a plurality, Harrison won the electoral vote. Personally honest, he was, nevertheless, unable to check the spoilsmen of
his own party. Harrison lost the reelection race to Cleveland in 1892,
and returned to his Indianapolis law practice.
        "Ex-Senator Bruce (colored)" was a reference to Blanch K. Bruce (see
Vol. III, note 19).

64   Frederick Douglass (see Vol. I, note 8) escaped from slavery in 1838
by successfully posing as a free sailor travelling from Baltimore to
New York. His intended wife, Anna Murray, a free black woman, followed
him to New York where they were married and subsequently had several
children. Years after the death of his first wife, Douglass shocked more

timid souls by marrying Helen Pitts, a white woman. According to Douglass, it was a sin for which "I was to be ostracized by white and black
alike." The daughter referred to in this passage was probably Rosetta,
whom Douglass employed in his office while he was Marshal and Recorder
of Deeds in Washington, D.C. Her husband, Nathan Sprague, disgraced
the family, and Rosetta frequently found herself and six children in
dire financial straits. Douglass gave Rosetta a position in his office
to provide her with a means of support.

65   James Zachariah George (1826-1897) was a U.S. Senator from Mississippi. Born in Georgia, he moved with his family to Mississippi when
still a boy, and attended school there. He served with the Mississippi
Rifles under Col. Jefferson Davis during the Mexican War. Afterward he
studied law, was admitted to the bar in 1847, and practiced in Carrollton. As a member of the Mississippi secessionist convention, George
voted for withdrawing from the Union. During the Civil War he rose to
brigadier general, and thereafter, became Chairman of the Democratic
State Executive Committee. Appointed judge on the state Supreme Court
in 1879, and then Chief Justice, finally he was elected to the U.S.
Senate for three consecutive terms between 1880 and 1897.

66   John Percival Jones (1829-1912), U.S. Senator from Nevada, was born
in England, and emigrated to America with his parents while still an
infant. From his home in Cleveland, Ohio, he and several other young
men sailed a vessel around Cape Horn and up to San Francisco to search
for gold. In Trinity County, California, he served as sheriff, state
legislator, and later lost a bid for the lieutenant-governorship. In
1867 he moved to Nevada and became part owner in the silver mine which
earned him a fortune. He was elected to the U.S. Senate in 1873 on the
Republican ticket and retained that seat for the next thirty years. As
might be expected, he was a champion of free silver.

67   James McMillan (1838-1902), a Canadian, came to Detroit in 1855 where
he became a contractor for the Detroit and Milwaukee Railroad, and the
manager of the Michigan Car Company, which built freight cars. Along
with John S. Newberry, he organized Newberry & McMillan, a highly successful railroad and ship-building enterprise. As Chairman of the
Republican State Committee, he reorganized the party in 1886 and thereby
insured himself of a political power base in the state. In 1889 he was
elected to the U.S. Senate where he served until his death in 1902.

68   Henry William Blair (1834-1920) was born in New Hampshire. After an
irregular elementary education, he read law and was admitted to the bar
in 1859. During the Civil War he rose to Lieutenant-Colonel in the New
Hampshire Volunteers, but a critical wound forced his discharge. Between
1875 and 1891 Blair served in the U.S. House and then the Senate. Upon
retirement he resumed his legal practice in Washington, D.C. A man of
strong humanitarian feelings, and firm religious convictions, he opposed
Chinese immigration, the sale of liquor, worked tirelessly for the
improvement of public education, supported woman suffrage, and had a
deep concern for the welfare of industrial laborers.

69   Leonidas Lafayette Polk (1837-1892) was born in North Carolina. Orphaned at fourteen, he became a farmer as his father had been. In 1860,
and again between 1865 and 1865, he served as a member of the state
legislature. After the Civil War Polk sat in the first state constitutional convention. A long-time advocate for the establishment of a
state Department of Agriculture, he was appointed its first commissioner
when that agency was founded in 1877. For a few years he also edited the
Raleigh News, and later began publishing the *Progressive Farmer* to teach
better agricultural methods and to promote the organization of political

clubs among farmers. Polk allied himself with the new Southern Alliance, and his paper became one of its official organs. In 1887 he became national Vice President of the Alliance, and two years later its President. Polk planned to attend the Omaha convention in July 1892, to nominate a Presidential candidate for the People's Party, but death suddenly terminated his career.

C. W. Macune was born in 1851 in Kenosha, Wisconsin. As a young man he drifted throughout the West, but finally settled in Texas. A highly versatile man of quick intelligence, he read law, practiced medicine, and was so well-informed on agricultural issues that in 1886 he was elected Chairman of the executive committee of the Texas State Alliance. Once he assumed the presidency of that organization, Macune did more than anyone to spread the Alliance across the South. In 1889 he became Editor of the *National Economist,* the major organ of the Southern Alliance. Macune was a gifted platform speaker, and never wanted for an idea to solve any problem. He founded a cooperative store for members, and was originator of plans for a farmers' cooperative insurance plan, and the sub-treasury plan (see Vol. III, note 52). When the Populists failed to gain the Presidency in 1892, Macune advocated a return to a non-partisan reform strategy. But his influence was now greatly curtailed. Charges that he and Benjamin Tillman (see Vol. III, note 60) had circulated a pamphlet denouncing James Weaver, the Populist Presidential candidate in 1892, undermined his effectiveness in the movement. Other embarrassing questions arose concerning the possibility of corruption which prompted his resignation. Thereafter Macune disappeared from public view.

William Alfred Peffer (1831-1912) was born and attended school in Cumberland County, Pennsylvania, and began teaching at fifteen. After serving in the Union Army during the Civil War, he settled in Kansas to practice law. Peffer also published three newspapers: the *Wilson County Courier,* the *Coffeyville Journal,* and the Populist *Kansas Farmer.* After a term in the Kansas State Senate, Peffer was elected in 1891 to the U.S. Senate as a Populist, but failed to be reelected. In 1898 he made an unsuccessful bid for the governorship.

70   Although "Culinary" is the preferred spelling, the sources consistently used "Cullinary."

Adams, Capt. C. H., 199, 200, 203, 206
Adams, Enoch, 148
Adams, John H., 265
Adams, Samuel B., 384
Adams, William, 231
Advocate, The Methodist, 409
Africa, 31, 281
A.M.E. Zion Church, 274
African Methodist Episcopal Church, 11
Africans, 413
African Union, 337
Afro-American Leagues, 143
Agnew, Thomas, 212-14
Agrarianism, 47
Akron, Ohio
Alabama Mirror, The, 296
Albert, A.E.P., 227-29
Allegheny, the steamship, 368, 370, 371, 378, 384, 389
Allen, George, 347
Allen, R. H., 205
Allison, D. B., 254
Amalgamated Association, 276
Amalgamated Association of Iron and Steel-Workers, 120
American Steam Fire Company, 221
Amsterdam, N.Y., 120
Anderson, Agent [of Ocean Steamship Co.], 370
Anderson, Alf E., 178
Anderson, Dolph, 179
Anderson, Wash, 178-79
Anglo-Saxon race, 27
Antoine, Augustave, 156, 232
Antoine, Lucien, 59
Antz, Master Mechanic, 403
Appeal-Avalanche, 349,358
Appomattox, surrender at, 249
Archery Club, 395
Armistead, William, 287
Armstrong, Mr. State Super-intendent, 15, 17, 18
Arthur, Chester A., 235, 318, 425
Arthur, Peter M., 48, 415
Atlanta University, 31
Attakapas Rangers, the 159, 164, 165, 167, 175-6, 179, 221
Auberry, Tom, 100
Aubert, L. C., 157
August, Charles, 156
Augusta, the City of, 400
Augusta, Ga., 25, 31, 123
Augustin, Judge, 65
Austin, Jr., E., 307, 309, 310
Austin, Osborn, 97
Austin, Texas, 73
Avery, Capt. Dudley, 162, 165, 166, 174, 176, 180, 182

Bailey, J. H., 152, 156
Bailey, J. T., 115
Bailey, W. H., 278

Ballard, John, 156
Baltimore, 45, 73
Baltimore Steamship Company, 370, 378, 389, 394
Banks, Christian, 192
Bannan, J. M., 260
Baptist Church, 8
Barnett, J. W., 164
Barrett, J. H., 121
Barrett, Wm. H., 129, 132
Barrett, W. J., 212
Bate, Senator, 329
Baton Rouge Fencibles, the, 169
Battle, Powell, 263
Beanham, Capt. W. H., 155, 161, 164, 165, 180
Beary, Thomas, 190
Beattie, Judge Taylor, 153, 155, 161, 165, 190-1, 197, 199, 202, 203, 204-5, 207
Beauregard, Gen., 164, 173
Bechel, E. L., 56
Bechel, M. A., 56
Bechel, P. A., 56
Beggs, James, 213
Belton, J. A., 256
Benedict, W. S., 163
Bennings, C. P., 158
Berger, Peter, 195
Bergman, Stevedore Frank, 399
Berwick, O. D., 154, 158
Bethencourt, Felice, 59
Bickerstaff, Andrew, 358
Bier, Henry, 213
Bing, Joseph, 158
Birmingham, the ship, 389, 393, 400
Birmingham, Ala., 11, 14, 17, 20, 23
Birr, Theodore, 407
Black and White [by T. T. Fortune], 93, 138
Black Belt, 301

Black, Charles S., 163
Black, D. H., 114
Black Diamond Steel Works, 276
"Black Maria," the, 69
Black workers: apprentices, 37; bartenders, 405-10; blacksmiths, 35; bricklayers, 23-24, 35-36, 43, 45, 50; carpenters, 20, 45, 50, 144; cigar makers, 35; in coal mines, 67, 70-72; contractors, 24; cotton pickers and choppers, 287-364 passim; in cotton yards, 66, 68; in domestic service, 10, 50; draymen, 68, 378-79; engineers, 143; farm laborers, 25, 29, 56, 65, 91, 145, 187; farmers, 6-7, 25, 29-30, 50-56; freight handlers, 77; hod carriers, 40-43; hoe hands, 144; iron heaters, 71; iron puddlers, 71, iron rollers, 71; laborers, 23-24, 29,

35, 43, 45, 67, 79, 89, 91-93,
137; longshoremen, 9, 68, 77,
84; mechanics, 35-36, 43, 45;
ministers, 9, 11; molders, 35;
newspaper editors 18; overseers,
144; in packing houses, 66;
plasterers, 35, 43; politicians,
12; railroad section hands, 85;
in saw mills, 24, 65; screwmen,
77; sleeping-car porters, 3;
sugar refinery hands, 144;
teachers, 5, 9, 15; teamsters,
66, 68; in tobacco factories,
10; tradesmen, 13, 37; warehousemen, 378-79; waiters, 405-
10; washerwomen, 251; wharf
workers, 367-405; conditions of
in the South, 2-33; should they
join ranks of labor, 34-50; unrest, 52-102; organize Knights
of Labor (K. of L.) lodges, 45,
71-76; and K. of L. strikes,
77-102; and K. of L. convention
of 1886, 104-34; and suppression,
136-42; and the 1887 Sugar strike,
143-240; and Terence V. Powderly,
240-70; and race relations within
the K. of L., 272-84; and deportation to Africa, 281-83; and the
National Alliance and Coopera-
tive Union, 286-363; and Savan-
nah Wharf Workers; Strike, 366-
404; and the Chicago Cullinary
Alliance, 405-10.
Blair, Henry W., 426
Blair, Senator, 326-29
Blenk, H. H., 209
Bodenhamer, J. A., 263
Bodin, Eugene, 158
Bond, Frank, 350
Bonham, Adjt. Gen., 141
Bosworth, Millard, 167, 170
Bostonians, the, 140
Boswell, T. J., 209
Bourbons, 113, 256
Boyd, Felix, 204
Boylan, T. N., 69
Bradstreets', 416
Breen, John, 214
Brooks, Mat, 203, 205
Brotherhood of Locomotive Engineers,
48, 415
Broughton, J. M., 251, 257
Brower, M. E., 212-13
Brown, Duncan, 358
Brown, Brother H. C., 405
Brown, Deputy Sheriff Duncan, 363
Brown, Henry, 219
Brown, Isaac, 397, 400
Brown, Jere A., 37
Brown, Jim, 144
Brown, J. L. 212
Brown, John, 128, 418
Brown, Dr. S. P., 209
Brown, Valeour, 59

Bruce, Blanch K., 71, 317, 416
Bryan, R. S., 407, 409-10
Bryan, William Jennings Bryan, 422
Bubbins, Dr. J. B. 281, 410
Bureau of Colored Knights, 127
Bureau of Engraving and Printing,
266-70
Burguires, J. M., 154, 158
Burns, George J., 214
Byram, E. E., 409

Cabell, R. B., 407-9
Cable, George Washington, 42, 281,
407, 415
Cade, Capt. C. F., 159, 164-65, 169,
176, 178-79, 180-81, 220
Caffery, Senator Donelson, 154, 158,
175, 177, 179, 180-81, 418
Cahill, Sam, 220
Caire, J. B., 56
Calder, D. R., 158
Calhoun and McDuffy doctrine, 279
Calhoun, John C., 421
Calhoun, Pat, 383
Cambias, Robert J., 214
Cambridge, Nathan, 156
Campbell, James, 213
Cann, Alderman, W. G., 376
Capren, J. D., 158
Carolan, Agent, J. J., 371, 377,
384, 397
Carpenters' and Joiners' Union, 35
Carpet-baggers, 248
Carr, Elias, 294, 305
Carter, J. W., 336-38
Catholic Church, 11
Catholic Irish, 280
Caucasian, The, 293, 423
Caucasian unions, 337
Cavanaugh, Hugh, 266-67, 269
Central Railroad, the, 367-405 passim
Chaffe, John, 158
Chandler, Senator William E., 217,
234, 419
Chappell, John T., 121
Charles Sumner Waiters' Union, 407,
409-410
Charpentier, J. M., 182
Chattahoochee, the ship, 370, 383-84,
389
Chesapeake and Ohio Railroad, 3
Chicago anarchist riot, 274
Chicago Colored Women's Club, 282
Chicago Waiters' Assembly, 407
Chicago Waiter's Union No. 1, 407,
409
"Chinaman", 26
Chinese, 38, 107, 414, 418
Christopher, C. C., 392
Chrisman, Dr. F. M., 94
Christopher, M. J., 400
Churchill, Gov. [ark.], 100
"City of Brotherly Love," 282
City of Macon, the ship, 370, 377,
383-84, 389, 393
Civil Rights Act of 1875, 413

Civil rights bill, the, 16, 19
Clairborn, Rev. C. H., 226
Clairville, Joseph A., 152, 156
Clarke, L. S., 154, 158
Claxton, Jesse, 20-21
Cleveland, Grover S., 219, 235, 247, 317-18, 425
Cleveland, Ohio, 35-36
Clinton Caucasian, The, 340
Coachmen's Union, 40
Cocke, Robert R., 158
Coffey, G. W., 287
Coker, Dr. J. H., 226, 228, 237
Coleman, A. J., 400
Coleman, Frank, 156
Coleman, John, 347
Collier, Joe, 397
Collins, Adam, 380
Colored Alliance of North Carolina, 294
Colored Craftsmen's Protective Union, 44
Colored Farmers' Alliance and Cotton Pickers' League, 337-38, 342-43
Colored Farmers' State Alliance of Tennessee, 295
Colored Female Assembly, Savannah, Ga., 257
Columbus, [Christopher], 27
Columbus Waiters and Bartenders' Association, 407
Colvin, Evan, 58
Comanches, 228
Comer, H. M., 375, 386, 387, 392, 399
Communism, 41, 47
Confederacy, 302
Confederate Congress, 413
Confederates, 247, 249, 250
Conners, J. H., 212
Connolly, Mr., 249
Connolly, Samuel, 397
Constitution, The Atlanta, 336
Constitution of the U.S., 227, 238
Convict lease system, 424
Convicts, treatment of, 290-91, 311-12
Conway, G. E., 121
Cooper, William, 178
Co-operative Soap Company, 75
Co-operative Workers of America, 141
Cotton Press Association, 375, 385
Cotton Yard Men's Benevolent Association of New Orleans, 212, 214
Councill, William H., 45-50
"Cox brothers," 209
Cox, Geo., 156
Cox, Henry, 157
Crane, H. A., 386
Crawley, N. C., 287
Cressey, J. M., 213
Crutcher, William, 374
Cunio, Thomas G., 197

Curley, Thomas, 252
Curtis, Mary, 419
Czolgosz, Leon F., 420

Daily American, the Baltimore, 44
Daily Picayune, the New Orleans, 145-46, 148
Dale, Dixon & Company, 402
Dallas Constitution, The, 333
Danville, Va., 3, 8, 9
Darly, Rev. Thomas, 274
Davidson, Hon. P. H., 274
Davis, Charlie, 390
Davis, James H., 58-59
Davis, Jefferson, 250, 317, 419
Davis, Miss Winnie, 317
Dayton, Robert D., 244
de Cair, Major A. J., 180
De Clay, Colonel, D. E., 121
Decuir, Major H. J., 158, 167, 170
Delaney, John, 212
Delhaye, Hubert, 158
Delhommer, Hon. Charles, 216
Delta Rifles, the, 169
Demas, Senator Henry, 54, 56, 63-65, 227
Democratic party, 22, 70, 105, 217-18, 224-25, 227, 233-37, 239, 247, 295-96, 299, 302, 318-19, 339, 345-46
Dennis, John Lucus, 276
Derbin, John, 265
Derrick, Sheriff W. B., 352-54, 356-57, 361-62
Deviesin, Auguste, 59
De Voto, Charles, 121
Dickinson, J. W., 216
Dickson, Phillip T., 156
Dismond, S. H., 121
District Assembly 102, 186-87
District 49 of New York, 105, 107-10, 112, 122-23, 128-31, 133
Donnelly, Ignatius, 422
Doswell, A. J., 307
Douglas, F. C., 154
Douglas, James, 213
Douglass, Frederick, 35, 71, 317-18, 414, 416, 425

Draymen's Labor Union Association, 378
Drew, Daniel, 415
Drury, Victor, 128, 418
Dubroca, Col. E. M., 147, 158, 167, 180-81
Duke M. E. Church, 275
Dunning, N. A., 405
Durand's Hotel, 166
Durant Commercial Co., 348
Dwyer, Mounted Officer, 390

East Atchison, Mo., 66
Economist, The, 295, 319
Edward, Gabriel, 152, 156
Edwards, James H., 108, 112

Edwards, Capt. J. W., 227
Egypt, 48
Election Bill, 296
Ellis, H. G., 255
Emile, Naquin, 161
England, 281
Equal Rights League of Columbus,
  Ohio, 125
"Equal rights to all, and special
  privileges to none," 302
Erie Railroad, 415
Escambia Rifles, 274
Estein, John, 407
Ethiopia, 27
Eustis, Senator, 234
Evans, Walker, 97
Evening Post, the New York, 93
Everglades, the, 182, 302
Exodus, the, 12, 413

Fabre, Archbishop, 119
Factors' and Employers' Union, 68
Fairfax, Jacob, 287
Fallon, L. J., 194
Farley, J. C., 128
Farmers and Laborers' Alliance, 289
Farmers' Alliance of Kansas, 299
Farmers' Mutual Benefit Association,
  289, 304
Federal Bureau of Labor Statistics,
  415
Ferrell, Frank, J. 104-34 passim,
  227, 418
Ferret, E., 56
Ferris, William L., 180
Fielding, N. R., 23-25
Fields, Daney, 355
Fields, W. W., 108
Fisher, Abe, 287
Fisk, James, 415
Fitzgerald, James, 213
Flannery, Capt. John R., 375, 387
Fleetwood, Dr. J. H., 76
Fleming, General Superintendent,
  371, 376, 384, 386, 389, 390, 397-
  98, 402, 404
Foner, Philip S., 413, 418
Foote, J. R. H., 146, 152, 160
Ford's Hotel, 116, 127
Foret, Nicholas, 161
Foret, Richard, 172, 174, 177
Fortune, T. Thomas, 294, 414
Fort Worth Gazette, the, 319
Foster, Hon. Charles, 266, 269-70,
  420
Foster, Murphy J., 158
Foster, Thomas J., 154, 158
Fowler, A. S., 95
"Fox brothers," 96-99
Fox, S. Andrew, 58-59, 61, 63
Frank, J. F., 148-54, 356, 361-63
Franklin, Henry, 156
Freedman's Bank, 15, 308, 413
Freedman's Bureau, 12
Freeman, The, 406, 408-9, 414

Freetown Riot, 220-21, 230, 236,
  238
Frere, A. G., 154
Frere, Sheriff, 180-82
Frost's Hotel, 157
Fulton, E. A., 94

Gallagher, Edward, 254
Galveston, Texas, 77-84
Galveston Typographical Union
  No. 28, 80
Gantt, M. A. B., 74
Gardemal, Sheriff, 218
Garnet, J. H., 115
Garrard, Col. William, 367
Gates, H. P., 159, 162, 164
Gaudet, Edward, 227
Gay, E. J., 156, 159, 164, 183-84
Gay, G. B., 181
Gay, S. R., 158
Gayaree, Hon. Charles, 213
Gazette, The, 101
Geddes, Hon. George D., 226, 228
Geddes Hall, 226-31, 237-38
George, Henry, 76, 142-43, 414
George, Senator James Z., 320-29,
  426
German Waiters and Bartenders
  Benefit Association, 407, 410
Gheens, John R., 180
Gibbs, M. W., 115
Gibson, Deputy Sheriff, N. M.,
  356-57
Gibson, Senator, 234
Gill, Hugh, 96-97, 100
Gill, Judge, R. D., 174
Gilligan, James J., 407
Globe-Democrat, the, 185
Glynn, Brig. Gen. John, 53, 173
Godchaux, Leon, 165, 183
Going, J. G., 21-23
Goins, A. B., 307
Golden, P. H., 77, 80-81, 84
Good Hope Baptist Church, 287
Gorman, John J., 191, 195, 199-200,
  204-5
Gould, Jay, 46, 325, 415, 417
Gould, Robert W. B., 209, 226, 231
"Gould system," 90
Grady, Henry Woodfin, 209, 302-3,
  424
Graham, P. A., 213
Grand Opera House, 212
Grangers, Northern, 291-92
Gray, Robert, 36
Gray, W. F., 195
Green, Eugene, 235
Green, General Manager, 383, 403-4
Green, H. C., 307
Green, Jeff, 209
Green, John P., 37, 414
Green, Chief of Police [Savannah],
  368-69, 371
Green, W. Paul, 227-28, 237
Grient, Ernest, 223

Grissmore, Major S. F., 190
Guano Association, 273
Guion, Lewis, 191, 196, 198
Gulf, Colorado and Santa Fe Rail-
  way Company, 78, 84

Hackney, J. H., 355
Hall, A. D., 115
Hall, Covington, 419
Halloway, Mr., 61-62
Hamilcar, 32
Hamilton, Ontario, 73
"Hamitic race," 27, 413
"Hamlet," 107
Hammond, William J., 212
Hannibal, 32
Harmon, Alderman R. F., 371
Harris, Rev. Alexander, 382
Harris, B. F., 154
Harris, Charles, 357-58, 362
Harris, J. L., 169
Harris, T. J., 53
Harrison, Benjamin, 219, 423, 425
Harrison, [William Henry], 317
Harriss, Albert, 219
Harris's Hall, 128
Hart, J. B., 407, 410
Hawkins, Ramie, 226
Hawley, Hon. R. M., 301
Hayes, Rutherford, B., 421
Hebrews, 279
Henderson, Jr., John, 158
Henry, John, 410
"Henry Georgeism," 47, 415
Herodtus, 27
Hickory, N. C., 141
Hilbert, Thomas H., 212
Hill, Henry, 97, 100
Hines, Y. E., 307
Hirst, James, 114
Hod Carriers' Union, 40
Hodges, Jessie, 353-54
Hoffman, Henry, 205
Holland, Bro. J. J., 263, 265
Hollier, Decliere, 218
Hollier, Detour, 218
Hollier, Vilmont, 218
"Home Club," 105, 117, 118, 122, 124,
  126, 128, 131, 133
Hooper, George H., 213
Hoover, Hiram F., 141, 143, 418
Horn, Fendel, 212
Hotel Waiters' Union, 40
Hottentots, 230
Houlgrave, Henry, 213
House of Representatives, 126
Howell, J. M., 191
Hudkins, Harry, 372
Hudson, Rev. J. W., 226
Hukless, R. S., 307
Humboldt, 27
Humphrey, R. M., 287, 297, 305-6,
  319-33, 336-45 passim, 423
Hureau, John F., 214

Iberia Guards, the, 162, 165, 174,
  175-6, 178, 182, 221
"Iberia riot," 220-21
Industrial Liberator, the, 74
Ingalls, Senator John J., 234, 299,
  423
Ingram, Jesse, 156
Ingram, Lenzy, 156
Inman, President John H., 383
International, the First, 418
International Typographical Union,
  215-16
International Workers of the World,
  419
Ireland, 281
Ireland, Gov. [Texas], 82
"Irishman," 26, 30
Irishmen, 282
Irons, Martin, 87, 417
"Israelites in Egypt," 27
Italians, 282

Jackson, Andrew, 280, 422
Jackson, Thomas Jonathan
  ("Stonewall"), 250, 420
Jackson, Gen. N. P., 413
Jacksonville, Fla., 65
James Lee, the steamer, 353, 357,
  359, 369, 362, 363, 364
Jarrett, John, 421
Jefferson school, the, 410
Jefferson, Squire, 178
Jenkins, W. D., 380
Jews, black, 27
"Jim Crow," 281
Johnson, Andrew, 314, 424
Johnson, Bradish, 54, 56, 58, 59
Johnson, Frank, 258
Johnson, Mit, 356
Johnson, W. W., 158
Jones, Early, 356, 361
Jones, John P., 426
Jones, "Uncle" George, 147
Jones, M. F., 306-7, 309
Jones, Mit, 354-55,
Jones, R. E., 121
Jones, Senator, 324, 326, 328-29

Kansas City, the ship, 370
Kansas Farmer, The, 427
Karow, Edward, 375
Kemp, A. J., 209
Kemper, W. P., 158
Kennedy, James D., 227, 231
Kennedy, Rev. P. H., 265
Kevlin, August, 215
Kewley, Joe B., 244
Keystone State, 250
Kilpatrick, Gen., 247
Kinckle, John H., 292, 397-99
King, Brother Charles C., 255
Kinkaid, Deputy Sheriff, 96-97
Kinney, J. T., 307

Knights of Labor: black workers, organize K. of L. lodges, 45, 71-76; and K. of L. strikes, 77-102; and K. of L. convention of 1886, 104-34; and suppression, 136-42; and the 1887 Sugar Strike, 143-20; and Terence V. Powderly, 240-70; and race relations within the K. of L, 272-84; and deportation to Africa, 281-83.
Knights of St. Crispin, 416
Knobloch, Lt. Gov. Clay [La.], 190, 199, 204-5
Knobloch Guards, the, 155, 168, 199, 206
Knoxville Tennessee Ironworks, 71
Kokee, Samuel, 235
Kramer, Rev. C. C., 221
Kremm, Thomas W., 418
Kruse, R. W., 255, 256

Labor Bureau, 68
Labor Men's Worlds Fair Committee, 410
Laborers' Union and Protective Association, the, 367-405 passim
Lacassagne, Paul, 169
Lagarde, Major, 190
La Grange, Ga., 9
Lambs, Thomas M., 407
Landaiche, L., 56
Landry, Adlard, 201
Landry, Odessa, 165
Langhenry, William, 407
Larkin, John, 100
Larouge, A. E., 212
Law and Order League, 110
Lawless, Phil, 205
Lawrence, William, 394, 400
Lazard, Major C., 156
Leche, Judge G., 55,64
Lee, Bill, 59, 63
Lee County, Arkansas, riots, 348-64
Lee, Governor Fitzhugh [Va.], 106, 110, 113, 121, 418
Lee, Green, 287
Lee, "Light Horse Harry," 419
Lee, Gen. Robert E., 250, 418-19
Lester, David, 213
Lewis, B. A., 407,409
Lewis, Col. James, 226
Lewis, Sidney F., 194
Libby Prison, 113
Liberia, 31
Lincoln, Abraham, 224, 300, 302
Litcheman, Charles H., 74, 169, 416
Little Rock, Ark., 91, 98-101
Livingston, Colonel, 333
Livingston, Jr., Ransom, 235
Lloyd, Charlie, 358
L. & N. R. R., 273
Locket, Miss S. A. E., 229
Longshoremen's Association, the 209
Louisiana Farmers' Alliance, 295

Louisianian, the, 67
Louisiana Rifles, 194-95, 197, 199-200, 203-6
Love, Rev. E. K., 392
Lowrey, H. S., 376, 382, 400
Lumber and Timber Workingmen's Union Association, 379-80
Lussian, Charles, 194
Lynch, Catherine, 414
Lynch, John R., 40, 414
Lynch, L. L., 121
Lynch, W. H., 253
Lynchburg, Va., 3-10
Lyon, Rev. Ernest, 226-29, 237
Lyon, Gov. [Ohio], 264

Macan, Dan, 209
Machinists' and Blacksmiths' Union, 416
Mason, James M., 418
Mc Bee, General Superintendent, 376, 387, 393, 397, 404
Mc Call, Richard, 201
Mc Clure, Col., 247
Mc Cormack, Andrew, 261
Mc Donough, John J., 367, 369, 376, 382, 384-85, 387-88, 394, 398, 404
Mc Duffie, George, 421
Mc Elroy, Capt. Frank, 60, 63
Mc Enery, Gov. Samuel D. [La.], 146, 158, 160, 186-89, 204-5, 207
Mc Gilbra, Israel, 287
Mc Guire, J. J., 120
Mc Guire, T. B., 123, 126
Mc Kay, J. P., 173
Mc Kinley, Jr., William, 267, 269, 420
Mc Laurin, Melton Alonza, 413
Mc Mahon, John A., 211-12
Mc Millan, Senator James, 325, 426
Mc Nair, Hillard, J., 262
Mc Neal, P. M., 252
Macune, C. W., 339, 405, 427
Mahon, James C., 158
Maier, First Lt. O. T., 199
Mallory, Henry R., 82
Mallory Steamship Company, 77-83
Manassas Railroad, 7
Mandingo, 31
Manson, R. A., 307, 309
Marsh, Fred C., 154, 165
Marshall, George, 163, 169
Marshall, John, 287
Martin, C. Fabe, 42
Martin, L. D., 56
Martin, R. B., 294
Martinet, L. A., 224, 226, 234, 238
Mason and Dixon Line, 114
Mason, Rev. M. C. B., 228, 231
"massa Powderly," 253
Matthews, C. S., 161, 165, 169
Maurice, E. J. E. B., 407
May, Capt. Eugene, 182
May, Henry, 59
Meat and Pastry Cook's Union, 407

Mehurin, C. C., 264
Mellaison, Henry, 193, 195
Merchants and Miners' Trans-
    portation Company, 371, 374, 376,
    377, 384, 394, 397-98, 402
Merchants Hotel of Richmond, 105
Merriman, G. W., 98
Meustin, C. V., 256
Mexicans, 343-44
Meyer, Brig. Gen. Adolph, 200
Michel, Antoine, 235
Midtown Express, 307
Miller, August, 214
Miller, Tom, 348-57, 363
Mills, Col. Anderson, 94,98
Mills, Frank, 353-55, 358, 362, 364
Minis, J. F., 386-87
Missouri Pacific Railroad Company,
    79, 86, 89, 416
Mitchel, E. A. F., 213
Mohammedan, 32
Molaison, Henry, 191, 199-200, 204-5
Montgomery, Ala., 9, 18
Montgomery, S. M., 287
Moody, W. L., 81, 84
Moore, Col. I. D., 191, 199
Moore, Rev. J. L., 301
Moore, Jr., Capt. John T., 169,
    170, 196
Morey, Gen. Frank, 177
Morris, D. B., 394-95
Morris, E. C., 115
Mosely, Dr. B. T., 224
Mott, Bro. G. Y., 263
Mozart Academy of Music [Richmond],
    107, 112, 120
Murphy, Sam
Murray, Charles, 213
Muse, Sergt., 375
Myers, Isaac, 44, 415

Nacoochee, the ship, 377, 384, 393
Naquin, Emile, 165
Naquin, Ozeme, 190
Nathaniel, W. N., 194
National Alliance, 288, 297
National Alliance, The, 288, 295,
    312
National Economist, The, 427
National Farmers Alliance and
    Industrial Union, 289, 296, 300,
    304, 404
National Guard of Louisiana, 155
"Negro Labor Problem," 49
Negro Masons, 121
Negro Press Committee, 115
Negro press, the, 39
Nelson, Lee A., 255
Nelson, Louis, 347
New Cotton Men's Executive Council
    and Trades Assembly, 212, 216
New Orleans, 3, 9-10, 58, 60, 65-67
New Orleans Picayune, the 314-15
New Orleans Pressmen's Union, 212
New Orleans Teamsters and Loaders
    Union Benevolent Association,
    212-16

New Orleans Typographical Society,
    215
"New South," 209
News and Courier, the Charleston,
    138, 141
Newsboys' Brass Band, 214
New York Central Railroad Co., 415
Nicholls, Gov. Francis T. [La.],
    225, 231, 237-38
Nichols, Willis, 287
Nihilism, 47
Nile Valley, 27
Nimrod, 27
"Noachian line," 28
Noah, 28
Nolan, Capt. John T., 201
Noop, Rev. Cleste, 117
Nora, Rev. H., 221
North American Review, 138
North Carolina Railroad, 246
Northen, Gov. [Ga.], 367
Norton, Dr. R. G., 394
Nugent, Patrick, 79

Ocala platform, 345
Ocean Steam ship Company, the, 367,
    386-89, 397, 404
Odeson, Landry, 161
O'Donnell, Will I. O., 212, 214
Oglesby, J. H., 158
Oliver, Newton, 397
Oliver, W. S., 95
O'Neill, John A., 151, 157
Opelousas Guards, 169, 172
O'Reilly, Tom, 253
Organ, Obadiah, 89
Oubre, A., 56
Oviatt, Second Lt. H. T., 199
Owens, Wyatt, 86
Oyster Dischargers' Union, 212, 215

Page, Morris, 198
Palfrey, Caaries, C., 158
Palm, C. S., 158
Parker, Albert, H., 164
Parker, C. A., 66
Parker, E. J., 407
Parkerson, Brig. Gen., 169
Parsons, J. O., 260
Patillo, W. A., 305
Pattell, M. W., 245
Patterson, Ben, 353, 355-59, 361-64
Patterson, Eli, 357-58, 362
Pattillo, Rev. W. A., 305
Payton, Ed., 358, 362, 364
Peffer, William A., 339, 427
Perry, H. H., 294
Peterford, Isaiah, 121
Peters, J. W., 287
Pharr, Capt. John N., 167, 175, 178,
    182
Phoenician, 32
Phoenix Bucket Fire Company, 221
Picot, Paul, 167, 170
Pierce, Gen. William, 172, 182
Pinckard, W. F., 200

Plaindealer, The Detroit, 35-36,
    39, 41-43, 313
Plate Printers' Assembly, 268
Pleasants, L. M., 392
Pledger, W. A., 392-93
Poindexter, James, 125
Polite, Isaac, 368
Polk, Leonidas, L., 339, 345, 405,
    426-27
Pomeroy, William C., 407-09
Populist Party, 422
Porcher, William, 149
Porter, Wilson, 347
Posey, Hon. W., 227
"Pottawatomie Massacre," 418
Powderly, Ala., 259
Powderly, Terence V., 73-74, 87, 90,
    105-34 passim, 242-70 passim, 416,
Price, Andrew, 158, 190, 202, 205
Price, William, 175
Progress, The, 225-26
Progressive Farmer, The, 340, 426
Pugh, James L., 15-17, 20, 25, 413
Pugh, Moses, 172, 174
Purse, Capt. D. D., 404
Putnam County Colored Farmers'
    Alliance, 302

Queen, B. F., 158
Quinn, Sr., James, 214

"Race Problem," the, 31
Raleigh Chronicle, The, 340
Ramsay, W. R., 210
Ray, John R., 246, 251, 258
Rebarer, Frank E., 376, 388
Record Review, the, 423
Reform Press, The, 340
Reid, Alderman William F., 402
Reilly, Col. Peter, 367
Rendville, Ohio, 126
Republican party, 16, 42, 76, 137,
    143, 208, 219, 227, 234-36, 239,
    274, 295, 299, 317-18
Retail Dry Goods Clerks Association,
    212, 215
Ricar, Marshall, 192
Richard, J. M., 156
Richard, Dr. M. V., 154
Richardson, Edward S., 336, 338
Richardson, Lt. Col. J. B., 200
Richardson, Gov. [S. C.], 141
Richmond *Dispatch,* 118, 121, 128
Richmond, Va., 3-4, 75
Riddle, J. T., 307
Rienze, Allen, 203
Risk, Capt. Sam J., 213
Rivers & Bidstrup, 158
Roach, James, 212
Robertson, J. W., 256
Rockwood, Gilbert, 244, 245
Rogers, Elizabeth, 120
Rogers, Col. H. P., 350-51
Rogers, J. J., 305-6
Roman Catholic Church, 119

Romans, 32
Rose, H. C., 158
Rosenbaum, Ben, 407
Ross, Prof. James, 392
Rousseau, P. O., 183-84
Roussel, O., 56
Russell, W. P., 139
Saddler, R. M., 287
St. Charles Hotel [Richmond], 108,
    112, 164, 201, 250
St. Cloud, V. E., 257
St. James Society, 68
St. Joseph Colored Society, 68
St. Martin, J. Emile, 201
St. Martin, Valcour, 53
St. Mary Local Aseembly No. 6205
    [La.], 146
Saint-Simon, Count de, 415
"Saint-Simonianism," 47, 415
Sanders, Dr. Henry J., 157-58, 177
Sanders, Shelby, 182
Santa Fe Railway, 81
Savannah Cotton Exchange and Board
    of Trade, 375-76
Savannah, Florida & Western Railroad,
    367-405 passim
Scannel, E., 158
Schaff, Henry, 201
Scheixnayder brothers, 56
Schriever, La., 152
Scott, Bud, 162
Scott, B. W., 150-51, 165, 261
Scott, James H. 17-20
Scott, Jim, 368
Scranton, Mr., 249
Screven, Wadley, 368
Screwmen Guards, 213
Screwmen's Benevolent Association
    of New Orleans, 211-16
Sealy, George, 81, 83
Searing, Samuel G., 266
Selma, Ala., 11
Senate Committee on Agriculture
    and Forestry, 319
Senate Committee on Relations Between
    Labor and Capital, 1883, 3-33
Shakespeare, Joseph A., 68-69
Shaw, G. W., 400
Sheridan, Gen. Phillip, 227
Sherman, Senator John, 269, 421
Sherman, William Tecumseh, 421
Ship Carpenters and Joiners Bene-
    volent Association, 212, 215
Shreveport plan, the, 294
Shuffer, J. J., 287-88
Simms, Marshall J., 229
Simms, M. J., 237
Simon, Edward, 220, 223
Simon, John, 235
Simon, Lewis, 220, 223, 235
Simon, Peter, 235
Simon, Thomas, 224, 235
Sims, Jim, 357-58
Sims, M.D., W. H., 257
Single tax part, 299, 423

Slaughter, Lon, 355
Smith, Andy, 223-24
Smith, E. Payson, 220
Smith, J. M., 66
Socialism, 41, 47
Sodoms and Gomorrahs, 230
Sons of Vulcan, 421
Sorrel, General Manager, 386, 398
Southern Alliance, 316
Southern Appeal, the, 264
Southern Confederacy, 126
Southwestern Christian Advocate, 186
Southwestern strike, 124
Sovereign, James R., 281, 422
"Sow-belly," 264
Spencer, H. J., 287-88
Spencer, John, 213
Sqan, E. S., 209
Stamps, Hon. T. B., 209
Stamps, Hon. T. B., 226-28, 231
Standard, the New York, 142
State Trades and Labor Assembly of Ohio, 36
"Stay in the Field Till the War is Ended," 378
Stevenson, John A., 56, 58-59
Stewart, Lewis, 121
Stewart, T. McCants, 44
Stewart, William J., 243
Stillwell, Miller & Co., 372
Stillwell, W. B., 387
Stock, B., 262
Street, J. Gordon, 37
Stritter, Otto, 407
Strong, Major, 53, 57-64 passim
Sub-treasury bill, 297-99, 315, 320-29
Sub-treasury plan, 423
"Sugar-Bowl," 143
Sugar Planters' Association, 157, 189, 198
Sullivan, Hon. E. A., 153
Sullivan, Hon. James J., 278
Sweet, S. F. S., 258

Taft, Alphonso, 413
Taney, Justice Roger B., 132
Taylor, Capt, E. Sumpter, 169, 172, 174
Taylor, Floren, 59
Taylor, Frank C., 226
Taylor, Robert, 121
Teachers' Institutes, 15
Teagle, C. A., 260
Teamsters' and Loaders' Union, 68
Teamsters' Union, 40
Tebo, W. B., 215
Teeley, Capt. John R., 161
Texas and Pacific Railroad, 90
Thompson, Capt., 180
Thompson, Rev. C. H., 209
Thompson, Daniel, 157-59
Thompson, First Lt. H. B., 155
Rhompson, Lazarus, 216

Thompson, Hon. L. D., 226
Thompson, Richard, 108
Thornhill, Floyd, 3-11
Tillman, Gov. Benjamin R. [S.C.], 314, 424
Tillman, J. F., 405
Time-Enterprise, 336, 338
Times-Democrat, the New Orleans, 147-48, 165, 170, 172, 179-81, 183, 192-93, 199, 200, 202, 216, 314
Times-Picayune, the New Orleans, 148
Todd, N. K., 158
Tomson, Organizer, 98
Toombs, Robert, 303, 424
Tounsend, J. M., 113
Trades and Labor Assembly of New Orleans, 211-12
Tudegar and Old Dominion Works, Richmond, Va., 71
Trosclair, L. A., 190
Trotter, James Monroe, 317, 425
Turner, Anthony, 287
Turner, Frederick W., 119, 124
Turner, Jacob, 156
Turner, J. H., 300, 405
Typographical Union of New Orleans, 212-14

Union Labor Party, 421
Union Pacific Railroad, 90
United Labor Party, 278
United Sons of Confederate Veterans, 419
United States, 297-98, 311, 319
United States Government, 29, 59
United States National Cemetery, 247
United States Senate, 225

Valden Negro newspaper, the, 348
Valere, Alexander, 235
Vallier, Alex, 224
Vallier, Edward, 224
Vanderbilt, Cornelius, 46-47, 325, 415
Vaudry Rifles, 62
Vice President of the United States, 126
Virginia Industrial, Mercantile and Building Association, 306, 309-10
Virginia Military Institute, 420
Virginian, the Norfolk, 113

Wade, J. D., 121
Wade, Superintendent, 385
Walker, Alexander, 254
Walker, G. G., 158
Walker, George P., 376, 387
Walker, Gov. Joseph [La.], 213
Walker, W. W., 419
Ward, Melvin, 313
Warmoth, Gov. [La.], 150
Warren, Col. J. L., 375, 386

Warwick, W. B., 409
Warwick, W. H., 307, 309
Washington and Lee University, 419
Washington and Lincoln, 313
Washington Artillery [La.], 62-64,
    164, 195, 197, 199-200
Washington, D.C., 3, 72, 74
Washington, Col. R. Q., 317-19
Waters, Chas. C., 95
Weaver, James, B., 422
Webre, John, 63
Webre, Sheriff, 63
Wehre, F., 56
Welch, F. M., 155
Wells, Ida B., 273, 421
Welsh, Rev. Isaiah H., 11-19
Wheeler, E. J., 407
White, Bob, 358
White, Charley, 275
White Folks Farmers' Alliance, 296
White, Judge E. D., 156, 161, 171,
    200
White, Rev. J. Wooford, 140
White, Richard H. 214
White, R. W., 392-93
Whitley, Washington, 156
White Virginia Knight, a, 116
Whitworth, Geo. W., 158
Wickham, T. W., 209
Wilkinson, Agent, 377, 383
William Lloyd Garrison Assembly
    8286 of the Knights of Labor,
    407, 410
Williams, F. H., 158
Williams, Frank, 177
Williams, George H., 259
Williams, George Washington, 309, 413
Williams, Capt. Ham, 100
Williams, James, 397
Williams, Jasper, 84
Williams, John, 379-397-98
Williams, N. S., 167
Williams, Sol, 148, 204, 206
"Williams's history," [George
    Washington], 32
Wills, Colonel, 159
Wills, Capt. W. H., 158, 164
Wilson, Charles B., 227-28
Wilson, Colonel, 128
Wilson, Patrick A., 212
Wilson, Samuel, 114
Wiltz, Gov. Louis A. [La.], 53-54,
    65
Windelkin, John H., 213
William Windom, 266, 268-69, 420
Winters, W. J., 256
Wise, Capt. W. H. P., 176, 182
Wood, James E., 355, 361
Woods, Mr. J. S., 40
Woodward, Rev. W. G. H., 255
Wormald, B. A., 161, 203
Worthen, Sheriff Robert W., 94,
    96-100
Wright, Brother, 243
Wright, R. R., 25-32

Wright, William, 120

Yarboro, C. E., 264
Yeiser, Magistrate J. G., 96
Youngblood, John, 369, 400

Zachry, Senator, 333
Zenor, George C., 177
Ziegler, F. M., 155
Zuberbier & Bran, 170